COMMONWEALTH CARIBBEAN CRIMINAL PRACTICE AND PROCEDURE

Fifth Edition

The fifth edition of this best-selling book has been thoroughly revised to take into account recent developments in the law in criminal practice and procedure across the region. As the only textbook to explore criminal practice and procedure as it relates to the Commonwealth Caribbean, the book clarifies the state law in each of 11 jurisdictions, while at the same time making it clear when laws are the same or similar and highlighting where differences among jurisdictions occur.

Both statute law and common law are examined in the relevant jurisdictions, which include Trinidad and Tobago, Guyana, Barbados, Jamaica and Grenada amongst others. The impact of statutory changes in the laws are analysed, as well as recent developments in the common law. Throughout the text the statutory law in the Commonwealth Caribbean is compared to similar English legislation, in light of the analysis of such legislation in English case law.

This book is the recommended textbook for all professional law schools in the Commonwealth Caribbean and is used at regional universities as a reference book for criminal justice students. In addition, as the only book that deals specifically with criminal practice and procedure in the regions, it has proved a valuable reference tool for legal practitioners, judicial officers and police officers.

Dana S. Seetahal SC was an attorney at law of over 30 years' experience. She was a private practitioner who appeared for both the defence and the State. She was also a public prosecutor for several years and a senior lecturer at the Hugh Wooding Law School, Trinidad and Tobago for 12 years. She held a Master of Science in Criminology from Florida State University and was a Fulbright scholar. Ms Seetahal wrote widely and presented numerous papers on criminal justice and related areas. She acted as a criminal justice consultant to governments across the region and various international bodies. Ms Seetahal was for eight years an independent senator in the Parliament of Trinidad and Tobago. In January 2006 she was appointed Senior Counsel.

Tragically Dana Seetahal was murdered in May 2014 at Woodbrook, Trinidad. Her untimely passing left relatives, friends and the legal fraternity in a state of shock at the callousness of her assassination. In 2011, when I, Roger Ramgoolam, assumed the post of Course Director of Criminal Practice and Procedure at the Hugh Wooding Law School, St Augustine, I quickly discovered that this excellent textbook, which was the backbone of the course, would serve as a valuable guide for both students and practitioners of criminal law. Subsequent to my appointment, Ms Seetahal released a revised fourth edition to the text that kept abreast of the latest developments in the law. I consider myself fortunate to have been asked by the publishers of the previous editions to do the honour of working on a new fifth edition of this text. It is my hope that the various updates I have inserted into the text will further enhance the quality of the text and ensure its continued status as an indispensable reference for all persons in the legal fraternity.

COMMONWEALTH CARIBBEAN LAW SERIES

The Commonwealth Caribbean Law Series is the only series of law books that covers the jurisdiction of the English speaking Caribbean nations. The first titles in the series were published in 1995 to acclaim from academics, practitioners and the judiciary in the region. Several editions followed, and they have now become essential reading for those learning and practising Caribbean law.

This must have series is required holdings for any law library specialising in Caribbean legal information.

Titles in this series include:

Commonwealth Caribbean Public Law
Albert Fiadjoe

Commonwealth Caribbean Tort Law
Gilbert Kodilinye

Commonwealth Caribbean Law of Trusts
Gilbert Kodilinye and Trevor Carmichael

Judicial Review in the Commonwealth Caribbean
Rajendra Ramlogan

Commonwealth Caribbean Administrative Law
Eddy Ventose

Commonwealth Caribbean Contract Law
Gilbert Kodilinye and Maria Kodilinye

Commonwealth Caribbean Employment and Labour Law
Natalie Corthésy and Carla-Anne Harris-Roper

Commonwealth Caribbean Tort Law
Gilbert Kodilinye

Commonwealth Caribbean Property Law
Gilbert Kodilinye

Commonwealth Caribbean Business Law
Natalie Persadie and Rajendra Ramlogan

Commonwealth Caribbean Corporate Governance
Edited by Suzanne Ffolkes-Goldson

Commonwealth Caribbean Family Law: Husband, Wife and Cohabitant
Karen Nunez-Tesheira

Forthcoming titles:

Commonwealth Caribbean Intellectual Property Law
Eddy Ventose

Commonwealth Caribbean Administrative Law (Second Edition)
Eddy Ventose

Commonwealth Caribbean Tort Law (Sixth Edition)
Gilbert Kodilinye

COMMONWEALTH CARIBBEAN CRIMINAL PRACTICE AND PROCEDURE

Fifth Edition

Dana S. Seetahal
with updates by Roger Ramgoolam

Routledge
Taylor & Francis Group
LONDON AND NEW YORK

First published 2019
by Routledge
2 Park Square, Milton Park, Abingdon, Oxon OX14 4RN

and by Routledge
52 Vanderbilt Avenue, New York, NY 10017

Routledge is an imprint of the Taylor & Francis Group, an informa business

First edition published by Routledge-Cavendish in 2001.
Fourth edition published by Routledge in 2014.

British Library Cataloguing-in-Publication Data
A catalogue record for this book is available from the British Library

Library of Congress Cataloging-in-Publication Data
Names: Seetahal, Dana S., author. | Ramgoolam, Roger, author.
Title: Commonwealth Caribbean criminal practice and procedure / by Dana S. Seetahal ; with updates by Roger Ramgoolam.
Description: Fifth edition. | Milton Park, Abingdon, Oxon ; New York, NY : Routledge, 2019.
Series: Commonwealth Caribbean law series | Includes bibliographical references and index.
Identifiers: LCCN 2018040525| ISBN 9781138590083 (hbk) | ISBN 9780367086947 (pbk) | ISBN 9780429955570 (epub) | ISBN 9780429955587 (adobe pdf) | ISBN 9780429955563 (mobipocket)
Subjects: LCSH: Criminal procedure—West Indies, British.
Classification: LCC KGL5971 .S44 2019 | DDC 345.729/05—dc23
LC record available at https://lccn.loc.gov/2018040525

ISBN: 978-1-138-59008-3 (hbk)
ISBN: 978-0-367-08694-7 (pbk)
ISBN: 978-0-429-95557-0 (ebk)

Typeset in Baskerville
by Swales & Willis Ltd

To my nieces and nephews who feel that I can do anything, to my students who made me realise the need for this text and to my colleagues who appreciated the first edition

CONTENTS

ACKNOWLEDGEMENTS

ACKNOWLEDGEMENTS TO THE FIRST EDITION

I wish to thank the following persons without whose contribution this book might not have been possible:

The Chairman of the Council of Legal Education, Mr Dennis Morrison, QC and the Principal of the Hugh Wooding Law School, St Augustine, Justice Annestine Sealey, who facilitated my writing of this book.

Justice of Appeal Rolston Nelson, Ms Sophia Chote, Mrs Patricia Khan, Mrs Beverly King and Ms Hannah Francis, all of whom assisted in proofreading the contents of the book.

The Director of Public Prosecutions of Trinidad and Tobago, Mr Mark Mohammed SC and his counterpart in the Bahamas, Mr Bernard Turner, who both willingly gave information and answered pointed questions on prosecution practice in their jurisdictions.

Justice of Appeal Lionel Jones, Justice Austin Davis, Principal of the Eugene Dupuch Law School, Mr Errol Mathews, Mr Doodnauth Singh SC (of the Guyana bar), Mr Israel Khan SC, Justice Alice Soo Hon, Ms Merlin Boyce and Mr Rikki Harnanan for their encouragement.

Senator Petrus Compton, Attorney General of St Lucia, who re-ignited my interest in writing this book when he commissioned me to do a project on the Criminal Law and Procedure in St Lucia.

Ms June Renie, Librarian at the Hugh Wooding Law School, Mr Amar Rampersadsingh and Mr Chandraban Maharaj, Library Assistants and the rest of the staff at the library who uncomplainingly and continually sourced materials and information for me.

Mrs Diane Gittens and her staff at the library at the Hall of Justice, Port of Spain for their assistance.

My colleagues, staff and students at the Hugh Wooding Law School for their unstinting support.

My many friends in the media for their generous support and encouragement.

The staff at Cavendish Publishing for demonstrating confidence in me.

My family, neighbours and others close to me who were always there to sustain me.

And finally and very significantly, Ms Diane Williams, Secretary at the Hugh Wooding Law School, not only for her typing and editing of the manuscript and intelligent deciphering of my handwriting, but more so for her unfailing good humour and confidence in me.

ADDITIONAL ACKNOWLEDGEMENTS TO THE SECOND EDITION

To the list of those persons mentioned in July 2001 I must add the following whom I sincerely thank:

The current Chairman of the Council of Legal Education, Mr Emile Ferdinand, for his support.

Mr Geoffrey Henderson, the current Director of Public Prosecutions of Trinidad and Tobago, for his assistance and encouragement.

And the Staff of the Library of Parliament of Trinidad and Tobago for so willingly and promptly sourcing material when requested.

Dana S Seetahal
July 2006

ADDITIONAL ACKNOWLEDGEMENTS TO THE THIRD EDITION

Reviewing this work with a view to producing a third edition has been particularly challenging in some ways, partially because I am no longer a full-time lecturer at the Hugh Wooding Law School and also given the constraints of my private practice.

In that regard the assistance of my in-service trainee students Imran Ali, Vanessa Knights, Leanna Seetahal, Shivani Jacelon and Cherisse Nixon has been valuable.

I also wish to express my gratitude to Justice Adrian Saunders of the Caribbean Court of Justice, Colin Williams, Director of Public Prosecutions of St Vincent, and the several other colleagues throughout the region who allowed me to impose on them to provide assistance in sourcing material.

Above all, I must acknowledge the valuable contribution of my associate David West in authoring the new Chapter 20 on 'Extradition'. His experience in this field is unparalleled in Trinidad and Tobago.

Finally, I wish to thank the Honourable John Jeremie SC, Attorney General of Trinidad and Tobago, for affording me the opportunity to make a direct impact in developing criminal practice and procedure in Trinidad and Tobago and ultimately in the region.

Dana S Seetahal SC
February 2010

ADDITIONAL ACKNOWLEDGEMENTS TO THE FOURTH EDITION

I am indebted to a number of my colleagues across the region and in Trinidad and Tobago for their invaluable help in providing assistance and/or clarification in sourcing new legislation of the various countries in the Commonwealth Caribbean. Among those I number:

The Attorney General and Minister of Legal Affairs of Guyana, The Honourable Mohabir Anil Nandlall
The DPP of Antigua and Barbuda, Mr Anthony Armstrong
The DPP of St Vincent and the Grenadines, Mr Colin Williams
Mr Damien Kelsick of the St Kitts and Nevis Bar
Mr Keith Scotland of the Trinidad and Tobago bar.

I also wish to express my gratitude to the staff of the libraries of the Hugh Wooding Law School and the Eugene Dupuch Law School.

I particularly thank Ms Ria Reyes and Ms Casandra Seetahal, young lawyers attached to my chambers, who devoted many hours in checking and cross checking material for this edition.

I must not forget to express my appreciation of the efforts of law students, Saddam Hosein, Aleema Ameerali and Ethlyn Mckenzie.

I continue to be grateful to my associate Mr David West for authoring Chapter 20 on 'Extradition' and updating the law in which field his experience remains unchallenged in Trinidad and Tobago.

Finally, I wish to thank the Honourable Anand Ramlogan SC, Attorney General and Mr Roger Gaspard SC, the DPP, both of Trinidad and Tobago, for affording me the opportunity to make a direct impact in the development of criminal practice and procedure in Trinidad and Tobago and ultimately in the region.

Dana S Seetahal SC
September 2013

ADDITIONAL ACKNOWLEDGEMENTS TO THE FIFTH EDITION

I wish to thank the publishers of this text for asking me to update this text. I consider it an honour and I dedicate this Fifth Edition to the memory of the late Dana Seetahal SC. I thank the dedicated staff at the Hugh Wooding Law School library for their professionalism and expertise in sourcing materials for the book. I also thank all the students of mine (both former and present) who sourced legislation from the various Caribbean territories. I wish to thank Attorneys-at-law Chris Selochan and Angelica Teelucksingh, as well as Magistrate Bramhannan Dubay, who all made valuable suggestions as to content. I especially thank Attorneys-at-law Russell Campbell and Susan Seecharan for their invaluable in-depth research. Attorney-at-law Aberlene Boodoosingh was instrumental in proof reading and organisation of content. I thank her and Justice Ronnie Boodsoosingh for their work as well as for their unflagging belief and support.

This book was updated when I was performing my duties as course director and tutor of both criminal practice and procedure and trial advocacy at the law school, which meant long hours out of my off time had to be sacrificed. The support of my family (especially my wife) and friends has been invaluable in keeping me going through the difficult times when energy was low and my patience was short.

I finally wish to thank my students, both past and present, who it has been my privilege to teach (and to learn from). Their eagerness to learn and to constantly push the limits of what is possible has been and continues to be a source of inspiration.

INTRODUCTION

This book constitutes an attempt to describe and analyse the law on criminal procedure and practice in the Commonwealth Caribbean as at 31 May 2018. In some instances the contents are circumscribed by the lack of material, such as local case law in some jurisdictions. In revising the text, ready availability of material, legislation and case law, in respect of some jurisdictions, continues to be the main drawback.

Despite this, I wish to assure the reader that I have accessed all available sources, including the regional libraries, online sources as well as practitioners, to ensure that the text represents the most accurate reflection of the current law. Any shortcomings or errors in this regard, however, are deeply regretted and are my sole responsibility.

The jurisdictions whose laws have been detailed here include 11 independent Commonwealth Caribbean countries, as follows:

Antigua and Barbuda – referred to as 'Antigua' in the book
the Bahamas
Barbados
Commonwealth of Dominica – referred to as 'Dominica'
Grenada
Guyana
Jamaica
Saint Christopher – referred to as 'St Kitts and Nevis'
Saint Lucia – referred to as 'St Lucia'
Saint Vincent and the Grenadines – referred to as 'St Vincent'
Trinidad and Tobago

In addition, reference has been made to the law of Belize and of Bermuda. Where appropriate, reference has also been made to English statute, both current and replaced, chiefly for purposes of comparing it with and also analysing existing legislation in the Commonwealth Caribbean, where criminal procedure statute is based to a large extent on old English statute.

The book is intended for both lawyers and law students. It serves as a text for students at the professional law schools of the Commonwealth Caribbean, who have already completed a law degree. At the time of writing the first edition in 2001, it was anticipated that, as a textbook in a field that was still academically largely unexplored in the region, it would provide a useful reference for legal practitioners. In fact, feedback from members of the judiciary and lawyers throughout the region attests to the fact that the text has surpassed the mission in that regard. Police officers and prosecutors have also indicated that they find the book valuable in developing a good understanding of how the criminal process works.

This edition of the book comprises some 20 chapters, beginning with 'Jurisdiction' and ending with 'Extradition'. The format represents an attempt to detail the criminal process from the time at which a criminal complaint surfaces. Jurisdiction must first be ascertained and so this is considered first, followed by the process bringing an alleged offender before the courts: arrest or summons. Thereafter, the book details the preliminary steps in a criminal trial until it diverges into summary trial and indictable trial processes, including appeals. Understanding the procedural differences in these two separate forms of trial – summary trial before a magistrate and indictable trial before a judge and jury – is crucial in appreciating how the criminal justice system operates. A new chapter on the criminal procedure rules has been added in view of the growing significance of these rules to the practice of criminal law. Issues in sentencing and the special trial of juveniles are then discussed. The final chapter relates to extradition, which may be perceived as an elaborate arrest procedure to remove a fugitive from one jurisdiction to another jurisdiction. Commonwealth Caribbean jurisdictions are increasingly faced with requests from foreign governments for the return of fugitives, so it has become relevant to appreciate the procedure that facilitates this.

Since the last edition written in 2013 several countries have introduced new laws in several areas while others have not only done so but have also revised their laws. This edition includes these changes as well as the developments in the common law across the region.

It should be noted that this book is meant to describe and analyse the existing law on criminal procedure and practice. The question of reforms in law and policy, and recommendations thereof, does not fall within the scope of this book and might well be the basis for another book entirely. Where necessary, however, some allusion is made to areas of uncertainty in the law that may need to be resolved.

TABLE OF ABBREVIATIONS

The following abbreviations are commonly used in this book:

AG:	Attorney General
Assizes:	Criminal High Court Board: Board of the Privy Council
CCJ:	Caribbean Court of Justice
DPP:	Director of Public Prosecutions
PC:	Privy Council
Privy Council:	Judical Committee of the Privy Council

In addition throughout the book:
'High Court' is used to refer to the first tier court if the Supreme Court across the region, which may be called Supreme Court in some countries or Circuit Court in others;
'Statute' to refer to statute law; and
'Defendant' to refer to any person charged with or convicted of a crime, whether a summary or indictable offence.

TABLE OF CASES

TABLE OF LEGISLATION

BARBADOS

GUYANA

JAMAICA

ST VINCENT AND THE GRENADINES

TRINIDAD AND TOBAGO

UNITED STATES

WEST INDIES

WINDWARD AND LEEWARD ISLANDS

CHAPTER 1

JURISDICTION

Before criminal proceedings may be commenced against anyone for any offence, it must first be ensured that the court before whom such proceedings are to be initiated has jurisdiction to hear the proceedings. Jurisdiction can refer to several matters, but in criminal proceedings it usually includes three things: physical jurisdiction; local jurisdiction, which determines which particular court within a country hears the case; and statutory limitation, which is effectively a denial of jurisdiction because of passage of time. The principles of abuse of process, which are discussed in Chapter 2, relate to situations where a court is asked to refuse jurisdiction to try a case because of the abuse of its process by prosecuting authorities.

PHYSICAL JURISDICTION

A State usually only has the ability to try offences that are committed within the boundaries of that State. The question of whether an offence is committed within a particular State depends not only on its physical boundaries, but also on legislation and legal principles that artificially extend those boundaries for jurisdictional purposes. In considering physical jurisdiction, the principles of both territoriality and extra-territoriality are relevant. As the names suggest, the former concerns matters within the State and the latter outside the boundaries.

Territoriality

The principles of criminal jurisdiction in the Commonwealth Caribbean courts are based on the English common law that is applicable across the region unless specifically overridden by statute law. The foundation of criminal jurisdiction is territorial, since it is regarded as one of the functions of the courts in a particular country to maintain peace by criminal process in that country.

In general, then, it is only conduct occurring within a particular State that is subject to prosecution by the agencies of that State: *Cox v Army Council* [1963] AC 48, HL. In that case the House of Lords considered the appeal of a British soldier from a conviction for driving without due care and attention contrary to the English Road Traffic Act. The incident itself occurred in Germany where the soldier was stationed. In upholding the conviction, Viscount Simonds emphasised, 'Apart from those exceptional circumstances in which specific provision is made in regard to acts committed abroad, the whole body of the criminal law of England deals only with acts committed in England'.[1] On the facts of this case, however, s 70 of the Army Act 1955, which decreed that a person 'subject to military law who commits a civil offence, whether in the United Kingdom or elsewhere' should be subject to punishment in accordance with the law of England, was applicable. This was an example of specific provision to which Viscount Simonds alluded. Once the constituents of the offence are

1 *Cox v Army Council* [1963] AC 48, HL, p 67.

committed by the offender in a particular State, the authorities may proceed to prosecute: *DPP v Stonehouse* [1977] 2 All ER 909, HL.

In *Stonehouse*, an English Member of Parliament was charged with attempting to obtain property by deception. He had insured his life with five insurance companies in England and then faked his death (in the US) the following month, September 1974. Subsequently, in December, he was found alive in Australia. His wife had meanwhile sought to cash in the policies. She did not know that his death was faked. He was extradited to England and prosecuted on several charges of dishonesty in seeking to enable his wife to obtain money by deception, contrary to s 15 of the Theft Act. On an appeal based on lack of jurisdiction, the House of Lords confirmed the convictions. The House held that it had jurisdiction, on the basis that Stonehouse's physical act (that is, his disappearance) wherever done would have caused the obtaining of property in England from the victim insurance companies. This was because Stonehouse had taken out the policies in England. Although the full offence was not completed he had performed sufficient of the actus reus in England to be liable in that country.

In *Liangsiriprasert v USA* [1991] 1 AC 225, PC, the Privy Council went even further in claiming jurisdiction for criminal process. The Judicial Committee held that on a charge of conspiracy to traffic in heroin, even though the agreement (the actus reus) may have been committed abroad, the conspirator was liable in the country where it was intended that the constituents of the full offence were to be committed. This was an extension of the earlier principles in *DPP v Doot* [1973] AC 807, HL, which had suggested that at least an overt act should have been done in the country claiming jurisdiction.

According to the House in *Liangsiriprasert*, the Hong Kong courts had jurisdiction to try the case even though the conspiracy itself had been entered in Thailand and no overt acts pursuant to it had yet occurred in Hong Kong. As Lord Griffiths stated,

> their Lordships can find nothing in precedent, comity or good sense that would inhibit the common law from regarding as justiciable in England inchoate crimes committed abroad which are intended to result in the commission of criminal offences in England.[2]

Presumably there was also nothing to inhibit as justiciable in Hong Kong an inchoate crime such as conspiracy committed in Thailand which was intended to result in a full crime, trafficking in heroin, in Hong Kong.

It follows, therefore, that an inchoate crime committed elsewhere is justiciable in any country in the Commonwealth Caribbean if the completed offence is to be committed in that country. The decision in *Liangsiriprasert* extended the principles of territorial jurisdiction set out in *Stonehouse*, which speaks to a rationale based on physical acts being done in the country that claims jurisdiction. In respect of inchoate crimes, however, since these by their very nature are incomplete, there is no requirement for physical acts to be done in the country. Once the result (the full crime) is intended in a given country, that country has jurisdiction to try the inchoate crime.

Extension of territory

The area of territory of a particular country can be extended to give jurisdiction to that country by prerogative of the executive head of the country or by Parliament. Thus,

2 *Liangsiriprasert v USA* [1991] 1 AC 225, PC, p 251.

although a State usually has jurisdiction only within its borders, those borders may artificially be extended by the decision of the Head of State or more usually by statute, as has been done in the case of territorial waters. In *R v Kent JJ ex p Lye* [1967] 2 QB 153, it was argued that the Red Sands Tower, in which the offence of unlawfully using wireless telegraphy apparatus was alleged to have been committed, did not fall within the county of Kent, England. The question then arose as to what 'territorial waters' meant in the absence of a definition in the relevant Act. It was held that these were waters over which the Crown, the English Head of State, declared sovereignty, invariably in conformity with international law. Nowadays, State boundaries are usually specifically extended by statute.

Territorial waters

In Commonwealth Caribbean jurisdictions, the State boundaries have been extended by statute, in most cases by 12 nautical miles.[3] This is called the territorial sea or territorial waters. Since most of the Commonwealth Caribbean territories are islands, this issue has more relevance than in larger countries where crime is concentrated in the landmass. Across the region there are statutory provisions that delimit the extent of the territorial sea.[4] An example of the common provision can be found in s 5(1) of the Grenada Territorial Sea and Maritime Boundaries Act (1989) Cap 318, which provides:

> Subject to subsection (2) and . . . the territorial sea of Grenada comprises those areas of the sea having, as their landward limit, the baselines and, as their seaward limit, a line measured seaward every point of which is twelve nautical miles distant from the nearest point of the baselines.

If one country is closer than 24 nautical miles to another, the territorial waters of each is determined by agreement.[5] In the absence of statute, common law prevails and at common law jurisdiction extends to three miles[6] from the nearest point of the baselines.

A ship that is within the territorial waters of a country is within that country's jurisdiction: *Pianka v R* (1997) 25 WIR 438, PC. In that case a boat registered in the US carrying US citizens was intercepted in the territorial waters of Jamaica with over 3,000 lbs of marijuana. Two US citizens were charged with possession of the drug. Upon conviction it was argued on appeal that the magistrate lacked jurisdiction. It was contended that the s 4 of the Jamaica Territorial Sea Act 1971, extending the territorial waters to 12 miles, applied to indictable offences only and this was a summary trial. It was held that the 1971 Act did apply to resident magistrates' courts and the extension of territorial waters of Jamaica was the same for jurisdiction as regards all offences.

This case also highlights some of the problems with territorial jurisdiction of summary courts where jurisdiction depends on the statute, that is, the relevant summary procedure legislation, since magistrates are creatures of statute. This compares to the High Court,

---

3 One nautical mile equals 6,080 ft, as compared with 5,280 ft for the usual mile.

4 See: Antigua: Territorial Waters Act, 18 of 1982; Bahamas: Archipelagic Waters and Maritime Jurisdiction Act, No 37 of 1993; Barbados: Territorial Waters Act, Cap 386; Dominica: Territorial Sea and Maritime Boundaries Act, Chap 1:11; Grenada: Territorial Sea and Maritime Boundaries Act 1989, Cap 318; Guyana: Maritime Boundaries Act, 10 of 1977; Jamaica: Territorial Sea Act 1971; St Kitts and Nevis: Maritime Areas Act, Cap 7:03; St Lucia: Maritime Areas Act, 6 of 1984; St Vincent: Maritime Areas Act, Cap 464; Trinidad and Tobago: Territorial Sea Act, Chap 1:51.

5 As indicated, for instance, in sub-s 5(2) of the Grenada Act, Cap 318.

6 *Pianka v R* (1977) 25 WIR 438, PC, p 443, letter C–H.

where judges have jurisdiction based on common law. Thus, in most summary procedure legislation in the region, there can be found a provision stating that for criminal acts committed within the territorial sea, or internal waters, the magistrate of the closest magisterial district has jurisdiction, or any magistrate[7] may have jurisdiction.

Extra-territoriality

On the face of it, it would seem that a State might not have jurisdiction over offences committed outside its land space or the territorial waters such as in the High Seas or airspace. However, international law has intervened to extend jurisdiction in specific situations, in respect of acts committed outside the boundaries or territorial waters of a particular State. This relates to both the High Seas and airspace. Statute also provides for a State to assist another in enforcing its jurisdiction by facilitating extradition of an offender to the latter State where the offence was committed.

High seas

The Convention on the High Seas (1958) specifies that a ship is subject to the jurisdiction of the State whose flag it bears.[8] Although this Convention was superseded by the United Nations Convention on the Law of the Sea (Law of the Sea Convention) the principle is restated in Art 97 of the latter. A ship may only fly one flag. It is subject to the exclusive jurisdiction of that State if it is on the High Seas. Most countries in the Commonwealth Caribbean are signatories to the Law of the Sea Convention, so the principles of international law should apply on such jurisdictional issues.

It must be noted that a ship may be subject to concurrent jurisdiction if not on the High Seas. It is subject to the jurisdiction of both flag State and the State in whose territorial waters it is: *Anderson* (1868) LR 1 CCR 161, *Anderson* [1861–1873] All ER 999.

Admiralty jurisdiction

English law[9] provides that courts may also rely on Admiralty jurisdiction in respect of ships in the High Seas. This jurisdiction stems in part from the inherent jurisdiction of the English High Court of Admiralty and also statute, the Administration of Justice Act 1956. The court is said to have inherent power to exercise jurisdiction in certain cases of injury to person or property on the High Seas. If a ship is owned by a British subject and is on the High Seas or foreign rivers (below bridges), it is subject to British law. Some countries have adopted this law on Admiralty jurisdiction.[10] It is arguable that in some other jurisdictions savings law

7 As in Magistrates' Courts Act 1996, s 15, Barbados, District Courts Act Chap. 2.02, section 6(2); St Lucia, Summary Courts Act Chap 4:20; section 10, Trinidad and Tobago.

8 Convention on the High Seas (Geneva, 29 April 1958), Art 6.

9 Administration of Justice Act 1956, esp. ss 1–8.

10 Pursuant to the Administration of Justice Act 1956, s 56, UK, the following orders were made:
Antigua: Admiralty Jurisdiction (Antigua and Barbuda) Order 1964, No 1659;
Bahamas: Admiralty Jurisdiction (Bahamas Is) Order (1965) Rev, kept in force by Act 1 of 1990;
Belize: Admiralty Jurisdiction (British Honduras) Order 1965, No 593, G 355/1965;
Dominica: Admiralty Jurisdiction (Dominica) Order 1964, No 1660, App 1964;

provisions,[11] which retain the common law, may operate to maintain such jurisdiction. However, this is not usually of importance given the adoption of the High Seas Convention whereby the criminal jurisdiction of a country extends over its ships, even private ships, usually when they fly the flag. Admiralty jurisdiction relates to ships whether they fly the flag or not.

In *Deokienanan v R* (1965) 8 WIR 209, the appellant was charged in the then British Guiana (now Guyana) with murder alleged to have been committed on board a ship in motion on the Corentyne river. This river, however, was not part of Guiana and there was no averment in the indictment that the offence was committed on the High Seas. There was also no evidence that the ship at the time of the incident was at any point on the river where 'great ships go', which would indicate the High Seas. It was held by the Court of Appeal that Admiralty jurisdiction extends to British ships on the High Seas and it was necessary for the indictment to aver 'High Seas' to fall within s 5 of the Criminal Law (Offences) Ordinance, Cap 10, and thus invoke Admiralty jurisdiction. The indictment was thus held to be a nullity and the conviction quashed. Subsequently the appellant was re-indicted and convicted. When the second case came up for appeal in *Deokienanan v R* (1966) 9 WIR 510, the court confirmed that a ship owned by a British subject, even though unregistered, was a British ship for the purposes of invoking Admiralty jurisdiction.

Airspace

Since the sovereignty of a State extends to its airspace as well as its land territory, as dictated by customary international law, there is no issue with jurisdiction as regards offences committed on board an aircraft flying in such airspace. There is no question of extra-territoriality really, as the airspace is regarded as territory in much the same way as the territorial sea. This basic principle has been encapsulated in the territorial waters legislation of some countries in the Commonwealth Caribbean.[12] The country in whose airspace the aircraft is flying has jurisdiction.

Different considerations apply if an aircraft is flying in open airspace. Usually, offences committed on board such aircraft may be prosecuted in the country in which the plane is registered. This is in keeping with the Tokyo Convention, which was signed in September 1963, which has been adopted to form part of the municipal law in most Caribbean jurisdictions.[13] In countries which have no specific law, reference may be made to the Convention on International Civil Aviation.

Grenada: Admiralty Jurisdiction (Grenada) Order 1964, No 1661, App 1964;
Guyana: Admiralty Jurisdiction (British Guiana) Order 1962, No 630;
St Vincent: Admiralty and Prize Jurisdiction Act, Cap 16, Act No 54 of 1989.

11 As in Barbados: Supreme Court of Judicature Act, Cap 117B, s 19; St Lucia: Supreme Court Ordinance, s 9; Trinidad and Tobago: Supreme Court of Judicature Act, Chap 4:01, s 12.

12 See, e.g., Grenada Territorial Sea and Maritime Boundaries Act, Cap 318, s 8(b).

13 See:
Barbados: Civil Aviation (Tokyo Convention) Act 1972, Cap 123B of 1972;
Grenada: Tokyo Convention Act, Cap 320;
Guyana: Fugitive Offenders Act, s 37;
St Kitts and Nevis: Tokyo Convention Act Cap 4:39;
St Lucia: Civil Aviation (Tokyo Convention) Act 13 of 1986;
St Vincent: Civil Aviation (Tokyo Convention) Cap 79;
Trinidad and Tobago: Civil Aviation (Tokyo Convention) Act, Chap 11:21.
The English Tokyo Convention Act 1967 gave effect to the Tokyo Convention to some overseas territories including the Bahamas, by virtue of the Tokyo Convention Act 1967 (Overseas Territories) Order 1968.

On the other hand, if an aircraft that is flying over one country's airspace is registered in another country, both countries may claim jurisdiction. This is an example of concurrent jurisdiction and it is usually resolved by agreement between the two countries as to who should prosecute.

The Trinidad and Tobago Civil Aviation Act, which was passed in May 1978, is typical of those in the region and gives rise to such instances of concurrent jurisdiction. Section 3(1) of that Act provides:

> ... an act or omission taking place on board a Trinidad and Tobago controlled aircraft while in flight elsewhere than in or over Trinidad and Tobago which, if taking place in Trinidad and Tobago, would constitute an offence under the law in force in Trinidad and Tobago constitutes that offence.

This means that an offence once committed on board a 'Trinidad and Tobago controlled aircraft' while that aircraft is in flight is deemed to have been committed in Trinidad and Tobago even when the aircraft is outside of Trinidad and Tobago airspace. A 'Trinidad and Tobago controlled aircraft' is not restricted to an aircraft registered in Trinidad and Tobago. As defined in s 2, the term includes aircraft hired out to a person who is qualified to be the legal/beneficial owner of an aircraft registered in Trinidad and Tobago and either resides there or has his principal place of business there. It also includes aircraft whose operator or owner is a person who is qualified as above and resides or has his place of business there.

Extradition

This is a field of growing importance today as offenders frequently seek to avoid prosecution by leaving the State in which they committed an offence. The question arises as to how they are to be tried, since the State to which they flee may have no jurisdiction to try the offence. The answer lies in extradition. By treaty, incorporated in local statute, States undertake to return or send offenders to the country that has jurisdiction. This is based on the principles of reciprocity and the Rule of Specialty. Reciprocity relates to the need for reciprocal legislation between the two countries that must also clarify which crimes are extraditable. The Rule of Specialty prohibits the receiving State from trying the returned offender for any offence other than that for which he was extradited.

Extradition is considered in detail in Chapter 20.

LOCAL JURISDICTION

Once it is established that a country has territorial jurisdiction to try an offence, the next question that must be determined is in which court the matter is to be heard. This question relates both to locality, the actual venue, and the nature of the court: should it be the Supreme/High Court or the magistrates' court?

Criminal proceedings must at least start in the magistrates' court, whether they are indictable or summary. If an indictable matter is being proceeded with indictably, the magistrate before whom the case is laid must first hold a preliminary enquiry, sometimes referred to as committal proceedings, to determine if a case fit for trial by jury is made out. If it is, the accused person is then 'committed to stand trial at the Assizes'. 'The Assizes' refer to the Criminal Assizes that are held in the High Court, or Supreme Court as it is called in some jurisdictions.

Indictable offences are those offences that are so designated by statute or the common law. The maximum penalty for such an offence is usually at least 12 months, since it was almost a rule of thumb that a summary offence is one where the maximum penalty is six months' imprisonment.[14,15] Indictable offences must be tried in the High Court unless there is specific statutory provision enabling a magistrate to hear the case.[16] This is usually permitted in respect of less serious indictable offences which are sometimes referred to as 'triable either way' offences or 'hybrid' offences. The magistrate is bound to follow the procedure specified to enable such trial, otherwise he will be held to have no jurisdiction[17] and the matter would be considered an indictable one to be tried in the Assizes, the Criminal High Court.

The High Court is what is termed a superior court of record over which judges who have many inherent powers, such as the power of contempt of court, sit.[18] Indictable offences are the only type of offences that are now tried by jury (in the High Court). In most instances in the Commonwealth Caribbean they are the only matters that are tried by juries.[19] Indictable offences include felonies[20] in those jurisdictions which retain the designation. Of course, indictable offences are not restricted only to felonies or arrestable offences, as the case may be, but include most serious offences. Non-indictable offences are 'summary' offences.

If the offence is summary, the magistrate is entitled to try the matter without a jury. Statute and common law has determined which offences are summary or indictable. Usually, this is specified in the statute creating the offence that will state, for instance, that an offence is punishable on 'summary conviction'. Otherwise, the maximum penalty will be a good indication. If it is a fine or six months' imprisonment or less, the offence is summary. Originally, all offences were tried by judge and jury before magistrates' courts were created.

Magistrates' courts

Magistrates' courts are created by statute.[21] It follows that magistrates are purely creatures of statute. Their jurisdiction originates and is founded in statute,[22] whereas judges derive much of their power from the common law, including the power to supervise and control the magistrates' courts and other 'inferior' tribunals. In *Johnson* (1875) LR 10 QB 544, it was confirmed that all jurisdiction in a magistrates' court must be conferred by statute and a

---

14 Consider, e.g., the St Vincent Criminal Procedure Code, Cap 172, s 137, which sets a statutory limitation for prosecution of offences 'punishable only by a fine or imprisonment for six months or less'.

15 In recent times the legislature has intervened to impose harsh sentences, sometimes up to 10 years, for offences that are purely summary in nature, such as breaches of the Customs law.

16 This procedure is discussed in Chapter 10.

17 *R v Tottenham JJ ex p Arthur's Transport* [1981] Crim LR 180.

18 See Richards, S, 'Reform in the magistrates' courts in Barbados', *The Lawyer*, July 1994, pp 33–34 for an analysis of the distinction between the higher and lower judiciary.

19 The only civil offence which still enjoys this distinction is defamation, and then in few territories, one of which is Barbados.

20 The distinction has been abolished in Trinidad and Tobago, Barbados and St Lucia, and replaced with 'arrestable' offences, where the penalty for the offence is mandatory or carries a penalty of at least five years' imprisonment.

21 In St Lucia, each district has a 'district court' that has both civil and criminal jurisdiction – s 4 District Courts Act Chap. 2:02. The magistrate is the sole presiding officer of each court – s 5 District Courts Act Chap. 2:02. In Jamaica, by virtue of Act No 6 of 2016, The Judicature (Resident Magistrates) Act has been re-named The Judicature (Parish Courts) Act. Under the new act, 'resident magistrates' are now called 'Judges of the Parish Court' and they have the jurisdiction to hear offences committed within the parish and one mile beyond.

22 *R v Horseferry Road Magistrates' Court ex p K* (1996) 160 JP 441, p 447.

magistrate (or justices as they were originally termed when sitting as a body of two or three) derives his powers purely from the enabling Act. The justices of Colchester in that case were held to have no power to convict for an offence committed in Kirkby Stephen, as the enabling Act did not permit this. In contrast, in *Cullen v Trimble* (1872) LR 7 QB 4, it was held, on a challenge to the jurisdiction of justices to summarily convict for exposing a diseased animal in a public place, that the Contagious Diseases (Animals) Act 1870 did confer this jurisdiction, although impliedly.

In *Agard v Assistant Superintendent of Police* (1964) 7 WIR 245, the Court of Appeal of the Windward and Leeward Islands considered an appeal against a magistrate's award of compensation in an assault case from Montserrat. The Court of Appeal held that the magistrate had no jurisdiction to award compensation on his own initiative as the empowering s 102A of the Magistrate's Code of Procedure Act only provided for award of compensation 'upon the application of the person aggrieved'. Since the victim had made no such application, the magistrate had acted ultra vires his statutory powers and so the award could not stand.

In Commonwealth Caribbean jurisdictions in general, magistrates and not justices[23] sit in the magistrates' courts. The magistrate is usually a trained lawyer and he sits as a one person tribunal, unlike justices in England. A magistrate is the judge of both fact and law in the summary courts.[24]

Lay magistrates

In 2009 Act No 25, the Summary Jurisdiction (Lay Magistrates) Act, was passed in Guyana creating lay magistrates' courts. A lay magistrate need not be a lawyer and qualifies for appointment if he is a fit and proper person with at least seven years' experience in a senior position in the public or private sector. The lay magistrate is assisted by a Clerk, appointed by the Chancellor, who advises him on the law and practice and procedure. Such a magistrate may not impose custodial sentences and is limited to imposing fines to a maximum of $10,000 (Guyanese dollars). The Act provides that the focus of the court is to promote reconciliation and encourage and facilitate the settlement of offences of 'a personal or private nature not amounting to a felony'.

The effectiveness of this system of lay magistrates in Guyana is, as yet, undetermined.

Districts

Most Commonwealth Caribbean countries are divided into magisterial districts by statute for the purpose of administering justice in the lower courts. The districts are those specified in the relevant summary procedure legislation. The number of districts obviously will depend on the size and population of the country so that St Kitts and Nevis has only three districts whereas Trinidad and Tobago has 12 magisterial districts. A magistrate only has jurisdiction

23 In Jamaica, there is separate statute creating the Justice of the Peace courts in the Justice of the Peace Jurisdiction Act and the Parish Courts in the Judicature (Parish Courts) Act. However, the Judge of the Parish Court has all the powers of a Justice of the Peace and in practice he exercises both jurisdictions. A judge of the Parish Court enjoys all the powers of a regular magistrate in the rest of the region, but may also try certain matters on indictment. Justices of the Peace still sit in the petty sessions to try very trivial matters.

24 As stated in *Peters v Peters* (1969) 14 WIR 457.

over cases which occur in the district in which he is sitting: *D'Oliviera, Comptroller of Customs and Excise v Chase* (1964) 7 WIR 18, unless statute provides otherwise.

In *D'Oliviera,* the Guyana Court of Appeal was emphatic that where a complaint alleges an offence in one judicial district, a magistrate of another judicial district has no jurisdiction to hear the complaint. This is so even though the evidence might disclose that the offence arose in the trial magistrate's district. In that case the complaint asserted that the defendants sold intoxicating liquor in the Blygezight, East Coast Demerara in the East Demerara judicial district. The matter was, however, laid before the magistrate in the Georgetown judicial district. In the course of the evidence it was given that Blygezight was in fact in the Georgetown district. The court upheld the magistrate's dismissal of the case on the basis that he had no jurisdiction to hear the case since the evidence was inconsistent with the allegation on the complaint. Furthermore, there could be no amendment of the complaint as this was an offence that required the consent of the Director of Public Prosecutions. While there had been consent to prosecute an offence committed in the East Demerara district, there was no such consent for the prosecution in the Georgetown district.

Section 10 of the Summary Jurisdiction (Magistrates) Act, Cap 3:05 of Guyana provides:

> Subject to any limitation of his jurisdiction under section 8, a magistrate may exercise and administer all jurisdiction and powers of a magistrates' court in any court within the area of Guyana to which he is appointed.

Having regard to *D'Oliviera,* this provision at least means that a magistrate has no jurisdiction to try cases arising out of other districts than that to which he is assigned. But can he be asked to sit in another district and try cases? The question arose in the Bahamas, where there is similar provision to the Guyana law in s 3(4) of the Magistrates Act, Ch 42. This section, in fact, is more emphatic in limiting jurisdiction to the magistrate of a particular district: 'The jurisdiction conferred on a magistrate by this or any other Act shall ... be exercised by him solely within his district'. The question came up for consideration in *Johnson v R* (1990) 56 WIR 23. In that case it was argued that a magistrate's jurisdiction (in the Bahamas) was limited to the jurisdiction to which he is assigned. The Bahamas Court of Appeal held that s 3(4) must be read in the light of s 12 of the Magistrates Act, which provided that any person appointed as a magistrate shall be a magistrate for 'the whole of the Bahamas'. Thus, a magistrate's jurisdiction is not limited to the district to which he is appointed. It seems that such a magistrate may be asked to sit in another district without having been assigned to that district.

Section 13 of the Barbados Magistrates' Courts Act is also quite specific in restricting jurisdiction of the magistrate to his district. That section stipulates that a magistrate has jurisdiction to try all summary offences committed within the district/s to which he is assigned. It seems based on *Johnson* (above) that this does not mean that he cannot be asked to sit in another district. However, while sitting in the district he may not try cases originating in another district. In contrast, the law[25] in Dominica and St Vincent specifically permits a magistrate sitting in any district to try matters committed in any part of the country. This is subject to the discretion of the court to transfer the case to the appropriate district if it finds it appropriate to do so.

On the question of evidence to establish local jurisdiction, it has been held that it is not necessary for a formal statement to be made in testimony that the locality of the offence is

25 Dominica: Magistrate's Code of Procedure Act, Chap 4:20, s 202(1) and (5); St Vincent: Magistrates Act, Cap 30, s 6(1).

'within this or that magisterial district': *Ram v Ramdass* (1975) 22 WIR 242.[26] The Guyana Court of Appeal chastised the presiding magistrate for allowing the prosecution to put words into the mouth of the 12-year-old victim to the effect that the offence took place in 'the East Demerara Magisterial District'. Instead, the court held that proof of locality required no set of formal words and could be established inferentially. Once evidence emerges that the matter is one within the magistrates' jurisdiction that is sufficient.

Districts and courts

It is important to note that there is a difference between a magisterial district and a magistrates' court. One district may have several courts: *Mark v Alexis* (1984) MA 123/84 (unreported), a magisterial appeal of Trinidad and Tobago. In this case the police appealed against the dismissal of a complaint by a magistrate. The latter ruled that the evidence before him disclosed that the offence was alleged to have been committed in Point Fortin, whereas the charge was brought in the Siparia magistrates' court. He stated that it should have been brought in the La Brea court where Point Fortin matters were usually heard. The Court of Appeal allowed the appeal holding that the magistrate's decision was misconceived since both courts, though located in different places, belonged to one magisterial district, that of Saint Patrick, as was specified in the Magisterial Districts Order made under the Summary Courts Act. In fact, in Trinidad and Tobago there were (at that time) 21 court locations in the then 12[27] districts.

In discussing *Mark v Alexis*, it would be remiss to fail to mention another point made by Warner J in that case, since it goes against the grain of the basic principles of the limits of local jurisdiction. In considering the argument that the matter was before the wrong court, he referred to the Summary Courts Act of Trinidad and Tobago, Chap 4:20. Section 8 of that Act provides:

> (1) The Chief Justice may assign one or more magistrates to a district or may assign a magistrate to more than one district.
> (2) Where more than one magistrate is assigned to a district each such magistrate shall exercise concurrent jurisdiction in that district with the other or others so assigned.
> (3) Every magistrate wherever assigned shall have jurisdiction throughout Trinidad and Tobago.

The judge considered that these words meant that where a complaint arose in one district but was brought before a magistrate in another district 'that magistrate would have jurisdiction, being a magistrate for the whole of Trinidad and Tobago'.[28] This statement seems to have been made without due consideration of the purpose of the section. It relates to assignment of magistrates to districts and the statement that a magistrate has jurisdiction 'throughout the country' should not be taken to mean without more that he can try any offence committed in any part of the country in any court. It simply means that a magistrate can be assigned[29] to any court/district from day to day. Were it otherwise, there would be

26 (1975) WIR 242, p 244.
27 There are now 13 districts.
28 *Mark v Alexis* (1984) MA 123/84 (unreported), p 3.
29 This is in effect what was held by the Bahamas Court of Appeal in *Johnson v R* (1990) 56 WIR 23.

no rationale behind the various provisions for transfer of cases from one magisterial district to another such as in s 56 of the Trinidad and Tobago Summary Courts Act, Chap 4:20:

> If upon the hearing of any complaint, it appears that the cause of complaint arose out of the limits of the district of the magistrate before whom such complaint has been made, the Court may direct the case to be transferred to the Court of the district wherein the cause of the complaint arose.

Thus, despite the judge's suggestion to the contrary in *Mark v Alexis* (above) it is suggested that the section does not confer on the magistrate a choice as to whether he can hear the case himself or transfer it to the correct district. If this were so, the section would have clearly so stated, as do the provisions of the Dominica and St Vincent statutes referred to above. It has been emphasised time and again that a magistrate's jurisdiction is stipulated and limited by statute, so if any particular power is to be conferred on him it is reasonable to presume that statute would have made this clear. The only discretion the magistrate could have possibly had in not transferring a case originating outside of his district then would be to dismiss it as was done in *D'Oliviera* (above).

It seems clear that if a magistrate purports to try a case outside his magisterial district, he acts without jurisdiction unless statute specifically permits otherwise, and the proceedings constitute a nullity. This is why the summary procedure legislation provides for transfer of cases and why magistrates in the Commonwealth Caribbean, even Trinidad and Tobago (despite *Mark v Alexis*), continue to ensure that the cases on their lists fall within the district in which they are actually sitting. Thus, if a complaint with regard to an offence allegedly committed in District A comes before the magistrate sitting in District B, he will transfer the case to the magistrates' court in District A.

Boundary

Where an offence is committed in two districts (a continuing offence), both districts will have jurisdiction. This general principle is contained in summary courts legislation of statutes in some countries[30] such as Dominica and Barbados. Even where such a provision is not encapsulated in statute, as it is not in Trinidad and Tobago, it is a basic rule of practice since the offence was committed in both districts. In such cases, the case will be heard in whichever district it is more convenient to so hear, having regard to the evidence and the witnesses.

It is a basic rule of law that one court cannot continue a matter begun by another. If a magistrate is transferred to another district, he must return to his previous district to complete any 'part heards' that he may have. Another magistrate cannot simply continue the matter, since the latter will not have heard all the evidence; this point was clearly brought home in *Pierre Simon Andre Sip Heng Wong Ng (alias Wong) et al. v R* [1987] 1 WLR 1356, PC. Similarly, if a magistrate retires or resigns from the bench, he may not continue a matter begun before he left even if he is subsequently reappointed: *Frederick v Chief of Police* (1968) 11 WIR 330.

The facts in *Frederick* were that a magistrate was appointed in Grenada to act as magistrate. He had begun hearing a case in June 1966 that he was unable to complete

30 Barbados: Magistrates' Courts Act 1996–27, s 14; Dominica: Magistrate's Code of Procedure Act, Chap 4:20, s 202(5) (c).

before his acting appointment was terminated. He was subsequently reappointed in December of that year as an additional magistrate to complete his 'part heard' cases in accordance with s 9(1)(e) of the Magistrates Act, Cap 177. Despite a submission by counsel for the defendant that the case should be begun de novo because he had become functus officio, the magistrate continued the matter and convicted the defendant. On appeal, it was held that the magistrate had become functus officio when his acting appointment was terminated and this was not cured by his subsequent reappointment. The reappointment did not confer on him any authority to resume the hearing of the case at the stage where it had been left incomplete in June 1966.

Committal proceedings

The issue arose in Trinidad and Tobago as to an enquiring magistrate's jurisdiction, during the course of an enquiry into certain offences, to hear evidence in relation to charges laid in another magisterial district. In *Application No 2 of 2008, In the matter of section 36(1) of the Supreme Court of Judicature Act* [judgment delivered on 16 January 2009] the DPP applied to the Court of Appeal, under a special provision of the Supreme Court of Justice Act permitting such a review, to review a magistrate's ruling that the prosecution, in adducing evidence in a preliminary enquiry into six charges against one FK, should confine itself to matters before the court and not lead evidence relating to five other charges against the accused, laid in other magisterial districts.

In holding that the magistrate was in error the Court of Appeal said, inter alia, that the Indictable Offences (Preliminary Enquiry) Act permitted an enquiring magistrate to hear matters wherever committed in Trinidad and Tobago. The legislation did not fetter the jurisdiction of a magistrate. Implicit in the judgment was the recognition that the division into magisterial districts in the Summary Courts Act was for jurisdictional purposes applicable to summary proceedings only. This did not constrain enquiring magistrates.

High Court/Supreme Court

In most of the countries of the Commonwealth Caribbean, there is only one High Court,[31] or Supreme Court as it is called in some jurisdictions. There is thus little problem with respect to locality in these jurisdictions. Thus in Barbados there is one High Court venue in which the Assizes are held regularly, although there may be more than one criminal court sitting at a time. The same is true of the Bahamas Supreme Court. In the smaller countries of the Eastern Caribbean States, there is not only one High Court, but the Assize sittings are in sessions which are not always continuous. The number of sessions is determined at the beginning of the court year. In some of these States, the sessions might be short and there might be perhaps only two per year. In others there may be several sessions which run over most of the year. The size of the country and the number of indictable trials listed will determine how often Assize sessions are held.

In Guyana, Jamaica and Trinidad and Tobago there are at least two localities in which the Assizes are held. In other words, Assizes are held at the same time in different court

31 Throughout this book 'High Court' will be used to describe the criminal court of first instance of the superior courts, although it may be referred to as Supreme Court or Circuit Court in some jurisdictions.

localities. In Jamaica, the Kingston Assizes are held daily and there are several Assize Courts sitting at the same time. There are also the Circuit Courts, where sessions are held in different parts of Jamaica at different times. In Trinidad and Tobago there are at least two permanent venues in which Assize Courts sit daily. These are in the two largest cities: Port of Spain and San Fernando. In Port of Spain, there are at least five such courts and in San Fernando, there are three.

As in the magistrates' courts it is expected that matters will be listed in the appropriate High Court locality in these countries. Unlike in the magistrates' courts, however, if a matter is fixed in one locality and it is felt that it would be preferable for the matter to be tried in another court locality because of possible bias of potential jurors, a judge may, on the application of either side, transfer the matter. This power stems from the inherent jurisdiction of a judge to ensure a fair trial[32] and it also can now be found in statute. In Trinidad and Tobago, it is not uncommon for murder trials from Tobago to be transferred for hearing to Trinidad upon assertions of possible bias against the defendant resulting from prejudice in the smaller community of Tobago.[33]

STATUTORY LIMITATION

It is a general rule of law and practice that there is no statutory limitation for prosecution of indictable offences. The rationale is that they are so serious that it would be against the public interest to allow a serious crime, which may have simply escaped detection or where the evidence was difficult to find, to go unpunished because a certain time period has elapsed from the date of its commission. Thus it is not uncommon to hear a statement such as 'the statute of limitations does not apply to murder'. While there may frequently be no specific statute of limitations today, there are provisions limiting prosecution by time, but they usually only apply to summary offences or where statute has specifically provided for this, as sometimes in the case of offences in relation to false tax claims. A person who is the subject of a very late prosecution on an indictable charge may nevertheless assert abuse of process of the court in trying him, but he must prove prejudice.[34]

Summary offences

For summary offences, statute provides that there is a specific time period within which a charge must be instituted. If the charge is laid outside that time period, then the court has no jurisdiction to hear it. In *R v The Network Sites Ltd ex p London Borough of Havering* (1997) CLR 595, the English courts had to deal with such an argument. The facts were that an offence was alleged to have been committed on 24 February 1995, but the valid information charging the summary offence was only laid on 28 September 1995 (two previous defective informations had been withdrawn), more than six months after the alleged offence had been committed. The appellant was convicted on this information, but appealed. It was held on appeal that the information was clearly out of time and statute-barred.

32 Discussed in *Nankissoon Boodram et al. v The State* [1996] 2 WLR 464, PC as an option open to the court on allegations of pre-trial publicity.

33 Tobago's population is less than one-twelfth of the over 1.2 million people in Trinidad.

34 This area is considered in Chapter 2.

In the Commonwealth Caribbean, the period of statutory limitation for prosecution of summary offences varies among the countries. In Grenada, s 69 of the Criminal Procedure Code, Cap 72B specifies that where there is no time specifically limited for making a statutory complaint for a summary offence, the complaint[35] must be laid within three months of the time when the matter arose. Larceny and kindred offences are, however, excepted and instead, six months is the limitation period specified for the prosecution of these summary offences. Similarly, in Trinidad and Tobago a special limitation period applies for larceny and kindred offences of a summary nature, but this exception is not stated in the general limitation provision, but is instead contained in the charging Act, the Summary Offences Act.[36] This is an example of where time is specifically limited for making a complaint and that time is 12 months. Otherwise, in Trinidad and Tobago the statutory time limit for laying summary charges is as provided in s 33(2) of the Summary Courts Act:

> (2) In every case where no time is specially limited for the making of a complaint for a summary offence in the Act relating to such an offence, the complaint shall be made within six months from the time when the matter of the complaint arose and not after.

In most other jurisdictions[37] the general limitation time for summary prosecution is, likewise, six months.

The Bahamas has amended s 213 of its Criminal Procedure Code by Act No 5 of 2011 to provide for the six month limitation time period to begin after the arrival of the vessel at the port of discharge in the Bahamas, where the offence in question is alleged to have occurred upon a vessel in the High Seas. This is undoubtedly in recognition of the fact that the country is a port of call to numerous cruise ships.

In St Vincent, the period of limitation for all offences where the punishment is 'only by fine or imprisonment for six months or less' is, except if a longer time is specifically provided, 12 months[38] from the date the matter arose or when it came to the knowledge of a competent complainant. This last qualification is not duplicated in the other territories, thus making the St Vincent legislation on statutory limitations the widest possible. It would mean that a summary offence, if committed against a child or otherwise incapacitated person, could still be prosecuted outside the limitation time if it was brought to the attention of a 'competent' complainant such as a parent after 12 months from the date of the incident.

In *Finbar Gangar v Her Worship Ejenny Espinet* [2008] UKPC 48, the Privy Council had to determine whether the limitation period of six months in s 33(2) of the Summary Courts Act applied to the Integrity in Public Life Act 2000 of Trinidad and Tobago where there was no time specified for the laying of a charge under that Act. In holding that it did not, the Privy Council considered ss 2 and 67 of the Interpretation Act. The latter section provided that where a written law declares an offence punishable on summary conviction the applicable procedure in trial or punishment of that offence was in accordance with the Summary

35 The terms 'complaint' and 'information' are used interchangeably in the Commonwealth Caribbean and both refer to the document laid before the court which contains the statement and particulars of a summary charge, or an indictable charge initiated in the magistrates' court.

36 Section 42 of Chap 11:02.

37 Antigua: Magistrate's Code of Procedure Act, Cap 255, s 75; Bahamas: Criminal Procedure Code, Ch 91, s 213; Barbados: Magistrates' Courts Act 1996, s 217(1); Dominica: Magistrate's Code of Procedure Act, Chap 4:20, s 68; Guyana: Summary Jurisdiction (Procedure) Act, Cap 10:02, s 6; Jamaica: Justice of the Peace (Jurisdiction) Act, s 10; St Kitts and Nevis: Magistrate's Code of Procedure Act, Cap 3.17, s 76; St Lucia: Criminal Code 2004, s 671.

38 St Vincent Criminal Code, Cap 172, s 137.

Courts Act. Section 2 of the Interpretation Act, however, provided that the Interpretation Act applied 'unless a contrary intention appears'. The Privy Council considered that it was clear that Parliament's intention was contrary to applying a time limit of only six months given that Parliament had amended the same Act to allow for inquiries into breaches of the Act to be made at any time. Parliament's aim, as the first instance judge [Bereaux J] had concluded, was to strengthen the legislation. Their Lordships endorsed his finding that no time limit applied in respect of offences under the 2000 Act.

This case makes it clear that courts will not simply enforce a generic statutory limitation period where no period is specified in the relevant charging legislation. They will consider the purpose of the law and the likely intention of Parliament where imposition of a standard limitation will make the legislation unworkable.

Counting the time

The Interpretation Act in most jurisdictions specifies how time should be calculated. The first day, that is, the date of the alleged offence, is not counted. The position is the same at common law, as was made clear in *Radcliffe v Bartholomew* [1892] 1 QB 102. In *Cross v John* (1964) 7 WIR 359, it was held by the Trinidad and Tobago Court of Appeal that an amendment of a defective complaint could be made outside of the limitation period. The charge as originally laid initiated the criminal proceedings and as this fell within the statutory period of six months, the proceedings were not statute-barred. The amendment did not create a new complaint.

If the offence is a continuing one, the statutory limitation does not generally apply, as it is considered that as long as the offence continues, it is repeated from day to day: *Rowley v TA Everton and Sons Ltd* [1940] 4 All ER 435. Therefore, in cases of regulatory offences, it is important to determine what is the offence. In *Rowley*, on appeal to the King's Bench Division from the magistrates' court, it was necessary for the court to determine if the offence charged was erection of dangerous machinery or failing to secure the machinery. If the former, then this would have been a finite offence committed on the day the machinery was installed, which would fall outside the limitation period. It was held that the offence was failing to fence the machinery properly and was a continuing offence as long as that circumstance existed. The proceedings were not statute-barred.

If a summary charge is laid within the statutory time, but the service of summons is delayed, it is possible for the defence to argue prejudice arising from abuse of process just as for indictable matters. It will not be possible to obtain dismissal of the case, since the matter is validly before the court, but the court can be urged to stay the matter.[39]

Indictable offences

Although there is no time limit for the laying of an indictable charge, if there is unusual delay in prosecution, the defence has the option to seek a stay on the basis that such delay will cause the defendant prejudice in defending the case. Abuse of process is an area of growing

39 See Chapter 2.

importance in the Commonwealth Caribbean in the trial of indictable matters in particular and thus justifies a chapter of its own.[40]

In any event, if there is an unusual delay in laying or prosecuting a charge, the judge ought to bring this to the attention of the jury and point out any possible resulting prejudice or unfairness to the defendant in the preparation of his defence: *DPP v Tokai* [1996] 3 WLR 149, p 157, PC. This is explored more fully in Chapter 2.

40 See Chapter 2.

CHAPTER 2

ABUSE OF PROCESS

It has been said that since early times, every court has had the inherent power to stay criminal proceedings on the basis that they are oppressive and constitute an abuse of its process.[1] The court effectively refuses jurisdiction in order to safeguard its own process from abuse. Despite this early recognition, it was not until *Connelly v DPP* [1964] AC 1254, HL that the discretion to stay proceedings was fully sanctioned with the House of Lords identifying the constituents of the plea of autrefois and the corresponding availability of a claim of abuse of process. Since then the concept has developed rapidly.[2] Although abuse of the process of the court should be raised as a preliminary issue, there is nothing to prevent it being raised during the trial. In fact in *R v Smolinski* [2004] 2 Cr App R 40, the English Court of Appeal suggested that the best time to make an application on the basis of delay should be after evidence is led so that a judge would be in a better position to assess whether it is unfair to try the defendant. However, a Court of Appeal will question it being raised for the first time on appeal.[3] On an abuse of process application the court, usually the court of trial, is asked to refuse to proceed with the case permanently and, if the application succeeds, it may make such an order, effectively blocking any further criminal proceedings in the matter.

Abuse of process defined

In *Connelly* (above), the House of Lords agreed that a court has a general power to safeguard itself from abuse of its process and a defendant from oppressive prosecution. An abuse of process was defined by the Privy Council as 'something so unfair and wrong that the court should not allow the prosecutor to proceed with what is in all other respects a regular proceeding'.[4] This power is wider than that of autrefois,[5] which relates to the allegation that a defendant has either been previously validly convicted or acquitted of the same or essentially the same offence and as such it would be unfair to retry him. This is really the rule against double jeopardy that was considered in detail in *Connelly*.

In *R v Beedie* [1997] 2 Cr App R 167, it was confirmed that if a plea of autrefois failed, a submission of abuse of process could nevertheless succeed, thus demonstrating that autrefois is narrower in scope than the doctrine of abuse of process. In that case, the defendant had been convicted for a summary offence under the Health and Safety at Work Act 1974 relating to a defectively installed gas fire. The Crown Prosecution Service subsequently prosecuted him for manslaughter, asserting the death of the victim and the same facts in the first charge. It was held on appeal that while the second charge was not based on exactly the same facts as the first, it would be an abuse of process to proceed when the accused person had already been convicted for an offence involving the defective state of the gas meter which had, in fact, caused the death that was the subject of the second charge.

---

1 Earl of Selbourne LC in *Metropolitan Bank Ltd v Pooley* [1885] 10 AC 210, p 214.

2 See analysis of Pattenden, R, 'Abuse of process in criminal litigation' (1990) JCL 341.

3 Per Lord Slynn in *Charles, Carter and Carter v the State* (1999) 54 WIR 455, PC, p 459.

4 Per Lord Lowry in *Hui Chi-Ming v R* [1992] 1 AC 34, PC.

5 This plea in bar is considered in Chapter 6.

In *DPP v Humphreys* [1977] AC 1, HL, the majority of the House of Lords, while emphasising that issue estoppel had no place in criminal proceedings, nevertheless confirmed that a trial judge has a discretion to prevent a prosecution if continuing it would be an abuse of the process of the court. Since then, there have been numerous cases in which the issue has been raised and this has led to the law in this area finally being defined with some clarity in the last 20 years (of the twentieth century).

The basic principle

The power of the court to stop a prosecution for abuse of its process arises in two categories of cases. They are:

- where it will be impossible to give the accused a fair trial;
- where it offends the court's sense of justice and propriety to be asked to try the accused in the particular circumstances of the case.

These are now the bedrock principles of abuse of process clearly enunciated in *R v Maxwell* [2010] UKSC 48 para 13).

In *Warren et al. v AG of the Bailiwick of Jersey* [2011] UKPC 10 the Privy Council emphasised that the two categories are distinct and should be considered separately. In the first category of case the court will stay the proceedings without more if it concludes that the defendant cannot receive a fair trial. In the second category the court is concerned to protect the integrity of the criminal justice system. Here a stay will be granted if the court concludes that in all the circumstances a trial will 'offend the court's sense of fairness and propriety' (*Bennett v Horseferry Road Magistrates' Court ex p Bennett* [1993] 3 All ER 138) or will undermine public confidence in the criminal justice system or bring it into disrepute (*R v Latif and Shahzad* [1996] 2 Cr App R 92, HL): Lord Dyson in *Maxwell*, para 13.

WHERE A FAIR TRIAL IS IMPOSSIBLE

The early cases which focussed on this issue were *R v Derby Crown Court ex p Brooks* (1985) 80 Cr App R 164, a decision of the English Divisional Court which was later followed by the Court of Appeal in *AG's Reference* (No 1 of 1990) (1992) 95 Cr App R 296 with a qualification as to the burden of proof. It should be for the defendant to show prejudice, especially where he alleges delay. Subsequently, the Privy Council in *Tan v Cameron* [1993] 2 All ER 493, PC approved the principles set out in *AG's Reference* (No 1 of 1990) (above).

Delay

Delay has been the most oft-cited ground in the Commonwealth Caribbean when asking the courts to invoke its power to stay proceedings for abuse of process. For that reason, it will be considered first. The leading cases are *Bell v DPP* (1985) 32 WIR 317, PC, *Tan v Cameron* (above), *DPP v Tokai* (1996) 48 WIR 376, PC, *Charles, Carter and Carter v The State* (1999) 54 WIR 455, PC, *Flowers v R* [2000] 1 WLR 2396, PC and *Prakash Boolell v The State* [2006] UKPC 46, all decisions of the Privy Council. In *Tapper v DPP* [2012] UKPC 26 the Board affirmed that the law on delay as summarised in *Boolell* (above) represents the law in Jamaica. By extension this would apply to the Commonwealth Caribbean. The Caribbean Court of

Justice considered the issue of delay in the appeal process in *Singh v Harrychan* [2016] CCJ 12 (AJ) and *Vishnu Bridgelall v Hardat Hariprashad* [2017] CCJ 8 (AJ).

Bell v DPP

In *Bell* (above), the applicant brought a constitutional motion against the DPP seeking a declaration that his right to a fair trial within a reasonable time, guaranteed under s 20(1) of the Jamaica Constitution, would be infringed by a prosecution in 1982 for offences allegedly committed in 1977. The Privy Council stated that, in determining if the defendant's right to a fair trial had been infringed, a court had to take into account the problems affecting the administration of justice in Jamaica; the length of the delay; the reasons put forward by the prosecution for the delay; and the prejudice to the accused person, among other factors.

The application was granted on the basis that when a retrial was ordered, delay would be less tolerated than the delay between arrest and trial. It was held that on the facts of *Bell*, the delay in seeking to prosecute the case in 1982, after an order for retrial made in 1979, was unfair. Although the defendant did not cite evidence of specific prejudice as a result of the delay, this did not mean that prejudice should be discounted.

Although *Bell* was decided on the basis of a breach of a fundamental rights provision in the Jamaican Constitution, its importance lies in the fact that it was then virtually unprecedented in the Commonwealth Caribbean for criminal proceedings to be stayed by reason of delay in prosecution. In addition, the Privy Council emphasised per curiam that apart from the Constitution, the common law of England prior to independence (which is applicable in criminal proceedings in the Commonwealth Caribbean) was not powerless to provide a remedy against unreasonable delay before trial. In other words, it was not necessary to rely on a constitutional right to seek to stay proceedings for delay in prosecution.

Specific prejudice/fair trial

The presumption of prejudice from the mere fact of delay alluded to in *Bell* was discounted in *AG's Reference* (above). In this case, the English Court of Appeal held that the jurisdiction to stay criminal proceedings on the ground of delay was exceptional even when it could be said that the delay was unjustifiable. Furthermore, such jurisdiction should rarely be exercised in the absence of fault on the part of the prosecution or its agents and should never be exercised if the delay was owing to the complexity of the case or at least contributed to by the actions of the defendant himself.

In *AG's Reference* (above) it was made clear that, contrary to what was said in *Bell*, it was for the defendant to show that he would suffer serious prejudice to the extent that no fair trial would be possible owing to the delay, so that the continuation of the prosecution amounted to an abuse of process. In *Tan* (above), the Privy Council, in applying *AG's Reference*, considered that it was unnecessary to refer to the burden of proof other than to stress that a heavy burden always rests on a defendant who seeks a stay on the grounds of delay. The court indicated that the essential question to be determined was whether, in all the circumstances, the delay was such as to make the prosecution unfair.

Following *AG's Reference* and *Tan*, the test to determine whether a prosecution should be stayed on the basis of delay has become much simpler and thus more certain in its application: can the defendant still obtain a fair trial?

In *Sieuraj Sookermany v DPP et al.* (1996) 48 WIR 346, the Trinidad and Tobago Court of Appeal considered an appeal in a constitutional motion in which the applicant sought a permanent stay of criminal proceedings for murder on the ground of delay that his right to a trial within a reasonable time was breached. S was charged in 1985 for the murder of his wife. At a preliminary inquiry held some months later, he was committed to stand trial for manslaughter (in 1986) and released on bail. Some years later, the DPP indicted S for murder and he was then rearrested in September 1993, after which the motion was brought. The appellant did not claim specific prejudice by the delay and he had been held in custody for only five months before his case was first listed for trial in the Assizes. The delay between his committal and the issue of the indictment was not atypical of the delays then current in Trinidad and Tobago.[6]

The Court of Appeal, while implicitly acknowledging the right of an accused person to be tried within reasonable time, indicated that such a right must be balanced against the public interest in having him tried. The court, in performing the balancing exercise, must take into account:

- the prevailing system of legal administration;
- the prevailing economic, social and cultural conditions; and
- the scarcity of financial resources.

The Court of Appeal followed *AG's Reference* and *Tan* in holding that even where delay was unjustifiable, a court should only in exceptional circumstances grant a stay on the basis of delay.

Constitutional issue or trial court

Immediately after the decision in *Sookermany*, the Privy Council had to consider the appeal in the matter of one Jaikaran Tokai. It was an appeal from a decision of the very Court of Appeal in a constitutional motion seeking a stay on the basis of delay which was said to constitute a breach of the appellant's right to a fair trial: *DPP v Tokai* (1996) 48 WIR 376, PC. The respondent, Tokai, in that case had been charged in 1982 for wounding with intent, but only committed to stand trial in 1986. He was in fact not indicted until February 1994, following which he brought the motion. The Privy Council, in reversing the decision of the Court of Appeal, held that where there is no express right to a speedy trial or trial within a reasonable time guaranteed in the Constitution, common law principles would be applicable in determining whether a trial was unfair. As such, it was for the trial judge (in the criminal courts) to decide whether criminal proceedings should be stayed, and not a court in constitutional proceedings. Only if the chance of a fair trial was totally destroyed would application to the High Court for constitutional relief on the basis of delay be entertained.

In Trinidad and Tobago, an application for a stay of prosecution on the basis of delay should be made before the trial court. The argument ought to be grounded on 'the discretionary power of the court to ensure that there should be a fair trial according to law, which involves fairness to both the defendant and to the prosecution'.[7] In respect of other jurisdictions where there does exist the constitutional right to a speedy trial, the Privy

6 In the Annual Report of the Judiciary of Trinidad and Tobago for the 1999–2000 law term (pp 46–47) it is claimed that the office of the Director of Public Prosecutions (DPP) is now able to maintain a record of two months for the time taken between the receipt of depositions from the magistrates' courts to the filing of an indictment in the High Court registry.

7 *AG's Reference* (No 1 of 1990) [1992] QB 630, Lord Lane, pp 641–42, cited with approval by the Privy Council in *DPP v Tokai* (1996) 48 WIR 376, PC.

Council had this to say: 'The ... right may be invoked by constitutional motion in advance of any trial'. The Privy Council, in a considered judgment in which all the leading English and Commonwealth Caribbean authorities were analysed, stated that:

The difference between the common law position and that where there is an express constitutional right to trial without undue delay or within a reasonable time, is that in the latter case complaint by way of constitutional motion can more readily be regarded as the appropriate remedy.

It is evident, then, that the Privy Council felt that there was no difference between the law on the impact of delay on a fair trial in the jurisdictions like Jamaica with express constitutional provisions for trial within a reasonable time and those like Trinidad and Tobago with none. It is merely the remedy that may be different. In other words, the same principles in deciding whether the accused suffered such prejudice as to render his trial an abuse of process will apply.[8] In considering the decision in *Bell* (above), the Privy Council said in *Tokai*: 'It may well be in similar circumstances that retrial of an accused person in Trinidad would not constitute a fair trial and that a stay would therefore be appropriate' (which was what was held in *Bell*).

The consequences of the decision in *Tokai* is that in jurisdictions such as Jamaica, it would not be inappropriate to come by way of constitutional motion to seek to secure a fair trial and prevent abuse of process by reason of delay. Where there is no specific constitutional right, but only a common law right to a trial within a reasonable time, it would be for the trial judge to take measures to protect common law rights such as the right to a fair trial. Such measures might even include the ordering of a stay in accordance with the principles of *AG's Reference* (above) or more usually the giving of special directions by the trial judge on the possible prejudicial effects of the delay.

Directions on delay

In *R v Hickson* [1997] Crim LR 494, the English Court of Appeal held that where specific aspects of disadvantage caused by delay had been raised by the defence, it was incumbent on the trial judge (if he did not grant a stay) to remind the jury of this and to point out the particular difficulties of which the defence complained. This was especially important if the defendant could not be expected to remember or was unable to recall what he was doing at a particular time. Similarly, where a constitutional motion made on the basis of denial of a fair trial because of delay is unsuccessful, it would be the duty of the trial judge to direct the jury accordingly.

In *Charles, Carter and Carter v The State* (1999) 54 WIR 455, PC, the Privy Council deplored the failure of the trial judge, after refusing to grant a stay, to give any assistance to the defence to counter the difficulties caused by the delay which had been 'considerable and disturbing'. In that case, the judge refused an application from the defence to be supplied with notes from a previous trial saying, somewhat inflexibly, that he was not concerned with any previous trial. In addition, the judge neglected to direct the jury on the specific prejudice which could accrue to accused persons who were being tried some nine years after the incident in respect of which they were charged with murder. This was in circumstances where, on the face of it, the delay was so great that even having regard to the public interest

8 De la Bastide CJ did, however, suggest in *Sookermany* (above) that where the right to a fair trial within reasonable time is expressly guaranteed by constitutional provisions, some limit might be imposed on the extent to which delays caused by inadequate resources could be relied on.

in convicting the guilty, it became 'an abuse of process and unacceptable for a prosecution to continue'.

In *Charles* (above), the deceased was shot dead in July 1987 and the appellants were arrested for murder on the following day. From that time until the Privy Council allowed their appeals in May 1999, they were in custody. They were committed to stand trial in 1988 but were first tried in November–December 1991. They were convicted, but their convictions were quashed in June 1994. They were retried in April 1995 but the jury failed to agree and, although a retrial was then ordered, it was not until September 1996 that the appellants had their third trial. It was in these circumstances that the Privy Council said that the delay was so considerable and disturbing that it would be unacceptable for the prosecution to continue.

It should be emphasised that in *Sookermany* (above), although the length of the delay was similar, the defendant was only in custody for a few months, first pending the preliminary inquiry and later, after the warrant of arrest was executed when the murder indictment was filed. He had not been prejudiced by the delay. Similarly, in *Tokai* (above), although the trial was delayed for an even longer time, the defendant was charged with wounding and was entitled to bail on that offence. In any event the issue in that matter was whether it was for the constitutional court or the trial court to make the decision of whether a stay should be granted in Trinidad and Tobago. In *Charles* (above) on the other hand, the application had come before the trial court and had been refused. Furthermore, in *Charles*, the court was also concerned with abuse of process arising from a third trial, a factor which was as equally relevant as delay in the decision to allow the appeal.

In the more recent case of *Flowers v R* [2000] 1 WLR 2396, PC, emanating from Jamaica, the Privy Council dismissed the argument made on behalf of the defence that the judge erred in failing to direct the jury on the significance of a delay of some seven years before the third trial. The Board stated that unlike *Charles*, there was no ossification of the evidence since the conflict between the police and the defendant was so stark that it was unlikely to be affected by the passage of the years.

The basic principles

In *Flowers* (above), the defence raised as a main ground of appeal the fact of the long delay in the trial of the defendant from April 1991, when he was arrested, to January 1997, when he was finally convicted. In two previous trials, the jury had failed to agree, the first being in December 1992.

In arriving at its decision, the Board considered its previous decisions from the Commonwealth Caribbean on the issue and dismissed the appeal, at the same time clarifying the following pertinent principles:

- In considering the defence submissions, the Board had to take into account the fact that no argument was advanced either at trial or at the Court of Appeal that the trial was an abuse of process on the basis of either delay or oppression. While in exceptional cases the Board would quash a conviction after earlier abortive trials on the grounds of delay or abuse of process, as in *Charles* (above), the failure to raise the issue previously must weigh against the defence.
- Issues relating to delay are matters for investigation by the local courts, more familiar with the conditions and problems existing in those jurisdictions. So submissions should first be raised at that level: *Bell v DPP* (above). The most serious aspect of prejudice to the defendant is the possibility that the defence will be unprepared. If the case is relatively straightforward, as this one, the possibility of prejudice is substantially discounted.

- The appellate court should take into consideration – if it is clear – from the facts, that the defendant is guilty of a very serious crime in deciding whether to quash a conviction merely because of delay.
- A Court of Appeal ought always to take into account any delay in the appellate process, which would deny the defendant the right to a trial within a reasonable time. Abuse of process was thus not successfully argued in *Flowers*. The Privy Council fully utilised the opportunity to set guidelines by which to determine arguments in the future, of abuse of process on the ground of delay.

The decisions of the Privy Council above, including *Flowers*, were considered by the Privy Council in *Prakash Boolell* [2006] UKPC 46, an appeal from Mauritius. This was a case where the appellant, a lawyer, had been charged in 1992 in respect of a 1990 transaction and was convicted only in March 2003. On his appeal before the Board the appellant relied on only one ground, breach of his constitutional right to a fair trial.

In considering the numerous cases on delay the Board approved the judgment of the House of Lords in *AG's Reference* (No 2 of 2001) 2003 UKHL 68 in which nine judges had deliberated; and stated that the resolution of the several issues on delay are to be found in that judgment. In that case the House endorsed a statement of a New Zealand court in *Martin v Tauranga District Council* [1995] 2 NZLR 419, 432: 'The right is to a fair trial without undue delay; it is not a right not to be tried after undue delay' in construing the constitutional right to be tried within a reasonable time. Lord Bingham confirmed, inter alia, that it would be inappropriate to stay or dismiss a prosecution unless (a) there can no longer be a fair hearing or (b) it would otherwise be unfair to try the defendant.

In *Boolell* the Board also endorsed the propositions material to determining the reasonableness of the time taken to complete the hearing in a criminal case, set out in the Scottish case of *Dyer v Watson* [2002] UKPC D1:

1. The first step is to consider the period of time which has elapsed. Unless that period is one which on its face and without more gives grounds for real concerns it is almost certainly unnecessary to go further.
2. The threshold to prove a breach of the reasonable time requirement is a high one not easily crossed.
3. If the period is one that on its face gives cause for concern then the court must look into the detailed facts and circumstances of the particular case including –
   (a) the complexity of the case
   (b) the conduct of the defence
   (c) the manner in which the case has been dealt with by the administrative and judicial authorities.

In *Tapper v DPP* (above) the Board affirmed that while the principles applied to post-conviction delay quashing a conviction is not a normal remedy, contrary to what was held in *Darmalingum v The State* [2000] 1 WLR 2303, PC, which significance as an authority has 'been reduced to almost vanishing point'.

In the Guyanese case of *Vishnu Bridgelal v Hardat Harriprashad* (above) the Caribbean Court of Justice (the CCJ) considered the issue of undue delay in the appeal process, where Article 144(1) of the Guyanese Constitution guaranteed the right to a fair hearing within a reasonable time. The State's appeal against the quashing of the appellant's conviction for trafficking cocaine was allowed by the Court of Appeal of Guyana six years and ten months after the grant of leave to appeal to the Court of Appeal and the appellant appealed to the CCJ. The court decided that the overall period of time that had elapsed (the appellant's case was before the courts for nearly ten years) was overly lengthy. The court held that the inadequacy of the administrative staffing of the Court of Appeal was not an acceptable excuse for what they considered to be clear breaches of the reasonable time guarantee. The appellant had already served half of his sentence so, as a remedy for the breach of his rights, the court stayed any further action against the appellant with respect to the enforcement of his prison sentence.

In the earlier case of *Singh v Harrychan* (above), the CCJ decided that the almost nine years that had elapsed between the incident leading to the defendant's charge and conviction, and proceedings in the CCJ, constituted unacceptable delay. The court ruled that the judicial system could not offer any justifiable explanation as to why preparation of the reasons for decision required three years and, furthermore, why a further 17 months was required to prepare the record and notify of its readiness. The CCJ noted that in cases of delay the appeal court could reduce the sentence or vacate a conviction. In the event, the appeal was brought by the State that the court could dismiss the appeal for want of prosecution.

Prejudicial pre-trial publicity

It may also be argued that a fair trial is no longer possible because of prejudicial pre-trial publicity and, as such, the proceedings should be stayed as an abuse of process. It is for the defendant to show on a balance of probabilities that it is impossible for him to have a fair trial.[9] In *R v Abu Hamza* [2007] 1 Cr App R 27 the English Court of Appeal held that the adverse publicity is not determinative of the issue. Once the trial judge concludes that a fair trial is possible with his assistance, and having regard to his experience and that of his fellow judges as to how juries perform their functions, including the fact that they usually abide by judicial directions on the issue,[10] a stay will not be granted.

It is very rare that a stay will be granted in respect of prejudicial pre-trial publicity having regard to the range of options open to the trial judge to ensure trial by an independent and impartial tribunal. These include an adjournment as a 'cooling off' period; challenges for cause to weed out jurors who may be prejudiced one way or the other; and directions that the judge himself may give to the jury.

Different considerations might apply when considering prejudicial publicity during the trial itself: *R v McCann* 92 Cr App R 239; *R v Taylor and Taylor* 98 Cr App R 361.

WHERE IT IS UNFAIR TO TRY THE DEFENDANT

It is now considered established that in the second category of cases where it offends the court's sense of justice and propriety to be asked to try the accused in the particular circumstances of the case the question of whether a fair trial is possible is not determinative. Even if a fair trial is possible the court may yet stay the trial.

In *Bennett v Horseferry Road Magistrates' Court ex p Bennett* [1993] 3 All ER 138, HL, the defendant claimed that he had been brought to England as a result of subterfuge and conspiracy between the English and South African police. He was to face a charge of

9 See Chapter 13 for further discussion on this issue.

10 See also Ruling by Mohammed J in *The State v Abu Bakr a/c Lennox Phillip* Cr No 75 of 2006 (unreported, Trinidad and Tobago).

obtaining a helicopter by deception in the English courts. He alleged that he was told that he was being repatriated to his country of citizenship, New Zealand, after he was arrested in South Africa, but was instead put on a flight via England simply to facilitate his arrest there. The Divisional Court held that it had no jurisdiction to inquire how the applicant came within the jurisdiction. In reversing this decision, the House of Lords held that it had jurisdiction so to inquire in order to maintain the rule of law. The House held that it was an abuse of process for a person to be forcibly brought into the jurisdiction in disregard of available existing procedures to face criminal charges. It was irrelevant that he could have a fair trial. Once there was evidence that there was a physical abduction of the defendant and prosecuting authorities were willing allies to the plan, any ensuing prosecution would fail. The public interest in the prosecution of crime would have to give way to the maintenance of the rule of law.

In *Beckford* [1996] 1 Cr App R 94 the English Court of Appeal following *Bennett* emphasised that that case had expanded the jurisdiction of the courts to protect its process from abuse: the court must consider whether in given circumstances it would be unfair to try the defendant.

In contrast to the decision in *Bennett*, the House of Lords in *R v Latif and Shahzad* [1996] 2 Cr App R 92, HL, came to a different conclusion on the facts of that case. It was held that the public interest in ensuring that those who are charged with committing grave crimes should be tried took precedence on the facts of that case. The House held that in the circumstances of the case where there was no abduction of the defendant to the jurisdiction (he came freely, although he was tricked into so doing), the integrity of the criminal justice system was not compromised. The court, in arriving at this conclusion, took into account the fact that the defendant had come into the jurisdiction to traffic heroin. Thus, it could not be said that the prosecution would be an affront to public conscience.

Latif set a limit to the decision in *Bennett* when the House stipulated the need for a balancing exercise between policy and justice considerations and suggested that in the absence of exceptional factors such as forcible abduction an application for a stay on the basis of abuse of process should be refused. In *Warren* (above) the Board of the Privy Council was faced with a situation where the crucial evidence on which the prosecution wished to rely had been obtained as a result of serious prosecutorial misconduct. The Board emphasised that fairness to the accused should not be the focus of this category of case. The particular circumstances of each case should be weighed carefully where there was a basis for concluding that the authorities had misconducted themselves. This involves a balancing exercise between the public interest in ensuring that those who are accused of serious crimes should be tried and the competing public interest in ensuring that executive misconduct does not undermine public confidence in the criminal justice system and bring it into disrepute. One of the considerations in engaging in this balance is whether the misconduct itself caused the defendant to act to his detriment. After considering all the factors that the Commissioner was entitled to consider, the Board in *Warren* actions held it could not find that his decision to refuse a stay was perverse.

Manipulation by the prosecution

The second ground cited in *Charles* (above), that it would be oppressive to try the defendant a third time, is an example of where it is contended that the prosecution have manipulated or misused the process of the court so as to deprive the defendant of the protection of the law or have otherwise acted unfairly. The appellants complained that it was wrong that they should be put on trial a third time after so many years in circumstances where one conviction had been quashed and one jury had failed to agree. The Privy Council held that, delay apart, it might be contrary to the principles of due process to allow the prosecution, having failed twice, to try to continue to secure a conviction. The appeal was thus allowed, and the convictions of the appellant quashed on the combination of this factor and the delay, the Board holding that the third trial should have been stayed by the trial judge at its commencement.

The decision in *Charles* on this point must be read in the light of the subsequent decision of the Privy Council in *Bowe v R* [2001] 58 WIR 1, PC. The Board considered that the English convention of not prosecuting a second retrial was not applicable to the Caribbean. Whether a second retrial should be permitted depends on a balance between the defendant's interests, whether his defence would be prejudiced, and the public interest in convicting the guilty. The overall consideration was whether a third trial would be oppressive and unjust.

It is apparent that the Board felt that in the circumstances of *Charles*, the prosecution had misused the process of the court. The situations in which a court may hold that the prosecution had misused/manipulated its process are not determinate. It goes without saying that there must be evidence of the actual misuse or manipulation of the process of the court.

In *Heron v DPP* (2000) 61 WIR 319 the Court of Appeal of Jamaica found that while the DPP had properly discontinued a charge of murder where three previous juries had failed to agree, an attempt to press for a fourth trial of offences based on the same incident amounted to an abuse of process. Having failed to achieve a conviction in the first two trials for murder the prosecution during the third trial then for the first time (four years later) filed an indictment for serious non-capital offences arising out of the same incident as the murder. They sought to proceed with them after the nolle prosequi had been filed. The Court of Appeal held that failure to prefer both indictments at the same time, contrary to the usual practice, and attempting to proceed with the second indictment after the accused had faced three trials for murder on the same facts amounted to oppressive conduct on the part of the prosecution.

The court does not take lightly any attempt to manipulate its process in order to secure a prosecution: *R v Brentford JJ ex p Wong* [1981] 1 QB 445. The court on a judicial review application was extremely scathing of the actions of the prosecution in laying an information only two days before the statutory limitation period of six months simply to gain time. The alleged offences had been committed on 30 January 1978 and informations for careless driving, inter alia, were laid on 28 July, although no decision to prosecute had actually been made. Such a decision was eventually made in October and a letter dated 28 October informed the applicant of the decision. Summonses were not served until December. On an application for prohibition, the court held that the actions of the prosecution amounted to a deliberate manipulation of the process of the court.

The question of abuse of process came up for consideration in *Nandlal v The State* (1995) 49 WIR 412, where the Trinidad and Tobago Court of Appeal castigated the actions of the Director of Public Prosecutions in bringing a second indictment against the appellant, in the circumstances of the case, as 'a clear affront to decency and fair play'. These may seem strong words, but the facts of the matter may have provided sufficient justification for them. A magistrate had solicited and received bribes of $440,000 and a motor car for the dismissal of three charges against the appellant. Both men had been indicted and convicted for corruption in respect of bribe by car when, 14 days after sentencing in that matter, the DPP served an indictment on them containing charges of conspiracy to pervert the course of justice and corruption in respect of the money bribe. Although the prosecution sought to argue that the charges were separate in that they related to dismissal of separate cases, the Court of Appeal was scathing in its dismissal of this argument since all the matters had proceeded on the basis that the money and the car constituted the 'full fee' for the dismissal of all the charges. They were all part of one transaction. The court, after considering all the leading authorities on abuse of process, in particular *Connelly v DPP* [1964] AC 1254, HL, held that it was a clear abuse of process to lay a second indictment in respect of offences that arose out of the same facts. The cases could have been joined in one indictment with one trial for each defendant, the court said.

It has been held that it will not always necessarily be an abuse of process to prosecute a person for an offence which could have been included in a previous indictment, in respect of which he was acquitted: *R v Southeast Hampshire Magistrates' Court ex p CPS* [1998] Crim LR 422. It depends on the fact situation, including whether the evidence is different or not. In *Nandlal,* not only had the appellant been convicted before of a related offence, but the evidence in both matters was essentially the same.

Promises not to prosecute

If the prosecution or their agents make an express or even an implied promise to a defendant not to prosecute and subsequently renege on the promise, a court may hold this to be an abuse of process if the defendant is induced to act on this promise to his detriment. In *R v Croydon JJ ex p Dean* [1993] 3 All ER 129, the applicant, a 17 year old, was arrested by the police in the course of a murder investigation and made certain admissions to the effect that he did certain acts with intent to impede the apprehension of another. He was later released on the basis that he would be a prosecution witness and would not be charged. He acted in accordance with that agreement in giving a statement to the police and assisting them otherwise. During the course of interviews which followed, the applicant was never told of a decision made by the prosecution to charge him with an offence consistent with his admissions. He was charged with the offence and committed for trial. On an application to stay the proceedings, it was held that the prosecution of a person who had received a representation that he would not be prosecuted could amount to an abuse of process. It was irrelevant that the police in this case did not have the power to make the promise or that they did not act in bad faith. On the facts of the case, especially having regard to the defendant's age, the court could find that the prosecution amounted to an abuse of the process of the court.

In another case, an implied suggestion by the prosecution that they would not prosecute was sufficient to ground an argument of abuse of process: *R v Liverpool Magistrates' Court ex p Slade* [1998] 1 All ER 60. In that case the defendant was charged with failing to keep his pit bull terrier muzzled. The case was dismissed on the basis that there was no evidence that the dog was of that breed. The day following the dismissal the police returned the dog to the defendant, allowing him to walk out of the police station with it unmuzzled in public. They later sought to charge him for a further offence in respect of that action. It was held on appeal that the police conduct must clearly have conveyed to the defendant that he would not be prosecuted for the action given the circumstances. The attempted prosecution was unfair.

In *R v Townsend and Others* [1997] 2 Cr App R 540, the English Court of Appeal made it clear that it is not every breach of promise not to prosecute that would give rise to an abuse of process. It could if circumstances have changed: for instance, if the defendant suffers prejudice because he acted on the promise. On the facts in *Townsend* the third appellant had, acting on the representation that he would be a prosecution witness, given witness statements implicating the first appellant. These were served on the first appellant who then made a statement implicating the third appellant. It was held that this amounted to serious prejudice that justified the granting of a stay of the prosecution of the third appellant for abuse of process.

The *Muslimeen* case

An offer of an amnesty which is acted upon by the defendants could operate to have a subsequent prosecution stayed: *AG of Trinidad and Tobago et al. v Philip et al.* (1994) 45 WIR 456, PC. In that case, insurgents, members of a religious sect, the Jamaat Al Muslimeen, held hostage most of the members of Trinidad and Tobago legislature, including the Prime Minister and other Cabinet members as well as private citizens, during the course of a failed coup bid. They were induced to free the hostages after negotiations, which involved amnesty in the form of a pardon from the Head of State. Although the pardon was held to be invalid by the Privy Council, the Board in delivering its judgment observed that it could constitute an abuse of process if any attempt were made to prosecute the insurgents who 'had relied on the offer of the pardon and had complied with the conditions subject to which that offer of promise or a pardon was made'. The Privy Council gave the following reasons why a prosecution would be improper:

- the insurgents had acted reasonably after the pardon;
- the (acting) President did not give any indication prior to their surrender that the validity of the pardon was in question;
- the negotiations which resulted in the release of the (majority of) hostages unharmed were conducted on the basis that they were entitled to the pardon;
- to prosecute the Muslimeen after their release on a habeas corpus action would be unfair since there was no appeal on such a matter and the only reason that the present matter had reached the appeal courts was because the constitutional motion had been consolidated with the habeas corpus.

As a result of the decision of the Privy Council, no attempt was made subsequently to prosecute the insurgents who had been previously released on writ of habeas corpus based on the presumed validity of the pardon.

Entrapment

In *R v Looseley* [2001] 4 All ER 897 the House of Lords, in confirming the established principle that entrapment was not a substantive defence to a criminal charge, held that a prosecution founded on entrapment may nonetheless be an abuse of the court's process. Their lordships considered that police conduct that brings about state-created crime is unacceptable and improper. To prosecute in such circumstances would be an affront to the public conscience.

The House recognised that it was not objectionable for the police to behave as an 'ordinary customer of a trade', lawful or otherwise, being carried out by the defendant. In determining whether the conduct of the police or other law enforcement agency amounted to 'state-created crime' the overall consideration is whether their conduct is so seriously improper as to bring the administration of justice into disrepute.

Repeated committal proceedings

It is trite law that a discharge in a preliminary inquiry is not an acquittal since there is no final adjudication at the committal stage. Accordingly the laying of a fresh information in respect of the same incident will not support a plea of autrefois: *R v Manchester City Stipendiary*

Magistrate ex p Snelson [1978] 2 All ER 62. In that case the applicant was charged with indictable offences under the Theft Act. On the first occasion, 8 December 1976, when the matter came up for hearing, the prosecution was not ready to proceed and an adjournment was granted until 13 January 1977. On that date they still had not completed their case, but the magistrate refused a further adjournment and, when the prosecution did not offer any evidence, discharged the applicant.

The prosecution commenced fresh committal proceedings shortly afterwards in respect of the same offences. On an application for prohibition, it was held that a magistrate had jurisdiction to hear fresh committal proceedings unless the prosecution abused this privilege by repeated committal proceedings which could be vexatious and amount to an abuse of process. On the facts there was no such abuse.

In *R v Horsham JJ ex p Reeves* (1982) 75 Cr App R 236, the position was different. After three days of hearing, the defence made a successful no case submission and the defendant was discharged. It was held that the laying of a fresh information in such circumstances would be vexatious and oppressive as the matter had already been fully considered by a court of competent jurisdiction. In a 1963 Trinidad case, *Cadogan v R* (1963) 6 WIR 292, the Trinidad and Tobago Court of Appeal took the same view, although they did not assert abuse of process. Indeed, it would have been passing strange if they had, since this concept was hardly acknowledged in these jurisdictions at the time. In that case, a magistrate had conducted a preliminary inquiry into murder against the appellant, after which he was discharged. Subsequently, another information was laid for the same offence and another inquiry was held at which medical evidence that was available, though not given at the time of the first inquiry, was led. The appellant was committed to stand trial, at which he was eventually convicted. It was held on appeal that since the additional evidence led at the second preliminary inquiry was not 'fresh', the inquiry, committal and all subsequent proceedings were invalid.

Therefore, although a fresh information may be laid after a discharge at committal proceedings, it is a power that should only be exercised in circumstances where there has not been a full or valid hearing in the matter (as in *Ex p Snelson*), otherwise its use may be vexatious and oppressive.

IN THE MAGISTRATES' COURTS

There has been much debate as to whether a magistrate, whether on summary trial or committal proceedings,[11] could exercise any discretion to stay a prosecution for abuse of process. This debate perhaps stemmed from the view that since magistrates are creatures of statute, they have no such inherent power. The debate may finally have been settled by the House of Lords in *Bennett*, but prior to that the position was far from certain.

The House of Lords itself appeared to be unsure when Lord Parker in *DPP v Humphreys* [1977] AC 1, HL doubted previous dicta in *Mills v Cooper* [1967] 2 QB 459 when he asserted that it would be 'fraught with considerable dangers' if the magistrates' courts were to have power to stay proceedings for abuse of its process. In *Mills*, Parker LJ had opined that every court had a right to decline to hear proceedings on the ground that they are oppressive.

Since then, it has been gradually acknowledged that magistrates' courts as well as the High Courts can protect themselves from abuse of process. In fact, in *R v Brentford JJ ex p*

11 Corre, N, 'Abuse of process and the power to stay a prosecution' (1991) 155 JPN 27 July 1991, p 469.

Wong [1981] 1 QB 445, the Divisional Court, although holding that the prosecution had attempted to manipulate the prosecution, declined to make an order itself for prohibition as the magistrates' courts 'had ample power' to deal with a matter that went to their jurisdiction. Still, it was uncertain how widely or sparingly this power should be utilised. In *R v Canterbury and St Augustine JJ ex p Klisiak* [1982] QB 398, it was held that the power should be utilised 'very sparingly' and only if otherwise it would be a 'blatant injustice' to do otherwise.

Finally, in *Bennett*, the House of Lords confirmed that magistrates in exercising both their summary jurisdiction and at committal proceedings have power to exercise control over their proceedings through an abuse of process jurisdiction. This power is, however, limited to matters relating to the fairness of the trial of the particular defendant before them, matters such as delay and unfair manipulation of the court process. Cases that do not belong to this narrow category would fail to be considered by the High Court with its wider responsibility for upholding the rule of law. Thus, where there are allegations of complicity in extradition matters, where lengthy submissions may be necessary or otherwise where the application (for a stay) is likely to be complex, the matter should be dealt with by the High Court.

CHAPTER 3

ARREST, SEARCH, AND SEIZURE

A person who, it is alleged, has committed an offence must be brought before the court to face trial. Powers are given at common law and statute to both police officers and private citizens to enforce compulsory attendance of suspected offenders before the courts. In the first instance this will inevitably be the magistrates' court, whether the offence is summary or indictable.

This chapter focusses on the power of the police and the citizen to enforce attendance at court, be it by summons or, more importantly, by way of arrest. The question of entry into private premises to effect an arrest will also be considered, as will the law on search and seizure. In respect of the latter areas, the law is largely statutorily based, since there is no general right of entry to anyone, including the police, into private property even to obtain evidence.[1]

ARREST

Summons or arrest

In general, a defendant is brought to the court by way of summons if the offence is a summary one or at least not a serious one. Before a summons can be issued, a complaint is made to the magistrates' court (in the relevant district). It may be on oath or not.[2] Subsequent to this, summons will be issued by the court, for attendance of the defendant on a specific date. The form of the summons is dictated by statute, but in general it should inform the defendant of the charge and the date and place of the alleged offence. The summons will be served by the police usually personally, or it may be left with an adult at his given address as stipulated by statute. It should be served at least 48 hours before the date of hearing so as to give the defendant sufficient notice.[3] Failure to do so will entitle the defendant to an adjournment and is even a valid excuse for non-attendance at the court.

Where a summons will do as a means of enforcing attendance, a warrant of arrest should not be issued: *O'Brien v Brabner* (1885) 49 JPN 227. This could be considered oppressive. For minor offences, therefore, a warrant should only be utilised in exceptional cases such as where the defendant appears to be avoiding service or is likely to flee. In such instances, it is reasonable to proceed by way of arrest, whether with or without warrant. Entitlement to arrest without warrant will depend on the powers (by common law or statute) granted to the police and private citizens.

What is an arrest?

An arrest is often defined as the seizing or touching of the person of an individual with a view to restraining him: *Alderson v Booth* [1969] 2 QB 216. In some cases, however, the

---

1 *Entick v Carrington* (1765) 19 State Tr 1029.

2 See, e.g., statute in Trinidad and Tobago, Summary Courts Act, Ch 4:20, s 39(2) and Indictable Offences (Preliminary Inquiry) Act, Chap 12:01, ss 6–7.

3 This period is particularised in statute in some jurisdictions such as Grenada, Criminal Procedure Code, Cap 72B, s 71, and Trinidad and Tobago, Summary Courts Act, Chap 4:20, s 42(1).

arrestor need not actually touch the person he has arrested; the arrest may be constructive. If the arrestee knows that he cannot leave, this may constitute an arrest. Tapping a person on the shoulder with a view to speaking to him, not to detain him, is not an arrest: *Donnelly v Jackman* [1970] 1 All ER 987.

Detention

It should be noted that at common law, there is no power of investigative detention short of arrest. There is no power to detain for questioning alone unless statute specifically permits this in particular circumstances. It is a well-established principle that to detain a person against his will without arresting him is an unlawful act: *Albert v Lavin* [1981] 3 All ER 878, HL. A detention per se, therefore, is really an 'arrest' which must be made in accordance with the law: *Ludlow v Burgess* [1971] Crim LR 238. After an arrest, a person may be detained in custody while he is under arrest.

The question may arise as to how long a person may be detained in custody after an arrest (without charge). It is clear that the lawfulness of continued detention raises different questions from those relevant to the arrest. In *Ramsingh v AG* [2012] UKPC 16 the matter arose at the Privy Council. The Board held that in the absence of statutory provision for continuing detention the common law would apply. To justify a continuing detention the detainer must have had reasonable grounds for believing that the appellant's detention without being charged was necessary to secure or preserve evidence relating to an offence for which he is under arrest or to obtain such evidence by questioning him. The Board found that the detention of the appellant at the police station, in the particular circumstances of the case, pending the arrival of medical information as to the condition of the alleged victim was not unlawful.

Constructive arrest

There may be an arrest by words alone only if the defendant submits. However, if a defendant is not physically detained and does not realise he is under restraint (he believes he can leave), he is not arrested: *Alderson v Booth* [1969] 2 QB 216. An invitation to accompany a police officer to the police station[4] is not an arrest once it is clear to the defendant that he may refuse. If it is brought home to him later that he will not be able to leave unless he does something, for example, provide blood, fingerprints and the like, he is now 'under arrest'. An order to go from one place to another may constitute an arrest since the arrestee can no longer be said to be acting on his own volition.

Arrest may be either with or without a warrant.

ARREST WITHOUT WARRANT

There are common law powers of arrest without the need for a warrant in both private citizens and police officers. In most Commonwealth Caribbean jurisdictions, statute has intervened to codify some of these powers and in all cases has extended them. In the absence

4 *Wood v Lane* (1834) 6 C&P 774.

of any express revocation of common law powers of arrest by statute, these powers are in addition to those conferred by statute.[5]

Common law powers

Powers of arrest at common law are enjoyed by both private citizens and the police. They arise in situations where a person has breached or is about to breach the peace.

In *Albert v Lavin* (above), the House of Lords held that it is the right and duty of every citizen in whose presence an actual or reasonably apprehended breach of the peace is being or is about to be committed to 'make the person who was breaching or threatening to break the peace, refrain from so doing', and if appropriate, to detain him against his will.

In that case the appellant, who caused a disturbance in a bus queue while attempting to board a bus, was arrested by an off duty policeman. He resisted the arrest apparently disbelieving that the officer was a policeman. The House held that even if his belief had been reasonable, this did not make his resistance lawful, since in the circumstances the arrest was lawful. This is because even a private citizen has the right to arrest someone who has committed a breach of the peace in his presence. Whether the person who arrested him was a police officer or a private citizen was thus irrelevant.

Furthermore, where the citizen reasonably believes that there is an imminent threat of a breach of the peace he is justified in arresting the person who threatens the peace: *R v Howell* [1981] 3 All ER 383. In *Howell*, the appellant (and others) caused a disturbance on the street after a 'West Indian' party. Following complaints from neighbours, the police arrived and asked the appellant to leave. He refused and continued to swear at the police, whereupon one of the officers took hold of his arm and a fracas ensued. The appellant appealed his conviction for assault occasioning actual bodily harm on the police officer on the ground that his arrest was unlawful and therefore, if he had struck the officer (which was not admitted), it would have been in self-defence in escaping an illegal arrest.

The English Court of Appeal held in a considered judgment in that case, per Watkins LJ, that the power of arrest without warrant for a breach of the peace existed where:

- a breach of the peace was committed in the presence of the person making the arrest;
- the arrestor reasonably supposes that such a breach would be committed in the immediate future by the person arrested even though at the time of the arrest he had not committed any breach; or
- where a breach of the peace had been committed and it was reasonably believed that a renewal of it was threatened.

The court felt, however, that it had to be established that the belief (that a breach was imminent) was both honest and founded on reasonable grounds.

What is a breach of peace?

In *Howell* (above), a breach of the peace was defined as 'An act done or threatened to be done, which either actually harms a person or, in his presence, his property; or is likely to cause harm; or which puts someone in fear of such harm being done' (Watkins LJ in *Howell*,

5 See the extract from *R v Podger* [1979] Crim LR 524 on this point, cited in *R v Howell* [1981] 3 All ER 383, p 387, letter j.

p 389). Clearly, then, at common law any person can arrest without warrant a person whom he sees committing a murder, wounding, malicious damage and such offences in his presence – or one who is about to do so. These seem to be obvious breaches of the peace. In addition, it seems a citizen may arrest a person for a disturbance arising from an act that is likely to cause fear that any such offence may occur. Other minor breaches would include fighting, using obscene language and the like.

Police officers have all powers private citizens have at common law to arrest without warrant. So, clearly at common law, both a constable and a citizen could always have arrested without warrant a person who commits murder, malicious damage and such offences in his presence, or one who is about to do so.

Statutory powers

To some extent statute has codified the common law powers of arrest,[6] but it has also granted much wider powers of arrest to police officers to arrest without warrant. As already emphasised, the statutory provisions do not derogate from the common law powers but add to them.

Private citizens

A consideration of the legislation of the Commonwealth Caribbean jurisdictions shows that a citizen's power of arrest (without warrant) has been amplified. In general, statute now enables a citizen to arrest anyone who has committed any indictable or arrestable (the latter in the case of Trinidad and Tobago and Barbados) offence in his presence or whom he reasonably suspects is the offender when such an offence has actually been committed.

There are variations of these powers in most jurisdictions. In St Vincent, for instance, s 32 of the Criminal Procedure Code, Cap 172, provides that:

> Any private person may arrest any person who in his view commits an indictable offence, or whom he reasonably suspects of having committed an offence punishable with imprisonment for three years or more (provided that such an offence has been committed).

This provision is repeated to varying extents in other Commonwealth Caribbean countries. In Guyana, for example, anyone may arrest a person 'found committing' an indictable offence.[7] In Trinidad and Tobago, the law as reflected in the Criminal Law Act, Chap 10:04, is similar to that of St Vincent except that the statute refers to 'arrestable offence'. The Barbadian legislation contained in the Criminal Law (Arrestable Offences) Act, 17 of 1992, is almost identical to that of Trinidad and Tobago on this power. Section 19(1) of the Bahamas Criminal Procedure Code, Ch 91, grants powers of citizen arrest in this way: 'Any person may arrest without warrant a person who in his view commits a felony or whom he reasonably suspects of having committed a felony, provided that a felony has been committed'.[8]

Trinidad and Tobago, Barbados and St Lucia to an extent, have reclassified criminal offences from felonies and misdemeanours to arrestable and non-arrestable offences. An

6 As shown in the subsequent discussion here.

7 Criminal Law (Procedure) Act, Cap 10:01, s 198. However, only police officers have such power in respect of summary offences.

8 See also in respect of St Lucia, Criminal Code 2004, s 570(4) and (6) which conveys a wider power to citizens.

arrestable offence is one for which the penalty is at least five years' imprisonment or fixed (mandatory) by law (as in murder). Thus, a private citizen may arrest anyone whom he suspects is in the act of committing an arrestable offence or has committed a particular arrestable offence. This is in addition to his common law power to prevent a breach of the peace.

It is clear that the powers of arrest conveyed to a citizen by statute are restricted to arrest (a) when a serious offence is committed in his presence or (b) when such an offence has already been committed and the citizen believes that he has found the culprit.

In addition, common throughout the region there is a specific entitlement to the owner of property or his agent to arrest any person whom he finds committing an offence against his property. Section 683 of the St Lucia Criminal Code is representative of the legislation of the Commonwealth Caribbean jurisdictions:

> Any person who is found committing any offence against property may be arrested by the owner of the property with respect to which the offence is committed or by his or her employee or any person authorized by him.

This power given to landowners possibly arose from the fact that most of the territories depended heavily on the plantation economy and many still do. The rights of landowners were highly respected and correspondingly assiduously protected.

Police officers

Police officers have all the powers of summary arrest (without warrant) granted to private citizens and more. These powers may be granted (1) in respect of indictable or arrestable offences, as the case may be; (2) in respect of summary offences; (3) under the relevant Police Act; and (4) under specific statutory provisions.

(1) In general, a police officer has the power to arrest without warrant anyone whom he suspects, with reasonable cause, is about to commit an indictable (or arrestable) offence or whom he suspects has committed such an offence.[9] This would obviously include someone whom he sees committing such an offence.

The arrestable/indictable offence need not actually have been committed to legitimise the arrest without warrant by a police officer. In contrast, the private citizen who does not actually see the offence being committed is only protected when he arrests a suspect if an indictable or arrestable offence has in fact been committed. In St Vincent, while police officers may arrest without warrant any person found committing an offence punishable by imprisonment, a private citizen, as indicated above, may only do so if the offence carries a penalty of at least three years' imprisonment.[10]

(2) Generally, only police officers have powers of arrest without warrant for summary offences. An officer may usually arrest any person whom he finds in the act of committing a summary offence. In *Bolai v St Louis* (1963) 6 WIR 453, the Court of Appeal in Trinidad and Tobago had to consider what the words 'found committing' in the Summary Courts Ordinance (now Act) meant.

In that case, the appellant was arrested at the direction of the respondent, a Superintendent of Police, for assisting at the fighting of gamecocks, a summary offence. At the time of arrest, he was sitting in a car parked on Poui Trace, the same Trace

9 As stated in Trinidad and Tobago Criminal Law Act, Chap 10:04, s 3 in relation to arrestable offences.
10 Cap 172, s 32.

where the fighting was alleged to have occurred. The police party had arrived on the scene at about 4 pm and the appellant was one of a number of persons seen coming from the direction of the ring where the fighting had been going on. He got into a car parked near the scene and was subsequently arrested there. On an action for false imprisonment for wrongful arrest, it was held that the appellant had not been found committing an offence since no police officer could say that he had actually seen the appellant at the ring at any time that afternoon. At most there was suspicion, but he had not been 'found committing any offence'.

If a person is arrested on the basis that he was 'found committing' an offence, then it stands to reason, if the offence is a summary one, that if he is not arrested at the time of the offence or immediately afterwards, then the police cannot proceed by way of arrest without warrant. The whole purpose of this power must have been to enable police officers to apprehend an offender immediately who might otherwise repeat the offence or flee. Delaying an arrest in such circumstances would mean that the police officer has lost the right to arrest granted by statute. The English courts have considered this issue and have held that when police power is conferred by statute to arrest someone 'found committing' an offence, the arrest must generally be contemporaneous or in fresh pursuit: *R v Howarth* (1828) 1 Mood CC 207, p 216; *R v Jones* [1970] 1 All ER 209, p 213. If the offence is indictable, the position is different, since for indictable offences there exist powers of arrest without warrant even where the offender is not caught in the act.

This general power of arrest without warrant granted to the police when someone is found committing a summary offence is common throughout the Commonwealth Caribbean. The Trinidadian provision in s 104 of the Summary Courts Act is fairly typical: 'Any person who is found committing any summary offence may be taken into custody, without warrant, by a constable.'[11]

St Lucia probably has the widest powers of arrest without warrant to police officers. Section 570 of the new Criminal Code 2004 enables every police officer to arrest without warrant any person whom he (the constable) has reasonable cause to suspect to be in the act of committing or about to commit any offence. In addition, where he with reasonable cause suspects any offence to have been committed he may arrest a suspect without warrant. The St Lucia legislation seemingly admits of no limitation to a police officer's power to arrest without warrant for any offence.

(3) It seems unnecessary to look to the Police Act for any additional power to arrest without warrant in St Lucia.

In the rest of the Commonwealth Caribbean this is not the case. In Jamaica, the Constabulary Force Act appears to be the source of several of the police powers to arrest without warrant. In the other jurisdictions, the powers in the relevant Police Act are merely supplementary to those contained in the summary procedure and criminal procedure legislation.

Most Police Acts grant the power of arrest without warrant against persons who resist arrest or commit aggravated assault. This may seem unnecessary since such actions should constitute breaches of the peace and would be covered by the common law. It may, however, be a means of communicating certainty to police officers as to their powers of summary

11 See the following: Antigua: Criminal Procedure Act, Cap 117, s 3; Bahamas: Penal Code, Ch 77, s 103; Barbados: Magistrates' Courts Act 1996 s 76(1); Dominica: Criminal Law and Procedure Act, Chap 12:01, s 8; Guyana: Summary Jurisdiction (Procedure) Act, Cap 10:02, s 70; Grenada: Criminal Procedure Code, Cap 72Bss 8 and 9; Jamaica: Constabulary Force Act, s 15; St Kitts/Nevis: Criminal Procedure Act, Cap 4:06, s 3; Trinidad and Tobago: Summary Courts Act, Chap 4:20, s 104.

arrest. One power granted by the Police Acts is that which allows the arrest of 'anyone who within the view of'[12] the particular police officer offends in any manner against the law and who either refuses to give his name and address or gives what is suspected to be either a false name or false address. This is a fairly general power of arrest, which is common throughout the region, but is circumscribed by two conditions: the act must be committed within the officer's view and the offender must refuse to give his name and address.

(4) There are additional powers of arrest granted to police officers as regards specific offences that are relevant in jurisdictions where police arrest powers without warrant are not as wide ranging as in St Lucia. In Jamaica, for instance, s 18 of the Constabulary Act permits arrest without warrant of any person 'known or suspected' to have in his possession (named) dangerous drugs or tickets to certain games of chance. The two offences seem very far apart in terms of their seriousness, but this is the way the legislation is framed.

In Trinidad and Tobago, s 38 of the Larceny Act, Chap 11:12 enables arrest without warrant of any person 'found committing' any offence under that Act, except for attempted extortion by means of a threat to publish. Thus, a person may be summarily arrested under this provision for offences ranging from simple larceny, obtaining by false pretences, to a variety of fraud offences. The Domestic Violence Act (1999) also grants to police officers powers of arrest without warrant for breaches under that Act.

There are undoubtedly other instances of police powers of arrest granted in relation to specific offences throughout the Commonwealth Caribbean. The above are merely examples of such instances.

Interpretation of statutory powers

As discussed above, 'found committing' in relation to an offence means that the offender must in effect be caught in the act of committing an offence to invoke the power of arrest without warrant. Therefore, it may be an attractive argument on behalf of a defendant who is later found not guilty of a charge to claim that, as a consequence, he was illegally arrested. If he is found not guilty then can it be said he was 'found committing' any offence? Nonetheless, as a matter of policy and common sense, the argument ought not to be upheld, since there are many reasons why a person may be acquitted. A police officer ought not to be deterred from exercising his statutory power to arrest a person who is 'found committing' an offence simply because it is possible that the offender may be acquitted of the offence. This issue has been dealt with by the English courts. In *Wiltshire v Barrett* [1965] 2 All ER 271, Lord Denning considered a section in the English Road Traffic Act empowering police officers to arrest without warrant anyone found committing an offence. He held that the words 'committing an offence' must mean 'apparently committing an offence'. Thus, if a police officer reasonably comes to the conclusion based on the conduct of the defendant that he was committing the offence, the arrest is lawful. A court may well baulk at interpreting the statute to authorise arrest without warrant of a person found committing 'any' summary or indictable offence, as the case may be. In *Hope v Smith* (1963) 6 WIR 464, the Trinidad and Tobago Court of Appeal was confronted with such a situation. The magistrate had dismissed charges of assaulting a police officer and resisting arrest against the respondent. He held that the power of arrest without warrant in s 104 of the Summary Courts Ordinance did not apply. This section granted the police the power to arrest anyone found committing any

12 For example, Bahamas Police Act, Ch 191, s 31.

summary offence. The court held that the word 'any' meant just that and should not be qualified in any way. The police had power to arrest anyone found committing any offence.

As discussed above, the police generally have statutory powers to arrest without warrant any person whom they suspect with reasonable cause has committed an indictable or arrestable offence. Questions may arise as to what 'reasonable cause' or 'reasonable grounds' for suspicion could be. The House of Lords in *O'Hara v Chief Constable of the Royal Ulster Constabulary* [1997] Crim LR 432, HL, considered this issue. They held that there must be sufficient material from which an inference could be drawn that the officer had reasonable grounds for his suspicion. It must constitute information known to him, though not necessarily from his own observation. He was entitled to form an opinion from what he had been told and it was not necessary that he prove that any of the facts on which he based his suspicions were true. The Court of Appeal of the Eastern Caribbean States in *Calliste (Devon) v R* (1994) 47 WIR 130 was of the view that the mere suspicion of a police officer or a 'hunch' that might connect a particular person with the commission of a crime does not in itself amount to 'reasonable grounds' that the person had committed the offence. It is obvious, therefore, that while the officer must have suspicion, the test of whether it is reasonably based is an objective one. He must have something solid on which to base the suspicion.

In Trinidad and Tobago and, to a lesser extent, in Barbados, there appears to be a lacuna in the law in respect of indictable offences that are non-arrestable. While statute in these jurisdictions enables arrest without warrant of a person found committing a summary offence and an arrestable offence, there is no similar general provision for other indictable offences. A police officer might conceivably find someone actually committing an indictable offence such as indecent assault, which carries a penalty of three years. Under the relevant statutory provisions, which pertain to only summary offences and arrestable offences, the police officer will have no power of arrest without warrant for such an offence. In practical terms this type of conduct could amount to a breach of the peace and will enable the exercise by a constable of common law powers of arrest. The fact remains, however, that legislation in Trinidad and Tobago is significantly silent on this point. Thus, for certain offences such as those of perjury under s 8 of the Perjury Act, Chap 11:14, the police will have no power at all to arrest without warrant. Even though the offences are indictable, the penalty for such offences is only two years' imprisonment, so they are not arrestable offences. In most other jurisdictions, the relevant legislation granting powers of arrest without warrant to police officers includes all indictable offences. Even the Barbados legislation provides to an extent for this.[13]

ARREST WITH WARRANT

Statute has intervened to give police officers powers of arrest with a warrant once a charge has been laid. A warrant of arrest may be obtained for any offence. Nonetheless, as pointed out above, it should not be utilised when summons will be equally effective to bring an alleged offender before the courts. To obtain a warrant of arrest a complaint (or information) in writing must be sworn to before a magistrate or a justice of the peace, judicial officers in the magistrates' court, where an offender must first appear.

13 Criminal Law (Arrestable Offences) Act, 1992–17, s 5.

The requirements throughout the Commonwealth Caribbean to obtain a warrant of arrest for either a summary or indictable offence are fairly similar and are stipulated in the relevant statutes.[14] There must first be a complaint (a charge), which must be on oath. The warrant must not be signed in blank and it may be directed to a named constable or constables generally. It should concisely state the offence for which it is issued and the name of the person to be arrested. The warrant orders the constable to arrest that person and bring him before the court to answer the charge. Usually there will be an endorsement as to whether bail is fixed such as 'No Bail' or 'On arrest, Bail with a surety in the sum of $10,000'.

In *AG v Williams et al.* (1997) 51 WIR 264, PC, the Judicial Committee of the Privy Council considered the prerequisites to obtain a search warrant in Jamaica. They held that the requirement that a search warrant be issued by a justice (or magistrate, as the case may be) is to interpose protection of a judicial decision between the citizen and the power of the State. If a police officer is authorised to act by virtue of a warrant granted by a justice, it is the function of the justice to satisfy himself that the prescribed circumstances exist. The court offered that:

> The law relies upon the independent scrutiny of the judiciary to protect the citizens from the excesses, which would inevitably flow in allowing an executive officer to decide for himself whether the conditions under which he is permitted to enter upon private property have been met.

The principle was enunciated in relation to the issue of search warrants, but it is suggested that it may equally apply to warrants of arrest. This is particularly so in relation to offences where a police officer would otherwise not have powers of arrest (such as for many summary offences not committed in the presence of a police officer). A magistrate or a justice ought not to be a mere rubber stamp in granting such a warrant, but should scrutinise the information sworn to before him by the police officer prior to issuing the warrant. It is possible that the magistrate will on occasion feel that the matter is not appropriate for arrest, since summons may be equally effective to bring the defendant before the court.

Sometimes the police may decide to proceed by warrant even though they may have powers of arrest without warrant. This is frequently the case where it is suspected that the offender may attempt to escape. The warrant enables police officers in any station to arrest the defendant with the security of knowing that a warrant has been issued. The particulars of the warrant also make it easier to inform the defendant of the cause of his arrest, without error. The police may also feel that the warrant gives legitimacy to any entry into private premises should that be necessary to effect the arrest.

Bench warrant

This is a special type of warrant of arrest, which may be issued by a court when a properly notified defendant fails to show up for his trial. The defendant may have been served by summons to attend court on a particular date. Alternatively, he may have been present in

14 In those jurisdictions where there is no one Criminal Code, there are separate but similar provisions for arrest by warrant in the summary procedure legislation and the indictable procedure legislation, e.g.: Trinidad and Tobago, Summary Courts Act, Chap 4:20, ss 106–07; Indictable Offences (Preliminary Inquiry) Act, Chap 12:01, ss 8–9.

court when the matter was adjourned to a fixed date. In either case, the court is empowered to issue a warrant for his arrest once a police officer swears in court to the contents of the complaint or information which initiated the charge.

If the defendant is already in custody, however, whether it is for the offence before the court or another, a warrant ought not to be issued.

EFFECTING THE ARREST

In effecting an arrest, the arrestor has certain duties as well as certain powers. The powers ancillary to arrest are usually granted to police officers under common law or statute, while the duties are attached to any person who arrests another.

Entry

At common law, a police officer has power to enter private premises to effect an arrest in limited circumstances. Force may only be used if entry is denied. Force may include breaking open the doors of a house, but this may only be done after permission to enter has been sought and refused. In *Burdett v Abbott* (1811) 104 ER 501, this issue came up for consideration where the then Speaker of the House of Commons issued a warrant of arrest for Sir Francis Burdett. In executing the said warrant, the Serjeant at Arms broke down the outer doors of the house. It was held that the officer had a right to break open the outer door, provided there was a request for admission first made for that purpose and an effective denial by the parties within. There has always been a common law right of entry to anyone to break open the door of a house to prevent a murder and to arrest the offender.[15] In *Swales v Cox* (1982) 72 Cr App R 171, p 174, the English Court of Appeal defined four situations at common law where the police may enter premises to effect an arrest. They are: (a) to prevent a murder; (b) to arrest a felon who has been followed into the house; (c) to prevent the commission of a felony; and (d) the right of police to follow an offender running away from an officer. The first three powers of entry are also enjoyed by citizens (at common law).

Statute has intervened to codify this power to an extent in some jurisdictions. Section 12 of the Bahamas Criminal Procedure Code Ch 91 and s 581 of the St Lucia Code specifically provide for power of entry to a police officer to effect an arrest and power to break down the door (or window) to effect the arrest if admission is refused or cannot be obtained. Section 3 (6) of the Criminal Law Act, Chap 10:04, of Trinidad and Tobago also contains this power in respect of arrest for arrestable offences. Forcible entry may be also utilised to effect the arrest by warrant for summary offences.[16]

To summarise, the power to enter private premises without a (search) warrant is limited. Anyone may enter private premises to prevent a serious breach of the peace, such as murder, and arrest the offender. Police officers may enter to effect a legal arrest for a serious offence and break down the outer door if entry is refused or cannot otherwise be obtained. This power of police officers is now encompassed in statute in most jurisdictions in the Commonwealth Caribbean.

---

15 A police officer may enter premises to prevent a breach of the peace: *Thomas v Sawkins* [1935] 2 KB 249.

16 See Summary Courts Act, Chap 4:20, s 108(5).

Search of the person

There is no general common law right to search a person who has been arrested, but a person may be searched if it is believed that he has a weapon or implement which may be utilised for escape. Additionally, he may be searched if it is believed that he has material evidence in his possession: *Elias v Pasmore* [1934] 2 KB 164. This power is codified in statutes in some Commonwealth Caribbean countries. Section 15 of the Bahamas Criminal Procedure Code, Ch 91, encapsulates the common law power almost word for word. Section 589 of the St Lucia Criminal Code allows anyone, not only police officers (as in the Bahamas), who arrests another to search that person and take possession of all articles he has, except for his apparel, into safe custody. The Jamaica law is more specific. Section 19 of the Constabulary Force Act enables a police officer to stop and search any vehicle suspected of carrying stolen goods, dangerous drugs and papers or tickets relating to certain games of chance. The officer may also search the vehicle, driver and any passenger in that vehicle.

In effecting a personal search, consequent on arrest the arrestor may use force only in exceptional circumstances, such as where the arrestee is resistant. In *Lindley v Rutter* [1980] 3 WLR 660, it was held that a policewoman used unnecessary force in searching a female suspect. On the facts, the defendant was arrested for disorderly conduct and taken to the police station. A policewoman attempted to search her and met with resistance. Thereupon two policewomen searched the defendant and removed her brassiere, as was the local practice. The Divisional Court confirmed that the right to search a person lawfully in custody is a very limited one. While it is necessary to search for evidence and remove objects which can be used as weapons, implements for escape, or to injure, it should not be used to subject a defendant to degradation. There was no need to remove the defendant's brassiere, which was normal clothing.

Section 588(2) of the St Lucia Criminal Code specifically requires that police officers should have regard to decency in searching a female. This presumably includes the need for a female officer to search a female suspect, which is the custom in police investigations in most jurisdictions in any event.

Thus there is no power to stop and search a person unless he has been legally arrested or unless statute otherwise provides,[17] as does the Jamaica Constabulary Force Act, discussed above.

Stop and question

The police are entitled to stop and question persons in the course of investigations and citizens are generally expected to assist the police. In some jurisdictions, statute even demands that citizens assist police in effecting an arrest if asked to do so. In *Rice v Connolly* [1966] 2 All ER 649, Parker LJ said (p 651) 'it is part of the obligation and duties of any police constable to take all steps which appear to him necessary for keeping the peace, for preventing crime or for protecting property from criminal injury'. In so doing, a police officer has a right to stop and question persons: *Donnelly v Jackman* [1970] 1 All ER 987. Nonetheless, a citizen is entitled to refuse to answer questions and if he does, the police officer has no power to detain him for questioning unless he makes a lawful arrest: *Kenlin v*

17 See *R (Gillan) v Commr of Metropolis* [2006] 2 AC 307 HL for an analysis of such powers under the UK Terrorism Act 2000.

Gardner[1967] 2 QB 510. In *Ludlow v Burgess* [1971] Crim LR 238, the defendant and a constable engaged in conversation and the defendant then turned to walk away. At this point the constable put his hand on the defendant's shoulder to detain him for further conversation and inquiries. It was held that this was an unlawful act and was not done in the execution of the officer's duty.

The reason for the arrest

An arrested person is entitled to be informed promptly of the reason for his arrest. This is a classic common law right which is now also included in some Commonwealth Caribbean constitutions. The locus classicus in this area of law is *Christie v Leachinsky* [1947] 1 All ER 567, HL, in which Viscount Simonds spelt out five basic propositions of law on the need to inform an arrested person of the reason for his arrest. In that case the appellant was discharged on a charge of unlawful possession of stolen cloth because, it was said, the police had decided to pursue the alternative charge of larceny. He was rearrested on leaving the court, but was never informed of the reason for his arrest. He sued for false imprisonment and on the issue of his re-arrest it was argued that he knew what was the offence for which he was being arrested. Viscount Simonds held that the authorities established the following principles:

- a police officer who arrests a person without warrant must ordinarily inform him of the true ground of the arrest;
- if the citizen is not so informed, the police officer will usually be liable for false imprisonment;
- if the circumstances are such that the arrested person must know the general nature of the alleged offence, the duty does not exist (such as where he is caught red-handed);
- the language need not be technical, but must convey the substance of the reason for his restraint to the arrested person;
- if the arrested person creates a situation (such as running away), which makes it impossible to inform him of the reason for his arrest, he cannot complain.

A police officer need only do what a reasonable person would do in circumstances to ensure that the defendant knows the reason for his arrest. If the person is deaf or cannot understand English, the police officer is not expected to anticipate this: *Wheatley v Lodge* [1971] 1 All ER 173. In that case the English Court of Appeal considered the situation where a defendant who was arrested never indicated to the arresting officer that he was in fact totally deaf. He could speak, although his speech was slurred and indistinct. The police officer on arresting the defendant told him that he was being arrested for driving while under the influence of drink. The defendant replied 'yes definitely' and accompanied the officer to the police station, although he had no idea he was under arrest. Subsequently he was taken to another officer to whom he indicated for the first time that he was totally deaf. At that stage he was processed under the Road Safety Act by means of written questions and responses. On his contention that his arrest and all that followed were unlawful, the Court of Appeal held that the arrest was valid. The court followed *John Lewis and Co Ltd v Tims* [1951] 1 All ER 814, HL, and held that the House of Lords in that case had recognised that there was a further exception to the general rule in *Christie* (above). It was that if a police officer arrests a deaf person or somebody who cannot speak English, all that he has to do to communicate the reason for the arrest is what a reasonable person would do in the circumstances.

Thus, if the police are unaware that the defendant is deaf and inform him in the normal way of his arrest, this would be sufficient. It follows that if they are aware or subsequently find out that he is deaf, they must act reasonably and ensure that the defendant is properly informed of the reason for his arrest.

Constitutional provisions

The duty to inform an arrestee of the reason for his arrest has been given statutory recognition in the fundamental human rights sections of most Commonwealth Caribbean constitutions. Section 13(2) of the Barbados Constitution states specifically: 'Any person who is arrested or detained shall be informed as soon as reasonably practicable in language that he understands, of the reasons for his arrest or detention'. Section 15(2) of the Jamaican Constitution is identical.

The Constitution of St Kitts and Nevis, on the other hand, while specifying that the arrested person is to be informed with 'reasonable promptitude', gives an upper limit of up to 48 hours after the arrest (s 5(2)). The St Lucia Constitution[18] in contrast sets a maximum time limit of 24 hours.

While these latter constitutional provisions may seem to extend the common law requirements, it must be remembered that these are really outside limits. It is still to be expected that the arrestee must be informed of the reason for his arrest as soon as is practicably possible. The Trinidad and Tobago Constitution is possibly more apposite, referring to the right of an accused person to be informed 'promptly and without delay of the reason for his arrest or detention'.[19]

Taking the arrestee before the authorities

An arrested person should be taken as soon as possible before the appropriate authorities. In the case of a citizen's arrest, the citizen must take the arrestee either to a police station or to the magistrates' court. This he must do as soon as he reasonably can, not necessarily immediately: *Lewis v Tims* (above).

The constitution and statute have set guidelines in most jurisdictions for bringing a person before the court. Most speak of the need to do so 'promptly'[20] or as soon as is 'reasonably practicable'.[21] The Constitution of St Kitts and Nevis gives an outside limit for this as 72 hours after arrest (s 5(3)) as does the St Lucia Code, s 584(1). It is obvious that a person arrested without warrant must either be charged within the stipulated time or released.

In *Dallison v Caffery* [1964] 2 All ER 610, which is now a locus classicus on the point, the English court confirmed that a constable has greater powers than a private citizen as to how long he may hold an arrestee before taking him to court. The constable who arrests someone without warrant (no charge having already been laid) can do what is reasonable to investigate the matter to determine whether his suspicions are justified. He can take the arrested person to his house to seek to recover evidence. He can take him to check up on his

18 Section 3(2).
19 Clause 5(2)(c)(i).
20 Trinidad and Tobago Constitution, cl 5(2)(c)(iii).
21 Barbados Constitution, s 13(3).

story. The police officer may also arrange for and place the suspect on an identification parade.

The court, however, disapproved of a deliberate detention of three days of an arrested person without bringing him before the magistrate. It would seem, therefore, that such a length of time is too long to hold an arrested suspect without charging him. If he is not charged, action may lie in habeas corpus proceedings to produce his body before the courts and justify his continued detention. In Trinidad and Tobago, a High Court judge disapproved of the detention of a suspect for six days without charge.[22]

Stollmeyer J said that while there was no statutory provision restricting the period of detention, he would use 48 hours as a guideline. This yardstick seems to be entirely in conformity with *Dallison v Caffery* (above). In St Lucia, statute has intervened to permit detention for a 'further period' not exceeding 72 hours where an investigation is incomplete.[23] This is upon application to a magistrate and for specified offences.

Once a suspect has been charged, he is invariably brought to court on the first court day after the charge is laid. In *Seeromani Maraj-Naraynsingh v AG of Trinidad and Tobago and The DPP* [2010] UKPC 19 the Privy Council held that the constitutional right to be brought promptly before an appropriate judicial authority relates on its face to a single time. It applies upon initial arrest or detention and not continuously during any period when a person is under arrest or detention.

Summary courts legislation in most jurisdictions grant to the police the right to grant bail to a person who has been arrested and charged for a summary offence, if he cannot be taken before the court without delay.[24] This will be considered in greater detail in the next chapter.

Right to an attorney

In two cases emanating from Trinidad and Tobago, the Privy Council affirmed the existence of the constitutional rights to an attorney and the right to be informed of the right to an attorney. In *Thornhill v AG* (1976) 31 WIR 498, PC, it was emphasised that the right to communicate with an attorney was granted to an arrested person both by the Constitution of Trinidad and Tobago and the common law. In several other Commonwealth Caribbean constitutions this right is clearly spelt out, as in St Kitts and Nevis[25] and Barbados.[26] The Jamaica Constitution does not specify this right. Even though this is not a constitutionally protected right in that jurisdiction, it would seem inarguable that an arrested person should enjoy the right to communicate with a legal advisor. In *Thornhill* (above), the Privy Council recognised that it was a right enjoyed de facto by private citizens before the Constitution which arose from settled practice in English law.

In Trinidad and Tobago, it has been held by the Privy Council, the Constitution demands that the police adequately inform an arrested person of his right to an attorney: *AG v Whiteman* (1992) 39 WIR 397, PC. The right to be informed of the right to communicate with an attorney is thus part of the constitutional protections guaranteed by the Trinidad and Tobago Constitution. The accused person must be so informed as soon as

22 *Trinidad Guardian*, 21 September 2000.
23 Section 595(1), Criminal Code.
24 As in Trinidad and Tobago Summary Courts Act, Chap 4:20, s 105.
25 Constitution of St Kitts and Nevis, s 25(2).
26 Constitution of Barbados, s 13(2).

possible and at least before in custody interrogations. This particular protection is not afforded in the constitutions of other jurisdictions.

More recently, in *Rajesh Ramsarran v AG of Trinidad and Tobago* (2005) 66 WIR 280, PC, the Privy Council affirmed a comprehensive rule that on any occasion that a person is arrested or detained he is entitled to the constitutional protections. It mattered not if the arrest was for nonpayment of a fine as opposed to arrest in the course of police investigations.

In effect, then, an arrested person has a constitutional right of access to legal advice in most jurisdictions. Where there is none, as in Jamaica, this is a right derived from settled practice. In Trinidad and Tobago, the right has been further enlarged as discussed above.

Breach of rights on arrest

If a police officer has no power to arrest without warrant, or where a warrant is improperly obtained, this will result in an illegal arrest. It is obvious that the officer will be acting illegally in either case, since he is acting without legal authority. In *Murphy v Richards* (1960) 2 WIR 143, it was held that the arrest was illegal in a case where a defendant in Jamaica had been arrested for unlawful possession. This was because the constable had no common law or statutory power to effect such an arrest without warrant and was acting illegally. However, in general this does not vitiate criminal charges, since arrest is merely the process by which the defendant is brought before the court.

In *R v Hughes* (1879) 4 QBD 614, a full court in England held that the arrest process was illegal since there was no written information nor oath to justify the issue of the warrant of arrest. Nonetheless, the court still had jurisdiction to hear the charge. The defendant had the option when he appeared in court to complain about the process and demand that he be properly brought before the court. If he did not object to jurisdiction he waived his rights: *Shepherd and Turner* (1864) 10 Cox CC 15. While the defendant may have been irregularly taken into custody, the court still has jurisdiction to proceed with the case. It has been suggested in *R v Kulnycz* [1970] 3 All ER 881 that if a defendant is unlawfully in custody and challenges that custody prior to the hearing of the case, he should be released and then be brought before the court by legal process.

If the charge is dependent on a legal arrest, however, the case may be dismissed if the arrest is illegal. Examples of such charges are resisting arrest or assaulting a police officer in the execution of his duty, the 'execution' of his duty being the arrest. In such circumstances, if a police officer does not tell the arrestee the reason for his arrest, the arrest becomes illegal and he is no longer acting on the execution of his duty: *Ludlow v Burgess* [1971] Crim LR 238. A charge founded on the arrest is thus invalid.

If the police have no valid power of arrest, the position is clear, but what about a situation where there is power to arrest but it is exercised wrongly? The arrestee has several rights on arrest and if any of these are breached it could lead to the arrest being deemed retroactively illegal. Failing to inform the arrested person promptly of the reason for an arrest may render an arrest illegal: *Christie* (above). Such a person will have grounds for an action for false imprisonment and probably assault as in *Murphy* (above). It is not as certain, however, whether a failure to grant the arrested person access to legal advice will make an otherwise legal arrest unlawful. It will be a breach of his constitutional right in most jurisdictions, other than Jamaica, and may lead to an award of damages for the breach on a constitutional motion. This denial of legal access, whether actual (as in *Thornhill*, above) or constructive (as in *Whiteman*, above), may lead to statements obtained from an accused person in such circumstances being held inadmissible.

Does a breach of a constitutional right which only arises upon arrest invalidate the arrest? It would seem probable, depending on the terms of the constitutional right. At least the continued detention of the arrestee will be illegal if this were to happen, even if the original arrest was authorised by law. The original legal arrest may become tainted by the subsequent conduct of the arresting authorities so as to make the entire transaction, the arrest, unlawful. If failing to inform an arrestee of the reason for his arrest, which is a common law right, makes the arrest unlawful, then breaches of constitutional rights, which arise upon arrest, may have the same result. It should be noted, however, that even if the arrest may be illegal by failure to inform the defendant of the reason for his arrest, the illegality can be cured if he is subsequently told of the reason: *R v Kulnycz* (above). Thus, by the time he appears in court, he will be in legal custody.

SEARCH AND SEIZURE

The police have power to search a person whom they have arrested for weapons or evidence connected to the suspected offence, as discussed above. They also have limited powers of entry into private premises to effect an arrest. In general, however, there is no right of entry into private premises to obtain evidence unless granted by statute or by consent of the occupier of the premises. In *Entick v Carrington* (1765) 19 State Tr 1029, the King's messengers entered the plaintiff's home and searched his papers under a warrant issued by a Government minister. In that case, Camden CJ stated: 'Our law holds the property of every man sacred so that no man can set foot upon his neighbour's home without leave; if he does, he is a trespasser'.

This common law protection of an individual from unlawful search is contained in the constitutions of the Commonwealth Caribbean which may speak generally of the right to 'protection for the privacy of his home and other property'[27] or, more specifically: 'Except with his own consent, no person shall be subject to the search of his person or his property or the entry by others on his premises'.[28]

The constitutional right to be free from illegal entry and search is not absolute. It is subject to exceptions which are necessary 'for the proper functioning of a democratic society', as Lord Hoffman acknowledged in *AG v Williams* (1997) 51 WIR 264, p 266, PC. The exceptions in relation to the search of private property are when a search warrant is obtained and where specified by statute.

Entry and search

Specific statutory provisions may enable police officers to enter private premises without warrant to search for evidence. There is not a wide variety of these provisions. In general, a search warrant is necessary for entry and search. Most of the powers of search without warrant granted by statute relate to where it is believed a person has in his possession stolen

27 Barbados Constitution, s 11(b).
28 Jamaica Constitution, s 19.

or uncustomed goods. For example, s 76(2) of the Barbados Magistrates' Courts Act 1996–27 provides:

> Every police or parish constable may stop, search and detain any vessel, boat, cart or carriage or other vehicle, in or upon which there is reason to suspect that anything stolen or unlawfully obtained may be found.

This provision is strikingly similar to others in the Commonwealth Caribbean such as s 632 of the St Lucia Criminal Code and s 38 of the Summary Offences Act, Ch 11:02, of Trinidad and Tobago. The Jamaica Constabulary Act provides for this power at s 17, which also includes the right to search any person found on board the ship or boat. In addition, s 19 enables a police officer to stop and search vehicles and their occupants without warrant in stated circumstances.

It should be noted that the statutory entitlements to police officers to search private premises without warrant do not generally include 'buildings'. It would seem that the legislature was clearly protective of homes and even offices. Search of such premises other than by invitation seems only legally possible with a search warrant.

Search warrant

At common law, a court had power to issue a search warrant on sworn information as to the suspicion of stolen goods on premises to search for such stolen goods: *Elias v Pasmore* [1934] 2 KB 164. This common law power has now been superseded by statute in relation to almost any offence. The typical provisions in the Commonwealth Caribbean are exemplified in s 10 of the Guyana Summary Jurisdiction (Procedure) Act, Cap 10:02, which states in part:

> Any magistrate who is satisfied, by proof upon oath that there is reasonable ground for believing that there is, in any building, ship, carriage, box, receptacle or place – anything upon or in respect of which any summary conviction offence has been or is suspected to have been committed for which according to any written law for the time being in force, the offender may be arrested without warrant; or
>
> anything which there is reasonable ground for believing will afford evidence as to the commission of that offence; or
>
> anything which there is reasonable ground for believing is intended to be used for the purpose of committing any offence against the person punishable on summary conviction, for which, according to any written law for the time being in force, the offender may be arrested without warrant,
>
> may at any time issue a warrant under his hand authorising some police or other constable named therein to search that building, ship, carriage, box, receptacle, or place for the thing and to seize and take it before the magistrate.

An identical provision is contained in s 50(1) of the (Guyana) Criminal Law (Procedure) Act, Cap 10:01, in respect of any indictable offences.

In Trinidad and Tobago the law is not restricted, in the case of summary offences, to only those for which the offender may be arrested without warrant as stated in s 10(1)(a) above of the Guyana law. In other words a search warrant may be issued to enter a building or other place to search for evidence in relation to any summary offence, not just those for which a person can be arrested without warrant. In St Vincent a search warrant is obtainable to search for 'any property whatsoever with or with respect to which an offence has been committed' in any place. The 'place' is the same as those identified in the Guyana law. The Bahamas provision[29] is as wide as those of Trinidad and Tobago[30] and St Vincent.[31] So too is the St Lucia law.[32] In contrast the Barbados law[33] is identical to that of Guyana.

Thus, a search warrant may be obtained to search for evidence in respect of the commission of any offence in those jurisdictions with the wider provisions. In the others, like Guyana and Barbados, a search warrant will not be issued in respect of summary offences for which a person cannot be arrested without warrant. These are usually such trivial offences that the omission is insignificant.

Grounds

In all jurisdictions a search warrant may be obtained upon information sworn on oath. There is no need to lay a charge first. Indeed, a search warrant usually is obtained for the purpose of searching for evidence in relation to a suspected offence.

Real evidence obtained from the search may then justify the charge. It has been held by the Privy Council that before a magistrate or justice issues a search warrant, the police officer must satisfy the magistrate or justice that he has reasonable cause to suspect that the circumstances exist to justify the issue of the search warrant. In *AG v Williams et al.* (1997) 51 WIR 264, PC, the Privy Council emphasised the need for the judicial authority issuing the search warrant to be satisfied that the applicant for the warrant has reasonable cause for suspicion. He should apply his mind to the matters on which the suspicion is based, the court said.

Although it is not expected for reasons of confidentiality that the information sworn to should state the grounds for suspicion, those must be disclosed to the issuing authority. The police officer must 'disclose all that the latter (the magistrate) needs to know in order to discharge his duty': *AG v Williams* (above). Sufficient information to establish grounds for suspicion to the magistrate's satisfaction must be stated on oath. It is not enough for the police officer to state on oath that he has reasonable suspicion. It is thus expected that magistrates and justices conform to their statutory duty to be 'satisfied on oath' before issuing a search warrant to enter private premises. This is to ensure that 'the protection of a judicial decision between the citizen and the power of the State is imposed'.[34]

Execution of warrant

The requirements as to the form of the warrant are specified by statute and are common throughout the jurisdictions. A search warrant may be addressed to a named constable or to any constable. If a specific constable is named, it has been held that he is the only one empowered to execute that warrant: *R v Rolda Ricketts* (1971) 17 WIR 306. In *R v Chin Loy* (1975) 23 WIR 360, the Jamaica Court of Appeal considered a provision in the Spirit License Law which authorised the issue of a warrant directed to 'any constable'. The search warrant was addressed to 'all members' of the Force of Cross Roads. The court held, on an appeal against conviction, that the warrant was unobjectionable since the statute did not

29 Ch 91, s 70.
30 Chap 4:20, s 41, and Chap 12:01, s 5.
31 Criminal Procedure Code, Cap 172, s 41.
32 Section 624 Criminal Code.
33 Magistrates' Courts Act 1996, s 4.
34 *AG v Williams et al.* (1997) 51 WIR 264, p 270, PC.

require a particular constable to be named. The principle is applicable to all jurisdictions, since they all have similar provision in this regard.

Common statutory provisions enable search warrants to be executed even on Sundays and at any hour of the day or night. At common law it was made clear that it was within the power of the police to break down the outer door of premises to execute a warrant: *Burdett v Abbott* (1811) 104 ER 501. This, however, is only permissible after a demand for admittance has been refused: *Lannock v Brown* [1819] 100 ER 482. Thus common law entitlement is contained in some statutory provisions such as s 42 of the St Vincent Criminal Procedure Act, Cap 172.

Although statute does not so stipulate, it is a usual practice to execute the search warrant (search the premises) in the presence of the occupier. If he is absent the search may be carried out in the presence of an adult on the premises. The police officer who executes the warrant will read it to the person who is on the premises. After the search, he should endorse on the back of the warrant what was found and seized, the name of the persons present and the time and date.

Seizure and retention

It is a common law right of the police to seize any items from premises that they have lawfully entered which may constitute evidence against a potential defendant: *Ghani v Jones* [1970] 1 QB 693. The evidence must be of the kind that will form material evidence on his prosecution for a crime. In *Ghani*, Lord Denning MR said (p 706):

> I would start by considering the law where police officers enter a man's house by virtue of a warrant, or arrest a man lawfully, with or without a warrant, for a serious offence. I take it to be settled law, without citing cases, that the officers are entitled to take any goods which they find in his possession or in his house which they reasonably believe to be material evidence in relation to the crime for which he is arrested and for which they enter.

If the goods found are not in relation to the offence for which the person was arrested or for which the police entered the premises, they may yet seize the goods. Lord Denning continued in *Ghani*:

> If in the course of their search they come upon any goods which show him to be implicated in some other crime, they may take them provided they act reasonably and detain them no longer than is necessary.

The police may thus seize goods in search of which they entered the premises, or any other goods pertinent to another possible crime. In *Chevalier v AG et al.* (1985) 38 WIR 240, the Trinidad and Tobago Court of Appeal considered the issue. The appellant's premises were lawfully searched by the police for US dollars. They found and seized both Venezuelan bolivars and US dollars. The appellant was later charged for breach of the Exchange Control Act for having in her possession unauthorised possession of foreign currency. The Court of Appeal confirmed that the police were entitled to seize the bolivars and to found a charge based on them notwithstanding that they were not mentioned in the search warrant. They clearly constituted material evidence in a crime.

It seems clear that seized goods, which constitute material evidence in a crime, may be retained as long as necessary for the prosecution of that crime.[35]

35 This common law principle is now contained in statute in some countries as in Bahamas Criminal Procedure Act, Ch 91, s 72.

Retention

The question of how far this prerogative should be extended, to include the power to retain goods which are not yet the subject of a criminal charge or not clearly necessary as evidence, has occupied the consideration of the courts.

In *Malone v Commissioner of Police* [1979] 1 All ER 256, the English Court of Appeal dealt with the issue. The police had entered the plaintiff's house under authority of a search warrant for stolen goods and found a large quantity of goods alleged to be stolen. They also found hidden in a cupboard a large quantity of banknotes to the value of £10,000. The plaintiff was charged for handling stolen goods, but no charge was proffered in relation to the banknotes. The plaintiff brought an action for detinue. The police argued that the banknotes could (a) constitute material evidence in prosecution of the offences for which the plaintiff had been charged, and could (b) be the subject of a compensation or forfeiture order under statute, hence their authority to retain it.

The Court of Appeal in *Malone* held that goods seized, if not stolen or the subject of any criminal charges, could not be retained unless the retention could be legally justified. Such a justification could be that the property was a 'reasonably necessary and valuable part of the evidence material to the charges against the accused'. It was in the public interest for the property to be retained at least until trial.[36] On the facts of the case it was probable that it might become necessary to produce the banknotes as evidence in the plaintiff's criminal trial. It was on that basis that the police had the authority to retain them. On the other hand, in the absence of specific statutory authority, there was no power for the police to retain money or property seized from a person solely in anticipation of compensation, forfeiture or retention order.

If no charge

It frequently happens that the police suspect that certain property is stolen, but they cannot prove it. This may occur where they observe that the engine or chassis number of motor vehicles have been tampered with. The alleged owner may have been a bona fide purchaser of the vehicle or at any rate may have no knowledge of any tampering. If the police lawfully seize such a vehicle on suspicion that it was unlawfully obtained, the question to be determined is for how long can they retain it in the absence of any charge being laid.

In the Trinidad and Tobago High Court, it has been held that detention of a vehicle, seized under the authority of a valid search warrant for about three years, was a contravention of the applicant's rights: *Deonanan Ramdial v Commissioner of Police and AG* HCA 542/99 (2000) (unreported).[37] The judge felt that three weeks was sufficient time for the police to complete their investigations in that case and return the vehicle if no charge was forthcoming.

On slightly different facts the Court of Appeal held in *Jaroo v AG* HCA No 78 of 1990 (unreported)[38] that a motor vehicle which was lawfully seized by the police was lawfully retained by the police. The vehicle was seized in August 1987 when the applicant went to the licensing office to have it inspected. There, the inspector observed that the chassis number appeared to have been tampered with. A subsequent examination by the Forensic Science Centre in June 1988 disclosed that both the engine and chassis numbers had been erased

36 If there is an appeal on conviction then the goods could be retained until the appeal is determined.

37 Judgment delivered, 17 June 2000.

38 Judgment delivered, 30 November 1998.

and new numbers stamped in their place. The Court of Appeal concluded that in the absence of criminal proceedings 'there would of necessity arise a time beyond which it would be unreasonable to detain the vehicle any longer'. On the other hand, a clear fetter on the ability of the police to restore the vehicle to the applicant existed since to do so would place the applicant in a position of breaking the law, by keeping a vehicle that was not qualified for registration (because of the fact that the tampering indicated that the particulars of the vehicle were false). Since the applicant had provided no assistance to the police which could lead to apprehension of those responsible for the tampering he could not complain of a failure by the police to actively pursue the (unidentified) culprits. In the circumstances of that case, there was no breach of his rights by the police.

The appellant appealed and the Privy Council affirmed the decision of the Court of Appeal in *Thakur Persad Jaroo v AG* (2001) 59 WIR 519 PC, following the principles in *Ghani* (above) and *Malone* (above). The Board, however, confirmed that the police had to show that in the first instance they had reasonable grounds for believing the property stolen and its continued detention was necessary to complete their investigations. Continued detention after a long period without any charges being proffered was unacceptable.

It is evident, then, that the police are entitled to seize and retain from a person goods that connect him to the crime being investigated. These may be retained as long as is necessary to prosecute a criminal charge. In respect of other goods, the police may seize anything which may be pertinent to any charge, but they may not retain them indefinitely if no charge is laid. They should be returned to the owner or person entitled to possession of it (*Jaroo*) unless there is some clear fetter on the power of the police to do so.

Illegal search

On a final note it should be pointed out that even if the police seize goods illegally, they are entitled to retain them once the goods constitute evidence in relation to a crime: *Kuruma v R* [1955] 1 All ER 236, PC. The law in Commonwealth Caribbean jurisdictions is in keeping with the English common law that illegally obtained evidence will not be deemed inadmissible merely because of that fact. In *Herman King v R* [1969] 1 AC 304, PC, the Privy Council considered an appeal from the Court of Appeal of Jamaica in which drugs were found on an appellant who was searched by the police acting under a search warrant which turned out to be illegal. It was confirmed that the evidence was not inadmissible merely because it was illegally obtained. Applying *Kuruma v R* [1955] 1 All ER 236, PC, it was held that the fact that the evidence was illegally obtained was no ground for disallowing it. This position is in striking contrast to that of the US, where this would constitute prima facie grounds for its exclusion: *Mapp v Ohio* (1961) 361 US 643.

In Commonwealth Caribbean jurisdictions, a person whose house or person has been illegally searched may have recourse to a civil action against the police (by suing the State or the Crown) for trespass, but the evidence will still be admitted.

CHAPTER 4

PROSECUTION AND BAIL

This chapter will focus on two separate areas that precede the actual trial process in the criminal court. The first is the prosecution powers of the main authority with the responsibility for prosecution, the Director of Public Prosecutions, and also the police and the private citizen. The second area is that of bail, which arises when a person is in custody having been arrested and charged with an offence.

PROSECUTION

Most Constitutions of Commonwealth Caribbean States establish the post of Director of Public Prosecutions (DPP). The Bahamas is a notable exception and while there is a DPP, that post is another public office and the Attorney General has control over prosecutions. In the other jurisdictions the post of DPP has constitutional protection, unlike most other public offices. By virtue of the different constitutions, the Director has power:

- to institute and undertake criminal proceedings against any person before any court other than a court martial in respect of any offence against the law;
- to take over and continue any such criminal proceedings that may have been instituted by any other person or authority;
- to discontinue at any stage before judgment is delivered any such criminal proceedings instituted by himself or any other person or authority.[1]

It would seem apparent from these provisions that the DPP has full control over all criminal proceedings in the countries of the Commonwealth Caribbean. Yet, within the constitutions themselves, there are specific limitations to that power. Additionally, the minister under whom the Department of Criminal Law falls (usually the Attorney General) may exercise some control over that Department.

The limits of the constitutional powers

While the relevant constitutions all say that 'the DPP shall not be subject to the direction or control of any other person or authority', some constitutions make this subject to powers

---

1 These clauses are identically reflected in the various Constitutions as follows:
Antigua, 88(1);
Barbados, 79(2);
Dominica, 72(2);
Grenada, 71(2);
Guyana, 187(1);
Jamaica, 94(3);
St Kitts and Nevis, 65(2);
St Lucia, 73(2);
St Vincent, 64(2);
Trinidad and Tobago, 90(3).

conferred on the Attorney General. In Antigua, for instance, the DPP's constitutional powers are subject to those of the Attorney General (AG) under s 89 of the Constitution. The AG in Antigua can give general or specific directions to the DPP as to the exercise of his constitutional powers in relation to offences against laws relating to official secrets, mutiny, or Antigua's rights or obligations under international law. The Barbados Constitution provides for even wider powers reserved for the AG to give directions to the DPP in the exercise of the latter's constitutional powers.[2] The AG may give directions in relation, inter alia, to offences of privacy, treason, sedition as well as official secrets, mutiny and the like. In Dominica, the AG may give directions to the DPP in relation to his power of discontinuance.

The powers of the DPP under constitutions such as those of Guyana, Jamaica and Trinidad and Tobago seem almost free from control. While in Trinidad and Tobago the exercise of his powers by the DPP is subject to the responsibility of the AG for 'the administration of legal affairs', this should not be taken to refer to interference with the prosecution of criminal matters. The issue came up for consideration in *AG of Fiji v DPP* [1983] 2 WLR 275, PC. In that case the Privy Council had to consider the provisions of a constitution which was identical to that of the Commonwealth jurisdictions but which, like Jamaica for example, included no reservation of power to the AG. Under constitutional provisions enabling the Head of State to assign responsibility of government departments to particular ministers,[3] the DPP's office was assigned to the AG. The DPP of Fiji initiated proceedings claiming that the assignment of responsibility to the AG was unconstitutional as it was in breach of the seemingly unrestricted powers of the DPP granted by the Fijian Constitution. The Privy Council held that it was indeed true that the constitutional functions and powers granted to the DPP by the Constitution and other laws were nonassignable (unless specifically stated otherwise). It was, however, permissible for the Head of State to assign to the AG such of the functions of the DPP as were not required by the Constitution or any other law to be exercised exclusively by the DPP. Areas of responsibility that could legitimately fall under the AG's general direction and control included matters of funding and accountability; accommodation; facilities and reviewing of the establishment of the staff of the department.

The Court of Appeal of Trinidad and Tobago in *The State v Seeromanie Maraj-Naraynsingh et al* Cr App No 5 of 2006 followed the Privy Council in *AG of Fiji v DPP* when a similar issue arose in that country. The Court of Appeal sitting in a panel of five judges confirmed that in the exercise of his prosecutorial powers under the Constitution the DPP is under no obligation to obey any instruction or direction from the Attorney General.

It would seem evident then that, while the AG may have more or less administrative powers of control over the department of the DPP and any other power reserved to him by the Constitution, the DPP acts independently in his actual control of criminal proceedings. Although the privilege of charging an offender lies within the domain of the police, the DPP is in charge of all prosecutions. As such, before charges are laid, the DPP may give advice to the police as to whether charges should be laid in any particular case. This will be especially true of cases of public interest and other serious matters such as murder cases and those that are complex. The police thus work closely with the DPP and must follow his advice, since he may step in at any time and 'take over' any criminal proceedings under his constitutional powers. He may direct the police to institute charges against any person before any court (other than a court-martial) and may also discontinue proceedings at any

2 Section 79A of the Constitution.

3 Identical to s 79(1) of the Trinidad and Tobago Constitution.

stage before judgment. Naturally, the DPP need not exercise all his powers personally, and constitutionally he may delegate the exercise of his powers to certain specified persons. Such persons, usually legal officers employed in the Office of the DPP, are, however, subject to the general or specific instructions of the DPP.

In *Benjamin (Steadroy) v Commissioner of Police and the AG of Antigua and Barbuda* [2014] UKPC 8 the issue arose as to whether the police were bound to follow the DPP's instructions not to lay a charge. In this case the appellant, the Leader of the Opposition, was, in August 2008, charged with a summary offence relating to an endorsement on an application form for a passport. The DPP had, however, previously instructed the police not to institute a criminal charge against the appellant. The police ignored the instruction and charged him. The appellant sought judicial review of this decision. At first instance the court refused the application. On appeal, the Eastern Caribbean Court of Appeal, by a majority, held that it would take an overly austere reading of the Constitution to hold that, notwithstanding the DPP's power to discontinue proceedings brought by the police, the DPP lacked the power to instruct the police not to institute criminal proceedings against an individual. The Privy Council allowed the appeal by The Commissioner of Police. The Board ruled that the DPP's Constitutional power under section 88 of the Constitution to institute criminal proceedings could not be construed as the power to prevent the police from initiating proceedings against an individual. The Board also disagreed with the majority opinion of the Court of Appeal, which held that implicit in the DPP's power under section 88(1)(c) of the Constitution to discontinue proceedings there lay a power to prevent the police from instituting criminal proceedings. The Board concluded that although the Director could not instruct the police not to institute proceedings he could still make such a request. In such instances, the police should act cautiously before deciding to reject such a request.

Consent of the DPP

While the police themselves lay charges and may initiate proceedings on their own initiative (subject to the control of the DPP, as discussed above) there are certain offences for which the consent of the DPP,[4] sometimes termed 'fiat', is required before proceedings are initiated. These offences are specified by statute in the various jurisdictions and unless specific consent of the DPP is given for their initiation, all ensuing proceedings will be null and void. The offences usually include corruption and certain types of perjury. It has been stated[5] that with regard to these types of offences, persons in high office are likely to be subject to accusations being made 'willy-nilly' by third parties, hence the protection afforded by the requirement for the consent of the DPP.

In *R v Waller* [1910] 1 KB 364, consent of the DPP was required for a charge of being a habitual criminal under the Prevention of Crime Act 1908. At the trial, no formal proof was given of the consent of the DPP to the charge although a written consent purporting to be signed by the DPP was produced. No evidence was given as to the authenticity of the signature and no objection was taken at trial as to the absence of that proof. The English Court of Appeal held that in the absence of an objection being taken, no formal proof of consent need be given. If objection is, however, taken then the court must satisfy itself that consent was given. In *Tappin v Lucas* (1973) 20 WIR 229, a case from the jurisdiction of

4 In the Bahamas, this falls within the domain of the AG, as reflected in the Criminal Procedure Code, Ch 91.

5 *Jagessar and Bhola Nandlal v The State (No 1)* (1989) 41 WIR 342.

Guyana, the Court of Appeal held that a letter to the court signed by the DPP was sufficient to comply with the Constitution empowering him to discontinue criminal proceedings when he chose to do so. It follows then that that letter should be equally sufficient to indicate consent of the DPP where such consent is necessary. Consent need not be given before the defendant is arrested for the offence or even charged. It has been said that such consent could be validly obtained up to the time the defendant appears in court.[6] In practice, the courts should not entertain the laying of a charge unless the consent, where necessary, of the DPP has been granted and is so indicated.

In *Angel* [1968] 2 All ER 607, the defendant was tried and convicted for gross indecency and buggery against a boy of nine. The Sexual Offences Act 1967 provided mandatorily that 'No proceedings shall be instituted except by or with the consent of the DPP against any man for the offence of buggery with, or gross indecency with, another man'. No consent had been obtained to the initiation of the proceedings. The court held that as a consequence the whole trial, including the committal proceedings, was a complete nullity. It had been instituted without the necessary consent. The conviction was therefore quashed. A similar decision was made in *R v Warn* [1968] 1 All ER 339 for a failure to observe the identical provision in another prosecution. An interesting application of the statutory requirement for consent by the DPP as it operated with various other statutes was considered by the Trinidad and Tobago Court of Appeal in *Jagessar and Bhola Nandlal v The State* (No 1) (1989) 41 WIR 342. To summarise the rather complicated facts: a magistrate and another were charged with various offences and the proceedings were laid in the magistrates' court as is usual. After a preliminary enquiry for conspiracy to pervert the course of justice, both parties were committed to stand trial for corruption, in accordance with the magistrate's power to commit 'for any indictable offence' disclosed from the evidence. The DPP, in accordance with her powers to indict for 'any offence' disclosed on the depositions, indicted for corruption. The defendants were convicted and appealed on the grounds, inter alia, that there had been no consent of the DPP to the institution of the prosecution as required by s 10 of the Prevention of Corruption Act under which provision the men were indicted.

The Trinidad and Tobago Court of Appeal dismissed the appeal and held that there had been no contravention of the spirit and intendment of the Corruption Act. The court distinguished *Warn*[7] (above) on the basis that in Trinidad and Tobago, all indictments must be signed by the DPP, whereas in England this need not be. Since the DPP had power to act as she did and did sign the indictment, it would be ridiculous to suppose that if she wanted to indict for corruption on proceedings for conspiracy to pervert she must start proceedings all over again. She would then be consenting to herself instituting proceedings. In all the circumstances the purpose and spirit of the law had been achieved.

Other powers

When the post of Director of Public Prosecutions was constituted constitutionally in the Commonwealth Caribbean, provision was made by statute to substitute the Office of the Director of Public Prosecutions for that of the Attorney General in the reference to certain legal functions related to criminal prosecutions.[8] As a result, the variety of functions which

---

6 *Whale* [1991] Crim LR 692.

7 *R v Warn* [1968] 1 All ER 339.

8 An example of such legislation is Cap 22:03 of St Kitts and Nevis.

must necessarily be performed by the public officer responsible for criminal prosecutions are now performed by the DPP. These include the power to file an indictment, refusal to file an indictment, order a further preliminary enquiry and in some cases direct the committal for trial of an accused person where the magistrate has discharged him. An example of a somewhat comprehensive, though not exhaustive, codification of the general powers of the DPP may be found in ss 647–653 of the St Lucia Criminal Code. In other jurisdictions these powers are located in several diverse pieces of legislation including the relevant Criminal Procedure Acts and the magistrates' or summary procedure legislation.

Nolle prosequi

At common law, the AG had power to stay indictable proceedings pending in every court by entering a nolle prosequi: *R v Dunn* (1843) 1 C&K 730. Since the DPP has (in general) assumed the functions of the AG in respect of criminal matters, this function now devolves to the former. While a nolle prosequi puts an end to proceedings, it does not operate as a bar or acquittal since there would have been no adjudication by a court of competent jurisdiction.

In most Commonwealth Caribbean jurisdictions, Barbados being a notable exception, the power to enter a nolle prosequi has been codified by statute. In jurisdictions where there is no statutory codification it would seem that the common law power would be enjoyed by the DPP, in the absence of any express abolition. It is, however, arguable whether this power adds anything to the express constitutional power of the DPP 'to discontinue at any stage before judgment is delivered any such criminal proceedings undertaken by him or any other person or authority'. This constitutional power is very wide. It is not limited, as is the power of nolle prosequi, which can only be entered in respect of indictable proceedings after preliminary enquiry. An example of its use in these jurisdictions is shown in *Tappin v Lucas* (above), where a discontinuance was entered by the DPP at the magistrates' court.

Some examples of the codification of the common law nolle prosequi may be found in s 13(1) of the Antiguan Criminal Procedure Act, Cap 117; s 114(1) of the Guyanese Criminal Law (Procedure) Act, Cap 10:01 and s 17(1) of the Criminal Procedure Act, Cap 4:06, of St Kitts and Nevis. These provisions refer to the exercise of the power after 'the receipt' of the depositions on committal to stand trial from the magistrates' court. The Trinidad and Tobago Criminal Procedure Act, Chap 12:02, s 11, speaks of a power of the DPP 'not to further prosecute' but only if the evidence is deemed to be 'insufficient'. Although the marginal note describes this as nolle prosequi and it is only exercised after a preliminary inquiry, the condition of its exercise, only on insufficient evidence, is not in keeping with the general concept of nolle prosequi.

It must be pointed out that in England, the Prosecution of Offences Act 1985, which establishes the prosecuting services of England and Wales, does not, in s 3, which describes the DPP's powers, include a general power of discontinuance like the West Indian constitutions. This may explain the continued use and importance of the power of nolle prosequi in England. It would seem hardly necessary for the DPP in Commonwealth Caribbean jurisdictions to have recourse to this power. One reason, however, why it may still be used is that there can be no argument that it gives rise to an acquittal or a bar to future proceedings. This was clear at common law and in fact, where there are statutory provisions codifying the power of nolle prosequi, this is stipulated.[9] It should be hardly less clear that a

9 As in Antigua, Guyana, St Kitts and Nevis, discussed above.

discontinuance is equally not an acquittal, but since this power has not frequently been the subject of litigation, office holders (in the post of DPP) may not want to test the waters.

Richards (Lloydell) v R (1992) 41 WIR 263, PC is an interesting example of the use of nolle prosequi in its widest sense. In a trial for murder in Jamaica, the prosecuting attorney indicated an acceptance of the plea to the lesser offence of manslaughter. The matter was adjourned for sentence and in the interval, the DPP stopped the proceedings by a nolle prosequi and started over again with the charge of murder. The defendant was convicted and appealed on an argument that this amounted to double jeopardy. The Privy Council held that there was no conviction if there had been no sentence. A plea of autrefois convict thus failed. The Privy Council appeared to see nothing wrong with the exercise of the power of nolle prosequi in the given circumstances so as to facilitate a prosecution of murder. The first proceedings were barred, but this did not prevent other proceedings based on the same evidence for the more serious offence of murder. The court even seemed to equate this exercise of the power of nolle prosequi with that of discontinuance when it said that the DPP 'in which power to discontinue any criminal proceedings, at any stage before judgment is delivered, is vested' decided to 'discontinue' the proceedings. This was said despite the fact that the Board recognised that on 3 October, a nolle prosequi was entered.

It would seem clear, then, that the power of discontinuance includes the power of nolle prosequi and it is now unnecessary for a DPP to resort to the latter to stop criminal proceedings.

Duties of the DPP

Attendant to his power to direct and control criminal prosecutions, the DPP has been held to have certain obligations to ensure a proper functioning of the administration of criminal justice. In *Boodram v AG of Trinidad and Tobago* (1996) 47 WIR 459, PC, the applicant, a murder accused, in a constitutional motion claimed that his right to a fair trial had been contravened by the failure of the DPP to stop prejudicial continuing press reports. Although the Privy Council dismissed the motion on the basis that prejudicial pre-trial publicity was not a proper ground for complaint under the Constitution, the Board had much to say of the DPP's failure to intervene. Given the flavour of the many news reports, which suggested that the applicant was involved in the local drugs mafia and had engaged in witness intimidation, the Board found it 'surprising, to say the least, that the director seems to have done nothing at all'[10] to alleviate the situation. They found that the DPP:

> by virtue of his position both as a participant in the criminal process and as an officer of the State with the authority and means to prosecute contentious issues, had a heavy responsibility towards the court, the defendants brought before it, and the community at large to play his part in keeping 'the springs of justice undefiled'.[11]

While he need not act on every trifling complaint, he must be alert to guard against any serious risk that trial by jury will develop into trial by media. This was seen as an important function of his office and it was opined that the DPP, in cases where the media carries prejudicial reports on criminal proceedings before the court, must act to give directions to the media to desist and/or must bring contempt of court proceedings as regards their publication. Such, then, are the types of responsibility that accrue to the office of the person who has control of all criminal proceedings in the particular jurisdiction.

10 *Boodram v AG of Trinidad and Tobago* (1996) 47 WIR 459, p 468, PC.

11 Ibid, p 472, PC.

Challenging the decision to prosecute or not

While the DPP has a discretion not to prosecute offenders in given cases, he must always act fairly. Although legislation and older cases, such as *R v Comptroller of Patents* [1899]1 QB 909, p 914, may suggest that the DPP's actions in deciding not to prosecute cannot be challenged, this seems no longer to be the case: *R v General Council of the Bar ex p Percival* [1990]3 All ER 137. Such a decision may be reviewable on the grounds of unreasonableness[12] of the conduct of a public authority. As has been discussed in Chapter 2, the trial courts will consider an application to stay unfair proceedings on the ground of abuse of process if it amounts to delay or manipulation of the process of the court. Alternatively, an application may be made for judicial review of the decision to prosecute if it is unfair or unreasonable, but this is less likely to succeed since the argument can be made before or at the trial itself. The Privy Council, however, emphasised in *Marshall v DPP* (2007) 70 WIR 193, PC that while the power to review a decision of the DPP not to prosecute is available in principle it is to be sparingly exercised. The DPP is not under a general duty to give reasons for a decision not to prosecute: *R v DPP ex p Manning* [2001] QB 330. It is, however, reasonable to expect in circumstances where a person had died in state custody and a coroner had concluded at an inquest that the killing was unlawful, that reasons be given for such a decision.

In *R (on application of F) v DPP* [2013] EWHC 945 (Admin) the English Divisional Court considered an application for judicial review of the decision not to prosecute in a case of rape, following 'a careful, detailed analysis' of the evidence and the relevant prosecutorial policies by the Deputy DPP. The Court focussed its consideration solely on whether the review was flawed and found that the decision was made on the basis of an error in law as to how 'choice' could influence 'consent' in an offence of rape. Judicial review was granted and the Court ordered that the decision not to prosecute should be reviewed on the basis of the legal principles on consent explained in the judgment.

This was a rare instance of a review being granted in respect of a decision not to prosecute. It may be explained on the basis that the one fundamental error in the law made (in the review of evidence) relating to the issue of consent, was in relation to principles of conditional consent to rape, which had not been fully developed at the time the decision was made by the Deputy DPP.

In *Satnarine Sharma v Carla Brown-Antoine and ors* (2006) 69 WIR 379, PC, the Privy Council examined the question of whether the decision to prosecute (as opposed to not prosecute) may be challenged by judicial review. The Board held that such a challenge should only be taken in rare and exceptional cases; that the criminal proceedings should generally be allowed to run the course, where all issues can be ventilated.

Private prosecutions

A private person may bring a criminal charge in his own name against a potential defendant.[13] This is in keeping with the general principle that a citizen's right to unimpeded access to the courts can only be taken away by express enactment: *Raymond v Honey* [1982] 1 All ER 756, p 762, HL. In that case, the House of Lords considered an application by the applicant, a prisoner, to commit the Governor of the prison at which he was an inmate for

12 See Hilson, CS, 'Discretion to prosecute and judicial review' (1993) Crim LR 737, pp 740–43.

13 See *Allman v Hardcastle* [1903] JP 440.

contempt. The Governor had stopped an earlier application by the applicant to the High Court for leave to commit the Governor for contempt. The House of Lords, in dismissing the Governor's appeal against a contempt finding, reiterated the right of every citizen to avail themselves of unimpeded access to the courts to have their legal rights and obligations ascertained. The prisoner had a right as a private citizen to bring an action for contempt.

The right to bring a private prosecution is limited in only two aspects, namely (1) where the prosecution is intended by way of an individual grievance only and (2) where the statute limits the right to prosecute to a particular person or party: *Safeway Access and Support Systems Ltd v Inspector of Factories* Civ Appeal Nos 229 & 218 of 2010 (Trinidad and Tobago) (unreported), following the English line of authorities.

Therefore, apart from the above limitations in Commonwealth Caribbean jurisdictions, anyone may file a criminal complaint in the magistrates' courts. In practice, however, this only happens if the police fail to do so and the complainant is dissatisfied. It is always preferable that the police lay the charge and they or the DPP prosecute the matter. This is so because the police have not only powers and duties to investigate and detect crimes, but also the resources to do so. These are not readily available to the private citizens. Invariably, then, private prosecutions occur only in respect of fairly trivial matters, breaches of peace as between neighbours, or where the complainant is seen by the police as a recurrent troublemaker and so they elect not to prosecute.

Interestingly enough, a private person in Trinidad and Tobago has the power[14] by statute to challenge the decision of the DPP to discharge a person who has been committed to stand trial. A judge may, on such an application, make an order to recommit a discharged person to stand trial and technically the complainant may be admitted to prosecute privately in the Assizes/High Court.[15] Nonetheless, since the DPP has the power to discontinue any criminal proceedings it is arguable that such an attempt to prevent a discharge may not get off the ground. An aggrieved complainant may have to resort to judicial review proceedings to challenge the actions of the DPP. In *Jewan Mohit v DPP* [2006] UKPC 20 (from Mauritius) the Board has to consider such an appeal. On the question of whether the power of the DPP to enter a nolle prosequi in a private prosecution is susceptible to judicial review, the Board held that while the Constitution gave the DPP control over (including discontinuing) criminal proceedings, there was no support for the contention that his power to enter a nolle prosequi cannot be challenged. If the DPP's decision is not subject to judicial review, the complainant may have no remedy against a suspected tortfeasor. The courts therefore have the power to inquire into the decision, as to whether it was made in a lawful or rational manner.

The foregoing on private prosecutions may be of academic interest, but in practical terms it has little impact in indictable trials. The Office of the DPP prosecutes such cases in the Assizes and the complainant is a witness. There has never been any instance of a person prosecuting privately in the Assizes.

Police prosecutors

Historically, police officers have prosecuted 'police cases' in the magistrates' courts, that is, criminal cases when they lay the charge (as distinct from private prosecutions). This is a common law practice which arose because of the insufficiency of lawyers in the prosecuting department and the relatively minor nature of the matters in the magistrates' courts. In fact

14 Criminal Procedure Act, Chap 12:02, s 10.

15 Indictment Rule 2(3), Chap 12:02 (above).

this practice is given specific recognition in the criminal procedure laws of some jurisdictions.[16] In St Lucia, the legislation requires that the police prosecutor should hold the rank of at least a corporal. In general, the Police Acts in other jurisdictions either expressly or impliedly recognise the practice of police officers prosecuting police laid cases.

Naturally, police prosecutors are subject to the overall control and direction of the DPP (and his delegated officers) in the prosecution of a case. This is because of the wide constitutional powers of the DPP to have and take control of all criminal prosecutions, as discussed above.

The Office of the DPP will itself prosecute in complex or capital matters in the magistrates' courts and in those which are of high public interest, depending on the availability of staff. It has been recommended that the use of police prosecutors be abolished[17] and that trained lawyers from the Office of the DPP, in the exercise of the ultimate control by that Office, replace them. It is recognised, however, that such a measure will depend on the availability of resources to expand the establishment of the Office of the DPP.

In summary, then, police officers by and large prosecute in the magistrates' courts while counsel from the Office of the DPP prosecute in the Supreme Court (the High Court and the Court of Appeal). In Jamaica, the position is slightly different in that a Clerk of the Courts, a trained lawyer, is empowered by the Judicature (Resident Magistrates) Act, as amended by Act No 6 of 2016, to prosecute in the Parish Courts. In these courts, specified indictable offences[18] are tried on indictment by the judge of the Parish Court. Such a Judge also has special statutory jurisdiction to try certain summary offences in which case the Clerk of the Courts will prosecute. A judge of the Parish Court also has all of the powers of a Justice of the Peace and in practice hears all summary matters. The Office of the DPP may also prosecute in the Parish Court as the DPP determines and will always prosecute in the Supreme Court.

Civilian representative

The summary courts legislation in some jurisdictions provides that while a complainant or defendant may represent himself or be represented by a lawyer, he may also be assisted by a relative (son, daughter, parent, spouse) or his employer.[19] The question of civilian representation came up for consideration in the English Court of Appeal in *McKenzie v McKenzie* [1970] 3 All ER 1034. In that case the trial judge in matrimonial proceedings refused to allow the husband litigant, who did not have legal representation, to be assisted in court by a non-practitioner in England (although he was a lawyer in Australia). The Court of Appeal sanctioned the obiter statement in *Collier v Hicks* (1831) 2 B&Ad 663 and confirmed that:

> Any person, whether he be a professional man or not, may attend as a friend of either party, may take notes, may quietly make suggestions and give advice; but no one can demand to take part in the proceedings as an advocate, contrary to the regulations of the court as settled by the discretion of the justices.[20]

16 St Lucia Criminal Code, s 653; St Vincent Criminal Procedure Code, Cap 172, s 66(2).

17 Report of Commission of Inquiry into Administration of Justice, June 2000–September 2000, Report submitted by Lord McKay, September 2000, p 7.

18 Judicature (Resident Magistrates) Act, as amended by Act No 6 of 2016, s 268.

19 Chap 4:20, as in Summary Courts Act, Trinidad and Tobago, s 5.

20 *McKenzie v McKenzie* [1970] 3 All ER 1034, p 1036.

It would seem that anyone then may sit with[21] a complainant or defendant in either a criminal or civil case and give advice or prompting. It is even possible, unless the practice of the court is otherwise, for such a person to appear as an advocate on his friend's behalf.

BAIL

Bail is defined as pre-trial release in criminal proceedings. It may be considered a contract whereby an accused person is released on certain terms from custody to his surety or sureties.[22] If granted bail, the defendant signs a bond in court offices or the prison, undertaking to appear for his trial. This is the contract, which is 'guaranteed' by a surety or sureties, as specified in the court order. The question of bail only arises if a person has been arrested. In respect of a person who has been summoned to court, no question of bail arises, since he is never in custody.

Once arrested, a person should either be released without charge or charged with an offence.[23] If he was arrested by warrant, the charge would have already been sworn to. If without warrant, the charge will follow arrest. As discussed in Chapter 3, the decision to charge or release must be resolved within a reasonable time, 48 hours being the usual outside limit.

If charged with a crime, an arrested defendant may be released from custody only on bail pending the determination of his case. Of course, a defendant may be released on signing his own bond, that is, with no surety, but this is not common practice and usually only occurs with trivial offences.

Constitutional right

The Trinidad and Tobago Constitution specifies in s 5(2)(f)(iii) that an arrested person has a right not to be deprived of 'reasonable bail without just cause'. Other Commonwealth Caribbean jurisdictions do not have this clearly expressed constitutional right. The right to bail must be elicited from the right to a trial within a reasonable time as in the Jamaican Constitution. Section 15 specifies in part:

> (3) Any person who is arrested or detained ... and who is not released, shall be brought without delay before a court; and if any [such] person ... is not tried within a reasonable time, then without prejudice to any further proceedings which may be brought against him, he shall be released either unconditionally or upon reasonable conditions, including in particular such conditions as are reasonably necessary to ensure that he appears at a later date for trial or for proceedings preliminary to trial.

The right to release on conditions or not which is equivalent to bail only arises if a trial within reasonable time has not been had by the defendant. This right would seem to be less protected than that in the Trinidad and Tobago Constitution, which grants the right to bail regardless of whether a speedy trial is achievable or not. Nonetheless, the Trinidad and Tobago provision itself permits the denial of the right if there is 'just cause'.

---

21 Ibid, p 1038, letter j.

22 Burke, J, *Osborne's Concise Law Dictionary*, 6th edn, 1976, p 42.

23 The exception is in the case of detention during a state of emergency, which is constitutionally permissible.

It seems clear, then, that the constitutional right to bail in the Commonwealth Caribbean is not open-ended. In these jurisdictions, the essential determination in granting bail and setting conditions is whether the defendant is likely to attend his trial. Factors which go towards making this assessment have been set down at common law in older English cases that are followed. Other principles in respect of the entitlement to bail and the procedure to apply for bail are contained in specific local enactments.

Statutory entitlement

Trinidad and Tobago,[24] the Bahamas,[25] Barbados[26] and Jamaica[27] have Bail Acts that are currently in force. While these Acts are based largely on the English Bail Act 1976, there are some differences.

The Bahamas Bail Act purports to 'consolidate the laws' relating to the release from custody of an accused in criminal proceedings. The Trinidad and Tobago Act, on the other hand, is said to 'amend the law' relating to the same circumstance. How far this has been done will be considered in the ensuing discussion. The Barbados Act merely seeks to 'make provision in relation to bail . . . and related matters'.

St Lucia does not have a separate Bail Act but has included in its Criminal Code 2004 extensive provisions codifying the principles relating to bail.[28] They are similar to the provisions of the Barbados Bail Act.

A defendant who has been refused bail by a judge may, however, reapply to the High Court for reconsideration of the issue on the basis of a change of circumstances since the refusal. These could include matters of health or even the delay in setting a trial date. Legislation in Trinidad and Tobago intervened in 2005 by the Administration of Justice (Miscellaneous Provisions) Act No 19 of 2005 (now section 11A of the Bail Act) allowing the applicant to appeal to the Court of Appeal on a judge's refusal to grant bail. The prosecution also may appeal to the Court of Appeal a decision of a trial judge to grant bail to an applicant. Similarly the Bail (Amendment) Act No 20 of 2010 of Jamaica allows the prosecution to appeal a Resident's Magistrate's (now a decision of a judge of the Parish Court) decision to grant bail. Previously only a defendant could appeal a decision on bail (a refusal).

The majority of the legislation in the other jurisdictions is piecemeal and far from comprehensive. They are similar in content[29] and merely set the outer limits for the grant of bail and in some cases the procedure. They allude to the discretion of the judge or magistrate to grant bail, but do not state the circumstances in which this discretion is to be granted, unlike the Bail Acts. The exercise of the discretion is thus determined by the common law. In general, all magistrates are prohibited from granting bail to a person charged with murder, treason or offences connected to treason. The general statutes leave open the question whether bail is grantable for such offences by a judge of the High Court. The Bail Act of

24 Act No 18 of 1994, the Bail Act 1994, now Chap 4:60.

25 The Bahamas Bail Act 1994.

26 Barbados Bail Act 1996–28 (proclaimed on 15 January 2001).

27 The Bail Act 2000 and Legal Notice 3/2002.

28 See Chapter 3, ss 591–613.

29 Compare, for instance: Antigua – Magistrate's Code of Procedure Act, Cap 255, s 62; Dominica – Magistrate's Code of Procedure Act, Chap 4:20, s 58; Grenada – Criminal Procedure Code, Cap 72 B, ss 47–49; Guyana – Criminal Law Procedure Code, Cap 10:01, ss 81–87; St Kitts and Nevis – Magistrate's Code of Procedure Act, Cap 3:17 s 66.

Trinidad and Tobago has established a total prohibition against the grant of bail for murder, treason, piracy or hijacking (s 5 read with the First Schedule, Part I).

The Barbados Magistrates' Courts Act 1996–27 provides that a person charged with high treason, treason or murder may be granted bail in accordance with the Bail Act. Section 5(4) of the Bail Act states clearly that only a judge can order bail to be granted to a person charged with murder, treason or high treason. The Jamaica Bail Act as amended by Act No 20 of 2011 at 3(4) and (4) A enables a judge or a resident magistrate (now a judge of the Parish Court) to do so but places the onus on the accused to satisfy the court that bail should be granted.

The St Lucia Criminal Code was amended in 2006 by Act No 11 of 2006 which repealed and replaced sub-section 593(4). The law now allows only a judge to entertain an application for bail for murder, treason, rape and a few other offences for which bail previously could not be granted. In Antigua Act No 13 of 2004 replaced section 62(3) of the Magistrates Code of Procedure to specifically prohibit a magistrate from granting bail to a person charged with murder, treason, certain offences against the Firearms Act and all offences under the Sexual Offences Act.

The separation of powers argument

The issue has arisen as to whether Parliament has the right to remove from the courts the jurisdiction to withhold bail in respect of certain offences – as is the law in many Commonwealth Caribbean jurisdictions. In *The State v Khoyratty* [2006] UKPC 13 the Board considered an amendment to the Mauritian Constitution which sought to deny the right to bail to persons charged with terrorism or drug offences. The Board held that the lower court was correct in holding that despite the fact that the law was a constitutional amendment it was still unconstitutional as it was in breach of the separation of powers doctrine underlying the Constitution. Bail was intrinsically within the domain of the judiciary and in a country founded on the rule of law and democratic principles it remained within that domain. The appeal by the State was dismissed.

It remains to be seen whether this decision will impact on the Commonwealth Caribbean in any way given the trend in the region towards legislative intervention to deny bail.

Who grants bail?

Bail may be granted by the police, a magistrate (or Justice of the Peace), a Judge of a Parish Court or a judge.

Police

In most jurisdictions, it is provided that where a person is arrested without warrant for a summary offence, the police may grant bail without bringing that person to court. If a person who is charged with a summary offence cannot be brought before the court within 24 hours, the police may grant bail.[30] These police powers are exercised more often in respect of breaches of the peace offences.

---

30 As in:
Barbados: Magistrates' Courts Act 1996–27, s 77;
Dominica: Magistrate's Code of Procedure Act, Chap 4:20, s 34;
Guyana: Summary (Jurisdiction) Procedure Act, Cap 10:02, s 71;
Jamaica: Justice of the Peace (Jurisdiction) Act, s 4;
Trinidad and Tobago: Summary Courts Act, Chap 4:20, s 104, which provision is saved by the Bail Act, s 21.

Magistrate

Since all offenders must first be brought before the magistrates' courts, magistrates are the authorities who mainly deal with bail applications. Other than where prohibited by statute (as in murder, treason, as mentioned above) a magistrate may entertain an application for the grant of bail for any offence. The application is made orally, usually on the first date of the appearance of the defendant. If bail is not granted, the defendant or his lawyer may re-apply for bail on subsequent hearings, then citing the length of time already in custody.

An application for bail may also be made before a Justice of Peace where a magistrate is unavailable. By statute, the former has power to grant bail, but will usually exercise it where it is expedient to do so, for trivial offences, or where the court may not sit for days.

Judge

All jurisdictions provide that where a magistrate refuses to grant bail, he must tell the defendant of his right to apply to a judge in chambers for bail. The Bahamas, Barbados, Jamaica, St Lucia and Trinidad and Tobago legislation all provide that a magistrate must supply reasons for his grant or refusal of bail so that either the defendant or the police may challenge his decision before a judge of the High Court. In the absence of statutory power, it would seem that the police have no right to apply to the High Court to challenge the decision of a magistrate to grant bail. Although High Court judges have inherent jurisdiction to grant bail, *Kray* [1965] Ch 736, p 741, it has been held that they have no power at common law to reduce the amount of bail fixed by a magistrate (exercising statutory powers): *Ex p Specular d* [1946] KB 48. In practice, however, persons frequently apply to the High Court for a reduction in bail set by a magistrate. Section 57 of the Grenada Criminal Procedure Code, Cap 72B, states that bail should not be excessive. The Bahamas, Barbados, Jamaica and Trinidad and Tobago Bail Acts allow this challenge as do the St Lucia provisions, enabling a defendant to ask for variation of the conditions. When bail is granted by a judge, he will usually direct that it be actually taken before a magistrate or Justice of the Peace.

The application

Applications for bail are made orally in the magistrates' court but in writing in the High Court. It is normal that the court in either case should be told of any previous convictions of the defendant whenever the police object to the grant of bail. In the High Court, this evidence is usually prepared beforehand and may be submitted in writing. The new Civil Rules of the Supreme Court of the Organisation of Eastern Caribbean States (OECS) specify the procedure to file an application to the Supreme Court on the hearing of a bail application (Part 58). Part 58 specifies, inter alia, the powers of the court to review the magistrate's decision. The practice in some jurisdictions is that bail applications in the High Court should be heard in camera as far as possible to prevent the prejudice that might occur if all and sundry were to hear of convictions of defendants before trial. It has been held to be desirable that in reporting cases, newspapers should refrain from mentioning previous convictions revealed in a bail application: *Ex p Specular d* (above).

It would seem obvious that a magistrate ought not to entertain an application for bail when a judge has refused a previous application. This, however, has not prevented lawyers from attempting to make a 'fresh application' for bail to a magistrate despite a refusal by the High Court in respect of the same defendant in the same matter.[31]

The principles

The general principles which a court must take into consideration in granting bail are set by the common law as reflected in *Archbold Criminal Pleading: Evidence and Procedure*, 38th edn, p 87. These are the matters which the court must consider in deciding whether to grant or refuse bail:

- the nature of the accusation;
- the nature of the evidence in support of the accusation;
- the severity of the punishment which conviction will entail;
- whether the sureties are independent or indemnified by the accused person.

The overall test is whether, should bail be granted, the defendant will appear to take his trial: *Re Robinson* (1854) 23 LJ QB 286. These common law principles are now more or less encompassed in statute in those jurisdictions that have a Bail Act.[32] In *Beneby v Commissioner of Police* (No 28 of 1995) (unreported), the Supreme Court of the Bahamas, in a considered judgment on the application of the common law vis à vis the Bahamian Bail Act, held that the Bail Act was really 'an enactment of the previous common law or some earlier statutory provision', in addition to the creation of new offences of absconding while on bail. Given that the Barbados, Jamaica and Trinidad and Tobago Bail Acts and the St Lucia provisions are in many ways very similar to that of the Bahamas, this would seem to be an equally adequate description of their contents.

The Privy Council has made it clear that the seriousness of the offence and the nature of the evidence do not constitute the essential determinant as to whether bail should be granted/ refused: *Hurnam v The State* [2005] UKPC 49. In that case the Board considered the Mauritius Bail Act 1999 which, like many Commonwealth Caribbean countries, is based on the English Bail Act 1976 and concluded that the magistrate had applied the right test in arriving at her decision to grant bail in circumstances where the offence was a serious one.

It is also an independent ground for refusal of bail if the defendant was already out on bail when he was charged with committing the current offence. This factor, now codified in the respective Bail Acts of the region, may ground the basis for a court refusing bail even if there is no likelihood of the defendant absconding.

Apart from those factors outlined above, which inform the decision to grant bail in all cases, the court may also refuse to grant bail in circumstances where the defendant has a bad criminal record, *Gentry* (1955) 31 Cr App R 195. This makes it likely that he may commit further offences of a similar kind while he is on bail or is likely to abscond without taking his trial: *R v Wharton* [1955] Crim LR 56, as recognised in *Beneby*.[33] Considerations such as whether the accused has a fixed abode, has ties with the community and is known to the

31 As reported in the *Trinidad Guardian*, 28 July 2000, p 4, headlined 'Kidnap accused fail again to get bail'.

32 The Bahamas Bail Act, Part A, First Schedule; Barbados Bail Act 1996–28, s 5(2); Trinidad and Tobago Bail Act, s 6(3)(4); St Lucia: Criminal Code 2004, s 593(2).

33 *Beneby v Commissioner of Police* No 28 of 1995 (unreported), the Bahamas, p 30.

police will also be taken into account. The Bail Acts of Trinidad and Tobago, Barbados, the Bahamas and Jamaica as well as the St Lucia bail provisions stipulate that the court should also consider whether the defendant, if released on bail, is likely to interfere with witnesses or otherwise obstruct the course of justice. In fact, this may be one of the determinants in the conditions set by a court in granting bail.[34]

The effect of these principles is that it is highly unusual to grant bail on charges of murder: *Re Barthelmy* (1852) 169 ER 636. This is so even in countries that do not completely prohibit the grant of bail for murder, as do Trinidad and Tobago and St Vincent.[35] A court will also place strong emphasis on previous convictions of the accused and his behaviour while out on bail on previous occasions. If he has a history of absconding, he is unlikely to be granted bail.

Constitution vs. the common law

In the absence of a total statutory prohibition on the granting of bail for specified offences, a court may review its own previous decision to grant bail if it appears that an early trial is unlikely. This is particularly true of those jurisdictions in which the constitutions, unlike Trinidad and Tobago, provide for the release of an accused person if he is not tried within a reasonable time.[36] In *Beneby* (above) the court held that this provision confers the primary right to a speedy trial (p 35), which, if not respected, leads to the constitutional right to bail. What is a 'reasonable time', however, may vary and the court held on the facts of that case that a preliminary enquiry scheduled to begin some three months after the charge was laid was reasonable.

In *Beneby* it was recognised that in the Bahamas, this constitutional provision has operated so as to permit the grant of bail to persons accused of murder because they were not tried in a reasonable time. This constitutional right can operate in an accused person's favour despite other negative factors, which would otherwise circumscribe the grant of bail. In Jamaica, this has occurred as well so that murder accused have been granted bail and it is an arguable entitlement in other jurisdictions, except for Trinidad and Tobago, which does not have such a constitutional right. Nonetheless, it would seem that once a preliminary enquiry is begun within a few months, the right to be tried within a reasonable time might be satisfied.

The surety

While bail may be granted on a defendant signing his own bond to appear for trial, on which failure he must pay the specified sum, this is usually only in respect of trivial offences. Otherwise, the accused person is granted bail on condition that he provides a surety. This is the usual primary condition: that the defendant must provide one or more surety or sureties for the purpose of securing his attendance to court when required. As such, the character and antecedents of the surety must be ascertained before he is accepted as such. The magistrate or justice accepting the surety may inquire as to both the sufficiency of the bail

34 As, e.g., in Bail Act 1996–28 of Barbados, s 12(4)(c).

35 St Vincent, Criminal Procedure Code, Cap 172, s 43, as amended by Act No 15 of 1993; Trinidad and Tobago, Bail Act 1994, s 5 and First Schedule, Part I.

36 Such as Jamaica, s 15(3). As indicated, this provision is common to most Commonwealth Caribbean constitutions.

and the means of the surety: *R v Saunders* (1849) 2 Cox 249, and this may be done on oath. The court ought to explain to the surety, and make sure that he understands, the obligation that he is about to undertake. If he fails to produce the defendant for his trial, or if any other condition is broken, the recognisance of the surety may be forfeited.

The recognisance

The surety will enter into a 'recognisance' by way of statutory declaration. This is the bond by which he undertakes the conditions of bail. The term 'recognisance' also refers to the sum which the surety pledges as an assurance that he will observe the conditions. This sum is also sometimes called the 'bond'. In general, the sum will be guaranteed by some property owned by the surety. In practice, a surety, or bailor as he is most often called, will guarantee the sum by a deed of title to property (or a certified copy of the same) or by cash. A certified cheque may also be accepted. The St Lucia Criminal Code enables a surety to deposit a sum of money as security. The Bahamas Act (Second Schedule) refers to financial assets including both movable and immovable property and bank balances as security for the recognisance. In Trinidad and Tobago s 4 of Act No 11 of 2017 creates a new s 4(A) which provides such diverse forms of security including cash or certified cheque, a bond issued by a licensed financial institution, and a charge on immovable property. The Act also allows the court the flexibility to order 'such other forms of security or combinations thereof as the Court sees fit'.

Other conditions

To ensure that the defendant shows up to take his trial, the court may impose such requirements or conditions as may appear necessary to secure that the defendant surrenders to custody when required.[37] Conditions other than the provision of a surety or sureties are specified by statute in some jurisdictions. The Trinidad and Tobago Bail Act[38] refers to three other conditions, namely, surrendering of the defendant's passport; informing the court if he intends to leave the State or reporting at specified times to any police station. The Barbados and Jamaica Bail Acts provide for similar conditions.[39]

An example of the type of conditions likely to be imposed in Jamaica, where the charge is murder, may be gleaned from the bail conditions imposed on one Ivan Taylor[40] charged with murder in June 2012. Granted bail a month later in the sum of $400,000 Jamaican dollars, he was also required to report to a Westmoreland police station three times a week and ordered not to interfere with witnesses. In addition a 'stop' order was placed in respect of him at all ports in Jamaica (including the airports).

The St Vincent Criminal Procedure Code, Cap 172[41] permits cash to be deposited in lieu of security at the discretion of the court. It further stipulates that conditions of bail may include not only the deposit of the accused passport and reporting to a police station, but also requiring the accused person to confine himself to a certain locality generally or during

37 *R v Wells Street Magistrates' Court ex p Albanese* [1981] 3 All ER 769, p 776.

38 Section 12(3).

39 Barbados Bail Act 1996–28, s 12, Jamaica Bail Act, s 6(2).

40 *Trinidad Guardian* 24 July 2012, p 13.

41 Section 34.

certain hours of the day or night. The Jamaica Bail Act stipulates the security as 'a payment of such amount as may be specified'. The Bahamas Act refers generally to 'conditions' of bail, which the court may impose. As in Trinidad and Tobago, those conditions may be imposed not only to prevent absconding, but also the possibility of interference with witnesses by the accused person.

Since the constitutions in most Commonwealth countries enable the granting of bail on 'reasonable conditions including in particular such conditions as are reasonably necessary to ensure'[42] the appearance of the defendant, it would seem that conditions in those jurisdictions without specific statute are not limited to the provision of a surety. In these jurisdictions, the courts on granting bail should have the power to call for the surrender of the passport of the accused person or for his reporting to the police, even if these conditions are not specified in legislation. The Constitutions seem to permit it.

Bail on appeal

'Bail' granted on appeal does not strictly conform to the usual definition of bail, which relates to pre-trial release. The defendant in such circumstances would have been convicted of the offence and would now be applying for bail pending the hearing of his appeal. The fact that he has been found guilty by a competent tribunal means that the defendant has lost his constitutional right, so to speak, to bail that attaches to a person arrested and 'charged' with an offence. In a considered judgement in *Sinanan et al v The State* (No 1) (1992) 44 WIR 359, the Trinidad and Tobago Court of Appeal considered the applications of several convicted murderers for bail pending their appeals. This was prior to the Trinidad and Tobago Bail Act, which prohibits the grant of bail for murder.

The court confirmed that in keeping with the common law, there was no inherent jurisdiction in the court to grant bail to a person who had been convicted of murder. They emphasised that the constitutional right to bail in Trinidad and Tobago was restricted to persons who had been arrested but not yet tried for an offence. Finally, the court reiterated that the granting of bail to persons who have been convicted by a jury is a facility that is sparingly and only in very 'exceptional circumstances' to be used. This, they held, was the approach of most if not all Commonwealth countries.[43] In this regard the court commended the principles stated by the Guyana Court of Appeal as to bail on appeal after conviction by a jury in: *State v Scantlebury* (1976) 27 WIR 103, pp 105–06. A convicted person who applies for bail in such circumstances is no longer presumed innocent and has no right to bail.

The possibility of success of an appeal is not sufficient by itself to constitute exceptional circumstances. Neither is delay in securing a hearing of the appeal. Bail should not be granted in the absence of any other special circumstances unless the court is convinced that the appeal will probably succeed. If the sentence is slight and the appeal cannot be brought on in good time so that the sentence might be served while awaiting the appeal, this may be considered an exceptional circumstance: *Scantlebury* (above). These general principles on what constitutes exceptional circumstances were outlined in *Sinanan* (above) as principles culled from the common law.[44]

42 As in s 15 of the Jamaican Constitution, which provision is common to most jurisdictions.

43 *Sinanan v The State* (No 1) (1992) 44 WIR 359, p 371.

44 *Sinanan v The State* (No 1) (1992) 44 WIR 359, p 373.

In summary matters

The question of bail on appeal in respect of summary convictions is somewhat different, fixed as it is by statute.[45] In most jurisdictions, a person who has been sentenced to a term of imprisonment in the magistrates' court and has appealed may be released from custody with or without sureties until the determination of the appeal.[46] While in the Bahamas this entitlement is contingent on similar considerations as general bail on appeal, in other jurisdictions, like Barbados,[47] once the defendant signs a recognisance to prosecute his appeal, if in custody he will be 'liberated'. Section 17 of the Jamaica Justice of the Peace (Appeals) Act makes similar provision. In Trinidad and Tobago, bail is automatically granted on appeal of a summary conviction if the sentence of imprisonment is three months or less.[48]

It would seem that as far as bail on summary conviction is concerned, once the sentence is anything less than a short term of imprisonment, there is apparently almost a right to be bailed if in custody when an appeal is pending, unlike on conviction by jury. The only necessary condition seems to be that the applicant must sign a recognisance to prosecute his appeal.

The St Lucia Criminal Code appears to treat with bail pending an appeal in the same manner as bail before conviction.[49]

So too does the St Kitts and Nevis law in Act No 25 of 2009 amending the Magistrate's Code of Procedure Act s 169. Further, only where the sentence does not exceed six months is an appellant entitled to bail.

Forfeiture of bond

If the bailed person fails to show up for his trial or if he breaks any other condition of his bail, the bond may be forfeited. Prior to that, however, if a surety feels that the defendant is likely to abscond or breach any other conditions of his bail, the surety may apply to the relevant court to be released from his obligations. The bailed person will then be rearrested.

The surety has a serious obligation when he takes bail, which the court (or other person granting bail) should make clear that he understands before accepting him as a surety. It is the duty of the surety to ensure that the defendant shows up for his trial. To do so, the surety ought to stay in touch with the defendant to ensure that he appears in court. It is thus also his duty to keep himself informed of the adjourned date of each hearing and not rely on the memory of the defendant or anyone else.[50] In *Zambar Baksh v The Magistrate First Court* (unreported) Mag Appeal No 107/82 (1982), the Trinidad and Tobago Court of Appeal considered an appeal by a bailor against an order of forfeiture of recognisance in the sum of $5,000 for failure to produce a defendant at the relevant date of hearing. In dismissing the appeal, the court held that the test in determining whether the bond should be forfeited was whether the bailor was guilty of a failure to show 'due diligence' in attempting to secure the appearance of the defendant. While the bailor did make efforts to secure the appearance of the defendant, he did not do all that he could, such as to keep personally in touch with her, to bring her before the court.

---

45 See Chapter 9.

46 See Bahamas Bail Act, s 3(2).

47 Magistrates' Courts Act 1996–27, s 246.

48 Summary Courts Act, Chap 4:20, s 133A.

49 See s 593(1) and (4) of the Criminal Code.

50 *Zambar Baksh v The Magistrate First Court* (unreported) Mag App No 107/82, Trinidad and Tobago, 10–13.

The court further confirmed that in the absence of express statutory provision that permitted forfeiture of part of the bond (as in England), the full sum must be forfeited.[51] The Bahamas, Barbados, Jamaica, and Trinidad and Tobago Bail Acts[52] and the St Lucia provisions now enable forfeiture of only part of the security.

The procedure for forfeiture

Where a bailed person fails to show up for his trial on the appointed day or breaks another condition, a warrant for arrest may be issued for him, in the absence of some reasonable excuse. Once a condition of bail is broken, the recognisance may be forfeited automatically unless statute says otherwise. This was the position at common law.[53] Section 49(1) of the St Vincent Criminal Procedure Code, Cap 172, is indicative of this. The bailor is then called upon to show cause why the recognisance should not be paid.

Under statute, however, the procedure may be reversed. Section 17(1) of the Trinidad and Tobago Bail Act provides that unless (the surety) has reasonable cause for his failure, the court may order forfeiture of the security.[54] This suggests that the bailor should be allowed to show cause before a forfeiture order is made. Even before this provision, the practice as described in *Zambar Baksh* (above) appears to have been to issue the summons to show cause to the bailor before declaring the recognisance forfeited.

In fact, this appears to be the preferred position sanctioned by the courts. In *Ralph v A Magistrate* (1967) 12 WIR 124, the then Chief Justice of Trinidad and Tobago (Wooding CJ) stated that 'it is contrary to natural justice to make any such order [of forfeiture] without first calling on the person concerned to show cause why it ought not to be made'. This despite the words of s 123(1) of the Trinidad and Tobago Summary Courts Ordinance, which suggested the forfeiture should be immediate. Wooding CJ held further that it was a judicial obligation on a magistrate, before committing any person to imprisonment for non-payment of the bond, to call upon him to show cause why he should not be committed for non-payment of the bond, which had been declared forfeited.

To summarise, therefore, in the absence of legislation specifically permitting otherwise, a forfeiture of the bond order should not be ordered without first giving the bailor an opportunity to show cause why it should not be made. In addition, a committal to prison for non-payment of the bond, after the forfeiture order, should not be ordered until the bailor has been given a separate opportunity to show cause why he should not be committed to prison.

A bailor's obligation in summary proceedings continues throughout those proceedings. In respect of indictable trials, however, the bailor's obligation is determined when the defendant surrenders to custody on arraignment (when the trial actually starts). The defendant remains in custody unless the judge grants bail to 'continue' at the end of each day during the trial: *R v Central Criminal Court ex p Guney* [1996] 2 All ER 705, HL. The further detention of the accused person is within the discretion and power of the judge. This principle is naturally subject to any statutory provision to the contrary. Such a provision is s 55 of the Grenadian Criminal Procedure Code, Cap 2, which holds that a bail bond shall be held to continue in force 'until the case is finally disposed of and the accused sentenced or discharged'.

51 *Bardoon v The Magistrate* (1965) 8 WIR 399.

52 Bahamas: Bail Act, s 14(1); Barbados: Bail Act, s 15(2); Jamaica: Bail Act, s 18(2); Trinidad and Tobago: Bail Act, s 17(2). St Lucia: Criminal Code, s 604.

53 *R v Southampton JJ ex p Green* [1976] QB 11, p 15.

54 Also in Barbados Bail Act, s 15(1).

CHAPTER 5

INITIATION OF PROCEEDINGS

All criminal proceedings are currently initiated in the magistrates' court, whether they are serious or minor. There are two types of offence, summary and indictable, the former tried in the magistrates' court and the latter by a jury before a judge. Even so, in respect of indictable offences, there must first be a preliminary enquiry in the magistrates' court in order for the magistrate to determine if the case should go up for trial to the High Court before a jury. Thus, both summary and indictable matters are begun in the magistrates' court with the laying of a complaint or information, as the case may be.

To determine whether an offence is summary and so triable in the magistrates' court, it is necessary to consider the statute which creates the offence or the penalty stipulated, if the offence is one at common law (not created by statute). As a general rule, all offences for which the maximum punishment is six months' imprisonment or less will be summary. A good rule of thumb is that all 'serious' offences are indictable. Historically, offences were separated into felonies, the really serious ones, and misdemeanours, the others.[1] Nowadays, this distinction is more academic than real and has been abolished in Trinidad and Tobago, Barbados and to an extent in St Lucia.

Offences may be classified into a possible third category: offences that are triable either way. These are indictable offences which, for convenience, it has been determined, could be tried summarily. The question of whether an indictable office is triable either way (or 'hybrid', as it is sometimes called) is determined by statute. This will be considered in greater detail in Chapter 10.

COMMENCEMENT OF PROSECUTION

As indicated in Chapter 3, the prosecution of an offence can be commenced in one of three ways:

- by an arrest without warrant followed by a charge and the laying of a complaint or information containing the charge;
- by the laying of a complaint or information on oath followed by the issue, based on the complaint/information, of a warrant of arrest for the named defendant;
- by the laying of a complaint, on oath or not, and the issue of a summons, based on the complaint, for the appearance of the defendant.

It should be noted that there is a tendency in some jurisdictions to refer to the complaint which begins indictable proceedings in the magistrates' court as an 'information'. In *AG v Williams et al* (1997) 51 WIR 264, p 272, PC, the Privy Council said, in passing, that the contents of the formal affidavit which is prepared in a form to be disclosed to the occupier of premises to be searched is sometimes described as 'the information'. This probably explains the origin of the use of the word information, now contained in some statutes, to actually describe the document containing the charge in the magistrates' court. In any event, the issue may be a moot one since the

---

1 Smith, JC, *Smith and Hogan, Criminal Law*, 8th edn, 1996, London: Butterworths, p 27.

interpretation section in most summary procedure legislation provides that complaint 'includes information'. Interestingly, in the Bahamas, 'information' is the term used for the formal document which is laid in the Supreme Court to initiate proceedings there. Section 138(1) of the Criminal Procedure Code, Ch 84 provides: 'Every person committed for trial before the Supreme Court shall be tried on an information preferred by the Attorney General'. In the Bahamas, trial before the jury is by information and not indictment, except in the case of a voluntary bill of indictment.

Summary level

Criminal proceedings are thus commenced by the prosecution presenting to the magistrate a complaint (or information, as it is called in some jurisdictions), alleging that the person named has committed some specific offence. If the complaint is not initially in writing, it should be reduced to writing. The complaint must specify the statement of the offence (the name of the offence) and sufficient particulars. The particulars will usually include the date and place of the alleged offence as well as the act complained of in succinct terms. These are requirements set by summary procedure legislation in most jurisdictions. Although statute in respect of preliminary enquiry proceedings may not set out the requirements of a complaint in such great detail in some jurisdictions,[2] the same constituents are expected in a complaint charging an indictable offence.[3] If the offence is one created by statute, a reference to the section creating the offence is expected to be included. In *Gould v Williams* (1962) 5 WIR 122, however, the Trinidad and Tobago Court of Appeal held that such a failure, in respect of a summary complaint at any rate, was not fatal to proceedings.

Indictable trial

In indictable trials by a jury before a judge, the 'indictment' is the document which is filed in court. In the Bahamas it is called the information, as indicated above. Thus, after the preliminary inquiry, if the Director of Public Prosecutions (or Attorney General in the Bahamas) wishes to proceed with the indictable charge, he must cause an indictment to be filed in the High Court. It is this indictment which initiates proceedings in the High Court. Various legislation and/or rules throughout the region determine the form of the indictment. These provisions are almost identical and are strikingly similar to the English indictment rules contained in the Indictment Act 1915 and the Indictment Rules 1971 made thereunder. Apart from the court in which they are filed, the difference between a complaint and an indictment is that in respect of the latter, the statement of offence and the particulars are separately laid out. This general form will be considered in Chapter 13.

More significant, however, is the fact that while one complaint is expected to contain one charge, an indictment in contrast may contain one or more counts. It is each count which represents a charge. A complaint and a count are really effectively the same, except the former is in the magistrates' court and the latter a charge in an indictment before the High Court.

Whether it is in respect of a complaint initiating criminal proceedings in the magistrates' court or an indictment initiating indictable trial in the High Court, there are certain

2 E.g., the Indictable Offences (Preliminary Inquiry) Act, Chap 12:01, s 6, Trinidad and Tobago is very general.

3 In some jurisdictions such as St Vincent, Dominica and St Kitts and Nevis, the provisions are the same for both a summary complaint and indictable charge.

common concerns which relate to such laying of charges. In general, a charge, whether contained in a complaint or in a count in an indictment, must contain only one offence. This is called the rule against duplicity, which is elaborated below. If a formal charge, the complaint or the count, is defective, it is possible to amend the charge. The circumstances and principles governing amendment are considered in detail below. Finally, the whole question of joinder is of paramount importance, as it relates to hearings at summary level as compared to indictable trials. Joinder, which refers to joint hearing of separately laid charges or of charges against different defendants, is determined by separate principles for summary hearings as compared to indictable hearings. These principles are hereinafter considered.

DUPLICITY

It has been said that duplicity is a matter of form and not evidence.[4] It arises where the form of a complaint or a count in an indictment discloses two or more offences. If it does, this means that the charge is double, it is duplicitous. If the form appears to be satisfactory, but from the evidence led it appears that the charge now relates to two offences, then it will be easier to amend the complaint or count to strike out the ingredients in the charge relating to another offence.

The rule

If a charge contains more than one offence, it is defective and considered 'bad for duplicity'. The rule against duplicity originated in the common law, although it is now entrenched in most summary procedure legislations in the Commonwealth Caribbean[5] which state quite simply: 'Every such complaint shall be for one offence only'. Just as one complaint must be for one offence, so must each count in an indictment be for one offence and one only.

The purpose of the rule against duplicity is to enable the defendant to know the case he has to answer so that he will not be prejudiced or embarrassed in the preparation of his defence. Such prejudice or embarrassment could result if the defendant is uncertain as to the specific offence for which he is charged in the complaint or count. The principle is designed to ensure fairness: *Gee v General Medical Council* [1987] 1 WLR 564, p 570, HL. The defendant must know which offence to defend and which not, so that his ability to plead should not be adversely affected. In other words, the defendant may wish to plead guilty to one of the offences contained in the duplicitous charge and not guilty to the other, but since only one plea is called for, he is prejudiced.

'One activity'

Sometimes it may be uncertain whether a charge is in fact duplicitous. Technically, perhaps, if circumstances relate to more than one act, they may give rise to more than one offence. If, however, these acts are part of one activity, they can be said to constitute one offence. In *Jemmison v Priddle* [1972] 1 QB 489, the English Divisional Court held that

4 *R v Greenfield* (1973) 57 Cr App R 849.

5 Examples are the Bahamas, Criminal Procedure Code, Ch 91, s 58(6); Jamaica, Justice of the Peace (Jurisdiction) Act, s 9; St Lucia, Criminal Code, s 665; Trinidad and Tobago, Summary Courts Act, Chap 4:20, s 39(4).

it was legitimate to charge as a single information one activity even if that activity involves more than one act. In *Jemmison*, the defendant was charged with the unlawful taking and killing of two red deer without a licence. The court considered that the defendant had been charged with the one activity of shooting red deer without a licence. The Lord Chief Justice said:

> although as a nice debating point it might well be contended that each shot was a separate act, indeed each killing was a separate offence, I find that all these matters, occurring as they must have done within a very few seconds of time and all in the same geographical location, are fairly to be described as components of a single activity and that made it proper for the prosecution in this instance to join them in a single charge.

Thus, separate incidents may constitute one charge if they form part of one activity and the rule against duplicity will not be breached. The House of Lords sanctioned this in *DPP v Merriman* [1973] AC 584, HL, when they approved the above principle in *Jemmison*. Lord Diplock said (*Merriman*, p 607):

> When two or more acts of a similar nature committed by one or more defendants are connected with one another in the time and place of their commission, or by their common purpose in such a way that they can fairly be regarded as forming part of the same transaction or criminal enterprise, they can be charged as one offence in a single count in an indictment.

This principle is, of course, also applicable to summary charges with modifications that may be dictated by statute. It is thus permissible to charge two or more acts as one offence in a complaint as long as they:

- are of the same nature (they must be acts of the same type of offence, such as stealing from different individuals);
- comprise one activity or criminal enterprise; and
- are connected in time and place of their commission.

Thus, a charge of manslaughter of two different victims by different acts is bad for duplicity: *R v Devett and Fox* (1838) 8 C&P 639. So, too, is a charge of incest on 'diverse days' as this suggests several separate activities on unknown days. Different acts of incest with the same victim might well constitute a series, but hardly one activity. They should be charged as separate offences. The offences may be of the same nature, but they do not comprise one activity. In contrast, libelling two people at the same time, in one speech, may give rise to one offence of criminal libel.

Similarly, uttering a number of forged documents together will amount to one activity and may justify one charge: *R v Thomas* (1800) 2 East PC 934.

In the Jamaican case of *R v Johnson and Brown* (1974) 22 WIR 470, the defendants each shot at two constables in the course of a police chase. They were charged together on single counts for the shooting of each constable. It was held that neither count was bad for duplicity since they related to one activity. The court followed the test first laid down in *Jemmison* (above). In *Ramjohn v Johnson* (1966) 10 WIR 159, the defendant was charged and convicted under s 66 of the Trinidad and Tobago Summary Offences Ordinance, which prohibited a person from 'having in his custody or possession any weapon, instrument, stick, bottle, stone or other thing intended for the purpose of committing' a crime. The defendant was charged for having both a stick and a cutlass in his possession intended for wounding Johnson. It was held that it was permissible to charge the defendant for both acts together. Although either one or the other of the two acts was adequate to constitute the offence charged, the defendant could be convicted of the offence as established by either act if they were from a single incident and were charged together. Where, however, the two acts were not contemporaneous, they should not be charged together even though the statute created only one offence.

Continuous offence

It is technically correct to charge a continuing offence in one complaint or count. In *Cullen v Jardine* [1985] Crim LR 668, it was held that charging the unlawful felling of a number of trees in one information did not offend against the rule against duplicity although the felling occurred over a number of different days. In practice, however, it might be fairer to the defendant in such a case, especially on a jury trial, to charge in separate counts for such different acts. Sometimes, however, as in *DPP v McCabe* [1992] Crim LR 885, the evidence is easy to constitute in one charge. In that case, 76 library books which were stolen over a period of time were found in the defendant's home. It was held to be appropriate to charge this as one offence of theft, although the books were taken from 32 branches of the same library. The substance of the offence was the same and the victim was one legal person. There could not be said to be any real prejudice to the defence.

Conjunctivity

The 'one activity' test may even be applied to situations where the defendant is charged for a statutory offence and the relevant provision of the statute creates two or more offences. This is the real basis of the conjunctivity principle referred to in *Ramjohn* (above). Here, the charge actually encompasses more than one of those offences. In the Trinidad and Tobago case of *Sookdeo v R* (1963) 6 WIR 450, the defendants were charged in one count in that they 'being armed with offensive weapons, to wit, two revolvers, together attempted to rob W'. The offence was contrary to s 24(a) of the Larceny Ordinance which stated: 'Every person who: (a) being armed with an offensive weapon or instrument, or being together with one person or more attempts to rob any person ... shall be guilty of a felony'.

It was held that even if the statute did create two separate offences, the indictment was not bad for duplicity since the offences were not charged in the alternative. They were charged together and both offences arose out of one act. The court followed *R v Clow* [1963] 2 All ER 216, holding that it is permissible to charge separate offences in one count of an indictment once they relate to one single incident and are charged conjunctively. In *Clow*, the defendant was charged with causing the death of one FC by driving a motor vehicle at a speed and in a manner which was dangerous to the public. It was held that although this related to two offences created by the statute, they could be charged conjunctively if the matter related to one incident. In the older case of *R v Jones et al* [1921] 1 KB 632, it was also held permissible to charge these two offences conjunctively where they related to one indivisible act of driving.

In a similar vein, the Trinidad and Tobago Court of Appeal in *Simon v Reid et al.* (1965) 8 WIR 166 has held that an information for assembling and gambling was not duplicitous because the two offences were charged conjunctively. The Guyanese High Court, in a magisterial appeal in *Doobay* (1968) 11 WIR 187, followed *Simon* on this point in respect of an offence of personation of a doctor under the Colonial Medical Services Ordinance, Cap 134. It is clear that the use of the word 'and' conveys one act or activity.

Alternative offences or modes

Conversely, if two or more offences are created by one section of a statute and they are not charged conjunctively but in the alternative, this will constitute a duplicitous charge. On the face of it, the defendant will have been charged with alternative and separate offences. The alternative nature of the charge makes it clear that one activity is not being alleged. In *Ware v Fox* [1967] 1 All ER 100 and *Fox v Dingley et al* [1967] 1 All ER 100 (both reported in the same page), the English Queen's Bench Division considered charges under s 5 of the Dangerous Drugs Act 1965. In the first case the defendant was charged with 'being concerned with the management of certain premises which were used for the purpose of smoking cannabis or cannabis resin or for the purpose of dealing in cannabis resin'. It was held that this section created two offences: (a) being concerned with the management of premises used for smoking cannabis; and (b) being concerned with the management of premises used for 'dealing in cannabis'. Thus, the charge was duplicitous as laid in the alternative and the conviction would be quashed.

The same court considered the same provision, s 5 of the Dangerous Drugs Act 1965, in *Fox v Dingley et al.* In this case the respondents were charged for being concerned in the management of premises used for smoking and dealing with cannabis. Since the two offences were charged conjunctively, the information was not duplicitous. As such the appeal was dismissed.

Frequently, the issue will arise as to whether a statutory provision creates two (or more) separate offences or whether it creates different modes of committing one offence. Clearly, if a complaint or count charges two or more offences in the alternative, as in *Ware v Fox* (above), it will be duplicitous. Equally clearly, if it charges different modes of committing one offence, this does not offend against the rule against duplicity once the wording of the charging section is adhered to. Summary procedure legislation in most jurisdictions gives statutory recognition to this latter principle. Section 665 of the St Lucia Criminal Code 2004 is typical of similar provisions in the region. It states in part that such complaint shall not be invalid if it describes:

> The offence or any material fact relating to the offence in alternative words according to the language of the enactment creating such offence.

The problem is in determining whether the statute creates one offence or more. In *Taylor v Khan* (1969) 15 WIR 254, the Trinidad and Tobago Court of Appeal considered a case where the defendant was charged on a summary complaint which alleged that he 'wilfully secreted or kept a postal package containing jewellery in the course of transmission by post'. This was said to be contrary to s 45(a) of the Post Office Ordinance which read as follows:

> Any person who fraudulently retains; or wilfully secretes or keeps or detains or when required by an officer of the Post Office, neglects or refuses to deliver up:
> (a) any postal package which is in the course of transmission by post . . . shall be guilty.

The magistrate had dismissed the complaint as duplicitous following a refusal by the prosecutor to amend it. He held that the section created two offences. The Court of Appeal held that the expression 'secreted or kept' which followed the language of the section strictly was alternatively descriptive of the nature of the offence. This was deliberately keeping a postal package which was not one's own in the course of its transmission by post. The charge related to one offence created by the section and reflected the wording of the statute. It was not duplicitous. It should be noted, nonetheless, that in *Ramjohn* (above) it was suggested that it was incorrect, though not duplicitous, to charge alternative modes conjunctively unless they originated from a single incident.

In *R v Russell and Russell* (1971) 16 WIR 151, the Jamaican Court of Appeal held that an indictment[6] in the resident magistrates' court charging the appellants with breaches of the customs law was not duplicitous. The allegation was that the count charged two offences, namely: (a) dealing with specified goods with intent to evade the prohibition on the importation of the goods without a licence; and (b) unlawful removal of the goods from the wharf. It was held that s 205 of the customs law created one offence of dealing with specified goods with intent to evade. The charge was conspiracy to commit that one offence and the question of unlawful removal was merely an overt act of the conspiracy. Thus, only one offence was charged in the count.

Two cases based on the English Road Traffic Acts 1930 and 1988 illustrate the difference between alternative offences and alternative modes of committing one offence. In *R v Wilmot* (1933) 24 Cr App R 63, the defendant was charged (under the 1930 Act) with driving 'a motor car recklessly or at a speed or in a manner which was dangerous to the public'. Although no objection to the charge was taken until after conviction, it was held that it was bad for duplicity and the resultant conviction must be quashed. The court held that the section obviously created more than one offence. The test, which the court appeared to use, was if 'a person may do one [act] without the other' it follows that the section creates different offences in relation to the different acts. A charge in the alternative, even citing the statutory provision, is thus bad because more than one offence is charged.

While the *Wilmot* decision may be in line with *Clow* (above), which considered similar legislation, the principle enunciated does not seem entirely consistent with *DPP v Bennett* (1992) 157 JP 493. In that case, the defendant was charged under s 170(2) of the 1988 Road Traffic Act with, inter alia, failing to stop and to give his name and address. Section 170(2) read:

> The driver of the motor vehicle must stop and, if required to do so by any person having reasonable grounds for so requiring, give his name and address and also the name and address of the owner.

It was held on appeal that this section created only one offence regardless of whether there was a stopping, but a failure to give name and address, or a failure to stop at all. However, if the test in *Wilmot* (above) were to be applied to this statute, that is, whether a person may do one with the other, it should follow that two offences were created. A person may fail to stop or he may stop and then refuse to give his name and address. These seem to be two separate acts.

It would seem then that the test in *Wilmot* is not exhaustive in determining if a section of a statute creates alternative offences or alternative modes of committing one offence. The best approach might be a consideration of the nature of the offence, which seemed to have been the determinant in *Bennett* (above) and even in *Taylor v Khan* (above).

The objection

An objection to a complaint or a count in an indictment on the basis of duplicity ought to be taken as soon as possible. It should be done before the defendant pleads. This was the decision of the Court of Appeal of the Eastern Caribbean States in *Social Security Board v Stout* (1986) 37 WIR 169. It was, however, acknowledged that the failure to take the objection

6 Resident magistrates (Now called judges of the Parish Court) in Jamaica have powers by statute to try certain offences on indictment.

earlier would not necessarily be fatal to an appellant's case where he relies on duplicity as the ground for his appeal against conviction: *Sharma v Leacock* (1970) 17 WIR 353, p 354.

In the Guyanese case of *Bhagwan v Chester* (1977) 25 WIR 189, the Court of Appeal confirmed that it was not too late to take an objection of this kind for the first time on an appeal. The court referred to the English cases of *R v Wilmot* (1933) 24 Cr App R 63 and *Ware v Fox* [1967] 1 All ER 100, where the point was taken on appeal in both cases. In both cases, the appeal against conviction was allowed because the complaint in each case was found to be duplicitous.

The procedure

It has been held that a duplicitous charge in itself is not enough to lead to the dismissal of a complaint. Summary procedure legislation in the Commonwealth Caribbean is very similar to s 1 of the English Summary Jurisdiction Act 1848, which stipulates that 'no objection is to be taken or allowed to any information for any alleged defect therein in substance or in form'.[7] In *Edwards v Jones* [1947] 1 KB 659, the English court considered the effect of this provision on an admittedly duplicitous information charging both dangerous driving and careless driving. Since summary courts legislation specifies that a complaint/information shall be for only one offence, it was held that if it is found to contain two, the prosecution must elect on which charge to proceed. The complaint/information must then be amended to strike out the second charge and the defendant should afterwards be called upon to plead on the one remaining charge. Legislation providing for no objection to be made to a defect in a complaint/information in substance or in form does not mean that a court can proceed on a duplicitous charge. The defect is too fundamental: *Bhagwan v Chester* (above), p 194. Even if the amendment is not made at the outset, it may be permitted later in the proceedings provided the defendant is allowed to plead afterwards: *Achim v Stephens* (1960) 2 WIR 359, p 361.

Effect on conviction

If there is no amendment of a duplicitous charge, then the charge is bad and should be dismissed: *Edwards* (above). It follows, then, that any conviction on such a charge must be dismissed, as was done in *Wilmot* (above), *Ware v Fox* (above) and other like cases. In *Hargreaves v Alderson* [1962] 3 All ER 1019, the English Queen's Bench Division (Lord Parker CJ) said that a duplicitous charge 'is not a mere irregularity. It is a matter that goes to jurisdiction'.[8]

---

7 See equivalent provision in: Antigua – Magistrate's Code of Procedure Act, Cap 255, s 230;
Bahamas – Criminal Procedure Code, Ch 91, s 208;
Barbados – Magistrates' Courts Act 1996–27, s 212;
Dominica – Magistrate's Code of Procedure Act, Chap 4:20, s 203;
Grenada – Criminal Procedure Code, Cap 72B, s 88(2);
Guyana – Summary Jurisdiction (Procedure) Act, Cap 10:02, s 95(2);
Jamaica – Justice of the Peace (Jurisdiction) Act, ss 2, 4;
St Kitts and Nevis – Magistrate's Code of Procedure Act, Cap 3.17, s 227;
St Lucia – Criminal Code, s 698;
St Vincent – Criminal Procedure Code, Cap 172, s 132;
Trinidad and Tobago – Summary Courts Act, Chap 4:20, s 118(3).

8 *Hargreaves v Alderson* [1962] 3 All ER 1019, p 1023, letter f.

It would seem reasonable that if duplicity goes to jurisdiction, then the court has no discretion to waive such a defect. This view is consistent with that of the Trinidad and Tobago Court of Appeal in *Achim v Stephens* (above) which followed *Edwards v Jones* (above). In that case the defendant was charged contrary to the Shop Hours Order 1928 for opening outside shop hours and allowing a transaction to be effected (a sale). It was held that the relevant statutory provision created separate offences involving separate activities of opening outside fixed hours and selling outside those hours. Therefore, the charge was duplicitous and since the amendment was only made after the defence case was complete, and no fresh plea was called for, the ensuing conviction was void. There was no proper plea to the 'new' charge and the defendant had had no opportunity to make a defence to it.

In *Bhagwan v Chester* (above), the Guyana Court of Appeal also followed *Edwards v Jones* (above), holding that a conviction on a duplicitous information could not be validated. There is nothing in statute to permit this, the court said. In fact, it was pointed out in *Hargreaves* (above) that the English Magistrates' Courts Rules 1952 specifically prohibited justices from proceeding on a duplicitous information. There appears to be no such clear prohibition in the Commonwealth Caribbean and so the issue must be determined by the courts and/or any relevant legislation permitting a valid conviction despite duplicity. For instance, s 701(1) of the St Lucia Criminal Code permits a magistrate to proceed notwithstanding any defect in the complaint. This may seem to permit conviction even on a duplicitous charge.

The Trinidad and Tobago Court of Appeal has also been more liberal in its application of the principle of duplicity. In *Sharma v Leacock* (1970) 17 WIR 353, the court seems to equate duplicity with any other defect which may be amended on application to the trial court or even on appeal. Phillips JA said, p 354:

> The principle underlying the question of duplicity in charges is that if it can be shown that the party might have been prejudiced or embarrassed in his defence then, of course, he is entitled to have the conviction quashed.

The court followed some older English authorities which suggested that the test as to whether the conviction should be quashed depended on if the defendant had been embarrassed or prejudiced in the preparation of his defence.[9] Once there was no prejudice, the conviction should stand. In *Sharma* (above), since the defence was fabrication, the defendant was held not to be prejudiced by a duplicitous charge. The conviction stood.

Once it is ascertained that a charge is indeed duplicitous, whether it is contained in a complaint or in a count, the validity of an ensuing conviction depends on the circumstances of the particular case. If objection is taken by the defence at the outset, but the prosecution still proceeds on the duplicitous charge, the conviction should be quashed: *Achim v Stephens* (above). If it is clear that no prejudice accrued to the defendant, the conviction should stand, as in *Sharma v Leacock* (above). This last proposition is subject to the position of the Guyanese courts as enunciated in the line of Guyanese cases specified in *Bhagwan v Chester* (above).

AMENDMENT

There are many other bases on which a charge may be considered defective other than that it is duplicitous. If so the charge may be amended. This is a general power of any court, which is now incorporated in statute in most jurisdictions in respect of both

9 *R v Thompson* (1914) 9 Cr App R 252, p 260.

summary court and indictable proceedings. They may be found in the respective summary procedure legislation[10] and the legislation[11] in respect of indictments and the attendant indictment rules.

A complaint or count may be defective for a variety of reasons which include:

- duplicity (as considered above);
- inaccuracies in date or place which do not conform with the evidence;
- the defendant, victim or other named party in the charge is incorrectly named;
- the incorrect value of an item is stated; and
- the wrong statute is cited or incorrectly named or the wrong section is stipulated.

The procedure

If any defect is noted, the prosecution may make an application to the magistrate or the judge, as the case may be, to amend the charge. It goes without saying that it is the prosecution who will be seeking any amendment, since they are preferring the charge. Most statutes provide that no objection shall be 'taken or allowed' for any defect in substance or form. This does not mean that an amendment should not be sought, but merely that objections to such defects will not usually be upheld.

If the amendment is allowed, and the charge accordingly amended, the defence is entitled to an adjournment (which is in fact stated in most summary procedure legislation). In any event, before the amendment is granted, the court should give the defence the opportunity to be heard: *Julian v R* (1969) 14 WIR 181. In this case, emanating from St Lucia, the Court of Appeal of the West Indies Associated States considered an amendment (of a count) granted to the prosecution during the judge's summing up. The count originally charged the defendant with 'unlawfully breaking and entering a dwelling house', but did not specify the purpose, one of the constituents of the offence. The Court of Appeal held that while the judge was given

10 Antigua – Cap 255, ss 230–32;
Bahamas – Ch 91, s 208;
Barbados – Magistrates' Courts Act 1996, s 212;
Dominica – Chap 4:20, ss 203–05;
Grenada – Cap 72 B, s88;
Guyana – Cap 10:02, s 95;
Jamaica – Justice of the Peace (Jurisdiction) Act, ss 2, 4;
St Kitts and Nevis, Cap 3:17 ss 226–28;
St Lucia – Criminal Code, ss 698–701;
St Vincent – Cap 172, s 132;
Trinidad and Tobago – Chap 4:20, s 118(3), Indictable Offences (Preliminary) Inquiry Act, Chap 12:01, s 11.

11 Antigua – Indictments Act, Cap 213, s 6;
Bahamas – Criminal Procedure Code, Ch 91, s 150;
Barbados – Indictments Act, Cap 136, s 6;
Dominica – Criminal Law Procedure Act, Chap 12:02, s 6;
Grenada – Criminal Procedure Code, Cap 72B, ss 128(2), 136–37;
Guyana – Criminal Law (Procedure) Act, Cap 10:01, ss 97, 99;
Jamaica – Indictments Act, s 6;
Judicature (Resident Magistrates) Act, as amended by Act No 6 of 2016 s 278;
St Kitts and Nevis – Indictments Act, Cap 4.14, s 6;
St Lucia – Criminal Code, ss 850, 860–62, 881–84;
St Vincent – Criminal Procedure Code, Cap 172, ss 167, 181;
Trinidad and Tobago – Criminal Procedure Act, Chap 12:02, s 14.

wide powers to amend a count in an indictment by virtue of s 927 of the Code, it was expected that the power would be exercised to cause no injustice to a defendant. The court had erred in two ways: by failing to grant the defendant an opportunity to be heard on the application, and by granting the amendment at such a late stage of the trial.

When an amendment is granted, it is expected that the charge should be read over to the defendant and that he be allowed to plead again if necessary. In any event, he should be granted an adjournment to obviate any embarrassment arising from the amended charge of which he would only now be fully seised.

The test

As suggested in *Julian* (above), it is of paramount importance that the court first considers any ensuing prejudice that may accrue to the defendant if the amendment is granted. If the accused person will be seriously prejudiced by the granting of an amendment to the complaint, count or indictment and this prejudice will not be cured by an adjournment, the amendment should not be granted. In *R v Fong* (1970) 16 WIR 156, the Jamaica Court of Appeal considered a case where the prosecution sought and was granted leave to amend a four-count indictment, one count alleging larceny, to include a fifth count alleging the alternative offence of receiving. This was done before arraignment and despite the objection of the defence counsel who requested that a new indictment be filed to include the additional count. On appeal, the court held that the original indictment was defective in that it failed to include the alternative (to larceny) charge of receiving as disclosed by the depositions. Since the amendment was granted before arraignment, no injustice had been done to the appellant as stipulated in the Indictments Law, Cap 158.

Similarly, in *State v Rohit Singh* (1978) 26 WIR 124, the Guyana Court of Appeal held that an indictment which failed to include a count for an offence founded on the facts disclosed in the depositions that could be lawfully joined in the same indictment was defective. In that case, the charge was larceny of a motor car contained in one count and the amendment was granted to include the alternative offence of receiving. As this was done before arraignment, no injustice was done to the appellant. The court emphasised the need for a trial judge to take great care in exercising his discretion to decide whether an amendment should or should not be granted so as to ensure that no prejudice resulted to the accused.

A noteworthy example of amendment on appeal is that in *DPP v Stewart* (1982) 35 WIR 296, PC. That case dealt with the special statutory entitlement in Jamaica of the resident magistrate to try certain matters on indictment. Section 302 of the Judicature (Resident Magistrates) Act granted wide powers to the Court of Appeal to 'amend all defects and errors in any proceedings in a case tried by a magistrate on indictment'. The Court of Appeal allowed an amendment to a count which cited the incorrect Part of the Schedule of the Act which was contravened. The Privy Council held that the original count was not a nullity since it contained a reference to the section which was breached and so the amendment was merely technical in nature. The defendant had full and correct notice of the facts alleged and no injustice had accrued to him. In general, then, while a court has wide discretion to amend a charge or even an indictment to include a new count (a charge), the overriding concern must be to ensure that the defendant suffers no injustice or prejudice.

The time for the amendment

It is apparent that the earlier an amendment is granted, the less objectionable it will be. This is particularly true of an amendment to a duplicitous charge as discussed in *Edwards v Jones*

[1947] 1 KB 659, and the line of cases on duplicity. If the amendment is merely technical (*Stewart*, above) it can be granted even on appeal. In short, there is no statutory deadline which determines when an amendment should be granted, although this should preferably be before the prosecution closes its case so that the defence will have full opportunity to answer.

In *Teong Sun Chuah* [1991] Crim LR 463, the prosecution was allowed to amend a count in an indictment to read 'obtaining property' by deception and not 'obtaining services'. Although these were separate offences under the (English) Theft Act, the evidence disclosed the former offence and not the latter for which the charge was laid. The Court of Appeal held that even though the amendment was made at a late stage, the substance of the case remained the same throughout and there was no prejudice to the defendant. In contrast, in *R v O'Connor* [1997] Crim LR 516, the prosecution sought and was granted an amendment on the 27th day of a manslaughter trial to add a seventh count for unlawfully killing a person unknown, the other six counts relating to named crew members. The appellant was eventually convicted on the seventh count alone. It was held that the amendment was unfair because its effect was to change the factual basis of the prosecution's case and to confront the defendant with a different and more difficult case. Previously, the allegation was that he had caused the six deaths by allowing a vessel to go to sea in an unseaworthy condition with no adequate lifesaving equipment. The new count alleged failing to take reasonable care of the safety of the victim. The defendant was thus deprived of an opportunity to mount a full and effective defence. The late amendment was unfair.

In *Tracey (Alphonso) and Downer (Andrew) v R* (1998) 53 WIR 242, PC, the Privy Council upheld the decision of the trial judge to allow an amendment on the fourth day of a capital murder trial in Jamaica. The charge of capital murder in the furtherance of an act of terrorism was amended (in accordance with s 6 of the Indictments Act) to include in the particulars, the alternative of murder in the course and furtherance of a robbery. The defence was given an opportunity to recall the key witness but declined to so do. On an appeal based in part on the lateness of the amendment, the Privy Council held that obviously no injustice accrued to the appellants by the amendment since, if it did, defence counsel would have taken the opportunity which he had to recall the witness. Furthermore, from the evidence it was obvious from the start that the murder took place in the furtherance of a robbery. The defence must have known this and they suffered no injustice or 'prejudice', as the trial judge said. The two words, the Privy Council indicated, meant the same thing, although the Jamaican Indictments Act referred to 'injustice'.

In general, then, an amendment at the discretion of the court may be made at any stage as long as the defendant suffers no real prejudice.

Types of amendment

As is clear from *Fong* (above) and *Rohit Singh* (above), an amendment will be granted even to add a new count in an indictment. This is in fact provided for in statute in the region which is based on s 5 of the English Indictment Act 1915. In respect of summary proceedings, however, such a situation would not arise, because a complaint stands alone and must contain only one offence. This is so despite provisions seemingly to the contrary in summary proceedings legislation in some jurisdictions. The Bahamas[12] statute provides for summary charges to be amended to 'alter or add' a charge at any time. Since the statute also mandates that a summary complaint must

12 Bahamas Criminal Procedure Code, Ch 91, s 208.

only contain one offence, it is difficult to see how an amendment can be effected to 'add' a charge to a summary complaint.

Altering the charge

In *Teong Sun Chuah* (above), the Court of Appeal sanctioned the altering of the charge from one deception offence to another, obtaining property to obtaining services.

It was said that the substance of the charge remained the same, presumably obtaining by deception. In contrast, in *Conliffe v Weekes* (1963) 5 WIR 180, a magistrate refused to amend a summary information on the basis that a different offence would be charged. Interestingly, in Barbados, there is no specific statutory provision allowing amendment at summary level. Nonetheless it seems clear that the general provision in the Magistrates' Courts Act 1996 which states that 'no objection shall be allowed to any information or complaint ... as to any defect in substance or in form or for any variance'[13] permits amendment in particular as to time (date) and place.[14] This section, however, does not permit an amendment to a different offence, as it seems this type of 'variance' is not covered by the section.[15]

In *Conliffe v Weekes* (above), the Barbados Court of Appeal considered that the English authorities on amendment at summary level were particularly applicable to Barbados as the legislative provisions in both countries were identical in respect of defects in summary complaints or information. As such, following certain English authorities, the court held that an amendment should not be granted to change the information charging 'unlawfully and maliciously inflicting bodily harm' to one charging 'wounding', the two being different offences under different sections of the Act. The Barbados court did recognise in its considered judgment that the facts in *Conliffe* were somewhat different from the English cases where the amendments concerned were in relation to different Acts, not just different sections. Nonetheless, the court held that an analogy could be drawn to adding a new count to an indictment after arraignment. The court followed a 1961 case[16] which held that 'it is doubtful whether a new count can be added' after arraignment, despite the wide provisions of the Indictment Rules. A similar view should then be taken with respect to amendment in summary proceedings, depending as it does on the limited provisions of s 109 (now 212).

The decision in *Conliffe v Weekes* would seem to be relevant chiefly to those jurisdictions such as Dominica, Antigua and St Kitts and Nevis which, like Barbados, do not seem to make specific provisions for amendment at summary level. Even these jurisdictions, however, have wider provisions than Barbados, enabling the magistrate to 'adjourn on such terms as he thinks fit' if there is a defect or variance. In contrast, jurisdictions like St Lucia and the Bahamas have very wide provisions of amendment, specifically allowing the charge to be altered.

It is also arguable whether the basis for the decision in *Conliffe* (above) in relation to amendment on indictment still stands. The test as to whether a new count should be included in an indictment is no longer whether it is sought before or after arraignment. The consensus of the authorities discussed in *Fong* (above), *Rohit Singh* (above) and *Teong Sun Chuah* (above) suggests that the determinant is really whether prejudice will accrue to the defendant or not.

In summary, then, it would seem that as far as altering a charge is concerned, this is permissible both at indictable trials and, depending on the provisions of the summary

13 Magistrates' Court Act 1996, s 212, then Magistrates' Jurisdiction and Procedure Act, Cap 110, s 109.

14 *Conliffe v Weekes* (1963) 5 WIR 180, p 181.

15 Ibid, p 182.

16 *R v Martin* [1961] 2 All ER 747.

procedure legislation, at summary level. Following the line of English authorities it may not be permissible, except in the case of broad legislation such as that of the Bahamas and St Lucia, to amend a complaint to state that it is contrary to an entirely different statute, as this may be unfair in not giving the defendant sufficient notice beforehand of the charge. It is, however, suggested that the decision in *Conliffe v Weekes* should not be conclusive. An amendment changing the section of a statute cited cannot in itself amount to the creation of a new offence. Where the particulars of the offence (unlike *Teong Sum Chuah* (above)) are different from that alleged and the section is also incorrectly stated, then any amendment to correct this could be said to create a new offence. The defendant will be prejudiced to an unacceptable level by the amended charge.

Technical defects

There can be no objection to the amendment of the date and place in a charge unless it will cause the defendant severe embarrassment. This will occur, for example, late in a trial when he is running a defence of alibi. In such latter case, the date of the incident is of essence. Where it is not, the court will always grant an amendment of this particular: *Joseph v The State* (1983) 32 WIR 225, a decision of the Court of Appeal of the Eastern Caribbean States. In that case, the date of the offence was amended to read 12 February 1981 instead of 12 May 1981. Such an amendment was also permitted in *Cross v John* (1964) 7 WIR 359, a decision of the Trinidad and Tobago Court of Appeal, when the date of the offence was wrongly stated in the complaint. Once the new date still shows that the complaint was laid within the statutory time period (in respect of summary matters), the amendment should be allowed.

Even the omission of key words in the particulars can be cured by amendment. In *Joseph* (above), the evidence on trial showed that the appellant was acting in concert. Accordingly, during the trial the words 'and others' were included in the charge on indictment after the appellant's name. It was held that this did not amount to an alternative to or revision of the substance of the charge.

Sometimes it may not even be necessary to amend the particulars of the offence if the statement of the offence itself is stated correctly. In *R v McVitie* [1960] 2 QB 483, it was held that the omission of the words 'knowingly' on a charge of possession of explosives contrary to s 4 of the relevant Act was not prejudicial to the defendant. The particulars of the offence were merely to be considered imperfect since the offence charged was known. An amendment was not even sought, but it is suggested it could well have been made even on appeal in the given circumstances. This position is in contrast to where the charge is so bad that it discloses no offence at all: *Garman v Place* [1969] 1 WLR 19. In such a case, the charge is void and there is nothing that can be amended.

Overall, then, a complaint, count or an indictment may be amended in accordance with the relevant statutory provisions permitting amendment and the general principles of law. The accused person must not be prejudiced or embarrassed in his defence as a consequence of the amendment so that the later the amendment is sought, the less likely it is to be granted. If the defect is merely technical, however, and the nature of the charge is clear, an amendment may be granted even on appeal as in *DPP v Stewart* (1982) 35 WIR 296, PC. In *Larry Joefield P.C. No. 17306 v Rupert Griffith* Mag. App. No. 097 of 2016 the defendant had been charged with 'using insulting language to the annoyance of persons on the road', contrary to the Summary Offences Act Chapter 11:02. At the close of the defence case the prosecutor invited the court to amend the complaint so that the charge would read that the defendant 'made use of insulting language with intent to or which might tend to provoke the appellant to commit a breach of the peace'. This wording would conform with the statutory wording. The court declined to exercise its discretion to allow the amendment on the basis that at that stage of the proceedings it would result in prejudice to the defendant. The court subsequently dismissed the charge against the defendant and the police appealed.

The Trinidad and Tobago Court of Appeal held that the defect in the complaint was merely technical in nature and was capable of amendment to bring it into accordance with the statute by which it was created. Moreover, from the questions put in cross examination of the complainant, the respondent always knew of the true nature of the charge he had to meet. The respondent was therefore not prejudiced by the amendment. Furthermore, even if the amendment was made, the factual basis of the prosecution's case remained the same. The respondent was not confronted with a different or more difficult case nor was he deprived of mounting a full and effective defence.

The Court of Appeal also decided that an amendment could be allowed despite the fact that the six-month limitation period to lay a charge had expired; even where the amendment alleged a different offence. This was provided that the new offence arose out of the same or substantially the same facts as the original offence. The most important consideration for the court in these cases is that the amendment must be made in the interests of justice.

JOINDER OF CHARGES

Joinder relates to the practice of hearing two or more charges at the same time (joinder of charges) or of holding the trials of two or more defendants together (joinder of parties). It does not refer to the laying of one charge which contains two or more offences. This latter situation relates to the problems of duplicity discussed above. In *Clayton v Chief Constable of Norfolk* [1983] 1 All ER 984, HL, the House of Lords said (p 989):

> The object of the rule against duplicity has always been that there should be no uncertainty as to the offence charged. But there is no such uncertainty where two or more informations are properly laid against an alleged offender.

Thus the rule against duplicitous charges does not prevent a court from hearing more than one charge at a time. A court may, thus, subject to legislative provisions to the contrary, hear 'matters which constitute the individual offence of the several offenders' together when the evidence is 'so related whether in time or by other facts that the interests of justice are best served by them being tried together': *R v Assim* [1966] 2 All ER 881, pp 887–89. The essence of the principles of joinder, then, is that it is permissible once the offences are based on evidence that is the same or related.

In general, statutory provisions in respect of joinder for summary offences are more restrictive than those for indictable offences in the Commonwealth Caribbean. There are few statutory provisions circumscribing the joinder of cases or parties at the preliminary enquiry.[17]

Joinder of summary charges

If statute does not require a magistrate to hear each information/complaint separately or that each defendant should consent to a joint hearing, then the court may adopt 'that

17 Discussed below.

practice and procedure best suited to contemporary needs'.[18] In several countries of the Commonwealth Caribbean, however, legislation specifically dictates the joinder of charges at summary level.

Consent

In Trinidad and Tobago, s 64(2) of the Summary Courts Act, Chap 4:20, provides:

> Where two or more complaints are made by one or more parties against another party or other parties and such complaints refer to the same matter such complaints may, if the court thinks fit, be heard and determined at one and the same time if each defendant is informed of his right to have such complaints taken separately and consents to their being taken together.

The Grenada provision[19] and that of the St Lucia[20] Criminal Code 2004 are identical. Thus, in summary proceedings in Trinidad and Tobago, Grenada and St Lucia, joint trials of defendants and joint hearings of offences are not automatic, as in England, for example, where there are no similar restrictive provisions. If two or more defendants are jointly charged with one offence in one complaint, a joint hearing follows. Where two or more complaints (charges) are laid the position, according to statute, is different. The offences must relate to the same matters if they are to be tried together. This would most likely mean that they must flow from the same incident. The more significant element in s 64(2), however, is the requirement for consent. Thus more than one charge against different defendants may not be heard together unless the defendants consent. Nor may different charges against a single defendant be heard together unless the defendant consents. The practice, therefore, is to lay separate complaints in respect of each defendant as well as each offence. The latter would be necessary in any event so as not to offend against the rule against duplicity. If the court does not obtain consent of the defendant or defendants (as the case may be) to the joinder, any ensuing conviction or convictions will be quashed. The hearing will be considered a nullity: *Quash v Morris* (1960) 3 WIR 45, following *St John v Washington* (1955) 15 Trin LR 7 on this point.

In *Quash*, the defendant and another were charged on separate complaints by one Morris. The charges were according to the record 'taken together by consent'. The Trinidad and Tobago Court of Appeal held that the record was prima facie evidence that the magistrate had complied with the statute in informing the defendant of her right to be tried separately. In other words, he was presumed to have informed her that the cases could only be tried together with her consent. The court followed its previous decision in *Lucky v IR Commissioner* (1960) 2 WIR 56, which had held that in the absence of any evidence to displace it, a statement by the magistrate that the matters were taken together with consent showed that the statute had been complied with.

The Trinidad and Tobago Court of Appeal in *Gocking and Gocking v Payne and Daniel* Mag. App. No P085 of 2014 decided that the right to have the charges heard together may be waived by the defendant. On the facts of this case this waiver was evinced by the deliberate absence of the defendants from the jurisdiction at the time of the trial and, also, by the silence of their legal representative on the issue of whether they would consent to joinder of charges when the matter was specifically raised by the magistrate. Accordingly, the magistrate was

18 *Clayton v Chief Constable of Norfolk* [1983] 1 All ER 984, p 990, HL.
19 Criminal Procedure Code, Cap 72B, s 80(3).
20 Criminal Code 2004, s 693(2).

correct to have proceeded to hear the complaints together in the absence of any express consent to do so.

'Same transaction'

Where the summary courts procedure legislation does not require that consent of the defendant must be obtained, then such consent is not necessary: *R v Bardon* (1964) 6 WIR 346. The Jamaica Court of Appeal considered s 22 of the Criminal Justice (Administration) Act, which provides for joinder of charges in summary cases. The provision stipulates in so far as is relevant:

> (2) Where in relation to offences triable summarily a person is charged with two or more offences arising out of acts so connected as to form the same transaction; or . . . such charges may be tried at the same time unless the court is of the opinion that such person is likely to be prejudiced or embarrassed in his defence by reason of such joinder.

The defendant was tried and convicted on five informations charging separate traffic offences. They were heard together and the defendant appealed on the basis, inter alia, that his consent to the procedure should have been obtained. The court dismissed the appeal, saying that the law was decisive on the point and since the charges arose out of the same subject matter and could be said to have formed the same transaction, they could be tried together. No consent was necessary.

The statutory provisions for joinder at summary trial in Jamaica are very similar to those for indictable trials and allow joinder of offences if they arise out of a series[21] as well as out of the same transaction. The Bahamas Criminal Code contains general provisions applying equally to summary trial as well as indictable.[22] They are as wide as those of Jamaica. The law in Barbados,[23] Guyana[24] and St Vincent[25] is similar in each case to that of Jamaica in that joinder principles at summary level are the same as for indictable hearings. The offences must be founded on the same facts or must constitute part of a series. The St Kitts and Nevis law[26] does not refer to 'part of a series', but is otherwise similar. In these jurisdictions, it also appears to be permissible to lay joint charges against defendants in accordance with *Assim* (above). Joinder of parties is considered below.

Specific provisions

Dominica[27] and Antigua[28] have identical laws which enable a magistrate to hear summary offences together 'where he considers necessary'. While these provisions may seem very wide ranging so as to permit possible hearing of entirely unrelated offences, they are not. The magistrate in both jurisdictions, as indeed in all jurisdictions, must ensure that the defendant is not prejudiced or embarrassed in his defence by the joinder. Furthermore, *Clayton* (above)

21 See Criminal Justice (Administration) Act, s 22(2), (6).
22 Criminal Procedure Code, Ch 91, ss 75–76.
23 Magistrates' Courts Act, 1996, s 40.
24 Summary Jurisdiction (Procedure) Act, Cap 10:02, s 29, as amended by Act No 21 of 1978.
25 Criminal Procedure Code, Cap 172, s 70 (6).
26 Magistrate's Code of Procedure, Cap 3.17, s 85 (3).
27 Magistrate's Code of Procedure, Chap 4:20, s 22.
28 Magistrate's Code of Procedure, Cap 255, s 25.

provides that even if there is no prohibition against joinder, a court must act in the interest of justice. Thus joinder will only be possible if the evidence is the same or related in respect of the different offences[29] even in these jurisdictions which have apparently wide-ranging provisions.

The St Lucia law on joint hearings at summary level was peculiarly restrictive. Section 1078(2) of the previous Criminal Code provided:

> Where there are similar separate complaints by one and the same complainant against separate defendants in respect of the same matter, the court may, if it thinks fit, hear and determine them at one and the same time.

The provision was considered in *Emmanuel v Cox* (1967) 10 WIR 560. In that case, the appellant was charged with three offences: (a) being armed with a dangerous weapon; (b) assaulting a police constable in the execution of his duty; and (c) resisting arrest. Another person was charged separately with three offences, one of which was assaulting a police officer in the execution of his duty, and two other different offences. The charges arose out of the same incident; the magistrate heard all six charges together and convicted the two men. It was held that the magistrate had no authority to hear all the complaints together since the offences were not 'similar'. Only the two cases of assaulting the police officer in the execution of his duty were properly heard together and so only these convictions would stand. Furthermore, the court suggested, the consent of the defendant should have been obtained to try their cases together, even though the legislation did not so specify. The Criminal Code 2004 effectively changed this restrictive law.

Cross charges

Sometimes a defendant in a summary case may file a cross charge against the complainant, whether a police officer or a civilian. This does not occur in indictable proceedings since the complainant would be the State or the Crown, against whom there could not be a complaint. Statutes in most jurisdictions enable such cross complaints, or cross charges as they are sometimes called, to be heard together for reasons of convenience. In the absence of enabling statutory provision, it is not possible to hear cross charges together: *R v Epsom JJ ex p Gibbons* [1983] 3 All ER 523. The parties must be the same and the complaint must in general relate to the same matter. In Grenada, consent of parties is required for this procedure.

The rationale for a single hearing of cross charges was discussed by the Trinidad and Tobago Court of Appeal in *Bally v Ninvale* (1964) 7 WIR 430. That court said that the statutory provision was designed to prevent a multiplicity of legal proceedings wherever possible. As cross charges by their very nature arise out of a single incident and have reference to the same matter, they should be taken together as provided by statute.

At committal proceedings

Except perhaps for the general provisions in the Bahamas Criminal Code[30] and the St Vincent Criminal Code[31] which apply to the initiation of all criminal proceedings in the magistrates' courts, there is little legislation determining joint hearings of cases at the

29 *R v Assim* [1966] 2 All ER 881.

30 Ch 91, s 75.

31 Cap 172, s 70.

committal stage. In *Clayton* (above), the House of Lords considered the situation where there is no statutory prohibition against joinder. In a considered judgment, the House found that since a trial judge could try any number of counts and offenders together in given circumstances on indictable trial, there was in principle no reason why a magistrate should be compelled to try each information/offender separately if the facts are closely connected. The House endorsed the practice recognised in *R v Assim* [1966] 2 All ER 881 and *R v Camberwell Green Justices* [1978] 2 All ER 377, which permits joint hearings once statute does not prohibit or restrict the procedure. In *Assim*, two defendants were tried in one indictment in separate counts for assaulting two different victims. The charges arose out of one incident. There was, however, nothing in the then Indictment Rules which provided for joinder of offences in relation to different accused persons. The relevant Rules spoke to joinder of offences against the same accused. A full Court of Appeal considered the appeal against the convictions in which it was alleged that in the absence of statutory authorisation for the joinder of parties, the entire proceedings constituted a nullity. The court in dismissing the appeal against conviction considered this irrelevant and held that:

> The question of joinder is a matter of practice in which the court has, unless restrained by statute, inherent powers to formulate its own rules and vary them in the light of current experience and the needs of justice.

Where the matters which constitute the individual offences of the several offenders are, upon the available evidence, so related in time or other factors, that the interests of justice are best served by their being tried together, they can be tried together. The principles in *Assim* seem to be quite expansive both in permitting joinder and disclaiming the need for statutory sanction of the procedure. How far they apply to committal proceedings as distinct from trials was answered in *R v Camberwell Green Stipendiary Magistrate* (above). In that case, a magistrate decided to hold one joint committal proceedings in relation to separate charges against separate defendants. The defendants did not wish to have joint committal proceedings. There was nothing in any legislation to indicate whether a magistrate had power to conduct concurrent committal proceedings.

The Chief Justice of the English Queen's Bench Division said that, in the circumstances, the procedure had to be determined by matters of practice as stated in *Assim* (above). He said that it was permissible to join in one committal proceedings two or more proceedings if those defendants could be joined in one indictment. Furthermore, where two offences could be tried together (on indictment), they could be the subjects of current committal proceedings as well.

Clearly, then, once there is no statutory provision to upset the practice, as there is not in the Commonwealth Caribbean, joinder is permissible at committal proceedings on the same basis as it could be on trial on indictment. The consent of the defendant or defendants is not required.

It has, however, been the practice in the Commonwealth Caribbean not to hold concurrent committal proceedings in respect of separate offences. Invariably, accused persons may be charged in one complaint if the evidence is that the offenders acted in concert,[32] but separate charges are not, in most jurisdictions, heard together in one set of committal proceedings. It seems apparent that this is not the best practice and the procedure endorsed in *Assim* (above) and *R v Camberwell Green Stipendiary Magistrate* (above) should be followed.

In any event, even if persons have been separately committed for trial for offences that may be lawfully joined in one indictment, the offences (and the persons) may be so joined:

32 As endorsed in *Assim*.

R v Groom (1977) 62 Cr App R 242. The English Practice Direction (Indictment – Joinder of Courts) (1977) 62 Cr App R 251 specifically permits this as follows:

> Where different persons have been separately committed for trial for offences which can lawfully be charged in the same indictment, it is permissible to join in one indictment the counts founded on the separate committals despite the fact that an indictment in respect of any one of those committals has already been signed.

Since the legislation in the Commonwealth Caribbean in respect of joinder of counts on indictment in general is identical to the English, this Practice Direction would be applicable. This position is now endorsed by the Court of Appeal of Trinidad and Tobago. The issue arose before an enquiring magistrate as to his jurisdiction, during the course of an enquiry into certain offences, to hear evidence in relation to charges laid in another magisterial district. In *Application No 2 of 2008, In the matter of section 36(1) of the Supreme Court of Judicature Act* [judgment delivered on 16 January 2009] the DPP applied for a review of the magistrate's ruling that the prosecution, in adducing evidence in a preliminary enquiry into six charges against one FK, should confine itself to matters before the court and not lead evidence relating to five other charges against the accused laid in other magisterial districts.

In holding that the magistrate was in error the Court of Appeal stated, inter alia, that the Indictable Offences (Preliminary Enquiry) Act permitted an enquiring magistrate to hear matters wherever committed. Where an offence is a continuing one or the offences are so closely related, although they may have been committed in different magisterial districts, the police should lay all the charges in one district. A magistrate has unfettered jurisdiction to hear evidence that discloses offences which may have been committed outside his magisterial district.

In the light of the English Practice Direction and *Application No 2 of 2008* it seems that a joinder is permissible of several informations where the offences are continuous or closely related.

Joinder of charges on indictment

The Practice Direction (above) also specifically states that two indictments can never be tried together. It is presumed that the charges in such indictments will be unrelated, since statute (in most jurisdictions) and practice permit 'charges for any offence to be joined on the same indictment if those charges are founded on the same facts, or form or are part of a series of offences of the same or a similar character'.[33] This follows the Indictment Rules, r 9, of England and is contained in the indictments procedure legislation of most Commonwealth Caribbean jurisdictions,[34] in either the substantive procedural law or the Indictment Act or the Rules.

Thus, different offences may be drafted as separate counts and charged in one indictment in accordance with the principles outlined above. Consequently, when the matter comes up for hearing at indictable trial, the cases are already 'joined' in one document: the indictment. There is then no need for the court to make an order, as for summary trial or in committal proceedings, to hear the matters together. The offences are joined in one indictment as different counts and are heard together (subject to any application made to the court for separation) at one hearing.

33 As in r 3, Indictment Rules Trinidad and Tobago, Criminal Procedure Act, Chap 12:02, s 832 St Lucia Criminal Code 2004.

34 See, e.g., r 3 of the Indictment Rules Jamaica, Indictments Act, Cap 158.

The tests

Charges may be joined if founded on the same facts or part of a series. As discussed above, in some jurisdictions this is also the determining test at summary level. It is the relevant test for all jurisdictions on indictable hearings. Offences are said to be 'founded on the same facts' if they have a common factual origin: *R v Barrell and Wilson* (1979) 69 Cr App R 250. In general, if the offences arise from the same incident or are based essentially on the same evidence, they may be said to be founded on the same facts. It is clear that the offences need not be similar. Thus offences of robbery and rape may be charged as separate counts in one indictment if they arise from one incident. Naturally, robberies of separate victims in one incident may also be heard together if charged in separate counts. As has been pointed out in the discussion on duplicity, it is theoretically possible to charge such acts of a 'similar nature' in the latter situation if they arise from one incident, as one offence, without offending the rule against duplicity: *DPP v Merriman* [1972] 3 All ER 42, HL. This is not the usual practice and instead, they will generally be charged as separate offences, but heard together.

Statute also permits joinder of 'a series of offences of the same or a similar character'. If the offences are admissible in proof of each other as evidence of similar fact, as determined in *DPP v P* [1991] 3 All ER 337, HL, then there is no doubt that they can be joined as counts on one indictment. It has been said, however, that the rule should not be given so restrictive a meaning: *R v Kray et al* (1970) 53 Cr App R 569. Once there is some nexus, some features of similarity which in all the circumstances of the case enables the offences to be described as a series, they may be tried together: *Ludlow v Metropolitan Police Commissioners* (1970) 54 Cr App R 233, HL.

In *Bhola Nandlal v The State* (1995) 49 WIR 412, the Trinidad and Tobago Court of Appeal considered at length the issues of joinder arising from a second indictment against the appellant. A money bribe had been made to a magistrate by the appellant via intermediaries, one of whom was SR. The magistrate also received the gift of a motor car paid for by the appellant. Both the bribe and the gift were for the dismissal by the magistrate of certain charges against the appellant. The DPP indicted, and the magistrate and the appellant were convicted, for corruption in relation to the car gift. The DPP later served an indictment against the appellant, the magistrate and SR for counts of conspiracy to pervert the course of justice and counts of conspiracy in relation to the money bribe. The magistrate was granted a separate trial while the appellant and SR were tried and convicted on this second indictment.

In a robust and sometimes scathing judgement, the Court of Appeal criticised the conduct of the DPP as being oppressive. The DPP, the court felt, had sought to take one transaction and split it in such a way that it could be susceptible to different indictments. The court endorsed the decision of *Ludlow* (above) in its interpretation of the English Indictment Act 1915 on joinder, the equivalent of which, it was pointed out, existed in Trinidad and Tobago. It held that the separation of the offences into two indictments was a contravention of r 3 of the Indictment Rules and had deprived the appellant of the opportunity of having all the charges against him considered together (in one indictment and at one trial) and in a manner that would not be oppressive. The court even pointed out that as a result, the defendant had to pay two sets of legal fees when he should have paid one.

In *Ferrell v R* [2010] UKPC 20 the Privy Council followed *Ludlow* and held that where a defendant had been found in possession of drugs, on the facts of that case money laundering charges in respect of unexplained deposits to his bank account could be properly joined and tried together with the drugs charges, all being part of a series of offences.

Capital offences

There is one significant exception to the principle that offences should be joined in one indictment if they are founded on the same facts or form part of a series in the Commonwealth Caribbean, and that is in respect of capital offences. By and large, the death penalty still exists in these countries and murder is one offence for which it is mandatory. It has been held that capital offences should not be tried with non-capital offences. This is because statute in general envisages different modes for trial of capital and non-capital offences: *R v McLeish* (1980) 31 WIR 317. A majority verdict is not accepted in a capital case, for instance. Furthermore, the number of jurors for murder or treason is generally 12 and for non-capital offences fewer. Thus a jury of 12 cannot sit on a non-capital offence where statute provides a different number of jurors for non-capital offences: *Seeraj Ajodha v The State* (1981) 32 WIR 360, p 373, PC. If a jury comprises a greater number of jurors in trying a capital offence than a non-capital offence, any ensuing conviction for such later offence by a jury selected to try the capital offence will, in the absence of permitting statutory provisions, be invalid.

In some jurisdictions, like the Bahamas and Guyana, the number of jurors is the same for capital and non-capital offences, but the practice in Guyana is at least still to try capital offences separately from non-capital even if they arise from the same incident. This may be because of the seriousness of the penalty. In St Vincent, statute creates a situation unique to the rest of the Commonwealth Caribbean. Section 13 of the Jury Act, Cap 28 confirms that a non-capital offence may be joined with a capital offence. That section makes provision for the taking of a majority verdict for the non-capital offence of 10 of the 12 jurors in the jury. Ordinarily, for trial of non-capital offences, nine jurors would have been selected.

Throughout the region, two murders arising from one incident may, however, be charged as separate counts in one indictment.

Misjoinder – the consequences

If offences are wrongly joined together and are heard together in one hearing, the question arises as to whether the entire proceedings will constitute a nullity. In respect of joinder of capital and non-capital offences which are misjoined because they should not be tried together, the Privy Council has said that conviction on only the misjoined noncapital offence will be void: *Cottle and Laidlow v R* (1976) 22 WIR 543, PC; *Seeraj Ajodha* (above). This is so once the proper procedure is followed for the count of murder (as in the correct number of jurors) and once the accused person is not prejudiced by the admissibility of the evidence on the other count.

Although it has been held in England that trial on a misjoined count in an indictment is a nullity, *Newland* (1988) 87 Cr App R 118, more recent cases such as *R v Smith* (BP) [1997] 1 Cr App R 390 suggest that *Newland* was wrongly decided. This is possibly because the Indictment Rules may be considered merely directory and not mandatory: *R v Laming* (1990) 90 Cr App R 450. The entire trial will not be considered a nullity. Conviction on the misjoined count will be deemed a nullity. The only issue will be for the court to decide which of the convictions should stand and which should go. In the final analysis, this should be for the court to determine having regard to the evidence and in the interest of justice.

As far as summary matters are concerned, *Quash and Morris* (1960) 3 WIR 45 confirms that lack of consent to joinder, when such consent is necessary, will result in the entire proceedings being deemed a nullity. This would seem to be because the requirement for consent to joinder at summary level in such jurisdictions as Trinidad and Tobago and Grenada is a condition precedent to the joint hearing. In contrast, where charges are wrongly joined simply because they do not conform to the statutory requisites for joinder, the entire proceedings will not be a nullity. An ensuing conviction may yet be considered valid: *Emmanuel v Cox* (1967) 10 WIR 560. Which conviction will stand is for the court to determine and this should depend on the evidence as to which is the essential charge.

JOINDER OF PARTIES

This relates to the practice of joining two or more persons in one charge – charging them together in one complaint or count. They may then be tried together. While some statutory provisions in the Commonwealth Caribbean[35] do provide for joinder of parties in one charge, this is really determined by practice. Section 73 of the Bahamas Criminal Procedure Code, Ch 84, provides, in so far as is relevant:

> The following persons may be joined together in one charge or information and may be tried together – persons accused of the same offence committed in the course of the same transaction persons accused of an offence and persons accused of aiding and abetting ... persons accused of different offences in the course of the same transaction persons accused of different offences all of which are founded on the same facts or form part of a series.

It appears that the above statutory provisions reflect the accepted principles for joint trials of different parties which were approved in *Assim* (above). In that case, the court held that although there was no specific indictment rule authorising joinder of parties in one count, it was definitely appropriate where the evidence was that the several offenders acted in concert. Joint trials were also permissible when the incidents were contemporaneous or linked in a similar manner. In practice, accused persons are charged in one count if they acted together. If the charges merely arise out of the same incident, they may be charged in one indictment (if it is an indictable matter) but in separate counts, as actually occurred in *R v Assim* [1966] 2 All ER 881. In *Nandlal v The State* (1995) 49 WIR 412, the Trinidad and Tobago Court of Appeal sanctioned the practice of a joint trial of defendants charged with offences arising out of the same matter. They held that it would have been acceptable to charge all the accused persons together in one indictment even if all three were not implicated in each count.

In respect of summary trials, the practice remains the same (as in *Assim*) unless prohibited by statute, as discussed above. The summary procedure legislation of Grenada and Trinidad and Tobago demand that different defendants must consent to more than one charge being taken together. However, if it is being alleged that the defendants acted in concert in relation to one offence (one complaint), consent is not necessary and it seems that the defendants may be charged jointly in one complaint. Generally, though, at summary level the prosecuting authorities in these jurisdictions tend to lay separate complaints against them. The legislation seems to contemplate that the charges against each defendant should be separately laid, although it does not so specify.

Separate trials

In *Assim* (above), the English Court of Appeal emphasised that it essentially remains a matter for the discretion of the trial judge whether several offenders should properly be tried together at the same time. The court thus recognised the general principle that even if

35 As in Bahamas Criminal Procedure Code, Ch 91, s 76; and Jamaica Criminal Justice (Administration) Act, s 22(1) (in respect of summary offences).

accused persons are properly charged jointly, separate trials may be ordered if a joint trial would embarrass or prejudice the fair trial of one defendant. This principle is contained in the legislation on indictment rules in most jurisdictions which enable an indictment to be amended to 'direct that the person should be tried separately for any or more offences charged in the indictment'.[36] In *Nandlal* (above), the Court of Appeal in the course of its judgment observed that one of the accused persons, the magistrate, had applied for and been granted a separate trial on the basis of possible prejudice.

The general rule is that it is in the public interest that defendants who are validly joined in an indictment or complaint should be tried together. This saves time, expense and makes for fairness in sentencing if the defendants are convicted. If it is anticipated that one defendant by his particular defence could incriminate or prejudice his co-defendant, the court must decide whether (in the case of a jury trial) directions to the jury will be sufficient to offset any latent prejudice. In *Moghal* (1977) 65 Cr App R 56, the English Court of Appeal disapproved of the fact that the trial judge had ordered separate trials of defendants who were jointly charged with participation in one offence, murder. It was stated that only in exceptional cases should an order for separate trials in such circumstances be made.

Severance

It is equally permissible to sever properly joined counts in an indictment. Severance refers to an order of the court permitting separate trials of properly joined counts (charges). This will, however, only be done if it is considered that the indictment is so overloaded that an unduly long and complicated trial will result: *R v Novac* (1977) 65 Cr App R 107. Such an order must be made with care, otherwise a defendant could possibly later claim that he suffered prejudice from two trials when there should have been only one: *Nandlal* (above). In *Ludlow v Metropolitan Police Commissioners* [1970] 2 WLR 521, p 575, HL, the House of Lords said: 'in most cases it would be oppressive to the accused as well as expensive and inconvenient for the prosecution to have two or more trials where one would suffice'.

The determinant then is whether one trial would suffice. Unless the joint trial of several, properly joined, counts can be shown to be prejudicial or embarrassing to the accused person, a judge should not order severance of such counts by directing separate trials of them. The overall consideration is the interest of justice. The question of severance of charges does not arise in summary proceedings, since complaints are never joined. Each complaint is in respect of only one offence. The magistrate must look into the question of prejudice to the defendant before he makes an order for the joint hearing of several offences. This compares to indictable trials where joinder of counts has already occurred when the indictment is drafted. Issues of possible prejudice are considered afterwards and then an order for severance of counts to be heard separately may be made by the judge.

36 In Criminal Procedure Act, Chap 12:02, s 14(3), Trinidad and Tobago.

CHAPTER 6

THE PLEA

A defendant who is on trial at the magistrates' court or the High Court is required to enter a plea to the charge before the trial can legitimately begin. This chapter focuses on the different types of pleas that are possible and the various issues, many of them problematic, which may arise in respect of each.

The accused person is usually present when a plea is taken since he is expected to make the plea personally. This is mandatory at indictable trial,[1] but not necessarily so in the magistrates' court. Statute in most jurisdictions enables a defendant to appear 'by' counsel[2] in respect of summary matters. In practice this is only done with permission of the court, which will usually be given if the defendant is pleading guilty to a minor offence such as a traffic violation. Otherwise, once a defendant is present, even at the magistrates' court he is expected to plead personally, although he is legally represented.

Where defendants are charged jointly, each defendant must plead, since liability is individual and the evidence against each defendant must be considered separately. Where a defendant is charged with more than one offence, he must plead to each offence. There should be no general plea and if there is, the court should not accept it, but should call on the defendant to plead to each charge.

FIT TO PLEAD

A defendant must be 'fit to plead'. If he is mentally incapacitated, it is apparent that he may not be able to give full or proper instructions to his lawyer, nor may he appreciate the consequences of a particular plea. A defendant is expected to understand what transpires at his trial (and at committal proceedings) so even if he is represented by counsel, if he is not fit to plead the trial may be a nullity. On indictable trial at the High Court, it is a jury decision[3] as to whether a defendant is fit to plead and the court will select a jury to try that issue before the real trial. This will be considered later in Chapter 13.

In summary trials there is no separate trial of the issue. It is generally inappropriate for a magistrate to hold a trial within a trial as he decides both the law and facts in any event. Nonetheless, the practice is that if there are doubts as to the defendant's fitness, the court may, in the interest of fairness, direct that he be medically examined. Even without specific provision permitting this, it seems to be entirely within a magistrate's discretion to do so in accordance with the principles of natural justice.

Some guidance as to how a summary court should proceed when dealing with a fitness to plead issue may be gleaned from *DPP v P* [2008] 1 WLR 1005, which concerned a decision of a youth court in England. In that case the Divisional Court considered an appeal from the DPP in respect of the decision staying charges against a 13-year-old youth. The latter was said to be of a low IQ and in 2004 several charges against him had been stayed by the Crown Court on the basis that he was unfit to plead. In 2005 he appeared before the

---

1 *R v Ellis* (1973) 57 Cr App R 571.

2 E.g., Summary Courts Act, Chap 4:20, s 60(1) of Trinidad and Tobago.

3 *R v Podola* [1960] 1 QB 325.

youth court and denied various criminal charges, thus implicitly accepting that he was fit to plead. The defence made a successful application to have those proceedings stayed as an abuse of process of the court, contending that the defendant did not have a sufficient level of maturity or intellectual capacity to understand and participate effectively in the proceedings and citing medical reports in support. In allowing the appeal the court held, inter alia that

(1) A court should only stay proceedings on capacity issues in exceptional cases where it was likely to affect the fairness of the trial.
(2) The fact that a court of higher authority had previously held that a person was unfit to plead did not make it an abuse to try that person for subsequent criminal acts. The issue of a defendant's ability to participate effectively had to be decided afresh.
(3) Medical evidence should be considered as part of the evidence in the case and not as the sole evidence on a freestanding application. It was the court's opinion of the defendant's level of understanding which had to determine whether a criminal trial was to proceed.
(4) If the court decided that it should call a halt to the criminal trial on the ground that the defendant could not take an effective part in the proceedings, it should then consider whether to switch to a consideration of whether the defendant had done the acts alleged. That decision was one for the discretion of the court, but the proceedings should be stayed as an abuse of process before fact finding only if no useful purpose could be served by finding the facts.
(5) It would be right for a court to stay proceedings at the outset if the defendant was so severely impaired as to be unable to participate in the trial and where there would be no useful purpose in finding the facts.

In *Taitt v State of Trinidad and Tobago* [2012] UKPC 38 the issue of fitness to stand trial was raised on appeal following a conviction for murder. The Board held that the fact that a person was of low intelligence did not operate as a bar to trial. It was where a person suffers from a severe physical or mental disability, which makes it impossible for him to understand what was going on or to give instructions, that the person can be held to be unfit to plead.

Where the individual is of borderline low intellectual capacity, whose level of impairment is such that he is likely to struggle to participate fully in a criminal trial, the court must consider the following:

a) Does the defendant understand the charges that have been made against him?
b) Is he able to decide whether to plead guilty or not?
c) Is he able to exercise his right to challenge the jurors?
d) Is he able intelligently to convey to his lawyers the case which he wishes them to advance on his behalf?
e) Is he able to follow the proceedings when they come to court?
f) Is he able, if he wishes, to give evidence on his own behalf?

The Board also emphasised that the quality of the accused's instructions to counsel or of any evidence that he may wish to give did not assist the court in deciding the issue of fitness to plead. Instead, the emphasis is on the accused's ability (or inability) to do the things mentioned in a) to f) above.

It was also decided in this case that only in an exceptional case would the Board entertain the argument that the appellant was not fit to stand trial due to low intelligence caused by a learning disability when the point was not taken on his behalf by counsel at his trial. The Board stated that it was the responsibility of counsel to assess whether his client was fit to stand trial since he was in the best position to judge at first hand whether his client was able to understand the charge that was brought against him and to give instructions for his defence. The attorney's conclusion that his client was fit to plead would normally be given great weight in such cases. The Board emphasised that the Privy Council would not permit the introduction of the issue for the first time at the final stage unless the evidence pointed very clearly to the fact that there was a miscarriage of justice.

In Dominica legislation in the form of the Criminal Law and Procedure (Amendment) Act No 2 of 2013, ss 36A to 36I was passed in 2013, reviewing that country's law on fitness to plead. The focus is on the 'decision-making capacity' of the accused and his fitness for trial is assessed on this basis, although the relevant factors in making such a determination are similar to those at common law. The new law provides for special measures that may be ordered to assist the accused in effectively participating in his trial. One such is through the use of an intermediary who communicates with the accused.

The charge is always read to the defendant before he is called upon to plead. The process for entering a plea in the High Court is called the arraignment and is more formal. For a defendant who is fit to plead there are three available options:

- guilty;
- not guilty;
- plea(s) in bar.

GUILTY PLEA

By such a plea the defendant allows the prosecution to dispense with the requirement to prove the offence. Since the defendant is giving up many of his rights when he enters a guilty plea, it is necessary that the plea be unambiguous and voluntarily given. Usually, he must plead personally as indicated above unless statute permits otherwise. A defendant who is charged with a trivial summary matter may plead guilty in absentia through his lawyer who appears. Practice and in some cases statute permit this.

In the High Court, the plea of guilty must be made personally by the defendant and in the magistrates' court, once the defendant appears, he himself should plead guilty. In *R v Heyes* (1951) 34 Cr App R 161, a statement by his counsel that the defendant wished to plead guilty was held to be insufficient. The plea of guilty was thus considered a nullity.

The procedure on a plea of guilty is that following the plea, the court invites the prosecution to give a summary of the facts, the case for the prosecution. The defendant then gives an explanation or a plea in mitigation. He is then sentenced if the plea is considered valid.

In the High Court the defendant who wishes to plead guilty may seek an indication from the court as to the maximum sentence the court will be minded to impose in the event the plea is actually entered. The case of *R v Goodyear* [2005] EWCA Crim 888 established the relevant principles to be applied in maximum sentence indications. These principles form the basis of Practice Directions in Trinidad and Tobago (dated 14 August 2015) and St Lucia (Practice Direction No. 4 of 2014). According to *Goodyear*, any advance indication of sentence to be given by the judge should normally be confined to the maximum sentence if a plea of guilty was tendered at the stage at which the indication is sought. Furthermore, the judge should not give an advance indication of sentence unless one has been sought by the defendant, though in an appropriate case the defence advocate may be reminded of his entitlement to seek an advance indication of sentence.

The judge retains an unfettered discretion to refuse to give an advance sentence indication or may choose to defer the giving of the same. Therefore, in a case involving a number of defendants, the judge may be concerned that an indication given to one defendant, who seeks it, may itself create pressure on another defendant. In these circumstances the judge may well decline to give the indication. Once an indication has been given, it is binding and remains binding on the judge who has given it. The indication also binds any other judge who becomes responsible for the case. If, after a reasonable opportunity to consider his position in the light of the indication, the defendant does not plead guilty, the indication will cease to have effect.

In Trinidad and Tobago it has been held that magistrates do not have the jurisdiction to entertain applications for a maximum sentence indication. In *Michael Murrell v Her Worship Gayle Gonzales Magistrate* Claim No. CV2016-00521, after a magistrate had refused to accept that summary courts could exercise such a jurisdiction, leave was granted for judicial review of this decision. The court in dismissing the application for judicial review, cited dicta in *Goodyear* that suggested that it would be impracticable for *Goodyear* indications to be extended to proceedings in the magistrates' court.

The court also noted that the Trinidad and Tobago Practice Direction only provided for an advance indication by a 'judge', with 'judge' being defined as a 'judge of the High Court' and 'court' as the 'High Court of Trinidad and Tobago'.

The court concluded that before *Goodyear* hearings at the summary level could be implemented, legislative amendments to summary procedure would be necessary. The most that magistrates would be allowed to give for the time being would be an advance indication as to whether or not a custodial sentence would be imposed.

The lesser charge

A defendant may by statute or common law plead guilty to a lesser alternative offence if the prosecution consents and the judge permits it. A plea of guilty to manslaughter on a charge of murder is thus permissible, since the former offence is encapsulated in the latter. Criminal procedure legislation in most jurisdictions recognises this principle and in any case at common law it is established that on indictment, a defendant may plead not guilty to the offence charged in the indictment, but guilty to another offence of which he might be found guilty on that indictment. It is not necessary that such offence be included as a count in the indictment.

It is up to the prosecution to decide if they are willing to accept the 'lesser' plea: *Hazeltine* (1969) 51 Cr App R 351. This will usually be determined by the strength of the evidence against the defendant. If the prosecution refuses to accept the lesser plea and the trial proceeds, they are prevented from resuscitating the guilty plea at a later stage in the trial. In *Hazeltine* the prosecutor refused to accept a plea of guilty to the lesser offence of unlawful wounding on a charge of wounding with intent. The trial proceeded with a not guilty plea being entered in respect of the wounding with intent. The jury returned a verdict of not guilty but were not asked about the lesser offence (which was not the subject of a separate count). The judge then proceeded to sentence Hazeltine for unlawful wounding. It was held on appeal that there was no power in the court to do so, since all that was before it then was a plea of not guilty to wounding with intent, the plea of guilty having been rejected.

It can be gathered from *Hazeltine* that there can only be one plea to one charge. On the charge of wounding with intent, the defendant had pleaded not guilty. On the lesser alternative he had pleaded guilty. Since that latter plea was rejected, only the first plea stood. Furthermore, it was made clear that both the prosecution and the judge must accept the plea to the lesser alternative offence. In *Emmanuel* (1981) 74 Cr App R 135, the judge withdrew his consent to a plea of guilty to the lesser charge after hearing the facts from the prosecution. This action was held to be valid on appeal.

When offences are tried in the magistrates' court, there is no common law entitlement for the court to accept a plea of guilty to what might be considered a lesser alternative offence. Magistrates are creatures of statute whose powers are circumscribed by statute. In most jurisdictions, however, statute does permit a magistrate to find a defendant guilty of a specific offence and not guilty of the offence charged. These are specified in summary courts legislation[4] and usually include such offences as receiving and larceny in the alternative or unlawful possession and larceny.

Unless it is clear that a lesser offence is constituted in the greater (as in manslaughter in murder), it is always permissible to charge both offences and leave it to the tribunal of fact to determine upon which to make a finding of guilt. This procedure also facilitates pleas of guilty to an alternative offence: *Yeardley* [2000] 2 Cr App R 141.

Unequivocal plea

The plea must be unambiguous. If a defendant says he is 'guilty with an explanation' this indicates that the plea is qualified. If, on listening to the explanation, the court forms the opinion that the defendant may have a valid defence, the court should record a not guilty plea and set the matter for trial. In *Lewis v Commissioners of Police* (1969) 13 WIR 186, a case from Grenada, a defendant was charged with assaulting a police officer. He pleaded guilty. The normal procedure was then followed in that the prosecutor stated the facts and the defendant then gave his explanation. It was held on appeal that the defendant's explanation amounted to a plea of not guilty and the court acted wrongly in choosing to believe the 'facts' alleged by the prosecution and proceeding to conviction. A plea of not guilty should have been entered.

The decision in *Lewis* is in line with previous English authority on point. In *Baker* (1912) 7 Cr App R 217, an unrepresented defendant pleaded guilty to a charge of having in his custody a mould under s 24 of the Coinage Offences Act 1861. On being asked for his explanation, the defendant for the first time said he only used the mould for medals. The relevant extract from the statutory provisions stated: 'Whoever without lawful authority or excuse ... shall have in his custody or possession any mould'. It was held that the defendant's explanation amounted to a defence of lawful excuse. His plea was thus either an incomplete one or equivalent to not guilty. Similarly, in *R v Ingleson* (1915) 11 Cr App R 21, it was held that a plea of guilty was bad. On charges of larceny and in the alternative, receiving, the defendant pleaded guilty to taking the horses in question 'not knowing they were stolen'. The Court of Criminal Appeal held that a plea of not guilty should have been entered.

Different facts

Even if the defendant's explanation does not amount to a possible defence, sometimes his version of the facts may be inconsistent with that of the prosecution. He may, for instance, gloss over or omit aggravating features of the offence. If the prosecution does not accept the defence account of the incident and if the discrepancy may significantly affect the sentence, though not the verdict, then the court should consider a *Newton* hearing. This is effectively a trial within a trial for the express purpose of resolving the differences. Evidence may be called by both sides to resolve the matter. The procedure for such a

4 As in the Summary Courts Act, Chap 4:20, s 76, Trinidad and Tobago.

hearing is set out in *R v Newton* (1983) 77 Cr App R 13 as elaborated in *Tolera* (1999) 1 Cr App R 29. It must be clear that the defendant's explanation does amount to an admission of guilt of the offence to which he pleads guilty and that the only conflict is as to the different accounts. In the magistrates' court, while no trial within a trial is held, the court may listen to evidence to resolve the issue.

Voluntary plea

A voluntary plea has two elements: the defendant must understand to what he is pleading; and he must make the plea of his own free will. He must not be pressured by anyone to plead guilty.

A defendant who through some disability, such as ignorance of the language or extreme youth, does not understand to what he is pleading cannot be said to have made a voluntary plea. His choice was not of his own free will. Here, the defendant is not suffering from a mental disorder, but at the time of his plea he was equally unaware of the nature and consequences of his plea. *R v Iqbal Begum* (1991) 93 Cr App R 96 is a good example of where the defendant did not know to what she was pleading. In that case the defendant, who was from Pakistan, understood very little English; although she had lived in England for a number of years, she had been virtually housebound. She was charged with murder and gave her instructions to her solicitor through a Pakistani accountant who acted as interpreter. She subsequently pleaded guilty to murder. On appeal, the defence contended that it was never made clear to her in language she understood, the difference between murder and manslaughter and she could have had a defence of provocation if she had understood. The Court of Appeal emphasised that it had often been pointed out that unless a person understands the full implication of the charge to which he pleads so that he can give instructions to his lawyer, the court cannot be sure that he pleaded with a free and understanding mind. On the facts of the case, the inadequacy of the interpretation was such that there was a lack of communication with the defendant. She did not fully understand what was said to her.

The defendant must not be pressured in any way into entering the plea. Such a plea will not be of his own free will. In *Peace* [1976] Crim LR 119, the Court of Appeal held that where counsel gave 'strong advice' to the defendant to plead guilty if it could be said he was not making a voluntary choice, then the plea would be a nullity. In that case, Peace applied to have his convictions for arson and conspiracy to defraud set aside on the basis that he pleaded guilty for fear that, if found guilty, he might get a harsher sentence, as his counsel had indicated. He contended that he was innocent. It was held that even though the defendant had pleaded guilty unhappily and regretfully, he still at the time had the power to make a voluntary and deliberate choice.

Peace was followed in *Simmons v Barker* (1983) 32 WIR 177, a decision of the Supreme Court of Bermuda. In *Simmons* the court held that the professional advice of counsel could not be regarded as improper or excessive pressure such as to vitiate the plea of guilty. At the time the plea was made, it represented the genuine intention of the appellant. Similarly, in *R v Herbert* (1992) 94 Cr App R 230, it was held that there are always pressures on an accused person and some factors may weigh in deciding how he pleads. Where, however, the course of events involves no fault on the part of anyone and the appellant had the benefit of the most conscientious advice, it was evident he had made his own free choice. In that case, the defendant was jointly charged with his wife for offences involving drug trafficking. He offered to plead guilty if the prosecution did not proceed against his wife. On his change of plea to guilty, the prosecution offered no evidence against his wife. It was held that his plea was not a nullity.

In contrast, a statement by the trial judge that the defendant was plainly guilty and was 'wasting' the court's time was improper: *Barnes* (1970) 55 Cr App R 100. Were a defendant to change his plea after such an intimation, the plea would be a nullity. In *Turner* [1970] 2 QB 321, it was made clear that a judge should not indicate the sentence which he is minded to impose if the defendant pleaded guilty, as against a different sentence if he is convicted on a not guilty plea. An intimation of sentence emanating from the judge, designed to encourage a guilty plea by threatening a harsher sentence otherwise, can amount to pressure to plead guilty.

Plea bargaining

The impact of *Turner* is also to disapprove of the practice of plea bargaining, which is part of the common law of the US. It is not part of English common law in its true sense, although there can be agreement by the prosecution and the defence that the former may accept a plea of guilty to a lesser alternative offence. This has sometimes been called implicit plea bargaining, but the difference is that in true plea bargaining the judge is empowered to indicate what sentence (or its range) he will give if a defendant pleads guilty.

In 1999 Trinidad and Tobago passed legislation recognising and legitimising the system of plea bargaining by means of the Criminal Procedure (Plea Discussion and Plea Agreement) Act No 11 of 1999, Chap 13:07. In December 2008, by virtue of Act 18 of 2008, similar legislation to that of Trinidad and Tobago was passed in Guyana. Its effect is yet to be assessed. At the time of writing the Jamaica Criminal Justice (Plea Negotiations and Agreement) Act of 2005, which was set to come into operation on a date to be appointed, had not yet come into operation. Its terms are identical in material aspects to those of the legislation of Trinidad and Tobago. Perhaps because of a lack of understanding of the system and how it operates in actuality, the practice of plea bargaining has not yet developed. It would seem in principle, however, that the arguments against pressure to plead guilty might be of less significance in Trinidad and Tobago in the future. The Act provides for the prosecutor and the accused or his attorney to engage in plea discussions. If an agreement is subsequently entered into the prosecutor is required to disclose to the Court in open court in the presence of the accused or his attorney the substance of, and reasons for, the agreement. The judge or magistrate is required to ensure that (a) no improper inducement was made to the accused person to enter into the agreement; (b) the accused person understands the nature, substance and consequences of the agreement; and (c) the offence to which the agreement relates adequately reflects the gravity of the provable conduct of the accused unless there are exceptional circumstances. In addition, the views of the victim are sought. In the final analysis the court may reject a plea agreement entered into between the prosecution and the accused person if he considers that it is not in the interest of justice to do so.

Withdrawal of guilty plea

An application to withdraw a guilty plea may be made at any stage before sentence is passed. Once sentence is passed, the court is functus officio; it cannot continue any further hearing in the particular case: *Beswick v R* (1987) 36 WIR 318, PC. In this Jamaican case a defendant was allowed to plead guilty to a minor traffic offence. The magistrate sentenced him, but subsequently ordered that summons should be reissued, effectively deeming that his sentencing order was null and void. The Privy Council held that once the magistrate had validly sentenced the defendant, he was functus officio and had no jurisdiction to order a subsequent reopening of the case. The same principle had been enunciated in an earlier English case of

R v Campbell ex p Hoy [1953] 1 All ER 684. In that case, it was held that a magistrate had no power to allow a defendant to change his plea to not guilty after the magistrate had sentenced him following a valid plea of guilty.

In *S (An Infant) v Recorder of Manchester* [1971] 1 AC 481, HL, the House of Lords confirmed that it has long been the law that when a man pleads 'guilty' to an indictment the trial judge can permit him to change his plea to 'not guilty' at any time before the case is finally disposed of by sentence or otherwise. The House also held that a summary court had a similar discretion. In *R v Richards* (1992) 41 WIR 263, PC, the Privy Council in considering a case from Jamaica followed *S (An Infant)* on this point. Even though the court may allow a withdrawal of a guilty plea before sentence, it should exercise this discretion with care. If the defendant did not really understand to what he was pleading or if his explanation renders the plea equivocal, the plea will amount to a nullity. In such circumstances, a plea of not guilty should be entered even if the defendant does not apply to change his plea. If the plea of guilty is entered as a result of a mistake or an improper understanding by counsel of the defendant's instructions, the court should allow the change of plea. The Court of Appeal will consider an appeal against conviction despite a guilty plea if it is contended that the plea was equivocal or made out of duress, as in *R v Crown Court at Huntingdon ex p Jordan* [1981] 2 All ER 872.

If, however, it is clear that the defendant pleaded guilty in circumstances where there was no possibility of a mistake, the court is not bound to allow a change of plea: *R v McNally* [1953] 1 WLR 933. Therefore, if it appears that a defendant simply fears, because of his attitude on hearing the facts, that the judge may give him a heavy sentence, a change of plea should not be allowed on this basis alone. Where a defendant after an adjournment, following a plea of guilty in the High Court, wishes to change his plea, it seems the court may hold an enquiry to determine if the accused person knew to what he was pleading. If the judge forms the opinion that the plea was unequivocal, he may decide not to allow the change. The enquiry need not be of a formal nature.

The attitude of magistrates is more liberal and an unrepresented defendant in particular will invariably be permitted to withdraw a guilty plea.

NOT GUILTY PLEA

When the accused person pleads not guilty, he puts the prosecution to proof of all the elements necessary to constitute the offence. Even if the defendant does not enter the plea personally, it is not a nullity, since he is not prejudiced by such a plea. Apart from a personal plea, a plea of not guilty is also entered if:

- the defendant refuses to plead;
- the defendant is mute of malice (as compared to by visitation of God);
- the trial is proceeding ex parte, as is permissible under summary procedure legislation in circumstances where a defendant who has been properly notified fails to attend court.

Mute defendant

If a defendant is mute, inquiries must be made as to whether he is mute by malice (refuses to speak) or by visitation of God (he cannot speak). In a jury trial, this may be decided by a jury as a preliminary issue. Frequently, a defendant may pretend to be unable to speak in the hope of causing a trial to be later declared null or simply to delay the trial. In the trial of the preliminary issue a jury is empanelled and the prosecution and defence may lead evidence on the issue and cross-examine as in a regular trial. The prosecution may seek to bring evidence of persons who have lately heard the defendant speak intelligibly. Medical evidence may also be called by either side. If the jury finds the defendant mute by visitation of God, they must specify what the 'visitation' is. If it is merely a physical problem, arrangements must be made for communication with the defendant such as through sign language or someone who understands his otherwise unintelligible speech. In any event, communication must be established with the defendant before trial begins.

If the defendant is found to be mute by visitation of God as a result of a mental situation, the jury must embark on trial of the issue of fitness to plead: *Podola* [1960] 1 QB 325. Unless the defendant is found fit to take his trial, the matter cannot proceed further.

In trial before the magistrates' court, the magistrate, as the arbiter of both facts and law, must come to a determination whether the defendant is mute by malice or not. This can be determined from medical evidence which may be obtained following an order for the defendant to be medically examined.

Effectiveness

A not guilty plea, once taken before a competent court, continues to be effective and need not be taken again. In *D'Aguiar v Cox* (1971) 18 WIR 44, the appellants pleaded not guilty before a magistrate in District G but the cases were transferred to the magistrate in District E. The latter did not take the plea again, but proceeded to hear evidence and eventually convicted the appellants. It was held on appeal by the Guyanese Full Court that the plea of not guilty continued to apply when the second magistrate heard the case. The usual practice, however, is to read the charge to the defendant again, in case he should change his plea to guilty.

The obvious rationale is that the defendant is not in any way prejudiced by this since the prosecution has to prove its case fully. Furthermore, a plea of not guilty, while it continues to be valid, does not begin a trial,[5] so the second magistrate may begin and continue the hearing of the case. The position is contrasted with a guilty plea in which case the matter must be continued before the same magistrate. This is because the plea of guilty begins the process of adjudication, as it were.

Change of plea

There is clearly no problem or issue with a defendant changing his plea to guilty at any stage of the trial. Even if the accused person has already been put in the charge of the jury in an indictable trial, this is acceptable. The special procedure to be followed outlined in *R v Heyes* (1951) 34 Cr App R 161 will be discussed in Chapter 13.

PLEAS IN BAR

A plea in bar may be taken before a defendant is called upon to plead at trial. In *Joseph v Mohammed* (1964) 7 WIR 96, the Trinidad and Tobago Court of Appeal in relation to autrefois stressed (p 97) that:

5 As stated in *R v Resident Magistrate for Saint Andrew and the DPP ex p Black et al.* (1975) 24 WIR 388, which was determined on the question of withdrawal of a charge.

> the procedure should be that at the beginning of the case, before any plea of guilty or not guilty, this plea of autrefois should have been taken on behalf of the defendant. All pleas in bar that are made in criminal trials appear to hinge on the general concept of abuse of process. This is excepting the plea of demurrer, which is an objection to the form or substance of the demurrer, with statutory provisions for amendments allowing defects to be corrected. This plea is almost defunct. It has been said that demurrer in criminal cases should be allowed to die naturally.[6]

Pleas in bar in modern times are of three types: pardon, autrefois acquit and autrefois convict and should be made before the defendant is called upon to plead further.[7] Since a plea in bar goes to the very root of its jurisdiction, a court has inherent jurisdiction to entertain such a plea at trial.

Pardon

An accused person is entitled to raise a pardon as a plea in bar to the prosecution of any offence. He may have been granted a pardon after conviction for an offence. The source of the power of grant was originally the royal prerogative of mercy which was initially delegated to Governors of British colonies.[8] This power of pardon is now exercised by the Head of State in Commonwealth Caribbean countries, on the advice of Cabinet, and is contained in the constitutions of such countries. It is usually referred to as the 'prerogative of mercy'. The Barbados constitutional provision is typical of most jurisdictions:

> 78 (1) The Governor General may, in Her Majesty's name and on Her Majesty's behalf –
>
> (a) grant to any person convicted of any offence against the law of Barbados a pardon, either free or subject to lawful conditions;
>
> (b) grant to any person a respite, either indefinite or for a specified period, from the execution of any punishment imposed on that person for such an offence;
>
> (c) substitute a less severe form of punishment for that imposed on any person for such an offence; or
>
> (d) remit the whole or part of any punishment imposed on any person for such an offence or any penalty or forfeiture otherwise due to the Crown on account of such an offence.

It is evident that the power of pardon envisaged in this constitutional provision relates to convictions. Essentially, a person may be pardoned for an offence for which he was convicted or for the whole or part of the punishment for a conviction. The consequence of such a pardon is not to eliminate the conviction so as to result in an acquittal.[9] It merely removes from the subject of the pardon 'such pains, penalties and punishments' that ensue from the conviction, as are stipulated in the pardon. In *R v Foster* [1984] 2 All ER 679, Foster had been charged with four counts in an indictment. He pleaded guilty in 1978 to two counts of rape and was sentenced to be detained in hospital under the Mental Health Act for those offences. Subsequently, in 1981, another man was arrested by the police on

6 Lord Parker CJ in *R v Inner London Quarter Sessions ex p Metropolitan Police Commissioner* [1970] 2 QB 80.

7 The Grenada Criminal Procedure Code, s 142(3) actually stipulates this.

8 *Re Royal Commissioner of Thomas case* [1980] 1 NZLR 602, 616.

9 *R v Foster* [1984] 2 All ER 679.

suspicion of indecent assault. He admitted those offences and a vast number of other offences against young girls including the two offences to which Foster had pleaded guilty. It eventually became clear that Foster, who was of very low intelligence, was innocent of the offences. In the circumstances, he received a free pardon from the Queen. Foster, however, wished to appeal against the conviction. The question arose as to whether he could appeal against a free pardon. It was generally thought at the time that a free pardon had the effect of quashing the conviction. The English Court of Appeal held that this was not so. A pardon did not result in an acquittal. The conviction in Foster's case was therefore still outstanding.

An accused person is thus entitled to use a 'pardon' as a plea in bar both on the basis that it is a pardon and also on the basis of autrefois convict. In rare instances, however, legislation may provide that a pardon may be granted even before trial. Such is the case in Trinidad and Tobago, where the Constitution provides:

> 87 (1) The President may grant to any person a pardon, either free or subject to lawful conditions respecting any offences that he may have committed. The power of the President under this subsection may be exercised by him either before or after the person is charged with any offence and before he is convicted thereof.

This power of pre-trial pardon is a new power under the Trinidad and Tobago Republican Constitution 1976 and is modelled on the pardoning power given in the US Constitution to the President of the US. It was utilised to pardon the late President Richard Nixon of possible crimes associated with the break-in at the Watergate Hotel in 1973. In *Phillip et al.* v *DPP et al.* (1991) 40 WIR 410, PC, this section was considered by the Privy Council.

Giving effect to pardon

The question arose as to how effect should be given to a pre-trial pardon. In 1990, 114 insurgents were charged in Trinidad and Tobago for various crimes ranging from murder to treason committed during the course of a failed coup attempt in July 1990. They claimed that they were the beneficiaries of a pre-trial pardon by the acting President. The applicants sought to raise this pardon as a plea in bar at the committal proceedings into the offences. It was argued that since pardon was a plea in bar, it could only be taken at trial, which was when a plea would be taken. The applicants brought habeas corpus proceedings and a constitutional motion claiming that their detention was unlawful. The proceedings were dismissed. They appealed and the appeal was argued on how effect could be given to a pre-trial pardon.

The Privy Council held that it would be oppressive to expect the applicants to wait until the trial, which might not be for years, to raise the plea. They had established a prima facie case of entitlement to a valid pardon under the Constitution. As such they were entitled to raise the plea on habeas corpus proceedings calling on the State to justify their detention. The matter was accordingly remitted to the High Court to determine the validity of the pardon before the committal proceedings could continue, if necessary. It is now well known that the Privy Council subsequently held that it would be an abuse of process to proceed with the prosecutions even though the pardon was technically invalid.[10]

Even though *Phillip v DPP* (above) was concerned with a pre-trial pardon, in principle it would seem that the same rationale should apply to all pleas in bar taken in respect of

10 *AG of Trinidad and Tobago et al. v Philip et al.* (1994) 45 WIR 456, PC.

indictable trials. It would seem equally oppressive to require any person charged with an indictable offence to have to await indictment before he can argue that he is the beneficiary of a plea of autrefois and should not be prosecuted.

Autrefois

It is a basic common law principle that a person may not be tried a second time for the same offence in respect of which he was in jeopardy of being convicted, was convicted or was acquitted on the first trial. This is sometimes referred to as the rule against double jeopardy, which is fundamental to English law and is in accordance with recognised constitutional principles of the right to due process. A person who is about to be tried a second time in such circumstances may raise a plea of either autrefois acquit or autrefois convict. If he raises autrefois acquit he is alleging that he was previously acquitted on the same charge and if autrefois convict that he was previously convicted on the same charge.

It has been settled in *Forbes v AG of Jamaica* [2009] UKPC 13 that the plea of autrefois can only be determined in criminal proceedings against the accused.

The scope of the plea

The scope of the plea of autrefois was considered in detail by the House of Lords in *Connelly v DPP* [1964] AC 1254, HL, which is the locus classicus on point. This case is recognised as the established authority on autrefois in the Commonwealth Caribbean.[11]

In *Connelly* (above) the House of Lords held that a person may not be tried for a crime in respect of which he has previously been acquitted or convicted. Furthermore, he may not be tried for a crime in respect of which he could at a previous trial have been lawfully convicted. For instance, on a charge of murder, the accused person can be convicted in the alternative for the lesser offence of manslaughter. If the jury return a general verdict of 'not guilty' on a charge of murder without saying anything more, the prosecution cannot come again on a charge of manslaughter. There would have been an implied not guilty verdict on the manslaughter. If, however, a jury acquit on the offence charged but are unable to agree on the statutory or common law alternative, this is not a bar to a further prosecution of the alternative charge: *DPP v Nasralla* [1967] 2 All ER 161, PC.

It has been confirmed that the suggestion in *Connelly* (the third principle) that autrefois can extend to situations where the first charge was in effect substantially the same is not valid. Neither is the fourth principle, which states that the test of autrefois is whether the evidence necessary to support the second charge or the facts necessary to constitute the second charge are the same as for the first charge: *R v Beedie* [1997] 2 Cr App R 167. These two latter principles are really part of the much wider doctrine of abuse of process, discussed in Chapter 2. Thus, where a person is charged with an offence which is substantially the same as a previous charge, it may be an abuse of process to try him again. In *Beedie*, a charge of manslaughter resulting from a defective gas installation was held to be an abuse of process where the defendant had already been convicted of a summary offence relating to the defective gas installation.

11 This is evidenced by the contents of the judgment in *DPP v Nasralla* [1967] 2 All ER 161, PC and *Nandlal v The State* (1995) 49 WIR 412.

The House of Lords in *Connelly* decided that a defendant who had been previously acquitted on a charge of murder could be subsequently tried on another indictment, charging robbery, arising out of the same incident. At that time in England, it was not the practice to try robbery on the same indictment with murder, which was then a capital offence. The doctrine of autrefois did not apply in *Connelly* and neither did the general principle of abuse of process, because the facts and evidence necessary to support a charge of robbery are different from those required for murder. In *Requena and Flores v R* (1981) 32 WIR 126, the Court of Appeal of Belize held on similar facts to *Connelly* that:

> there was no rule or principle that evidence which had been adduced by the prosecution on a charge in respect of which a person had been acquitted (murder) could not be adduced at his subsequent trial on a different charge arising out of the same facts (robbery).

In *Lewis v Irish* (1966) 10 WIR 500, the respondent was charged with unlawful possession. Hearing was begun in the matter and the case was then adjourned. In the meantime, further inquiries were made and a charge of larceny of the same property was laid, in part founded on the new evidence acquired after the first charge. The magistrate dismissed the charge of unlawful possession and subsequently accepted a plea of autrefois acquit based on s 73(5) of the Summary Courts Ordinance. The Trinidad and Tobago Court of Appeal allowed an appeal by the prosecution holding that on the facts, the defendant was never in jeopardy of being convicted of larceny on the unlawful possession charge. On the facts of that case, the evidence was not sufficient to 'establish the commission of the offence of larceny' as stipulated in s 73(5). The plea of autrefois acquit should not have been accepted.

The Court of Appeal of Trinidad and Tobago in *Walker v Feese* Magisterial Appeal No. 96 of 2009 considered whether a dismissal of a charge of trafficking cocaine under the Dangerous Drugs Act Chap.11:25 would entitle the defendant to raise a plea of autrefois acquit on subsequent charges of importing and attempting to export prohibited goods under the Customs Act Chap. 78:01.The court held that regarding the offences before the court there was a similarity in intention, possession and penalty and thus the elements of importing and exporting and trafficking, as well as the evidence necessary to prove the offences, were the same. The magistrate was therefore correct in concluding that the three offences were substantially the same and entitled the defendant to rely on autrefois acquit.

Nullity

In *Haynes v Davis* [1915] 1 KB 332, Lush J, in his dissenting judgment, sought to define what being 'in jeopardy' meant. This was in relation to a plea of autrefois acquit but the principle is of general application. A defendant would be in jeopardy if: (a) the court was competent to try the defendant for the offence; (b) the trial was on a valid indictment (or charge) and (c) (in relation to acquittals) the acquittal was on the merits. The latter point meant that the acquittal must not be on some technical ground indicative of the fact that an ensuing trial would have been a nullity. There must have been a proper adjudication.

There are many examples of cases in which the court has held that the previous trial was a nullity for one reason or the other. In *R v West* [1962] 2 All ER 624, the justices purported to try summarily a charge of being an accessory after the fact and dismissed the charge. They had no power to try such an offence summarily. Subsequently, a second information was laid in respect of the charge and despite a submission of autrefois acquit, committal proceedings were embarked upon and the defendant committed. The Court of Criminal Appeal held that the first 'trial' was a nullity as the court was not competent to try the defendant for the offence. Furthermore, in respect of indictable proceedings, it is for the trial court to decide on a plea of autrefois, not examining justices (or a magistrate, as the case may be). Similarly, in *Stoute v Braithwaite* (1962) 4 WIR 391, the Barbados Supreme Court held that a dismissal of a charge for want of jurisdiction was not a bar to a later charge for the same offence. Want of jurisdiction indicated that the first trial was a nullity. The court followed the English authority *R v Marsham ex p Pethick Lawrence* [1912] 2 KB 362 in which it had been held that where evidence was given unsworn, when not permitted by statute, the entire proceedings amounted to a nullity. A subsequent trial was valid.

If a defective information was so flawed that any ensuing proceedings must constitute a nullity, the defendant was not placed in jeopardy: *DPP v Porthouse* (1989) 89 Cr App R 21. In *Williams v DPP* [1991] 3 All ER 651, the Queen's Bench Division stated that the imperfections of the original proceedings meant that the charge was bound to fail and thus amounted to a nullity.

In *Harrington v Roots* [1984] 2 All ER 474, HL, the prosecutor sought an adjournment of charges against the respondent. The defence did not object, but indicated they wished a date other than that suggested by the (justices) magistrates. The latter refused to allocate another date and instead, without calling upon the prosecution to proceed, dismissed the charges forthwith. The House said that the magistrates' dismissal was a nullity as they acted in breach of their statutory duty to give the prosecution an opportunity to proceed. Since it is also a requirement in the summary procedure legislation in Caribbean Commonwealth jurisdictions to allow the prosecution to be heard, the same principle would apply. Both sides must be given an opportunity to be heard. The House in *Harrington* (above) emphasised that for purposes of the rule against jeopardy, jeopardy only arises after a lawful acquittal or a lawful conviction. The acquittal had been in breach of statutory requirements and was unlawful.

Dismissal on merits

If the previous proceedings constitute a nullity, it is clear that any ensuing acquittal would not have been on its merits. There are, however, instances where it is not as obvious and this may occur when a court dismisses a charge without hearing any evidence or when the prosecution 'offers no evidence'.

There are various cases in which the issue arose as to whether a dismissal of a charge in the magistrates' court was effective as having resulted from an adjudication.

In *R v Pressick* [1978] Crim LR 377, it was held that where there has been an 'adjudication, whether or not there was a trial on the merits, the decision is binding and the matter cannot be prosecuted again'. The test seems to be then whether there was a (valid) adjudication according to *Pressick* (above). The commentary on that case in the *Criminal Law Review* states: 'where the prosecution offers no evidence there is "no trial on the merits", but it is clear that the acquittal is a bar to a further charge'.

In contrast, in the Guyanese case of *Bowen v Johnson* (1977) 25 WIR 60, the Court of Appeal held that a dismissal on no evidence being offered is a dismissal on its merits and thus a bar to a further charge. It is, however, interesting to note that in both cases the defendants had pleaded before the prosecution had offered no evidence. In the circumstances in each case, it is arguable that the defendant was put in jeopardy and the subsequent dismissal of the charge amounted to a valid adjudication even though no evidence had been led. It seems irrelevant to distinguish between dismissed 'on the merits' and a valid adjudication for purposes of a plea of autrefois acquit. In fact, in a considered judgment in *De Gannes v Maharaj* Mag App No 124 of 1979 (unreported), the Trinidad and Tobago Court of Appeal seemed to use the question of whether or not a plea was taken as the litmus test for both.

The court quoted Lucie Smith CJ in *Joseph v Douglas* [1914] 2 SC Trinidad and Tobago 285, p 287 where he said: 'The magistrate had done nothing to exhaust his jurisdiction, the person charged did not plead and the magistrate did not adjudicate'. There was thus no dismissal on the merits (adjudication) to justify a plea of autrefois acquit.

In *De Gannes* (above) the court said (p 12):

> Where a defendant had appeared before a court of competent jurisdiction to answer a charge and pleaded not guilty and indicated his readiness to proceed with the hearing, if the prosecution offers no proof of their case ... and the magistrate dismisses the complaint this is an acquittal on the merits and a bar to a subsequent prosecution.

The view expressed in *De Gannes* is consistent with the English case of *Williams* (above) in which it was held that since the defendant had never entered a plea, he was never in peril of being convicted. It would seem, then, that if a court dismisses a charge when the defendant has not pleaded, such a dismissal does not amount to an adjudication or a dismissal on the merits. The defendant was never in jeopardy of being convicted.

It follows, then, that the discharge of a defendant on committal proceedings does not operate as a bar to any subsequent proceedings. He would never have pleaded and there would have been no trial of the issues. Such a defendant is not in jeopardy at committal proceedings: *R v Manchester City Stipendiary Magistrates ex p Snelson* [1977] 1 WLR 911.

In *R v Benson* (1961) 4 WIR 128, the then Supreme Court of British Guiana emphasised that a magistrate has no power to 'withdraw' a prosecution. Such an order was in effect a dismissal. What seems to emanate from the decision in that case is that if the prosecution purport to withdraw a charge, they are offering no evidence on it. Thus if the defendant has already pleaded to the charge, an ensuing dismissal will amount to an adjudication and will give rise to a successful plea in bar of autrefois acquit.

A decision which seems to be contrary to this is the Jamaican case of *R v Resident Magistrate for St Andrew and the DPP ex p Black et al.* (1975) 24 WIR 388. In that case two of the three judges who heard the (joint) appeals felt that since a trial did not commence on a plea of not guilty, the magistrate had the discretion to permit the prosecution to withdraw a summary case in order to lay an indictable charge. Smith CJ in his dissenting opinion stated that the magistrate had no power to allow the prosecution to withdraw the charges without their consent, since by their plea of not guilty an issue had been joined that they were entitled to have determined.

In *R v JFJ* [2013] EWCA Crim 569, a decision of the English Court of Appeal given in April 2013, the court reviewed *Connelly* (above) and most of the English authorities on the issue of what is a dismissal on its merits. On the facts of the case the prosecution had offered no evidence on a charge of common assault in order to proceed with an indictable offence of assault occasioning actual bodily harm. At trial the defence pleaded autrefois and the trial judge ruled in their favour. The Court of Appeal held that the plea of autrefois should be confined to a narrow basis and further concluded that, whatever may have been the position in the 1990s, the pre-trial procedures in the magistrates' courts and the Crown Court have much in common. Just as in the Crown Court, even though a plea may be taken before directions and other hearings but the trial is not considered to have begun until the accused is put in charge of the jury, in the magistrates' court a trial does not begin when an information is put and the plea made.

It was held that a defendant can be in peril only when the magistrate is at the hearing for the purpose of determining whether the defendant is guilty. The court said that can be the first hearing when the plea is put, 'but these days it is more likely to be the date fixed for summary trial'. Accordingly on the facts of the case the appellant was not in peril at the time, the prosecutor offered no evidence and the charge was dismissed both because the defendant had not objected to the reorganisation of the way the prosecution was to put its case and, in any event, a stage in the proceedings had not yet been reached where he could be in peril.

In a trial on indictment in the High Court, if the prosecution offers no evidence after an accused is put in charge of the jury on a plea of not guilty, the accused has been put in peril. However, it is the jury that must return the verdict of not guilty. This is because it is the jury and not the judge who adjudicates in an indictable trial. If the judge, on the prosecution offering no evidence, himself directs that a verdict of not guilty be entered, the verdict is a nullity: *R v Griffiths* (1981) 72 Cr App R 307. Legislation in line with s 17 of the (English) Criminal Justice Act 1967 may intervene to permit the court to order that a not guilty verdict be recorded without putting the defendant in the charge of the jury.

Alternative offence

As indicated above, an autrefois plea is available in respect of a crime on which a defendant could, on a previous trial, have been convicted or was impliedly acquitted. If, however, the jury express themselves unable to agree on the alternative offence, the plea of autrefois will fail on retrial: *DPP v Nasralla* [1967] 2 All ER 161, PC. In this case a Jamaican jury on a trial of murder brought in a verdict of not guilty for murder. They were unable to agree on the manslaughter and did not return a verdict in respect of that alternative charge. On an application by the accused person that he should be entitled to maintain a plea of autrefois acquit on the manslaughter charge, the Privy Council allowed the appeal of the DPP and dismissed the application. The Board held that the jury had not returned a verdict on manslaughter and so there was no acquittal on which to find a plea of autrefois acquit. If the jury had brought in a general verdict of acquittal on the indictment, a plea of autrefois could have been maintained. In like vein the Guyana Court of Appeal held in *Lawrence v The State* (1999) 59 WIR 239 that where an alternative verdict of manslaughter, delivered after less than two hours retirement on a murder charge, was a nullity this was no bar to the appellant being retried for manslaughter.

At common law, conviction of a lesser offence than that charged is permissible provided that the greater offence necessarily includes the lesser offence and that both offences are of the same degree: *R v Woodall and Wilkes* [1872] 12 Cox 240, *R v Kelly* (1964) 48 Cr App R 1. Both offences must be felonies or both misdemeanours in jurisdictions which retain that distinction. The common law principle has been encapsulated in statute in relation to indictable trials in the relevant criminal procedure legislation in most jurisdictions. It is clear that murder would include the alternative of manslaughter; wounding with intent, unlawful wounding; rape, indecent assault; and robbery, theft (or larceny). It is equally clear that before the jury can consider the lesser alternative offence they must first find the defendant not guilty on the greater offence: *R v Saunders* [1988] AC 148, HL.

Legislation may intervene to enable the jury to find a defendant guilty of a lesser summary offence on trial for an indictable offence. This is the case with motor manslaughter, resulting from driving recklessly or dangerously, and the summary offence of dangerous driving. Legislation throughout the Commonwealth Caribbean enables a conviction for dangerous driving on a charge of manslaughter as discussed in *Mohammed v R* (1965) 8 WIR 169.

It follows, therefore, that a person who is convicted for dangerous driving cannot later be tried for manslaughter on the same facts. The plea of autrefois convict will apply. In *Mohammed*, the appellant was charged indictably with manslaughter, and summarily with dangerous driving arising out of a motor vehicle accident. Following committal proceedings on the manslaughter charge, the appellant was discharged. He was then convicted, on his plea of guilty, of dangerous driving. A judge's warrant was then obtained in accordance with statutory provision for the arrest and committal of the appellant for manslaughter. On his arraignment, the appellant pleaded autrefois convict in bar to the manslaughter proceedings but this was rejected by the trial judge. The Trinidad and Tobago Court of Appeal held that, following *Connelly* (above), a plea of autrefois should have been upheld since on a trial for motor manslaughter, conviction on the lesser offence of dangerous driving was permissible by statute. Thus a conviction of this lesser offence was a bar to prosecution for the greater, there being no new evidence which resulted in the manslaughter charge.

It would seem there is no reason why the common law rule (that conviction on a lesser offence is permissible on a charge for a greater offence which includes the lesser) should not equally apply to summary cases. This has, however, not been the practice. In *Joseph v Mohammed* (1964) 7 WIR 96, the defendant was charged for dangerous driving and careless driving in different complaints in respect of the same incident. He was acquitted of the dangerous driving and the prosecution then sought to proceed on the careless driving. He pleaded autrefois. It was held by the Trinidad and Tobago Court of Appeal that the defendant was not in jeopardy of being convicted of careless driving on the dangerous driving charge since the statutory provision did not provide for this. The court seemed to suggest that in relation to offences created by statute (which most summary offences are), a court is not empowered to convict a defendant of a lesser offence on a charge for a greater unless statute so specifies. This seemed to have been the view of the court in *Lawrence v Same* [1968] 2 QB 93, although the court did feel that there seems no reason why in logic and common sense magistrates should not have the same power for summary offences as a jury had in respect of indictable offences.

A 'new' offence

In *Lewis v Irish* (above), the Trinidad and Tobago Court of Appeal held that even where the law permits conviction on an alternative offence, this does not mean that in all cases prosecution of an alternative offence will be barred if there is conviction on a particular charge. In that case, the defendant was charged for unlawful possession and the Summary Courts Ordinance permitted the conviction of the alternative offence of larceny if 'the evidence established the commission of the offence of larceny'. The defendant was acquitted of the unlawful possession charge, and the prosecution sought to pursue a larceny charge in respect of the same incident. The case was, however, partially based on evidence obtained after the unlawful possession charge. It was held that the second charge of larceny was not barred, since the evidence was different and obtained after the charge for the first offence.

It was also recognised in *Connelly* (above) that autrefois does not apply to prevent a trial for murder or manslaughter where the victim dies after proceedings for another offence not involving death has commenced. The offences will not have arisen out of the same or even substantially the same set of facts. The death changes everything.[12] It was confirmed in *R v Beedie* [1997] 2 Cr App R 167 that such a prosecution will not even constitute an abuse of the process of the court. In that case, however, the principle of abuse of process applied because the different offences did arise from substantially the same facts. It is then possible that if the prosecution proceeds with the first charge after they have evidence of the second

12 See also discussion in *Mohammed v R* (1965) 8 WIR 169 and cases cited therein.

and the defendant is convicted on the first, it may be an abuse of process to proceed with the second, more serious charge.

If the defendant is acquitted in the first proceedings and the victim later dies, the death changes nothing. The acquittal will bar subsequent proceedings: *R v G* [2001] 2 Cr App R 31.

Using previous acquittal

It has been held that the doctrine of autrefois does not prevent the use of evidence led in a previous trial which resulted in an acquittal, at a subsequent trial for another offence: *R v Z* [2000] 3 WLR 117, HL. This is so even though the prosecution uses the evidence to indicate guilt of the previous offence. In a considered judgment in *Z*, the House of Lords held that when the prosecution adduces such evidence in a criminal trial for a second offence, the purpose is not to prove that the defendant was guilty of the first offence, but for the purpose of proving that the defendant is guilty of the second offence. Once the defendant is not placed in double jeopardy, evidence once relevant is not inadmissible simply because it shows that the defendant was in fact guilty of the earlier offence of which he was already acquitted.

In *Z* the defendant had been tried for four offences of rape, but convicted of only one. The prosecution sought to call all four previous complainants to give evidence as similar fact evidence in a new trial for rape in order to rebut the defence of consent. The trial judge refused to admit the evidence of the three complainants in respect of whom the defendant had been acquitted. The prosecution appealed against the judge's ruling (as they became entitled to under the Criminal Procedure and Investigations Act 1996). The House considered all the previous authorities on point and held the evidence was admissible once it was relevant and the probative value outweighed its prejudicial effect. The rule against double jeopardy was not breached since the defendant was not, in the new proceedings, at risk of being convicted on the previous charges.

In so holding, the House distinguished the older authority of *Sambasivan v Public Prosecutor of Malaya* [1950] AC 459 which had been considered the established law on this issue. The House restricted that decision to its facts. It held that *Sambasivan* was correct to the extent that a person should not be tried a second time where the first and second offences were in fact founded on the same incident and where a conviction on the second offence would be manifestly inconsistent with a previous acquittal. In *Sambasivan* the defendant was charged for possession of a firearm and of ammunition, offences which arose out of one incident (in the first trial). Since the allegation had been that the revolver carried ammunition, the issue of possession of ammunition, for which he had been acquitted, should not be raised again on the second trial for possession of a firearm.

A conviction on the firearms offence would be manifestly inconsistent with an acquittal on the ammunition offence. Raising the issue of possession of the ammunition again in the circumstances could breach the principles against double jeopardy, as the facts were intertwined and related to one incident.

Autrefois convict

A defendant may not be tried again in respect of an offence for which he was previously convicted. Issues may arise as to (a) whether there was in fact a previous conviction; or (b) whether the defendant was indeed convicted of essentially the same offence. As already discussed above, conviction of a lesser alternative offence, permissible under law, is sufficient to ground a successful plea of autrefois convict: *Mohammed v R* (above).

A conviction[13] has been held to include both a finding of guilt and a sentence: *Richards (Lloydell) v R* (1992) 41 WIR 263, PC. Therefore, although a magistrate might be functus officio in respect of a finding of guilt over which he deliberated, as held in *Paynter v Lewis* (1965) 8 WIR 318, a decision of the Court of Appeal of Trinidad and Tobago, the finding is not a conviction. In *Richards*, the appellant was charged with murder. When he was arraigned, he pleaded guilty to manslaughter and the prosecutor accepted this. The case was adjourned for character evidence. On its resumption, the DPP of Jamaica entered a nolle prosequi following which the appellant was charged again with murder. He was convicted and appealed, pleading autrefois convict. The Privy Council, overruling older authorities on point, held that a plea of autrefois convict could only be sustained on proof that the defendant had been subjected to a complete adjudication on the previous charge, amounting to a conviction. Such an adjudication must comprise both the decision establishing guilt and the final disposal of the case by passing sentence (or making an order such as an absolute discharge). On the facts, then the plea could not succeed and the murder conviction stood.

It might be argued on these facts whether a submission of abuse of process based on manipulation of the prosecution might not have succeeded. The Privy Council itself said (p 271): 'in all the circumstances ... it would be wholly inappropriate that the death sentence should not be commuted'. The Board itself must have had some concerns about the fairness of the actions of the prosecution.

Where a court stated after a no case submission 'there will be a conviction', this was held not to be a true conviction: *R v Midhurst JJ ex p Thomson et al.* [1973] 3 All ER 1164. The court had realised its mistake soon enough and had attempted to rectify it. There had been no final adjudication on the matter. In any event, the statement, coming when it did, before the defence was heard, was not an effective order of conviction and was a nullity.

Where a defendant is charged for essentially the same offence under different statutes, a conviction or acquittal under one is a bar to proceedings on another. In *Wemyss v Hopkins* (1875) LR 10 QB 378, the defendant was charged under one Act for striking a horse ridden by the victim and causing 'hurt and damage' to the victim. He was convicted and fined for this offence. Several weeks later he was charged for unlawfully assaulting, striking or otherwise abusing the victim under a different statute. It was held that the two offences were essentially the same, in effect assaulting the victim. The first conviction was thus a bar to the second.

Disciplinary offences

If a person is acquitted or convicted of a disciplinary offence of a similar nature to a subsequent criminal charge, he may plead double jeopardy. He is entitled to allege that his common law right not to be placed in jeopardy twice in respect of the same offence has been violated. In *Lewis v Morgan* [1943] 2 All ER 272, it was made clear that a conviction on a disciplinary offence will not be a bar to later proceedings in a criminal court if the disciplinary offence did not necessarily include the criminal charge. In that case the defendant was charged and convicted in domestic proceedings by a master of a ship that he was absent without leave and a forfeiture of wages ordered. He was subsequently charged

13 This is relevant mainly to the plea of autrefois; some statutes still refer to 'conviction' in its narrow meaning – mere pronouncement of guilt.

before a court of summary jurisdiction under the Defence (General) Regulations in that he 'being lawfully engaged to serve on a requisitioned ship' was absent without leave. It was held that the second charge was different from the first, being in effect a war offence – it was laid by the Ministry of War Transport. The first offence was a domestic matter under the Merchant Shipping Act.

Similarly, in *R v Hogan and Tompkins* (1960) 44 Cr App R 255, the defendants, prison escapees, were punished under the Prison Rules for breaches of discipline. The defendants were later charged criminally for escaping by force and simple escape (from a prison). It was held that the principle of double jeopardy did not apply as the first 'offence' was really just for breaches of discipline and was not dealt with as an escape.

In a more recent civil appeal, *Re Barings plc et al.* (No 2) [1999] 1 All ER 311, the English Secretary of State for Trade and Industry issued proceedings against the applicant B and others seeking disqualification orders under the Company Directors Disqualification Act 1986. The applicant applied for a stay of these proceedings, contending double jeopardy in that he had already resisted disciplinary proceedings by the Securities and Futures Authority (SFA) in respect of the same or similar charges. It was held that the issues the court would have to adjudicate on, in respect of the disqualification proceedings, were not the same as those already adjudicated by the SFA. The SFA proceedings related to allegations that B had failed to act with due care and attention of a prudent manager. On the current proceedings, the relevant question was whether B's conduct as a director had fallen far short of the competence required of a company director. The latter proceedings related specifically to B's responsibility for the insolvency of the company.

The Barings principle, it would appear, is equally applicable to criminal matters since the issue at all times was one of double jeopardy.

The procedure to plead autrefois

It used to be thought that in magistrates' courts, the plea of double jeopardy was not strictly a plea of autrefois: *Flatman v Light* [1948] 2 All ER 368. The reason given was that such a plea is not pleaded formally in writing as required for indictable trial. Despite this, many subsequent cases have referred to a plea of autrefois in the magistrates' court. In *Joseph v Mohammed* (1964) 7 WIR 96, p 97, Phillips JA said in respect to this procedure in the magistrates' court: 'this plea of autrefois should have been taken on behalf of the defendant'.

This is explicit recognition of the fact that autrefois may be pleaded in the magistrates' court and it need not be done formally. In contrast, for the High Court, the same procedure as in England is endorsed by statute in Commonwealth Caribbean jurisdictions. Criminal procedure legislation throughout the region specifically recognises the plea of autrefois in indictable trials. Some jurisdictions provide that the plea in such cases should be made in writing.[14] In practice, the judges of the High Court do not appear to hold this requirement as mandatory. Furthermore, even though there may exist statutory provisions that a jury may be empanelled to try any issue of fact[15] (and this is so at common law)[16] arising from the

14 As in, Criminal Procedure Code, Cap 72 B, s 142(5); and Trinidad and Tobago, Criminal Procedure Act, Chap 12:02, s 32.

15 As in Criminal Procedure Code, Ch 91, s 158(3), the Bahamas.

16 As evidenced in *R v Rodriguez* (1973) 22 WIR 504, a decision of the Court of Appeal in Trinidad and Tobago, and *R v Couglan* (1976) CLR 631.

plea of autrefois, in practice it is the judge who determines the validity of the plea.[17] The jury will be selected to try the issue, but they will usually heed the judge's direction as to whether the plea should succeed or not. This may be because rarely will there be disputed issues of fact on a plea of autrefois.

Although it is expected that a plea in bar should be taken before actually pleading, it can even be entertained after a plea of guilty: *Cooper v New Forest District* [1992] Crim LR 877. It is considered that the rule against double jeopardy is so fundamental that once there are grounds on which a plea of autrefois can be sustained, the court should inquire into it.

There appears to be no reason why a person charged with an indictable offence should wait until trial to test the validity of a plea of autrefois. It would seem that, just as with a plea of pardon, he may come to the court on habeas corpus proceedings contending that his detention is illegal: *Phillip et al. v DPP et al.* (1991) 40 WIR 410, PC. The illegality cited in this instance will be that he was previously convicted or acquitted of the same offence, or could have been on the previous charge.

---

17 As is clear from the judgment of the Court of Appeal of Trinidad and Tobago in *Nandlal v The State* (1995) 49 WIR 412, commenting on the trial judge's determination of the issues in that case.

CHAPTER 7

SUMMARY TRIAL

All summary offences are tried in the magistrates' courts. In addition, statute provides that certain indictable offences may be tried summarily.[1] When this procedure is invoked, the matter is thereafter tried in the same manner as a summary offence. Summary proceedings are governed almost exclusively by statute as magistrates (and Justices of the Peace) are creatures of statute.[2] The legislative provisions and magistrates' powers have been considered and interpreted by the courts over time and case law now serves to amplify statute in respect of summary proceedings. Once a summary complaint is laid before a magistrates' court, the attendance of the defendant must be secured and then summary trial may commence. In St Lucia, Trinidad and Tobago and Belize Criminal Procedure Rules also govern both summary and indictable procedure. The rules are discussed in more detail in Chapter 8.

PRELIMINARIES

The complaint

The complaint is the document which initiates proceedings in the magistrates' court. The term 'complaint' includes information in most jurisdictions. In some jurisdictions like Trinidad and Tobago and St Lucia, complaint is what is used, whereas the legislation in Barbados and Jamaica refers to an information. In the Bahamas, unusually, 'information' is used to refer to an indictment. It seems that historically, the term 'complaint' described the initiatory step in summary civil proceedings, whereas information meant the initiatory step in criminal proceedings.[3] This distinction is no longer valid; complaint will be used to describe the initiatory step in criminal proceedings generally and will include an information.

A complaint must contain 'a statement of the specific offence with which the accused person is charged together with particulars as may be necessary for giving reasonable information as to the nature of the charge'.[4] If the offence charged is one created by statute, as most summary offences are, the statement of offence should contain a reference to the section and statute that is breached. In *Gould v Williams* (1962) 5 WIR 122, it was held to be immaterial that the statutory section creating the offence was not stated since sub-s 35(4) of the Summary Courts Ordinance provided that the charge was valid once it would have been sufficient before the legislation (s 35(2)), requiring that the statute be cited, came into effect. In considering an identical section in the Justice of Peace Jurisdiction Act (s 64), the Jamaican Court of Appeal in *R v Ashenheim* (1973) 20 WIR 307 decided that it was irrelevant that the section cited was incorrect. Section 64 is identical to s 35 of the Trinidad and Tobago Summary Courts Ordinance (now s 35 of the Summary Courts Act) and states:

---

1 This procedure is discussed in Chapter 10.

2 Richards, S, 'Reform in the magistrates' courts in Barbados', *The Lawyer*, July 1994, p 31.

3 *Re Dillon* (1859) 11 ICLR 232 (IR).

4 As stated in Summary Courts Act, Chap 4:20, s 38(1), Trinidad and Tobago.

(4) Any information, complaint, summons, warrant or other document to which this section applies which is in such form as would have been sufficient in law if this section had not been passed shall notwithstanding anything in this section, continue to be sufficient in law.

The court held that, since prior to this section coming into effect it was unnecessary to refer to the section of the statute creating an offence, it followed that even if the wrong section was cited (one creating no offence) the charge was still valid. The real issue was whether the defect had misled the defendant in any way.

In respect of any challenges to the form of a complaint then the essential determinant is whether the alleged defect misled the defendant in any way so as to affect his fair trial. In *Williams v Daniel and Bobb* (1968) 13 WIR 490, the issue came up for consideration in the summary trial of an indictable charge (which was triable summarily by statute). The defendant was charged under the (then) Criminal Offences Ordinance of Trinidad and Tobago which stipulated that a clerk or servant in the public service who 'wilfully and with intent to defraud' made certain false entries was guilty of an offence. In the particular charge against the defendant, the word 'wilfully' was omitted. It was held by Wooding CJ that the omission of this word from the charge did not make the complaint invalid. Similarly, in *Ludwis Wheatley et al. v Commissioner of Police* [2006] UKPC 24, the Privy Council held that where the language in the complaint did not mirror the words in the statute creating the offence the charge was not invalidated as long as the defence could discern the gravamen of the offence.

A complaint may be unsworn, complaint without oath; or sworn, complaint upon oath. A complaint is made on oath in summary matters if a warrant of arrest is sought.

Summons

A summons is, in effect, a notice to a person to appear at a certain place and time. In general, summons and not a warrant will issue to enforce the appearance of a defendant in summary criminal proceedings. Such summons is issued after the complaint is laid since the particulars contained in the summons will be based on the complaint. A summons will be issued either by the magistrate or Justice of Peace in the area where the complaint is laid. The complaint will be laid in the administrative office of the magistrates' court in the district where the offence occurred. The chief administrative officer there, sometimes called the Clerk of the Peace, will usually be ex officio a Justice of the Peace and will generally issue the summons before the matter comes before the court for hearing. He will set a date for the first hearing. The summons will be headed 'Summons to the Defendant' and will inform him of the charge and the particulars and the date of hearing. It must usually be served on the defendant at least 48 hours before the date of hearing. Police officers will serve the summons giving it personally to the defendant or by leaving it with an adult at his known address. This is usually stipulated in statute.[5]

Questions have arisen as to whether a magistrate, or a Justice of Peace as the case may be, should give judicial consideration to the complaint in order to determine whether he should in fact make an order for the issue of the summons for attendance of the defendant. In *Vysick v Commissioner of Police* (1971) 17 WIR 391, it was held that a magistrate must see the complaint before he authorises the issuing of summonses for the defendant. The Court of

5 See, e.g., Summary Courts Act, Chap 4:20, ss 42–3, Trinidad and Tobago; Magistrate's Code of Procedure Act, Chap 4:20, s 25, Dominica; Justices of the Peace (Jurisdiction) Act, s 2, Jamaica.

Appeal of the West Indies Associated States followed Lord Goddard CJ in *R v Wilson* [1947] 2 All ER 509, p 570 in holding that

> a summons is the result of a complaint which has been made to a magistrate on which a magistrate must bring his judicial mind to bear and decide whether or not, on the complaint before him, he is justified in issuing the summons.

The court suggested that it was necessary for the magistrate to consider the complaint because he was exercising a discretion. Indeed, s 74(1) of the Grenada Criminal Procedure Code, Cap 77, which was being considered, authorised the issue of the summons but did say that 'it shall be lawful for the magistrate in his discretion to issue his summons'.

The Dominica[6] legislation specifically provides that a magistrate may refuse to issue any summons: 'Nothing hereinfore contained shall oblige any magistrate to issue any summons'. The section, however, also provides that an aggrieved person may apply to the High Court to require the magistrate to issue the summons. In jurisdictions like Jamaica, Trinidad and Tobago, Barbados and Guyana there is no like specific provision allowing a magistrate a discretion in the issuing of a summons for the defendant upon complaint. At the same time there is no mandatory requirement to do so.

Despite the decision in *Vysick* it appears that in practice, a magistrate or justice rarely gives any judicial consideration to the merits of a complaint before issuing a summons for the appearance of the defendant. In fact, it has been stated categorically in the English case of *R v Clerk to the Bradford JJ ex p Sykes and Shoesmith* (1999) 163 JP 224 that there is no obligation on a magistrate or his clerk to make inquiries to satisfy himself that it would not be vexatious to issue a summons. While it is true that the function of a magistrate in determining whether a summons should be issued is a judicial one, the magistrate must only bring his mind to bear to decide whether or not on the material before him he is justified in issuing the summons. He may consider the complaint in order to determine whether: (a) the allegation is an offence known to law; (b) the offence is not out of time; (c) the court has jurisdiction or (d) the complainant has any necessary authority to prosecute.

At this stage, however, a court should not inquire into the merits of the case. That issue is properly for trial or even an application for a stay on an abuse of process (per Collins J in *R v Clerk to the Bradford JJ*). It is also unnecessary for a complaint to bear the signature of either the magistrate or the justice before whom it is instituted: *D'Oliveira v Singh* (1963) 6 WIR 193. The Supreme Court of (then) British Guiana stated that the affixing of the signature of the magistrate is only an administrative act and did not affect the merits of the complaint. In contrast, it seems that it is necessary for the complainant to sign the complaint.

Not only will a defendant be required to appear for trial, but so will the witnesses for the prosecution and the defence. Summonses will also be issued through the court for the attendance of such witnesses.

AT THE HEARING

At the date set for hearing of the case, the parties are expected to appear before the court. The magistrate is the judicial officer who hears cases in the summary courts. He is the tribunal of both law and fact. He hears preliminary submissions, sits on the trial, renders a

6 Magistrate's Code of Procedure Act, Chap 4:20, s 24.

verdict and passes sentence. The magistrate must ensure that the correct and proper procedure is followed throughout the hearing of the case and above all that the defendant is treated fairly.

Opportunity to be heard

The defendant must be given full opportunity to be heard on the charge. Part of the opportunity is the right to legal representation. As will be seen, this does not necessarily mean that a defendant must be legally represented. In fact he may choose not to be, but he must be allowed the time to obtain legal advice and get his witnesses. Denial of an adjournment to do so in certain cases may amount to a denial of the opportunity to be heard: *Aris v Chin* (1972) 19 WIR 459. In that case the appellant, a solicitor in Jamaica who was on a disciplinary charge, requested an adjournment of two weeks and produced a medical certificate in support of his request. The Committee refused and granted an adjournment of only one week to facilitate the complainant's giving of evidence. On the adjourned date the solicitor again asked for an adjournment after the complainant gave evidence to prepare himself to give his own evidence. This was refused. The Court of Appeal held that in the circumstances the Committee had denied the appellant a full and fair opportunity of being heard in answer to the charge.

In *Allette v Chief of Police* (1965) 10 WIR 243, a defendant who was arrested and charged on 3 August (in Grenada) appeared in court the next morning to answer the charge. He sought an adjournment on this first appearance to brief counsel and summon his witnesses. His request was refused and the magistrate proceeded to hear the case. The defendant refused to participate. He was eventually convicted and appealed on the sole ground that he did not receive a fair trial. The Court of Appeal of the Windward Islands allowed the appeal and strongly emphasised that the denial to a defendant of the opportunity to retain and instruct counsel or to summon witnesses was a 'clear denial of natural justice'.

Denial of an application for an adjournment made by the prosecution is in itself not a basis for dismissal of the case. The prosecution must yet be given the opportunity to be heard and failure to do so will render any dismissal a nullity: *Harrington v Roots* [1984] 2 All ER 474, HL.

In deciding whether to grant an adjournment, a court should consider the adverse consequences likely to accrue to the person seeking the adjournment: the convenience of the court, the importance of the proceedings and the extent to which the applicant has been responsible for the circumstances leading to the application: *R v Kingston upon Thames JJ ex p Martin* (1993) *The Times*, 10 December. In *Green v Springer* (1976) 28 WIR 9, the (then) Divisional Court of Barbados considered *Allette* but held that whether an adjournment should be granted in any particular circumstances is a matter for the discretion of the magistrate. In this case, the party which sought the adjournment was the complainant, the Comptroller of Customs, not the defendant. Since the magistrate had given reasons at the time he refused each application for the adjournment (which was sought in order to retain counsel) it was evident that he had deliberated on the exercise of his discretion. The appeal against the dismissal of the Customs charges was disallowed.

The courts tend to be more reluctant to uphold a refusal to grant an application for an adjournment to the defendant, even if it appears to be an abuse. In *R v Bolton JJ ex p Merna et al.* (1991) 155 JP 612, the defendant claimed that he was too ill to attend trial. It was held that the principal consideration in deciding whether to proceed ex parte is fairness. Even if the court suspects that the reason for requesting an adjournment is spurious, it should express its doubts and grant the adjournment, giving the defendant the chance to provide professional support for his claim.

In *Jahree v The State* [2005] UKPC 7 the Privy Council had to decide whether a magistrate's refusal to grant an adjournment to an unrepresented defendant amounted to a breach of his constitutional rights including his right to defend himself by a legal representative. Having considered the established authorities of *Robinson v R* (1985) 32 WIR 330, PC; *Dunkley and Robinson v R* (1994) 45 WIR 318, PC, and *Mitchell v R* (1999) 55 WIR 279, PC, the Board felt that it could be inferred that the magistrate, especially by her reference to an abuse of his right to counsel, concluded that the appellant knew that there were difficulties about his representation but took no action to secure the services of counsel. That being so, it was within her discretion to refuse to adjourn the trial and to require the appellant to proceed without legal representation.

The Board, however, observed that in most cases it would be incumbent upon the court, faced with an unrepresented defendant on a serious charge, to make proper inquiry about the reasons and, if deciding to proceed, to ensure that the defendant has been able to read the case papers or is given sufficient time to allow him to do so. It would also be prudent to ensure that such steps are properly noted in some official form.

Ex parte trial

Summary courts legislation in most jurisdictions provides that where a defendant who has been properly notified of the date of hearing fails to appear for his trial, the magistrate may proceed ex parte.[7] Alternatively, the magistrate may issue a warrant for the arrest of the defendant. He cannot do both: *Perreira v Cato* (1979) 28 WIR 169. In that case the appellant failed to appear for her summary trial for wounding on six occasions between 17 August and 20 December. She had been previously served to appear and a warrant was issued as a result of her failure to appear on 29 November. The magistrate did not, however, await the execution of the warrant of arrest, but proceeded to hear the matter ex parte (in the absence of the defendant) on 20 December. It was held on appeal by the Guyana Full Court that the legislation did not envisage that the court should pursue more than one course of action at a time. The ex parte trial was in lieu of the issuance of a warrant.

Similarly, in *Wilson v Gellizeau* (1971) 17 WIR 175, the Court of Appeal of the West Indies Associated States held that under s 1075 of the St Lucian Criminal Code, the magistrate was required to elect one of the options available on non-appearance of the defendant on the specified date. Section 1075 provided for ex parte trial; issue of a warrant or simply an adjournment in the alternative in each case. In addition, on the facts of that

7 See: Antigua: Magistrate's Code of Procedure Act, Cap 255, s 77;
Barbados: Magistrates' Courts Act 1996, s 33;
Dominica: Magistrate's Code of Procedure Act, Chap 4:20, s 70;
Grenada: Criminal Procedure Code, Cap 72B, ss 73, 78;
Guyana: Summary Jurisdiction (Procedure) Act, Cap 10:02, ss 13, 25;
Jamaica: Justices of the Peace (Jurisdiction) Act, ss 3, 12;
St Kitts and Nevis: Magistrate's Code of Procedure Act, Cap 3:17, s 78;
St Lucia: Criminal Code, s 690;
St Vincent: The Criminal Procedure Code, Cap 172, s 122;
Trinidad and Tobago: Summary Courts Act, Chap 4:20, ss 44, 60.
The Bahamas legislation alone – Criminal Procedure Code, Ch 91, s 198 – suggests that the defendant must consent to ex parte trial.

case, as the defendant had been in prison on the date of the ex parte trial and no effort had been made to bring him before the court, an ex parte trial was unfair.

If a court wishes to either proceed ex parte or issue a warrant for non-appearance, it is necessary that it be first established that the defendant was properly notified of the hearing. If it is the first date of hearing and process is by summons, proof must be offered that the defendant was properly summoned. This is provided for in summary procedure legislation in all jurisdictions. The issue also came up for consideration in *R v Appeal Committee of County of London Quarter Sessions ex p Rossi* [1956] 1 All ER 670. In that case, the defendant was served to appear, but the summons was returned endorsed 'no response'. On the specified date, the co-defendant appeared and the matter proceeded ex parte. It was held that since the defendant had not been properly served, the proceedings in relation to him constituted a nullity. He had not been served in accordance with statutory provisions.

Legislation throughout the region also provides that ex parte trial is possible on an adjourned date once the defendant knew of the date and fails to appear: *Wilson v Gellizeau* (above). There must be satisfactory proof that the adjournment was made in the presence and hearing of the defendant or his representatives. Where the adjournment is in the absence of the defendant or his lawyer, notice of the adjourned date must be given to the defence: *R v Seisdon JJ ex p Dougan* [1983] 1 All ER 6. Any purported trial of the defendant in absentia without such notice will constitute a nullity.

In *Bharath v Cambridge* (1972) 20 WIR 450, a defendant attempted to argue on this basis that the requirements for an ex parte trial under the Trinidad and Tobago Summary Courts Ordinance had not been fulfilled. He contended that the previous hearing had been adjourned in his absence and in the absence of any counsel retained by him and he had been served no notice of the date of the adjourned hearing. It transpired that the matter had been first adjourned in the presence of a lawyer who had been asked to hold a brief for the defendant's own lawyer. On the next occasion, counsel had again appeared for the defendant who was absent, but it was difficult from the court records to ascertain who was the counsel. The Court of Appeal held that once the matter had been adjourned in the presence of a lawyer who stated that he appears for the defendant (whether he was holding a brief or not), the defendant was deemed to have notice of the adjourned date. The defendant thus was afforded an opportunity to be heard, but made no use of it. A conviction after an ex parte hearing would only be set aside if there had been no culpable neglect on the part of the defendant. On the facts, there was such culpable neglect and the conviction stood.

The questions of culpable neglect had arisen earlier in *Spencer v Bramble* (1960) 2 WIR 222, a decision of the Trinidad and Tobago Supreme Court. In that case, the defendant and his lawyer were present when the magistrate adjourned his case (two traffic charges) to a fixed date for trial. On that date the defendant did not appear and no explanation was forthcoming as to his absence. The magistrate proceeded ex parte. The defendant later appealed against his convictions on the basis that he was genuinely mistaken as to the adjourned date. The court held that the defendant had been given every reasonable opportunity to be heard. Through his own fault he had failed to grasp that opportunity. Being mistaken as to the date fixed for trial did not mean that he was not at fault. The court went on to say that if the defendant is without fault in his non-appearance then he is not guilty of 'culpable neglect'. Such an instance would be where on his way to court he is injured in an accident. In this situation, the defendant would be entirely without fault. There can be no suggestion of carelessness or lack of diligence. Even though a magistrate who is ignorant of these circumstances will be within his rights to proceed ex parte, a Court of Appeal may set aside an ensuing conviction in the interest of justice.

This brings us to an issue that may arise if a magistrate were to proceed ex parte and during the course of the hearing the defendant appears. The question to be determined then is whether the magistrate should proceed with the defendant now participating or restart the matter. In *Agdoma v Tomy* (1968) 12 WIR 296, a magistrates' court in St Lucia embarked on a summary trial where a properly served defendant failed to appear (proof upon oath having been given). The magistrate proceeded to hear the complaints, adjudicated and convicted the defendant on both charges. In the afternoon of that day the defendant and his lawyer appeared and submitted a medical certificate for the defendant's non-appearance earlier that day. The magistrate purported to set aside the earlier convictions and then referred the matter to the High Court for opinion on a certified question.

The court held that since the magistrate in hearing the complaints had jurisdiction to do so, the matter was not a nullity. The magistrate was functus officio and could not set aside the convictions. It is possible on the basis of *Spencer v Bramble* (above) that the Court of Appeal could set aside the conviction in its general jurisdiction in the interest of justice, but this was not an issue.

It was still left open whether a magistrate who had not yet convicted could have rescinded his earlier decision. In *R v Dewsbury Magistrates' Court ex p K* [1994] *The Times*, 16 March, the defendant appeared before conviction but after the court had reached a guilty verdict in respect of his ex parte trial. The defence applied for a rehearing under s 52 of the English Magistrates' Courts Act, but was refused. On appeal it was held that in the particular circumstances of the case and the fact that the matter was a serious one the interest of justice demanded that the case be reheard.

Although similar statutory provision for rehearing is uncommon[8] in the region, it seems only reasonable that if it appears that the defendant's failure to attend court in time was not intentional, a court could rehear the case. This is so since the Court of Appeal would, in such circumstances, allow a defence appeal: *Spencer v Bramble* (above). Furthermore, even a court that is not yet functus impliedly has jurisdiction to make any legitimate order and an order to stop the hearing of a case in the interest of justice may arguably be valid. The problem, however, is that there is no statutory power specifically empowering a court to do so.[9]

The first hearing in any event will not lead to a valid plea of autrefois as there would be no adjudication. It is suggested that even where a defendant culpably appears late, the court should facilitate him by recalling witnesses, rereading the evidence if necessary and permitting cross-examination. The court may have acted within its jurisdiction, but should still be as fair to the defendant as is possible.

In summary, then, the court has jurisdiction to proceed on an ex parte trial or to issue a warrant for the non-appearance of a defendant if it is so empowered by the legislative provisions. In this regard, the relevant Barbados statute[10] specifies that no sentence of imprisonment should be imposed on an ex parte trial. Although no such restriction appears to exist in most of the other jurisdictions, it might be inappropriate for a court to proceed ex parte on a matter which is being tried summarily, such as possession of illegal narcotics, where the penalty is likely to be a period of imprisonment. If there is an ex parte trial, a warrant of arrest may be issued to execute the sentence of the court whether it is a fine (if no time to pay is allowed) or a sentence of imprisonment.

Bias in magistrates' courts

It is perhaps more likely in the magistrates' courts that issues of bias may arise, since the court is both the tribunal of law and fact. In small countries such as those of the

8 See Barbados Magistrate's Courts Act 1996, s 228 as an exception.

9 For further consideration of this issue see discussion on Functus officio below.

10 Magistrates' Courts Act 1996, s 33(3).

Commonwealth Caribbean it is not unlikely that a magistrate in a particular district may be friendly with counsel on either side or may know the defendant. In conjunction with this fact there exists a basic principle that a tribunal ought not to sit on any matter in which it or any of its members has a personal interest. The well-known maxim 'justice must not only be done, but must be seen to be done' applies.

A personal interest may be financial or may stem from a relationship between the parties or particular knowledge by the tribunal of fact which may result in prejudice. It is now settled law that the test to be applied in cases of apparent bias by a jury, arbitrator, magistrate or other tribunal members is whether there is a real danger that injustice will occur as a result of the alleged bias: *R v Gough* [1993] AC 646, HL, adjusted by *Porter v Magill* [2002] AC 357, HL. The issue is whether a fair-minded and informed observer would conclude that there is a real possibility that the tribunal was biased. If, therefore, a magistrate knows of previous convictions of the defendant, has tried him before or has a particular friendship with the prosecutor, the question arises as to whether he should disqualify himself from hearing the matter.

In a magistrates' court it is not unlikely that the magistrate of a particular district may have tried or convicted the defendant before. In smaller countries, he may even know the defendant or the alleged victim by reputation. In the English case of *R v McElligott ex p Gallagher and Seal* [1972] Crim LR 332, the defendants appeared before the respondent magistrate charged with loitering. When the matter was called, their lawyer asked for the case to be tried before another magistrate since they had been tried and convicted before the respondent magistrate previously. The magistrate refused. The defendants applied for an order of prohibition. The Queen's Bench Division refused the application holding that there was no proposition of law that a defendant whose past record was known to a magistrate should not be tried by him. While it may be desirable to have another magistrate try the case, this statement 'could not be elevated to a point of law'. The order was refused.

In the commentary of the case in the *Criminal Law Review* (1972, pp 333–34), the authors recognised the apparent conflict in treatment of cases where a jury might have heard of the defendant's previous convictions. They suggest that the explanation as to why a magistrate who is familiar with a defendant's convictions might still try him is perhaps historical: 'In small communities all the magistrates would inevitably come to know the persistent offender. He could not be tried in the locality at all except by those who knew him'. This historical explanation perhaps is still relevant in small Caribbean countries today.

In any event it was recognised in the commentary that magistrates may be more capable of excluding from their minds improper considerations than jurors who have little experience of the criminal justice system. In the Jamaican case of *R v Ruel Gordon* (1969) 14 WIR 21, the point was well made. On facts not unlike those of *McElligott* (above), the defence submitted that there was a breach of natural justice by a magistrate trying a defendant whom he had previously convicted. The Court of Appeal dismissed the appeal, holding that where a magistrate is a trained lawyer he must be taken to have disabused his mind from any latent prejudice of a previous trial. It was expected that he would apply himself to the issues in the subsequent case.

It follows that the same expectations would arise where a magistrate may know the counsel or the alleged victim in the matter. If the defence, however, raise the question of bias as emanating from any circumstance outside of the norm (not merely trying a previous case or knowing counsel), the court must give serious consideration to the allegations. If the alleged bias is such that there is a real danger of injustice, the case should be transferred if possible, or another magistrate should be brought in to hear it. The last is not an uncommon occurrence in some jurisdictions, especially if the case is of great public interest and the local magistrate lives in the community.

Notes of evidence

It is necessary that a record be taken of what transpires in court in respect of every matter. An appeal court will look to the record not only to ascertain what evidence was given at the hearing, but also to determine what happened prior to or after the actual hearing. By far the most important part of the record is the 'notes of evidence', which is a record of the facts and circumstances connected with the charge whether taken on oath or not: *Sam v Chief of Police* (1965) 10 WIR 245. In that case the Court of Appeal of the Windward Islands and Leeward Islands considered an appeal from Grenada in which a magistrate had failed to take any notes on a plea of guilty. The court held that a magistrate (in Grenada) is under a statutory duty to take notes in writing of the evidence and 'evidence' means a record of the facts and circumstances connected to the charge. The court confirmed that a magistrate must take notes in every case and the duty is 'not whittled down' because the defendant has pleaded guilty.

In most jurisdictions, a magistrate has a statutory duty either to take notes of the evidence himself or to cause notes to be taken of the evidence. It is apparent that even if statute were not to require that a record of the evidence given at a hearing be taken, it must be a mandatory practice, since on appeal an appellant is entitled to consider and utilise the evidence given at trial to argue his appeal. In some jurisdictions such as Guyana, the magistrate takes the notes himself, while in others like Trinidad and Tobago a clerk does so. In either event, the magistrate usually must sign daily the record book of proceedings. This contains the record of all the proceedings in the court during each day, including the record of the evidence.

In *Canterbury v Joseph* (1964) 6 WIR 205 (which was followed in *Sam* (above)), the British Guiana Supreme Court emphasised that on a plea of guilty, it was insufficient for the magistrate's notes to record 'Deft pleads guilty' and the sentence. His duty to take notes of evidence extended to recording facts narrated by the prosecutor as well as the statement made by the defendant afterwards. The record of the proceedings is usually considered conclusive evidence of what transpired at any hearing, even if statute does not so stipulate, as do ss 11–12[11] of the Trinidad and Tobago Summary Courts Act, Chap 4:20.

PROCEDURE

Trial in the magistrates' court, as in the High Court, is in 'open court' unless the court decides to clear the court room for special reasons. In the magistrates' court, such situations will usually be dictated by statute, as in the hearing of juvenile matters or sexual offence cases. This procedure is usually referred to as a hearing in camera. In the Barbados Magistrates' Courts Act 1996, for instance, s 209(1) provides that the summary trial must be in open court, but this is subject to:

> the provisions of any law conferring power on a magistrate to sit in camera and to any enactment relating to domestic proceedings or affiliation proceedings or in a juvenile court.[12]

11 Such notes were held to be conclusive proof in *Bharath v Cambridge* (1972) 20 WIR 450, the Trinidad and Tobago Court of Appeal considering ss 11–12 of the (then) Summary Courts Ordinance.

12 Magistrates' Courts Act, 1996, s 209(2).

Section 23 of the Jamaica Criminal Justice (Administration) Act is similar in effect and applies to all criminal proceedings. Interestingly, s 23(1) specifies that the 'public shall in the interest of public morality be excluded during the hearing' of specified offences. The Trinidad and Tobago Summary Courts Act, Chap 4:20, in this regard seems to confer on magistrates powers as wide as those of a judge's inherent power to run his court. In respect of summary offences:

> a Magistrate or Justice may, on special grounds of public policy, decency or expediency, in his discretion exclude the public at any stage of the hearing; and in every such case shall record the grounds on which such order has been made.[13]

It is of interest to note that this power exists apart from those in respect of juveniles and existed before the Sexual Offences Act 1986 introduced in camera hearings for sexual offences.

Appearance of parties

In the magistrates' court there is a case list in which all the matters for the particular day are listed. Courts usually begin sitting at 9.00 am (as is sometimes stipulated in the relevant regulations or Orders) and the defendant and complainant are expected to be present at that time on the date fixed for hearing. They will have been notified of the particular court to attend within the specified magisterial district. Witnesses who have been summoned are also expected to attend.

When the case is called, if the complainant, the person who laid the charge (the complaint), does not appear but the defendant appears, the court may dismiss the charge or adjourn the case at its discretion. Summary procedure legislation in all jurisdictions gives the magistrate this prerogative. Many factors will influence a court's decision to adjourn or not, not the least of which is whether it is the first time that the matter is called or whether there is a valid excuse for lateness or absence of the complainant. In most jurisdictions of the Eastern Caribbean, the relevant legislation refers to non-appearance of 'the person making the charge'.[14] Usually this will be taken as referring to the police officer who actually lays the charge. Police officers generally do in respect of prosecutions that are not private prosecutions, unless power to lay charges is given to precepted persons, such as customs officers or game wardens for specific offences. It would seem unfair that a prosecution should be dismissed if the police complainant fails to appear in a case where the alleged victim and other witnesses are present and ready in court. In such circumstances, the court should exercise its discretion to adjourn.

Similarly, if both the complainant and the defendant fail to appear, the court has a discretion to dismiss or adjourn the case. Even though the alleged victim and witnesses might be present, the magistrate cannot embark on ex parte trial for failure of the defendant to appear unless statute so provides. Statute provides in several jurisdictions that a magistrate may proceed with the further hearing of an adjourned summary trial if neither party appears on the adjourned date.[15] This is, however, not permissible on the day set for first appearance of the parties. On that date, if neither party appears, the magistrate must carefully exercise

13 Chap 4:20, s 54(2).

14 As in Magistrates' Code of Procedure, Cap 255, s 78, Antigua.

15 See, e.g., Summary Courts Act, Chap 4:20, s 66(4), Trinidad and Tobago; Magistrate's Code of Procedure Act, Chap 4:40, s 73, Dominica; Magistrates' Courts Act 1996, s 38, Barbados.

his discretion in determining if to adjourn or dismiss the case. It is interesting to note that legislation does not specifically include the issue of a warrant as an alternative when both parties fail to appear. It is arguable that the general provisions permitting the issue of a warrant for the arrest of a defendant for failure to appear apply in such circumstances.[16] The magistrate may issue a warrant for the defendant in keeping with the other requirements of the statute, such as proof that the defendant had notice of the date of hearing.

Both parties appear

Once both parties appear, the magistrate may embark on the trial. This is of course in addition to his powers to proceed on ex parte trial as discussed above. Before the trial can proceed, the charge must be read to the accused person and he is then asked to plead. If the defendant pleads guilty, the prosecutor will read a summary of the facts of the case. The defendant is then asked by the magistrate for his reply to the facts. As stated in *Sam v Chief of Police*[17] (above), the position is somewhat similar to the allocutus on indictable trial, where the prisoner is asked why the court should not proceed to pass judgment against him. Once the defendant's reply does not show the plea to be equivocal, the magistrate will then proceed to sentence or may, in extenuating circumstances and if legislation permits, make an order of an absolute discharge. The effect of such a discharge is that no conviction is recorded against the defendant. Even a defendant who is found guilty after a full hearing may benefit from an order of absolute discharge.

If a plea of not guilty is recorded on behalf of the defendant, the prosecution is then put to proof of all the elements necessary to constitute the offence. The plea of not guilty itself does not actually begin the trial, i.e., the determination of guilt or innocence,[18] although the defendant is considered to be in jeopardy[19] from that time. It continues to be a valid subsisting plea even if the case is adjourned or transferred.[20]

Delay

Often trials at magistrates' courts are delayed simply because of the number of cases listed before these courts which, it is said, deal with more than 90 per cent of all criminal cases. Arguments to stay proceedings on the ground of delay, while they may be entertained by magistrates, appear to be rare.

The legislature in St Lucia has, however, intervened to treat delays in magistrates' courts in Rule 7.4 of the Criminal Procedure Rules. That Rule provides that the court shall dismiss any summary case if the charge has been pending for more than 180 days and the trial has not commenced. The caveat is that the delay must not have been occasioned by the defendant nor are there exceptional reasons for not dismissing the case. This provision was tested in *Ludovic v Magistrate Velon John and the AG of St Lucia* SLUHCV 2011/1151 on judicial review of the magistrate's decision to allow the case against the claimant to continue. The court held that where the delay was not occasioned by the defendant and there was no

16 Such as the Summary Courts Act, Chap 4:20, ss 44 and 66(5), Trinidad and Tobago.

17 At page 247.

18 *R v Horseferry Road Magistrates' Court ex p K* (1996) 160 JP 441, p 445.

19 As discussed in Chapter 6.

20 *D'Aguiar v Cox* (1971) 18 WIR 44.

indication of any exceptional circumstances by the magistrate, the decision to continue was illogical and in breach of the statutory rules.

The course of the trial

The basic procedure for trial is set down in the summary procedure statutes throughout the region, although such legislation does not usually specify that preliminary submissions or a no case submission may be made. These are necessary options of any hearing, so they must form part of the process regardless of whether specified in statute or not. The basic procedure for making preliminary submissions is the same for any trial.

Once the court indicates that the matter will start, defence counsel may make any preliminary submission at this stage. Once entertained, this will have the effect of starting the 'trial process' even though no evidence is yet given: *R v Horseferry Road Magistrates' Court ex p K* (1996) 160 JP 441. The prosecutor, too, may make preliminary submissions such as to seek an amendment of the charge. After the preliminary submissions are dealt with, the actual hearing will commence. Although statute provides that the prosecutor may make an opening address, this is rarely if ever done in a summary trial. Instead, the prosecutor will call his first witness.

Trinidad and Tobago passed legislation by Act No 15 of 2005 amending the Summary Courts Act to allow proof by formal admissions in a summary criminal trial without the need to call witnesses to these admissions. The defence must agree to such formal admissions which may be made before the proceedings or in court.

When the case is about to start, witnesses in the case will be sent out of court and hearing and in Commonwealth Caribbean jurisdictions this usually includes expert evidence whose evidence might be critical. It should be emphasised that the court has the power to issue a warrant for any witness who has been properly notified of the date of hearing (whether by service of summons or by being present in court on the previous occasion) and fails to appear. In practice, this rarely occurs in summary trials. If it is the alleged victim who is absent, the court may require the prosecution to proceed on what evidence it has. If the case is not proved, then the matter will be dismissed. Otherwise, the case may be 'part heard' with what witnesses are present, or may be simply adjourned and a fresh summons issued for the attendance of the absent witnesses.

All witnesses must give sworn evidence at trial except for children (in general, persons under 14) in certain circumstances. Any unsworn evidence otherwise given for the prosecution constitutes a nullity; it is as if no evidence was given. In *R v Marsham ex p Pethick Lawrence* [1912] 2 KB 362, it was held that a trial of assaulting a police constable, where the victim policeman gave evidence unsworn, was a nullity. A witness may be sworn in any manner which is recognised as binding on his conscience: *R v Hines and King* (1971) 17 WIR 326. It is no longer necessary to prove that he recognises the divine sanctity of an oath.

The prosecutor will call each of the prosecution witnesses in time to give evidence following which the defence may cross-examine the witness. A witness is permitted to remain in court after having given evidence or may be relieved from further attendance at the discretion of the court.

Opposing counsel will usually challenge the evidence of witnesses that directly conflicts with his client's case. It is generally expected where a witness's veracity is being questioned that this should be made clear to the tribunal of fact. Nonetheless, it has been held that in the magistrates' court, frequently one party or the other may be represented by a person who is not a qualified professional advocate. Such a person might be insufficiently skilled to appreciate the necessity of putting matters that are challenged clearly to the witness for the other side: *O'Connell v Adams* [1973] Crim LR 113.

In that case, on a summary trial of a defendant for permitting his taxicab to be used with defective tyres it was the police prosecutor who failed to suggest to defence witnesses that any part of their evidence was untrue. On appeal against conviction, the defence contended that this unchallenged evidence must be regarded as credible. In dismissing the appeal, the court held that allowance must be made for the inexperience and lack of qualification of the representation in the magistrates' courts.

It is, however, suggested that in the Commonwealth Caribbean, where magistrates are trained professionals (unlike the English justices) just as are trial judges, they may intervene to bring it to the attention of a delinquent party that he has failed to challenge key evidence of the other side. In *O'Connell*, although this practice by justices was disapproved, it was on the basis that they should not interfere in proceedings in the same way that 'a professional judge' could. This finding is largely irrelevant to the Commonwealth Caribbean.

After the prosecution closes its case, the defence may make a no-case submission. If the magistrate finds a prima facie case is made out, the defence must be given an opportunity to answer the charge. This is premised on the basic natural justice principle that both sides must be heard, or at least given such opportunity. The defence may choose not to call the defendant or, for that matter, any witnesses. The defendant has a right to refuse to give evidence but in most cases failing to do so may put him at a disadvantage, as the court will not have the opportunity of hearing his side of the story. If the defendant chooses to give evidence, he is the first witness to be called by the defence. If a court makes a pronouncement 'There will be a conviction' after the prosecution has closed its case and before the defence is allowed to present its case, this will be of no effect: *R v Midhurst JJ ex p Thompson et al.* [1973] 3 All ER 1164. It will not be an order of conviction, because the court has acted without jurisdiction in proceeding to convict without giving the defence an opportunity to reply, in accordance with the rules of natural justice and in breach of statutory provisions.

In like manner, it has been held that a decision to acquit without calling on the prosecution to lead its evidence is a nullity: *Harrington v Roots* [1984] 2 All ER 474, HL. In that case the prosecution sought an adjournment because the complainant was away on holiday. The justices (magistrates) at first agreed to the adjournment, but when the defence objected to the suggested date, they dismissed the charge without at least calling upon the prosecution to proceed on the evidence that was available. The House of Lords said that the justices acted in breach of their statutory duty (to hear the prosecution) and the acquittal was a nullity.

Although neither the prosecution nor the defence makes an opening address in summary trial, each party is entitled to make a closing address and usually does so. This is at the end of the case when both sides have presented their respective cases. The order of addresses depends on what is stipulated in the relevant statute. In Trinidad and Tobago, s 65 of the Summary Courts Act, Chap 4:20, provides that the defendant 'shall be entitled to address the court at the commencement or the conclusion of his case as he thinks fit'. In *Bascombe v Commissioner of Police* (1970) 17 WIR 361, the Court of Appeal of the West Indies Associated States considered an identical section in the Grenada Criminal Procedure Code, Cap 77 (now Cap 72B). The court held that the right of a defendant in the magistrates' court to address the court is (in Grenada) statutory, and as the defence had not addressed the court at the commencement of their case, they were entitled to do so at the close. The complainant is allowed to reply on the conclusion of the case at the magistrate's discretion if the defence presents witnesses. In practice, once the defendant gives evidence, the magistrate will allow both sides to address him, the order dependent on statute or the practice in the High Court in that jurisdiction.

The closing address in the magistrates' court is usually fairly short, especially if the issues are purely factual. Both counsel will attempt to point out to the magistrate the discrepancies in the case of the other side and the strength of their own case. A closing address takes the form of a short summary of the pertinent matters of which each side seeks to remind the court.

Unlike jury trials, both sides may also address on the law since the magistrate decides on both fact and law: *Peters v Peters* (1969) 14 WIR 457. After the closing addresses, the magistrate will render a verdict. This is generally done immediately, since the matter is after all of a summary nature. If the defendant is found guilty, he will be allowed a plea in mitigation which will be made by his lawyer if he is represented. Sentence will then be passed. In summary courts, the maximum sentence is specified by statute and, unless the matter is an indictable case being tried summarily,[21] is generally six months' imprisonment.

Disclosure

Until 2004 in the Commonwealth Caribbean there was no statute on disclosure in criminal proceedings as there is in England.[22] This was somewhat altered by s 704 of the Criminal Code of St Lucia which requires the defence to disclose any special defences and information that might be of 'assistance to the complainant'. In 2013 Dominica also passed legislation in sections 31B to 31F of the Criminal Law and Procedure (Amendment) Act No 2 of 2013 providing for disclosure by both the prosecution and the defence.[23] The law on disclosure in Trinidad and Tobago has also been altered with the advent of the Criminal Procedure rules (discussed in Chapter 8). In general throughout the region, there are no administrative guidelines pertaining to disclosure in summary proceedings. Most of the case law on disclosure relate to indictable trial. The matter has, however, been considered by the courts.

The basic principles enunciated in *Dallison v Caffery* [1964] 2 All ER 610 are still applicable. If the prosecuting attorney knows of a credible witness who can speak of material facts which can assist the defence, he must either call the witness himself or make his statement available to the defence. In *R v Leyland JJ ex p Hawthorn* [1979] 1 All ER 209, the defendant was tried for driving without due care and attention as a result of a collision in which he was involved. Two witnesses had given the police statements whose contents were helpful to the defence. These were, however, only given to the defence after the defendant had been convicted. It was held that the conviction must be quashed. The defendant was denied natural justice. Any witness, who appears credible and who can be helpful to the defence, must be made available to the defence as soon as possible. Furthermore, the prosecution must disclose any previous statement of a prosecution witness which is inconsistent with the witness's evidence at trial. This is part of the elementary rule of fairness.

Other than the above, there is no general obligation on a prosecutor to disclose witness statements in advance of a summary trial: *R v Kingston upon Hull JJ ex p* McCann (1991) 155 JP 569. McCullough J expressed this opinion, p 572:

> I do not assert to the general proposition that for a man accused of a summary offence to have a fair trial it is necessary for the prosecution to disclose to the defence in advance of the trial, the statements which the witnesses have made.

---

21 Discussed in Chapter 10. Offences involving illegal narcotics, firearms and the like may carry sentences of up to ten years, even when tried in the magistrates' courts, in jurisdictions such as Trinidad and Tobago.

22 Criminal Procedure and Investigations Act 1996.

23 See Chapter 14 for further discussion on this.

It seems that while it may be advisable for prosecution to disclose such statements where there are likely to be conflicts between the prosecution evidence and the statements, it would be oppressive to expect the prosecution to disclose all the statements they obtain in the vast multitude of summary offences. The cost and time attendant with such demands might be prohibitive.

However, the courts have recognised that if the offence is 'serious' or complex, albeit a summary offence, disclosure of witness statements should be afforded the defence: *Franklyn and Vincent v R* (1993) 42 WIR 262 PC.

The Jamaican Court of Appeal has considered the question of disclosure at summary trial several times.[24] Its current practice is based on that laid down in *Franklyn and Vincent v R* (above). In that case Lord Woolf said in contrast to the trial of complex cases: 'In the converse situation, where the offence is trivial, to be dealt with summarily, where the issues are simple, the provision of statements before trial is less important'. The Privy Council recognised that the resident magistrates' court in Jamaica does try serious offences, including specified indictable offences which are by statute permitted to be tried by a resident magistrate (as distinct from a Justice of Peace under the Justice of the Peace Jurisdiction Act). The court considered previous decisions of the Jamaican Court of Appeal and concluded that in summary trials, if a request is made by the defence, the provision of the statements of prosecution witnesses to the defence is a facility that ought to be afforded to them in order to assist the defence in the preparation of its case. The exceptions are in the case of petty offences or where the prosecution is of the view that it is necessary to withhold the statement for the protection of a witness. The disclosure must be made in ample time to ensure fairness.

In other jurisdictions of the Commonwealth Caribbean, magistrates do not have the power to try as of right indictable offences. Nevertheless, it would seem that where indictable offences triable either way are in fact tried summarily, the prosecution should disclose witness statements in circumstances as suggested by the Jamaican Court of Appeal. It is suggested consistent with *Franklin* that the greater the penalty on summary trial, the more onerous the obligation to disclose. In Guyana, advance disclosure in such cases (summary trial of indictable offences) is mandatory.[25] The prosecution is required to file witness statements with the court and for service to the defendant before the hearing begins. In the case of pure summary offences, the position should be determined on the basis of elementary fairness as discussed above.

No-case submission

It is the right of the defendant to make a no-case submission at the end of the case for prosecution if he feels that such a submission is justified. If he chooses to do so, it is not proper for the magistrate to ask him to elect whether he is going to stand by his submission and call no witnesses: *Bascombe v Commissioner of Police* (1970) 17 WIR 361, p 303. In criminal cases, a defendant cannot be called upon to elect between making a no-case submission and calling witnesses.

The defendant will be contending that the prosecution has not established a prima facie case sufficient to call upon him to answer. The grounds on which a no-case submission may be made in the magistrates' court (and indeed in any criminal proceedings) were set out in

24 As in *Williams et al v R Mag Crown* App Nos 24–26/95 (unreported).

25 Summary Jurisdiction (Procedure) Act, Cap 10:02, s 61, as amended.

the English *Practice Note* [1962] 1 All ER 448 which was adopted by the Trinidad and Tobago Court of Appeal in *Riley v Barran* (1965) 8 WIR 164. The *Practice Note* stipulates that:

> a submission of no case may properly be made and upheld:
> (a) when there has been no evidence to prove an essential element in the alleged offence; or
> (b) when the evidence adduced by the prosecution has been so discredited as a result of crossexamination or is so manifestly unreliable that no reasonable tribunal could safely convict.

The *Practice Note* reflects the law on no-case submission which was subsequently developed in relation to indictable proceedings in *R v Galbraith* (1981) 73 Cr App R 124. *Galbraith* was followed by the Privy Council in *Daley v R* [1994] 1 AC 117, PC, an appeal from Jamaica, thus confirming its applicability to the region. In Guyana, which does not have the Privy Council as its final court of appeal, the Court of Appeal in *DPP's Reference* (No 2 of 1980) (1981) 29 WIR 154 confirmed that the test in deciding whether to uphold a no-case submission is (a) whether all the constituent elements of the offence are proved or (b) whether the evidence was so weak or manifestly unreliable as a result of crossexamination that no reasonable tribunal could safely convict on it (pp 167–68).

It has been suggested that because a magistrate is both a judge of facts and the law he has more discretion[26] in determining when the prosecution's case is manifestly unreliable, than a judge who must leave issues of fact to the jury. Even if there is some evidence at the end of the prosecution's case which, if accepted, would entitle a reasonable jury to convict, a magistrate may have the right (as a jury would) to acquit if he does not accept the evidence. The authors of both *Archbold* and *Emmins* contend that at this stage, since the magistrate himself is assessing the evidence, he can make a decision in determining whether to accept the prosecution's evidence or not. *Archbold* suggests that the *Practice Note* (above) should be qualified to this extent in relation to magistrates' courts.

This argument was made by counsel for the respondent in the Trinidad and Tobago case of *Hernandez v Brooks* Mag App No 333 of 1969 (unreported). The Court of Appeal rejected the submission that the magistrate is empowered at the close of the case for the prosecution to accept or reject some of the evidence in order to determine if a prima facie case is established. The court said

> it is not the duty of a magistrate at that stage to determine which, if any, of the witnesses have spoken the truth or whether there are discrepancies in the evidence, except where the evidence is of such a quality that no reasonable tribunal might consider it in any sense worthwhile.

The court confirmed its reliance on *Riley v Barran* (above) which had followed the *Practice Note.* The court felt that at the stage (of the no-case submission) the magistrate must determine whether there is evidence which, if believed, supports the charge. If there is, the no-case submission should be rejected.

It would seem that the procedure in *Hernandez* is not a practical or realistic one in relation to magistrates' courts. Since the particular magistrate is the tribunal who at the end of the case would have to assess the evidence to determine if it should be believed, it would be an exercise in artificiality to ask the court to postulate on whether another reasonable tribunal might believe the evidence. To refrain from upholding a no-case submission at the end of the case for the prosecution on this artificial basis when the very court finds the

26 *Emmins* (7th edn) para 9.7.3; *Archbold* (1999 edn) para 4–296.

evidence manifestly unreliable and then to ask the court to return to considering the same issue at the end of the defence case is pointless. Since it is the duty of the prosecution to prove its case beyond reasonable doubt, if the magistrate finds the case not proven at the end of the case for the prosecution, he should at that stage be entitled to dismiss the charge, regardless of whether a mythical tribunal might believe the evidence or not. The magistrate is after all the tribunal of both law and fact, and must act as such in relation to all aspects of a summary trial.

After the defence makes its submission of no case, the prosecution will reply to the submission. The magistrate will then rule on the submission. If the submission is upheld, the case is dismissed and the defendant acquitted. If the submission is overruled, the defence has the option to call evidence. The court will usually ask defence counsel or the defendant (if unrepresented) what he intends to do. In the Bahamas, s 204 of the Criminal Procedure Code, Ch 91 sets out the procedure[27] that a magistrate must follow in explaining the options to an accused person. In general, however, the procedure at summary trial in other jurisdictions is much less formal. As long as the defendant is made aware that he may elect to give evidence or not, this will be sufficient.

Functus officio

A court or tribunal may sometimes come to a decision that, as a result of subsequent events, it may desire to change. Questions may arise as to whether the court or tribunal has power to effectively rescind its decision. If the court has discharged all judicial functions in a matter it is said to be functus officio: *R v Camberwell Green Magistrates' Court ex p Brown* (1983) 4 FLR 767.

If a court has acquitted a defendant, it has discharged all its functions in the matter in that it has adjudicated fully in the matter. Thus a magistrate cannot revisit his dismissal in a case. In *R v Midhurst JJ ex p Thomson et al.* [1973] 3 All ER 1164, it was held by the English Divisional Court that a court retained full jurisdiction over all matters until final adjudication of the matter. In *R v Richards* (1992) 41 WIR 263, p 270, the Privy Council confirmed that a verdict of not guilty is a final adjudication and disposal of the case. Once a court of competent jurisdiction returns a not-guilty verdict, it is functus officio in respect of the case.

Furthermore, where a court has convicted and sentenced a defendant, it has no further jurisdiction to deal with the matter: *Beswick v R* (1987) 36 WIR 318, PC. In that case Lord Griffiths said (p 32): 'Once he had recorded the conviction and sentence (the magistrate) had exhausted his jurisdiction to deal with the offence and was functus officio'. A conviction comprising both a decision establishing guilt and the sentence is a final adjudication: *Richards v R* (above). Commonwealth Caribbean courts in general do not have the statutory power granted to English justices by virtue of s 142 of the Magistrates' Court Act 1980 to rescind and vary sentences. In the absence of such power, the conviction is final. Section 228 of the Barbados Magistrates' Courts Act 1996–27[28] contains a provision similar to that of s 142. A magistrate may reopen a case after conviction to vary or rescind the sentence or order made. He may also decide to remit a case in which he has found a defendant guilty for trial by another magistrate. Both of these provisions must be exercised within 28 days of the order.

27 As discussed in *Outten v Ferguson* (1990) 55 WIR 1.

28 Proclaimed in January 2001.

There can be little argument with the fact that a magistrate's functions have expired on full adjudication of a matter upon an acquittal or sentence. The situation is less certain where the court has adjudicated on a matter and finds a defendant guilty following a plea of not guilty. In *Paynter v Lewis* (1965) 8 WIR 318, the Trinidad and Tobago Court of Appeal, purporting to follow *R v Sheridan* [1937] 1 KB 223 said: 'Once a magistrate has accepted a plea of guilty or has adjudicated and finds a defendant guilty or not guilty, he is functus officio as regards the commission or non commission of the matter'.

The court in *Paynter* was equating a plea of guilty with a finding of guilty on an adjudication. In *Richards*, however, the Privy Council categorically stated that a court of summary jurisdiction, having once accepted a plea of 'guilty', had jurisdiction to allow the defendant to change his plea to 'not guilty'. The court did not follow the *Sheridan* line of authorities and adopted the reasoning of the House of Lords in *S (An Infant) v Recorder of Manchester* [1971]1 AC 481, HL. It seems clear from *Richards*, then, that on a plea of guilty a magistrate is not functus officio and may allow the defendant to change his plea at any stage before sentence.

The Board of the Privy Council left open the question of whether the court could have changed its own decision if it had adjudicated on the question of guilt. Furthermore, although the Board overruled the decision of *Sheridan*, that decision hinged on whether a finding of guilt was sufficient for a plea of autrefois convict. Since a finding of guilt in itself is not a complete conviction if no sentence is passed, the Board rightly held that it was not sufficient for a plea of autrefois convict. This is entirely in keeping with earlier decisions such as *R v Manchester JJ ex p Lever* [1937] 3 All ER 4 (cited in *Paynter*), which had held that a finding of guilt and imposition of fine amounted to a conviction. Similarly in *Agdoma v Tomy* (1968) 12 WIR 296, the High Court of St Lucia held that where a magistrate had proceeded ex parte to conviction and sentence, he was then functus officio and could not rehear the complaint.

In *Paynter* (above), the Trinidad and Tobago Court of Appeal held that where a magistrate had, on a plea of not guilty, adjudicated and found the defendant guilty, he could not recall the 'conviction' (finding of guilt). Although the court based its decision on *Sheridan, Paynter* did not hinge on an issue of autrefois convict. The issue was squarely one of functus. It is thus arguable that the principle in *Paynter* should still hold despite the fact that *Sheridan* was overruled. A finding of guilt after deliberation does not support a plea of autrefois convict since there has been no conviction as contemplated in *Richards* (above). It may, however, be sufficient to deem the magistrate functus as regards the commission or non-commission of the offence.

The question of functus with regard to a jury was considered by the Trinidad and Tobago Court of Appeal in *Cummings et al v The State* (1995) 49 WIR 406. In that case a jury had failed to agree on a decision in respect of any of the three accused, whereupon the trial judge ordered a new trial. The foreman then persuaded the trial judge to allow the jury further time. He did, and the jury eventually returned verdicts of guilty in respect of all three accused. The Court of Appeal found that the jury became functus officio when the trial judge made the order for a retrial. In its judgment the Court of Appeal applied *Paynter* (above) and quoted the (by then) overruled case of *Sheridan* (above). The court did not seem to have considered *Richards* at all.

Nonetheless, the decision in *Cummings* (above) seems correct on its facts since it is clear that the jury must be considered to have discharged all its functions when the judge ordered the retrial. In relation to *Paynter* (above), the Court of Appeal (in *Cummings*) identified the issue in that case to be whether 'a magistrate could order an acquittal after a conviction of the defendant had been pronounced'. The 'conviction' here referred to a conviction in its narrow sense, a pronouncement of guilt.[29] The Court of Appeal felt that just as a jury was functus officio having made a determination, so too was a magistrate.

It would seem that the decision in *Paynter* can on its facts still be considered good law. While 'an adjudication' leading to a finding of guilt is not a full conviction (for the purposes of autrefois) it is nevertheless an exhaustion of the magistrates' function as far as the determination of guilt is concerned. A magistrate is not functus officio the entire case because he will still have functions to perform such as hearing a plea in mitigation and sentencing. He is, however, functus as regards any further decision as to whether the defendant has committed or not committed the offence. He cannot reverse his finding of guilt which he has made following a full hearing.

The question which follows from the above analysis is whether a magistrate having, after deliberation, pronounced guilt on a defendant must proceed to making an order of sentence (or absolute discharge). If the hearing was a nullity where the court had acted illegally in proceeding, as in *R v Seisdon JJ ex p Dougan* [1983] 1 All ER 6, then the court may refuse to proceed to sentencing and instead may rehear the case. Otherwise there seems to be no basis on which a magistrate can refuse to proceed to sentencing.[30] The summary courts procedure legislation in the region does not contemplate such a course. If a defendant arrives late to court after an ex parte trial, as happened in *Agdoma v Tomy*, it would seem the court cannot consider the defendant's excuse unless it relates to jurisdiction. If there has been a conviction made up of pronouncement of guilt and sentence, the defendant can only put forward his excuse on appeal, as suggested in *Spencer v Bramble* (1960) 2 WIR 222, as a ground of appeal on the basis that he is not guilty.

If prior to sentencing the magistrate reviews his earlier finding and now believes the defendant should not be convicted, the magistrate may request the DPP (or the Attorney General in the Bahamas) to discontinue proceedings. This was done by the DPP in Jamaica in *Richards* (above) on indictable trial in a converse situation where a guilty plea had been accepted. If the proceedings are discontinued, the matter may then be reheard. There is, however, in general no statutory power for a magistrate to order a rehearing of a matter which has been validly heard. In the absence of a discontinuance, it seems that a magistrate who has adjudicated and found a defendant guilty at a valid hearing must proceed to sentence the defendant or make some other order, such as one for absolute discharge. The Barbados Magistrates' Courts Act 1996 has provided that in that jurisdiction, a magistrate may, in the interests of justice, even after a finding of guilt, ask that the case be reheard by another magistrate. This provision is unique to the region and qualifies the general common law principles of functus officio as they apply in Barbados.

Where a defendant pleads guilty to an offence and in mitigation disputes some of the prosecution facts, a magistrate has no jurisdiction to dismiss the charge once the defendant clearly accepts he committed the offence: *PC Dass v Dexter Danclair* Mag Appeal No 70 of 2002 (unreported), a judgment of De la Bastide CJ.

29 *S (An Infant) v Recorder of Manchester* [1971] 1 AC 481, HL.

30 The English case of *R v Leighton Buzzard Justices ex p DPP* 1990 Vol 154 JP 41 supports this position, holding that on a plea of guilty a magistrate has no power to dismiss the case. While not functus he only has statutory jurisdiction to proceed to sentence or other order.

CHAPTER 8

CRIMINAL PROCEDURE RULES

Criminal procedure rules are rules of procedure intended to improve efficiency in the workings of the criminal justice system. At present, criminal procedure rules only apply to three jurisdictions: Trinidad and Tobago, St Lucia and Belize. This chapter attempts to set out the main rules in each of the three jurisdictions above, and then examines how the courts have interpreted the rules in actual practice.

TRINIDAD AND TOBAGO

Introduction

The Criminal Procedure Rules 2017 came into effect in April 2017. These rules introduced new procedural elements into summary and indictable procedure (Rule 4.1). The overriding objective (Rule 3.1) of these Rules is that criminal cases 'be dealt with justly'. Dealing with cases 'justly' includes dealing with the prosecution and the defence fairly, ensuring the protection of all the rights of an accused person, considering the interests of the accused, witnesses, victims and jurors and keeping them informed of the progress of the case as necessary, and dealing with the case efficiently and expeditiously (Rule 3.3).

Overview of the rules

Bail hearings before the magistrate (Rule 6)

Where the magistrate remands the accused into custody for the purpose of considering bail, the magistrate is allowed to grant a single adjournment for a period not exceeding two days.

Initial details of the prosecution case in summary courts (Rule 7)

In summary proceedings, the complainant is required to serve initial details of the prosecution's case on a person designated as the 'court officer' no later than the commencement of the first hearing. The 'initial details' must include, inter alia, a summary of the evidence on which the prosecution's case will be based and any document or extract setting out facts or other matters on which that case will be based. A failure to comply with these requirements could lead to 'comments' being made by the court.

Case management in the High Court and summary courts (Rule 8)

Under this rule the court is mandated to further the overriding objective by 'actively managing' the case, which includes the early identification of all possible legal issues, ascertaining the nature of the defence, setting a timetable for progress of the case, ensuring that evidence is presented in the shortest and clearest way, discouraging delay and giving any direction appropriate to the needs of that case as early as possible.

Court directions (Rule 10)

The court may give certain directions so that cases can be effectively managed. Directions can be given without a hearing (Rule 10.1) as well as via telephone, letter or other electronic communication (Rule 10.1). Failure to comply with a rule or a direction gives the court the power to fix, postpone, bring forward, extend, cancel or adjourn a hearing, or even to impose other sanctions. In practice, various directions, such as directions to file a list of witnesses, a certificate of readiness and a hearing questionnaire, are given by the judge or magistrate at a case management conference.

Disclosure of material (Rule 14)

Directions given by the court pursuant to rule 10 should include fixing a date by which the prosecution must make all relevant disclosure to the defence. A date should also be fixed for disclosure to the defence of any material in the prosecution's possession that they do not intend to use at trial which materially weakens the prosecution case or assists the accused.

Practice direction on defence disclosure (practice direction dated 14 December 2017, *Trinidad and Tobago Gazette*, Vol 56, No 138)

Within 56 days of the prosecution complying with its disclosure obligation under the rules, the defence must file a defence statement signed by the accused and his attorney-at-law. This statement should, inter alia, set out the nature of the accused's defence, and should indicate the matters of fact upon which he intends to take issue with the prosecution.

The court is allowed to impose sanctions upon the accused for certain matters such as where the defence advanced at trial is different in nature to that set out in the defence statement, or where the defence statement is disclosed late, provided that the late service is relevant to the defence's credibility or adversely affects the prosecution's ability to investigate the defence.

In these instances the court or prosecution may make comments, or the court or jury may draw proper inferences relevant to the accused's guilt.

Trial management (Rule 16)

In order to establish the disputed issues the court must consider setting a timetable that takes account of the disputed issues. Parties to the case may be required to identify such items as: which witnesses are being called to testify; what arrangements or special measures are desirable to facilitate the giving of evidence by a witness; what written or other evidence a party intends to introduce; and what facts and evidence can be agreed between the parties. The court can also limit the examination, cross-examination or re-examination of a witness as well as the duration of any stage of the hearing.

Application to withdraw a guilty plea (Rule 17.8)

Where the accused wants to withdraw a guilty plea, an application must be made as soon as practicable after becoming aware of the reasons for doing so and before sentence. The application must explain why it would be unjust not to allow the accused to withdraw the guilty plea.

Procedure if the court convicts (Rule 17.9)

Where the magistrate or jury convicts the defendant, the court may request a statement of the accused's financial circumstances as well as a pre-sentence or probation report. The prosecution must also provide information relevant to sentence, including any statement of the effect of the offence on the victim, the victim's family or persons connected to the victim or the offence.

ST LUCIA

Introduction

The overriding objective, Rule 1.1(1) of the Criminal Procedure Rules, is virtually identical to that expressed in the Trinidad and Tobago Rules, which is to enable the court to deal with criminal cases 'justly'.

Overview of the rules

Case management (Part 7)

The 'Criminal Division' is responsible for case management. Case management incudes matters dealt with in Rules 8 and 16 in the Trinidad and Tobago CPR above. The court may exercise case management powers, which include the appointing of a case manager who is responsible for managing cases, conducting omnibus conferences and giving directions.

Conduct of trials (Rule 7.4)

The rules regarding the conduct of trials are essentially captured by Rule 16 of the Trinidad and Tobago Rules (see above) which deal with trial management.

Summary court procedure (Rule 6.1(1))

Summary cases are multi-staged, comprising:

a. an orientation session;
b. an initial hearing;
c. a pre-trial case management;
d. an omnibus conference, and
e. a trial.

The orientation session (Rule 6.2)

This is conducted by a member of the Criminal Division case management team and includes:

a. taking attendance;
b. noting requests for adjournments;
c. verifying the defendant's address and contact information; and
d. acquainting a defendant with the Court's procedures.

The initial hearing in summary matters (Rule 6.7)

At the initial hearing the magistrate must take crucial steps including:

a. verifying the defendant's identity and contact information;
b. reading the charges to the defendant and explaining his rights;
c. explaining the plea process to the defendant;
d. considering the grant of bail.

The magistrate may conduct a trial at this stage but only where the defendant or the prosecution requests an immediate trial and the defendant consents. The court at the initial hearing must make a scheduling order (Rule 8.1) that sets out the dates for matters such as:

a. when the prosecution is required to make disclosure;
b. when the defence must disclose his alibi or any special defences;
c. the omnibus conference;
d. the trial.

The omnibus conference (Rule 8.3)

This conference is conducted by the magistrate on a date specified in the Scheduling Order. At this conference the court can:

a. review the status of disclosure;
b. discuss trial readiness issues;
c. set out issues to be resolved at trial;
d. set a firm trial date;
e. set down for hearing by a magistrate any legal issues that must be resolved prior to the trial.

The initial hearing in indictable matters (Rule 6.8)

For indictable matters the magistrate is responsible for all of the matters included in the initial hearing for summary matters save that the defendant does not enter a plea and the case is forwarded to a judge or master. The magistrate makes a scheduling order that fixes dates, including dates for:

a. the sufficiency hearing;
b. a date by which the defendant should retain an attorney-at-law.

The sufficiency hearing (Rule 10.3)

Within 60 days of the initial hearing or such other 'reasonable time' fixed by the court, a judge or master must conduct a sufficiency hearing. This hearing is to determine whether the prosecution has met the required standard of proof (prima facie proof) to justify the case proceeding to trial before a judge and jury. Witness statements are admissible in evidence at the hearing (Rule 10.4). At the conclusion of the hearing parties on both sides are allowed to make submissions.

The court has the power to commit the defendant where the prosecution had established a prima facie case, or otherwise discharge the defendant where the prosecution had failed to establish its burden.

High court procedure

Trial management (Rule 13.3)

In order to manage a trial the court may require a party to identify certain items such as:

a. the witnesses intended to be called to testify;
b. the written evidence intended to be introduced;
c. whether any point of law will be raised that could affect the conduct of the trial or appeal;
d. the timetable a party intends to follow.

Arraignment (Part 11)

Upon the arraignment the judge must enter a scheduling order that outlines the next steps to be taken, such as the date for disclosure to be made by the prosecution and the defence and the date for the omnibus conference. The judge must also advise the accused of such matters as the right to know the maximum penalty and any mandatory minimum penalty for the offence, and the right, prior to entering a plea, to be given an indication of the sentencing options available to the court (Rule 11.2). Where the accused wishes to plead guilty, the judge must inter alia first ensure that the plea is voluntary and made with knowledge of the consequences of the plea (Rule 11.3). Early pleas of guilty may result in a reduction of sentence except in cases where the law carries a mandatory minimum sentence (Rule 11.4). Where the plea is not guilty the judge may schedule a case management conference (Rule 11.5).

The case management conference (Part 12)

The judge at the case management conference must make an order that schedules certain events such as the date:

a. by which the DPP must provide any outstanding disclosure;
b. by which the defence must plead alibi or any special defence;
c. by which any pre-trial motions must be filed;
d. for the holding of the omnibus conference;
e. for the projected trial.

Mutual disclosure (Rules 12.2 and 12.3)

Within 14 days of the indictment being preferred the prosecution must make all relevant disclosure, including any possibly exculpatory material that the prosecution does not propose to use. The defendant must give the prosecution notice of any special defence as well as notice of any alibi. Particulars of witnesses who will be called in support of the defence must be given to the prosecution by a particular date set by the court. (See also Sections 908–912 Cap. 3:01 of the St Lucia Criminal Code.)

The omnibus conference (Rule 12.5)

This may be conducted by a judge or a master and is heard on a date set in the scheduling order. Its purpose includes:

a. reviewing the status of disclosure;
b. setting out issues to be resolved at trial;
c. setting a firm trial date.

BELIZE

Introduction

The overriding objective (Rule 1.2)

This states that the duty of the Court and all parties and participants, where the context so requires, is to further the overriding objective, which is that criminal cases be dealt with justly and expeditiously.

Overview of the rules

Time limits (Rule 2.1)

The rules establish a time frame for the disposal of cases. In cases where a summons has been issued, the first hearing must take place within 28 days of the date of the summons. In cases where a defendant is brought before the court after charge, the first hearing must proceed immediately. Subject to Rule 2.8 (custody time-limits), every matter to be tried before a magistrates' court shall be concluded within a period not exceeding 39 weeks (nine months) from the date of the first hearing. In the event of conviction, the defendant must be sentenced by the court before which he was convicted within a period not exceeding 21 days from the date of conviction, save only in the case of exceptional circumstances.

Failure to comply with time limits (Rule 2.15)

Save only in exceptional circumstances, where there has been an unreasonable failure by the prosecution to comply with any of the time-limits prescribed, the court must order that the case immediately proceed to trial or that the matter be dismissed. The Office of the Director of Public Prosecutions or Prosecution Branch must be given notice and an opportunity to be heard before an order under Rules 2.15 and 2.16 is made. The court in such instances of failure to comply may also consider making a costs order in accordance with Rule 4.9.

Adjournments (Rules 3.1–3.4)

Adjournment applications must not be considered by the court unless notice is filed with the court 14 days prior to the hearing in respect of which the application is made and a copy served upon all other parties, except where it can be shown that the grounds for the application could not reasonably have been known before the application is made. Subject to Rule 3.3, adjournments shall be granted only if the court is satisfied that:

a. there is good cause for an adjournment; and
b. an adjournment is necessary in meeting the interests of justice.

Applications for adjournments should be rigorously scrutinised and certain factors should be taken into consideration including:

a. summary justice should be speedy justice;
b. delays are scandalous;
c. the more serious the charge, the more the public interest demands that a trial take place.

Case management (Rules 4.1–4.5)

The court's case management function includes:

a. the early identification of the issues;
b. the early identification of the witnesses and their needs;
c. ensuring that the evidence is disclosed as speedily as possible and is presented in the most concise and comprehensive manner.

Pursuant to its case management function, the court is also empowered:

a. to appoint a case manager to monitor the progress of and manage cases;
b. to list cases for case management hearings to monitor the progress of cases;
c. to issue a direction on its own initiative or on the application of any party;
d. for the purpose of giving directions, to receive applications and representations by fax, email, telephone or by any electronic means and conduct a hearing via such means;
e. to fix, postpone, bring forward, extend or cancel a hearing.

Wasted costs orders (Rules 4.9–4.10)

The court has the power to order that the costs of and associated with a wasted hearing are to be borne by a particular person or party involved with the proceedings. The court is only able to make a wasted costs order where the wasted hearing has resulted from the improper, unreasonable or negligent act or omission on the part of any person or party involved with the proceedings.

Disclosure (Rules 5.1–5.10)

At every first hearing, the prosecution must serve on the court and the defendant a copy of the summons/charge sheet and a fact sheet outlining the nature of the case against him (the fact sheet is a document for administrative purposes only and is not admissible in evidence at a subsequent trial or voir dire. Its contents should not form part of the magistrate's consideration at preliminary inquiry). The prosecution must then provide disclosure to the defendant:

a. in the case of summary only matters, within eight weeks from the date of the first hearing;
b. in the case of hybrid matters triable summarily, within 16 weeks from the date of the first hearing; and
c. in the case of indictable matters, 14 days before the preliminary inquiry; and once the matter has been committed to the Supreme Court, within 14 days before the arraignment hearing.

Disclosure means providing every defendant with a copy of the case file, except for any material that is administrative in nature, legally privileged or that is covered by public interest immunity.

The defence may also make a written application for disclosure and, when the court is satisfied that there is material that is relevant to the case in possession of the prosecution that has not been disclosed, the court must order the disclosure of that material. Any such order is to be complied with within 14 days of the court's decision. The court may order that any disclosure provided for by the Rules be denied or deferred. The application for denial or deferral must be made in writing and good cause for the deferment or denial must be shown.

Where the defendant intends to plead an alibi, he is required to give notice of the particulars of this defence within seven days from the preliminary inquiry or service of the notice of additional evidence as appropriate.

Application for bail (Rules 6.1–6.4)

At the first hearing or at the time of issuing an arrest warrant the court must consider the issue of bail. Upon receipt of a bail application, the court must:

a. immediately send a copy of the application to the Office of the Director of Public Prosecutions or Prosecution;
b. fix a date, time and place to hear the application; and
c. give notice of the date, time and place to the appropriate parties, such as the applicant and the prosecutor.

Procedural stages of trial in the magistrates' court (Part 8)

The first hearing in each case shall be conducted by a magistrate and must take place no later than 28 days from the date of issue of the complaint/summons/information. The first hearing is used for such matters as:

a. verification of the defendant's identity, current address and contact details;
b. providing details of the defendant's representation if any;
c. reading of the charges by the magistrate and reading of the fact sheet summarising the evidence by the prosecutor; and
d. considering bail.

A plea is also entered at the first hearing for summary-only matters. For hybrid matters, the defendant is required to enter a plea immediately if the court determines that it is to be tried summarily. For indictable matters, the defendant must be asked whether or not he wishes to indicate a plea at the start of every hearing in the magistrates' court.

Where a hybrid offence is to be tried, a magistrate conducts a venue hearing (Rule 8.3) and, wherever possible, this should be done at the same time as the first hearing. The purpose of the venue hearing is to determine whether the matter should be tried or sentenced, as appropriate taking into account any plea indication, in the magistrates' court or the Supreme Court.

Following a plea of not guilty in a summary matter, the magistrate must complete a case management form that includes the following:

a. witness requirements;
b. the date and method by which prosecution disclosure will be provided (in accordance with Rules 5.2 and 5.4);
c. any issues of fact and law to be resolved and whether or not a pre-trial hearing can be listed to determine these.

Listing for trial (Rule 8.6)

The magistrate must list the matter for a trial to take place as soon as reasonably practicable, having regard to the seriousness and complexity of the case and, in any event, within the time limits prescribed in Rules 2.1 (iii) and 2.8 (six months if person is in custody and nine months in all other cases).

Accepting guilty pleas (Rule 8.8)

Before accepting a plea of guilty, the magistrate must be satisfied that the defendant committed the alleged offence, that the plea is entered voluntarily and that it is made with an appropriate understanding of the consequences.

Preliminary inquiries (Rule 8.11)

The defence must notify the prosecution if the preliminary inquiry is to be contested at least seven days before it is due to be heard. Having determined that the case should be committed to the Supreme Court, the court must inter alia:

a. identify the next practicable sitting within which the case might be heard;
b. give directions in respect of the date and method for prosecution disclosure (in accordance with Rules 5.2 and 5.4);
c. consider the issue of bail;
d. inform the defendant of his right to require the attendance of any witnesses not being called to physically give evidence and the procedures involved for enforcing such attendance.

The magistrates' court is required, within 14 days of the date upon which a case is committed to the Supreme Court, to send the case file to the Office of the Director of Public Prosecutions and the Supreme Court (Rule 8.13).

Supreme court procedural stages (Part 9)

Priority cases

Upon receipt of a case file, the Supreme Court and the Office of the Director of Public Prosecutions must consider whether a case is a priority for the purpose of its listing for trial. Certain factors should be considered in this regard:

a. whether the defendant is on remand or on bail;
b. if on remand, the length of time the defendant has been awaiting trial;
c. the age and mental state of the defendant.

Rule 9.2 provides that the Director of Public Prosecutions may either prefer an indictment or decline to do so. All indictments must be preferred and filed with the court as soon as reasonably practicable, and in any event not later than three days before the arraignment hearing.

Assignment of counsel (Rule 9.6)

In cases where counsel is to be assigned to the defendant, this must be done by the Supreme Court within 14 days of the receipt of the case file from the magistrates' court. Once counsel has been assigned to a case, recusal may only take place following a hearing if the court is satisfied that both reasonable grounds exist and a suitably qualified alternative counsel can be secured without delay.

Arraignment (Rules 9.8–9.9)

The arraignment of all defendants committed to that sitting takes place on the first day of each Supreme Court sitting. Before arraigning the defendant, all parties must indicate their readiness for arraignment through the completion of a case management form. At the arraignment the judge must inform the defendant of certain matters, including:

a. if appropriate, the right to legal representation, bail and/or an interpreter;
b. the plea process and the right to reduction in sentence for a guilty plea;
c. the right to receive an indication of the applicable range of sentences available.

Procedure where plea of not guilty is entered (Rule 9.11)

If a not guilty plea is entered, certain matters must be addressed through the completion of a case management form including:

a. in capital cases, the progress of assigning counsel to the defendant;
b. the date and method for prosecution disclosure (in accordance with Rules 5.2 and 5.4);

c. the particulars of an alibi defence;
d. any issues of fact and law to be resolved and whether or not a pre-trial hearing can be listed to determine these matters.

Procedure where guilty plea is entered (Rule 9.13)

Before accepting a plea of guilty the judge must be satisfied either by

a. questioning the defendant personally, or
b. by calling upon counsel to lead the questioning,

that the defendant committed the alleged offence, that the plea is entered voluntarily and that it is made with an appropriate understanding of the consequences.

APPLICATION OF THE CRIMINAL PROCEDURE RULES

The overriding objective

The overriding objective that demands that criminal cases should be dealt with justly includes considering the interests of the accused, witnesses and victims. It is also in the public interest that charges against accused persons be dealt with as soon as is reasonably possible, thus saving time and resources and promoting public confidence in the administration of criminal justice. In *PC Sheldon Callendar v Kevon Neptune* Mag App No S 083 of 2016 the appellant appealed against the decision of a magistrate to dismiss a charge against the respondent for want of prosecution. In dismissing the appeal, the Trinidad and Tobago Court of Appeal emphasised that in order to facilitate the more expeditious hearing of matters, police complainants should not allow matters to 'slide'.

The purpose of the Criminal Procedure Rules is to deal with matters of procedure and in so doing the court has to keep in mind the overriding obligation to deal with cases justly. This does not, however, affect the way in which the substantive law is to be interpreted. In *Hubner v District Court of Prostejov Czech Republic* [2009] EWHC 2929 (Admin) the appellant appealed against a decision to extradite him, submitting that the UK Criminal Procedure Rules required the court to have regard to the overriding objective that required cases be dealt with justly. The court held that in this case it could not allow the overriding objective to affect how the Extradition Act 2003 was interpreted.

Judicial intervention may be done in furtherance of the overriding objective. This intervention will often extend to correcting an advocate on a matter of law or procedure, to ensure proper, relevant and appropriate examination of a witness, or to elicit further information or explanation from a witness. This is done in order to gain an understanding of the evidence or to assist the jury to do so, or to cure or prevent confusion between the witness and the advocate (*R v Ian Frances Berry* [2010] EWCA Crim 313). The court in *Berry* also stated that it was no part of the trial judge's task to intervene in the presentation of the evidence for the purpose or with the effect of imposing upon the trial his own view of the merits of that evidence.

The court in *Berry* stressed that this type of repeated intervention will give rise to the danger either that the judge would actually prevent a fair trial, or at least give the appearance of preventing a fair trial. In *Berry* the judge had intervened on several occasions with the effect of diminishing the appellant's evidence in the eyes of the jury. He also expressed personal opinions in the absence of the jury that he then reinforced during the evidence, partly in the form of leading questions and partly in the form of comment. As a result the impartial onlooker would not have received the impression that the appellant had received a fair trial.

Case management

The trial judge in managing the trial has to be alert to the needs of everyone involved in the case, including the defendant, the prosecution, the complainant, witnesses, the jury, jurors in waiting and, finally, the community's interest that justice should be done without unnecessary delay. A fair balance has to be struck between all these interests. In *R v Chaaban* [2003] EWCA Crim 1012 the appellant criticised the way in which the judge managed the trial, which included a claim that the imposition by the judge of a timetable on the trial led to a sense that everything was being rushed. It was held that the judge should, as part of his trial management function, exercise firm control over the timetable where necessary, making clear in advance and throughout the trial that the timetable would be subject to appropriate constraints and, furthermore, the judge is entitled to direct that the trial is expected to conclude by a specific date and to exercise his powers to see that it does.

Active case management in furthering the overriding objective that cases be dealt with justly includes the power to impose 'proportionate' procedural sanctions, meaning sanctions that provide for no more than what might reasonably be required for the proper working of a rule. Court orders, such as, for example, unconditional orders for disclosure of privileged material as well as an order that absolutely prohibited a party – with no discretion in the trial court – from calling a witness whose identity he had not disclosed in advance, would exceed the requirements of a reasonable regulatory regime.

The right to a fair trial does not entitle either or both sides to take as much time as they like in conducting their respective cases: *R v Jisl and others* [2004] EWCA Crim 696. The court in *Jisl* emphasised that every day unnecessarily used at trial represents wastage of scarce resources as well as another day's stressful waiting for the remaining witnesses and the jurors in that particular trial. Just as important, delay in the progress of a trial results in continuing and increasing tension and worry for another defendant or defendants, some of whom are remanded in custody. In order to make sensible use of time there is a need for judicial management and control.

To enable the trial judge to manage the case in a way that is fair to every participant, the potential problems as well as the possible areas for time saving should be canvassed pre-trial. The Court of Appeal noted in *Jisl* that if proper principles of time management had been utilised in the trial, it would be inconceivable that the trial would have taken 70 days before the jury reached its verdict. Equally, with proper time management, it was doubtful whether the repeated recall of prosecution witnesses, some twice, several three times, would have taken place, or that the judge would have been invited time after time to break off the hearing of the evidence in order to give legal rulings.

Breach of the rules

A judge may exercise his discretion to refuse to grant leave to admit certain evidence when there is a breach of procedural rules. Such a situation arose in *R v Musone* [2007] EWCA Crim 1237. In *Musone*, the judge refused an application by the defendant to admit bad character evidence, on the grounds that the application was late and without notice and therefore in breach of the rules. On appeal against conviction, the court stated that the procedural rules should not be used to discipline one who has failed to comply with them in circumstances where unfairness to others may be cured and where the interests of justice would otherwise require the evidence to be admitted. However, there would be cases in which the judge can properly refuse to allow evidence, not merely as a matter of discipline but to prevent substantive unfairness. The court emphasised that cases in which a breach of the procedural rules will entitle a court to exclude evidence of substantial probative value will be rare. The more credible the evidence, the less likely it is that the judge will exclude it on grounds of a breach of a procedural requirement.

In certain circumstances the court may even stay proceedings where the rules have been breached. In *R v LR* [2010] EWCA Crim 924, the trial judge ordered the prosecution to provide copies of certain photographs (which were to be used as evidence in the case) to be shown to the defendant, subject to appropriate undertakings as to safe custody and control of the photographs. The prosecution refused to provide the copies in accordance with order on the ground inter alia that to do so would be illegal and appealed the judge's subsequent decision to stay the proceedings due to non-compliance with the order.

In dismissing the appeal the Court of Appeal stated that the normal consequence of disobedience by the prosecution to an order made by the judge in the interests of a fair trial is either the exclusion of any evidence to which the order relates, or a stay would be ordered by the judge.

Time limits

The objective of the Criminal Procedure Rules 'to deal with all cases efficiently and expeditiously' depends upon adherence to the timetable set out in the rules. The court may, however, exercise its discretion to shorten a time limit or to extend it even after it has expired. In the exercise of that discretion the court will take account of all the relevant considerations, including the furtherance of the overriding objective. The court's discretion to extend time is not fettered by a rule that time should only be extended in exceptional circumstances.

Where a time limit is imposed by the court to complete a procedural step and a sanction is attached for breach of that time limit, the court has the power to waive the sanction: *R v Owens and another* [2006] EWCA Crim 2206. In *Owens*, the court waived the sanction of exclusion of the proposed evidence. The Court of Appeal decided that it would be in the interests of justice to waive the sanction of exclusion of the prosecution's evidence. The judge was entitled, having satisfied himself that there was ultimately no unfairness and no undue prejudice in the service of the evidence on the defence, to waive the sanction of exclusion.

In *R (on the application of Robinson) v Sutton Coldfield Magistrates' Court* [2006] 4 All ER 1029, the prosecution's application to extend the time to file and serve a notice of intention to adduce bad character evidence was allowed. The claimant was found guilty and, upon his application for judicial review, he submitted inter alia that, having regard to the overriding objective in the CPR to 'deal with cases efficiently and expeditiously', the court should only exercise its discretion to extend time under the CPR in exceptional circumstances, where it had been provided with sufficiently good reasons as to why the prosecution could not comply with the mandatory time limit.

The court held that in the instant case there were two principal material considerations:

1. The reason for the failure to comply with the rules; a party seeking an extension must plainly explain the reasons for its failure.
2. Whether the claimant's position was prejudiced by the failure.

On the facts of the case, although the court had 'reservations' for the explanation that was offered, what was material was the fact that the claimant was not prejudiced and, accordingly, it dismissed the application for judicial review.

Adjournments

In *The DPP v Radziwilowicz* [2014] EWHC 2283 (Admin), the District Judge in the magistrates' court refused the prosecution's application for an adjournment and dismissed the charges. The prosecutor was not authorised to prosecute the case and necessary evidence was unavailable. The court dismissed the case pursuant to its powers under the CPR. On the case stated, the court held that at the hearing there was no obligation on the prosecution to have their witnesses available. Furthermore, the District Judge well knew that the prosecutor was not authorised to conduct trials. The decision to refuse the adjournment was 'purely disciplinary'. Those persons who complained about the conduct of the defendants had been deprived of their opportunity to pursue the matter in a way and at a time that was unjustified.

In *R v Phillips* [2007] EWCA Crim 1042, the Court of Appeal held that judges should be robust in case management decisions since active hands-on case management, both pre-trial and during the trial, is an essential part of the judge's task. This notwithstanding, the court criticised the trial judge's decision to proceed with a trial even where the prosecution had failed to make full disclosure to the defence. The Court of Appeal stated that it would have been preferable if the defence had been granted some more time to peruse and absorb the late disclosure made by the prosecution. In opting to start the case, the trial judge had placed defence counsel in considerable difficulties and distracted him from the primary task of conducting the defence.

Judge's intervention in the trial

In *R v Perren* [2009] EWCA Crim 348, the Court of Appeal held that a judge should be particularly careful about refraining from intervening during a witness's evidence in-chief, except insofar as it is necessary to clarify, to keep the evidence moving on and, if necessary, to avoid prolixity or irrelevancies. On the facts of the case, the nature and extent of the judge's interventions during the appellant's evidence in-chief deprived the appellant of the opportunity of having his evidence properly considered by the jury in keeping with his right to a fair trial

Defence statement

In *Sexius v AG of St Lucia* [2017] UKPC 26, the issue of whether the provisions of the St Lucia Criminal Code 2004 and Criminal Procedure Rules 2008, concerning the requirements for a defence statement to be filed in advance of a criminal trial, were consistent with the Constitution of St Lucia was considered. The Privy Council held that the impugned provisions did not impact on the appellant's right to silence at trial since he was not compelled to give or to call evidence. If he otherwise intended to give or to call evidence the defendant, according to the rules, is required to give advance notice of the nature of his defence and the issues raised. If his advance notice of the nature of his defence is inconsistent, whether within the defence statement or with evidence at trial, he may be called to account at trial. However, this did not amount to a limitation on the right not to be compelled to give evidence.

Furthermore, since the onus of proof remained on the prosecution throughout, the requirement for advance disclosure of any positive case that was to be made was, similar to advance notice of 'special defences', entirely consistent with the presumption of innocence. The Privy Council concluded that, insofar as the relevant provisions involved a qualification of pre-trial silence (which in any event was not the case), the provisions were reasonably directed towards a clear and proper public objective and represented no greater qualification than the situation called for.

CHAPTER 9

SUMMARY APPEALS

This chapter focusses on the law in relation to appeals from trials in the magistrates' court. Such appeals are, in general, in respect of trials of summary offences. In certain specified cases and circumstances, however, a magistrate may have statutory power to try some indictable offences.[1] When this occurs, appeals in respect of such trials are usually dealt with in the same manner as appeals in purely summary matters. In exceptional instances they may be treated differently in some particular way. In Jamaica, for example, appeals in matters tried on indictment, or by this special statutory summary jurisdiction by a resident magistrate (now District Court judge), lie to the Court of Appeal.[2] Other appeals from summary trials in the magistrates' court lie to the Circuit Court (High Court) of the particular parish.

TO EXERCISE THE RIGHT

Who can appeal?

In general, any person dissatisfied by a conviction or order in the magistrates' court may appeal. Thus a complainant may appeal against the failure of the court to make a conviction or a defendant may appeal against a conviction or order made against him.[3] In Dominica s 141 of the Magistrates' Code of Procedure Chap 4:20 provides there shall be no appeal where the complaint has been dismissed, although the DPP may refer a point of law by case stated. The respective St Vincent[4] and Antigua[5] legislation have been amended to make it clear that the prosecution may now appeal a magistrate's decision. Although the Antiguan provision speaks to appeal only on a point of law, this is not as restrictive as it appears since most appeals are based on points of law. Statute in some jurisdictions[6] even provide that where a defendant pleads guilty, he may only appeal against sentence and not conviction. Nonetheless, where a plea of guilty is a nullity, it seems that this prohibition cannot stand.

In most jurisdictions a magistrate, on the application of either party, may apply to the High Court or the Court of Appeal, whichever is stipulated by the relevant law, for a case to be stated on a point of law. Any decision given by the appellate court in respect of a case stated will not affect the actual decision of the magistrate, but will provide guidance on the law and practice. Sometimes a magistrate on his own initiative can refer the case for an opinion. In *Agdoma v Tomy* (1968) 12 WIR 296, a magistrate, having established that a defendant had been properly served, embarked on summary trial ex parte on his failure to appear. Subsequently, after conviction, the defendant appeared and submitted a medical certificate as to his earlier absence. At first the magistrate decided that the conviction could

1 See Chapter 10.
2 Judicature (Resident Magistrates) Act, as amended by Act No 6 of 2016, s 293, Jamaica.
3 As provided in Summary Courts Act, Chap 4:20, s 128, Trinidad and Tobago.
4 Act No 13 of 2007 providing for a new s 212A of the Criminal Procedure Code, Cap 172.
5 Act No 13 of 2004 creating a new Pt VIIIA of the Magistrate's Code of Procedure Act.
6 As in Barbados: Magistrates' Courts Act 1996–27, s 238(2), and Bahamas, Criminal Procedure Code Ch 91, s 233.

not stand, but then opted to refer the case to the High Court, as provided in the St Lucian Criminal Code, for an opinion on a question of law: 'whether on the above statement of facts the District Court came to a correct decision in point of law in setting aside the convictions and sentences and acceding to a rehearing of the case'. The High Court answered the reference 'in the negative', but did not itself affirm the conviction. It was for the magistrate to then apply the law as stated by the High Court.

Magistrate's reasons

Once an appellant appeals against an order, be it a conviction or dismissal by a magistrate, the latter must supply reasons for his decision. Statute in some jurisdictions such as Barbados, Dominica, Grenada and Trinidad and Tobago now provides for this.[7] In Barbados, the legislation even provides that if a magistrate does not fulfil his statutory obligation to supply reasons within 21 days, he may be summoned before the Court of Appeal, presumably to explain his delinquency. Even without statutory requirement, it has been authoritatively affirmed that it is of 'fundamental importance' that reasons be furnished, especially in circumstances where the deprivation of liberty is at stake.[8] In a Trinidad and Tobago case, *Aqui v Pooran Maharaj* (1983) 34 WIR 282, the Court of Appeal ordered a new trial in a magisterial appeal where no reasons had been provided by the magistrate. The court considered that without reasons, the decision of the magistrate could not stand. It was held that although no statutory provision (at that time) expressly required a magistrate to state the reasons for his decision, the practice of doing so had grown up and had been adhered to over the years so that it was now properly regarded as a rule of law. The court considered that it is a fundamental principle of justice that parties to litigation are entitled to know the reasons for the decision of a court of law.

In *Alexander v Williams* (1984) 34 WIR 340, the Court of Appeal of Trinidad and Tobago followed its own previous decision in *Aqui*. For over four years a magistrate failed to provide reasons for the conviction of the appellant, which entailed a term of imprisonment. The Court of Appeal was faced with an ironic situation in that the matter was not listed earlier because the lack of the magistrate's reasons rendered the record of proceedings incomplete. In a robust judgment the Court of Appeal, in quashing the conviction, applied *Aqui* and reiterated that it was a rule of law that in criminal proceedings a magistrate must provide his reasons when the defendant lodges an appeal against conviction. Furthermore, the court held, in cases involving the liberty of the subject, the furnishing of reasons by a magistrate in cases in which appeals have been lodged was an indispensable requirement of due process.

Following *Alexander*, the Trinidad and Tobago legislature amended the Summary Courts Act, Chap 4:20 to require every magistrate to submit reasons for his decision within 60 days of an appeal.[9] Despite the passage of this legislation, the Trinidad and Tobago Court of Appeal was faced with the same problem in *Forbes v Maharaj* (1998) 52 WIR 487, PC, which was eventually determined by the Privy Council. The magistrate in that case had convicted the appellant for possession of marijuana and sentenced him to five years' imprisonment against which conviction he appealed. The magistrate never submitted any reasons and the

7 Magistrates' Courts Act, 1996–27, s 241, Barbados; Magistrate's Code of Procedure, Chap 4:20, s 146, Dominica; Magistrates' Judgments (Appeals) Act, Cap 178, s 15(3), Grenada; Summary Courts Act, Chap 4:20, s 130A, as amended by Act No 13 of 1986, Trinidad and Tobago.

8 *Forbes v Maharaj* (1998) 52 WIR 487, PC.

9 Act No 13 of 1986, creating a new s 130B.

appellant remained in custody for 19 months until he was bailed pending the appeal. The Court of Appeal eventually heard the appeal in March 1997 and varied the sentence to 18 months' imprisonment, which was the maximum sentence permitted under the then law. Although the appellant had already been in custody for 19 months, the Court of Appeal ordered that the sentence should commence on the day the appeal was determined.

The Privy Council, while raising the question of the propriety of this course of action by the Court of Appeal, did not comment on it because the matter was argued on the effect of the failure of the magistrate to state his reasons. The Board of the Privy Council endorsed the judgments of the Court of Appeal in *Alexander* (above), which clearly recognised the fundamental importance of the furnishing of reasons. The Board also observed: 'without the statement of reasons it will usually be impossible to know whether the magistrate has misdirected himself on the law or misunderstood or misapplied the evidence'. An appellant would in such instances be justified in arguing strongly that there was no sound basis for the magistrate's decision.

In all cases of appeal, therefore, whether statute so requires or not, it is evident that a magistrate ought to give reasons for his decision. Failure to do so is unfair to an appellant and in cases where the liberty of the citizen is at stake, it is usually considered necessary that a court should justify its decision to convict. The Privy Council in *Forbes* therefore allowed the appeal, deciding that the Court of Appeal was in error in reviewing the record of the hearing to 'see if there was sufficient evidence upon which the magistrate could have come to the decision', which he did. This was too low a threshold upon which to decide to uphold a conviction in the absence of reasons of the magistrate. While the absence of reasons will not always mean that an appeal against a magistrate's decision will be allowed, such absence will make it very difficult to support a conviction and sentence of imprisonment.

An exception to the general rule is *Cedeno v Logan* (2000) 58 WIR 411, PC in which a magistrate having convicted the defendant of larceny retired without giving reasons. Recognising that there might be cases where no reasons are given because a magistrate died or retired, the Privy Council upheld the conviction stating that the basis for the magistrate's decision was obvious. The magistrate had rejected the contention that the identification was mistaken.

In contrast, the Court of Appeal in Guyana in *Griffith v Niewenkirk* (2004) 67 WIR 142, in a case involving convictions for embezzlement where neither the notes of evidence nor the reasons of a magistrate who had emigrated were available, held that the interests of justice demanded that the appeal be allowed.

It has been held[10] that a written decision explaining his ruling in the case is sufficient to constitute a 'statement' of the magistrate's reasons. A decision which shows that the magistrate considered the relevant points and submissions made by parties in the matter is enough. It is unnecessary to prepare a separate statement of reasons for purposes of the appeal if this type of decision was forthcoming.

The appellate court

In general, an appeal from the magistrates' court is to the Court of Appeal.[11] For magisterial appeals the composition of the Court of Appeal may vary, consisting of one or two judges instead of the usual three, which constitutes a sitting Court of Appeal for appeals from the High Court.

10 *D'Aguiar v Cox* (1971) 18 WIR 44.

11 E.g., Barbados: Magistrates Courts Act, 1996–27, s 238; Dominica: Magistrates' Code of Procedure, Chap 4:20, s 141; Trinidad and Tobago: Summary Courts Act, Chap 4:20, s 128.

In some jurisdictions, the law varies depending on the nature of the offence. In Guyana, appeals from the decisions of magistrates are usually to the Full Court of the High Court (three judges of the High Court).[12] If the decision is in relation to an indictable matter which is tried summarily, however, an appeal will lie to the Court of Appeal.[13] In the Bahamas, Act No 25 of 1996 amended s 234 of the Criminal Procedure Code is in relation to appeals from magistrates' courts. If the case involves an indictable offence for which the offender is liable to imprisonment for at least one year and the matter was tried summarily, appeal lies to the Court of Appeal. Act No 26 of 1996 also amends the law in relation to appeals from magistrates' courts by amending the Court of Appeal Act, Ch 40. Now, all appeals in respect of scheduled indictable offences tried summarily lie directly to the Court of Appeal. In other instances, if the matter was tried by the Chief Magistrate; Deputy Chief Magistrate; a senior stipendiary and circuit magistrate or a circuit justice on circuit, appeal will lie to the Supreme Court. Any of these magistrates or a circuit justice may hear other appeals from the magistrates' courts. Those latter provisions are peculiar to the Bahamas, and probably result from the expanse of the islands of the Bahamas of which about 30 are populated. For reasons of convenience, it may have been deemed necessary to allow appeals to magistrates from hearings by Justices of the Peace (which, under the Magistrates Act, is permissible in exceptional cases).[14]

In Jamaica, appeal lies to the Circuit Court[15] of the parish in which the summary matter was tried. If the matter is one tried under the Resident Magistrates' Act as amended by Act No 6 of 2016 by a resident magistrate (now District Court judge), appeal lies to the Court of Appeal as mentioned earlier. Such matters are usually in relation to indictable matters tried summarily by virtue of that Act or by the special statutory jurisdiction of the resident magistrate to try summary matters.

PROSECUTING THE APPEAL

The provisions governing the procedure for appeals from the magistrates' court are outlined in the relevant Acts throughout the region, which may be either the summary procedure legislation or specific summary appeals legislation. Such legislation specifies, inter alia, the requirement for:

- making the appeal including the signing, giving and service of notice of appeal and also notice of the grounds of appeal;
- recognisance or giving of security to prosecute the appeal;
- the hearing of the appeal and judgment including the need for appearance of the parties; the question of amendment of defects in the proceedings, and the statutory grounds of appeal.

Notice of appeal

The giving of notice of appeal is a condition precedent to the initiation of the appeal. The notice initiates the appeal. All jurisdictions specify that notice of appeal must be given within

12 Summary Jurisdiction (Appeals) Act, Cap 3:04, ss 2 and 3.

13 Administration of Justice Act No 21 of 1978, s 7(1).

14 Magistrates' Act, Ch 42, s 8.

15 The Justices of the Peace (Appeals) Act, s 3.

a specified statutory time period. While notice may be given orally, it must be reduced to writing within that time period. If notice is not given or if the notice of appeal is invalid, there can be no appeal. This is a mandatory statutory requirement. In *Rochester v Chin and Matthews* (1961) 4 WIR 40, the Jamaica Supreme Court considered an appeal where the notice of appeal was served outside the statutory time limit. The court held that the giving of a notice of appeal is a condition precedent to the hearing of the appeal. The performance of this condition founded the jurisdiction of the appellate court to hear the appeal. It was not a mere formality which could be waived by the court. The appeal was out of time and therefore would be dismissed. Although this case related to a civil appeal where notice was required to be made to the respondent, the principle applies to criminal appeals.

In fact, s 130(1) of the Summary Courts Act Chap 4:20 of Trinidad and Tobago specifically provides: 'An appeal shall be commenced by giving to the clerk notice of the appeal'. Whomever the statute stipulates must be served notice of the appeal and whatever period is stipulated must be followed. The time period for serving notice varies among the jurisdictions. In the Bahamas and Barbados the period is seven days, whereas in most other jurisdictions it is 14 days.[16] In St Lucia it is 15 days. In St Vincent it is 21 days. The Interpretation Acts make it clear that whenever a statutory time period is stipulated as seven days, only working days will be counted. Where the period is 14 days or longer however, all days, including Sundays, must be counted in computation of the period: *Reynolds v Yarde* (1962) 4 WIR 268. In that case an appellant in (then) British Guiana filed an appeal 16 days after the magistrate's decision. It was held that the Sundays occurring in the period of 16 days were correctly included in the computation. The appeal was outside the 14-day limitation period for appeals.

In most jurisdictions, the magistrates' courts provide printed notice of appeal forms to facilitate the filing of appeals.

Extension of time

Unless statute so provides, there can be no extension of the statutory time period to file a notice of appeal. In some jurisdictions this has resulted in defendants filing for judicial review or a constitutional motion if a good ground of appeal is discovered after the expiration of the time for appeal. Other jurisdictions, however, specifically provide for the grant of extension of time to appeal. Such application is usually made to the court to which the appeal lies.[17] In the Bahamas, Grenada, Guyana, St Lucia and now Trinidad and Tobago, leave to appeal out of time may be sought. The court will carefully consider the circumstances before granting such leave to ensure that the appellant is not abusing the process.

In *Partin v D'Oliveira* (1977) 24 WIR 261, the Court of Appeal of Guyana was faced with an application for extension of time in respect of an appeal from the Full Court's dismissal of an appeal in a summary matter. The applicant, a foreign national, had left Guyana illegally while his appeal against conviction and a $67,500 fine was still pending. He was still outside the jurisdiction when he sought the extension of time to appeal from the Full Court to the Court of Appeal. In refusing the application for extension of time the court held, inter alia, that the fact that an appellant had absented himself from the jurisdiction of the court without

16 By Act No 6 of 2004, Trinidad and Tobago changed the time limit from 7 days to 14 days in amending s 130(3).

17 As in the Bahamas, Criminal Procedure Code, Ch 91, s 235(2); Grenada, Magistrates' Judgment (Appeals) Act Cap 178, s 13; Trinidad and Tobago, Act No 6 of 2004 creating s 130A of Chap 4:20.

permission is a relevant factor for the court to take into account in exercising its discretion whether to grant the extension. Furthermore, it was an abuse of process for the appellant to seek to put the appeal machinery of the court into motion and at the same time show no intention of returning to the jurisdiction. These are some of the matters a court will take into account in granting an extension of time. A simple test is: did the appellant abuse the appeal machinery? In *Jonathan Eaton Vyse v Cpl Warwick* (unreported) Mag Appeal No 14 of 2009, JA Soo Hon sitting in the Trinidad and Tobago Court of Appeal Chamber Court granted an extension of time to the appellant to appeal his conviction after a period of several months. The appellant, a foreigner, had been arrested on a ship before he had even entered the country and left the day after his conviction, two days after his arrest. The day after his arrival home in the US he took steps toward effecting an appeal. The Court found that the appellant had formed an early intention to appeal and had pursued that intention with due diligence.

Signing the notice

Even if oral notice of appeal is given, a written signed notice of appeal should be submitted to the relevant clerk in the magistrates' court where the appeal is made. In some jurisdictions, statute speaks of notice to the magistrate, but in practice it is sufficient to notify the court officials. There is usually a standard form of notice of appeal prepared by the magistrates' court. Statute now permits the appellant or his lawyer to sign the notice to effect the appeal. This is so in most jurisdictions where signing of the notice by the appellant is necessary to effect the appeal process. A failure to sign the notice could render it invalid: *Stanley v Andrews* (1963) 5 WIR 457. In that case, the appellant gave verbal notice of appeal in March. It was reduced to writing, but was not signed by the appellant until some six months later. The Trinidad and Tobago Court of Appeal held that the appeal was void, since the law required that a verbal notice of appeal should be reduced to writing and signed by the appellant as a necessary condition of its efficacy. That was not done. The notice was invalid if it was not signed within the statutory time specified to file it. Wooding CJ pointed out that it was vital that Clerks of Peace should promptly discharge their statutory duties in this regard. If verbal notice of appeal is given by anyone (entitled to appeal), that person must see to it that the notice is reduced to writing in the correct form and signed 'forthwith'. He added: 'And "forthwith" means precisely what it says, forthwith'.

In *Samuel v Karan Mag* App No 98/86 (unreported), the Trinidad and Tobago Court of Appeal followed *Stanley* and held an unsigned notice of appeal to be a nullity. In an earlier case of *George v Darlington* [1954–1955] 15 Tri LR 53, the complainant in a traffic offence appealed against a failure to convict. He had filed the notice of appeal but not the notice of reasons (grounds). The court confirmed that the notice of reasons did not specifically require the appellant's signature and could be signed by the court prosecutor. Although the headnote in that case speaks of 'Notice of Appeal', the judgment makes it clear that it was the notice of reasons that was not signed by the appellant. This was not fatal to the appeal.

The requirement for signing the notice of appeal raises an interesting dilemma that has been faced in some countries of the Commonwealth Caribbean. As stated above, the prosecution is entitled to appeal in most jurisdictions in respect of a failure of the magistrate to convict. However, in some jurisdictions the relevant statutory provision provides that 'the complainant' may appeal. This is so in Trinidad and Tobago, Barbados, St Lucia and Antigua[18] among others. It appears that if the police officer who laid the charge, the complainant, does not actually sign and file the notice of appeal against a failure to convict, there will be no valid appeal.

18 Antigua, s 167 Cap 255; Barbados, s 238(1)(a) MCA 1996; Trinidad and Tobago, s 128(1) Chap 4:20.

This is the stance that was taken by the Trinidad and Tobago Court of Appeal based on the wording of the statute. No matter how serious the summary offence was or how minor a role the complainant may have played in the prosecution of the offence, he was the person required to appeal. Following the dismissal of a number of appeals on this basis the law was changed. 'Complainant' now includes Director of Public Prosecutions.[19]

Such a situation may frustrate the attempts of the Director of Public Prosecutions or even a police prosecutor to take a matter from the magistrates' court to the appellate court. Conversely, a police complainant may waste time and unnecessarily invoke the appellate process by filing an undeserving appeal himself. Although the Director of Public Prosecutions (or his officers) appears at the appeal hearing, the complainant could engage in a frolic of his own before that time. It would appear that the law in the relevant jurisdictions should be corrected, perhaps along the lines of the Grenadian Magistrates Judgment (Appeals) Act, Cap 178, which at s 3(b) provides that no appeal lies from a dismissal of a criminal case in the magistrates' court, 'save by leave of the Director of Public Prosecutions'. Thus, the DPP is brought in at the initial stage of the appeal. In some other jurisdictions like Jamaica and Guyana it appears that anyone aggrieved[20] or dissatisfied[21] with a decision on a summary trial may appeal. This entitlement appears to be very wide as there may be many people unconnected with the case who may be dissatisfied with the decision. Nevertheless, it is expected that only persons who have locus standi in the matter would be able to appeal. It is arguable that the DPP in such a case, and not just the police complainant, as the public officer who is in charge of all criminal prosecutions (except in the Bahamas) should be able to appeal as a person 'aggrieved' or 'dissatisfied' if he in fact is.

The recognisance

The 'recognisance' referred to in summary appeals statute is a bond to prosecute the appeal. In general, an appellant must enter into such a recognisance with or without securities within a specified time following filing of notice of appeal. Although bail pending appeal is alluded to in statute in some jurisdictions, it is provided in several Commonwealth Caribbean jurisdictions that an appellant who is in custody shall be 'liberated' once he signs the recognisance to prosecute the appeal.[22] It appears that in such a case the recognisance is the bail bond. Interestingly, it is almost universally provided in the region that in lieu of a recognisance the appellant may give security by way of deposit of money to prosecute the appeal. The payment of specified security in such cases is sufficient to enable the release of an appellant who is in custody.

In general, an appellant who remains in custody need not enter into a recognisance or pay a security to prosecute the appeal.[23] This does not, however, appear to be the case in Guyana, St Vincent and the Bahamas. The St Vincent Criminal Procedure

19 Act No 6 of 2004, s 3 amending s 2 of Chap 4:20.

20 Justices of the Peace (Appeals) Act, s 3, Jamaica, permits any person aggrieved or affected by the judgment to appeal.

21 Summary Jurisdiction (Appeals) Act, Guyana, Cap 3:04, s 3, allows 'anyone dissatisfied with a decision of the magistrate' to appeal.

22 St Vincent and the Bahamas are notable exceptions.

23 Antigua: Magistrate's Code of Procedure Act, Cap 255, s 173; Barbados: Magistrates' Courts Act 1996–27, s 247; Dominica: Magistrate's Code of Procedure Act, Chap 4:20, s 145(2); Grenada: Magistrates' Judgments (Appeals) Act, Cap 178, s 7; Jamaica: Justices of the Peace (Appeals) Act, ss 13–7; St Kitts and Nevis: Magistrate's Code of Procedure Act, Cap 3:17 s 168,170; Trinidad and Tobago: Summary Courts Act, Chap 4:20, s 136(1).

Code (s 216) and the Bahamas Criminal Procedure Code (s 236) both provide that where the complainant acts on behalf of the police, the Crown or the DPP (or Attorney General in the case of the Bahamas) no recognisance is needed. Otherwise, every appellant must enter into a recognisance. In Guyana,[24] an appellant who remains in custody is, instead of a recognisance, required to pay a small deposit to prosecute the appeal. In St Lucia, the magistrate may release an appellant who is in custody if he enters into a recognisance.[25]

It would seem that a complainant who appeals on a failure to convict should not be required to enter into recognisance since he has not been convicted. In Jamaica, however, the Justices of the Peace (Appeals) Act states otherwise. Section 13 provides that the appellant in the case of dismissal or refusal to adjudicate must deposit a sum sufficient to cover the costs of dismissal that may be awarded and costs of appeal. In Barbados, Antigua and St Kitts and Nevis the legislation specifically states that all appellants (except those who remain in custody) must enter into a recognisance. The Trinidad and Tobago Summary Courts Act specifically provides otherwise.[26] An appellant who appeals on a failure to convict need not enter into a recognisance. This type of provision seems to make it clear that a recognisance to prosecute an appeal is not the same as a bail bond, despite how it is treated in practice, but is really an undertaking to commit to the appeal. In fact, it has been held that once the defendant does not remain in custody, the entering into a recognisance is a condition precedent to the prosecution of an appeal from the magistrates' court: see *Tai v Charles* (1959) 1 WIR 346, a decision of the Trinidad and Tobago Full Court. This is so regardless of whether he was sentenced to a custodial sentence or not, which would be the only situation where bail should be needed. In the St Lucia case of *Tomy v Agdoma* (1968) 12 WIR 490, the High Court of St Lucia emphasised the separate nature of a recognisance to prosecute an appeal by holding that one recognisance could not be entered into in respect of appeals against two convictions, although the cases were heard together. In contrast, in respect of bail, it is not unusual to have one bail bond to cover more than one offence.

In Jamaica, the Court of Appeal dismissed the suggestion that the deposit of security in lieu of a recognisance was a mere formality: *Patterson and Nicely v Lynch* (1973) 21 WIR 378. It was held that it was a condition precedent to the jurisdiction of the court and failure to conform to the statute within the required time rendered the appeal invalid. Section 5 of the Guyana Summary Jurisdiction (Appeals) Act, Cap 3:04 specifically states: 'if the appellant fails to make the deposit the notice of appeal shall be of no effect'.

Bail

It is evident, then, that a recognisance to prosecute an appeal is not the same as a bail bond. The confusion, such as it is, has arisen in those jurisdictions which suspend the requirement for the recognisance if the appellant remains in custody and/or conversely enable his liberation if he does enter into a recognisance. Nevertheless, the St Vincent and Bahamas statutory provisions make it emphatically clear that bail is separate from recognisance. Even if an appellant enters into a recognisance or pays a security in these jurisdictions, once he is

24 Summary Jurisdiction (Appeals) Act, Cap 3:04, s 5(4).
25 St Lucia, Criminal Code, s 733(3).
26 Summary Courts Act, Chap 4:20, s 133A.

in custody he must separately apply for bail[27] since he is not 'liberated' merely by virtue of entering into the recognisance.

In contrast, the Trinidad and Tobago Summary Courts Act, Chap 4:20 actually seems to equate bail with the entering of a recognisance by a defendant who is sentenced to imprisonment. Section 133A provides:

> (1) Where an appellant who is sentenced to a term of imprisonment for less than three months has given notice of appeal then if he is in custody the magistrate ... shall grant him bail.
>
> (2) Within nine days after the pronouncement of the decision an appellant to whom sub-section (1) applies, shall, unless he remains in custody under Section 136, enter into a recognisance.

Section 136 dispenses with the requirement for a recognisance if the appellant remains in custody and s 135 provides that the court 'shall release the appellant from custody once he gives notice of appeal and enters into the recognisance'.

The real contention with the Trinidad and Tobago legislation is that it seems to dispense with a requirement for a recognisance if a defendant is not sentenced to imprisonment. In actuality, this is not so. The magistrates' courts require any appellant who is sentenced even to pay a fine to enter into a recognisance. The rationale is that once such an appellant appeals and does not pay the fine, he is liable to serve the alternative term of imprisonment. As a result he is required to enter into a recognisance before he is released.

In the final analysis it seems that a convicted defendant who appeals must enter into a recognisance to prosecute his appeal. In most jurisdictions this will dispense with a separate requirement for bail.

Grounds for appeal

Statute provides that an appellant must serve notice of 'reasons' for his appeal shortly after he gives notice of appeal. The time period for so doing varies among the countries of the region. Usually it is within the same time period for filing the notice of appeal, but in some jurisdictions the time is enlarged. For instance, in Barbados, where the notice of appeal must be filed within seven days, the time period for serving the notice of reasons is enlarged to 10 days and 14 days respectively. However, it appears that the time for filing a notice of reasons is not mandatory as the time for filing a notice of appeal usually is. It is not unusual to be granted an extension of time to serve a notice of reasons.[28] Like the notice of appeal, the notice of reasons must be served not only on officials at the relevant magistrates' court, but also on the respondent.

In most jurisdictions, the reasons or grounds of appeal are stipulated by statute and are very wide. They include grounds such as that the magistrate had no jurisdiction or exceeded it; inadmissible evidence was admitted; the decision was unreasonable or the magistrate made an error of law. The jurisdictions with statutory grounds include Antigua, the Bahamas, Barbados, Guyana, St Kitts and Nevis and Trinidad and Tobago. Although the statutes in these jurisdictions suggest that the appellant should be limited to arguing the reasons enumerated in his notice of reasons, the Court of Appeal will usually grant leave to

27 Criminal Procedure Code, Cap 172, s 218, St Vincent; Criminal Procedure Code, Ch 91, s 238, Bahamas.

28 In *Spencer v Bramble* (1960) 2 WIR 222, p 226, the appellate court acknowledged this.

amend the reasons to include others: *Richardson v Emmanuel* [1954–1955] 15 Tri LR 33. This is so as not to deny an appellant the opportunity to be fully heard.

In some jurisdictions like Jamaica and St Vincent, there appear to be no statutory grounds stipulated for appeal from the magistrates' court. The grounds may thus be very general. Even in jurisdictions where reasons or grounds are detailed to include such matters as 'the court has no jurisdiction in the case',[29] in practice the appellant need not specify the details of his reasons in his original notice of reasons. He may, nearer to the date of hearing of the appeal, amend his notice to include the basis for his allegation as in: 'The court had no jurisdiction because the matter originated in District A and not District B in which it was tried'. These are sometimes referred to as 'perfected' grounds. A notice of reasons or grounds might even include many matters which are not pursued at the hearing of the appeal. The appellant may merely have included them at the outset out of an abundance of caution so as to avail himself of many options.

The reasons or grounds for the appeal usually relate to matters of law, like most appeals. The Court of Appeal will not lightly interfere with or overrule the trial court's findings of fact: *Peters v Peters* (1969) 14 WIR 457. In that case, the Trinidad and Tobago Court of Appeal held that where a magistrate has made findings of fact in accordance with his functions, and there is evidence to justify his findings, it is not the function of the Court of Appeal to interfere by substituting its own view of the facts. If it is alleged, however, that the magistrate's decision is totally unreasonable, having regard to the evidence, the appellate court will review the finding of facts: *Bracegirdle v Oxley et al.* [1947] 1 KB 349.

Appearance

If statute provides that the appellant must appear, he must do so personally unless statute permits appearance through counsel as in Guyana.[30] In general, on summary appeal, the legislation must be strictly followed and the requirements for appearance are considered mandatory. In *Bach v Ferreira* (1965) 9 WIR 282, the appellant, a national in France, was out of the country at the date of the hearing of the appeal. The Trinidad and Tobago Court of Appeal held that 'appears' in the statute means 'appear in person' and an appellant, though represented by counsel, must personally appear to prosecute the appeal. In the circumstances, the appeal was struck out.

An appeal will be dismissed if the appellant, having been served properly, personally at his home or by registered mail, fails to appear without a valid explanation (such as medical excuse). In jurisdictions which allow appearance by counsel without the need for personal appearance of the appellant, one or the other must appear. In a magistrates' court appeal, it is not unusual for an appellant to argue his own case.[31] If a properly served respondent does not appear, the appellate court may hear the matter in his absence once the appellant is present.

Fresh evidence

The appellate court has power throughout the region to hear fresh evidence on appeal. This will usually constitute material evidence that was either not known of at trial or was otherwise

29 As in Summary Courts Act, Chap 4:20, s 132(a), Trinidad and Tobago.

30 Summary Jurisdiction (Appeals) Act, Cap 3:04, s 19.

31 Justices of the Peace (Appeals) Act of Jamaica, s 29, supports this.

unavailable. The evidence may be given by means of affidavit or even orally. In *Spencer v Bramble* (1960) 2 WIR 222, p 226, the Supreme Court construed the relevant provision in the then Trinidad and Tobago Summary Courts Ordinance which enabled the taking of fresh evidence by affidavit. The court then sought to set out the procedure for taking fresh evidence. It stated that the proper procedure was to make an application to the appellate court by way of motion seeking leave to file affidavits or otherwise adduce evidence. To the application should be exhibited a statement of the evidence sought to be adduced. The court will be moved to consider whether or not leave should be granted. If the necessity for adducing evidence only arises during the hearing of the appeal, the court may make any order that the justice of the case required.

The hearing

Section 29 of the Jamaica Justices of the Peace (Appeals) Act sets out the detailed procedural steps for the hearing of an appeal by listing them 'first' to 'fourth'. In that jurisdiction, it is necessary that the appellant first prove service of his notice and grounds of appeal as well as having entered into a recognisance. All of these appear to be conditions precedent to the hearing of the appeal. In general, in other jurisdictions, the procedure is not so rigid. Only if it appears that there are procedural issues will the point be taken by the respondent or even the Court of Appeal.

In arguing the appeal, the appellant must go first. If fresh evidence is to be called, this will be given before any legal arguments. The appellant should have served the court and respondent with relevant legal authorities, but since the matter is of a summary nature the requirement is not as strict as for indictable appeals and may be waived. The judge or judges of the appellate court may ask questions of the appellant during his submissions. If the appellant has not raised any viable argument, the Court of Appeal may not even call upon the respondent. This depends on the complexity of the case and the arguments. After the appellant has argued his grounds, the respondent may be called upon to reply in whole or in part (some grounds may not be viable). After the respondent makes his submission, the appellant usually has a right of reply in respect of new matters raised by the respondent.

The judgment

The powers of the Court of Appeal in giving judgment in respect of a magisterial appeal are specified in the summary procedure legislation in the region. The court may affirm the magistrate's decision, be it a dismissal or a conviction, by itself dismissing the appeal if it finds that it is without merit. This is what happened in *Spencer v Bramble* (above), where it was held that the appellant had been given an opportunity to be heard.

The appellate court may modify or amend the decision in whole or in part. It may also substitute another sentence for the original sentence if it thinks that is warranted. In *D'Aguiar v Cox* (1971) 18 WIR 44, the Guyana Full Court, although it dismissed the appeal and affirmed the conviction, varied the sentence by reducing the costs payable. The court may allow the appeal and in doing so may simply reverse the decision. This is what was done in *Riley v Barran* (1965) 8 WIR 164, where the Court of Appeal of Trinidad and Tobago allowed an appeal against the magistrate's decision to uphold a no case submission and dismiss the case. More usual, however, when the appeal is allowed the Court of Appeal may, under its statutory power, order that a new trial be held, unless it would be unfair to the defendant. In *Lewis v Commissioner of Police* (1969) 13 WIR 186, the Grenada High Court allowed the appeal against conviction on an equivocal plea of guilty and ordered that the case be remitted to the magistrate for trial de novo. A similar order was made by the Court of Appeal in *Allette v Chief of Police* (1965) 10 WIR 243 when it was held that the appellant had been denied an opportunity to be heard at trial.

Apart from the orders mentioned above, the Court of Appeal may 'make such an order for disposing of the case as the justice may require' or refer the case back to deal with as the court thinks fit (instead of simply to rehear it). An example of a different type of order is that in *Williams v Daniel and Bobb* (1968) 13 WIR 490, where the order was 'Appeal allowed, case remitted to the magistrate to call on the respondents for their defence and thereafter to adjudicate according to law'. In *Paynter v Lewis* (1965) 8 WIR 318, where the complainant appealed against a decision of the magistrate to recall a conviction, the appeal was allowed. The Court of Appeal of Trinidad and Tobago further ordered that a conviction of larceny be entered against the respondent and the case remitted to the magistrate to pass sentence. It should be remembered that the Court of Appeal also decides points of law on case stated. Its order in such an 'appeal' relates specifically to the question of law posited.

In *Agdoma v Tomy* (1968) 12 WIR 296, the High Court of St Lucia considered a question submitted by a magistrate as to whether he had made the 'correct decision in point of law in setting aside the convictions and sentences and acceding to a rehearing of the cases'. The order of the Court of Appeal was 'Reference answered in the negative'. Thus the convictions stood without the need for any further order. Summary procedure legislation throughout the region provide that the appellate court may order either party to pay costs both at the summary court level and the Court of Appeal. Such costs may be awarded even if the appeal is abandoned or withdrawn. The awarding of costs in criminal cases is not usual, and the power to do so is dependent on statute. These costs are, however, determined by the Court of Appeal at the time it makes its order. The costs are thus not 'taxed' and are fairly minimal, and in some jurisdictions the amount is fixed by statute.

In *Bharath v Cambridge* (1972) 20 WIR 451, the Court of Appeal dismissed the appeal against conviction 'with costs' emphasising that the appellant had been 'culpably negligent' in failing to appear for his trial. In general, however, costs are granted as the Court of Appeal 'may think just'.[32]

Appealing from the Court of Appeal

While an appellant does not need leave to appeal from a decision of a magistrate, if he wishes to appeal from a dismissal of his appeal by the Court of Appeal he must obtain leave to do so. The Privy Council is still the final Court of Appeal in most jurisdictions. Leave to appeal to the Privy Council in respect of a magistrates' court matter is not frequently sought, perhaps because such matters are not perceived as involving serious penalties or major issues of law. Nonetheless, it may be sought and granted. In *Beswick v R* (1987) 36 WIR 318, PC, the appellant appealed to the Privy Council against the dismissal of his appeal by the Jamaica Court of Appeal. Although the offence involved was a minor traffic offence, the issue of law revolved around the interesting question of whether the convicting magistrate had been functus officio. Since 2005, final appeal lies to the Caribbean Court of Justice in Barbados and Guyana.

32 Summary Courts Act, Chap 4:20, s 152, Trinidad and Tobago.

CHAPTER 10

TRIABLE EITHER WAY

Every offence is either summary or indictable. In Chapter 7, the procedure relating to the trial of summary offences was discussed. In general, an indictable offence is tried by a jury, following the preferring of an indictment, before a judge in the High Court. Statute may nevertheless provide that some indictable offences in given circumstances may be tried summarily in the magistrates' court. This is usually referred to as 'triable either way' matters. In Jamaica, the procedure is somewhat different in that such matters are tried on indictment but in the Parish Court.[1]

The power of magistrates to try these indictable offences emanates wholly from statute, so it is mandatory that the statutory procedure is followed otherwise the court will be acting without jurisdiction. Even if the court breaches the set procedure with the acquiescence of the defendant, this will not validate the procedure: *R v Kent JJ ex p Machin* (1952) 36 Cr App R 23. In this case the defendant elected summary trial on a triable either way offence of larceny. He was told of his rights to trial by jury, and right to consent or not. He was not, however, told of his liability after trial to be committed to the Assizes for sentence under the relevant statute if the magistrate felt that his punishment powers were inadequate.[2] In holding that the court acted illegally, Lord Goddard CJ said:

> The justices took it upon themselves ... to try offences without strict compliance with the provisions of the Act which alone allows an indictable offence to be dealt with summarily.

In the Commonwealth Caribbean there are four instances in which indictable offences may be tried summarily. They are:

- where the offences are 'scheduled' or specified by statute;
- where the offence itself may be charged indictably or summarily;
- where the offence is one in respect of which the inquiring magistrate feels that the evidence establishes a summary offence of a 'like kind'; and
- where a juvenile (usually a person under 16) is charged with a non-capital offence.

Throughout the region, legislation permits that a child may be tried by a magistrate for a noncapital indictable offence and this will be considered in a later chapter. The other instances, however, are not necessarily all applicable to every jurisdiction. In Grenada, for example, there exists no provision for 'scheduled offences', a list of offences which may be tried summarily.

SCHEDULED OR SPECIFIED OFFENCES

In general, summary courts legislation in the various jurisdictions will enable a court:

---

1 Judicature (Resident Magistrates) Act, as amended by Act No 6 of 2016, s 274, Jamaica.

2 This is a requirement before proceeding with summary offences triable either way in some Commonwealth Caribbean jurisdictions such as Barbados, Magistrates' Courts Act 1996–27, s 47(2)(b); St Vincent, Criminal Procedure Code, Cap 172, s 12(2)(b).

> at any time during a preliminary enquiry if it appears to the court, having regard to any representations made in the presence of the accused by or on behalf of the prosecutor or made by the accused, and to the nature of the case, that the punishment that the court has power to inflict under the section would be adequate and the circumstances of the case do not make the offence one of serious character and do not for other reasons require trial on indictment, the court may proceed with a view to summary trial.[3]

The legislation specifies a list of offences that is usually contained in a schedule[4] to the Act in respect of which summary trial may be available. The consent of the accused person to summary trial is invariably a condition precedent to the summary trial except in Guyana.[5] The legislation will specify the procedure to be followed if the court is to proceed summarily in respect of these scheduled offences. The substituted[6] s 46 of the Magistrate's Code of Procedure of Antigua specifies that: where an indictable offence prescribes a penalty that does not exceed a fine of $10,000 or a term of imprisonment of 24 months and the accused either (1) pleads guilty or (2) consents to summary trial the matter may be dealt with summarily. Thus there are no offences listed and the provision is clearer, based simply on penalty.

The procedure

Once the offence is one listed in the relevant schedule, either party, the prosecutor or the defence, may make representations to the court as to why the offence is more suitable for summary trial. In some jurisdictions, like St Vincent and Barbados, the statute[7] stipulates in detail the procedure and the matters to which the magistrate must have regard. The Barbados legislation contains separate provisions enabling the magistrate to decide which mode of trial to embark on before the hearing actually begins (s 46 of the Magistrates' Courts Act 1996) and during the hearing after the preliminary enquiry has begun (s 52(3) and (4) of the Magistrates' Courts Act 1996). The factors which are taken into account, however, are similar. In other jurisdictions the statutory provisions are much more succinct and in Dominica, for example, the court is merely required to 'have regard to all the circumstances of the case'.[8] Representations are usually made before the hearing of the matter actually starts, although statute in Trinidad and Tobago suggests that submissions for summary trial can be made 'at any time during the enquiry'. In St Lucia the procedure is essentially the same, although the references in the statute have now been amended by Act No 11 of 2008 to stipulate 'sufficiency hearing'.

3 Summary Courts Act, Chap 4:20, s 100(2), Trinidad and Tobago. Similar provisions exist in:
Bahamas: Criminal Procedure Code, Ch 91, s 214;
Barbados: Magistrates' Courts Act 1996,as amended by Act 2016–15, s 46;
Dominica: Magistrate's Code of Procedure Act, Chap 4:20, s 43;
Guyana: Summary Jurisdiction (Procedure) Act, Cap 10:02, s 61, as amended by Act 21 of 1978;
St Kitts and Nevis: Magistrate's Code of Procedure Act, Cap 3:17, s 51, s 50;
St Vincent: Criminal Procedure Code, Cap 172, ss 9–12.

4 In the St Lucia Criminal Code 2004 the offences are listed in s 775(9) of the Code.

5 *Kwame Apata v Roberts* (No 1) (1981) 29 WIR 69, p 82.

6 Substituted by s 11 of Act No 13 of 2004.

7 See, e.g., Magistrates' Courts Act 1996, as amended by Act 2016–15, s 46(3), Barbados; Criminal Procedure Code, Cap 172, s 11, St Vincent.

8 Dominica Magistrate's Code of Procedure, Chap 4:20, s 43.

In the final analysis it is for the magistrate, as statute specifies, to make the determination whether the scheduled offence should be tried summarily or not. He will usually consider the nature of the offence; whether the circumstances of the case suggest that the offence is one of a serious character; and the adequacy of the punishment if the (indictable) offence is tried summarily. In *R v Horseferry Road Magistrates' Court ex p K* (1996) 160 JP 441, the English Queen's Bench considered ss 19 and 20 of the Magistrates' Courts Act, the provisions of which are very similar to legislation in the Caribbean. The court concluded that the decision of the magistrate must rest on chiefly 'offence-related' matters, although there is allowance for consideration of the offender in 'any other circumstances of the case'.

In many jurisdictions there is a caveat on the magistrate's exercise of his power to try scheduled indictable offences summarily. The DPP has what may be termed veto powers in insisting that the matter must be tried indictably.[9] In practice, the magistrate will inquire whether the DPP objects before embarking on summary trial even without statutory requirement. There is an acknowledgment of his constitutional powers to take over prosecutions and his power of reversion even when summary trial is embarked upon. This will be discussed below.

Once the magistrate has considered the matters and forms the opinion that the case is more suitable for summary trial, he should explain his decision to the accused person.

Consent

Except in Guyana, generally throughout the region statute provides that before the court can hear a scheduled offence summarily it must obtain the consent of the defendant. Requirement for consent of the accused was abolished in Guyana by s 4 of the Administration of Justice Act No 21 of 1978[10] and the decision to hear the case summarily or not is solely at the discretion of the court.

The defendant is usually asked whether he wishes to be tried by the magistrates' court or by a jury before a judge. It is important that the magistrate explain in ordinary language to a defendant, in particular one who is undefended, what the consequences of the two options are. The Barbados and St Vincent legislation even demands that the court explain to the accused person that, even after he has been found guilty on summary trial (if he chooses summary trial) the magistrate may, exceptionally, commit him for sentence to the High Court if he feels that the antecedents of the defendant indicate that a greater punishment than the magistrate can give is justified. Section 50 of the Barbados Magistrates' Courts Act 1996 enables consent of the accused person to be given by his counsel and even allows the court to proceed in the absence of the accused person once he is legally represented.

If the defendant does not consent or is not given the option to elect his mode of trial in respect of scheduled offences when legislation demands his consent, any ensuing trial will constitute a nullity. In *George v Francois* (1969) 15 WIR 394, a defendant was charged for the indictable offence of assault with intent to rape. The Attorney General felt the matter should have been dealt with summarily. Under his statutory power in Trinidad and Tobago (which is now reserved to the DPP), he referred the case to the magistrate to deal with the case 'accordingly'. The magistrate heard the case summarily without the consent of the defendant. The Trinidad and Tobago Court of Appeal held that the statute required the

9 As in Magistrates' Courts Act 1996, as amended by Act 2016–15, s 46, Barbados.

10 As explained in *Apata v Roberts* (No 1) (1981) 29 WIR 69 and *Apata v Roberts* (No 2) (1981) 32 WIR 219, both decisions of the Court of Appeal of Guyana.

magistrate to consider the matter in accordance with the provisions of the Summary Courts Ordinance enabling summary trial of an indictable offence. The offence was a scheduled offence and the procedure for scheduled offences should have been followed. Since no consent of the defendant was obtained for the hearing of the matter summarily, the court acted without jurisdiction. The conviction and sentence were set aside.

If two or more defendants are jointly charged on one complaint for an indictable offence in respect of which consent is needed for summary trial, they each have a separate right of election: *Nicholls v Brentwood JJ* [1991] 3 All ER 359, HL. In that case, three defendants were jointly charged for an indictable scheduled offence. After representations were made by both sides, the court decided that the matter was suitable for summary trial. The defendants were then put to their statutory election of summary trial or trial by jury. Nicholls and another defendant elected summary trial, but the third stated that he wished to be tried on indictment. The court decided that once one defendant elected indictable trial, all the defendants must be tried indictably and thus proceeded to committal proceedings. The applicant Nicholls sought judicial review to quash the order of committal. The House of Lords reversed the decision of the Queen's Bench Division and held that the right of election as to mode of trial is given to each defendant individually and not collectively to accused persons, even if they are jointly charged. Where one accused person elects summary trial and the co-accused elects trial on indictment, the court should try summarily the accused who elects summary trial and should hold committal proceedings in respect of the accused who elects trial on indictment.

Statute can, however, intervene to change this, as has been done by s 16 of the St Vincent Criminal Code, Cap 172. The section states that where two or more accused persons are jointly charged for a scheduled offence, if one elects indictable trial, then the matter in respect of both must be proceeded with indictably. By the same token, if an accused person is charged with more than one offence which could be tried together on indictment, the offences must all be tried together. The accused person cannot elect summary trial in respect of only one. In such a situation, all offences will be tried on indictment. Otherwise, the accused must elect summary trial in respect of all.

Re-election

Sometimes, a defendant who has elected summary trial in accordance with the relevant statute may seek to withdraw his consent and opt for trial by jury. It has been held by the English courts that a magistrate has a discretion to allow a defendant to withdraw his consent to summary trial: *R v Southampton City JJ ex p Briggs* [1972] 1 All ER 573 following *R v Craske ex p Commissioner of Police of the Metropolis* [1957] 2 All ER 772. In *Ex p Briggs*, the applicant, who was unrepresented, elected summary trial on three charges when the election was put to him by the court. Subsequently, he sought to elect trial by jury on one charge. The court refused on the basis that they had no power to consent to the withdrawal of the defendant's earlier election for summary trial. The Queen's Bench Division held on an application by the defendant for mandamus that the court had a discretion to permit withdrawal of consent and granted mandamus to require the court to exercise that discretion.

In *R v Birmingham JJ ex p Hodgson et al.* [1985] 2 All ER 193, the Queen's Bench was called upon to decide on the magistrate's refusal to allow the defendants to re-elect their mode of trial. They initially elected summary trial when unrepresented. On a subsequent day, their lawyer submitted that the original election had been made by mistake, a failure on the defendants' part to appreciate they had a defence. The defendants had pleaded guilty, but this plea was rejected by the magistrate on hearing the plea in mitigation, which was that they believed that the wood which they were charged with stealing was abandoned. The magistrate had entered a not guilty plea but refused to allow them to re-elect. The Queen's Bench held that the magistrates, having given no reason why they refused to allow the withdrawal, had exercised their discretion improperly.

The court said that the test to be applied by a court in determining whether a defendant should be allowed to re-elect was whether the defendant had properly understood the nature and significance of the choice which he had made when he elected summary trial. The Queen's Bench found that although the defendants in the particular case may have understood the choice they were being asked to make (summary trial or trial by jury), they did not appreciate its significance to them. Since they had intended to and did initially plead guilty to the offence, they were concerned with sentence and did not consider the consequences of the election. In the circumstances of the case in *Ex p Hodgson*, the defendants should have been allowed to withdraw their consent to summary trial and re-elect.

In *Chadee v Santana* (1987) 42 WIR 365, the Trinidad and Tobago Court of Appeal considered an appeal against conviction for possession of cocaine where Dole Chadee, the defendant, was tried summarily. Initially the defendant, represented by junior counsel, had elected summary trial (and pleaded not guilty) in accordance with s 100 of the Summary Courts Act, Chap 4:20. Subsequently the defendant was represented by senior counsel. On his advice the defendant told the court that he wished the case to be tried on indictment. The magistrate refused, saying that the defendant had already elected summary trial on a previous occasion. The defendant was convicted after the ensuing summary trial. The Court of Appeal allowed the appeal and followed *Craske* (above), in which Lord Goddard CJ had said that 'one should not lightly deprive persons of their right to be tried by jury'. The court considered other English authorities where the courts had interpreted the consent requirement in s 25 of the English Magistrates' Court Act 1925, which the court said was analogous to s 100 of the Summary Courts Act.

The Court of Appeal confirmed that the magistrate had a discretion to permit re-election by the defendant. In a 'proper case if the magistrate finds that a defendant is deliberately delaying his trial'[11] he is entitled to take this into account in exercising his discretion to permit re-election. There was no such evidence in the instant case and the magistrate had made no enquiry as to the reason for the withdrawal of consent to summary trial. The case was sent back to the magistrates' court for re-hearing.

Even if a defendant pleads guilty after electing summary trial, he may revisit his consent to summary trial. This in fact did happen in *Ex p Hodgson* (above), but it was the magistrate who had directed that not guilty pleas be entered after hearing the defendants' explanation. The plea was in fact equivocal. Nevertheless, even on an apparently unequivocal plea, the defendant may be permitted to withdraw his consent to summary trial. He may only do this, however, if he first obtains leave to withdraw his guilty plea. In *R v Highbury Corner Magistrates' Court ex p Ali* (unreported, 22 May 1984), cited in *Ex p Hodgson* (above), an unrepresented defendant elected summary trial and pleaded guilty to malicious wounding and the matter was adjourned. On the adjourned date he was allowed to withdraw his plea of guilty on his request, but not his election for summary trial.

It was held on appeal that once a defendant is allowed to withdraw his guilty plea, as he is entitled to do any time before sentence: *S (An Infant) v Recorder of Manchester* [1971] 1 AC 481, HL, he must be permitted to re-elect. His earlier election was not relevant to the not

11 *Chadee v Santana* (1987) 42 WIR 365, p 370.

guilty plea. At the time he elected, he would not have been thinking about where he would be tried, since he knew he intended to plead guilty (per McCullough J in *Ex p Hodgson*).

To sum up, then, a defendant who has consented to summary trial of a (scheduled) indictable offence in accordance with statute may be permitted to withdraw that consent. The magistrate may allow this withdrawal or not at his discretion, but this discretion must be exercised fairly and depends on whether the defendant properly understood the nature and significance of the choice he made. Even a defendant who pleaded guilty may re-elect provided he is allowed to withdraw his guilty plea first. In the latter circumstances, the magistrate really has no discretion, but must permit re-election.

Jamaica procedure provisions

The Jamaica legislation in respect of summary trial of indictable offences is unique in the Commonwealth Caribbean. The relevant legislation is the Judicature (Resident Magistrates) Act, as amended by Act No 6 of 2016, in particular ss 267–305, which deals with the criminal jurisdiction of the judge of the Parish Court. Although each judge of the Parish Court is also ex officio a Justice of the Peace and generally presides over most Petty Sessions (pure summary matters) throughout Jamaica as such, the Judicature (Resident Magistrates) Act as amended by Act No 6 of 2016 confers special powers on him to try indictable offences. The judge of the Parish Court is empowered to try within his parish certain indictable offences indictably. The Parish Court is peculiar in the jurisdiction, since it is not restricted to trying offences summarily as in other jurisdictions. For example, in Trinidad and Tobago, when a magistrate decides to try a scheduled indictable offence and obtains the consent of the accused person, he 'shall proceed to the summary trial[12] of the complaint'. This is so in all jurisdictions other than Jamaica, where a judge of the Parish Court hears an indictable matter in the Parish Court.

Section 268(1) of the Jamaica Act lists a variety of indictable offences which the judge of the Parish Court may try. They range from wounding and related offences; assaults; certain kinds of larceny; offences under the Forgery Act to offences under the Perjury Act. The procedure preliminary to the trial of these offences by the particular judge of the Parish Court is laid down in ss 272–75 of the Act. If a person appears before the judge charged with a listed indictable offence, the judge makes a determination whether he should try the offender or whether he should hold committal proceedings with a view to committal to trial in the Circuit Court (the High Court equivalent).

In making the decision, the judge determines whether his power of punishment is adequate to deal with the offence charged. A judge of the Parish Court is entitled generally to sentence a defendant to as many as three years' imprisonment for an indictable offence, which he tries under his statutory power. For some offences, he may even sentence a person up to four or even five years (such as uttering a forged document) under s 268(2) of the Act.

Having made up his mind to try the offence, the judge then directs the presentation of an indictment for any offence or offences disclosed in the information which is before the court. The information would have been laid for the purposes of committal proceedings into the (indictable) offences charge. The Clerk of the Courts,[13] who is a lawyer assigned to each resident magistrates' court and acts as the prosecutor and chief administrative officer, actually prefers the indictment in the court against the accused person. He opens the case

12 Summary Courts Act, Chap 4:20, s 100(4).

13 Judicature (Resident Magistrates) Act as amended by Act No 6 of 2016, s 16, Jamaica.

for the prosecution by outlining briefly the facts on which they rely and then asks for an order for trial on indictment before the resident magistrate.

Unless any preliminary objection is upheld, the order will be granted. As indicated before, the order may include a direction to include charges not actually specified in the information. The judge must sign the order set out on the information. Before the indictment is drafted, the order is supposed to be recorded on the information before the court. The judge must sign this order before the Clerk of the Courts signs the draft indictment, since it authorises the Clerk to draft the indictment. Failure of the judge to comply with these requirements will result in an ensuing trial being deemed a nullity: *R v Stewart* (1971) 17 WIR 381. The Clerk then signs the actual indictment, thus preferring it before the court for trial. The accused person is after this called upon to plead.

What follows thereafter is the usual procedure for summary trial in terms of the calling of evidence and the making of submissions. Section 282 of the Judicature (Resident Magistrates) Act as amended by Act No 6 of 2016 provides:

> Save as is hereinafter expressly provided, the procedure before any court at the trial of any indictable offence shall be the same, as near as may be, as in the case of offences punishable summarily.

One of the major differences to other jurisdictions, as has been already alluded to, is that the case is tried on indictment and the trial is not a summary one. There are distinct provisions for amendment (s 278), but the powers of adjournment and remand are the same as for preliminary inquiries (s 279). A major difference is that appeal from indictable trial by a judge of the Parish Court is to the Court of Appeal (s 293). This compares with where a judge tries a case under his Petty Sessions jurisdiction when appeal is to the Circuit Court, as provided for in the Justice of the Peace (Jurisdiction) Act.

While in other jurisdictions the procedure to try scheduled/listed indictable offences is essentially dependent on representations, the magistrates' agreement and the consent of the accused, in Jamaica the statutory provisions, while including these matters, are much more detailed and all-encompassing. Furthermore, the indictable offence does not lose its true nature as in the other jurisdictions where the offence is, in the final analysis, 'tried summarily'. In Jamaica, the offence is tried on indictment, but by the judge of the Parish Court and not a jury and judge.

HYBRID OFFENCES

Statute creating particular offences may sometimes stipulate that a person found guilty of the offence may 'on summary conviction' be liable to a particular sentence and alternatively 'on indictable conviction' may be liable to a different sentence. These offences are sometimes termed 'hybrid' offences. It has been conclusively held that such an offence is really an indictable offence because the prosecution has the choice to proceed on indictment: *Hastings and Folkestone Glassworks Ltd v Kalson* [1948] 2 All ER 1013. In that case the defendant was charged for breach of certain Defence (General) Regulations. These provided that a person who contravened any of them should: '(a) on summary conviction be liable to imprisonment ... or to a fine ... or (b) on conviction on indictment, be liable to imprisonment.' The defendant had pleaded guilty before a court of summary jurisdiction and the question arose as to whether he was convicted of an indictable offence. The English Court of Appeal held that the offence was indictable at the time of commission once the prosecution could proceed with it on indictment.

This case was subsequently followed by the Guyana Court of Appeal in *Apata v Roberts* (No 1) (1981) 29 WIR 69, *Apata v Roberts* (No 2) (1981) 31 WIR 219 and *R v Guildhall JJ ex p Marshall* [1976] 1 All ER 767. These authorities seem to confirm that, in respect of hybrid offences, the prosecution alone has the right to elect the mode of charge and trial. In fact in *Apata v Roberts* (No 2), both the majority opinion (Crane C, p 225) and the dissenting opinion (Luckhoo JA, p 237) envisage that the prosecution elects on such cases whether to lay a summary charge or an indictable charge. In respect of summary-laid charges, the magistrate has no power to proceed to indictable trial. Similarly, on an indictably laid charge of a hybrid offence the court had no power (in the absence of statute) to deal with it summarily. In fact, in *Apata v Roberts* (No 2), Crane C specifically said that even if such a practice existed, there is 'no warrant for it'.

Statute may, however, intervene to permit the court to hear an indictably laid hybrid offence summarily. In Trinidad and Tobago, this has been accomplished by the inclusion in the Second Schedule of 'Indictable Offences for which Adults may be tried by Consent by a Summary Court' to the Summary Courts Act, Chap 4:20. These offences are listed in the Second Schedule from 1–33, which include:

> 30 Any offence that is by virtue of any written law both an indictable offence and a summary conviction offence.

In Guyana, the amended[14] First Schedule specifies that 'all indictable offences against any law' with specified enumerated exceptions may be tried summarily. This obviously includes all hybrid offences which have been held to be indictable offences: *Apata v Roberts* (No 2).

The St Vincent Criminal Procedure Code, Cap 172 in like manner provides that the same procedure will apply where the offence is a scheduled offence or one 'which under any other law is triable summarily or on indictment'.[15] Section 45 (as amended in Act No 13 of 2004) of the Magistrate's Code of Procedure, Cap 255, Antigua, allows the prosecution to elect mode of trial in relation to an offence that is 'by virtue of any enactment both an indictable offence and a summary offence'. Presumably, this refers to 'hybrid' indictable offences. This replaced section no longer allows the magistrate to later switch to a summary trial on representation made by either party.

It thus appears that in the above jurisdiction, indictable 'hybrid' offences are treated in the same manner as indictable scheduled offences for purposes of summary trial. This is made possible by statutory intervention outlined above. In those jurisdictions where statute has not intervened, the procedure must be as discussed in *Apata v Roberts* (No 1) and (No 2). The prosecution must elect whether to charge the offence summarily or indictably. Once summary trial is selected, the matter must be proceeded with summarily. By the same token, if the charge is laid indictably, the matter must be proceeded with indictably unless it is discontinued and a summary offence charge laid. There can be no switching to summary trial on an indictably laid charge of such a type in those jurisdictions which do not by statute provide for summary trial of such offences.

This is indicative of the fact that the whole process of summary trial of an indictable offence must be strictly grounded in statute: *R v Kent JJ ex p Machin* (1952) 36 Cr App R 23. In practice, hybrid offences, where the statutory provision provides for summary conviction and indictable conviction, are charged indictably and a switch to summary trial may then occur only if possible under statute.

14 Amended by Act No 21 of 1978.

15 Criminal Procedure Code, Cap 172, s 9(1).

LIKE OFFENCES

There is in some jurisdictions additional power granted to a magistrate to switch from committal proceedings to summary trial. Section 94(1) of the Summary Courts Act, Chap 4:20 of Trinidad and Tobago is reflective of this power:

> Where, upon the holding of any preliminary enquiry on a charge of an indictable offence, the Magistrate is of the opinion that the evidence establishes, or appears likely to establish, the commission of a summary offence of a like kind to the offence charged, the Magistrate may if he thinks fit, and unless the Director of Public Prosecutions otherwise directs, inform the accused person accordingly, and all further proceedings in the case thereafter shall be the same as if a complaint had been made against such persons for such latter offence.

An identical provision appears in s 6 in the Grenada Criminal Procedure (Preliminary Inquiries) Act No 35 of 1978. In fact in Grenada, this is the only statutory entitlement for a court to hear an indictable matter summarily. There are no provisions as in the rest of the region listing scheduled offences which may be tried either way.

The Magistrate's Code of Procedure Acts of both Antigua and St Kitts and Nevis also provide for like offences in identical sections.[16] The Summary Jurisdiction (Procedure) Act, Cap 10:02 of Guyana contains (s 33) a provision identical to that of Antigua and St Kitts and Nevis. These provisions are similar to that of Trinidad and Tobago except that there appears to be no veto power of the DPP to direct otherwise, as in the Trinidad and Tobago section. The Dominica law reflected in s 6 of Act No 14 of 1995 is the same as that of the Trinidad and Tobago law except in one material aspect. The statute refers to 'the commission of a summary offence similar to the offence charged' rather than 'of a like kind to the offence charged'.

Effect

In the final analysis, however, these provisions are basically the same in their effect, which is to allow a magistrate the power to stay the preliminary enquiry into an indictable and proceed to summary proceedings. The difference between this procedure and that where an accused person elects summary trial of a scheduled offence is that the summary proceedings under this law need not be for the same offence. The law authorises the magistrate to switch to summary proceedings if he believes the evidence establishes the commission of a summary offence 'of a like kind' or of a similar kind, as the Dominican law states. This would clearly suggest that the magistrate is proceeding on a similar but different offence, the essential difference being that it is summary.

One effect of the like/similar offence provisions is that a magistrate may switch from holding a preliminary enquiry from a purely indictable offence to summary proceedings. This is possible once he believes that the evidence justifies it. The original offence itself need not be a triable either way offence and neither the prosecution nor the defence are required to make representations or consent to the ensuing summary trial. In *Robbles v Glanville* (1964) 7 WIR 220, a case from Trinidad and Tobago, the appellant was charged with unlawful wounding, which was a triable either way offence. Although the defendant was offered

16 Magistrate's Code of Procedure Act, Cap 255, s 48, Antigua, is identical to Magistrate's Code of Procedure Act, Cap 3:17, s 53, St Kitts and Nevis.

summary trial under the scheduled offences provisions, he refused to consent. The magistrate nonetheless determined that the offence was not of a serious character and decided to proceed under the 'like offence' provision. He called upon the defendant to answer a charge of assault occasioning a wound. The defendant refused to plead on this charge: a plea of not guilty was entered and he was convicted after trial.

The defendant appealed and contended that the magistrate had no jurisdiction to act as he did, since assault occasioning a wound was not of a like kind to the indictable offence of unlawful wounding. It was also suggested that the magistrate acted as he did under prompting by the prosecution and this was improper. In the Court of Appeal, Wooding CJ held that when acting under s 91 (now s 94(1)) of the Trinidad and Tobago Summary Courts Ordinance, the magistrate was free to act upon representation or application by either side, even though neither side is bound to make such representations. The magistrate may also act upon his own initiative and in any event the final decision is his.

In respect of whether the assault was a like offence, the court followed the English case of *Re Black Bolt and Nut Association of Great Britain's Agreement* (No 2) [1961] 3 All ER 139. The court held that 'like' is not synonymous with identical, and 'offences may be like offences if they have essential features in common'. If the essential constituents of the offence are in substance the same, the two qualify to be classified as being of a like kind. The appeal was dismissed and the conviction affirmed.

The procedure

Provision for switching to summary proceedings for a like offence (to the indictable charge) is only available in particular jurisdictions. Furthermore, they are invoked only rarely, except perhaps in Grenada where there are no other provisions for summary hearings of indictable matters. Nonetheless, if a magistrate wishes to convert a preliminary hearing to a summary trial under his 'like offence' power in Antigua, Dominica, Grenada, Guyana, St Kitts and Nevis, and Trinidad and Tobago he should have regard to *Robbles v Glanville* (above). The statute suggests that the conversion should be done upon the holding of the preliminary enquiry and it is suggested that this means before the defence is called upon. This is so because the defence should be asked to plead to the substituted like summary offence as was done in *Robbles v Glanville* (above). The magistrate must inform the defendant that he intends to deal with the matter summarily under his statutory power and without defence consent. If the defendant is not allowed to plead again, the ensuing proceedings may amount to a nullity.

It is necessary that a 'like' offence of a summary nature actually exists in order to utilise the statutory provision. In *George v Francois* (1969) 15 WIR 394, the Trinidad and Tobago Court of Appeal made it clear that a magistrate on invoking s 91 (now s 94(1)) must find a like offence to the indictable offence charged. The Court of Appeal said that there was no summary offence akin to assault with intent to commit rape with which the defendant was charged indictably. The only offences of a like kind to it were indictable offences. Thus, s 91 could not be invoked.

After the magistrate informs the defendant of his decision and specifies the summary offence which he intends to substitute, the defendant should plead again. It does not appear necessary for the prosecution to lead the evidence again from the start. The tenor of the statutory provision suggests that the magistrate merely continues the hearing, albeit for a new (summary) offence. *Robbles v Glanville* (above) also suggests that this is the proper procedure. It may be so because the evidence up to the time of conversion would have 'established the commission' of the summary offence in respect of which the court now chooses to proceed.

It is thus apparent that the 'like offence' provisions do not really permit offences to be tried either way, but authorises a special procedure to be invoked if the evidence at the preliminary enquiry appears to establish not the indictable offence charged, but a similar or like summary offence.

REVERSION

Legislation in several jurisdictions permits either the magistrate or the DPP or both to revert to indictable proceedings in respect of an indictable offence in which it was originally decided to proceed summarily. Sometimes the legislation may even go so far as to permit the court or DPP to stay any summary hearing of a complaint and proceed with the matter indictably.[17] This power is, however, usually only exercised in relation to triable either way offences.

Thus, if an indictable matter is being heard summarily in accordance with the relevant statute, the presiding magistrate or the DPP has the option to change his original decision to hear the matter summarily. This is only possible if statute grants this power to the magistrate and/or the DPP. It appears that in some jurisdictions, such as St Kitts and Nevis, there is no provision specifically authorising reversion by the magistrate or the DPP. Where this occurs, the DPP may act under his constitutional power to discontinue the summary proceedings before the case is completed and direct that charges be re-laid to proceed indictably in accordance with the principles in *Richards (Lloydell) v R* (1992) 41 WIR 263, PC.

The magistrate

In the Bahamas, Barbados, Grenada, Guyana, St Lucia and Trinidad and Tobago[18] where a court during the summary hearing of a case feels that the matter should be heard indictably, it may stay the summary proceedings and hold a preliminary enquiry. The Bahamas provision allows the magistrate to act 'before or during the course of the trial'. In Barbados, the magistrate may discontinue the summary trial 'at any time before the conclusion of the evidence for the prosecution'. The law in the other jurisdictions suggests that the switch to indictable proceedings must occur 'upon the hearing of the complaint'. In St Lucia the provision reads 'at any time during a sufficiency hearing'. In Jamaica[19] 'at any stage of the trial' prior to the defence case, a judge of the Parish Court may switch from trying a listed indictable offence to holding committal proceedings pursuant to trial by the Circuit Court, if he thinks the nature of the proceedings demand it.

But for the Bahamas, then, it appears that the magistrate must act after the hearing has started. In *R v Birmingham Stipendiary Magistrate ex p Webb* (1992) 157 JP 89, the English Queen's Bench considered s 25(2) of the Magistrates' Court Act which allows a magistrate to switch to indictable proceedings. Section 25(2) stipulates in part:

17 As in Grenada, Criminal Procedure Code, Cap 72B, s 85; Trinidad and Tobago, Summary Courts Act, Chap 4:20, s 55.

18 Bahamas: Criminal Procedure Code, Ch 91, s 215; Barbados: Magistrates' Courts Act 1996, as amended by Act 2016–15, s 52(2); Grenada: Criminal Procedure Code, Cap 72B, s 85; Guyana: Summary Jurisdiction (Procedure) Act, Cap 10:02, s 34; St Lucia: Criminal Code 2004, s 775(2); Trinidad and Tobago: Summary Courts Act, Chap 4:20, s 55.

19 Jamaica, Judicature (Resident Magistrates) Act, as amended by Act No 6 of 2016, s 275.

> Where the court has begun ... to try the information summarily the court may, at any time before the conclusion of the evidence for the prosecution, discontinue summary trial.[20]

In that case the magistrate decided to deal summarily with a charge of supplying controlled drugs. On the adjourned date, the matter came up before a stipendiary magistrate who decided that the case was better suited for indictable trial. The court (Mann LJ) held on an application for judicial review that the power of the court to switch did not arise until after the court had begun to try the case. It follows, then, that in those jurisdictions which specify that the magistrate must act only during the 'hearing' or the trial that the magistrate cannot switch until the trial has actually started.

Nonetheless, this does not mean that the magistrate can only act after the hearing of evidence in such cases. While the entering of a plea of not guilty does not begin the trial process, a court may begin a trial without hearing evidence, such as where it entertains preliminary submissions: *R v Horseferry Road Magistrates' Court ex p K* (1996) 160 JP 441. In that case the Queen's Bench confirmed that the jurisdiction of the magistrates' court in respect of re-opening the mode of trial is entirely statutory. If the legislation says or suggests that a magistrate can only switch when the trial has started, it must be strictly complied with. The court, however, held that there are a number of possible circumstances in which, after a plea of not guilty and before the commencement of the evidence, it can become apparent that the court had embarked upon the trial process. One such circumstance is where the defence makes and the magistrate considers submissions in support of a preliminary ruling.

In Dominica the magistrate's power to switch only applies where the magistrate has reduced the indictable charge to summary where the evidence appears to establish a summary offence 'similar to the offence charged': s 6 of the Criminal Procedure (Preliminary Inquiries) Act 14 of 1995. After reducing the charge to a summary one, the court may thereafter still deal with the offence as an indictable one if it thinks fit to do so. It appears that the power is exercisable once the offence is 'being dealt with'.[21]

Even though the power of the magistrate to switch in such a jurisdiction is more limited than in Trinidad and Tobago and similar jurisdictions, it appears that in the final analysis the power must be exercised when summary trial has begun. This may be so because it is only then that the court might be able to determine that the matter is more suitable for indictable proceedings and 'ought to be tried'[22] as an indictable offence. Despite the fact that the magistrate's discretion to switch to indictable proceedings appears to be unfettered (once he acts after the trial has started), it has been held that the court ought not to act unreasonably: *R v West Norfolk JJ ex p McMullen* (1992) 157 JP 461. In that case, two co-accused elected trial by jury on a charge of theft. The defendant elected summary trial and the case proceeded as such in recognition of the decision in *Nicholls v Brentwood JJ* [1991] 3 All ER 359, HL, that each co-accused has an individual right of election. Nonetheless, after the first witness for the prosecution had given evidence, the prosecution asked the magistrate to exercise his discretion to discontinue the summary trial and proceed with committal proceedings, since it was preferable that all the accused be tried together. On a judicial review application, the Queen's Bench held that this would be an improper exercise of its jurisdiction by the court since it was designed to get around the difficulty in *Nicholls* (above).

20 Barbados Magistrates' Courts Act, as amended by Act 2016–15, s 52(2) is identical to this. It is patterned on this section.

21 Act No 14 of 1995, s 9.

22 As stated in relevant statutory provisions of the Bahamas, Grenada, Guyana and Trinidad and Tobago.

Thus a court must have good reason to exercise its discretion to switch from summary trial to indictable proceedings (a preliminary enquiry).

DPP's power

In some jurisdictions, the DPP has specific powers under the relevant procedure legislation to direct the magistrate to switch to indictable proceedings. This is so, for instance, in Grenada, Guyana, Jamaica, and Trinidad and Tobago. In Guyana the DPP has the same power as the magistrate under s 34 of the Summary Jurisdiction (Procedure) Act, Cap 10:02 on the hearing of the complaint. Section 277 of the Jamaica Judicature (Resident Magistrates) Act as amended by Act No 6 of 2016 gives the DPP power 'at any time before' the defence case to require the judge of the Parish Court to deal with a case as one for indictable trial in the Parish Court. In Trinidad and Tobago, the DPP may 'at any time before decision' in the case require the magistrate to revert to indictable hearing in respect of an indictable offence which is being proceeded with summarily: s 95 of the Summary Courts Act, Chap 4:20.

In Grenada there exist two provisions for the DPP to direct a switch to indictable hearing. He may act under s 85 of the Criminal Procedure Code, Cap 72 B with the same power as a magistrate (identical to Guyanese s 34) or under s 7 of Act 35 of 1978. The latter power is only in respect of 'like' offences where the indictable charge was reduced to a like summary offence under that Act. This s 7 power of the DPP is identical to that of the DPP in Dominica, which also is solely in respect of 'like' offences: s 8 of Act No 14 of 1995. Both the s 8 provision in Dominica and the s 7 power in the Grenadian statute may be invoked 'at any time before a decision'.

In invoking his power to direct the magistrate to switch, the DPP must usually proceed in writing and this is stipulated in most statutes. The magistrate will usually adjourn if the prosecution asks for an adjournment to ask the DPP to invoke his statutory power to require the magistrate to deal with the case as one for indictment. In fact, some statutes specify this. In *DPP v Sullivan* (1996) 54 WIR 256, the Full Court of Guyana considered the extent of the DPP's power under s 34 of the Summary Jurisdiction (Procedure) Act, Cap 10:02.

In that case a defendant was charged with conspiracy to defraud, a scheduled offence triable either way. Summary trial was suggested by the prosecution, the defence agreed and the magistrate decided to deal with the offence summarily in accordance with his statutory power under s 61 of Cap 10:02. About a year later, counsel for the prosecution made an oral application to switch the mode of trial. The magistrate refused and, some weeks after, the DPP wrote to the magistrate intimating that he wished to exercise his power under s 34. This section states:

> If upon the hearing of a complaint it appears to the court that the cause ought to be tried as an indictable offence before the High Court or if the Director of Public Prosecutions intimates to the court his opinion in writing to that effect, further proceedings in the case as for a summary conviction offence shall be stayed, and depositions taken and the case shall in all other respects be dealt with as if the charge had been originally one for an indictable offence.

The Full Court held that the DPP had wide powers both under the Constitution and under s 34 to review an earlier decision and direct the magistrate as he did to proceed indictably. Once the DPP acted within the ambit of his statutory powers, as he did here by intimating his wishes in writing, the section is mandatory and the magistrate is bound to comply with his direction to stop the summary proceedings. It should be noted that although no evidence had been taken, the defendants had pleaded and statements filed in accordance with s 61 of Cap 10:02. It would seem that the hearing had commenced within the ambit of the principles laid down in *Ex p K* (above). The power of the DPP to direct the magistrate to switch is in addition to his constitutional power to discontinue any criminal proceedings, as was made clear in *Sullivan* (above). So, in those jurisdictions where there is no specific statutory provision for switching, the DPP may invoke his general statutory powers to discontinue and relay indictable charges. Furthermore, this power to switch is separate and apart from the power of the DPP, after committal on a preliminary enquiry, to direct that the case is suitable for summary trial. This provision is contained in the relevant criminal procedure provisions[23] of most jurisdictions. It is, however, exercisable only if the offence is one triable either way: *George v Francois* (1969) 15 WIR 394. In that case, the Attorney General, under his statutory power (now enjoyed by the DPP), directed the magistrate to deal with an offence summarily in accordance with the law. The Trinidad and Tobago Court of Appeal held that the magistrate could only proceed summarily under the relevant statutory provisions permitting an indictable offence to be tried summarily. For the offence of assault with intent to rape, a scheduled offence, to be dealt with summarily the accused had to consent.

On plea of guilty

Where the power of switching to indictable proceedings, whether by the DPP or the magistrate, is exercisable after the trial has started, it cannot be exercised after a plea of guilty has been taken: *Chief Constable v Gillard* [1985] 3 All ER 634, HL. In that case the House considered the English s 25(2), which allows a magistrate to discontinue summary trial 'where the court has . . . begun to try the information summarily'. The court held that once an accused person had pleaded guilty on a triable either way matter and the plea had been accepted, it could not be considered that there was an actual trial. The plea of guilty disposed with the need for the prosecution to prove its case and thus no evidence need be led. It could not be said that the prosecution had begun to 'try' its case on a plea of guilty as 'trial' denotes the process of determining the guilt or innocence of the accused person. Thus, where a defendant pleaded guilty after summary trial was decided upon, the court could not revert to indictable proceedings, unless statute clearly suggested otherwise. The time for reversion had passed.

The legislation in most of the Commonwealth jurisdictions which permits reversion suggests that a trial must have begun. Phrases such as 'upon the hearing' of the complaint and at 'any stage of trial' (Jamaica) are clearly indicative of this.

THE PROCEDURE

In respect of all indictable offences, whether triable either way or not, the procedure in the magistrates' court is at the outset as if the offence is to be dealt with as an indictable offence. The magistrate will usually read the (indictable) charge to the accused person and inform him that he is not called upon to plead.

Once the court assumes the power to deal with the matter summarily (after following the statutory requirements), the procedure from that moment is the same as for trial of a summary offence.[24] The defendant will be called upon to plead, and if he pleads not guilty

23 E.g., Magistrates' Courts Act 1996 as amended by Act 2016–15, s 27, Barbados.

24 This is specifically detailed in some jurisdictions such as Antigua, Magistrate's Code of Procedure, Cap 255, s 238; Dominica, Magistrate's Code of Procedure, Chap 4:20, s 211; St Lucia, Criminal Code, s 773(a).

the trial will commence as soon as the court can begin the hearing. If the hearing had already begun before it is decided to proceed summarily, it is not necessary to take again the evidence of a witness who already gave evidence. Instead, such witness will be recalled for cross-examination by the defence.

In Guyana, statute has outlined a unique procedure following the decision to deal with the matter summarily. Act 21 of 1978 amending s 61 of the Summary Jurisdiction (Procedure) Act, Cap 10:02, specifies at s 61(6) to 61(10) that the prosecution must provide advance information to the defence. This is accomplished by the filing of copies of statements of all prosecution witnesses with the Clerk of the Courts. The accused will be entitled to copies of these statements and the prosecution cannot call any witness whose statement has not been so filed. Thus statute in Guyana has intervened to ensure disclosure to the defence (and the court) in the same way that depositions would have been disclosed had the indictable offence (now tried summarily) been tried indictably.

Sentence

In most jurisdictions, statute does specify an increased sentence where an indictable offence is tried summarily. This is usually subject to special provision in relation to certain offences where the statute creating the offence specifies a particular penalty upon summary conviction. Such offences include possession of illegal narcotics, trafficking in illegal narcotics and illegal possession of firearms. Penalties on summary conviction for those offences are usually greater than those for other indictable offences tried summarily.

In general, summary offences carry a maximum penalty of six months' imprisonment or a suitable alternative fine (depending on the value of the dollar in the different countries). When an indictable offence is tried summarily, however, the maximum penalty may be increased to two years' imprisonment as in Barbados.[25] In Trinidad and Tobago[26] the maximum penalty was increased to five years in 2004. Section 59 of the new Magistrates' Courts Act 1996 of Barbados provides for a wide range of sentencing in the case of indictable offences tried summarily; for instance, on a second conviction an offender may be liable to imprisonment for five years. In other jurisdictions it may be as many as five years even on a first conviction; the Bahamas, s 7 of the Criminal Procedure Code, Ch 91, now provides that the magistrate must comply with sentencing guidelines in relation to sentencing of indictable offences tried summarily.

In Jamaica[27] the maximum penalty for these offences is three years generally, four years for certain larceny offences and five years for certain offences under the Forgery Act. By virtue of Act 2 of 2000, the alternative maximum fine is now one million dollars. In St Vincent[28] the maximum is five years or $15,000 and the court even has a discretion to send the matter for sentence to the High Court if it is felt that heavier punishment is necessary. Section 61 of the Guyanese law as amended by Act 21 of 1978 provides that the maximum penalty for indictable offences triable summarily is three years or $15,000. Section 775(5) of the St Lucia Code provides similarly but for two years or $2,000.

In other jurisdictions where no special sentence is provided the penalty will be the same as for a summary offence.

---

25 Magistrates' Courts Act 1996, s 59(a), for first conviction.

26 Chap 4:20, s 100(5), amended by Act No 6 of 2004.

27 Judicature (Resident Magistrates) Act, as amended by Act No 6 of 2016, s 268.

28 St Vincent Criminal Procedure Code, Cap 172, ss 17 and 19.

Appeals

In general, there is no difference between appeals from the magistrates' court where indictable offences are tried in that court as compared to appeals in relation to pure summary offences. In both situations, appeal is to the Court of Appeal, just as is an appeal from the High Court.

In Guyana and Jamaica there is a difference in procedure. This stems from the fact that usual summary appeal is not to the Court of Appeal. In Guyana it is to the Full Court of the High Court and in Jamaica it is to the Circuit Court (High Court). Where indictable matters are tried in the Parish Court, however, appeal in both jurisdictions is to the respective Court of Appeal.[29,30] Presumably, this is in recognition of the fact that these matters are more serious than trivial summary offences.

29 As provided in Judicature (Resident Magistrates) Act, as amended by Act No 6 of 2016, s 293, Jamaica; Summary Jurisdiction (Procedure) Act, Cap 10:02, s 61(12) as amended by Act 21 of 1978, Guyana.

30 Any offence that is by virtue of any written law both an indictable offence and a summary conviction offence.

CHAPTER 11

COMMITTAL PROCEEDINGS

Unlike summary trials, indictable trials[1] consist of a two-stage process:

(a) the preliminary enquiry[2] (or inquiry); and
(b) the trial by jury before a judge.

The first stage, which is sometimes called the committal proceedings, is presided over by a magistrate in the magistrates' court. The magistrate sits as an enquiring magistrate whose function it is to determine at the end of the proceedings whether a prima facie case is made out against the accused person to justify his trial by a jury.

Indictable trials are held in respect of:

- offences which are triable only indictably by a jury before a judge such as murder, treason, manslaughter and rape among others; and
- those indictable offences which may be tried by a magistrate, as discussed in Chapter 10, but where the final decision is to proceed indictably to trial in the High Court.

This chapter focusses on the rationale for committal proceedings, the procedure to be followed in the preliminary enquiry (including the need for strict compliance with the relevant statute) and the effects of a committal to trial or a discharge by the magistrate.

THE BACKGROUND

Committal proceedings are the creation of statute. The function of these proceedings has historically been to allow examining justices (now the magistrate in the Commonwealth Caribbean) to decide whether the evidence adduced by the prosecution establishes a prima facie case that the defendant has committed an indictable offence. No one should stand trial by a jury for such an offence unless a prima facie case against him has been made out by the prosecution: *R v Epping and Harlow* [1973] 1 All ER 1011. Although it has been said that committal proceedings are not intended to allow an accused person to explore the evidence as a rehearsal for trial,[3] this statement was made in the context of the application of s 1 of the English Criminal Justice Act 1967. That section introduced the alternative procedure of committal without consideration of the evidence, which committal evidently was not meant to be a rehearsal for trial.

---

1 This is of course except in Antigua and St Lucia which at the time of writing had effectively abolished preliminary enquiries. In Jamaica, the Committal Proceedings Act No 24 of 2013 abolished preliminary enquiries in favour of new style 'committal proceedings' (discussed later in this chapter). Old-style preliminary enquiries are still being conducted in certain instances. Also in Jamaica, committal proceedings are not held for those indictable offences, specified in the Judicature (Resident Magistrates) Act, as amended by Act No 6 of 2016 s 268, which are tried on indictment by a judge of the Parish Court. In Barbados, committal proceedings are conducted under the provisions of either the old Magistrates' Courts Act 1996–27 or the amended Magistrates' Courts Act (amended by Act No 15 of 2016 discussed later in this chapter).

2 The spelling of the word varies among the jurisdictions.

3 *R v Grays JJ ex p Tetley* (1979) 70 Cr App R 11.

In Commonwealth Caribbean jurisdictions, however, where full committal proceedings are still more common than any form of paper committal, it is considered, in line with the older English authorities, that depositions are taken to enable the person charged to know what might be proved against him: *R v Stiginani* [1867] 10 Cox CC 552. The object is to allow the accused to prepare to defend himself adequately, in any way he thinks fit, against a serious indictable charge. It has also been opined that depositions, evidence documented usually in written form at the preliminary enquiry, are taken because of the possibility that a witness might be unable to attend the trial through death or otherwise: *R v Ward* (1848) 3 Cox CC 279.

In the Commonwealth Caribbean region, the consensus appears to be that the prosecution is not entitled to keep evidence up its sleeve to create an element of surprise at trial. In *R v Gomes* (1962) 5 WIR 7, the Supreme Court of Guyana (then British Guiana) endorsed statements of Lord Devlin to this effect in his book *Criminal Prosecution of England*, p 93. The Supreme Court felt that the preliminary enquiry serves the dual purposes of making the person aware of the case he has to meet as well as giving him an opportunity to probe and counter it. This, it is suggested, appears to be the rationale for full committal proceedings which are still the norm in the Commonwealth Caribbean. It seems that the chief purpose is to allow full disclosure of the prosecution's case to the defence. Support for this view may be had from the very fact that in England, where full committal proceedings were effectively abolished by the Criminal Procedure and Investigations Act 1996, that very Act provides for a detailed system of pre-trial disclosure. For the first time, disclosure has been made a requirement by statute, at the same time that the taking of oral evidence at committal proceedings was abolished.

While there have been frequent suggestions that preliminary enquiries should be abolished,[4] it is unlikely that this will be achieved unless detailed pre-trial disclosure of all the evidence of the prosecution, which is now achieved by the preliminary enquiry, is made mandatory. In the Commonwealth Caribbean, while in some cases disclosure is recognised as necessary prior to trial at indictable level, it is not a mandatory pre-trial condition. This fact has not generally proven to be detrimental because of the disclosure afforded by the preliminary enquiry, but if this were abolished the defendant would be adversely affected.

In these jurisdictions, therefore, where paper committals, even when permitted by statute, are rare, full committal proceedings maintain their essential and original nature. They are to permit the accused person to know the case he has to meet and to allow the magistrate to decide whether a prima facie indictable case has been made out against the accused person.

THE DUTIES OF THE PROSECUTION

Arising from the accepted functions and purpose of the preliminary enquiry, as outlined above, the prosecution in committal proceedings has certain consequential duties.

Leading all the evidence

If the accused person is not to be surprised at trial, the prosecution should produce all the evidence at the preliminary enquiry that is to be led at trial. This requirement may not be as stringent in respect of preliminary enquiries conducted by paper committals (*Ex p Tetley*

4 Richards, S, 'Reform in the magistrates' courts in Barbados', *The Lawyer*, July 1994, p 41.

(above)) because this type of committal proceedings is designed as a shortcut to a full committal hearing.

In *Gomes* (above), the Supreme Court of Guyana considered an objection to the admissibility of fresh evidence of a material nature at a rape trial. The evidence contained in a statement to the police had been available to the prosecution at the time of the preliminary enquiry. The court considered then (in 1962) English authorities relating to full committal proceedings and held that where evidence is available to the prosecutor at the time of the preliminary enquiry and is not led, such evidence is inadmissible at the trial in the Supreme Court. This is so even if the prosecution at trial files notice of additional evidence and serves the notice on the defence, as was provided[5] for in s 151 of the Criminal Law (Procedure) Ordinance.[6] Even though common law[7] also sanctions the admissibility of such fresh evidence at trial, the court in *Gomes* was of the opinion that the additional or fresh evidence must not have been available at trial.

Support for this proposition can be found in *Cadogan v R* (1963) 6 WIR 292. In that case, the appellant had been discharged by the magistrate at the conclusion of a preliminary enquiry into a charge of murder against him. The prosecution thereafter caused another information to be laid against him for the same offence and a further enquiry was held, at the conclusion of which the appellant was committed to stand trial. In this second enquiry, two witnesses were called who were not called in the first preliminary enquiry, although they had been available to give evidence at the time. After the appellant had been tried and convicted, he appealed. The Trinidad and Tobago Court of Appeal held that the second committal proceedings were invalid, since evidence which had been available initially ought not to have been called as 'additional' or fresh evidence in the later proceedings.

In *Abdool Salim Yaseen and Thomas v The State* (1990) 44 WIR 219, the Guyana Court of Appeal re-examined *Gomes* and the whole history involved on the issue of evidence not led at the preliminary enquiry, although in the possession of the prosecution, now sought to be admitted at trial (esp. 253–55).

The court commended the principles in *Gomes* as a sensible balance between two legitimate interests – the public interest that the guilty be brought to justice as against an accused person's right to full disclosure of the case he has to meet. While the court declined to amend the judgment, it recognised that had the practice in Guyana been as in England to furnish an accused person with copies of statements of all witnesses on whom they intend to rely the position might have been different (at 255). It was key to the fair trial of an accused person that he was assured of adequate time and facilities for the preparation of his defence.

In summary then, if the only means that an accused person has of knowing the case he ultimately has to answer is the evidence given at the preliminary enquiry (there was no previous disclosure), it would follow that evidence not led at the preliminary enquiry, which was in the prosecution's possession, ought not to be admitted at trial. If the prosecution had disclosed all witness statements to the defence, evidence of a witness not given at the preliminary enquiry would be allowed, consistent with earlier authorities.

It has been suggested that if the prosecution intends to call a witness at trial who did not give evidence at the preliminary enquiry, it needs simply to serve notice of intention to do so along with a copy of the witness statement to the defence: *Berry (Linton) v R* (1992) 41 WIR

5 There are statutory provisions for additional evidence at trial in some other jurisdictions such as the Bahamas: Criminal Procedure Code, Ch 91, s 166; Barbados: Magistrates' Courts Act 1996–27, s 26(3); St Kitts and Nevis: Criminal Procedure Code, Cap 4:06, s 29; St Vincent: Criminal Procedure Code, Cap 172, s 191.

6 Now the Criminal Law (Procedure) Act, Cap 10:01.

7 See *Berry (Linton) v R* (1992) 41 WIR 244, p 249, PC.

244, PC. While this may represent the practice in Jamaica, if available evidence is inadvertently not led at the preliminary enquiry, it is suggested that this does not represent the practice in the rest of the Commonwealth Caribbean. In jurisdictions other than Jamaica, there is provision for the prosecution through the DPP (or Attorney General in the Bahamas) after the committal proceedings to refer the case back to the magistrate, directing him to reopen the inquiry to take further evidence.[8] This is a special power given when there has been a committal for trial, but the DPP considers that all the available evidence has not been led by the prosecution.

It was held in *Gomes*, p 11 (above) that the availability of this procedure ensured that the prosecution does not suffer where a prosecutor by careless omission fails to lead certain available evidence. On the directions of the DPP, the magistrate may reopen the enquiry and take evidence of a witness either who did not give evidence, although his statement is on the prosecution file, or who gave incomplete evidence. This procedure is effectively a continuation of the preliminary enquiry after which the accused person must again be committed to stand trial.

In Jamaica, there appears to be, following committal for trial, no power of referral back by the DPP to cause the Judge of the Parish Court to reopen the enquiry. Accordingly, it is arguable that the rule requiring that the prosecution produce all its available evidence at the preliminary enquiry may be applied less strictly here. *Berry* (above) seems to suggest that such evidence may yet be admitted at trial. Thus in Jamaica, once notice of additional evidence is served, a court is more inclined than not to allow additional evidence of a witness to be given at trial which was not given at the preliminary enquiry even though available then. This would cure a situation where a prosecutor inadvertently omits to lead material evidence which was contained in his brief. It should be noted that it is now the practice in Jamaica to disclose statements of all potential witnesses at the preliminary enquiry stage.

It seems that in most Commonwealth Caribbean jurisdictions the prosecution is expected to disclose its entire case against the accused person at the committal stage. If this is not done, evidence which was available at the preliminary enquiry stage, but was not called, may in general not be produced at the trial stage.

Disclosure

It has been settled that a magistrate's function as an examining magistrate does not include a determination whether the prosecution has provided adequate disclosure: *DPP v Chief Magistrate (No 2)* (2003) 67 WIR 240. The only determination the magistrate makes is whether a prima facie case has been made out. While the magistrate does not make the determination on disclosure, however, the principles of fairness, as reflected in the common law on disclosure that has developed in the region, determine what disclosure is required of a prosecutor at the preliminary enquiry stage.

Apart from producing all its proposed evidence at the preliminary enquiry, the prosecution, when fairness demands, may be required to make other material available to the

8 Bahamas: Criminal Procedure Code, Ch 91, s 138;
Barbados: Magistrates' Courts Act 1996–27 as amended by Act 2016–15, s 26;
Dominica: Criminal Law and Procedure Act, Chap 12:01, s 15(6);
Grenada: Criminal Procedure Code, Cap 72B, s 112;
Guyana: Criminal Law (Procedure) Act, Cap 10:01, s 77;
St Kitts and Nevis: Criminal Procedure Act, Cap 4:06, s 14;
St Vincent: Criminal Procedure Code, Cap 172, s 160;
Trinidad and Tobago: Indictable Offences (Preliminary Inquiry) Act, Chap 12:01, s 27.

defence. Such material may include original statements given to the police by persons who have been called as witnesses at the preliminary enquiry. In England, where oral evidence is no longer given, such a statement will constitute part of the 'bundle' served on the defence. In the Caribbean region, where paper committals are still a rarity, the real evidence is given viva voce and an original statement need only be disclosed if it is at variance with the oral evidence: *Milton (Audley) v R* (1996) 49 WIR 306, PC. In that case the evidence given by two prosecution witnesses at the preliminary enquiry and later the trial was substantially different from the contents of their statements made to the police. The prosecution did not disclose the original statement of these witnesses, Gayle and Anderson, and the discrepancies only came to the attention of the defence prior to the hearing of the appeal at the Privy Council. In allowing the appeal, the Board held that, given the serious discrepancies between the statements and the evidence, the statements should have been shown to the defence at or even before the preliminary hearing. It seems apparent that the defence was treated shabbily, in that it was deprived of the opportunity to cross-examine crucial witnesses (in a murder case) on their previous inconsistent statements.

Because of the strong words of censure used by the Privy Council against the prosecution in *Audley* (above) and the earlier case of *Berry (Linton) v R* (1992) 41 WIR 244, PC, a practice in Jamaica has evolved of disclosing all original statements of prosecution witnesses to the defence. This seems rather unnecessary and the multitude of paper may even cloud the fact that a few witnesses may have, at the enquiry, departed from their original statements. More importantly, the practice begs the question of whether in such circumstances it is necessary to have any oral hearing at all. One of the purposes of a preliminary hearing would have been defeated, that of making the prosecution's case known to the defence.

Nevertheless, the law, as distinct from practice, recognises that at the very least previous inconsistent statements of the witnesses must be disclosed to the defence: *Berry* (above). Furthermore, it has always been recognised that the prosecution must either call all credible witnesses itself or make them available to the defence: *Dallison v Caffery* [1964] 2 All ER 610; *John v R* (1965) 8 WIR 302. It was held in *John* that the prosecution need not make available the statements of all witnesses it does not call, only of 'credible' witnesses. It would seem, however, that it ought not to be up to the prosecution to make a judgment call of who is or is not credible unless there can be no doubt as to his complete unreliability. The defence should be entitled to make its own decision as to whether a witness is or is not 'credible'.

At the actual trial, the duty to disclose by the prosecution is more expansive, including as it does material relating to the background of prosecution witnesses and the like. Sometimes such information may be requested at the preliminary enquiry stage, but it is more critical at trial. This will be considered later in discussion of indictable trials. In the final analysis, the stage at which disclosure is necessary and the substance of the disclosure required will be determined on the basis of the elementary right of the defendant to a fair trial.[9]

Admissibility

An examining magistrate is expected to accept and consider any admissible evidence that is put before him. He has no power or right to exercise any discretion to reject evidence: *R v Horsham JJ ex p Bukhari* (1982) 74 Cr App R 291.

9 As recognised by the House of Lords in *R v Brown* [1997] 3 All ER 769, HL, considering common law disclosure principles prior to the English 1996 Criminal Procedure and Investigations Act which now prescribes the principles of disclosure in England.

Such a magistrate has no discretion to determine if legally admissible evidence, such as dock identification, should be excluded: *R v Highbury Corner Magistrates' Court ex p Boyce* (1984) 79 Cr App R 132. In that case, the defence sought to prohibit the admission of dock identification evidence at a preliminary enquiry, contending it was unreliable. The judicial review application was refused by the English Divisional Court on the basis that the examining justices were not entitled to reject legally admissible evidence. Thus, while a trial judge will have to determine whether dock identification is more probative than prejudicial, it is not for the committing magistrate to make such a determination. He must allow the evidence because he is not trying the case.

In the Trinidad and Tobago case of *The Director of Public Prosecutions v Magistrate Her Worship Cardenas-Ragoonanan* Application No. P 014 of 2015 the magistrate had refused to allow the prosecution at committal proceedings to call certain evidence on the basis that the evidence was likely to be more prejudicial than probative. On an application for judicial review the court held that, inasmuch as the magistrate at committal proceedings was entitled to rule on relevance, she could only do so after she had heard the evidence. The magistrate could not properly rule on the issue of relevance if she chose not to hear the evidence at all. The magistrate had therefore acted erroneously in refusing to allow the prosecution to call the evidence.

In the Commonwealth Caribbean, examining magistrates act in accordance with this practice on the basis that disputed admissibility questions are for the trial court. At committal proceedings, therefore, a confession of the defendant will be tendered into evidence since its actual admissibility on the basis of voluntariness can only be determined on a voir dire hearing at trial. Until then it constitutes legal evidence. Where the evidence is, however, legally inadmissible, it is wrong to admit it in breach of the rules of evidence. Nonetheless, even if inadmissible evidence is admitted, committal proceedings will not be considered invalid merely on this ground: *R v Norfolk Quarter Sessions ex p Brunson* (1953) 37 Cr App R 6. There must, however, be other evidence, apart from the inadmissible evidence which may yet support a conviction. In *R v Bedwellty JJ ex p Williams* [1996] 3 WLR 361, HL, the House of Lords held that a committal order may be quashed where it is found that there is no admissible evidence justifying the committal. In addition, the committal will be quashed where the evidence led is not reasonably capable of supporting the committal. If the committal is quashed, this means that an indictment founded on it is invalid. In the circumstances of *Bedwellty JJ*, the House of Lords suggested that no evidence existed to justify an indictment.

THE PROCEDURE

Since committal proceedings are the creation of statute, the procedure stipulated by relevant statutes of Commonwealth Caribbean jurisdictions must be strictly followed. Failure to do so may result in the proceedings being declared a nullity,[10] as happened in several cases considered hereinafter.

Just as for a summary charge, an indictable offence is initiated by the laying of a complaint. The accused person is brought to the court usually by way of arrest, given the serious nature of the offence. Once the offence is being proceeded with indictably, as is the case for offences that are not triable either way or where triable either way offences are not being heard summarily, the accused is not called upon to plead. The magistrate will read the charge and inform the accused that he is not called upon to plead (since the proceedings do not constitute a trial). There is

10 As in *R v Gee et al.* (1936) 25 Cr App R 198.

provision for a magistrate to deem that committal proceedings should not be in open court if he thinks fit, but most magistrates will not choose to proceed in camera merely on the ground that they are holding a preliminary enquiry.

Presence of accused

The preliminary enquiry must be held in the presence of the accused and this is stipulated in the relevant statutory provisions[11] across the region. In Trinidad and Tobago there is provision that if evidence at the preliminary enquiry is taken in the absence of the accused person, it may be read over to him in the presence of the witnesses and the proceedings continued as legislation permits. Otherwise, if any evidence is taken in the absence of the accused, the committal proceedings will be held to be invalid: *R v Phillips and Quayle* [1939] 1 KB 63.

In that case, two accused persons were charged with several offences of conspiracy and obtaining by false pretences. The preliminary enquiry proceedings commenced against Q alone and some 35 witnesses were called. Thereafter, P was joined as a co-defendant. The witnesses were recalled, but were not asked to give their evidence again. They merely confirmed in P's presence that their earlier evidence was correct following which P was given the opportunity to cross-examine. The proceedings continued and both defendants were committed to stand trial and later convicted for several offences. On appeal it was held that the procedure adopted in respect of P was irregular and not in compliance with s 17[12] of the Indictable Offences Act 1848. Accordingly, the committal based on such procedure was unlawful and an indictment based on the committal was bad. P's conviction could not stand. Since Q's committal was separate and distinct and the procedure in so far as he was concerned was proper, his committal was valid.

It is of note to mention that the procedure in relation to P would in Trinidad and Tobago be valid because s 16(2) of the Preliminary Inquiry (Indictable Offences) Act permits this. It is also noteworthy that s 17(2) of the Magistrates' Courts Act 1996–27 as amended by Act 2016–15 of Barbados provides that evidence may be given before an examining magistrate in the absence of the accused person if he behaves in a disorderly manner or where the court considers it necessary in a hearing for a sexual offence involving a child's evidence or where the accused consents in writing to the procedure and he is legally represented.

The depositions

Statute provides that the evidence given in a preliminary enquiry must be recorded in the form of depositions. This really refers to the form in which the evidence is recorded at a

11 Bahamas: Criminal Procedure Code, Ch 91, s 119(1);
Barbados: Magistrates' Courts Act 1996–27 as amended by Act 2016–15, s 17(2);
Dominica: Magistrate's Code of Procedure Act, Chap 4:20, s 48;
Grenada: Criminal Procedure Code, Cap 72B, s 102(2);
Guyana: Criminal Law (Procedure) Act, Cap 10:01, s 64(2);
Jamaica: Justices of the Peace Jurisdiction Act, s 34 (now repealed and only applies to matters not done under the provisions of Act No 24 of 2013).
St Kitts and Nevis: Magistrate's Code of Procedure Act, Cap 3:17, s56;
St Vincent: Criminal Procedure Code, Cap 172, s 142(1);
Trinidad and Tobago: Indictable Offences (Preliminary Inquiry) Act, Chap 12:01, s 16(2).

12 The relevant statutory provisions (cited in footnote 11 above) of Commonwealth Caribbean jurisdictions are based on this provision.

preliminary enquiry (as distinct from what occurs at trial). Statutory provisions[13] throughout the region provide that the evidence of each witness must be taken down in writing by the magistrate or his clerk. After each witness has been examined and cross-examined, his (recorded) evidence is read over to him in the presence and hearing of the accused person. The witness has the opportunity to make any corrections of any errors in the recorded evidence. He must then sign the deposition. Following this, the deposition must be authenticated by a certificate signed by the examining magistrate. The certificate is to the effect that the evidence was read over to the witness in the presence of the accused and he (the witness) indicated that it was correct. In some jurisdictions, such as Trinidad and Tobago, statute[14] even provides that where a witness refuses to sign his deposition, he may be committed to prison for such refusal.

In *Bramble v R* (1959) 1 WIR 473, the Court of Appeal for the Windward and Leeward Islands considered an appeal from Antigua concerning the admissibility in evidence at trial of a deposition given at the preliminary enquiry of a witness who had since died. The court considered all the requirements that are necessary to constitute a valid deposition and held that a deposition must conform to the provisions of the relevant statute. The court emphasised that evidence taken down at a preliminary enquiry does not become a deposition until it has been read over and signed by the witness. Any failure to adhere to the statutory requirements will invalidate the deposition.

The importance of recording the evidence as a deposition at the preliminary enquiry stage stems from the fact that a valid deposition may be tendered as evidence at the actual trial of the defendant. This is permissible when the witness is ill or out of the country or dead, and in circumstances provided in the relevant statute[15] throughout the region. The exercise of this discretion will be considered hereafter in discussing the course of an indictable trial. In any event, before the court may even consider the exercise of that discretion, it must ensure that the deposition was recorded as provided by statute.

In *Bramble* (above) it was held that the evidence as recorded did not constitute a deposition which could be given in evidence in the absence of the witness. It did not conform to the statutory requirements. In *La Vende v The State* (1979) 30 WIR 460, the Trinidad and Tobago Court of Appeal held that once the deposition is in order, the certificate of the magistrate may be admitted together with it. It need not be proved separately and independently that the examining magistrate had certified the deposition. In effect, the certificate speaks for itself.

In the English case of *R v Edgar et al.* [1958] 2 All ER 494, where the magistrate signed some depositions and not others, it was held that only the evidence in the signed depositions could be considered for committal. The evidence in the unsigned 'depositions' could not be used to justify the committal. The court thus had to consider whether the committal could be supported by the evidence in the valid depositions.

Other irregularities

While irregularities in the form of a deposition may have serious consequences if the deposition itself is sought to be tendered as evidence, there are other more significant

13 In Barbados, the requirement is contained in the Magistrate's Courts (Criminal Procedure) Rules 2001 (r 21), as compared with the other jurisdictions, where it is in the substantive law.

14 Indictable Offences (Preliminary Inquiry) Act, Chap 12:01, s 16(5).

15 As, e.g., in the Indictable Offences (Preliminary Inquiry) Act, Chap 12:01, s 39, Trinidad and Tobago; and Justice of the Peace (Jurisdiction) Act, s 34, Jamaica (now repealed, see footnote 11 above). This is discussed further in Chapter 14.

breaches of the statutory provisions which may invalidate the entire committal proceedings. This is where the procedural requirements for the actual hearing are breached, such as in *Phillips and Quayle* (above).

Evidence of witnesses must be given orally in the presence of the magistrate, except if proceeding by way of the alternative procedure of 'paper committal'.[16] Otherwise, if an examining magistrate does not actually hear the evidence, the ensuing committal may be invalid and any ensuing conviction from an invalid committal may be void: *R v Gee et al.* (1936) 25 Cr App R 198. In that case, committing justices failed to comply with s 17[17] of the then Indictable Offences Act 1848 in taking the evidence of witnesses. Instead of the magistrate or his clerk recording the evidence, the clerk signed pre-typed statements on the basis of which the witnesses were examined by the police prosecutor. The defendants were not even given copies of these statements. They were committed on the 'evidence' in these pre-typed statements and later indicted on the statements which were regarded as the 'depositions'. In quashing the ensuing convictions, the Court of Appeal held that, there being no compliance with the requirements for the taking of evidence as prescribed by statute, the committal was unlawful and no valid bill of indictment could be founded on it. That being so, the trial was a nullity.

Similarly, in Trinidad and Tobago, the trial judge upheld a motion to quash an indictment on the basis that it was founded on an unlawful committal: *State v Latiff Ali et al.* HCA 118 of 1990 (unreported). The facts were similar to *Phillips and Quayle* (above) in some respects. Here, several witnesses gave evidence before a magistrate at a preliminary enquiry into a charge of conspiracy to kidnap. Before the enquiry was completed, the magistrate retired. Another magistrate was assigned to hear the matter and, to avoid delay occasioned by the repetition of all the evidence that had gone before, he decided to follow the procedure endorsed in *Ex p Bottomley et al.* [1909] 2 KB 14. That case supported the view that where a magistrate starts fresh committal proceedings, he may utilise depositions given at an aborted preliminary enquiry. Each witness must be individually recalled and sworn in the witness box.

The deposition would then be read over to the witness by the clerk and asked by the magistrate if it was true and correct and if he wished to make alterations or corrections. The prosecuting attorney would be allowed to examine the witness further if he wished, and the defence allowed to cross-examine the witness further.

This procedure was followed in *Latiff Ali* (above) and the accused committed for trial. The trial judge, however, considered that the second magistrate had committed serious breaches of the procedure set out in the Indictable Offences (Preliminary Enquiry) Act. He declined to follow *Bottomley* (above) and expressed the view that it was wrongly decided. The judge felt that it was important that the magistrate hear all the evidence orally as this was what the statute envisaged. He emphasised that procedures in criminal prosecutions that have been statutorily enacted must be strictly followed. Accordingly, he quashed the indictment.

General matters

During the course of an enquiry, just as in a trial, the defendant is entitled to have legal representation and the opportunity to obtain such representation. A refusal to grant a

16 This was introduced by statute in some jurisdictions and is discussed in Chapter 12.

17 Equivalent provisions in the Commonwealth Caribbean are based on this section.

reasonable request for an adjournment may similarly be considered a breach of natural justice.[18] The accused person thus has all the rights in this respect that he enjoys at trial. Although statute may not specifically so provide for them, these are all part of the rights of a defendant included in a fair hearing.

In respect of preliminary hearings, statute provides, in contrast to trials, that there should be no publicity of the evidence given at committal proceedings. This stems from the fact that the preliminary enquiry is merely to decide if a prima facie case is made out and not a trial. Possibly the legislature wanted to prevent, as far as possible, witnesses from being informed of the evidence of other witnesses so as to synchronise new evidence at trial. More probably, however, the reason may be to avoid prejudicing potential jurors by making known to them the evidence before the actual trial.

Finally, statute throughout the region provides that every witness who has given evidence for the prosecution must sign a bond to appear and give evidence at trial.[19] A witness who refuses to sign (or otherwise endorse) the bond may be committed to prison until trial or until he does.

No-case submission

The defence is entitled to make a no-case submission at the end of the case for the prosecution on the basis that a prima facie case has not been made out. The test is essentially the same as that at summary trial: *Practice Direction (Summary Trial)* [1962] 1 WLR 227 handed down by Lord Parker CJ. The defence may argue: (a) that no evidence has been led to prove an essential element of the alleged offence; or (b) the evidence adduced by the prosecution has been so discredited as a result of cross-examination or is so manifestly unreliable that no reasonable tribunal should safely convict on it.

It is obvious that at this stage, the examining magistrate is not to be concerned with questions of credibility (unless the evidence is really worthless) since the magistrate is not the final arbiter of the facts, as at summary trial. If a reasonable jury properly directed on the law and the facts could possibly convict on the evidence of the prosecution, the no-case submission should not be upheld.

It is necessary that the magistrate, in considering a no-case submission in committal proceedings, keep in mind that statute may enable him to commit the defendant for trial for any indictable offence disclosed from the evidence, not just for the offence charged. This is specifically provided for in statute in jurisdictions such as Barbados, Guyana, Jamaica and Trinidad and Tobago.[20] In such cases, the magistrate must consider whether there is evidence on which any reasonable jury properly directed could convict for any indictable offence. It has been held that where a no-case submission is made by the defence and there exists the possibility of committal for a different offence instead of the original charge, the defence should be given the opportunity to address the court on those possibilities: *R v Gloucester Magistrates' Court ex p Chung* (1989) 153 JP 75. In *State v Mc Lennon* HCA No 18 of 2003 the High Court of Guyana had to address this issue in a fact situation where a

18 *Aris v Chin* (1972) 19 WIR 459, which principles apply to all criminal or quasi-criminal hearings.

19 As in Indictable Offences (Preliminary Inquiry) Act, Chap 12:01, s 21(4), Trinidad and Tobago; Justices of the Peace (Jurisdiction Act), s 38, Jamaica.

20 Barbados: Magistrates' Court Act 1996–27 as amended by Act 2016–15, s 19;
Guyana: Criminal Law (Procedure) Act, Cap 10:01, s 69;
Jamaica: Justice of the Peace (Jurisdiction) Act, s 43 (now repealed, see footnote 11 above).
Trinidad and Tobago: Indictable Offences (Preliminary Inquiry) Act, Chap 12:01, s 23(2).

magistrate had committed for murder an accused charged with manslaughter. The court held it was procedurally unfair and irregular for the DPP to indict for murder when the accused was charged with manslaughter and invited to lead a defence to that offence, a defence that did not support the offence of murder.

In ruling on a no-case submission, the examining magistrate is entitled to indicate that at that point he finds that a prima facie case is made out: *Berry* (1947) 32 Cr App R 70. In that case, the appellant argued on appeal that his conviction should be overturned because the committal order made by the examining justices (magistrates) was bad. The defence contended that in overruling the no-case submission, the court had ruled that 'there is sufficient prima facie evidence to justify us in committing the accused for trial'. This, it was said, indicated that the magistrates had made up their minds to commit the accused to stand trial without giving him an opportunity to be heard. The relevant statutory provision, like those in the Commonwealth Caribbean, entitled the court to commit an accused person for trial if at the end of the case for both the prosecution and the defence it found that a prima facie case was made out.

The English Court of Criminal Appeal held that the ruling of the court was merely indicative of the fact that at that moment, at the end of the case for the prosecution, there was sufficient evidence to commit the prisoner. The words were intended to indicate that they did not agree with the no-case submission. From the facts, it was clear that the appellant had been given an opportunity to be heard, although he had not taken it. The appeal was dismissed. *Berry* was followed in *Vishnudath Rooplal* [1993] HCA 929 of 1992 (unreported) judicial review proceedings before the High Court of Trinidad and Tobago. In that case a similar argument was made, that a decision of the magistrate on the committal was bad, on identical facts. The application was refused, the court citing the principles in *Berry*.

It has been held that if there is any ambiguity in the prosecution's evidence made apparent by the no case submission, the court may grant the prosecution the opportunity to resolve this, if it overrules the submission. In *R v West London JJ ex p Kaminski* (1983) 147 JP 190, the court held that this should be done before calling on the defence. It seems that there can be no objection to this in principle once there is sufficient other evidence to justify overruling the no-case submission.

THE DEFENCE

Unless the magistrate discharges the accused person he is required, at the end of the case for the prosecution, to administer to him a caution in a form specified in the relevant statute of each jurisdiction. The form of the caution in general is based on old English statute and is along the following lines:

> Having heard the evidence do you wish to say anything in answer to the charge? You are not obliged to do so unless you desire to do so but whatever you say will be taken down in writing and may be given in evidence upon your trial. And I give you clearly to understand that you have nothing to hope from any promise of favour and nothing to fear from any threat that may have been held out to you to induce you to make any admission or confession of your guilt, but whatever you now say may be given in evidence on your trial notwithstanding such promise or threat.[21]

21 The now repealed s 56 of the Magistrate's Code of Procedure Act, Cap 255, s 56, Antigua which is reflected in identical provisions in Dominica: Magistrate's Code of Procedure Act, Chap 4:20, s 52; and St Kitts and Nevis: Magistrate's Code of Procedure Act, Cap 3:17, s 60. The Justice of the Peace (Jurisdiction) Act of

In some jurisdictions the caution is specified in a more shortened form[22] but conveys that the defendant may make a statement or give evidence on oath although he is not obliged to say anything and that the statement or evidence will be recorded and may be used at his trial. In general, the accused person has the option to remain silent, make an unsworn statement or give evidence on oath. In St Kitts and Nevis, the right to make an unsworn statement in any criminal proceedings was abolished in s 33 of the Criminal Procedure Act, Cap 4:06. The accused person may remain silent or elect to give evidence on oath.

In Trinidad and Tobago, the right of an accused person to make an unsworn statement at committal proceedings was specifically abolished by Act No 8 of 1990 which amended the Indictable Offences (Preliminary Inquiry) Act, Chap 12:01. The magistrate must now, after the close of the case for the prosecution, inform the accused that he 'is entitled to give evidence on oath or to remain silent'. Only if the accused person indicates that he wishes to give evidence need the magistrate administer the caution.[23] The Indictable Offences (Preliminary Enquiry) Amendment Act No 8 of 1990 replaced the older statutory caution with a new shortened version (similar to that of Grenada). This new caution in Trinidad and Tobago, unlike those of other jurisdictions, includes a warning that the accused person may only give evidence on oath upon which he may be cross-examined.

In jurisdictions where the accused person is entitled to make an unsworn statement in his own defence, this must be made clear to him. The magistrate must indicate to him that he is entitled to remain silent or to give evidence on his own behalf. In general, however, an accused person will not give evidence at the preliminary enquiry except for strategic reasons. Since it is not the function of the examining magistrate to determine issues of credibility, where the court rules on a no-case submission that there is sufficient evidence at that time for a reasonable tribunal to convict, it might be considered of little use for the defence to call evidence. It would be almost impossible for a magistrate who has ruled that there is sufficient evidence to go to the jury at the end of the case for prosecution to find otherwise because the defence has given evidence. For the magistrate to do so would mean that he has acted as a fact-finding tribunal and considered issues of credibility.

Nevertheless, the magistrate cannot refuse to hear the defendant after rejecting a no-case submission: *R v Horseferry Road Magistrates' Court ex p Adams* [1977] 1 WLR 1197. In this case, the examining magistrate rejected a no-case submission by the defence at the close of the case for the prosecution. He then refused to allow the defendant to give evidence on the ground that it was not his function to determine the issue of credibility. The defendant applied for certiorari to quash his ensuing committal. The Queen's Bench, in granting the application, held that the general rule in criminal trials, that a defendant is entitled to call evidence even after the rejection of a no-case submission, applied equally to committal proceedings. The magistrate acted unlawfully in delaying the defendant his right.

The right of the defendant to be heard includes his right to cross-examine fully any prosecution witness, although he may choose not to exercise that right. In *Roulette v R* [1972] 4 WWR 508 (Canada), the presiding magistrate in a preliminary enquiry told the defence counsel, after a long period of cross-examination of a medical witness, that 'he only had half an hour more'. It was held that the accused person has the right to cross-examine a witness on all relevant matters, no matter how long such cross-examination may take.

Jamaica, s 36, (now repealed, see footnote 11 above) while not identical, contains the full substance of these words. The caution does not apply to matters done under Act No 24 of 2013.

22 As, e.g., Criminal Procedure Code, Cap 72B, s 103(1), Grenada.

23 Chap 12:01, s 17(2) (as amended).

The right to call witnesses and procedural errors

The right to call witnesses is indubitably a part of the right to be heard and statute throughout the Commonwealth Caribbean region provides that an enquiring magistrate must inform the defendant of his right to call witnesses. This is after the magistrate has informed the defendant of his own right to give evidence or after the defendant gives evidence. In considering similar legislation in Canada, a court in that jurisdiction held that on a preliminary enquiry it is mandatory for the magistrate to ask an accused if he wishes to call any witnesses and give him the opportunity to do so: *R v Feener* [1960] 129 CCC 314. Another Canadian court held that where a magistrate not only failed to ask the accused whether he wished to call any witnesses, but refused to allow him to do so, an ensuing committal was void and must be quashed: *Brooks v R* [1964] 49 WWR 638.

The statutory provisions in the region requiring the magistrate to inform the accused person of his right to call witnesses seem free from ambiguity and hardly likely to be the subject of controversy. Nevertheless, this turned out not to be the case in Trinidad and Tobago when the courts had to consider the effect of s 18(1) of the Indictable Offences (Preliminary Inquiry) Act, Chap 12:01 as amended. This section reads in part: 'After the proceedings required by s 17 are completed the Magistrate shall ask the accused person if he wishes to call any witnesses'.

In 1998 several indictments were quashed by judges of the High Court on the basis that the relevant committal proceedings were invalid, as the records displayed a noncompliance with s 18. In these cases, there was no record that the magistrate had in fact informed the accused person of his right to call witnesses. There was a record of the caution being put to the accused in a form provided for that purpose, but nothing else. As a result several judges considered that there was a breach of s 18 and that the committal proceedings amounted to a nullity in each case. The unreported judgment of Archie J in *State v Roger Hinds*, Trinidad and Tobago, HC No S 365/97 is reflective of the ruling of many judges.

On the other hand, other judges and commentators felt that where the accused had stated 'I reserve my defence' in answer to the statutory caution, that clearly indicated that he wished to reserve his entire defence: including his right to call witnesses. The magistrate's reiteration after this of his right to call witnesses seems wholly redundant. By Act No 32 of 1998, the Trinidad and Tobago Parliament sought to rectify the situation calling for the magistrate to record both the response of the accused on his being advised of his right to give evidence, and his response when informed of his right to call witnesses. Furthermore, even if there has been a procedural breach during the preliminary enquiry, the Amendment Act provides that the DPP may still prefer a valid indictment with the consent of a High Court judge. Fortunately, in terms of wider legal concerns, the matter was considered by the higher courts. On 15 November 2000, the Privy Council rejected a petition for leave[24] of Arnold Ramlogan, convicted by a Trinidad and Tobago court for murder. Three judges considered the petition for leave which included as one ground the fact that the magistrate had failed to inform the defendant of his right to call witnesses at the preliminary enquiry. This, it was claimed, was a serious flaw which would render the committal and the indictment based on it invalid. In dismissing the petition, Lord Steyn is reported to have said that the submission was 'the most misconceived argument' that he had heard for some time. He stated that even if there was a breach, it could not

24 There is usually no written judgment of a rejection of an application for leave to appeal to the Privy Council (Trinidad and Tobago).

possibly affect the fairness of the trial as long as the defendant knew that he could call witnesses at trial.

It would seem that the Privy Council took a practical view of the situation recognising the fact that accused persons rarely, if at all, call witnesses at the preliminary enquiry stage. In a judgment given on 1 December 2000 after the Ramlogan petition, although the appeal was heard before, the Trinidad and Tobago Court of Appeal dismissed the appeal of Charles Matthews[25] for murder. The main ground of appeal appeared to be a failure to comply with s 18. At his committal hearing the defendant had appeared, represented by counsel. He elected to remain silent when asked if he wished to give evidence or to remain silent. He was then committed for trial. He argued that his committal was bad as he was not informed of his right to call witnesses, as was mandatory under s 18.

The Court of Appeal dismissed his appeal indicating that the consequences of the procedural breaches in respect of s 18 must be considered on a case-by-case basis. If the consequences were not grave, the committal would be valid. The Court of Appeal considered and held that *Roger Hinds* had been wrongly decided. In delivering the judgment of the court, De la Bastide CJ said that where the defendant indicated that he 'reserved' his defence, s 18 becomes otiose and does not affect the validity of the committal. If, on the other hand, the defendant gives no indication that he is 'reserving' his defence but simply indicates he does not wish to give evidence, different considerations apply. If he is represented by counsel, it would be 'inconceivable that his attorney would not at that stage have been aware that the appellant was entitled to call witnesses if he chose'. In contrast, if the defendant is unrepresented, it would seem that there is a heavier burden on the magistrate to inform the defendant of his right.

The Court of Appeal considered that failure to inform the accused of his right to call witnesses was not fatal as would have been a failure to inform him of his right to give evidence. In the first scenario, the defendant must show he suffered prejudice. The court distinguished *Feener* (above) on its facts, which included that the defendant was unrepresented. It held that on the facts of Matthews, since the defendant was legally represented and there appeared to be no witnesses whom he could have called in any case (he called none at trial), he had suffered no prejudice by the magistrate's failure to inform him of his right to call witnesses.

Subsequently, the Privy Council had occasion to directly confront the issue in *Leslie Tiwari v The State* (2002) 61 WIR 452, PC. The Board held that failure to comply with the statutory provision (to inform the defendant of his right to call witnesses) does not necessarily render a subsequent conviction a nullity. The court agreed with the reasons of De la Bastide CJ given in the *Charles Matthews* appeal.

Defence witnesses

The prosecution is of course entitled to cross-examine any defence witness. Since the purpose of the preliminary enquiry is to assess the strength of the case against the defence and the magistrate is not called upon to determine issues of credibility, the prosecution may opt not to cross-examine at this stage. Like the evidence of the defendant, the evidence of his witnesses at this stage might have little impact on the decision to commit. Nevertheless, if a witness is likely to be unavailable at trial, the defence may choose to call him at the preliminary enquiry. As in the case of a prosecution witness, the evidence of a defence witness may be tendered as a deposition at trial once the statutory requirements are met.

25 *Matthews (Charles) v The State* (2000) 60 WIR 390.

Except for character witnesses any defence witness must, like the prosecution witnesses, sign a bond to give evidence at trial. His failure either to sign the bond or to give evidence later will meet with the same consequences as for prosecution witnesses: he may be committed to prison until trial or until he does sign.

Notice of alibi

In general, the accused person has no obligation to give evidence or, as is now the law in England, to disclose his defence. In one regard, however, statute has intervened to change this in some jurisdictions. In the Bahamas, Barbados, St Kitts and Nevis, St Vincent and in Trinidad and Tobago,[26] statute has intervened to require the defence to give notice of alibi. The accused person is told of this requirement on committal and in some jurisdictions such as the Bahamas, St Kitts and Nevis and Trinidad and Tobago he is given a deadline of some days after committal by which he must serve notice of alibi. In St Vincent, notice need not be given until trial.

Notice of alibi is only required in respect of matters which are to be tried indictably after there has been a committal. The defence must supply the names and addresses of potential alibi witnesses or other means of identifying them to the prosecution. The prosecution will then be better prepared to check the alibi evidence and find rebuttal evidence if necessary. If there is no rebuttal evidence, then the defence may argue that they have a stronger case. If the defendant does not give notice of alibi as required by statute, he must seek leave of the court to run a defence of alibi at trial. A court will usually give such leave to a defendant who was unrepresented at trial or where a refusal might seriously prejudice the defence.

THE DECISION

A magistrate has two options in committal proceedings. He may either discharge the accused person or commit him for trial. In some jurisdictions[27] statute refers to the power of the magistrate to 'dismiss the charge'. Despite the use of the term 'dismiss', the effect is not that of the dismissal at summary trial and must be the same as a 'discharge' in the other jurisdictions, since both relate to a determination in committal proceedings.

The discharge

Statute provides that the magistrate may discharge the defendant if he is of the opinion that no sufficient case is made out against him. This is the same as saying that no prima facie case[28] is made out, that is, no case which can be successfully impugned on the basis that no reasonable tribunal properly directed can convict upon it.

26 Bahamas: Criminal Procedure Code, Ch 91, s 123(4); Barbados: Evidence Act 1994–4, s 17, Magistrates' Courts Act 1996–27 as amended by Act 2016–15, s18F; St Kitts and Nevis: Criminal Procedure Act, Cap 4:06, s 33; St Vincent: Criminal Procedure Code, Cap 172, s 198, s 150(2); Trinidad and Tobago: Indictable Offences (Preliminary Inquiry) Act, Chap 12:01, s16A.

27 Magistrate's Code of Procedure, Chap 4:20, s 54, Dominica; Magistrate's Code of Procedure Act, Cap 3:17, s 62, St Kitts and Nevis.

28 This is the term used in Indictable Offences (Preliminary Inquiry) Act of Trinidad and Tobago, s 23(1), which was amended in 1979 to substitute 'prima facie case' for 'sufficient case'.

This is not to say that a discharge at a preliminary enquiry may not be effected before the end of the prosecution's case. The magistrate may discharge the defendant prior to that, for instance, after a successful preliminary submission that the complaint is bad in law. In addition, magistrates have been known to discharge accused persons when the prosecution is unable to proceed on a particular date for one reason or another. More common, however, is the discharge of an accused person on a successful no-case submission at the end of the prosecution's case. Even if the no-case submission is overruled, the court may reconsider its decision after all the evidence has been given and after the accused has been permitted the opportunity to be heard.

The effect

A discharge (or dismissal) at a preliminary enquiry is not an acquittal.[29] Apart from the fact that the enquiry is not a trial, the defendant would not have even pleaded. In *R v Manchester City Stipendiary Magistrate ex p Snelson* [1978] 2 All ER 62, it was specifically held that a discharge at a preliminary enquiry is not an acquittal. A court thus has the jurisdiction to entertain fresh committal proceedings in respect of a charge on which the defendant has been discharged whether as a result of offering no evidence or after a hearing. As a result, there are several options open to the prosecution after a discharge to still proceed to trial without any suggestion that the defendant will suffer double jeopardy. The prosecution may: (a) relay the charge; (b) if statute specifies, hold a further enquiry on the discovery of additional evidence; (c) obtain a committal otherwise or (d) proceed by way of voluntary bill.

Relaying the charge

Where the prosecution offers no evidence at a preliminary enquiry it is entitled to come again in subsequent proceedings, be they indictable or summary: *R v Canterbury and St Augustine's JJ ex p Klisiak* [1981] 2 All ER 129. In that case, the court confirmed that there was no question of autrefois acquit, since there was no adjudication. The accused had never been in jeopardy. The prosecution was entitled to proceed on another charge in respect of the same matter. Similarly, where earlier proceedings constituted a nullity, the court is entitled to proceed to hold a preliminary enquiry in respect of the same charge: *R v West* [1964] 1 QB 15. In that case, the magistrate purported to hear and acquit an accused on a charge which was triable only indictably. It was held that the purported acquittal was a nullity, as the magistrate had no jurisdiction to try the matter. The court could thereafter proceed to hold committal proceedings.

Despite the fact that the prosecution may come again after a discharge it has been held that the repeated use of the procedure may become vexatious and while not amounting to double jeopardy, could constitute an abuse of process: *R v Horsham JJ ex p Reeves* [1981] CLR 566. In that case, after some 14 witnesses had given evidence and been cross-examined in committal proceedings over three days and some seven witness statements read, the defendant was discharged on a no-case submission. The preliminary enquiry had been held in respect of some 24 indictable charges of theft and handling. After the discharge, the prosecution preferred five fresh charges of an identical nature to some of the earlier indictable charges. The defendant sought judicial review. The Divisional Court granted prohibition on the basis that the latter proceedings were oppressive. The court was clearly

29 In some jurisdictions statute indicates this as, e.g., Criminal Procedure Code, Ch 91, s 125, the Bahamas.

moved by the fact that there had been a full hearing on the merits (unlike in *Ex p Snelson*) of the committal proceedings. The prosecution could have been said to be seeking to manipulate the process of the court.[30]

In contrast, where the accused person had been discharged merely because the prosecution was not yet ready to proceed, they could come again unless the delay in the proceedings is shown to be exceptional: *R v Grays JJ ex p Graham* [1982] 3 All ER 653. Furthermore, if new evidence is discovered after the discharge on the first hearing, the prosecution would not be acting improperly if they re-laid the charges.

Additional evidence

In Trinidad and Tobago, statute provides that following a discharge, if 'additional evidence of a material nature in support of some offence becomes available, a further enquiry may be held in the like manner ... as if it were an original preliminary enquiry'.[31] This power is clearly ancillary to the power of the prosecution to relay a charge as discussed above. This provision covers the situation where there has been a full hearing at the original preliminary enquiry upon which the defendant was discharged. If additional evidence subsequently becomes available and a fresh preliminary enquiry is held, the latter will not constitute an abuse of process. It would seem that even without this specific provision it is permissible to relay a criminal charge upon a discharge where additional evidence is discovered after the discharge since this involves new evidence.

In *Cadogan v R* (1963) 6 WIR 292, the Trinidad and Tobago Court of Appeal made it clear that the statutory provision that enabled a further enquiry when additional evidence 'becomes available' did not convey on the prosecution the unrestricted right to proceed again on evidence at a second preliminary enquiry which had been available at the time of the first. In that case a magistrate conducted a preliminary enquiry into a charge of murder against the defendant. After witnesses for the prosecution had given evidence, the accused person was discharged. The prosecution re-laid the charge and at the second preliminary enquiry called medical evidence which had not been called at the first proceedings. The appellant was committed to stand trial and was eventually convicted on the evidence. On appeal, it was shown that this evidence had been available at the time of the first preliminary enquiry. It was held that the statute would only apply if new evidence emerged after the discharge or became known to the prosecution only after that date.

Having regard to the interpretation given to the statutory provision, it would seem that it adds nothing to the power of the prosecution to proceed to fresh committal proceedings after a discharge. Even without statutory statement, it seems only reasonable that the prosecution should be able to relay charges if fresh evidence subsequently becomes available since the discharge is not, after all, an acquittal. Nonetheless the Court of Appeal did suggest that the section limits the power to relay only to situations where there is fresh evidence.

Power of the prosecution on discharge

If there has been a discharge by a magistrate but the prosecution believes that sufficient evidence has been led to disclose a prima facie case, they may act to proceed with the

30 See Chapter 2.

31 Indictable Offences (Preliminary Inquiry) Act, Chap 12:01, s 23(8), Trinidad and Tobago.

matter without the necessity of laying a fresh charge. Statute has provided that the DPP may in some jurisdictions move to obtain a committal on the evidence given or in other jurisdictions proceed by way of voluntary bill of indictment.

In Guyana and St Kitts and Nevis,[32] the relevant statute provides that the DPP, if he is of the opinion (based on the evidence given at the preliminary) that the defendant should have been committed for trial, may remit the case to the magistrate with the appropriate directions. Section 72(2) of the Criminal Law (Procedure) Act of Guyana specifically provides that the DPP can direct the magistrate to 'reopen the enquiry and to commit the accused for trial'. It was, however, held in *R v Hussain ex p DPP* (1964) 8 WIR 65, in interpreting this section, that before such a magistrate commits he must comply with the rest of the requirements of the section which includes first giving the accused person a right to be heard, to give evidence or call witnesses. Statute in St Kitts and Nevis does not clearly specify any similar requirements but states that the DPP may remit the matter to the magistrate with suitable directions to deal with it. It is suggested that such directions ought to include allowing the accused person the opportunity to be heard before committing him. It has also been held by the Court of Appeal of Guyana that a direction given by the DPP to a magistrate (which is authorised by statute), such as to reopen the preliminary enquiry, is mandatory: *Re Williams and Salisbury* (1978) 26 WIR 133.

Statute in Dominica, Grenada and Trinidad and Tobago[33] provides for another procedure to secure a committal for trial after a discharge. Here the DPP, after considering the evidence given in the committal proceedings, applies[34] to a judge of a High Court to obtain a warrant for the arrest and committal of the discharged defendant. The DPP will annex to his application a copy of the record of the proceedings in the magistrates' court inclusive of the evidence. The judge performs a judicial function in considering the proceedings, since he may only issue the warrant if he 'is of the opinion that the evidence, as given before the Magistrate, was sufficient to put the accused person on his trial'.[35]

The Trinidad and Tobago provisions (similar to those of Grenada and Dominica) were considered in *AG v Aleem Mohammed* (1985) 36 WIR 359. In that case, the Court of Appeal held that the accused was not entitled to be heard before the judge issues his warrant of committal. The court held that the procedure was ex parte just as is a hearing for the preferment of a voluntary bill of indictment. The accused was not deprived of his right to a fair hearing, which he could enjoy at trial. Further, the statute did not contemplate, since it did not include, a right of the accused person to be heard at the time of the issue of the judge's warrant. In Trinidad and Tobago since 2005 the Indictable Offences (Preliminary Enquiry) Act (s 23G) now permits the DPP to appeal the refusal of a High Court judge to issue a warrant on committal and arrest of the discharged defendant.

32 The relevant statutory provisions are:
Guyana: Criminal Law (Procedure) Act, Cap 10:01, s 72(2);
St Kitts and Nevis: Criminal Procedure Act, Cap 4:06, s 15.

33 The relevant statutory provisions are:
Dominica: Criminal Procedure Act, Chap 12:01, s 17;
Grenada: Criminal Procedure Code, Cap 72B, s 105;
Trinidad and Tobago: Indictable Offences (Preliminary Inquiry) Act, Chap 12:01, s 23(5)–(7).

34 In Trinidad and Tobago the application must be made within six months of the discharge: s 23(7) (above).

35 Indictable Offences (Preliminary Inquiry) Act, Chap 12:01, s 23(6), Trinidad and Tobago.

Voluntary bill

In those jurisdictions[36] which do not have statutory provision allowing the prosecution to go behind the discharge of a magistrate and obtain a committal on the same proceedings, the prosecution has statutory power to proceed by way of voluntary bill of indictment. In these jurisdictions the relevant statute allows the DPP (or AG in the Bahamas) to seek permission from a High Court judge to prefer an indictment without a committal. The judge may do so only if there is sufficient evidence supporting the charge contained in the draft bill of indictment.

In *Brooks v DPP et al.* (1994) 44 WIR 332, PC, the Privy Council discussed the general nature of a voluntary bill. In considering the Jamaican statute, which is unique in the region in that it allows both the DPP and a judge to consent to a voluntary bill, the Privy Council held that even though he had the power himself to consent to a bill, the DPP was entitled to seek the direction and consent of a judge as to whether or not an indictment should be preferred.

In respect of the general nature of a voluntary bill, the Board confirmed that it is just a preliminary step in the initiation of proceedings for trial at the High Court and, accordingly, prior notice to the defendant (that he was considering a voluntary bill) was unnecessary. The judge, however, did have residual discretion to require notice to the defendant in exceptional cases if he felt it necessary. That could apply in situations where the judge did not have a magistrate's court proceedings before him. In such instances, presumably the defence may be heard before consent to the bill of indictment is given.

The grant of a voluntary bill of indictment as provided for by statute is not an abuse of process even in respect of a matter where the magistrate held a full hearing before discharging the accused. In *Brooks*, the Privy Council considered that once the DPP and the judge had paid due respect to the decision of the magistrate, the bill of indictment could be granted if there was evidence justifying the charge.

Where a voluntary bill is sought after a discharge on a preliminary enquiry, it is usual for the prosecution to file with its application the proceedings at the magistrates' court, as was done in *Brooks*, so that the judge could properly consider the evidence and the basis for the magistrate's decisions. Where a voluntary bill is otherwise obtained without any committal proceedings having been held at all, different considerations apply. For example, witness statements will be served on the defence and the court. In such a case it is only reasonable that the defence should be notified of the voluntary bill.

In Trinidad and Tobago, Section 23(8) of the Indictable Offences (Preliminary Enquiry) Act Chap. 12:01 has intervened to permit the DPP to prefer an indictment without holding a preliminary enquiry at all in five stipulated instances. These are: where an inquest was already completed in the matter; where a co-accused is arrested after a preliminary enquiry was held in respect of the other accused and it is desired to join the co-accused in the trial of the others; where a magistrate who began a preliminary enquiry cannot complete it; in cases of serious or complex fraud; and where the offence is of a violent or sexual nature involving children or threatened witnesses.

36 They include: Bahamas: Criminal Procedure Code, Ch 91, s 258A; Barbados: Criminal Procedure Act, Cap 127, s 4; Jamaica: The Criminal Justice (Administration) Act, s 2; St Vincent: Criminal Procedure Code, Cap 172, s 162.

Committal

At the end of all of the evidence given at the preliminary enquiry, the magistrate may commit the accused for trial. This, of course, may only be done after the accused has had an opportunity to be heard: *Matthews (Charles) v The State* (2000) 60 WIR 390.

In Barbados, Guyana, Jamaica and Trinidad and Tobago[37] statute specifically provides that the magistrate may commit the accused person for any indictable offence disclosed from the evidence given at the proceedings. Thus in *Jagessar and Bhola Nandlal v The State* (No 1) (1989) 41 WIR 342, the Court of Appeal in Trinidad and Tobago endorsed the decision of the enquiring magistrate to commit the accused persons for corruption on a preliminary enquiry into a charge of conspiracy to pervert the course of justice. The court held that the power to commit for any indictable offence, having been conferred by statute, in this case s 23(2) of the Indictable Offences (Preliminary Enquiry) Act, Chap 12:01, gave the magistrate the authority to commit even for an offence which required the consent of the DPP for its initiation. Thus there can be no doubt that, regardless of the indictable offence in respect of which the preliminary enquiry was held, the magistrate in the above named jurisdictions can commit for any offence justified by the evidence.

Where the statute is less clear and simply states that the magistrate 'shall commit [the accused] for trial' there is no clear indication whether such committal must refer only to the offence charged. It may well be argued that the examining magistrate may only commit for the offence charged. If no prima facie case is made out for that offence, he should discharge the defendant. This was the contention in the old Guyanese case of *Clarke v Vieira* (1960) 3 WIR 19. In that case the court considered legislation which existed prior to the current s 71 of the Criminal Law (Procedure) Act, Cap 10:01. The old s 71, which was amended by Act 22 of 1961 (after *Clarke v Vieira*), stated that if the magistrate was of the opinion that a sufficient case was made out against the accused person, he should 'commit him for trial'. The Court of Appeal rejected the submission that this provision meant that the magistrate could only commit for the offence charged. The court felt that since the Attorney General (now DPP) could indict for any offence disclosed from the evidence at the preliminary enquiry, it would put too narrow a construction of (then) s 71 to hold that the magistrate could only commit for the particular charge laid. Therefore 'if by legally admissible evidence the commission of some other indictable offence is disclosed then ... the magistrate may commit the accused person for trial': *Clarke v Vieira*, p 27. The court felt that the accused person could be committed for the offence charged (as in the instant case) once a prima facie case is made out even if for another offence. In any event, the magistrate could commit for any offence disclosed by the evidence.

It would seem that despite the different statutory provisions, in both instances, a magistrate may commit for any indictable offence disclosed from the evidence. It should be noted, however, that following *Clarke v Vieira*, the Guyana legislature amended s 71 to permit committal for 'any indictable offence', as it now reads. In the interest of clarity this might be an advisable amendment for other jurisdictions which still have the vague provision allowing the magistrate merely to 'commit for trial'.

The 2004 Antiguan Amendment Act No 13 of 2004, through a new s 48(1), clearly permits a magistrate in committal proceedings to commit an accused person for trial for

37 Barbados: Magistrates' Courts Act 1996–27 as amended by Act 2016–15, s 19;
Guyana: Criminal Law (Procedure) Act, Cap 10:01, s 71;
Jamaica: Justices of Peace (Jurisdiction) Act, s 43 (now repealed, see footnote 11 above).
Trinidad and Tobago: Indictable Offences (Preliminary Inquiry) Act, Chap 12:01, s 23(2).

what is termed an indictable offence 'of a like kind' to that charged. This is where the magistrate is of the opinion that the offence of the 'like kind' is established as distinct from the offence charged.

Referrals back

As stated in the discussion on 'leading all the evidence' above, throughout the region except for Jamaica, relevant statute[38] enables the DPP to refer the case back to the magistrate even after committal. This is to facilitate the taking of evidence inadvertently omitted from the case for the prosecution. In referring the case back to the magistrate, the DPP will usually specify the witnesses whose evidence must be amplified or the names of those who have not called but whom he wishes to be called to give evidence at the preliminary enquiry. Sometimes, the DPP may indicate generally the evidence he wishes to be taken. In some jurisdictions[39] statute provides that the DPP will direct the magistrate specifically on what points he wishes the further evidence to be taken.

After the evidence is taken the accused person will be given the opportunity to cross-examine again. The magistrate must again commit the accused person to stand trial. It is also advisable to read the statutory caution to him before the committal even though this was done on the initial committal.

Appeal

Since a preliminary enquiry is not trial, there is usually no appeal as there is no conviction or refusal to convict against which to appeal. Nevertheless, legislation [Act No 13 of 2004] in Antigua has intervened to permit this. The DPP may appeal to the Court of Appeal against a dismissal on committal proceedings on a point of law.[40]

An accused person may in exceptional circumstances challenge the decision of the magistrate to commit him to trial by way of judicial review: *Neill v North Antrim Magistrates' Court* [1992] 1 WLR 1220, HL. This decision came long after *Clarke v Vieira* (above) in which the Guyana Court had followed old English authority in holding that certiorari does not lie to remove a decision of a magistrate to commit an accused person for trial.

The law has since developed, but the High Court will still only sparingly exercise its review powers in respect of committals. The committal must have been based on evidence which it is certain would not support a finding of guilt: *R v Bedwellty JJ ex p Williams* [1996] 3 WLR 361, HL. It is possible that in old style committals, where a magistrate can and will refuse to admit inadmissible evidence and may uphold a no-case submission, the situation may rarely arise as it could more often in the case of 'paper committals' where the evidence would be in

38 Bahamas: Criminal Procedure Code, Ch 91, s 138;
Barbados: Magistrates' Courts Act 1996–27 as amended by Act 2016–15, s 26;
Dominica: Criminal Procedure Act, Chap 12:01, s 15(6);
Grenada: Criminal Procedure Code, Cap 72B, s 112;
Guyana: Criminal Law (Procedure) Act, Cap 10:01, s 77;
St Kitts and Nevis: Criminal Procedure Act, Cap 4:06, s 13;
St Vincent: Criminal Procedure Code, Cap 172, s 160;
Trinidad and Tobago: Indictable Offences (Preliminary Inquiry) Act, Chap 12:01, s 27.

39 As in the Bahamas: Criminal Procedure Code, Ch 84, s 135; and Guyana: Criminal Law (Procedure) Act, Chap 10:01, s 77.

40 See new Section 191 B.

the form of written statements that may not be as carefully scrutinised by the examining magistrate. Such was the case in *Bedwellty JJ*, where the committal was declared invalid. Another option open to the defence, if it is contended that the committal was bad, or if there was insufficient evidence, is to write to the DPP asking him to review the evidence and exercise his constitutional power to discontinue the proceedings.

Abolition of preliminary enquiry

The Antigua Magistrates' Code of Procedure (Amendment) Act No 13 of 2004 became law in November 2004. It provided for substantial changes in procedure in the magistrates' court. Among them was the effective abolition of preliminary enquiries which are now replaced by what are termed 'committal proceedings'. A new s 42A was created which provides that all committal proceedings in respect of public prosecutions[41] shall be instituted under the direction of the Director of Public Prosecutions by the filing of (a) one or more written statements of witnesses in support of the charge; and (b) a list of exhibits, if any. As was recognised by the Privy Council in *Hilroy Humphreys v the Attorney General of Antigua and Barbuda* [2008] UKPC 61, there is now no longer any right to oral hearing of evidence or cross examination. The defence only has an option, after being served with the evidence, to make submissions in law. The magistrate makes the decision to commit based entirely on written statements and exhibits of the prosecution and the accused, if he wishes.

In *Hilroy Humphreys* the Privy Council affirmed that the abolition of preliminary enquiries was not unconstitutional. The issue was whether the new system was fair. It was held that it was. The new 'committal proceedings' operated as a filter system after which the accused person was entitled to his fair hearing at trial where he could cross examine and give oral evidence.

In Jamaica, Act No 24 of 2013 (The Committal Proceedings Act, 2013), which became law in January 2016, abolished the preliminary enquiry. In its stead the Judge of the Parish Court holds committal proceedings for indictable offences. Act No 24 of 2013 applies to matters which were yet to be started at the commencement date of the act (January 2016) or where the accused, in a part-heard matter commenced prior to the commencement date, elects to continue the matter under the provisions of the act. Other matters would continue to be conducted under the provisions of the old legislation (Justice of the Peace Jurisdiction Act). Under the new law, committal proceedings may be conducted wholly on the basis of written statements but the court can authorise the taking of oral evidence where the court deems it necessary to do so. The accused has the option to: give oral evidence, tender a witness statement, make an unsworn statement or remain silent.

In St Lucia the legislature has gone one step further and removed any decision-making authority from the magistrate. By Act No 11 of 2008 St Lucia amended the Criminal Code to create one Criminal Division. The Amendment Act, in creating a new s 570A, also enabled the Chief Justice to make rules of practice and procedure in criminal matters. Further, a new s 779A is created which stipulates that the procedure relating to indictable offences shall be as provided for in the Rules, made pursuant to s 570A, and shall include an 'initial hearing by a Magistrate and sufficiency hearing by a Judge'. Throughout the Code references to 'an inquiry' are replaced with 'sufficiency hearing'.

These amendments convey the essence of the new procedure that replaces committal proceedings. There are no longer committal proceedings in the magistrates' court. In St

41 as amended by Act No 7 of 2005.

Lucia all criminal proceedings are initiated by a complaint filed in the Criminal Division, whether they are summary or indictable. The provisions that previously provided for committal proceedings, ss 797 to 802 of the Code, have all been repealed and replaced with provisions requiring a magistrate to conduct an initial hearing in accordance with the Criminal Procedure Rules at which a date for a sufficiency hearing before a judge is fixed. The relevant rules are discussed in Chapter 8.

The new procedures replacing the cumbersome preliminary enquiry in Antigua and St Lucia have revolutionised the procedure leading to indictable trial. Matters are being listed before a trial judge within months of the commission of the offence. It is as yet uncertain whether this may create a back-up of cases for trial in the Criminal High Court itself.

An attempt to abolish preliminary enquiries in Guyana in respect of sexual offences was held to be unconstitutional by the Chief Justice of the High Court in the matter of a reference by the Chief Magistrate in *PC Anthony Branche v Leonard Singh* CJ 2509/2011 (unreported), judgment delivered August 2012. The First Schedule to the Sexual Offences Act No 7 of 2010 purported to create a system of paper committal whereby only evidence from the 'prosecution shall be allowed'. The court held that the paper committals under the Act were unlawful in that the accused was denied the right to adduce any evidence in response to that adduced by the prosecution. This was held to be not in accordance with the fair trial rights guaranteed under the Constitution.

The situation with paper committals for sexual offences has now changed with the advent of the amended First Schedule to the Sexual Offences Act Cap 8:03, which now gives both the prosecution and the defence the right to lead 'credible evidence' at committal proceedings.

The accused must file in the court registry all defence evidence for the purposes of a paper committal not later than 45 days after the date on which the magistrate reopened the paper committal. Items of both prosecution and defence evidence which are admissible in paper committals under the act include written statements, relevant documents or other exhibits and depositions. Section 12 of the First Schedule allows the magistrate, where satisfied that all the evidence tendered by or on behalf the prosecutor and the accused is admissible, to commit the accused for trial without consideration of the evidence unless the accused is unrepresented or where the accused requests the court to consider a no-case submission.

It should be noted that in both the Antigua and St Lucia legislation abolishing preliminary enquiries, the accused has the right to file evidence (written) in response to that of the prosecution.

In Barbados the Magistrates' Court Act 1996–27 was amended by Act 2016–15, which altered the procedure for committal proceedings. The amended legislation applies to committal proceedings for offences committed after the commencement date. From the commencement date (1 February 2017) committal proceedings for existing charges must only be conducted in accordance with the provisions of the amended legislation where at the commencement date the proceedings had not started. For proceedings commenced before the commencement date, the accused may apply to the court for the proceedings to be continued in accordance with the amended provisions.

Under the amended provisions, evidence, whether for the prosecution or the defence, shall consist of written statements. These statements are admissible into evidence in the same manner as oral evidence where certain statutory formalities are followed. Notwithstanding the admission of written statements, the accused is still allowed to make a no-case submission.

The magistrate may authorise the taking of oral evidence at the proceedings from any person other than the accused, whether or not a statement from that person has been tendered into evidence, and that witness may be cross-examined. The accused may elect to tender his own written statement into evidence or give oral evidence or an oral statement. Following the close of the prosecution's case, the court may be required (where necessary) to give the accused an alibi warning, as prescribed by rule 22(4) of the Magistrates' Court (Criminal Procedure) Rules 2000.

The accused who intends to rely on an alibi at his trial must give notice of alibi at the committal proceedings, failing which he will not be permitted to raise alibi at the trial. The examining magistrate, after a consideration of the evidence whether written or oral, may, based on the sufficiency of evidence, either commit the accused for trial or discharge the accused.

CHAPTER 12

PAPER COMMITTALS AND COMMITTAL FOR SENTENCE

'Paper' committals and committal for sentence are two types of procedure, created by statute in some jurisdictions, that may be utilised instead of the full oral hearings in a preliminary enquiry discussed in Chapter 11. These specialised types of hearing result in the shortening of the otherwise lengthy procedure at the preliminary enquiry into an indictable charge. This short chapter focusses on the circumstances in which each procedure may be utilised and the law in the jurisdictions that provide for one or the other or both.

PAPER COMMITTALS

The English precedent

The English Criminal Justice Act, passed in 1967, introduced, in s 1, an alternative procedure by which magistrates in committal proceedings could commit an accused person for trial without consideration of the evidence at the preliminary enquiry. That section was later re-enacted in s 6(2) of the Magistrates' Courts Act 1980, whereas s 6(1) dealt with committal on consideration of the evidence. In both cases the prosecution must establish a prima facie case before the magistrate. Section 6(2) of the 1980 Act provided:

> A magistrates' court inquiring into an offence as examining justices may, if satisfied that all the evidence before the court (whether for the prosecution or the defence) consists of written statements tendered to the court under section 102 below, with or without exhibits, commit the defendant for trial for the offence without consideration of the contents of those statements, unless (a) the accused or one of the accused is not represented by counsel or a solicitor; (b) counsel or a solicitor for the defendant, or one of the defendants, as the case may be, has requested the court to consider a submission that the statements disclose insufficient evidence to put that defendant on trial by jury for the offence.

Section 102 of the 1980 Act dealt with the admissibility of written statements in lieu of oral evidence as depositions in a preliminary enquiry as follows:

> (1) In committal proceedings a written statement by any person shall, if the conditions mentioned in subsection (2) below are satisfied be admissible as evidence to the like extent as oral evidence to the like effect by that person.

The conditions in sub-s (2) relate to requirements that the statement: must be signed by the maker; must contain a declaration by the maker to the effect that it is true (which if false is subject to criminal prosecution) and that a copy of the statement must first be served on the opposing party along with a notice that he could object to the admissibility of the statement. It appears, therefore, that once these conditions are satisfied, a written statement may be admitted as a deposition in a preliminary enquiry without the need for oral evidence. This is, of course, subject to the right of the court or the defendant to require the person who gave the statement to attend for cross-examination. If this happens, then the magistrate can no longer commit without consideration of the evidence, since all the evidence would no longer consist of written statements.

The purpose of the law in the English Magistrates' Courts Act 1980 was to enable preliminary enquiries to be expedited. Because of the emphasis on written statements, this permissible alternative procedure was referred to as the system of 'paper committals'. Several jurisdictions in the Commonwealth Caribbean have enacted statute patterned on s 6(2) and s 102 of the English Magistrates' Courts Act 1980 or on s 102 alone.

Local legislation

Statutory provisions in this regard in Barbados, Dominica, Grenada, Guyana and Trinidad and Tobago are very similar to those of the English Magistrates' Courts Act 1980. These jurisdictions provide both for the admissibility of written statements as depositions (s 102 of the 1980 English Act) and committal without consideration of the evidence (s 6(2) of the 1980 Act). In each case[1] the legislation provides for committal without consideration of the evidence 'where all the evidence before the courts consists of written statements'. This is, however, not possible if the defendant is unrepresented or his lawyer wishes to make a no case submission. In these situations, the magistrate must consider the evidence before committal.

In *R v Grays JJ ex p Tetley* (1980) 70 Cr App R 11, the English Divisional Court made it clear that the procedure allowing committal without consideration of the evidence does not give the defence the right to have witnesses whose statements the prosecution does not tender called as witnesses. While the defence has a right to seek to cross-examine witnesses whose witness statements are to be tendered as evidence, it cannot demand to cross-examine witnesses who are not tendered by the prosecution. Once the court is satisfied that the prosecution evidence consists wholly of written statements, it may commit the defendant subject to the right of the defence to call evidence. It is not subject to their right to require the prosecution to call additional witnesses.

The procedure for tendering the written statements before committal without consideration of the evidence is set out in statute. These statements are usually read aloud at the preliminary enquiry proceedings immediately before committal.

The Guyanese Criminal (Procedure) Act amended by Act No 17 of 2008 is in contrast. It permits a magistrate holding a preliminary enquiry to admit as evidence 'statements, documents, writings and other articles' in the absence of the witness and to commit an accused for trial if he finds that a prima facie case is made out on the basis of these materials 'on consideration'.[2] So, while the legislation is similar to the original English law in that a committal may be had only on written material (and exhibits), in Guyana the magistrate must consider the evidence before committal. There is no committal without consideration of the evidence and if an accused person wishes to cross examine or call witnesses he may do so. Oral evidence, in short, is still the order of the day.

---

1 Barbados: Magistrates' Courts Act 1996–27 s 20 and Rule 24 of the Magistrate's Courts (Criminal Procedure) Rules 2001 (applies only to matters done under the old law, for the procedure under the amended law see Chapter 11);
Dominica: Act No 14 of 1995, the Criminal Procedure (Preliminary Inquiries) Act 1995, s 2, amended by Act No 1 of 2004; Grenada: Act No 35 of 1978, Criminal Procedure (Preliminary Inquiries) Act, 1978, s 2;
Trinidad and Tobago: Act No 23 of 2005, s 10, creating a new Section 23A to Chap 12:01;
Guyana: Sexual Offences Act Cap 803, First Schedule s 12.

2 New s 71A(2) created in Act No 17 of 2008, the Criminal Law (Procedure) (Amendment) Act 2008.

Written statements

To enable a committal without consideration of the evidence it must be shown that all the evidence before the court consists of written statements. Following s 102 of the English Magistrates' Courts Act 1980 those jurisdictions with the alternative procedure made provision for the tendering of written statements[3] as depositions.[4] Interestingly, written statements may be used as depositions as long as the statutory conditions for admissibility (mentioned above) are satisfied. The statute in the regions is similar in this regard to s 102 of the English Magistrates' Courts Act 1980 as evidenced by s 3 of Act No 35 of 1978 of Grenada:

> (1) In a preliminary inquiry a written statement by any person shall, if the conditions mentioned in the next following subsection are satisfied, be admissible as evidence to the like extent as oral evidence to the like effect by that person.
>
> (2) The said conditions are:
>
> (a) the statement purports to be signed by the person who made it;
>
> (b) the statement contains a declaration by that person to the effect that it is true to the best of his knowledge and belief and that he made the statement knowing that, if it were tendered in evidence, he would be liable to prosecution if he wilfully stated in it anything which he knew to be false or did not believe to be true;
>
> (c) at least two days before the statement is tendered in evidence, a copy of the statement is given, by or on behalf of the party proposing to tender it, to each of the other parties to the inquiry; and
>
> (d) none of the other parties, before the statement is tendered in evidence at the preliminary inquiry, objects to the statement being so tendered under this section.

Thus, even if the committal is with consideration of the evidence, the magistrate may still admit written statements. If the defendant is unrepresented, while the magistrate may not commit without consideration of the evidence, he may yet allow written statements as depositions in these jurisdictions.[5] He considers the evidence in the written statements. In *R v Bedwellty JJ ex p Williams* [1996] 3 WLR 361, HL, the House of Lords considered whether the magistrates had been at fault in performing their functions under s 6(1) of the Magistrates' Courts Act 1980 which simply deals with the general power of the magistrate to commit (on consideration of the evidence) once a prima facie case is made out. In that case, it was clearly accepted that, at a preliminary enquiry in which the evidence is being considered, written statements are admissible once certain conditions are satisfied, 'to the like extent as oral evidence' would have been in the preliminary enquiry: *Ex p Williams*, p 366. The examining magistrates therefore had to

3 Barbados: Magistrates' Courts Act 1996–27 s132 (now repealed by Magistrate's Courts (Amendment) Act, 2016–15 and only applies to matters not done under the amended provisions of Act 1996–27).
Grenada: Act No 35 of 1978, s 3.
Trinidad and Tobago, Act No 23 of 2005, s 4, creating new sections 16C and 16D.

4 In Guyana, however, Act No 17 of 2008 makes no such provision: see new s 71A(1). See also Sexual Offences Act Chap 8:03 First Schedule s 6.

5 Antigua, Barbados, Grenada and St Lucia.

consider the question of the admissibility of hearsay evidence in the written statements. In that case it was held that the committal was bad because the written statements consisted mostly of inadmissible evidence. Nevertheless, it was clear that the written statements could constitute depositions where there was committal on consideration of the evidence.

The value of admitting written statements as depositions is that this practice will serve to expedite the hearing of the preliminary enquiry. In at least three Commonwealth Caribbean jurisdictions, legislation has been passed simply to permit the admissibility of written statements. This is so in the Bahamas by the virtue of the Preliminary Inquiries (Special Procedure) Act, Ch 85, which was passed solely to establish a procedure to expedite the hearing of preliminary enquiries. While s 3 of that Act does allow the magistrate to make a determination on whether to commit or not based on the evidence in the statements, there is no provision for committal without consideration of the evidence. Similar legislation exists in St Vincent by virtue of s 142 of the Criminal Procedure Code, Cap 172. As mentioned above, in Guyana by Act No 17 of 2008, statements, documents and writings of a witness may be put in evidence in the absence of the witness and while there may be a committal simply on this evidence it must be after consideration of the evidence.

The Jamaica statute, s 31C of the Evidence (Amendment) Act 1995, is not patterned exactly on s 102 of the English Magistrates' Courts Act. It does, however, enable the admissibility of written statements as evidence in 'any criminal proceedings' provided certain conditions similar to those in s 102 of the English Magistrates' Courts Act 1980 are satisfied.

The use of procedure

The provisions for written statements in these jurisdictions, which are based on the English law, seek essentially to avoid the long drawn out preliminary enquiry process. While the use of the written statements procedure has been reasonably successful in some countries, in others it is yet to get off the ground. Although its use got off to a slow start in Trinidad and Tobago, more and more written statements are being tendered as evidence in chief in preliminary enquiries. Since the majority of defendants at committal proceedings are undefended, it is unlikely that the existing procedure of committal without consideration of the evidence can be resorted to as often as may be desired by the prosecution. In contrast, the practice of tendering written statements in lieu of, or along with, oral evidence at a preliminary enquiry may be more successfully utilised. It shortens the process without denying the defendant the right to make a no case submission or to have the evidence considered by the magistrate. This practice may in time replace oral hearings entirely as has been done in England by virtue of the Criminal Procedure and Investigations Act 1996. That Act prohibits the giving of any oral evidence on a preliminary enquiry. The decision on whether to commit or not is based solely on written statements.

In several Commonwealth Caribbean jurisdictions full oral hearings still predominate at preliminary enquiries. In the absence of radical legal reform, this is unlikely to change in the near future.

The Antigua position

As discussed in Chapter 11, Antigua abolished preliminary enquiries with the passage of the Magistrate's Code of Procedure (Amendment) Act No 13 of 2004 which became law in

November 2004. They were replaced by what are termed 'committal proceedings' which involve consideration by a magistrate of documentary evidence and exhibits only: there is no option to cross examine and there is absolutely no oral evidence. A new s 42A (as amended by the Magistrate's Code of Procedure (Amendment) Act 2005) was created and provides:

(1) All committal proceedings in respect of public prosecutions shall be instituted under the direction of the Director Public Prosecutions.

(2) Committal proceedings shall be commenced by the filing of –

(a) one or more written statements of witnesses in support of the charge; and

(b) a list of exhibits, if there are any which the prosecutor intends to produce in connection with the proceedings.

(3) The prosecutor shall, as soon as practicable, cause the documents filed under subsection (2) to be served on the accused person.

In *Hilroy Humphreys v the Attorney General of Antigua and Barbuda* [2008] UKPC 61 the Privy Council recognised that there is now no longer any right to oral hearing of evidence or cross examination. The defence has an option after being served with the prosecution evidence to serve its own statements and exhibits and may make submissions to the magistrate seeking a dismissal of the charge. Thereafter, pursuant to Section 42C:

> A Magistrate holding committal proceedings may commit an accused person for trial by jury on a charge of an indictable offence if he is satisfied that either the charge supported by the evidence in the documents filed ... alone or in conjunction with any documents filed ..., establish or are likely to establish the indictable offence charged or an indictable offence of a like kind which is not otherwise within his jurisdiction to deal with summarily.

The Privy Council affirmed that the abolition of preliminary enquiries was not unconstitutional. It was held that the new system was fair and the new 'committal proceedings' operated as a filter system after which the accused person was entitled to his fair hearing at trial, where he could cross examine witnesses and give oral evidence.

COMMITTAL FOR SENTENCE

Even though a defendant is not called upon to plead at the holding of a preliminary enquiry, he may still indicate that he is guilty. In such a case the magistrate may, if statute provides, proceed to commit the defendant 'for sentence' rather than 'for trial'. Statute in most jurisdictions, Guyana and Jamaica being notable exceptions, enable the magistrate to accept a guilty plea even to a matter triable only on indictment and thereafter to commit the defendant to the High Court for sentence. The Antigua Criminal Procedure (Committal for Sentence) Act, Cap 118 was repealed by s 30 of Act No 13 of 2004, which also abolished preliminary enquiry proceedings.

Matters tried summarily

This power is different from that of a magistrate in some jurisdictions who, having tried an indictable matter summarily, decides that his sentencing powers are insufficient. In such cases he refers the matter to the High Court for sentencing. Section 65 of the Barbados Magistrates' Courts Act 1996–27 as amended by Act 2016–15 reads:

> Where, on the summary trial of an offence triable either way, a person who is not less than 16 is convicted of the offence, then if, on obtaining information about his character and antecedents, the magistrate is of the opinion that they are such that greater punishment should be inflicted for the offence than he has power to inflict, he may commit him in custody to the High Court for sentence.

Similar provisions exists in the Bahamas and St Vincent.[6]

At the preliminary enquiry

In contrast, where a preliminary enquiry has begun in respect of any indictable offence other than murder, treason or genocide, statute in many jurisdictions permits the magistrate to commit the accused person for sentence if he wishes to plead guilty. The rationale for excluding murder and the like is presumably because they are capital offences and the courts will not lightly consider a plea of guilty where the penalty could be death.

Otherwise, where the accused person admits his guilt, the court will take all the depositions in accordance with the statutory procedure and then commit for sentence. The prosecution then must present all its evidence so that the High Court judge may determine for himself if there is evidence of a prima facie case, despite the guilty plea. In those jurisdictions where statute provides for deposition by way of written statements, the magistrate may short-circuit the lengthy oral hearing process and accept such statements as evidence, since there is unlikely to be any objection from the defence on the basis that they wish to cross-examine the witness.

Even if statute does not explicitly state that all the evidence must be led despite an indication of guilt by the defendant at committal proceedings, it is apparent from the context of the provisions that this must be so. For example, the Barbados Magistrates' Courts Act 1996 as amended by Act 2016–15 provides, s 21:

> Except where the charge is one of treason, high treason or murder, where an accused person in any written or oral statement made to the examining magistrate says or admits that he is guilty of the charge, then the magistrate shall commit him for sentence.

This section does not require that depositions be taken, but s 24, which deals with speedy trial of persons committed for sentence, clearly states, s 24(3):

> (3) Where an accused appears or is brought before the High Court pursuant to this section and enters a plea other than that of guilty or where he pleads guilty but the court is satisfied from examination of the depositions that some other plea should be entered, the court shall commit the accused for trial at the next sitting of the High Court either in custody or on bail.

It emerges from this section that the magistrate must still take depositions in cases where an accused person pleads guilty at the preliminary enquiry. The Trinidad and Tobago legislation is more explicit on the point at s 27A of the Indictable Offences (Preliminary Inquiry) Act, Chap 12:01. The admission of guilt is actually only recorded after the prosecution has completed the case and the accused person informed of his rights. It is recorded as what the accused person says after the statutory caution is read to him. In Trinidad and Tobago,

6 Bahamas: Criminal Procedure Code, Ch 91, s 218; St Vincent: Criminal Procedure Code, Cap 172, s 19.

although unsworn statements are no longer permitted, statute enables the magistrate to accept an admission of guilt (not on oath) by the defendant at committal proceedings.

The relevant statute[7] in each jurisdiction stipulates the respective procedure for committal for sentence, but in practice it is similar. After the admission of the defendant is recorded and he is given the opportunity to call witnesses, he is committed to the Assizes for sentence. The witnesses are usually bonded to give evidence in respect of their depositions should the matter come to trial.

Speedy trial

An accused person who admits he is guilty on a preliminary enquiry is usually assured of a speedy trial. Statute in some jurisdictions, such as Barbados,[8] provides for this, but even where the law does not so specify, the prosecuting authorities are under a duty to ensure that this is done. One of the reasons for this is the fact that the accused person is proposing to dispense with the requirements of proof at trial and save the prosecution time, expense and the uncertainty of a trial. It is only fair, then, that in recognition of this he should be given the opportunity to be sentenced early so as to begin serving his sentence without delay. Related to this is the fact that most defendants who have admitted guilt are committed to custody pending the listing of their case in the High Court. This seems to be on the assumption that the accused person will obtain a speedy hearing of his case at the Assizes. If he does not, then bail is usually granted, but the failure to grant a defendant who has admitted guilt a speedy trial would serve to defeat the purpose of the statute.

In such a case, an accused person may very well withdraw his admission of guilt, possibly because of subsequent advice, but more likely as a consequence of the delay.

Withdrawal of admission

A defendant is entitled to request a trial at the High Court even though he has been committed for sentence. This will occur when he enters a plea of not guilty instead of the expected guilty plea when he is arraigned at the Assizes. An accused person is, after all, free to enter any plea that he wishes. Statute in some jurisdictions specifically provides for this change of plea even after committal for sentence.

If a defendant does so, however, he runs the risk of his admission of guilt at the magistrates' court being used in evidence against him. The documentary record of that admission will have been made by the magistrate and the defendant may be cross-examined on it. Even so, the prosecution has to await the defence choosing to give evidence (in the witness box) to seek to elicit this information in cross-examination. However, the prosecution may seek to lead evidence to prove the admission as was emphasised in the English case of

7 Barbados: Magistrates' Courts Act 1996–27 as amended by Act 2016–15, ss 21–4;
Dominica: Magistrate's Code of Procedure Act, Chap 4:20, s 52; Criminal Law and Procedure Act, Chap 12:01, ss 18–23, 58;
Grenada: Criminal Procedure Code, Cap 72B, ss 115–25;
St Kitts and Nevis: Magistrate's Code of Procedure Act, Cap 3:17, s 60, and Criminal Procedure (Committal for Sentence) Act, Cap 4:07;
St Vincent: Criminal Procedure Code, Cap 172, ss 19, 146–47, 171–76;
Trinidad and Tobago: s 3, Act No 20 of 1994, providing for new ss 27A–27C of Chap 12:01.

8 Magistrates' Courts Act 1996 as amended by Act 2016–15, s 24.

Barker [1951] 1 All ER 479. A witness who was present in court when the defendant's admission of guilt was made, followed by committal for sentence by the magistrate, may give evidence to that effect. This admission will constitute evidence in the same way that a confession would, except that the defendant will have greater difficulty in denying or explaining an admission made before a court. Probably he may successfully do so only if he was unrepresented at the time of the preliminary enquiry. In such a case, the trial judge may exercise his discretion to refuse to allow the evidence of the admission.

On sentencing, following a committal for sentence to the High Court, the defendant will be subject to the same penalty as if the matter had been tried. Invariably, however, the court will take his admission of guilt, given as early as the preliminary enquiry, into account as an important mitigating factor. The prosecution itself may recommend this. In consequence, the sentence of the defendant may be significantly reduced.

CHAPTER 13

PRELIMINARIES TO INDICTABLE TRIAL

The trial of indictable matters in the High Court is initiated by the filing of an indictment.[1] The indictment is an essential preliminary step to commence indictable trial (in the High Court): *Da Costa v R* (1990) 38 WIR 201, PC. The actual trial only commences with the arraignment[2] of the accused. Institution of proceedings with a view to trial on indictment is accomplished by means of filing a charge before the magistrate who may commit the accused person after committal proceedings or, in some jurisdictions, by preferring a voluntary bill of indictment.[3] The trial of an indictable matter itself must be initiated in the High Court and this is by way of indictment, or information as it is called in the Bahamas. After the indictment is filed, a copy is served on the defendant and statute specifies this must be done at least a few days before the trial date. A copy of the record of the preliminary enquiry proceedings will also be served on the defendant. On the day fixed for trial, the defendant appears, usually represented at this level, and at that stage preliminary issues are in general dealt with before the arraignment of the accused person. Upon arraignment, the accused will plead, and it is at this stage that the trial begins: *Da Costa* (above), at p 208.

THE INDICTMENT

The indictment is preferred by the Director of Public Prosecutions[4] (or the Attorney General[5] in the Bahamas). The document is really the printed accusation of the crime or crimes made at the suit of the State, or the Queen, depending on the jurisdictions. In most Commonwealth Caribbean jurisdictions, Dominica, Guyana and Trinidad and Tobago being notable exceptions, the Queen of Great Britain and Northern Ireland is still the Head of State, as these jurisdictions are constitutional monarchies.

Statute may provide that the indictment may be signed on behalf of the DPP by a legal officer acting on his behalf.[6] In some jurisdictions, like Dominica[7] and Jamaica,[8] statute enables a person 'authorised' by the DPP to prefer an indictment on his behalf. In Barbados, although the DPP prepares and files the indictment, it appears that the Registrar may sign

---

1 In the Bahamas, trial of indictable matters is initiated by preferring an information, which appears to be in all material respects the same as an indictment. The only difference is the name.

2 For the process of arraignment, see later in this chapter.

3 See discussion in Chapter 11.

4 See Antigua: Criminal Procedure Act, Cap 117, s 15;
Dominica: Criminal Law and Procedure Act, Chap 12:01, s 24, as amended by Act 13 of 1993;
Grenada: Criminal Procedure Code, Cap 72 B, s 128;
Guyana: Criminal Law (Procedure) Act, Cap 10:01, ss 92, 95;
St Lucia: Criminal Code, ss 841, 843;
St Vincent: Criminal Procedure Code, Cap 172, ss 161–67, 242;
Trinidad and Tobago: Criminal Procedure Act, Chap 12:02, Indictment Rules thereto, r 12.

5 Criminal Procedure Code, Ch 84, s 138(1).

6 As in St Kitts and Nevis, by Act 12 of 1967, s 3, now Cap 22.03.

7 Criminal Law and Procedure Act, Chap 12:01, s 24, as amended by Act 13 of 1993.

8 Criminal Justice (Administration) Act, s 2(2).

it.[9] If the officer of the court designated by statute to sign the indictment does not sign the indictment, it will be invalid, and no proper trial can emanate from such an indictment: *R v Morais* (1988) 87 Cr App R 9. Where an indictment is not served on the defendant in accordance with the requirements of the relevant statutory provisions and he has no notice that he would be tried until the day on which he is called upon to plead, any ensuing conviction must be quashed: *Lester v The State* (1996) 50 WIR 452.

'Any offence' disclosed

The charge or charges contained in the indictment may be for any indictable offence or offences disclosed in the depositions, the evidence of the witnesses given at the preliminary enquiry. Statute thus enables the prosecuting authority, the DPP (or the Attorney General in the Bahamas), to charge for an offence notwithstanding that the defendant may not have been committed for such offence. In some jurisdictions, the statute clearly states that the charge on the indictment may be for 'any indictable offence'[10] disclosed in the evidence given at the preliminary enquiry. In others the relevant statute generally allows the DPP to institute such criminal proceedings as he thinks 'proper'.[11] In yet other jurisdictions, the DPP is entitled to file charges in an indictment for any offences founded on the facts disclosed in the depositions.[12]

Once a charge in an indictment is for an indictable offence and it can be supported by the evidence disclosed in the depositions, it is a valid charge. In *R v Manning* (1959) 2 WIR 111, the British Guiana (now Guyana) Supreme Court considered the meaning of the words 'institute those criminal proceedings ... which to him seem legal and proper' in determining the powers of the prosecuting authority to indict for offences. The court held that the words must be given a wide interpretation, since the history and general scheme of the legislation demonstrated an intention to confer upon the Attorney General (now DPP) wide powers to bring persons to trial for indictable offences. The court held that even if the legislation did not specifically say so, the Attorney General had power to indict for any offence disclosed from the legally admissible evidence given at the preliminary enquiry.

Thus interpretation is, of course, entirely consistent with the constitutional power of the DPP to 'institute and undertake criminal proceedings in respect of any offence against law'.[13] More recently the Trinidad and Tobago Court of Appeal considered this power of the DPP in *Jagessar and Bhola Nandlal v The State* (No 1) (1989) 41 WIR 342. In that case the appellants had been charged with conspiracy to pervert the course of justice and the preliminary enquiry had been held in respect of that charge. The DPP indicted them for corruption contrary to the Prevention of Corruption Act, which stipulated that initiation of proceedings under that Act must be with the express consent of the DPP. The court held that the DPP had acted properly in accordance with her powers under s 25(3) of the Indictable Offences

9 Criminal Procedure Act, Cap 127, s 4.

10 As in: St Lucia, Criminal Code, s 842; Trinidad and Tobago, Indictable Offences (Preliminary Inquiry) Act, Chap 12:01, s 25(3); Bahamas, Criminal Procedure Code, Ch 91, s 141(3).

11 Antigua: Criminal Procedure Act, Cap 117, s 14; Dominica: Criminal Law and Procedure Act, Chap 12:01, s 24(2); Grenada: Criminal Procedure Code, Cap 72B, s 148; St Kitts and Nevis: Criminal Procedure Act, Cap 4:06, s 18.

12 Barbados: Criminal Procedure Act, Cap 127, s 4(3); Guyana: Criminal Law (Procedure) Act, Cap 10:01, s 113(2); St Vincent: Criminal Procedure Code, Cap 172, s 161; Jamaica: Criminal Justice (Administration) Act, s 2(3).

13 As discussed in Chapter 4.

(Preliminary Enquiry) Act, Chap 12:01, to indict for 'any offence ... which in the opinion of the DPP is disclosed by the depositions'. Since the depositions disclosed the corruption offence, the DPP had power to indict for that offence despite the fact that no express consent had been obtained from the DPP for the preliminary enquiry proceedings on which the corruption charges were founded.

Form of the indictment

The form of the indictment is specified by statute in the relevant Act or Indictment Rules. The indictment comprises: (a) a commencement; (b) a statement of offence and (c) particulars of offence. In most jurisdictions of the Commonwealth Caribbean, the indictment is brought in the name of the Queen, who is the constitutional Head of State. In other jurisdictions, such as Dominica, Guyana and Trinidad and Tobago, which are not constitutional monarchies, the indictment is brought in the name of the State as in 'The State v Defendant X'. In all indictments the name of the accused person must be stipulated as part of the heading to the indictment. The commencement of the indictment is strikingly similar in most jurisdictions as stipulated in the requisite Indictment Act or Indictment Rules. In these jurisdictions the indictment begins 'Indictment by the Director of Public Prosecutions'. As indicated already, in the Bahamas the indictment (information in that jurisdiction) is filed by the Attorney General.

The relevant statute in the various jurisdictions include draft precedents of indictments, which in Barbados, Guyana, Jamaica and Trinidad and Tobago are included in each case in an Appendix either to the Indictment Act or Indictment Rules. These precedents are identical and are based on the English forms of indictment. In one jurisdiction, St Lucia, the form of the indictment as reflected in Forms 88 and 90 to the Criminal Code is unique. The commencement to the indictment is 'The Director of Public Prosecutions presents that the accused ...' rather than simply 'Indictment by' the DPP. In addition, there are no separate subheadings for Statement of Offence and Particulars of Offence as in the other jurisdictions. Each indictment contains at least one count. Each count comprises its separate: (a) statement of offence and (b) particulars of offence. A 'count' is a charge. An indictment may contain several counts once they are founded on the same facts or form part of a series of offences. In respect of each count the defendant must plead separately: *R v Boyle* (1954) 38 Cr App R 111, since they are separate offences. In that case the defendant was charged with four counts: larceny, forgery, uttering and obtaining property by a forged document, all arising out of one incident. The indictment was put to the defendant as a whole and he entered a plea of guilty. The English Court of Criminal Appeal disapproved of the then prevailing practice by the courts of taking general pleas.

The statement of offence specifies in short the name of the charge and must include the statutory provision that is allegedly breached if the offence is a statutory offence, as most are. This requirement is provided for by statute. Thus, a statement of offence may simply read 'Murder', which is still a common law offence or 'Robbery with aggravation contrary to s 100 of the Larceny Act, Chap 10:00', the latter an offence created by the Larceny Act. In *Nelson* (1977) 65 Cr App R 119, the appellant was charged with possession of an offensive weapon as count 7 in an indictment. However, the statement of offence failed to state the statute which the appellant was alleged to have contravened (s 1(1) of the Prevention of Crime Act 1952). At the end of his trial, counsel moved for an arrest on judgment on the ground that the indictment was defective and null and void. The Court of Appeal held, though allowing the appeal on other grounds, that the indictment was not a nullity, though it was defective. In *Molyneux and Farmborough* (1980) 72 Cr App R 111, the Court of Appeal took a similar position where a statutory conspiracy was misdescribed as a common law conspiracy and thus no statutory provision was cited. The court held that the indictment was not a nullity, but was merely defective, since the particulars of the offence described the statutory offence of conspiracy to rob. It was not a case of the count disclosing no offence known in law, in which case the count would have been void.

The particulars of the offence are thus vital to the allegations in the count. They must include the place of the offence, the date and what exactly is being alleged against the defendant in succinct terms. The particulars must be sufficient to convey to the accused exactly with what offence he is being charged and in respect of whom, if there is a victim. If it is felt that the particulars of a charge in an indictment are insufficient, the judge on his own motion or on the application of the defence may order the prosecution to give further particulars to the defence: *R v Savage, DPP v Parmenter* [1991] 4 All ER 698, HL. As discussed previously,[14] no count must contain more than one offence unless they are charged conjunctively as arising out of a single incident. To do otherwise would be sanctioning a duplicitous charge, which would be prejudicial to the fair trial of the defendant.

Joinder

As discussed in Chapter 5, one indictment may contain several counts, several offences, as long as they are founded on the same facts or form part of a series of offences. Every count is really equivalent to a separate indictment,[15] but may properly be heard together as counts in a single indictment in one trial because they satisfy the statutory requirements. These requirements are the same in the jurisdictions of the Commonwealth Caribbean.

Offences which are founded on the same facts are said to be those which have a common factual origin: *R v Barrell and Wilson* (1979) 69 Cr App R 250. The facts needed to prove each offence need not be identical, nor need they have arisen contemporaneously as long as they can be regarded as forming part of the same transaction. In the alternative, although offences are not part of the same transaction, they may be joined in one indictment if they may be regarded as being sufficiently similar[16] so that evidence in respect of one is admissible in the trial of the other offence, on the basis that it is more probative than prejudicial: *DPP v P* [1991] 3 All ER 337, HL. Two offences are sufficient to satisfy the requirement of constituting a 'series' within the meaning of the statute: *Ludlow v Metropolitan Police Commissioners* (1970) 54 Cr App R 233, HL.

As discussed in Chapter 5, despite the English principle to the contrary, it is not usual in the Commonwealth Caribbean to join counts of murder with other offences[17] even if they arise from the same incident: *Cottle and Laidlow v R* (1976) 22 WIR 543, PC; *Seeraj Ajodha v The State* (1981) 32 WIR 360, HL. This is because of the fact that in these jurisdictions, murder still carries a mandatory death penalty, and as such it is preferable to try that offence by itself.

The prosecution has the sole discretion to join charges on one indictment. They may also opt to join parties in one indictment if it is alleged that the parties are acting in concert

14 See, 'Duplicity' in Chapter 5.
15 *R v Boyle* (1954) 38 Cr App R 111, p 115.
16 This relates to the principles of admissibility of 'similar fact' evidence.
17 Except in St Vincent, reading the Jury Act, Cap 28, s 13, together with the Criminal Procedure Code, Cap 172, s 165, and in the Bahamas, where 12 jurors sit in all cases.

or their offences arise out of one incident. There is no question of consent by the defendant. In fact, if the prosecution deliberately fails to join offences arising out of one incident and seeks to hold separate trials thereof, this may constitute an abuse of process: *Bhola Nandlal v The State* (1995) 49 WIR 412. Nevertheless, the prosecution should not overload an indictment so that the trial is unfair to the defendant. Factors which must be taken into consideration include the complexity of the matter, the number of charges, the number of defendants and the probable length of trial: *R v Novac* (1977) 65 Cr App R 107. These are the matters which must determine whether charges which may be joined should be so joined. In *Novac* the English Court of Appeal strongly criticised the overloading of the indictment which contained 19 counts, and had already been reduced from 38 counts. The charges were against four defendants and led to a long and complex trial, over 47 working days, and one which had put an immense burden on the judge and jury. The court in *Novac* opined that this would have been a proper case for severance either of charges or accused.

Separate trials

Novac illustrated a situation where severance of properly joined charges is permitted in the interests of fairness to the defendant or defendants. Severance is generally at the discretion of the trial judge. Sometimes, a defendant may apply for a separate trial from a co-defendant on the basis that his fair trial will be prejudiced by the case of his co-defendant: *R v Lake* (1977) 64 Cr App R 172; *Grondkowski* [1946] KB 369. Possibly his co-defendant may run a 'cut-throat' defence, by which he seeks to incriminate the defendant. Such was the case in *Grondkowski* where each accused, charged with murder on the basis of a common enterprise to rob, sought to put the blame for the actual shooting on the other. In such a situation, in the interest of fairness, the trial judge has a discretion to grant separate trials and the Court of Appeal will not lightly interfere with the exercise of that discretion.

Generally, however, where it is alleged that the accused persons were accomplices in respect of one criminal activity, it is inappropriate and contrary to the due administration of justice to grant separate trials. In Trinidad and Tobago, courts have granted separate trials seemingly on the barest of rationales as occurred in the trial of the defendant in *Allie Mohammed v The State* (1998) 53 WIR 444, PC. In that case, the defendant was charged along with three others for murder. The defendant was the only one who gave an incriminating statement, in which he admitted he was a secondary party to the offence assisting the others. Despite the fact that there was ample other evidence, the judge granted the three other defendants a separate trial from the defendant. In *R v Moghal* (1976) 63 Cr App R 56, the English Court of Appeal emphasised that once the prosecution is alleging that the accused persons engaged are in a joint enterprise, only in exceptional cases should separate trials be ordered. Indeed, where the evidence against the accused reflects essentially one incident, the savings in time, expense and convenience would generally outweigh any possible prejudice to a defendant who has the protection of the judge's directions to look forward to in order to ensure his fair trial.

Duplicity and amendment

Issues of duplicity and amendment arising from the form of an indictment may be determined in accordance with the law and principles discussed at length in Chapter 5. It should be noted that in most jurisdictions in the region, specific statutory provision is made with respect to amendment of an indictment. Generally, the rules favour the granting of an amendment of the indictment where appropriate unless the defendant will be seriously prejudiced by it.

Powers of the DPP/AG

As indicated in Chapter 4, the Director of Public Prosecutions (or the Attorney General in the case of the Bahamas) has power to institute criminal proceedings as well as to discontinue such proceedings at any stage before judgment. Thus, even when a magistrate has committed an accused to stand trial at the Assizes, the DPP may decide not to proceed with the proceedings. He may in such a case enter a nolle prosequi instead of filing an indictment. The effect of such a decision is that the DPP indicates that he is proceeding no further at that time with the proceedings. This does not mean that the defendant cannot afterwards be prosecuted in respect of the matter, since there is no acquittal: *R v Richards* (1992) 41 WIR 263, PC. In some jurisdictions, the DPP may even enter a nolle prosequi after he has filed an indictment, as was done in *Richards*. In such instances, however, his constitutional powers of discontinuance may be more appropriate, since it is much wider than a nolle prosequi. In Trinidad and Tobago, for instance, a nolle prosequi may be granted only if the DPP considers that there is insufficient evidence[18] to prosecute the defendant further. The power of discontinuance is not so constrained.

Undertaking

The DPP may also give an undertaking not to prosecute or further prosecute a suspect or a person who has been charged. This immunity is usually granted in the case of an accomplice who engages to give evidence for the prosecution against fellow conspirators in a criminal case: *R v Turner* (1975) 61 Cr App R 67. The terms of the undertaking may specify that it may be withdrawn if the beneficiary does not give the evidence in accordance with his statement given to the prosecution. Immunity from prosecution should never be given by the police: *R v Croydon JJ ex p Dean* (1993) 98 Cr App R 76, and should be granted only sparingly by the DPP.

THE START OF THE HEARING

When the case is called, the defence may make preliminary submissions to seek to have the matter determined in their favour before trial. These may include a motion to quash the indictment or an application to stay the proceedings. After the preliminary submissions are dealt with, if none is resolved in the defendant's favour, the arraignment process will commence. At this stage, any issue of the defendant's fitness to plead may be raised. The defendant is expected to be present at his trial on indictment before the jury. There is no ex parte trial at this level.

18 Criminal Procedure Act, Chap 12:02, s 11.

As compared with summary trial

Indictable trials originated at common law. Consequently, the practice and procedure in general is founded in the common law and not statute. Judges and juries are not 'creatures of statute' as are magistrates. While much of the law in respect of indictable trial has now been codified (and even revised), custom and practice may be resorted to when there is no statutory provision on point.

Furthermore, statute in most Commonwealth Caribbean jurisdictions provides that where legislation is silent on some procedure for indictable trial, the English common law is applicable,[19] once there is no conflict with local statute or case law. A general provision to such effect may even be found in the relevant Interpretation Act in some jurisdictions.

Motion to quash

Before the trial begins, the defence may take an objection to the indictment or any count therein. The most usual method is by way of motion to quash. While the defence may also object to the indictment, requesting a stay of proceedings or making a plea in bar, a motion to quash seeks to have the indictment itself quashed, declared void. Although the proper time to take the objection is before the defendant has pleaded, this does not preclude the defence from raising the objection at a later time: *R v Thompson* (1914) 9 Cr App R 252. That case dealt with the contention by the defence that the indictment was bad for duplicity as it alleged an offence as having been committed on 'divers days'. The contention was upheld and the indictment quashed.

The most usual ground for submitting that an indictment should be quashed on the basis that it is void is that it charges no known offence. In some jurisdictions this ground is contained in statute, as in the Bahamas, St Lucia and St Vincent.[20] It may also be contended that the indictment is so defective that it cannot be cured. For instance, it may be alleged there has been misjoinder of counts or that a count is duplicitous, as in *Thompson* (above). Since an unsigned indictment is a nullity, *R v Morais* (1988) 87 Cr App R 9, an application may be made at any time to quash such an indictment and thus any ensuing conviction based on it.

In recent times, the most common basis on which the defence has moved that an indictment should be quashed is that the committal on which the indictment is founded was defective for failure to follow the prescribed statutory procedure at the preliminary enquiry. Since it is only on a valid committal for trial that an indictment can be founded if a committal is invalid, the indictment constitutes a nullity and is liable to be quashed: *R v Gee et al.* (1936) 25 Cr App R 198. In that case it was alleged that the preliminary enquiry was not held in accordance with the statutory provisions which stipulated the procedure. The committal was thus invalid. In Trinidad and Tobago[21] in 1998–2000, in a spate of cases before the High Court, it was alleged that the indictments should be quashed because the committals were defective for non-compliance with the statutory procedure for the holding of

19 As, e.g.: Antigua, Criminal Procedure Act, Cap 117, s 23(1); Bahamas: Criminal Procedure Code, Ch 91, s 145; Barbados: Criminal Procedure Act, Cap 127, s 3; St Kitts and Nevis: Act No 3 of 2005, s 4; Trinidad and Tobago: Criminal Procedure Act, Chap 12:02, s 7.

20 See Bahamas, Criminal Procedure Code, Ch 91, s 151(1); St Lucia, Criminal Code, s 859; St Vincent, Criminal Procedure Code, Cap 172, s 182.

21 See Chapter 11 on this point: 'The right to call witnesses'.

a preliminary enquiry. It was contended in each case that the record of the committal proceedings did not show that the defendant had been told of his right to call witnesses at the preliminary enquiry. In several cases, including *State v Roger Hinds* (1998) T&T HC No S 365/97 (unreported), the courts held that the committal in each case was bad as a consequence and so the indictment was invalid. This matter has now been resolved following *Charles Matthews v The State* (2000) 60 WIR 390,[22] a decision of the Trinidad and Tobago Court of Appeal.

It used to be thought that a court should not examine the evidence in the depositions to determine if it could support a valid committal. This, it was felt, could be the subject of a no case submission at the appropriate time on trial. Thus a motion to quash an indictment founded on the argument that the depositions disclosed no or insufficient evidence to justify a committal would not be entertained: *R v Central Criminal Court and Nadir ex p Director of Serious Fraud Office* (1993) 96 Cr App R 248. The position has changed to some extent following *Neill v North Antrim Magistrates' Court* (1993) 97 Cr App R 121, HL, and *R v Bedwellty JJ ex p Williams* [1996] 3 WLR 361, HL.

Although both cases arose from judicial review proceedings, the House of Lords in each case sanctioned the exercise by the trial court of its discretion to quash an indictment which was founded in a committal that was based largely on inadmissible evidence. Such an indictment would be void because the committal would constitute a really substantial error as it would be based on little or no admissible evidence sufficient to support a charge. It is apparent, then, that a committal based on inadmissible evidence such as the evidence of a child taken without any enquiry as to competency[23] would be void if there was insufficient other evidence to justify the committal and charge.

Where an indictment is quashed by the judge on a successful motion, the prosecution is free to come again with a fresh indictment since there has been no determination of the case on its merits. If the indictment itself is defective, a new indictment will suffice based on the same committal proceedings. If the indictment is deemed void on the basis that the committal was bad, then the prosecution must embark on fresh committal proceedings so as to obtain a valid committal on which to found the indictment. In those jurisdictions where there is provision for a voluntary bill of indictment, usually granted by a judge, the prosecution may seek to obtain a bill of indictment without the necessity of a committal. There must, however, be sufficient evidence filed in the statements before the judge to justify the preferring of the indictment.

Stay of proceedings

It is open to the defence at the start of the trial to seek a stay of the proceedings from the trial judge on the basis that it will be unfair to try the defendant or that he will not be able to obtain a fair trial. In such cases, the proper way to challenge the indictment is not by way of motion to quash, but by seeking a stay of it: *R v Central Criminal Court ex p Randle and Pottle* (1992) 92 Cr App R 323. This is because the submission is not made on the basis that the indictment itself is invalid, but simply that the trial is unfair.

The Privy Council has stipulated that, contrary to the then growing practice, it is not a proper use of the protection afforded by the Constitution to seek a stay of criminal

22 Discussed in Chapter 11.

23 *Fazal Mohammed v The State* (1990) 37 WIR 438, PC. Statute in some jurisdictions specify the need for such an enquiry as in Trinidad and Tobago, the Children Act, Chap 46:01, s 19 as amended by Act No 28 of 1996.

proceedings by way of constitutional motion, on the basis of breach of the right to a fair trial: *DPP v Tokai* (1996) 48 WIR 376, PC. It was held in that case that in respect of an appeal from the Trinidad and Tobago Court of Appeal, it is for the trial judge in the criminal court to decide whether criminal proceedings should be stayed on the basis of abuse of process or on any other ground. This point should be taken as a preliminary point in the trial rather than form the basis of a separate action, such as a constitutional motion, which was utilised in *Tokai.* Only if the chance of a fair trial were totally destroyed should an application to the High Court for constitutional relief on this basis be entertained.

The defence may argue that the trial should be stayed because it would be an abuse of process to permit the prosecution. This contention may be grounded on: (a) undue delay or (b) manipulation of the process of the court. Delay was the ground argued in *Tokai* (above). The principles enunciated by the courts in determining whether a prosecution should be stayed for abuse of process were fully examined in Chapter 2.

Prejudicial pre-trial publicity

In addition, the defence may seek a stay on the basis that a fair trial is no longer possible because of prejudicial pre-trial publicity.[24] In *Boodram v AG of Trinidad and Tobago* (1996) 47 WIR 459, PC, the Privy Council decided that any such application should be made as a preliminary motion at the trial. Nevertheless, the Privy Council found that on the facts as alleged:

(a) The pre-trial publicity was prejudicial. Among other things it suggested that the defendant was a notorious drug smuggler; that he has been previously charged with murder; that the higher rate of witness mortality was in relation to the appellant's family; that the appellant was involved in the killing of a State witness in the criminal case and the appellant and his brother were engaged in systematic witness intimidation.

(b) The Director of Public Prosecutions (DPP) had a duty to take measures to protect the administration of justice from abuse such as prejudicial pre-trial publicity. As the public authority in charge of prosecutions, he has the power and means to prosecute contemnors, those who are in contempt of court for adversely affecting the administration of justice by prejudicial pre-trial publicity.

Although the media in Trinidad and Tobago had not been deterred by the threat of contempt in this case, the Privy Council affirmed the availability of the power of contempt to ensure a fair trial. The Board of the Privy Council emphasised that the onus is on the DPP, the authority constitutionally in charge of all prosecutions, to enforce this power of protection. This power exists apart from those of a trial court to ensure a fair trial by measures only it can take. If the DPP fails to protect the fair administration of justice by dealing with contemnors, then he leaves the way open for unbridled prejudicial publicity which can so negatively affect a subsequent prosecution that it can lead to a permanent stay of prosecution. Such a stay was initially granted by the Canadian courts[25] in *Vermette* [1984] 15 DLR

24 See Seetahal, Dana S, 'Pre-trial publicity and a fair trial', *Caribbean Journal of Criminology and Social Psychology*, Vol 4, Nos 1 and 2, January/July 1999, p 192.

25 This was reversed by the Supreme Court of Canada in *R v Vermette* [1988] 1 SCR 985.

(4th) 218 but was later reversed by the Supreme Court, which held that it was premature and could only be determined when the jury was selected.

Despite the fact that the Privy Council refused to grant the stay sought in the constitutional motion in *Boodram*, the application was made at the trial of the appellant, Nankissoon Boodram (along with nine others), in June 1996. At that time the trial judge refused to grant the stay sought by the defendants, but did utilise several of the procedures suggested by the Privy Council in *Boodram* (above) to protect the integrity of the trial even in the face of prejudicial pre-trial publicity. The measures endorsed by the Privy Council included:

- sequestration of the jury;
- challenge for cause in the selection of the jury by permitting questioning of the jurors to determine if they were prejudiced, which challenge usually is restricted to circumstances where the defence establishes a foundation of fact to support the ground in respect of individual jurors challenged;
- jury instructions as to what matters the jury should consider and what to ignore;
- adjourning the case;
- change of venue.

At the trial Nankissoon Boodram and his co-accused were convicted and, on appeal, the Court of Appeal[26] commended the trial judge for his handling of the case and the steps he took to protect the integrity of the jury by sequestration among other measures. In 1998 the Privy Council refused leave to appeal the convictions; thus affirming that a fair trial was in fact obtained despite the prejudicial pre-trial publicity.

Presence of defendant

At an indictable trial before a judge and jury, there is no statutory provision for the trial to be started in the absence of the accused person as there is for summary trial. If the defendant has been properly served[27] with the indictment personally or at his last given address and does not appear, a warrant may issue.[28] Otherwise, the matter will in general be adjourned and a subpoena will issue for the attendance of the defendant. Defendants who are in custody will be brought to court from the prison at which place the defendant will have been sent the indictment.

Once there is no statutory power permitting an ex parte trial, the usual principles of fairness apply and these demand that an accused person must be present at his trial for a criminal offence. He is expected to be present during the entire trial, both when submissions in law are being made, when the jury is absent and when evidence is being led. In *Lee Kun* (1915) 11 Cr App R 293, Lord Reading CJ said, p 300:

> The reason why the accused should be present at the trial is that he may hear the case made against him and have the opportunity, having heard it, of answering it. The presence of the accused means not merely that he must be physically in attendance, but also that he must be capable of understanding the nature of the proceedings.

26 *Boodram et al v The State* (1997) 53 WIR 352.

27 E.g., as required by Indictment Rules to the Criminal Procedure Act, Chap 12:02, r 14(1), Trinidad and Tobago.

28 See, for instance – St Lucia Criminal Code provisions at s 876.

Lord Reading CJ, however, conceded: 'No trial for felony can be had except in the presence of the accused unless he creates a disturbance preventing the continuance of the trial'. In *Jones* (No 2) (1972) 56 Cr App R 413, the Court of Appeal approved the recommendation of the Criminal Law Revision Committee that there be no difference in the application of these principles to felonies or misdemeanours. In effect, then, in respect of all indictable trials, each accused person should be present for his trial, but occasionally it may be 'convenient that the trial may continue in the absence of one or more of them, especially if it is a long trial and there are several accused'. Obviously, the power to continue a trial in the absence of the accused should be used sparingly and only when this would not prejudice the defence. Roskill LJ in *Jones* considered this recommendation of the Committee to be an impeccable statement of the law.

The trial of an accused person can therefore proceed where he deliberately absconds during his continuing trial. He is then considered to have waived the right to be present: *Jones* (No 2). The judge has a discretion to allow the trial to proceed in his absence. Similarly, where a defendant creates such a disturbance that the trial cannot proceed, the judge may fine him for contempt and continue the trial in his absence rather than threaten force: *R v O'Boyle* (1991) 92 Cr App R 202.

In the case of *Patrick and Small v R* (1974) 26 WIR 518, the Trinidad and Tobago Court of Appeal approved proceeding in the absence of a defendant who had to be removed from court for violent behaviour.

The question of convenience referred to in *Jones* (above) must give way to fairness to the accused person where appropriate. In *R v Howson* (1982) 74 Cr App R 172, the English Court of Appeal considered the effect and extent of the decisions in *Lee Kun* and *Jones No 2*. *Howson* was concerned with the trial of 29 members of the All England Chapter of 'Hell's Angels' for offences arising out of the unprovoked attack on another Chapter. The trial spanned some 48 working days, but because of an operation, the appellant missed the first day and several other days of the trial (some 15 days). During the days that he was present, he was under medication. Upon conviction, the appellant appealed, citing as a ground that the trial judge should not have continued the trial in his absence. The jury should have been discharged from returning verdicts in his case. The appeal court confirmed that the judge's discretion to continue a trial in the absence of the defendant was not limited solely to cases where the defendant had abused his right to be present or had voluntarily agreed to the trial going on in his absence. In an appropriate case the judge also 'had a discretion to continue a trial in the absence of one of the accused through illness'. The court, however, held that that discretion must be sparingly exercised, and never if it would prejudice the accused's defence.

In *Howson*, the appeal was allowed because the defendant had missed much of the trial because of ill health and had not been fit enough to give evidence. In the circumstances, the continuation of his trial in his absence was thus not a fair exercise of the judge's discretion.

The principles established in *Lee Kun*, *Jones (No 2)* and that line of cases must now be considered in the light of the House of Lords judgment in *R v Jones* [2002] 2 All ER 113 HL. In that case the House sanctioned the decision by a trial judge to try a defendant who had voluntarily absented himself. The House set out certain guidelines for ex parte trial (at page 139) acknowledging that a defendant can waive his right to be present at his trial wholly or in part. If knowing, or having the means of knowledge, as to when and where his trial is to take place, he deliberately and voluntarily absents himself and/or withdraws instructions from those representing him, he wholly waives this right. The judge may exercise his discretion to try the defendant entirely in absentia on such circumstances.

Arraignment and plea

A defendant is formally arraigned on trial on indictment. This is done before the jury is selected. An arraignment consists of three ingredients (*R v Central Criminal Court ex p Guney* [1996] AC 616, HL):

(a) calling the prisoner to the bar;

(b) reading the indictment to him; and

(c) taking the plea, which consists of asking him if he is guilty or not guilty.

The defendant must plead separately to each count: *R v Boyle* (1954) 38 Cr App R 111. In that case it was also held that if the counts are in the alternative and the accused person pleads guilty to the first count, there is no need to put the alternative count to him.

The initial arraignment must be conducted by the Clerk of the Court and the defendant himself. The defendant must plead personally to the arraignment and the plea cannot be made through any other person on his behalf: *R v Ellis* (1973) 57 Cr App R 571. If the plea is one of guilty, an ensuing conviction will be vitiated if the plea was not personally made by the defendant. Where, however, the trial proceeded on the basis of a not guilty plea, which reflected the intention of the defendant but was not formally made by him, the ensuing proceedings would be deemed valid once they followed the same course as they would have had there been a formal arraignment: *R v Williams* [1977] 1 All ER 874. It was held in that case that the defendant suffered no prejudice from the failure to formally arraign him. Waiver of the arraignment could be considered to be implied given the presence at trial of the defendant and his counsel.

If a defendant pleads guilty upon arraignment before he is put in charge of the jury, the judge may accept the plea once it is shown to be voluntary and unequivocal. The prosecution is then invited to give a summary of the facts and the defence will, after this, make their plea in mitigation and call character witnesses if necessary in support thereof. If the defence version of facts differs significantly from that of the prosecution, the judge may proceed to hold a *Newton* hearing[29] to resolve the issue. This will be an option once it is clear that in law, the defendant's explanation amounts to an admission of guilt to the offence to which he pleads guilty.

It has been held that if a person accused of a capital charge pleads guilty to the charge, the trial judge must satisfy himself that the accused person is fit to plead before accepting the plea, regardless of whether the accused person is represented: *Habib v The State* (1989) 43 WIR 391. In that case, the defendant pleaded guilty to a charge of murder upon arraignment. The Court of Appeal of Trinidad and Tobago recognised the fact that in that jurisdiction, the penalty for the plea, if accepted, is death by hanging. A person may plead guilty to a capital charge for several reasons: out of bravado; because he truly wishes to confess or because at the time he was unfit to plead. It was the duty of the trial judge before accepting the plea to rule out the possibility that the defendant was unfit to plead.

If a defendant pleads not guilty to the charge (count) or any of the counts in the indictment, a trial will ensue. A jury is chosen in accordance with the law in that respect and he is then put in their 'charge'. The charge of the jury is to enquire whether he is guilty or not guilty (as stipulated in the Juror's Oath).

29 See under 'Guilty plea' in Chapter 6.

Change of plea

Where a defendant pleads guilty and wishes to change his plea to one of not guilty, the judge can permit him to do so at any time before the case is finally disposed of by sentence or otherwise: *S (An Infant) v Recorder of Manchester* [1971] 1 AC 481, HL, followed in *R v Richards* (1992) 41 WIR 263, PC.

In *R v Drew* [1985] 2 All ER 1061, the Court of Appeal followed *S*, confirming that even where the defendant had pleaded guilty after being put in the charge of the jury, which had then returned a formal verdict of guilty, this was not a bar to a change of plea. This was because a guilty verdict returned on the direction of the judge was no more than a formality. Accordingly, this did not prevent the judge from exercising the similar discretion that he had to allow a change of plea at any time up to the passing of sentence, if no verdict was returned by the jury.

Although the judge has the power to allow the change of plea, only rarely would it be appropriate for him to exercise his undoubted discretion in favour of an accused person who seeks to change an unequivocal plea of guilty to one of not guilty. This is particularly so in cases where the defendant has throughout been advised by experienced counsel and where, after full consultation, he has already changed his plea to one of guilty at an earlier stage of the proceedings: *Drew* (above). In *Drew* the defendant had sought and been refused a separate trial from his co-accused. He then changed his plea to guilty. His sentencing was adjourned. His co-accused were then tried and while the jury were considering their verdicts, the defendant applied to change his plea. The court refused. On appeal, the Court of Appeal held that in the circumstances it was evident that the defendant's desire to change his plea was merely a ruse to obtain the separate trial which had been previously refused. There was no evidence that the plea had been involuntary as alleged and accordingly the request was refused.

Where a defendant pleads not guilty after being put in the charge of the jury he is, of course, entitled to change his plea to one of guilty. When this happens, however, the finding of guilty must be returned by the jury in whose charge he has been put: *R v Heyes* [1951] 1 KB 29. This is so because a prisoner who is in the charge of the jury can only be convicted by a verdict of the jury. If there is no such verdict, the trial is a nullity. The proper procedure then is to re-arraign the defendant in the presence of the jury. Once the jury hears the defendant plead guilty, the correct course is for the court to ask them to return a formal verdict of guilty before proceeding to mitigation and sentencing.

Fitness to plead

It is an essential element of a fair trial that a defendant must be fit to plead. He must be capable of understanding the nature and effect of his plea. It may happen that a defendant is insane at the time of his trial, or he is otherwise incapable of pleading or taking his trial.

Where a defendant remains mute at the time he is asked to plead, statute throughout the region[30] provides that a plea of not guilty must be entered on his behalf. It is evident that such a plea which prefaces the trial ought only properly to be entered after it has been ascertained that the defendant is mute by malice, that is, he is deliberately refusing to plead.

30 E.g.:
Antigua: Criminal Procedure Act, Cap 117, s 20;
Barbados: Criminal Procedure Act, Cap 127, s 7(2);
Jamaica: Criminal Justice (Administration) Act, s 11;
Trinidad and Tobago: Criminal Procedure Act, Chap 12:02, s 30(1)(c).

This is so although statute in general refers to the entering of a not guilty plea if the accused person 'stands mute of malice or will not answer'.

In *R v Scheleter* (1866) 10 Cox 409, it was held that where a defendant is silent when called upon to plead, the court itself may not determine whether he is mute of malice or by visitation of God. A jury must be empanelled to determine this issue. In respect of the selection of such a jury, there is no right of challenge, since it is generally accepted that the right of challenge in the Jury Acts exists after the accused person has been arraigned:[31] *R v Paling* (1978) 67 Cr App R 299. Both sides may call evidence on trial of the issue. The prosecution goes first and may, for instance, call evidence to show that, just prior to the trial, the defendant was capable of speaking and did speak. The defence may choose to call evidence, for instance, to show that the defendant has always been deaf and dumb. This was done in *R v Dyson* (1831) 7 C&P 305 and, in that case, the jury found the defendant to be mute by visitation of God. A similar finding was made in *Pritchard* (1836) 7 C&P 303 in respect of a defendant similarly handicapped.

If the defendant is found to be mute by visitation of God then the same jury must be sworn again to determine the separate issue of whether 'the prisoner has sufficient understanding to comprehend the nature of the trial so as to make a proper defence to the charge': *Dyson* (above). In both *Dyson* and *Pritchard*, the defendants were found unfit to take their trials and thus 'insane'. In Dyson, it was, at that time, considered that if the defendant could not understand or make his defence, he was to be adjudged insane. It is suggested that this would not be enough to determine fitness to plead today, where physically incapacitated persons through the provision of interpreters and the use of standard sign language may be capable of making a proper defence to a criminal charge.

On the other hand, a defendant who is insane at the time of trial is in general considered unfit to plead by reason of mental incapacity. In most jurisdictions, there are identical statutory provisions for trial of this issue.[32] Even if the accused person has already pleaded, it may become apparent during the course of his trial that he is mentally incapacitated so that he is unable to appreciate what is happening. He may be shown to be incapable of giving proper instructions. In such a case, the jury chosen for the trial will be asked instead to determine the issue of fitness for trial (instead of guilt or innocence). Statute throughout the region specifies this.

Otherwise a jury will be specially selected to try the issue of fitness to plead and the question to be determined is whether the jurors are satisfied that the accused person is insane so that he cannot be tried on indictment: *R v Podola* [1960] 1 QB 325. This issue is clearly different from a defence of insanity, which relates to insanity at the time of the incident in respect of which the charge is laid. A defendant may have been insane at that time, but may have become well enough to understand what is happening at the time of trial. Conversely, a defendant who showed no signs of insanity at the time of the incident may have been reduced to such a state at the time of trial.

If the defence alleges unfitness to plead, the burden on the defence is only to satisfy the jury that on a balance of probabilities the defendant is not fit.[33] On the other hand, where the prosecution alleges and the defence disputes that the defendant is insane at the time of trial, the burden on the prosecution is to satisfy the jury of this beyond reasonable doubt: *R v Robertson* [1968] 3 All ER 557.

31 As in Juries Act, Cap 115B, s 28, Barbados; Jury Act, s 33 (as amended by Act No 13 of 2016), Jamaica; Jury Act, Chap 6:53, s 23, Trinidad and Tobago.

32 As in Antigua: Criminal Procedure Act, Cap 117, ss 51–52; Bahamas: Criminal Procedure Code, Ch 91, s 155; Grenada: Criminal Procedure Code, Cap 72B, s 180; Jamaica: Criminal Justice (Administration) Act, s 25.

33 *R v Dyson* (1831) 7 C&P 305, pp 350–51.

The procedure at the trial of the issues involved in assessing a defendant's fitness to plead is similar to the trial procedure for the general issue (the offence) except that the issues are not related to guilt or innocence, but pertain as the case may be to: (a) whether the defendant is mute by malice or visitation of God or (b) whether he is insane in that he does not have the proper understanding to comprehend his trial so as to make a proper defence. In addition, as compared to trial of the general issue, the jury is usually selected without challenge by either side (*Paling*, above) in keeping with the premise that it is not yet determined that the defendant is capable of giving instructions in relation to challenge.

In contrast, when a jury is selected to try a special plea in bar such as autrefois, defence counsel may use his right of challenge. This was done in *R v Rodriguez* (1973) 22 WIR 504. It was held in that case by the Trinidad and Tobago Court of Appeal that where the right of challenge is exercised when selecting the jury for trial of an autrefois plea and the defence does not object to the same jury trying the general issue, the trial will not be held to be void. This is in keeping with the statutory provisions, s 21 of the Jury Act, Chap 6:53 of Trinidad and Tobago (then s 18 of the Jury Ordinance), which allows that 'where no objection is made' any case may be tried with the same jury that was previously drawn for the trial of any other cause. Similar provisions[34] exist in most jurisdictions, such as those in the Bahamas, Guyana and St Lucia. It was emphasised in *Rodriguez* that this provision may only be operational if the right to challenge had been known and available at the trial of the first preliminary cause.

In *DPP v P* [2008] 1 WLR 1005 the Divisional Court found that an appeal by the DPP against a decision staying charges against a 13-year old youth who was found unfit to plead gave some guidance on how the issue of fitness to plead could relate to an application to stay proceedings. The court, inter alia, held

(1) A court should only stay proceedings on capacity issues in exceptional cases where it was likely to affect the fairness of the trial.
(2) The fact that a court of higher authority had previously held that a person was unfit to plead did not make it an abuse to try that person for subsequent criminal acts. The issue of a defendant's ability to participate effectively had to be decided afresh.
(3) Medical evidence should be considered as part of the evidence in the case and not as the sole evidence on a freestanding application. It was the court's opinion of the defendant's level of understanding which had to determine whether a criminal trial was to proceed.
(4) It would be right for a court to stay proceedings at the outset if the defendant was so severely impaired as to be unable to participate in the trial and where there would be no useful purpose in finding the facts.

Legislation was passed in Dominica in the Criminal Law and Procedure (Amendment) Act No 2 of 2013, ss 36A to 36I, reviewing that country's law on fitness to plead. The focus is on the 'decision-making capacity' of the accused and his fitness for trial is assessed on this basis, although the relevant factors in making such a determination are similar to those at common law. The new law provides for special measures that may be ordered to assist the accused in effectively participating in his trial. One such is through the use of an intermediary who communicates with the accused.

34 Bahamas: Criminal Procedure Code, Ch 91, ss 157–58; Guyana: Criminal (Procedure) Act, Cap 10:01, s 41; St Lucia: Criminal Code, s 947.

CHAPTER 14

THE COURSE OF AN INDICTABLE TRIAL

In the Commonwealth Caribbean jurisdictions, the existing system of criminal justice is the adversarial system.[1] In essence this involves pitting two advocates[2] (representing different sides) against each other in a trial where evidence, having been gathered by the police or the defence counsel as the case may be, is presented and tested.

It is also expected that each side will advance all tenable arguments to promote the interests of that side. In an indictable trial, a disinterested finder of fact, the jury, considers and evaluates the evidence according to rules of law, the applicability and determination of which are decided by a judge, who presides over the trial. It is the jury who, at the end of the trial, decides on guilt or acquittal, and the judge who determines and pronounces sentence if guilt has been found.

ADVERSARIAL PROCEEDINGS

At an indictable trial in the High Court (or Assizes, as the criminal High Courts are traditionally called), the prosecution is always represented by counsel and the defendant usually is. It has been emphasised time and again that the prosecutor is a minister of justice[3] and must do all he can to assist in the administration of justice. In *Allie Mohammed v The State* (1998) 53 WIR 444, p 456, PC, the Privy Council endorsed the view expressed by the Trinidad and Tobago Court of Appeal that there exists a 'cardinal rule that the prosecuting attorney must not unduly press for a conviction'. Even though decisions[4] of the US Supreme Court might suggest otherwise in seeming to promote partisan advocacy, the American Bar Association has emphasised that 'it is the duty of the prosecutor to seek justice, not merely to convict'.[5] The Code of Ethics to the Legal Profession Act of Trinidad and Tobago, Act No 12 of 1986 is even more explicit. Rule 14 of Part A stipulates:

> When engaged as a public prosecutor the primary duty of an attorney-at-law is not to secure a conviction but to see that justice is done and to that end he shall not withhold facts tending to prove either the guilt or innocence of the accused.

It is suggested that this statement captures the essence of the duty of the prosecution in a criminal trial across the Commonwealth Caribbean. It provides the underpinning for the law as regards the role of the prosecutor in respect of the general conduct of the case for the prosecution (including disclosure which is discussed hereinafter).

In *Randall v R* (2002) 60 WIR 103 PC, the Privy Council had occasion to consider the behaviour of a prosecutor over the course of a protracted trial in the Cayman Islands. The appellant cited as his main ground of appeal unfairness in the trial resulting from misconduct

---

1 As emphasised by the Privy Council in *Wallace and Fuller v R* (1996) 50 WIR 387, PC.

2 As described in Acker, JR and Brody, DC, *Criminal Procedure, A Contemporary Perspective*, 1999, Gathersbury, MD: Aspen, p 499.

3 Avory J in *Banks* (1916) 12 Cr App R 74.

4 As in *Herring v New York* (1975) 422 US 853, p 862.

5 American Bar Association Standards Relating to the Administration on Criminal Justice, 3rd edn, 1992.

by the prosecutor, who was at times supported by the judge. While recognising that a contested criminal trial on indictment is adversarial in nature and that tempers may become frayed during a long trial, the Privy Council reiterated that the duty of the prosecutor is not to obtain a conviction at all costs. They found that by his running comments, interruptions and prejudicial references the prosecutor conducted himself as 'no minister of justice should'. Furthermore the judge failed to control the proceedings or to enforce proper standards of behaviour. He had so allowed himself to be overborne that the resulting departures from good practice in the course of the trial denied the appellant a fair trial.

Similarly, after this decision in *Benedetto v R* (2003) 62 WIR 63 PC, the Privy Council had to comment on the conduct of a prosecutor during the course of a criminal trial. The court considered that his behaviour was 'wholly at variance with the way in which prosecuting counsel as a minister of justice should behave'. His attacks on the credibility of the defence witnesses were laced with xenophobia and directed to prejudice the jury against the witnesses. His comments were often sweeping and not founded on facts.

The appeals of both appellants were allowed.

In contrast to the prosecutor, the defence counsel's primary duty is to his client and this is so even at the risk of judicial disfavour or public unpopularity. He should represent his client fearlessly, regardless of his private interests. Rule 20 of the Trinidad and Tobago Code of Ethics,[6] Part A specifies: 'An attorney-at-law in undertaking the defence of persons accused of crime shall use all fair and reasonable means to present every defence available at law'. One result of the difference between the duties of the prosecutor and the defence counsel is that the latter has no duty of disclosure except as statute specifically provides which in the region is usually limited to notice of alibi in only some countries.[7] In fact the defence counsel is generally bound by legal professional privilege not to reveal anything his client has disclosed to him (except as is necessary in presenting his defence).

As in most adversarial systems, trial is in 'open court' (just as it is for summary trial). There are exceptions to this rule where statute provides that certain trials should be in camera, such as those involving sexual offences or where children are the defendants.

THE START OF THE CASE

After the accused person is arraigned, if he pleads not guilty, a jury is selected and empanelled to try him. It is the role of the jury to determine issues of fact. The judge determines issues of law including admissibility of evidence. He also rules on any submissions made by either counsel.

The defendant is put in the charge of the jury, after the members are sworn, in that they are 'charged' to determine whether he is guilty or not guilty by harkening to the evidence. The indictment is read to the jury before the defendant is put in their charge. It is for the Clerk of the Court to ensure that the trial judge has the actual indictment before him. The prosecutor must make himself aware of the indictment, the document on which he is founding his case: *Olivo* (1942) 28 Cr App R 173. In that case, by inadvertence, three indictments were tried together and as a consequence the trial was deemed a nullity. The English Court of Criminal Appeal emphasised that while the three charges could have been included in one indictment and tried

6 To the Legal Profession Act, No 12 of 1986.

7 The St Lucia Criminal Code 2004 now provides for disclosure by the defence. See discussion on the 'Duty to disclose' later in this chapter.

together, since they were in fact charged in separate indictments they could not be tried together. It is elementary, the court said, that only one indictment may be tried at a time.

Sworn evidence

As in a summary trial, only sworn evidence can be given in an indictable trial unless specifically provided for at common law or by statute. Children are permitted to give unsworn evidence, but only after an enquiry is held by the judge in the presence of the jury to determine the capacity of the child to give evidence.[8] In many Commonwealth Caribbean jurisdictions an accused person is still permitted to give unsworn evidence in the dock in his defence. Other than these instances any evidence given unsworn will constitute a nullity: *R v Marsham ex p Pethick Lawrence* [1912] 2 KB 362. In giving sworn evidence a witness is entitled to be sworn in the form which he declares to be binding on his conscience: *R v Hines and King* (1971) 17 WIR 326. In that case the trial judge refused to allow Hines to take the oath in accordance with his beliefs as a member of the Rastafarian faith and required that he swear in accordance with the Jamaica Oath law, by which the commencement of an oath was 'I swear by the Almighty God'. The Court of Appeal considered that Hines had been deprived of his right to give sworn testimony on his own behalf and quashed his conviction.

Use of unsworn statements

Legislation has been passed in at least some jurisdictions to permit the admissibility of written statements 'in criminal proceedings as evidence of any fact of which direct oral evidence by him would be admissible if it is proved to the satisfaction of the court that such person' is, inter alia, dead; unfit, by reason of his bodily or mental condition, to attend as a witness; outside of the country or kept away by threats. The statute in Jamaica, Evidence (Amendment) Act 1995, in Trinidad and Tobago, the Evidence (Amendment) Act 2007 and in Antigua, ss 37–38 of the Evidence (Special Provisions) Act No 5 of 2009, is in each case based on the English 1988 and 2003 Criminal Justice Acts and is much wider than the law that permits the admission of depositions given at a preliminary enquiry. Apart from providing for the admissibility as evidence of unsworn statements the law also applies to preliminary enquiries and summary proceedings. Thus the statement of a witness to a crime may be tendered in evidence at the preliminary enquiry and used at trial or admitted as evidence at a summary trial, even if he never attends court and has never been cross examined. In *Grant v R* (2006) 68 WIR 354 PC, the constitutionality of the Jamaican legislation was challenged on the basis that an accused person was, among other things, denied adequate protection of the law, including his right to cross-examine and hear live witnesses. The Privy Council rejected the contention and held that an accused was entitled to a fair trial, had no right to confrontation and there were adequate safeguards in the legislation to secure his rights. These include an enhanced power to challenge the credibility of the author of a hearsay statement and what appears to be a wider discretion for a court to exclude such evidence.

Where a witness who has given evidence at a preliminary enquiry trial is unavailable at trial, it is now no longer necessary to tender his evidence as a deposition. The prosecutor, or

8 *Fazal Mohammed v The State* (1990) 37 WIR 438, PC.

defence counsel as the case may be, has options and may choose to tender the evidence under whichever law makes compliance easier.

THE PROSECUTION

The prosecution have to establish a prima facie case before the defendant can be called upon to answer. Thus the prosecution must present their case first. This they do by calling witnesses to give evidence to prove the charge against the accused person. However, before the prosecutor calls witnesses, he will 'open' his case.

The opening address

After the defendant is put in the charge of the jury, the judge invites the prosecutor to begin. This he does by opening his case with a short address to the jury. In that address the prosecutor will give a summary of the facts of his case and explain to the jury how he is going to prove it. The prosecution ought only to refer to admissible evidence. Furthermore, challenged evidence ought not to be referred to as facts, for example, the contents of a confessional statement, when its admission is expected to be objected to on the ground of involuntariness.

A prosecutor must be careful in his opening address not to refer to matters as facts which may not be borne out by the evidence. In *Leslie Joseph Carr* [2000] 2 Cr App R 149, the defendant was charged with murder. He had been a 'bouncer' in a night club which the deceased and his friends had attended on the night of the incident. Following a fracas in the club the deceased and his party were ejected. After the ejection, the deceased was assaulted and fell to the ground. As a result of his fall the deceased sustained injuries to his skull and brain, from which he died. In his opening address the prosecuting counsel contended that the prosecution case was that the defendant delivered a karate kick to the head of the deceased using unreasonable force and the deceased died from the injuries sustained from the kick. The defence asked for particulars as to the way in which the prosecution case was to be put, but this application was refused. At the trial, the prosecution adduced evidence which suggested that the defendant had inflicted a blow with his fist on the deceased. It was held by the English Court of Appeal that it was a matter of importance to the defence how the assault occurred. If it was by a kick, the only issue would be identity; if by the fist, self-defence would also arise. The defendant was prejudiced by the failure of the prosecutor to give particulars and the fact that 'having nailed its colours to one version of the events in opening' the prosecutor had been permitted to depart from that position during the trial. The appeal against conviction for manslaughter was allowed.

The prosecutor as a minister of justice should, in his address, avoid the use of emotive language, calculated to stir up sympathy for the victim or animosity for the defendant: *Banks* (1916) 12 Cr App R 74; *Randall v R* (2002) 60 WIR 103 PC. Furthermore, while the prosecutor may refer to the legal basis on which the case is to be proven (for example, that the accused persons were acting in concert) if it will assist the jury in understanding the evidence, no reference to cases or statute should be made. This will at this stage unnecessarily confuse the jury and will also constitute a usurpation of the function of the judge, which includes advising the jury on the law when he delivers the summing up.

Regardless of the number of accused persons tried jointly or the number of offences joined in the indictment, the prosecutor only has one opening address in the trial. Where two or more accused persons are tried together, the prosecutor will usually suffer no hardship in his address in this regard since the evidence will invariably concern one incident.

Leading the evidence

The trial is in open court, so the evidence is given in court to which the public has access, and the proceedings may be published. If statute provides otherwise, then the matter may be heard in the absence of members of the public, such as in sexual offence trials in some jurisdictions. There is, however, usually no restriction of reporting in such cases unless statute also specifies.[9]

It is the duty of the prosecutor to ensure that all witnesses who gave evidence for the prosecution at the committal proceedings and whose names appear on the back of the indictment are present at the trial: *R v Oliva* [1965] 3 All ER 116. The prosecution, however, have a discretion whether or not to call those witnesses and, if called, whether to examine them or merely to tender them for cross-examination. This discretion must be exercised in a manner calculated to further the interests of justice and the fair trial of the defendant. Thus the prosecution ought to call those witnesses whose evidence is capable of belief even if the evidence is inconsistent with the case for the prosecution. Where, however, a witness has shown himself to be unreliable, the prosecution need not call that witness. In *Oliva*, where two prosecution witnesses had given evidence at the committal proceedings which was in conflict with earlier evidence in one case and in conflict with an original statement to the police in another, it was held that the prosecutor was entitled merely to ensure that the witnesses were present at the trial. There was no duty to call them.

If the prosecution make all efforts to secure the attendance of a witness who gave evidence at committal, but are unable to do so, they may proceed with the case without that witness: *R v Cavanagh and Shaw* [1972] 2 All ER 704. In that case the defendants were charged with robbery of T and B and wounding of B. T and B as well as a third witness, M, were Indian seamen who were not readily available to give evidence. When the matter came up for trial, contrary to expectations, B was not present, as he was unable to sail from India because of illness. The prosecution, even though they regarded B as reliable, were prepared to proceed in his absence. They did not seek to have his deposition read, but proceeded with the other witnesses. The defendants were acquitted of the robbery, but convicted of wounding. The Court of Appeal upheld the decision of the trial judge to allow the trial to continue in B's absence. The court held that no injustice could be said to have been done to the defendants since, on balance, they benefited from the absence of B.

Convictions of prosecution witness

As a minister of justice, the prosecutor is expected to inform the defence of the convictions of any prosecution witness so that the defence may have the opportunity to cross-examine on credibility if they wish. Statutory provisions[10] throughout the region enable a cross-examining party to prove the convictions of any witness if the witness denies them. In the case of prosecution witnesses, proof of any convictions must be made known to the defence to facilitate such cross-examination.

9 This may be non-publication of the name of the victim, for instance.

10 As, e.g., Evidence Act Cap 5:03, s 78, Guyana; Evidence Act Chap 7:02, s 8, Trinidad and Tobago.

In *Paraskeva* (1983) 76 Cr App R 162, the English Court of Appeal confirmed that it was the duty of the prosecution to inform the defence of any convictions of prosecution witnesses. In that case the (virtual) complainant had a conviction for theft, but this was unknown to the defence. The court held that the defence would have been able to challenge the credibility of the complainant as a person who had a previous conviction as against that of the defendant, who was of previous good character. Failure to make known the conviction was a material irregularity in the trial which resulted in the conviction being quashed.

In *Glenroy Bishop v The State* (2000) 60 WIR 370, the Trinidad and Tobago Court of Appeal was faced with a similar situation. The appellant had appealed to the Privy Council from a previous judgment of the Court of Appeal against the affirmation of his conviction for murder. At the Privy Council, it was disclosed that the two main prosecution witnesses, Singh and Jacobs, had previous convictions. The Privy Council quashed the conviction and remitted the case back to the Court of Appeal to decide if a retrial was appropriate. At the Court of Appeal, fresh evidence was led to show that in fact the eyewitness, Singh, had no previous conviction. Nevertheless, the Court of Appeal held that the failure to disclose the previous convictions of Jacobs was unpardonable. The court confirmed that the prosecution's duty to disclose previous convictions entailed a duty to make 'the necessary enquiries to ascertain whether its witnesses have any convictions'. The defence have no corresponding duty to make enquiries. Having regard to the fact that the case against the appellant appeared to be strong and that the lapse of time in hearing the case and appeal was not inordinate, the Court of Appeal ordered a retrial. *Paraskeva* and *Bishop* serve to emphasise the importance which the courts attach to the duty of the prosecutor to disclose previous convictions of its witnesses so as to ensure the fair trial of a defendant.

Tendering a deposition

It may sometimes transpire that a witness who gave evidence at the committal proceedings may be unable to give evidence at trial. This may occur if the witness is dead, ill, insane, out of the country or cannot be found. In any such situation the prosecution may seek to tender the deposition of the absent witness as evidence in the trial (at the High Court). Statutory provisions[11] throughout the region enable the tendering of depositions at trial if certain conditions are met. Invariably these conditions include proof that the defence must have had full opportunity to cross-examine the witness and that the deposition itself must have been taken in accordance with the statutory requirements. The relevant Grenada statutory provision, in s 198 of the Criminal Procedure Code, is representative of those in the region. It reads:

11 Antigua, Magistrate's Code of Procedure Act, Cap 255, s 197;
Bahamas, Criminal Procedure Code, Ch 91, s 168;
Barbados, Criminal Procedure Act, Cap 127, s 25;
Dominica, Magistrate's Code of Procedure Act, Chap 4:20, s 170;
Grenada, Criminal Procedure Code, Cap 72B, s 198;
Guyana, Evidence Act, Cap 5:03, s 95;
Jamaica, Justice of the Peace (Jurisdiction) Act, s 34; applies only to committals not done under the Committal Proceedings Act, 2013.
St Kitts and Nevis, Magistrate's Code of Procedure Act, Cap 3,17, s 194;
St Lucia, Criminal Code, s 894; St Vincent, Criminal Procedure Code, Cap 172, s 193;
Trinidad and Tobago, Indictable Offences (Preliminary Inquiry) Act, Chap 12:01, s 39, as amended by Act No 8 of 1990.

(1) A deposition taken against or for an accused person may be produced and given in evidence at his trial if it is proved, to the satisfaction of the Judge –

(a) that the deponent is dead, or so ill as not to be able to travel, although there may be a prospect of his recovery; or

(b) that the deponent is kept out of the way by the prosecutor or the accused; or

(c) that the deponent is too mad to testify; or

(d) that the deponent is beyond the jurisdiction of the Court; and if

(i) the deposition purports to be signed by the Magistrate before whom it purports to have been taken; and

(ii) it is proved by the person who offers it as evidence that it was taken in the presence of the accused person or the prosecutor, as the case may be, and that he, or his counsel, had a full opportunity of cross-examining the witness; or, in cases where the deposition was taken after committal, that notice of the examination was given, as provided in this Code, to the party against whom the deposition is proposed to be given in evidence.

(2) If the deposition purports to be signed as aforesaid, it will be presumed, in the absence of evidence to the contrary, to have been duly taken, read, and signed.

In some jurisdictions such as Antigua, Barbados, Dominica, Jamaica[12] and St Kitts and Nevis, the legislation specifies that the deposition 'shall' be admitted in evidence. There appears to be no statutory discretion in the court to determine if the deposition should be admitted or not. In the other jurisdictions, the legislation admits of a discretion in stipulating that the deposition 'may' be admitted as evidence. It has nevertheless been held that even in those jurisdictions where there is no statutory discretion bestowed on the trial judge, there exists at common law a power in a judge to refuse to allow the prosecutor to adduce the deposition as evidence: *Barnes, Desquottes and Johnson v R; Scott and Walters v R* (1989) 37 WIR 330, PC. That case dealt with the decision of the respective trial judge in each case to admit a deposition of a dead witness in two separate trials for murder in Jamaica. The Privy Council considered the relevant Jamaican statute, s 34 of the Justices of the Peace Jurisdiction Act, which provided that a deposition of a dead witness 'shall' be admitted in evidence. The Board nevertheless held that the discretion of a judge to ensure a fair trial includes a power to exclude the admission of a deposition although: 'It is however a power that should be exercised with great restraint'. The court considered that if courts are too ready to exclude the depositions of a deceased witness, it may well place the lives of witnesses at risk, particularly in cases where only one witness has been courageous enough to give evidence against the accused person or where only one had the opportunity to identify him.

Barnes and Scott is considered the landmark case in the region on this issue and has been followed in the Commonwealth Caribbean and in England. The Board of the Privy Council attempted to lay down some principles to guide a judge when admitting a deposition. He must:

12 In Jamaica there is a proviso to s 34 (above) which provides that depositions of persons who are 'absent from the Island or insane' may only be admitted with the consent of the trial court. Otherwise, if the witness is dead or ill, the deposition 'shall' be admitted into evidence: *Barnes and Scott* (below).

- warn the jury that they have not had the benefit of hearing the evidence of the deponent tested in cross-examination and must take this into account in assessing the weight to be given to the evidence;
- point out particular features of the evidence in the deposition which are in conflict with other evidence and which could have been explored in cross-examination; and
- scrutinise the deposition carefully so as to exclude inadmissible evidence or evidence that is more prejudicial than probative.

As long as such precautions are taken, only rarely should a deposition tendered on one of the statutory grounds (the witness is dead, too ill, etc.) be excluded. The court considered that in determining admissibility, neither the inability to cross-examine, nor the fact that the deposition contained the only evidence against the accused person, nor that the evidence is identification evidence, will itself in each case justify exclusion of the evidence. What is important is the quality of the evidence in the deposition.[13] For instance, if the deposition contains identification evidence that is weak, then the judge may justifiably exclude the deposition. The Privy Council seemed to consider that the decision to exclude in such a case should be based on factors similar to those that would inform a decision to withdraw a case from the jury where the identification evidence is weak.

In the English case of *Filip Dragic* [1996] 2 Cr App R 232, the Court of Appeal considered the admissibility of a witness statement (similar to a deposition) where the witness was too ill to give viva voce evidence. The evidence was sought to be admitted under s 23 of the Criminal Justice Act 1988, s 26 of which provided for a statutory discretion of the trial judge to refuse to admit the statement. Despite this clear statutory discretion, the Court of Appeal considered the principles in *Barnes and Scott* (above), in relation to the common law discretion to exclude a deposition, to be applicable. The court endorsed the view that the fact that there was no ability to cross-examine; that the testimony of the witness who was absent was the only evidence against the accused person; and that his evidence was identification evidence, were not sufficient reasons to render the admission of the written evidence contrary to the interests of justice.

Similarly, in *Nankissoon Boodram et al. v The State* (1997) 53 WIR 352, the Trinidad and Tobago Court of Appeal followed the learning in *Barnes and Scott* (above). The court recognised that in Trinidad and Tobago there existed a statutory discretion, unlike Jamaica, to refuse to allow the deposition of a dead (or ill) witness to be admitted in evidence. Nevertheless the court considered that the statutory discretion in the Trinidad and Tobago legislation is simply a restatement of the common law and must be exercised in the same way and in accordance with the same principles enunciated in *Barnes and Scott*. De la Bastide CJ considered that the warning of the Privy Council in that case, that courts should not be too ready to exclude the deposition of a deceased witness or they may well place the lives of witness at risk, 'has a special piquancy in a jurisdiction like ours in which witnesses are murdered or refuse through fear to testify, with alarming frequency'.[14]

The courts in the region have been of late more willing to admit the depositions of witnesses who are unable to give evidence at trial whether because they are ill, dead or out of the country. In *Donason Knights v R* (1998) 53 WIR 125, PC, the Privy Council considered the Grenada statutory provision (spelt out above) which provides that in certain circumstances a deposition 'may be produced and given in evidence'. While holding that the admissibility of a deposition in Grenada is very much a matter for the discretion of the trial judge, the Privy Council endorsed

---

13 See also on this issue *Smith v R* (2008) 74 WIR 379, PC.

14 *Nankissoon Boodram et al. v The State* (1997) 53 WIR 352, p 383.

the applicability of the principles of *Barnes and Scott* by the trial judge in *Knights* in admitting the deposition of a prosecution witness who was at the time out of the country.

It is evident, therefore, that *Barnes and Scott* (above) was the turning point in the law in the region as to the admissibility of depositions at trial. A deposition of a witness who is dead; so ill as not to be able to give evidence; insane; out of the country or cannot be found, is admissible at trial once certain conditions are met. The primary consideration is that the defence must have had full opportunity to cross-examine the deponent, whether they took advantage of it or not: *Cauldero and Francois v The State* [1999] UKPC 44. The deposition must also have been taken in accordance with the statutory requirements which make it a deposition[15] and must have been certified by the magistrate. It will be presumed that the signature at the bottom of the deposition, identified as the signature of the magistrate at the preliminary enquiry, is in fact the signature of such magistrate, without formal proof: *La Vende v The State* (1979) 30 WIR 460, p 464, a decision of the Court of Appeal of Trinidad and Tobago.

It is the practice for the party seeking to tender the deposition to prove the fact of the absence of the deponent through a person who has personal knowledge of the reason for the absence of the witness, such as his death or the fact that he is out of the country. The deposition itself may be tendered through a witness who is familiar with the signature of the deponent or one who was in court when the deposition was recorded and signed by the deponent. This may be a Clerk of the Courts or even the committing magistrate, as was done in *Knights* (above). It is clear from the statutory provisions, however, that the certificate of the magistrate is proof enough that the deposition was taken in the presence of the accused person or his lawyer during the preliminary enquiry. All that is necessary to tender the deposition is identification of the signature which is accomplished as described above.

Once all of the conditions for admissibility are met, the trial judge has to determine whether the admission of the deposition of the absent witness would be likely to produce injustice of a kind inconsistent with a fair trial: *Barnes and Scott* (above, p 339), adopting the test stated in the Guyanese case of *Sutherland v The State* (1970) 16 WIR 342, to guide the trial judge's exercise of his discretion to exclude a deposition.

Using a deposition in another matter

A deposition taken in committal proceedings in respect of one charge may sometimes be used in a trial of another charge. While at least three Commonwealth Caribbean jurisdictions have specific statutory provisions permitting this, in other jurisdictions it is a matter of interpretation of the general provision relating to the tendering of depositions. Section 33 of the Antigua Criminal Procedure Act, Cap 117 is an example of a specific statutory provision.[16] The section states:

> Depositions taken in the preliminary or other investigation of any charge against any person may be read as evidence in the prosecution of such person for any offence whatsoever, in all respects, as they may, according to law, be read in the prosecution of the offence with which such person was charged when such depositions were taken.

It would seem that this provision enables the use of a deposition, of which the evidence is relevant, in any other trial. Thus where a defendant is charged with wounding and a deposition is taken from the victim in committal proceedings for that offence, that deposition

15 As discussed in *Bramble* (1959) 1 WIR 473.

16 An identical provision exists in the Dominica Criminal Law and Procedure Act, Chap 12:01, s 41 and the St Kitts and Nevis Criminal Procedure Act, Cap 4.06, s 41.

may subsequently be used in committal proceedings and later in the trial for murder of the same defendant, if the victim dies.

The question arises, however, as to whether a deposition may be similarly used in jurisdictions which do not have this specific permitting provision. While this issue has not been the subject of judicial consideration in the Commonwealth Caribbean, it has arisen for consideration by English courts. In *R v Beeston* (1854) 6 Cox CC 425, the prosecutor sought to use upon a trial for murder a deposition made by the deceased before his death on a charge of wounding with intent against the same accused person arising out of the same incident. The court in that case considered the provision of s 17(b) of statute 11 & 12 Vict c 42, which allowed a deposition to be read at trial. That provision is identical to the current s 34 of the Justice of the Peace (Jurisdiction) Act of Jamaica (applies only to committals not done under the Committal Proceedings Act, 2013).

The court considered the meaning of the words:

> and if upon the trial of the person so accused as aforesaid [the person accused of the indictable offence], it shall be proved by the oath or affirmation of any credible witness that any person whose deposition shall have been taken as aforesaid [in the manner stipulated for taking a deposition] is dead or so ill as not to be able to travel ... it shall be lawful to read such deposition as evidence in such proceedings.

In *Beeston*, the court considered that according to the literal meaning of these words, the deposition taken on the wounding charge was clearly admissible in a murder trial, arising out of the same circumstances as the wounding, once the statutory conditions were fulfilled. The conditions are those for tendering a deposition in trial for the same offence as discussed in *Barnes and Scott* (above) in which s 34 of the Jamaican Justices of Peace Jurisdiction Act was interpreted. In *R v Abbatto and Healey* [1955] Crim LR 645, the court considered the same English provision (11 & 12 Vict c 42, s 17(b)) re-enacted in s 13(b) of the Criminal Justice Act 1925, and concluded that the deposition taken in committal proceedings for an assault charge was admissible in a murder trial. In that case the accused person was charged with assaulting H with intent to rob and causing grievous bodily harm. H gave evidence from his hospital bed and died a few hours after the accused person was committed for trial. The court held that the statutory requirements having been complied with, the deposition was admissible, and fell within the precise meaning of the statute.

It would seem reasonable, then, that the same principle should apply to Jamaica. It should also apply in other Commonwealth Caribbean jurisdictions once there is no stipulation in the relevant statute that a deposition is admissible only in a trial for or an offence arising out of the same proceedings in respect of which the preliminary enquiry was held. There appears to be no such restriction in the relevant provisions throughout the jurisdictions. In fact, the provisions in some jurisdictions stipulate that a deposition may be read at trial of an accused person committed for trial: 'on the trial of that person, whether for that offence or for any other offence arising out of the same transaction or set of circumstances as that offence'.[17] There is no restriction stipulating that the trial must be in relation to the same proceedings, merely that the trial must be for an offence arising out of the same circumstances. While it may be argued that these words contemplate perhaps different counts in an indictment based on a committal in the same proceedings, the words of the statute are clearly not so restrictive. They may be

17 A similar provision for reading a deposition in evidence exists in such jurisdictions as: Bahamas: Criminal Procedure Code, Ch 91, s 168; Guyana: Evidence Act, Cap 5:03, s 95; St Vincent: Criminal Procedure Code, Cap 172, s 193; Trinidad and Tobago: Indictable Offences (Preliminary Inquiry) Act, Chap 12:01, s 39, as amended by Act No 8 of 1990.

given the meaning suggested in *Beeston* (above) or *Abbatto and Healey* (above). In *Abbatto*, the deposition given in the committal proceedings for the assault charge was tendered as an exhibit in committal proceedings for murder (arising out of the same incident) through the Court Clerk (in the committal proceedings for the assault). It was then read as evidence at the trial for murder.

While the foregoing may be considered beneficial to the prosecution in assisting in the successful prosecution of an accused person where the alleged victim dies, it must be remembered that the courts reserve a discretion to exclude a deposition if its admission will affect the fair trial of the accused person. It is possible to argue that the defence was denied full opportunity to cross-examine at the hearing of a charge of murder when at the time of taking the deposition the charge was for a non-capital offence. It will be of interest to see what the courts say if the relevant provisions for admitting depositions are tested in this manner in the region.

Use of transcript

Where a witness has given evidence in a previous trial, or where his evidence has been electronically recorded and he is no longer available at trial, the question may arise as to whether the transcript of his evidence, which is unsigned by the witness, is admissible as evidence. In *R v Hall* [1973] QB 496 the English Court of Appeal considered whether a transcript of a witness's evidence given at a trial was admissible at a subsequent trial. The court recognised that there was no statutory provision that allowed this and sought the guidance of the common law. The court concluded that

> a deposition properly taken before a magistrate on oath in the presence of the accused and where the accused had the opportunity of cross examination was at least since 1554 admissible at common law in a criminal case if the deponent was dead despite the absence of opportunity to observe the demeanour of the witness.

The court went on to observe that 'the only difference between such a deposition and the transcript of evidence given at a previous trial is that the transcript is not signed by the witness'. It was held that provided it is authenticated in some other appropriate way, such as by calling the shorthand writer who took the original note, there seemed to be no reason to think that such a transcript should not be equally receivable in evidence.

In *R v Thompson* [1982] QB 647 it was held that a transcript of evidence of a witness was admissible on a retrial of the same defendant on the same charge if the witness was unable to attend the retrial through death or illness, or if the witness was incapable of being called.

Following these cases Mohammed J, in the High Court of Trinidad and Tobago, in *State v Dane Lewis* (unreported), March 2009 held that the same reasoning would apply to an electronically recorded transcript of evidence. Once the transcript was authenticated, by proving that the recording was accurate, there was nothing to prevent its admissibility.

Duty to disclose

In its Criminal Code 2004 St Lucia passed legislation for the first time in the region codifying principles of disclosure applicable at an indictable trial.[18] The statute codifies the general

18 St Lucia: Criminal Code ss 908–11.

common law principles and as well provides for modes of disclosure (copies, inspection, etc.). In addition, just as in the English Criminal Procedure Investigations Act 1996, an onus is placed on the defence to disclose defences and contentious issues.

It is also arguable that, with the passage of Act No 3 of 2005 in St Kitts and Nevis, amending the Criminal Procedure Act, the English law on disclosure applies by virtue of the amended s 53A. That provision states that any matter of procedure not expressly provided for in the Act shall be regulated by the law and practice in England.

Substantial amendments to criminal procedure were made in Dominica in 2013 by the Criminal Law and Procedure (Amendment) Act No 2 of 2013. Among other things, the Act created several new sections in s 31B to 31F, providing for disclosure by both the prosecution and the defence. The prosecution's duty under the statute is similar to that at common law, to disclose any material 'which might undermine the case for the prosecutor against the accused', as well as expert witness reports and the like. The defence now have a corresponding duty to disclose what the nature of the defence is in general terms and the matters that the defendant takes issue with in the prosecution case. They must also indicate what defence witnesses are to be called in support of any special defence such as alibi, duress or necessity, among others. Should the defence fail to make such disclosure or put forward a defence different to that disclosed, the court or the prosecution, with leave, is entitled to make appropriate comment on the issue and the jury is entitled to draw adverse inferences from the circumstances.

Otherwise, as was discussed in Chapters 7 and 11, in the rest of the region the prosecution's duty to disclose in criminal proceedings in general is determined by the common law. The essential determinant is fairness to the defendant and it is clear that the prosecutor as a minister of justice must disclose all material which may be of assistance to the defence.

There is no longer any issue as to whether the prosecution must disclose previous inconsistent statements of their witnesses to the defence at, or even before, the preliminary enquiry: *Milton Audley v R* (1996) 49 WIR 306, PC. Questions have arisen, however, as to how far the prosecutor must go in assisting the defence case and how much material should be disclosed. For instance, should the prosecutor turn over all original witness statements before the preliminary enquiry (which in the region usually constitutes a full oral hearing) to the defence, and how far in their investigation of the defendant himself need they go? These questions have come up for consideration in many English courts (before the passing of the 1996 Criminal Procedure and Investigations Act) and Commonwealth Caribbean courts. The following principles emerge from those cases:

- The rules of disclosure owe their origin to the elementary right of every defendant to a fair trial: *R v Brown* [1997] 3 All ER 769, HL.
- There is no express right of disclosure under the Constitution but the duty to timeous and fair disclosure is adequately covered by the common law and general guarantees under the Constitution: *Ferguson v AG* (2001) 58 WIR 446 PC.
- The prosecutor must disclose the criminal record of all prosecution witnesses to the defence and, in the case of police officers or like witnesses, such as Justices of the Peace, must disclose whether disciplinary proceedings are pending against them: *Glenroy Bishop* (above) and *Everald Lawrence*, unreported decision of the Trinidad and Tobago Court of Appeal, 21 January 1998. The prosecutor should investigate the background of prosecution witnesses to give effect to this duty.
- The prosecution has a duty to the defence to disclose any medical records in the hands of the prosecution or its agents: *Winston Solomon v The State* [1997] UKPC 59, PC. It is irrelevant if the prosecutor himself does not know of the records; he must enquire of his

agents and is responsible for any delinquency in this regard. In *Browne v R* (1998) 56 WIR 95, the Court of Appeal of Barbados quashed the conviction for murder of the appellant because of failure of the prosecution to disclose psychiatric evidence that the appellant was suffering from a mental illness.

- Disclosure must be made of any material discrepancy between the witness's statement to the police and his evidence, as well as any other matters, such as descriptions of the suspects (where identification is in issue), that might be useful to the defence: *Audley* (above) and *Cauldero and Francois v The State* [1999] UKPC 44, PC.
- Where a prosecution witness has been granted an immunity from prosecution to give evidence, this must be made known as soon as possible to the defence, as early as the preliminary enquiry if possible: *Boodram et al. v The State* (1997) 53 WIR 352, p 381.
- The prosecutor must always make available to the defence statements of persons not called as witnesses for the prosecution which may be helpful to the defence, whether the witness is, in the opinion of the prosecutor, credible or not: *R v Mills* [1997] 3 All ER 780, HL; considered in *Ferguson v AG of Trinidad and Tobago* (1999) 57 WIR 403, CA. In *Hall v R* [1997] UKPC 223, PC, the Privy Council felt that the rule in *Mills* may not be applicable to Jamaica with its history of witness intimidation. Thus the courts would not frown upon the failure to disclose the statements of witnesses that are not credible or not helpful to the defence: *Hall.* The Board of the Privy Council expressed the view that there existed the possibility that some defendants may seek to use the information to intimidate such a (non-credible) witness to give evidence beneficial to the defence, thus subverting the criminal justice system. The recommended practice in Commonwealth Caribbean jurisdictions, then, may be that the prosecution need not disclose the statements of witnesses who have shown themselves not to be reliable: *Hall* (above) and recognised in *Ferguson* (above).
- In recent cases the Privy Council has confirmed that the prosecution has a duty to disclose material which implicates key prosecution witnesses in conduct which affects their credibility. In *Ashook Kumar v The State* (2000) 56 WIR 503, PC, the accused person was convicted of murder based largely on five confessionary statements. Three of these statements had been certified by KJ, a Justice of the Peace who, at the time of trial, had been removed from his office by the President. This was not disclosed to the defence. Although the charges against KJ were subsequently dismissed for want of prosecution, he had not been reinstated. The Privy Council held that KJ's 'credibility could well have been seriously affected or even destroyed if the defence had been aware of the nature and seriousness of the charges against him and that as a consequence of the cloud hanging over him he had been removed from office'. KJ might no longer have appeared to be of the character to be expected of a Justice of the Peace and qualified to certify a confession. The jury could have been told that although KJ might or might not have committed the crimes (for which he was then facing charges) in assessing his evidence, the jury was entitled to have regard to the fact that serious allegations involving dishonesty had been made against him. In the circumstances of the non-disclosure, the conviction was quashed.

In *Krishna Persad and Ramsingh Jairam v The State*, PC (2001) 58 WIR 433 PC, the Privy Council confirmed that the prosecution may have a duty to disclose to the defence information bearing on the reliability of a prosecution witness. The test is whether it is necessary to do so to secure a fair trial. In that case, the Board confirmed:

- that the misconduct must not be a matter of mere complaint or speculation;
- where there has been some finding in the past that a police officer has been guilty of malpractice in a way which may bear upon the reliability of his evidence regarding past behaviour, that finding may be admissible to challenge his reliability. If it was shown that he lied or fabricated evidence or committed either malpractice, the conduct may be raised;
- where a defendant in another trial had been acquitted on rejection of a statement taken by the police witness who gives evidence of oral and written admission made to him by the defendant currently on trial, the conduct in the first matter should be disclosed.

There are some recognised exceptions to the requirement for disclosure (*Mills*, above). These include:

- Matters which only go towards the credibility of defence witnesses. In *Brown* (above) the House of Lords emphasised that the prosecution ought not to be expected to conduct investigations searching for evidence for the defence.
- Non-material matters. These could include criminal records or charges pending against deceased victims (who are not witnesses) unless shown to be relevant and material. They may also include reports of enquiries into the criminal conduct of prosecution witnesses which do not give rise to disciplinary charges. Were it otherwise, the prosecution would be required to make extensive checks as to any enquiries in matters in which a prosecution witness may be involved, however remotely. This clearly constitutes a 'fishing' expedition and can place untold hardship on the prosecution and State resources.
- Matters protected by public interest immunity at common law[19] or by statute. An informant's identity is sometimes protected by anti-drugs legislation in the region so as to facilitate police investigations. In addition, documents or records held by the State could be protected by national security interests. These could include reports sent to the DPP by the police: *Evans v Chief Constable of Surrey* [1988] QB 588.

Thus there can be no right in a defence counsel to see the personal file or employment record of a witness unless the public interest in the due administration of justice can be said to override the public interest in promoting police investigations or protecting national security. If there is challenge by the defence on a prosecution failure to disclose a document on the basis of public interest immunity, the judge[20] will make the final decision in balancing the competing interests and taking into account the relevant issues in the case: *Agar* (1990) 90 Cr App R 318.

---

19 *Marks v Beyfus* [1890] 25 QB 491; *Agar* (1990) 90 Cr App R 318 and *Savage v Chief Constable of Hampshire* [1997] 2 All ER 631.

20 The principles and extent of public interest immunity are more comprehensively dealt with as issues of criminal evidence.

While the prosecutor must at all times seek to ensure fairness to the accused person in performing his duty to disclose, there is in general no corresponding duty on the defence.

Fresh evidence

Statute in some jurisdictions[21] and common law sanction the admissibility of evidence at trial that was not led at the preliminary enquiry by the prosecution. In *Berry (Linton) v R* (1992) 41 WIR 244, p 249, PC, it was suggested that if the prosecution intend to call a witness at trial who did not give evidence at the preliminary enquiry, the prosecution need simply serve notice of fresh evidence, along with a copy of a statement of the proposed evidence, to the defence. While the procedure itself is appropriate and is utilised throughout the region, it is doubtful whether merely fulfilling the procedural requirements will be sufficient to justify the actual admission of the fresh evidence in most jurisdictions.

In fact, in *R v Gomes* (1962) 5 WIR 7, the Supreme Court of Guyana specifically held that where evidence in respect of an indictable matter is available to the prosecutor at the time of the preliminary enquiry and is not led, such evidence is inadmissible at the trial at the Assizes. It does not constitute 'fresh' evidence, that is, evidence of matters that arose after the preliminary enquiry or was unknown to the prosecution then. The court suggested that to allow evidence that is not 'fresh' to be given by the prosecution for the first time at trial would be defeating the purpose of a preliminary enquiry (where full oral hearings are still the norm in Commonwealth Caribbean jurisdictions).

This position was taken by the court in spite of the provisions of s 151 of the Criminal Law (Procedure) Act which recognised the fact that evidence not given at the preliminary enquiry may be given at trial. *Gomes* qualified the section to mean only 'new' evidence. It would seem that this is the interpretation[22] which should, in the interests of fairness to the accused person, be given to both the statutory and common law discretion to call fresh evidence at trial. The Trinidad and Tobago case of *Cadogan v R* (1963) 6 WIR 292, discussed in Chapter 11, seems to support the proposition. In that case, the court held that 'additional' evidence means fresh evidence, not available at the earlier time. So even in those jurisdictions where statute permits the calling of 'additional' evidence by the prosecution, such as the new s 28A of the Criminal Procedure Act of St Kitts and Nevis, created by Act No 10 of 1998, the evidence should be that which was previously unavailable.

The fact that statute in most jurisdictions permits the DPP to refer a case back[23] to the magistrate, even after a committal, to receive evidence inadvertently admitted by the prosecution at committal proceedings, lends support to this view. It appears that only in Jamaica does no such provision exist, which would explain the stance taken by the trial courts in that country in permitting witnesses to either enlarge upon evidence given at the preliminary enquiry or give evidence other than that given at the preliminary enquiry, merely by giving to the defence notice and a copy of the new evidence. The courts in Jamaica may be of the opinion that the prosecution should not be made to suffer because evidence may have been inadvertently omitted by an inexperienced prosecutor at the preliminary enquiry. This position is understandable in Jamaica, since there is little that the prosecuting authorities can do about evidence omitted at the preliminary enquiry before trial, unlike in the other countries of the Commonwealth Caribbean.

---

21 As in the Bahamas: Criminal Procedure Code, Ch 91, s 166; Guyana: Criminal Law (Procedure) Act, Cap 10:01, s 151; St Kitts and Nevis: Cap 4:06, s 29; St Vincent: Criminal Procedure Code, Cap 172, s 191.

22 Subject to the caveat raised in *Abdool Salim Yaseen and Thomas v The State* (1990) 44 WIR 219 – where the prosecution disclosed the evidence at the preliminary enquiry stage to the defence although it was not led. Exceptionally in such circumstances a trial judge may allow the 'new' evidence (see Chapter 11).

23 As discussed in Chapter 11 under 'Leading all the evidence'. See statutory provisions at fn 5 of that chapter.

In general, then, fresh evidence is admissible at trial once it pertains to relevant, usually material matters that were not available at the preliminary enquiry.

Timing of prosecution evidence

The prosecution begins to adduce evidence by calling the first witness. After the witness gives evidence in examination-in-chief, the witness may be cross-examined by the defence and usually prosecutor, as the party calling the witness, is entitled to re-examine the witness to resolve any ambiguity that may have arisen during cross-examination. Following this, the witness may remain in court, having completed his evidence. The next witness for the prosecution will then be called and the process is repeated until all the prosecution witnesses have given evidence. The case is adjourned at the end of the sitting of the court for that day. The time varies in the different jurisdictions, but this is at least by 4.30 pm. Unlike hearings in the magistrates' court, an indictable trial usually continues from day to day, as there is a jury sitting to hear the matter and it may be prejudicial, not to mention impractical, to have piecemeal hearings of the case over an uncertain period of time. In fact, legislation[24] in some jurisdictions suggest that the jury ought not to even separate, unless the judge permits, until the case is finished.

In general, the prosecution is expected to adduce all the evidence on which it intends to rely before the close of the case for the prosecution: *R v Rice* [1963] 1 All ER 832. There are, however, three recognised exceptions to this rule of practice. They are:

(a) where any matter arises ex improviso which the prosecution could not foresee, evidence may be given in reply to this new matter;
(b) where the evidence is a mere formality; and
(c) in very exceptional cases in the light of the facts of the particular case: *R v McKain* (1994) 47 WIR 290. In that case, the Jamaica Court of Appeal considered the English authorities on point in a fact situation where the prosecution had been allowed to lead what was essentially rebuttal evidence after the defendant had given evidence. The court held that the evidence did not arise ex improviso and the other two exceptions ((b) and (c)) did not apply.

It is clear, then, that the mere fact that evidence is rebuttal evidence is not by itself sufficient reason for the judge to allow its admissibility after the prosecution has closed its case. If the evidence was available to the prosecution at the time that the prosecution evidence was being adduced and it was obvious that it would be relevant (for instance, to rebut a defence) the court should not exercise its discretion to admit such evidence: *R v Cleghorn* (1967) 51 Cr App R 291. It would have been obvious that the evidence would be relevant. If, however, the evidence was either not available at the time or its relevance was unknown to the prosecution, the evidence will be admitted. In *R v Doran* (1972) 56 Cr App R 429, which was applied in *McKain* (above), the prosecution was allowed, after the defence case, to call two witnesses of whose existence they had only become aware after they had closed their case. The evidence had arisen ex improviso.

As regards the prosecution adducing merely formal evidence after the defence case, it has been held that the trial judge should sparingly exercise his discretion in the prosecution's favour if it will prejudice the defence: *R v Francis* (1990) 91 Cr App R 271. In that case, the prosecution mistakenly assumed that identity was not an issue and did not lead evidence that the defendant had been the

24 E.g., Jury Act, s 47(1), Jamaica; Jury Act, Chap 6:53, s 26(1), Trinidad and Tobago.

person picked out in an identification parade. The Court of Appeal held that the prosecution should not have been allowed to rectify what was an essential error after it closed its case. If the evidence had been non-controversial, the position might have been different.

In *R v McDonald* (1971) 18 WIR 89, the Court of Appeal of Jamaica considered a case where the scientific analyst in a trial for possession of ganja had been allowed to give evidence for the prosecution after the defendant gave evidence. The defence had indicated a desire to cross-examine the analyst. The court confirmed that it was a rule of practice and not law that all evidentiary matters on which the prosecution intend to rely should be adduced before the prosecution closed their case. In the circumstances of that case the departure from the usual practice did not prejudice the fair trial of the defendant.

Issues of admissibility

Issues of admissibility of evidence are dealt with by the trial judge as they arise during the course of the trial. If, however, the prosecution case depends substantially on evidence which may be challenged as being inadmissible, it might be more practical to deal with such issues before the prosecution open their case: *R v Hammond* (1941) 28 Cr App R 84. This may be done as soon as the trial starts, after the defendant has been put in charge of the jury, where the challenged evidence consists of an alleged confession of the defendant which constitutes the only or the primary evidence against him. The court may hold a voir dire, a trial within a trial, before any evidence is led. In such a situation, the prosecutor would otherwise be unable to explain his case in his opening address if he could not mention the contents of the challenged statement in his opening: *Seeraj Ajodha v The State* (1981) 32 WIR 360, p 372, PC.

A voir dire to determine the admissibility of evidence may be held in cases other than where the admissibility of a confession is an issue. Where there are issues of fact to be decided which will determine the admissibility of the challenged evidence, the judge may hear evidence in a voir dire to enable him to make an informed decision as to admissibility. This may occur, for example, in relation to tape recordings where the authenticity is questioned.

After all the prosecution witnesses have given evidence, the prosecutor concludes his case, sometimes by indicating simply to the jury and the court: 'This is the case for the State/ Crown'. At this point, if there is no submission of no case to answer by the defence, the defence will be called upon to answer the case for the prosecution. If there is a no-case submission that is overruled, the same procedure then follows in calling the defence to respond.

THE DEFENCE CASE

In the trial of an indictable matter at the Assizes, the accused person is usually represented. The right to legal representation, however, is not absolute even in trial for a capital offence: *Robinson v R* (1985) 32 WIR 330, PC. Thus a defendant is not entitled to repeated adjournments to secure that right. Other relevant considerations, such as the availability of witnesses, must be taken into account. An accused person tried on indictment has the same rights as a person tried summarily of an opportunity to be heard, including the time to retain counsel and prepare his case. He is also entitled to call witnesses. He should not be denied a reasonable application for an adjournment to ensure these rights: *Willoughby, Reeves and Goddard v R* (1996) 54 WIR 57; *Dunkley and Robinson v R* (1994) 45 WIR 318, PC.

Defence counsel will test the prosecution's case in cross-examination and, where appropriate, he will challenge the evidence of the witnesses for the prosecution as to their version of the facts when it contradicts the defence case. The defendant may or may not give evidence. In any case, he is entitled to call witnesses as to the issues in the case or simply as to his character if this is relevant.

Where two or more defendants are tried together, each may be separately represented. If the case for each defendant is in conflict with the other, this is advisable. Each defendant has a separate right of cross-examination and to lead evidence. The first defendant will be called upon first and will present his case before the second defendant, and the second will be called next and the process is repeated. It is important that the judge at the appropriate time should tell the jury that a statement of one defendant made out of court is not evidence against a co-defendant: *R v Gunewardene* (1951) 35 Cr App R 80. In contrast, evidence given on oath by one co-defendant may constitute evidence against the other, but the judge must warn the jury to exercise caution in accepting such evidence because the co-defendant may have his own interest to serve.

Unrepresented defendants

Statute in some jurisdictions stipulate that for capital cases, the accused must be represented.[25] Otherwise it is a matter of practice[26] facilitated by legal aid legislation[27] whether a trial should proceed with an unrepresented defendant. This will rarely occur on a capital charge.

An accused person who is unrepresented will usually be granted an adjournment to secure the services of counsel. Where it appears, however, that the defendant in a non-capital case is prepared to conduct his own defence, the judge may proceed to hear the case: *R v Mings* (1976) 27 WIR 12. In that case, on a trial in Barbados for entering a dwelling house, defence counsel withdrew after the judge refused his request for an adjournment. The defendant requested copies of the deposition and with the assistance of the trial judge proceeded to defend himself. It was held on appeal that there was no breach of the constitutional right of the defendant to have adequate time and facilities to prepare his defence, nor of his right to have a legal representative of his choice to represent him. He had that opportunity, but the counsel of his choice chose to withdraw.

It is the duty of the trial judge to ensure that an unrepresented defendant is afforded a fair trial. This includes informing the accused person of his right to give evidence or to remain silent and always to call witnesses.[28] In jurisdictions where the law permits, he must be informed of his right, alternative to giving evidence, to give unsworn evidence from the dock. This duty of the trial judge exists at common law. In the English case of *Carter* (1960) 44 Cr App R 225, the convictions of the unrepresented defendant on two charges of receiving were quashed because of failure of the trial judge to inform him of his right to call witnesses on his behalf.

In *Willoughby, Reeves and Goddard v R* (1996) 54 WIR 57, the three defendants who were unrepresented were given copies of the depositions on the morning of the trial. In each case the defendant sought an adjournment to allow him to study the depositions and prepare his defence. It was refused. The Barbados Court of Appeal, in quashing the convictions, held that the refusal of the adjournment infringed the right of the defendants to a fair trial guaranteed under the Constitution. Each defendant was forced to conduct his defence himself in circumstances in which he was clearly unprepared. Similar observations were

---

25 E.g., Grenada: Criminal Procedure Code, Cap 72B, s 200; Bahamas: Criminal Procedure Code, Ch 91, s 194.

26 In some jurisdictions legal aid legislation entitles persons accused of serious crimes to legal aid if they cannot afford a lawyer. In many other jurisdictions, legal aid is a right only in capital cases.

27 Explained in *Habib v The State* (1989) 43 WIR 391 in respect of Trinidad and Tobago.

28 In *Tiwarie v The State* (1990) 43 WIR 406, the Court of Appeal of Trinidad and Tobago said per curiam that a trial judge should ensure that a note is made of whatever he says to an unrepresented defendant by way of informing him of his rights, advising him or assisting him in the course of a trial and of anything that the accused may say in response.

made by the Barbados Court of Appeal in *Cumberbatch v R* (2004) 67 WIR 48. In contrast, in *The State of Dominica v Newton* (1985) 35 WIR 184, the Court of Appeal of the Eastern Caribbean States dismissed the appeal of the first appellant, who argued that the judge did not perform his duty in informing him of his right to challenge an alleged confession. The Court of Appeal held that the appellant, Newton, had insisted on conducting his own defence and was obviously a man of intelligence. This was not a case of an accused who merely happened to be unrepresented, where the judge's duty is clear. Here N 'deliberately and consistently' refused legal representation. The court said that the judge could have done no more than he did short of taking upon himself the conduct of N's defence.

In *Jahree v The State* [2005] UKPC 7 the Privy Council considered whether a magistrate's refusal to grant an adjournment to an unrepresented defendant amounted to a breach of his constitutional rights, including his right to defend himself by a legal representative. The Board noted that there was no absolute right to legal representation. The Board however observed that in most cases it would be incumbent upon the court, faced with an unrepresented defendant on a serious charge, to make proper inquiry about the reasons and, if deciding to proceed, to ensure that the defendant has been able to read the case papers or is given sufficient time to allow him to do so. It would also be prudent to ensure that such steps are properly noted in some official form.

Representation in capital cases

As indicated above, practice, and in some cases statute,[29] dictates that a person charged with a capital offence should be represented at trial. In *Habib v The State* (1989) 43 WIR 391, the Trinidad and Tobago Court of Appeal held that, despite the repeal of a statutory provision which required a person on a capital charge to be represented by an attorney, the need for such representation still obtained in accordance with the scheme and spirit of the Legal Aid and Advice Act which repealed the provision. The court continued (p 392):

> The necessity for an accused person on a capital charge to be represented by an attorney from the outset of his trial, and indeed on his arraignment, exists even if the accused person when he is arraigned before the court volunteers information to the court that he wishes to take a certain course.

Thus even, or especially, if a person on a capital charge indicates that he wishes to plead guilty, he ought to be represented.

Although a defendant is entitled to defend himself by a legal representative of his choice, even a defendant on a capital charge cannot have his trial delayed indefinitely in the hope that he will be able at some indefinite time in the future to raise sufficient money to do so: *Robinson v R* (1985) 32 WIR 330, PC. The right merely means that the State should not prevent the accused person from exercising his right. If such a defendant cannot afford a lawyer, the State (in capital cases at least) is under an obligation to provide legal representation. Where, however, the defendant rejects legal aid, he is not entitled to repeated adjournments to secure that right: *Robinson* (above). It would follow, then, that a defendant who cannot himself retain his own counsel is not entitled to legal representation of his own choice to be paid for by the State. He must accept the legal aid that is provided or himself retain and pay for his counsel.

Sometimes during the course of a trial, a defendant may lose confidence in his lawyer or for some other reason the lawyer may wish to withdraw. This situation has been considered by the

29 As in Grenada: Criminal Procedure Code, Cap 72B, s 200; Bahamas: Criminal Procedure Code, Ch 91, s 194.

Privy Council in a series of cases arising from Jamaica. It has been held that where counsel, appearing for a person accused of a capital charge, seeks leave to withdraw during the course of a trial, the judge should do all that he can to persuade the lawyer to remain: *Dunkley and Robinson v R* (1994) 45 WIR 318, PC. If the proposed withdrawal arises out of an altercation with the trial judge, the judge should consider adjourning the case for a cooling off period. Leave to withdraw should only be granted if the judge is satisfied that no prejudice will accrue to the defendant. If counsel still insists on withdrawing, the judge should consider whether the trial should be adjourned to enable the defendant to obtain alternative counsel. Where, through no fault of his own, a defendant on a capital charge is left unrepresented there should, in all but the most exceptional cases, be a reasonable adjournment to enable him to secure alternative representation.

In *Dunkley*, following an altercation with the trial judge concerning the admissibility of identification parade forms, defence counsel told the judge: 'if your Lordship is not hearing me on my objection, I ask that I be withdrawn from this case'. The judge in response twice told him: 'You may do as you please'. Despite the fact that the defendant indicated in clear words on several occasions that he was not capable of representing himself, the judge insisted on proceeding with the trial. It was held by the Privy Council that the defendant's trial was prejudiced by absence of counsel which had occurred through no fault of his own. The judge should have allowed him the opportunity to retain alternative counsel. The conviction was therefore quashed.

An exceptional case of the type referred to in *Dunkley* was that of *Ricketts v R* (1996) 55 WIR 269, PC. In that case, the defendant, who was charged with murder, was assigned counsel by the legal aid authorities. The defendant refused to instruct his attorney. A jury was empanelled to determine if he was mute by malice and they found that he was. Counsel sought leave to withdraw since he could not properly challenge the prosecution case, nor put forward a defence without instructions. The trial continued with the defendant being unrepresented. He was convicted. On appeal, the Privy Council confirmed that circumstances had existed to justify the judge in exercising this discretion to allow the trial to continue. This was a case where the accused by his own conduct deliberately denied himself of the opportunity to be represented. He had not been deprived of his right to a fair trial. The conviction was affirmed.

In *Mitchell v R* (1999) 55 WIR 279, PC, the Privy Council considered the newer authorities on representation on trials for capital offences (in Jamaica): *Robinson* (above), *Dunkley* (above) and *Ricketts* (above). The Privy Council approved the principles enunciated in *Dunkley*. The Board distinguished *Robinson* and *Ricketts* as examples of cases where the accused persons had effectively deprived themselves of lack of representation by their own intransigence in each case. The facts in *Mitchell*, on the other hand, were different. The defendant had lost confidence in the attorneys assigned to him by the legal aid authorities and the attorneys, the Board found, expressed the clear desire to withdraw because they were professionally embarrassed by differences with the defendant. The Board held that although the defendant was prevented from voluntarily changing counsel assigned to him under a legal aid certificate (by the Rules to the relevant Act), the authorities did have a discretion to change counsel, especially in circumstances like those existing in the case. The judge should have granted an adjournment for the purpose of allowing the defendant to secure alternative legal representation. The case was not so exceptional as to make an adjournment unnecessary, since the withdrawal of counsel was not through any fault of the defendant. The defendant suffered prejudice as a result of not being legally represented. His conviction was accordingly quashed.

Inexperience

The Privy Council has stressed that a defendant charged with a capital offence should be defended by counsel of some experience. In *Wilberforce Bernard v The State* (2007) 70 WIR 255, PC the Board emphasised that a defendant in a criminal trial is entitled to a fair trial at common law as well as the constitutional right to due process of law and the protection of the law under s 4 of the Constitution of Trinidad and Tobago. Inadequate representation could infringe these rights. They found that it could never be justifiable to appoint counsel of three months' standing to defend a client on his own in a capital murder trial. Even when one could not readily point to specific matters with which he failed to deal effectively, it could not be supposed that he had

> the maturity of judgment and experience of tactics, handling of evidence and presentation to be able to make correctly the myriad of necessary decisions in the course of a major trial, many of which require instant and sure reaction for which experience alone fits an advocate.

In that case, as a consequence, the Board allowed the appellant's appeal against his conviction for murder.

Duties to client

It is the duty of defence counsel in defending an accused person on a criminal charge to present the defence fearlessly and without regard to personal interest. This is the position at common law and is now endorsed in the Code of Ethics in relevant Legal Profession Acts throughout the Commonwealth Caribbean.

To carry out his duty effectively, a defence counsel should take written instructions from his client: *Bethel v The State* (1998) 55 WIR 394, PC. In that case,[30] defence counsel was appointed by the Legal Aid and Advisory Authority of Trinidad and Tobago to defend an accused person charged with murder. At the January 1996 trial, the defendant was convicted. Following a dismissal of his appeal by the Court of Appeal, the defendant sought leave to appeal to the Privy Council. At issue in the leave application was whether his lawyer had ever spoken to the defendant before trial. The defendant contended that although he had seen him, they had never spoken. The defence lawyer responded that not only had he spoken to the defendant on a number of occasions before trial, but on two occasions the defendant had confessed his guilt to the crime. In the circumstances he advised the defendant not to give evidence of a 'contrived story', which the defendant wished to do at trial.

The Privy Council, while confirming that it was impossible for them to investigate such conflicting allegations, nevertheless observed that there were two areas where counsel had failed in the performance of his duty. The first was the 'apparent absence of any documentation concerning the instructions which [defence counsel] obtained from his client'. The Board expressed the view that defence counsel should, as a matter of course, make and preserve a written record of the instructions he receives from his client. The Board emphasised the absolute necessity for counsel to protect themselves from baseless allegations through this means.

In addition the Board observed that defence counsel should have sought to withdraw from the case when the defendant made a full confession of the crime to him. Such a confession must place counsel in a gravely embarrassing position in the conduct of his defence. In such circumstances, counsel should advise his client that his position is compromised and that he, the defendant, should be represented by someone else. From the facts of *Bethel* it was evident that the defence lawyer must have been affected in the conduct of the defence by what the defendant told him, particularly as it impacted on the confessionary statement and the desire of the defendant to give evidence.

Defence counsel is expected to challenge the evidence of prosecution witnesses which is inconsistent with the defence case. In *Warren Thomas Jackson v The State* (1998) 53 WIR 431 PC the Privy Council endorsed the comment by the trial judge:

30 See also the subsequent decision of *The State v Muirhead* (2008) 74 WIR 394, PC where this point was reiterated.

> Now the rules of procedure require attorney to put material things to an opposing witness to give the witness an opportunity to say yes or no or to explain.

The learned trial judge went on to comment on the failure of defence counsel in that case to put several material aspects of the defence case, as given in evidence by the defendant, to the prosecution witness. These aspects of the evidence were inconsistent with the prosecution case. The Privy Council held that the comments by the trial judge were not unfair. The Board said that the matters upon which the defence counsel omitted to cross-examine the prosecution witnesses were important and the omissions were 'quite properly' raised by prosecuting counsel in his address. In the circumstances and in the absence of any explanation by defence counsel, the judge had to deal with the omissions as best he could. In *Kurt Fabian Ebanks v R* (2006) 68 WIR 249, PC the Board stated 'Legal principle dictates that counsel's duty is to put the defendant's case, whether or not he intends to call evidence to support it'. The Board recognised that there may have been widespread misunderstanding in Commonwealth Caribbean countries that if the defendant did not give evidence it would be improper for his counsel to put to the police that they had fabricated evidence against him. The Board was of the opinion that the failure of counsel to put instructions in such a case would deny the defendant a fair trial.

Where a defendant is merely disappointed that trial counsel's strategy did not result in his acquittal, then this would not be a basis of appeal on the grounds of counsel's incompetence where it could not be said that, on the evidence, competent counsel would have succeeded in achieving a different outcome. This was the decision of the Caribbean Court of Justice in the case of *Lashley and Campayne v Cpl Winston Singh* [2014] CCJ 3 (AJ). The court noted in its decision that a high threshold must be met to set aside a criminal conviction on the basis of the incompetence of counsel. Obvious examples of a trial being conducted by incompetent counsel would be if the accused had been represented by counsel whose judgment had been impaired by senility, drugs or some mental disease or if counsel conducted the defence without having taken his client's instructions. In the instant case trial counsel had opted not to contest the real evidence preferring instead to put the prosecution to proof of its case. Counsel also did not lead any sworn evidence. These matters notwithstanding, the court concluded that the appellants were granted the full panoply of their rights at trial.

Unless the appellate court has some lurking doubt that injustice has been done by the flagrant incompetence of counsel (*R v Ensor* [1989] 1 WLR 497), the court will assume that the conduct of a case by an advocate has been in accordance with the instructions of the client: *Harewood v R* (1994) 48 WIR 32, a decision of the Court of Appeal of Barbados. In that case, the defence counsel failed to object to the admissibility of the evidence of a complainant in a charge of wounding against the defendant. There being no indication that he was acting contrary to his client's instructions, the Court of Appeal refused to grant leave to appeal. The Privy Council has shown, however, that it is not averse to admitting evidence (even at that stage) of convicted persons to show otherwise, as was the case in *Warren Thomas Jackson* (above). These cases emphasise the necessity on the part of defence counsel to take written instructions and to act on those instructions. If counsel finds that he cannot do so, he must so indicate and seek leave to withdraw from the defence.

It may transpire that sometimes the misconduct of defence counsel is so extreme that it is beyond flagrant incompetence and may have resulted in the defendant being denied due process. In such a situation an examination of the impact of counsel's conduct on the result of the case is no longer necessary: *Boodram v The State* (2001) 59 WIR 493 PC endorsing *Bethel v The State (No 2)* (2000) 59 WIR 451 CA. The determinant is simply whether the defendant had a fair trial.

In *Boodram* the Privy Council considered a situation where defence counsel had not even realised he was engaged in a retrial. This led to multiple failures in his conduct of the case; he failed to object to an alleged confession that had been deemed inadmissible at the first trial. The Board held that counsel's failure to carry out his duties was of so fundamental a nature that the defendant had been denied due process. The appeal was allowed.

In 2005 the Privy Council considered and applied the test formulated by de la Bastide CJ in *Bethel v The State (No 2)* in two cases emanating from the region. In *Bally Sheng Balson* (2005) 65 WIR 128 PC, an appeal from Dominica, the appellant contended that the defence had been conducted improperly. Counsel, it was said, had failed to take proper instructions as a result of which there was a failure to insist on a voir dire in respect of questions and answers of the defendant recorded by a police officer. The Board considered that this was not a case of denial of due process. The defendant was a difficult client who refused to take what amounted to unpalatable advice from his counsel and was reticent in his dealings with him. He had had two other counsel in the matter with whom his current counsel had conferred so as to advance his defence. The Board even held that the omission to lead good character evidence on the part of the defence would have made no difference to the case. The conviction stood.

In contrast in *Mark Teeluck and Jason Ellis John* (2005) 66 WIR 319 PC the Privy Council considered that the failure of defence counsel to adduce evidence of good character of the appellant John rendered his conviction unsafe. The omission of counsel in a situation where the defendant was of good character and the prosecution case rested on alleged confessions was crucial. Authenticity and reliability of the confessions were strongly contested so the credibility of the defence was a fundamental issue. The conviction was quashed.

Options of the defendant

At the close of the case for the prosecution or after a no-case submission has been overruled, the defendant is called upon to answer[31] the case for the prosecution.

This the judge will do by inviting the defendant to choose one of three, or two options as the case may be. The defendant is told that he may remain silent and say nothing in response to the case for the prosecution or he may give evidence in the witness box, in which case he may be cross-examined by prosecuting counsel.

In many jurisdictions, the accused person still has a third option, the right to make an unsworn statement[32] from the dock on which he cannot be cross-examined. Such a statement does not have the same effect as sworn evidence, but the jury must take it into account.[33] The trend in the region is now to abolish this right, as has been done in England.[34] There is a growing recognition by courts and the legislature that some accused persons may take advantage of the fact that they would not be cross-examined on an unsworn statement to use it to cast imputations on the police and other prosecution witnesses or speaking of their own good character. The most that the prosecution could hope for in such cases is to call specific rebuttal evidence to disprove a defendant's assertion in the dock of good character: *R v De Vere* (1981) 73 Cr App R 352. Consequently, jurisdictions such as the Bahamas, St Kitts and Nevis, St Vincent and

31 In the Bahamas, the options are stipulated in statute: Criminal Procedure Code, Ch 91, s 170.

32 For the history of this right, see *DPP's Reference* (No 1 of 1980) (1980) 29 WIR 94, pp 99–105.

33 *R v Frost and Hale* (1964) 48 Cr App R 284; *R v Couglan* (1977) 64 Cr App R 11.

34 Criminal Justice Act 1982, s 72.

Trinidad and Tobago have abolished[35] the right of a defendant to make an unsworn statement in the dock.

Where an accused person chooses to remain silent, this failure to testify in the Commonwealth Caribbean may not be commented upon by the prosecutor although the judge in his discretion may make appropriate comment as long as he ensures that the trial is fair: *R v Sparrow* (1973) 57 Cr App R 352.

The defendant should always be informed of his right to call witnesses other than himself, and this is mandatory if the defendant is unrepresented: *Carter* (1960) 44 Cr App R 225. In such a situation, an ensuing conviction may be quashed for failure of the trial judge in that regard. If the defendant chooses to give evidence, he should do so before his other witnesses.

Defence opening address

In general, the defence may open their case to the jury with an address similar to that of the prosecution in opening. This prerogative was granted by s 2 of the English Criminal Procedure Act 1865 (Denman's Act) at a time when the defendant could not give evidence. That Act was later amended by the Criminal Evidence Act 1898, which granted the right to an accused person to give evidence at his trial.

In Commonwealth Caribbean jurisdictions through the various Criminal Procedure and Evidence Acts, the legislature adopted the provisions of Denman's Act and the 1898 Act that deal with the right of the defendant to give evidence and the order of speeches. The effect of this has been somewhat confusing, as shown by way of example in s 23(1) of the Antigua Criminal Procedure Act, Cap 117 which provides:[36]

> (1) Upon any trial, the addresses to the jury shall be regulated as follows: The counsel for the prosecution, in the event of the defendant, or his counsel, not announcing, at the close of the case for the prosecution, his intention to adduce evidence, shall be allowed to address the jury a second time at the close of such case, for the purpose of summing up the evidence; and the accused, or his counsel, shall then be allowed to open his case, and also to sum up the evidence, if any be adduced for the defence, and the right of reply shall be in accordance with the practice of the Courts in England.

It is clear that this provision, which is taken from the 1865 Denman's Act, does not recognise the right of the defendant himself to give evidence and speaks of a prosecution right to address the jury a second time before the defence opens. In practice, the prosecutor only addresses at opening and in closing after the defence have completed their case. Furthermore, s 23(2) of the Antigua Criminal Procedure Act continues:

> (2) Where the only witness to the facts of the case called by the defence is the person charged he shall be called as a witness immediately after the close of the evidence for the prosecution. In cases where the right of reply depends upon the question whether evidence

35 The Bahamas: Criminal Procedure Code (Amendment) Act No 35 of 2011 (amending s 170 of the principal Act);
St Kitts and Nevis, Criminal Procedure Act, Cap 4:06, s 32.
St Vincent: Criminal Procedure Code, Cap 172, s 196 and s 12A of the Evidence Act as amended by Act No 9 of 2007, the Evidence (Amendment) Act;
Trinidad and Tobago: Evidence Act, Chap 7:02, s 13B.

36 Identical provisions exist in: Dominica, Criminal Law and Procedure Act, Chap 12:01, s 32(1); St Kitts and Nevis: Criminal Procedure Act, Cap 4:06, s 28(1).

> has been called for the defence, the fact that the person charged has been called as a witness shall not of itself confer on the prosecution the right to reply:
>
> Provided that the right of reply shall be always allowed to the Director of Public Prosecutions, or to any counsel acting on behalf of the Crown.

This provision is a direct copy of ss 2 and 3 of the English 1898 Criminal Evidence Act and has also been adopted in many jurisdictions across the region.[37] It has been held that the phrase 'he shall be called as a witness immediately after the close of the evidence for the prosecution' means that there is no right to the defence to make an opening speech when the only witness to the facts for the defence is the defendant himself: *R v Hill* (1911) 7 Cr App R 1. In that case, the English Court of Criminal Appeal confirmed, following the passing of the 1898 Evidence Act, that in any case where counsel for the defence is calling witnesses other than the prisoner, he has a perfect right to open his case before calling evidence. It follows, then, that if the converse occurs, there is no such right to open. Thus in those jurisdictions where the only provisions on the address by counsel are based on the Denman's Act and ss 2 and 3 of the 1898 English Criminal Evidence Act, the defence has no right of an opening address where there is no witness but the defendant for the defence. This seems to be the case in Antigua, Dominica and St Kitts and Nevis.

In many jurisdictions, however, there is a specific right of the defence to make an opening address granted by statute. Section 171 of the Bahamas Criminal Procedure Act, Ch 91 specifically provides that after his options are made known to him and the defendant elects (whether to give evidence, remain silent or otherwise), 'the accused person or his counsel may then open his case'. The Grenada[38] and St Lucia[39] Codes refer to the right of the accused person to open his case. The Guyana[40] and Trinidad and Tobago[41] statutes state that the defence counsel shall be allowed to open his case 'if he thinks fit'. The choice seems, then, to be left with the defence if they wish to open or not.

By contrast, the St Vincent Criminal Procedure Code, Cap 172 is very clear in restricting the right of the defence to open their case 'if, and only if witnesses for fact other than the accused himself are to be called for the defence'. Although this provision is the same in effect to s 2 of the English 1898 Criminal Evidence Act as interpreted in *Hill* (above), the St Vincent provision very clearly leaves no room for doubt.

The savings provision in s 3 of the Barbados Criminal Procedure Act, Cap 127, provides that the proceedings in the High Court for trial on indictment shall be subject to the practice applicable in England. Since there is no distinct provision in that Act for opening by the defence, the English procedure would be applicable. No opening address is available to the defence if the defendant calls no witness but himself.

Although a defence opening address is in practice rare, this may more likely result from the fact that the defendant is often the only defence witness and so the English practice has been followed. Nonetheless, if an opening address is made, the defendant or his counsel may outline the case for the defence as well as criticise the evidence for the prosecution.[42] Like the prosecutor, defence counsel must be careful of stating as facts matters which comprise his instructions but of which there is no evidence in support.

---

37 As e.g.: Bahamas, Criminal Procedure Code, Ch 91, ss 97–98; Dominica, Criminal Law and Procedure Act, Ch 12:01, s 32(2); Jamaica, Evidence Act, ss 10–11; St Kitts and Nevis, Criminal Procedure Act, Cap 4:06, s 28(2, (3)); Trinidad and Tobago, Evidence Act, Chap 7:02, s 15.

38 Criminal Procedure Code, Cap 72 B, s 163.

39 Criminal Code, s 917.

40 Criminal Law (Procedure) Act, Cap 10:01, s 148.

41 Criminal Procedure Act, Chap 12:01, s 39.

42 This principle is well encapsulated in the Bahamas Criminal Code, Ch 91, s 171.

Interaction with court

Since trial is meant to be in open court (subject to certain exceptions)[43] and in the presence of the accused person, interaction between judge and counsel in chambers (privately) is discouraged. This is particularly important in jurisdictions where there is no judicial recognition of the practice of plea bargaining: *R v Coward* [1980] Crim LR 117. It should be noted that only in Trinidad and Tobago is there statutory recognition of plea bargaining by means of the Criminal Practice (Plea Discussion and Plea Agreement) Act No 11 of 1999. Even so, this Act has been rarely utilised and unless it is, the common law position with respect to interaction between counsel and the court in the absence of the defendant must prevail.

In *R v Turner* [1970] 2 QB 321, p 326, the English Court of Appeal laid down some guidelines as to how counsel, the defendant and the court should interact in respect of any in-chamber discussions as to a plea by the accused person. They are:

- Counsel must be completely free to do what is his duty, namely to give the accused person the best advice he can and, if need be, advice in strong terms. This may include advice that a plea of guilty might be appropriate.
- The accused person must have complete freedom of choice to determine whether to plead guilty or not guilty.
- There must be freedom of access between counsel and judge. Counsel for both sides must be present at any such discussions. Freedom of access to the judge is important because there may be matters calling for communication or discussion which are of a nature that counsel cannot in the interests of his client mention in open court. An example of such a discussion would be whether the judge would consider in a proper case a plea to a lesser offence.
- A judge should never indicate the sentence that he is inclined to impose if the defendant were to plead guilty or if he were convicted by the jury. The judge may, however, indicate that regardless of what happens, the sentence will not be of a particular kind, for example, a fine or custodial sentence.

The Court of Appeal in *Turner* was at pains to point out that it is imperative that, so far as possible, justice must be administered in open court. Furthermore, where any discussions on sentence have taken place between judge and counsel, counsel for the defence should disclose this to the accused person and inform him of what took place.

The principles in *Turner* (above) are generally followed throughout the Commonwealth Caribbean where the courts have always emphasised that justice must be administered in open court. In that regard it is stressed, as indicated in *Turner*, that counsel should ask to see the judge only when it is felt to be necessary. In *Plimmer* (1975) 61 Cr App R 264, p 266, the English Court of Appeal expressed the view 'that this practice of going to see judges is in general an undesirable one, that it should be reserved for exceptional cases and that it is apt to produce very embarrassing situations'.

Such an embarrassing situation occurred in *R v Preston et al.* [1993] 4 All ER 638, HL. In that case five defendants were charged with conspiracy to import prohibited drugs into Britain. They were convicted and appealed against the conviction arguing, inter alia, that the holding of private

43 Such as those identified in the Criminal Justice (Administration) Act of Jamaica, s 23, which includes trial for sexual offences such as rape.

discussions between the judge and counsel to determine the admissibility of details of intercepted telephone calls of the defendant was a material irregularity. Evidence of the telephone calls was admitted, but no evidence was given as to how they were intercepted. In addition, the judge had held part of the trial in camera and had ruled that the individual defendants should not be informed about the nature of what had taken place in chambers. The House of Lords, while dismissing the appeal, held that the trial judge was wrong to hold so much of the trial in private and to prevent defence counsel from telling their own clients of what went on in the judge's room. This was a serious irregularity although it had not affected the outcome of the trial. The House confirmed that discussions between the judge and counsel in the judge's private room in private are objectionable in principle and in practice, as it militates against the essence of the adversarial process that a party, such as the defendant, should hear what his opponent has to say and how he said it.

Any complaints that the defence wish to make about the trial should as far as possible wait until after the trial, unless the fair trial process itself will be affected. In the same vein a judge should wait until after the trial is concluded to deal with any issues of contempt of court that may have arisen during the course of the trial from the behaviour of counsel or other participants. In *State v Solomon* (1982) 32 WIR 149, the Court of Appeal of Guyana stated that if counsel wishes to complain about any aspect of a trial which has concluded, he should approach the trial judge through the Court Registrar and not directly. If possible counsel should contact the other party to the proceedings to see if they could agree on the content of a note to be submitted to the trial judge for his consideration. Counsel should ask the judge for his recollection of what happened and/or his approval or disapproval. He may then pursue the matter, as he sees fit, to appeal or otherwise.

NO-CASE SUBMISSION

A submission of no case may properly be made by the defence at the close of the case for the prosecution. The defence are asking the judge to rule as a matter of law that the prosecution have not established sufficient evidence to call upon the defendant to answer. If the judge so decides, he will ask the jury to give a directed verdict of not guilty. They will not be required to deliberate, but must return the verdict of not guilty as directed by the trial judge.

Origin

In *Daley v R* [1993] 4 All ER 86, PC, an appeal from Jamaica, the Privy Council acknowledged (p 90) that it has for many years been recognised that 'the trial judge has power to withdraw the issue of guilt from the jury if he considers that the evidence is insufficient to sustain a conviction'. The Board recognised that while the judge had the power to so intervene on his own motion, more commonly a formal submission on this basis is made by counsel for the defence at the close of the prosecution case.

Significantly, the Board pointed out that while the practice has no statutory basis, the background to its exercise was that provided by the 1907 English Criminal Appeal Act which (s 4 (1)) 'required the Court of Criminal Appeal to quash a conviction "if they think that the verdict of the jury should be set aside on the ground that it is unreasonable or cannot be supported having regard to the evidence"'. The Board stated that this provision was understood to mean that an appellate court would intervene only if there was no evidence on which (if uncontradicted) a properly directed jury could convict. Against this background, then, the practice developed that a trial judge should intervene to stop a case only in situations where, if the jury had convicted, the verdict would have been quashed on appeal.

It seems clear, then, that the practice of the courts in considering and upholding no-case submissions stems from the fact that an appeal against conviction may be allowed if there is insufficient evidence to support the conviction. The rationale must have been that it would be unfair to the defendant to allow the matter to go further and possibly allow a tribunal of fact to pronounce guilt even in the absence of sufficient evidence. Thus in the interests of ensuring a fair trial, a court must have power to entertain a no-case submission.

Commonwealth Caribbean jurisdictions followed the 1907 Criminal Appeal Act of England in enacting legislation regarding grounds for criminal appeals from conviction on indictable trials at the High Court. Some jurisdictions, such as Trinidad and Tobago and Jamaica, still retain appellate powers in terms of the 1907 Act which includes the right of the Court of Appeal to quash a conviction if it is unreasonable having regard to the evidence. In England, this Act was repealed and replaced to include a different factual ground in s 2(1) of the Criminal Appeal Act 1968, which stated that the court was required to quash a conviction if under 'all the circumstances of the case it was unsafe or unsatisfactory'. In most jurisdictions in the Commonwealth Caribbean, other than the Bahamas,[44] Guyana,[45] Jamaica[46] and Trinidad and Tobago,[47] s 2(1) has been incorporated into the law in respect of criminal appeals of the respective jurisdictions,[48] replacing their equivalent to s 4(1) of the old Criminal Appeal Act 1907. Whether this change in statute made any difference to law on no-case submissions will be considered in discussing the test in determining a no-case submission.

The test

It has not been doubted that the grounds upon which no-case submissions may be properly made and upheld are still those contained in the *English Practice Note* [1962] 1 All ER 448 which has been followed across the region[49] and confirmed by the Privy Council in *Daley v R* (above), p 93, letter j. The test is the same for all criminal trials. A submission of no case may be upheld: (a) when there has been no evidence to prove an essential element of the alleged offence; or (b) when the evidence adduced by the prosecution has been so discredited as a result of cross-examination or is so manifestly unreliable that no reasonable tribunal could safely convict on it. In respect of the first ground, there may be little conflict in that there is either evidence or there is not. There has, however, been much judicial discussion as to how the second ground may be applied as regards an indictable trial where the judge is not allowed to usurp the function of the jury to decide on issues of credibility of witnesses. A difficulty arises as to how a judge is to determine that no reasonable tribunal could properly convict on the prosecution evidence.

The matter was considered at length by the English Court of Appeal in *R v Galbraith* [1981] 2 All ER 1060, which is now considered the locus classicus on point for English courts. The Court of Appeal held that a judge should approach a no-case submission in this way:

- if there is no evidence that the crime alleged has been committed by the defendant there is no difficulty;

---

44 Court of Appeal Act, Ch 40, s 12(1).

45 Court of Appeal Act, Cap 3:01, s 13.

46 Judicature (Appellate) Jurisdiction Act, s 14(1), analysed in *Daley v R* [1993] 3 All ER 86, p 92.

47 Supreme Court of Judicature Act, Chap 4:01, s 44.

48 As, e.g., in the Criminal Appeal Act, Cap 113A, s 4(1)(a), Barbados; Eastern Caribbean Supreme Court (Dominica) Act, Chap 4:02, s 38(1).

49 *Sangit Chaitlal v The State* (1985) 39 WIR 295, p 298, a decision of the Trinidad and Tobago Court of Appeal and *DPP's Reference* (No 2 of 1980) (1981) 29 WIR 154.

- if there is some evidence, but it is of a tenuous character, either because of inherent weakness or vagueness or because it is inconsistent with other evidence:
  - (a) where the judge comes to the conclusion that the prosecution evidence, taken at its highest, is such that a jury properly directed could not properly convict on it, it is his duty, upon a submission being made, to stop the case;
  - (b) where, however, the prosecution evidence is such that its strength or weakness depends on the view to be taken of a witness's reliability, or other matters which are generally speaking within the province of the jury and where on one view of the facts, there is evidence upon which the jury could properly come to the conclusion that the defendant is guilty, then the judge should allow the matter to be tried by the jury.

In arriving at this approach, the English Court of Appeal rejected the alternative approach that the judge should stop the case if in his view it would be unsafe or unsatisfactory for the jury to convict. It had been previously argued that because s 4(1)(a) of the Criminal Appeal Act 1966 (which was repealed and replaced by the consolidatory provisions of the Criminal Appeal Act 1968) required the Court of Appeal to allow an appeal if they were of the opinion that the verdict was, under all the circumstances, unsafe or unsatisfactory, this should change the approach of the trial judge to a submission of no case. A practice had grown up of (English) counsel inviting judges to make a judgment that it would be unsafe for a jury to convict on the prosecution evidence.

The Court of Appeal in *Galbraith* roundly rejected this approach for the reason that it would be unwise to allow a judge to make a determination that a conviction would be unsafe or unsatisfactory. To do so would authorise the judge to apply his own views as to the weight to be given to the prosecution evidence and the credibility of their witnesses. This was clearly not permissible. Thus the Court of Appeal upheld the test that had existed prior to the 1966 provision (later incorporated in the Criminal Appeal Act 1968) and sanctioned the approach highlighted above. The determinant was whether an ensuing conviction would be unreasonable or cannot be supported having regard to the evidence.

Applicability of *Galbraith*

Given that the English Court of Appeal rejected the suggestion that the new appellate provision (holding a conviction to be unsafe and unsatisfactory) should make a difference in the approach to a no-case submission, the reasoning of the Trinidad and Tobago Court of Appeal in this regard in *Sangit Chaitlal v The State* (1985) 39 WIR 295 is difficult to follow. In that case, the Trinidad and Tobago Court of Appeal held that since *Galbraith* was based on English statute, to wit the Criminal Appeal Act 1966 (later s 2 of the Criminal Appeal Act 1968), it was inapplicable to the Trinidad and Tobago jurisdiction where the statute as regards appellate powers refers to a verdict as being unreasonable having regard to the evidence (the 1907 provision) as distinct from being unsafe and unsatisfactory. Since the English Court of Appeal has clearly said that the new statutory provision did not change the approach to a no-case submission, this rationale cannot stand. The 'unsafe and unsatisfactory' test for criminal appeals makes no difference to no-case submissions.

The court in *Chaitlal* appeared to be concerned with the suggestion of the English court in *Galbraith* that the judge should only stop a case if the evidence taken at its highest is such that 'a jury properly directed could not properly convict on it'. It appears that the Trinidad and Tobago court was unduly concerned since the detailed approach specified in *Galbraith*, discussed above, makes it clear that a no-case submission will only be upheld where there is no evidence upon which 'a jury properly directed could convict' (the words used in *Chaitlal*, p 312). It is suggested that the words 'properly convict' used in *Galbraith* makes the difference, and this is what gives rise to the detailed approach to submissions of no case at indictable trials, sanctioned in *Galbraith*.

The matter was considered in *Daley* (above), a case emanating from Jamaica, where the appellate powers have continued to be expressed in terms of the 1907 Act just as in Trinidad and Tobago. Ironically enough, the Privy Council suggested that there was a wider view of the judge's powers in considering a no-case submission in England, as a result of the later provision. In contrast, the court in *Chaitlal* seemed to suggest that the 1968 Act must have left the trial judge with narrower powers than previously. It would seem that the Privy Council's implicit conclusion in *Daley* (which endorsed the reasoning in *Galbraith*), that the change in appellate powers made no difference, is reasonable. In *Daley*, the Board recognised that the approach in *Galbraith* had been consistently applied in Jamaica. In a subsequent case of *Taibo v R* (1996) 48 WIR 74, PC, from Belize, the Privy Council applied the principles in *Galbraith*. These two Privy Council cases would seem to suggest that the principles in *Galbraith* should be equally applicable to Trinidad and Tobago given the similarity in appellate legislation. It also follows that the *Galbraith* principles must also apply to the Bahamas and without doubt in all those jurisdictions which have legislation identical to s 2 of the English Criminal Appeal Act 1968. As for Guyana, the principles will be of persuasive authority, since that jurisdiction no longer retains the Privy Council as the final court of appeal.

The grounds for making a submission of no case then remain as outlined in the 1962 *Practice Note* [1962] 1 All ER 448. The approach in determining the success of either ground is that outlined in *Galbraith* and followed in *Daley* and *Taibo*.

Withdrawal of the jury

A no-case submission must be made in the absence of the jury. This custom was laid down as a rule of law in *Crosdale v R* (1995) 46 WIR 278, PC, which is now followed across the Commonwealth Caribbean. In that case, the Privy Council decisively stated that a judge should require the jury to withdraw during the hearing of a submission that the defendant has no case to answer. This is so whether the defence seek their absence or not. Furthermore, the jury should never be present when the judge delivers the ruling, nor should they be informed of the reasons for any decision he might make on the submission. The Privy Council did concede that, in exceptional circumstances, the judge may accede to a defence request that the submissions should be made in the presence of the jury. Since the rationale for the withdrawal of the jury is to protect the interests of the defendant, it is hard to imagine a situation where the defence would request the presence of the jury while they make a submission which may be rejected. As the Board said in *Crosdale*, there is no legitimate advantage to be gained by allowing the jury to remain.

Nonetheless, the Board found that on the facts of *Crosdale* there was no real risk of prejudice arising from the presence of the jury during the submission since, in the circumstances of that case, the submission that there was no case against *Crosdale* 'was hopeless'. In contrast, in *Neil v R* (1995) 46 WIR 307, PC, a case, like *Crosdale*, emanating from Jamaica, the Privy Council gave judgment on the same day as *Crosdale* and, following the principles expounded in that judgment, allowed the appeal. The Board confirmed that the jury should be made to withdraw during the submission of no case. In that case a submission made on behalf of the co-accused in the presence of the jury was upheld. None was made on behalf of the appellant. The Privy Council was of the opinion that, despite the fact that the irregularity was understandable, as part of the then existing practice in Jamaica, there were real doubts as to whether or not it prejudiced the fair trial of the appellant. This was so because the arguments at the hearing of the submission were made on the assumption that the appellant had done the shooting which resulted in the homicide. Thus, when the submission of no case made on behalf of the co-accused was upheld, this would necessarily have been damaging to the defence case. The jury could possibly see confirmation that the appellant did the shooting in the upholding of the submission. The Board quashed the conviction. The facts in *Neil* amply demonstrate why it is infinitely preferable that the hearing of a submission of no case should be in the absence of the jury.

The submission

On a no-case submission, the question to be decided by the trial judge is whether a properly directed jury could convict on the evidence given on behalf of the prosecution at the close of its case. The judge does not have to find at that stage that the prosecution has established the ingredients of the offence beyond a reasonable doubt. This is never a determination for a judge to make on an indictable trial. It remains the function and prerogative of the jury, who is the tribunal of fact.

As stated by the Privy Council in the Belize case of *Taibo v R* (1996) 48 WIR 74, PC, the criterion to be applied by the trial judge is whether there is material on which a reasonable jury could be satisfied of the guilt of the defendant. In other words, the judge is merely to consider whether a prima facie case has been established by the evidence of the prosecution. The Board applied *Galbraith* in maintaining that once there is credible material, even if the prosecution case was 'very thin', the trial should proceed.

Insufficient evidence on the greater offence

It may sometimes transpire that there might be insufficient evidence on the offence charged, but enough evidence of the lesser alternative charge. For instance, if a defendant is charged with one count of murder but the evidence at the end of the prosecution case discloses that there is no proof of the required mens rea (intention to kill or to do grievous bodily harm), the question may arise as to what the trial judge must do. Upon occasion, judges have held that if there is no alternative count of manslaughter charged in the indictment, a submission of no case to answer must be fully upheld as regards the charge of murder. A judge may then direct the jury to return an unqualified verdict of not guilty.

Common sense alone should dictate that in such a case, if there is evidence of recklessness, the accused person should be called upon to answer the implicitly included alternative charge of manslaughter. In fact in *R v Saunders* [1987] 2 All ER 973, HL, the House of Lords held that there is no legal principle which prevents the trial judge from removing for consideration of the jury the major offence. The jury may be discharged from the obligation of returning a verdict on the major offence if the justice of the case so requires. The House confirmed that it is not desirable to abandon the long-established practice of indicting only for murder in cases where manslaughter may be left to the jury.

Although the House of Lords in *Saunders* was sanctioning the practice of discharging the jury from the obligation of returning a verdict at the time of his summing up, in principle the judge should be entitled to make a similar decision when ruling on a no-case submission, where the circumstances merit it. Further, if a judge can do this when a count for manslaughter has been separately included in the indictment, then he is equally entitled to do so on a single count of murder. This is because, as has long been established, at common law, a charge of murder necessarily includes in its definition the alternative offence of manslaughter: *DPP v Nasralla* [1967] 2 All ER 161, p 165, PC. In other words, murder and the unstated lesser alternative of manslaughter are comprised in the one count.

This practice would apply to all other offences which include unstated lesser alternatives in the count for the greater offence, such as wounding with intent and unlawful wounding; or robbery with violence and robbery simpliciter. An accused person thus is not entitled to a full acquittal on a no-case submission once there is sufficient evidence of an alternative, even though unstated, offence which is implicitly contained in the count charged.

CLOSING SPEECHES

After the defence close their case, or in the case of more than one defendant after the last defendant has closed his case, counsel for each party is entitled to address the jury in an attempt to persuade its members to his point of view. Since the defence generally bear no burden of proof[50] in a criminal case, defence counsel need not attempt to persuade the jury that the defence version of the facts is true, but merely that the prosecution have not proved their version, their case, beyond a reasonable doubt so that the jury can feel sure that the accused person is guilty.

Historical background

Under s 2 of the English Criminal Procedure Act 1865 (Denman's Act), the prosecutor had both a right to address the jury to sum up the evidence against the defendant before the defence case, and the right of reply to the defence address. This practice was the source of detailed judicial consideration in *DPP's Reference* (No 1 of 1980) (1980) 29 WIR 94, pp 108–09, 113, 116–21 by the Court of Appeal of Guyana. The learning in this case has been followed in other jurisdictions such as Trinidad and Tobago in *Allie Mohammed v The State* (1996) 51 WIR 320, and acknowledged by the Privy Council in *Allie Mohammed v The State* (1998) 53 WIR 444, p 456, PC.

In the *DPP's Reference*, the Guyanese Court of Appeal pointed out that there was a distinction between the prosecution's right to sum up the evidence, created by s 2 of Denman's Act, and the right of reply, acknowledged by the closing lines of the section. Some jurisdictions[51] in the Commonwealth Caribbean still retain this provision of Denman's Act (which had been incorporated in statute in those jurisdictions) in spite of the fact that the English Criminal Procedure (Right of Reply) Act 1964 reduced to one the number of addresses that the prosecution could legitimately give at the end of the evidence.

---

50 Except for insanity at common law or where statute specifically places an onus on the defence: *Woolmington v DPP* [1935] AC 462, p 481, HL.

51 Such as:
Antigua: Criminal Procedure Act, Cap 117, s 23;
Dominica: Criminal Law Procedure Act, Cap 12:01, s 32;
St Kitts and Nevis: Criminal Procedure Act, Cap 4:06, s 28(3);
In the St Lucia Criminal Code, s 918, s 2 of Denman's Act has merely been paraphrased.

Nevertheless, in the twentieth century, despite such statute, the practice developed for the prosecution to only address once. This observation was made by Watkins J in *R v Bryant* [1978] 2 All ER 689, p 695:

> during this century what used at one time to be separate prosecution speeches of summing up and reply have merged into one closing speech.

In *DPP's Reference* (above) the Court of Appeal of Guyana stated that this observation supported the view that ss 147–49 of the Guyanese Criminal Law (Procedure) Act were enacted to avoid a local repetition of the problems revealed in s 2 of Denman's Act, and to cut down the number of speeches by prosecuting counsel. The Guyanese provisions are identical to those of Trinidad and Tobago, ss 39–40 of the Criminal Procedure Act, Chap 12:02. Even were this not so in those jurisdictions, it would seem that, having regard to what was said in *Bryant* (above), whether or not statute conveys more than one right of address to the prosecution, since the twentieth century this has merged into one closing speech. This practice is followed throughout the Commonwealth Caribbean even in those countries which retain Denman's Act.[52]

Order of the addresses

In all cases, the defence have a right to address the jury after all the evidence has been given, to sum up their evidence to the jury. To that address the prosecution had a right of 'reply' in the past only if the defence called evidence: *DPP's Reference* (above), p 113. Thus the prosecution had the conditional right to have the last word. Where, however, the two addresses for the prosecution have been merged into one closing speech, the entitlement to make this speech should not be dependent on the defence calling evidence. In fact, in general in the Commonwealth Caribbean this is not so. Relevant statute is specific in most cases that the prosecutor has the right of reply 'in all cases' or 'always', as the case may be.[53] The prosecutor may therefore address last in these jurisdictions.

In St Vincent,[54] the relevant legislation confers a general right of the prosecution to make a closing speech to which the defence have the right of reply. Similar to the English practice, then, in these countries the prosecutor addresses first and the defence have the last word. In Barbados, the relevant statutory provision is less direct. Section 8 of the Criminal Procedure Act, Cap 127 provides that the 'right of reply and practice and course of proceedings' shall be as at present in England, which would be in 1992 (when the section was amended by Act No 17 of 1992). In Barbados, then, the defence have the right of reply to the prosecution address.

In Jamaica, the prosecutor has the right of reply, although this is not clearly spelt out in the criminal procedure legislation. However, s 11 of the Evidence Act implicitly recognises this right in that it states that the fact that the defendant 'has been called as a witness shall not in itself confer on the prosecution the right of reply'. If there is to be a closing address by the prosecution at all, then, it is apparent that this will come in reply, after the defence address.

---

52 See fn 49 above.

53 Antigua: Criminal Procedure Act, Cap 117, s 23(2);
Dominica: Criminal Law Procedure Act, Chap 12:01, s 32(2);
Grenada: Criminal Procedure Act, Cap 72B, s 164;
Guyana: Criminal Law (Procedure) Act, Cap 10:01, s 149;
St Kitts and Nevis: Criminal Procedure Act, Cap 4:06, s 28 (3);
St Lucia: Criminal Code 2004, s 918(3);
Trinidad and Tobago: Criminal Procedure Act, Chap 12:01, s 40.

54 Criminal Procedure Code, Cap 172, s 107(3).

If there is more than one defendant charged, the defence in each case have a separate right to a closing address. The first named defendant will address first, then the second defendant, and so on. The prosecution may make only one address in respect of the case against all the defendants.

It has been suggested time and again that those jurisdictions which still permit the last word to the prosecutor should consider the abolition of the practice: *DPP v Daley* [1979] 2 WLR 239, p 245, PC. The Court of Appeal in *DPP's Reference* (above) drew attention to the statement by the Privy Council in *Daley* querying the propriety of the continued preservation to the prosecution of the right of reply in that jurisdiction. The court pointed out that, having regard to the superior facilities at the disposal of the prosecution and law enforcement agencies, the retention of the last word by the prosecution may be considered unfair and a disadvantage to the defence and unnecessarily oppressive. It is nevertheless possible that this disadvantage may be offset by the heavy burden placed on the prosecution to prove their case as well as the duty of full disclosure which is not shared by the defence in these jurisdictions. Even so, it is debatable whether the prosecution really has an advantage simply because of a right of reply. No scientific study in these jurisdictions in comparing, for example, what occurs in St Vincent or the Bahamas as against the other countries has as yet been done.

The issue, however, was raised in the Court of Appeal of Trinidad and Tobago in *Burnett v The State* (2007) 72 WIR 348. In that case a police officer had been convicted of murder. Although neither side had made a closing address at the trial, it was argued on appeal that the prosecution's right of reply, conferred in statute, was both prejudicial to the defendant and a breach of his constitutional right to a fair trial. The court held that there was no unconstitutionality in the provision which was clear and unambiguous and any change in the law was a matter for the legislature. Although the matter was appealed to the Privy Council, which reduced the conviction to manslaughter on other grounds, the argument was not pursued before the Board.

Conversely the Bahamas in 2011, by Act No 35 of 2011, repealed and replaced s 176 of the Criminal Code switching the order of addresses. The prosecution in that jurisdiction now has the last word, being entitled to address the court 'after the accused person, or his counsel, has made his address'.

Discretion to address

The defence always has the right of a closing address. This right is exercised by defence counsel if the defendant is represented and by the defendant himself if he is unrepresented. While the relevant statutory provisions in most jurisdictions, as discussed above, suggest that the prosecutor always has a right to make a closing address, practice and procedure dictate otherwise.

The exercise by the prosecution of the right of reply was closely examined in *DPP's Reference* (No 1 of 1980) (1980) 29 WIR 94 by the Court of Appeal in Guyana. The court held that while the Guyana statute[55] gives prosecuting counsel the power to reply in all cases, the prosecutor should not do so in every case. The prosecutor should not address the jury in reply in the following cases:

55 The Criminal Law (Procedure) Act, Cap 10:01, ss 148 and 149, which has identical counterparts in Grenada (Cap 72B, ss 163–64) and Trinidad and Tobago (Chap 12:02, ss 39–40).

- where the defendant is unrepresented (*DPP's Reference*, p 121, j) and calls no witnesses except himself. It does not matter if the defendant addresses the jury;
- where a represented defendant calls no witnesses and his counsel does not address the jury. This is so even if the accused person gives evidence or (in those jurisdictions where it is permitted) makes an unsworn statement.

The second instance was highlighted by the Court of Appeal of Trinidad and Tobago in *Allie Mohammed v The State* (1996) 51 WIR 320, p 325. In that case the defendant was charged with murder. He gave evidence, but called no witnesses. His counsel did not address the jury. Prosecuting counsel was, nevertheless, allowed to address the jury at length at the conclusion of the evidence. The defendant was convicted and appealed on the ground, inter alia, that the prosecutor should not have been allowed to make a closing address. The Court of Appeal considered and applied the principles in *DPP's Reference* (above). The court held that where the right given (to the prosecutor) by statute is a right of reply, where there is no address by or on behalf of the accused person and no witnesses are called except the defendant, the prosecution really have nothing to reply to except the testimony of the defendant. Since statute throughout the region, as well as common law, specifies that the fact that the defendant gives evidence does not in itself confer on the prosecution a right of reply, the prosecutor ought not to have exercised that right. The Privy Council accepted this as a correct statement of the law in *Allie Mohammed v The State* (1998) 53 WIR 444, p 456, PC.

Even without clear statutory provision to this end, as exists for instance in Trinidad and Tobago[56] and Jamaica,[57] qualifying the right of reply, it is clear from the tenor of *DPP's Reference* (above) that the court felt that the prosecutor is wrong to insist on his right of reply where defence counsel does not address and does not call witnesses other than the defendant. There will, indeed, be nothing to which to reply.

It would seem that, where an accused person is represented, once his lawyer addresses the jury, prosecuting counsel still has the right to a closing address, even if the defence call no witnesses at all, not even the defendant. In *R v Bryant* (1978) 67 Cr App R 157, the English Court of Appeal held that, in such circumstances, the speech should be brief.

In the Bahamas and St Vincent, where the defendant goes last, so the prosecution does not have the right of 'reply', statute makes provision restricting the right of the prosecution to address. Section 176 of the Bahamas Criminal Code Ch 91 stipulates the circumstances in which counsel for the prosecution can address the jury after the close of the evidence. He may address if 'the accused person is represented by counsel, or when he is not so represented but calls witnesses as to fact in his defence'.

In a similar vein, s 107(3) of the St Vincent Criminal Procedure Act, Cap 172 denies the prosecution the right to address 'in a case where the accused is not represented by counsel and has not called witnesses to the facts other than himself'. On the other hand, the accused person or his counsel may address the court whether the prosecutor has addressed or not. It would seem that in the Bahamas and St Vincent, there is nothing to prevent the prosecutor from making a closing address in cases where the defendant is represented or has called other witnesses of fact, even if the defence indicates they will not address. Since the defence would have the last word in these jurisdictions, it is unlikely that they will not respond.

---

56 Evidence Act, Chap 7:02, s 15(2).

57 Evidence Act, s 11.

Content of closing address

A closing address by counsel is an address on the evidence in the case. Each counsel has the opportunity to talk directly to the jury and seek to persuade its members that they should acquit or convict the defendant as the case may be. As such, a closing address should, in general, not contain advice to the jury on the law in the matter since this remains the domain of the judge. Sometimes counsel may, with express or implied leave of the judge, mention basic principles of law so as to make his closing address more comprehensible. The final word on the law is with the judge in any event, and this should be made clear to the jury. The following are relevant principles as to the content of a closing address by counsel:

- All the evidence: counsel is entitled to found his address upon all the material then before the court: *R v Bryant* (above). The object of an address is for counsel to take the evidence of the other side and comment upon it and so to show that the effect of the evidence given by (or the case for) the side addressing ought to be accepted: *R v Gardner* [1899] 1 QB 150, p 156.
- No law, speculation: the addresses should relate strictly to the evidence and the inferences which may be drawn from it. Speculation has no place in a closing address. Furthermore, while counsel may refer in general terms to basic matters like the burden and standard of proof, no references should be made to cases or even statute.
- Sentencing: there should be no references to the consequences of a conviction. In *AG for the State of Southern Australia v Brown* [1960] AC 432, PC, the Privy Council stated that they had been informed that it was common practice for counsel in South Australia in their addresses to juries in murder trials to refer to the consequences of their verdict. The Privy Council emphasised that if such a practice is permitted, it is incumbent on the trial judge to instruct the jury that such matters are not their concern and are completely irrelevant to any issue they have to determine. The trial judge in that case had in fact done so and the Privy Council considered that the trial judge's emphasis to the jury that sentencing was not their concern was not open to objection. It is obvious, therefore, that it is far preferable for counsel not to refer to issues of sentencing to the jury as this falls within the province of the judge. It is in fact improper for counsel to do so, and he should be stopped by the judge from venturing into this area.
- Personal views: arising from the principle that an address should relate to the evidence, it is considered unacceptable style for counsel to boldly voice his own opinions of the evidence, since these are matters for the jury. He should desist from prefacing his comments with 'I believe' or 'I think'. The personal views or experiences of counsel are really irrelevant and if he ventures too much along that line, he may be seen to be attempting to give evidence himself. Instead, counsel should make suggestions or statements inviting the jury to adopt the comments he makes.
- Silence: in Commonwealth Caribbean jurisdictions, no comment is allowed by the prosecutor on the failure of the accused person or his spouse[58] to give evidence.[59] However, a co-defendant

58 Act 28 of 1996 of Trinidad and Tobago, which amended the Evidence Act, Chap 7:02, s 13 now permits comment, if desired, on the failure of the spouse to give evidence.

59 This is based on statute by which jurisdictions in the region adopted the English Criminal Evidence Act 1898, s 1 (b). See, e.g., Evidence Act, s 9(b), Jamaica; Evidence Act, Chap 7:02, s 13(1)(b), Trinidad and Tobago.

may do so. In remaining silent, the defendant is seen to be merely exercising his statutory or common law right to remain silent. This is somewhat different from a comment which may be made if the defence has cross-examined along a certain line and suggested certain things as fact to witnesses but called no evidence in support thereof. In such a case it is permissible to comment that there is no evidence called to support the suggestions which, if denied, do not themselves constitute evidence.

- The prosecutor's role: a prosecutor should not press for a conviction. In *Allie Mohammed v The State* (1996) 51 WIR 320, p 325, the Trinidad and Tobago Court of Appeal considered as inappropriate and unbecoming, both in style and content, the address by the prosecutor at the trial. The court considered that there were several criticisms of the address by the prosecutor which 'clearly infringed the cardinal rule that prosecuting counsel must not unduly press for a conviction'. The court felt that the prosecutor apparently 'did not properly appreciate that restraint and detachment should characterize the performance of his role. The nature and length of his address confirm this impression'.

Misconduct of prosecutor

Although the Court of Appeal in *Allie Mohammed* did not allow the appeal despite this irregularity, on further appeal to the Privy Council, the Board allowed the appeal on this single issue. They found that the prosecutor had erred in several aspects: *Allie Mohammed v The State* (1998) 53 WIR 444, p 457, PC:

> The prosecutor informed the jury of his view that the appellant was plainly guilty. He made emotional appeals for sympathy for the deceased and his family. He demanded that the jury should not let the appellant 'get away with it'. He repeatedly 'urged' the jury to convict. His speech contained many inflammatory passages. The prosecutor had commenced his speech by saying 'I am a minister of Justice'. The contrary is the case; the prosecutor made a wholly improper speech. The judge's interventions during the speech were perfunctory. And in his summing up the judge did not direct the jury to disregard the speech. The judge told the jury in general terms not to be swayed by emotion but he said nothing to counteract the prejudice which the speech of the prosecutor was calculated to generate in the minds of the jurors.

In *Benedetto v R* (2003) 62 WIR 63 PC, the Board reiterated that, especially in his closing address, a prosecutor must demonstrate he is a minister of justice. In that case it was said that while there was nothing wrong in a robust speech, one which went beyond this to being xenophobic and inflammatory was objectionable.

In subsequent cases the Privy Council had cause to re-emphasise the duty of the prosecutor as a minister of justice. In *Ramdhanie et al. v The State* (2005) 67 WIR 340, PC, the Privy Council advised that while allowances must be made for context and environment there were fundamental limits which must be observed by prosecuting counsel in their closing address, especially where the prosecutor had the right of reply. Where the prosecutor's speech contained emotive and unjustified comments on the defence case, and where the prosecutor improperly vouched for the prosecution case this amounted to a material irregularity. The appeal was allowed. Subsequently the Board in *Huggins v The State* (2008) 73 WIR 420, PC, in reviewing most of the authorities on the issue, reiterated the need for prosecuting counsel to observe proper standards of decorum and courtesy in their conduct of the case. The court emphasised that where there have been departures in good practice the test in determining whether the appeal should be allowed was whether they were sufficient to deny the appellant of the substance of a fair trial.

Just as in *Huggins* the Board later, in *Smith v R* (2008) 74 WIR 379, PC, held that while the behaviour of the prosecutor was not that expected of a minister of justice it was not so gross, persistent or prejudicial to render the conviction unsafe.

It is evident, then, that the prosecutor bears a heavy burden in delivering his closing address. He must be careful to act with circumspection, for if a jury fails to convict because of irregularities in the defence address, there is no appeal on this basis; but if the jury convicts where the prosecutor's address has been improper, an ensuing conviction may be quashed on this basis alone. The judge's subsequent warning to the jury or admonitions to counsel as to the impropriety may not be considered sufficient to ensure a fair trial.

JUDGE'S FUNCTIONS

In *Wallace and Fuller v R* (1996) 50 WIR 387, PC, the Privy Council, in an appeal from Jamaica, reiterated that a criminal trial is adversarial by nature. In doing so, the Board said it is for the advocates to decide what evidence is adduced, what cross-examination is made, what objections are taken and what points of law are raised. In all of this, the judge's task is essentially to hold the scales. In doing so he must control the proceedings and cannot abdicate this role to either counsel: *Randall v R* (2002) 60 WIR 103 PC.

In *Crosdale v R* (1995) 46 WIR 278, PC, the Privy Council emphasised that a judge and a jury have separate but complementary functions in a jury trial. The court stated: 'The judge has a supervisory role', in which he carries out, among other things, a filtering process to decide what evidence is to be placed before a jury. A judge will thus rule on objections to the admissibility of evidence during the course of trial if it is alleged that the rules of evidence are breached. He will determine admissibility of specific items of evidence such as confessional statements in a voir dire: *Chan Wei Keung v R* [1967] 2 AC 160, PC; *Seeraj Ajodha v The State* (1981) 32 WIR 360, PC.

In *Krishna v The State* [2011] UKPC 18, the Privy Council, in a late appeal in 2010 in respect of a 1988 conviction, ruled in favour of the appellant where the trial judge following the then practice referred to his ruling in the voir dire that he had determined the appellant's confessional statement was voluntary. This was held to constitute a material irregularity. This case emphasises that a judge should not comment on rulings on admissibility of evidence made in the absence of the jury.

A judge is also required, as discussed above, to consider on a submission of no case to answer whether the prosecution has produced sufficient evidence to justify putting the issue to jury. After both sides have made their closing addresses, the judge must sum up the case to the jury so as to enable the jurors to make a sound determination in applying the relevant law to the issues of fact in the case. Finally, if the defendant pleads guilty or is found guilty, the judge has to decide upon and pronounce sentence.

During the trial

The judge should be present at every stage of a trial, including a view of the locus in quo by the jury: *R v Hunter* [1985] 2 All ER 173. It is irrelevant whether the view is a simple one without witnesses being present or a view with witnesses present who give evidence or a demonstration.

A judge has a limited right to call witnesses himself.[60] This is a right that is rarely exercised, but, if it is, it should not be done so as to assist the prosecution's case: *R v Tregear*

60 This power is contained in statute in some jurisdictions: Criminal Procedure Code, Cap 72B, s 167, Grenada; Criminal Procedure Act, Chap 12:02, s 41, Trinidad and Tobago.

(1967) 51 Cr App R 280. The chief determinant is whether this course is necessary in the interests of justice. Where the judge takes such a course, he should allow both sides to cross-examine the witness if the witness gives evidence that is adverse to one party. The judge may also question any witness called by either side. In doing so, however, the judge must not be seen to be descending into the arena and performing the functions expected of counsel for the defence or the prosecution. Thus a judge should not interrupt a witness so frequently that he makes it difficult for counsel properly to adduce evidence or cross-examine the witness. On the other hand, questions which are clearly designed merely to resolve ambiguities or to confirm salient points are perfectly in order.

During the trial, the judge should refrain from making comments on the defence case. Such comments are objectionable if they are likely to influence the jury or even the defendant. In *Barnes* (1970) 55 Cr App R 100, the trial judge during the trial, but in the absence of the jury, told the counsel for the defence: 'I think I should tell you in the presence and hearing of your client that I take a very serious view indeed of hopeless cases, without the shadow of a defence, being contested at public expense'. Counsel offered to withdraw in the light of advice he had given to the defendant, to which the judge replied that any other counsel would be bound to give the same advice. The defendant was eventually convicted and, on appeal, the English Court of Appeal held that the judge had put extreme pressure on the defendant to plead guilty (although the defendant in fact did not). Furthermore, he had attempted to interfere with the independence of counsel in his duty to give the defendant the best advice. The conviction was quashed because of the impropriety of the trial judge. Similarly, in *Randall v R* (2002) 60 WIR 103 PC, the Privy Council criticised the judge for allowing his antipathy to both the appellant and his counsel to be only too manifest.

The principle that the judge should not enter into the arena applies equally to making determinations on procedural issues which might be advantageous to the defendant. In *Wallace and Fuller* (above), the appellants complained that they should have had separate trials, although it was never raised at trial. The Privy Council said that while there may be moments when a trial judge simply has no choice but to take the initiative, these are few. Otherwise, if the judge enters into the arena, the shape of the trial is distorted. Since no one sought a separate trial, it was not for the trial judge to impose it on any party.

Bias

It follows that a conviction will be quashed if it is shown that a trial judge may have been biased against an accused person. The test in determining bias is whether from the circumstances a fair-minded and informed observer would conclude that there is a real possibility of bias on the part of the judge: *R v Gough* [1993] 2 All ER 724, HL as adjusted by *Porter v Magill* [2002] AC 357, HL. The bias may arise from many reasons not connected to financial interests. In *R v Bow Street Metropolitan Stipendiary Magistrate et al. ex p Pinochet Ugarte* (No 2) [1999] 1 All ER 577, HL, the House of Lords considered the allegations of possible bias on the part of one of its own members in a previous hearing of the same matter. The case resulted from extradition proceedings brought against Pinochet, who was the former Head of State of Chile. On an appeal to the House of Lords on the question of the scope of the immunity of a former Head of State from arrest and extradition proceedings, Amnesty International (AI) was granted leave to intervene in the proceedings. The appeal was allowed by a majority of three to two in the House of Lords, thus paving the way for the continuation of the extradition proceedings. After the judgment, it was discovered that Lord Hoffman, one of the judges who was in the majority, and his wife both had ties with AI. Lord Hoffman was in fact a director of its charitable trust, while his wife was a programme assistant at AI.

The result was a second petition to the House of Lords for a rehearing of the case. The House granted the petition and set aside its previous decision.[61] The House confirmed that a judge could be disqualified from hearing a matter in his own cause not only in those cases where he had a pecuniary interest in the outcome, but where his decision could lead to a promotion of a cause in which the judge was involved together with one of the parties. Since the Law Lord was a director of a charity closely allied to AI, he was automatically disqualified from hearing the appeal.

It was in somewhat unusual circumstances that the defence in a re-sentencing hearing in the Bahamas challenged the impartiality of the judge in *R v Jones* (2007) 72 WIR 1. The contention was that the trial judge was constitutionally infirmed as a result of a publication in the press by the AG of a 'report card' on judges' performance; a statement by the AG that judges were accountable to the public and the failure of the Government to appoint an independent commission to determine judges' remuneration and pension. It was held that the circumstances were not such that a fair-minded and informed observer would conclude that there was a real possibility that the trial was not independent and impartial given the tradition of judicial independence in the Bahamas and the fact that judges were appointed by an independent commission and were accountable only to the Constitution.

The law on apparent bias has evolved to the extent that, in determining the propriety of a court's action in continuing to sit on a matter, the appellate court would assess the matter both prospectively and retrospectively. In *Lesage v Mauritius Commercial Bank Ltd* [2012] UKPC 41 the Privy Council allowed an appeal against a decision of a two-judge panel giving judgment against the appellant who had been sued for fraud to the value of hundreds of millions of rupees. The Board, applying *Porter v Magill* [2002] AC 357, emphasised that the notional observer must be presumed to have two characteristics: full knowledge of the material facts and fair-mindedness. Applying these qualities to the consideration of the issue he must ask himself whether there was a real possibility that the decision maker was biased. Where one of the judges had received a letter from the appellant containing privileged information prior to the hearing of the case and had not even raised it with the parties, the Board would examine the conduct of the judges during the trial to see if it supported the suggestion of the appearance of possible bias. The Board held that the informed observer would be bound to conclude that the court was not alert to the need for vigilance to ensure that the information did not have an unintended effect on its view of the credibility of the appellant's case. The possibility that the judges would be influenced to a subconscious disposition against the appellant's case was inescapable. The Board found that this view was reinforced by the conduct of the trial by the judges overall.

Bias application

In *R v Lewis* (2007) 70 WIR 75, CCJ (AJ), the CCJ advised on how a trial judge should treat an application to recuse himself:

> The first is the question whether in criminal trials an application to the judge to recuse himself should be made in open court or in chambers. We recommend the adoption in such circumstances of the following procedure. Counsel for the party wishing to object to the judge sitting should ask to see the judge together with counsel on the other side in the judge's chambers before the court sits. He should there indicate his objection to the judge and explain

61 *R v Bow Street Metropolitan Stipendiary Magistrate, ex p Pinochet Ugarte* (No 1) [1998] 4 All ER 897, HL.

> the reasons for it. If the judge is then persuaded that he should recuse himself, the case is called in open court and either adjourned or transferred to another court. The judge should indicate in open court, at least in general terms, the reason for the adjournment or transfer. If, however, the judge is not then so persuaded, the application for his recusal should be made in open court. Before the objection is heard, however, the court should be cleared of all jurors in waiting and if anything is said in the course of the objection which is prejudicial to the accused, the judge should warn any members of the media present not to report the prejudicial matter before the conclusion of the trial, or risk being charged with contempt of court. The judge's ruling on the objection and a brief statement of his reasons should be given by him in open court. In recommending this procedure we have in mind the importance of conducting judicial proceedings, particularly those which involve a person's liberty (or life), in public.

Notes and reasons

It is imperative that a transcript of the evidence given at an indictable trial and the summing up must be recorded even though this duty may not be incorporated in statute (as it is for the magistrates' courts). Without the judge's summing up, in particular, it will be highly impossible to ground an appeal. In *Williams* [1994] 99 Cr App R 163, p 165, the English Court of Appeal considered an appeal which had to be conducted without any transcript of the relevant evidence or 'more importantly the judge's summing up'. It appeared that the tapes which had been used to record the evidence and the summing up had been lost. The court expressed concern for the absence of transcripts, but felt that the very clear handwritten notes made by the judge provided sufficient information on the facts of that case to enable it to reach a proper decision. Both counsel for the prosecution and the defence had agreed to this beforehand.

In the absence of such agreement as occurred in *Williams*, it would be highly unusual for a court to proceed without the record of the summing up, on an appeal from an indictable trial. The summing up is, after all, the written record of the matters of law that the jury would have been told were relevant to the facts in the case and which they must apply to those facts. In most jurisdictions, the summing up is taped and otherwise recorded, in some cases by computer-aided transmission. In many jurisdictions, however, notes of evidence are still recorded by hand by the trial judge. They are also so recorded by defence and prosecuting counsel. Nevertheless, this proliferation of note-taking may assist in the event that official notes of evidence are lost. On a retrial a duty rests on the court system to ensure that defence counsel is provided with the transcript of the first trial or the relevant part of it: *Boodram v The State* (2001) 59 WIR 493 PC. A residual duty also lies on the prosecution to ensure that this is done. If the defence is not so provided with the transcript of a first trial, this could successfully ground an appeal: see also *Charles v The State* (1999) 54 WIR 455 PC at 463.

It was also argued in *Wallace and Fuller v R* (1996) 50 WIR 387 PC that the failure of the trial judge to give reasons why he ruled in favour of the admissibility of confessional statements was irregular. The defence contended that a trial judge should always express his reasons for any procedural ruling given during the trial. The Privy Council disagreed. The Board held that in each case it is a matter for the trial judge to decide whether the interests of justice call for the giving of reasons and, if so, with what degree of particularity. There will be occasions when good practice requires a reasoned ruling, such as when a judge decides a question of law. In such a case sufficient must be displayed of his reasoning to enable a review on appeal. In addition, if the issue concerns the exercise of a discretion, this may call for an account, however brief, of the judge's reasoning as to his exercise of that discretion.

If, however, the only question is whether the judge believed one set of witnesses or the other in a voir dire, reasons are unnecessary. Here, no principle of law is in issue and no discretion is to be exercised. There was nothing to recommend that the trial judge should proceed to give reasons as to why he decided to admit the confessional statement of an accused person once he found it to have been given voluntarily. For the judge to expand in detail his reasons for preferring one story to the other would wholly unbalance the proceedings, since the reasons would have to be given in the presence of the public, the advocates and the accused. It is clear that the Board in *Wallace and Fuller* felt that the giving of reasons in such a situation could be prejudicial to the fair trial of the defendant.

The summing up

This comes after the closing addresses. The summing up is an address by the judge to the jury in open court in which the judge gives directions in law and analyses the evidence, if necessary. A summing up need not follow a prescribed format once overall it is fair to the defence: *Walters v R* (1968) 13 WIR 354, PC. By the time he sums up, the judge will have had an opportunity of observing the jurors and it is best left to his discretion to choose the most appropriate set of words to make that jury understand that they must not return a verdict against a defendant unless they are sure of his guilt. It is the overall effect of the summing up that matters.

The Privy Council in *Huggins v The State* (2008) 73 WIR 420, PC endorsed the decision of the trial judge to correct the misstatements of prosecuting counsel prior to beginning her summing up after the addresses of counsel for the defence and prosecution. The Board observed: 'This was done in a separate segment of the trial, so that it had maximum impact and it could not become submerged in the content of the long and detailed summing up'. The Board endorsed the opinion of the Court of Appeal that this 'corrective statement' removed a good deal of the potential unfairness of the prosecutor's comments. It is evident then that the practice of actual summing up following addresses of counsel can make way for matters such as these which are necessary for a fair trial.

A judge usually begins his summing up by explaining the respective roles of judge and jury in particular at that stage of the trial. He should indicate to the jury that they must take the law as he directs and apply it to the facts as they find them. Some judges may explain the functions of the respective counsel as well.

A judge must tell the jury that it is for the prosecution in a criminal trial to prove the case and that they must do so beyond reasonable doubt. Failure to give these essential directions on the burden and standard of proof in a criminal trial will almost always result in the quashing of any ensuing conviction. Furthermore, where the defence raises special pleas such as self-defence or provocation, a general direction on the onus of proof is insufficient: *R v Cameron* [1973] Crim LR 520. The judge must specifically tell the jury where such defence is expressly raised that it is for the prosecution to negate the defence and not for the defendant to prove it. While a judge is entitled to comment on the failure of the defendant to give evidence, he must be careful not to suggest that the defendant has any obligation to do so: *R v Sparrow* [1973] 1 WLR 488.

The judge is required to direct the jury on the elements of the offence or offences charged. He must explain what the prosecution must prove in order to establish a case against the defendant. It is usual practice for the judge at this time to refer to points in the evidence which may go towards either proving or raising a reasonable doubt as to some ingredient of the offence. The judge may at the same time identify the defences raised from the evidence led either by the defence or arising from the case for the prosecution.

Where any special issues arise from the evidence, the judge must address the jury on them. If there is any question as to how an issue is to be addressed or whether certain matters should at all be dealt with, the judge should first resolve these with counsel before he starts the summing up. In *Crosdale v R* (1995) 46 WIR 278, PC, the Privy Council followed *R v Cristeni* [1987] Crim LR 504 in holding that a trial judge ought to raise with counsel in the absence of the jury points which were not actively canvassed in the trial but which he intends to introduce in his summing up. In *Crosdale*, the judge did not do so in respect of an issue of fact, but mentioned the matter to the jury anyway. The Board of the Privy Council considered that this was an error.

There are many questions of law that may arise from evidential issues. Such a question may include whether corroboration directions are necessary in those situations where suspect witnesses (such as accomplices) or children give evidence. The judge may wish to consult counsel as to whether there is any evidence of corroboration at all or what format a warning in respect of the evidence of a suspect should take: *R v Makanjuola* [1995] 2 Cr App R 469. Special directions must also be given as to certain types of evidence such as visual identification if the correctness of an identification is in issue: *R v Turnbull* [1977] 1 QB 224; Res Gestae[62] or Dying Declaration[63] evidence. In addition, whenever statute or common law dictate that special directions are necessary, the trial judge is bound to give such directions in his summing up. Failure to do so will amount to an error in law or a misdirection.

It is important that the judge advise the jury on how to treat the evidence where more than one defendant is being tried. He must tell the jury that they must consider the evidence against each defendant separately and that, even though they are being tried together, each is entitled to a separate verdict. The judge should make an effort to compartmentalise the evidence against each accused person. If there have been confessional out-of-court statements made by co-defendants which implicate each other, it is vital that the trial judge emphasise that such statements constitute evidence only against the maker and not the co-defendants: *R v Gunewardene* (1951) 35 Cr App R 80.

In most cases in his summing up to the jury, the judge is expected to deal with the actual evidence adduced. If, however, the issues are simple and the case is a short one, it is not a fatal defect for the evidence not to be reviewed in the summing up: *R v Attfield* [1961] 3 All ER 243. A judge's summing up should not be long and repetitive, and long and involved sentences should be avoided: *R v Francisco De Freitas* (1970) 15 WIR 217. In that case, the Guyanese Court of Appeal held that the summing up was replete with 'diffused statements of law'. The trial judge in that case used what was considered circumlocutory language that may well have caused confusion and disarray in the minds of the jury. The whole object of a summing up, the Court of Appeal said, is that real issues must be left to the jury in language that they can follow. Similarly, in the English case of *R v Charles* (1976) 68 Cr App R 334, the Court of Appeal stated that the practice of some judges, in long cases, of reading out their notes to the jury is one which is most unsatisfactory. The issues should be analysed and the evidence related to them. Lengthy summings up are more likely to confuse rather than assist a jury.

The judge should always ensure that he puts the defence to the jury fairly and adequately, however weak it may appear: *David Watkins v R* (1966) 11 WIR 37, a decision of the Court of Appeal of Trinidad and Tobago. He must put the nature of the defence, reminding the jury shortly of what the evidence is. In *Mears v R* (1993) 42 WIR 285, PC, the Privy Council, on an appeal from Jamaica, held that while a judge is entitled to comment on the evidence in his summing up, he must clearly leave the determination of facts to them. Comments which fall short of usurpation may nevertheless be so weighted against the defendant as to leave the jury with little choice other than to comply with what are plainly the judge's views. In that case, the

62 As stipulated in *R v Andrews* [1987] AC 281, HL.

63 See *Nembhard v R* [1982] 1 All ER 183, PC.

case for the prosecution depended largely on the evidence of one S, who said that the defendant had confessed to her that he had killed the deceased. The defence challenged the evidence of the witness yet the trial judge, in commenting on her evidence said, inter alia, 'I recoil to think that any human being could be so degenerate, so wicked that they would concoct a story like this, especially a woman who has borne from a womb a child for a man'. The Board of the Privy Council considered that such comments went beyond the proper bounds of judicial comment. Taking this into account as well as the fact that the judge had effectively neutralised the defence case by telling them it was irrelevant if the body examined by the pathologist was that of the alleged victim, it was held that the summing up was unbalanced and unfair.

In *Crosdale v R* (1995) 46 WIR 278, the Privy Council held that the judge's criticism of the defence case as 'lacking in sincerity' was unfair to the defence. The Board said that even a defendant against whom the cards are stacked is entitled to have his defence fairly presented to the jury. Applying *Mears* (above), the Privy Council held that the defendant could not be said to have had a fair trial. In contrast in *Warren Thomas Jackson v The State*, (1998) 53 WIR 431, an appeal from Trinidad and Tobago, the Privy Council held that the judge's comments in that case were not unfair. The Board compared the facts of that case to those of *Crosdale* and held that, unlike *Crosdale*, there was no need to raise any special issues on the evidence with counsel before the summing up. The decision of whether to address the discrepancies in the defence case fell clearly within the judge's discretion. The discrepancies had been raised by the prosecutor in his closing address when he commented that defence counsel had omitted to cross-examine prosecution witnesses on important matters raised by the defendant in giving evidence. The judge, in the absence of any explanation by defence counsel, was entitled to and had to deal with the matters raised as best as he could in his summing up. His summing up was not unfair to the defence.

During the course of the summing up it is not expected that counsel will interrupt the judge. If there is any omission or misdirection that needs to be brought to the attention of the judge this may be done at the end of the summing up: *Randall v R* (2002) 60 WIR 103 at 109 PC. It is usual for the judge to ask counsel at the end of his summing up if there is anything they wish him to add or clarify. In fact in *Jackson* (above), the Board pointed out that at the end of his summing up the trial judge had invited defence counsel to address him further if he so wished. Defence counsel had declined the invitation and so lost an opportunity to complain about the judge's comments or clarify his position in respect of them. If there is any error in the summing up, the law or analysis of facts, the prosecutor has a duty to assist the judge in this regard: *R v McVey* [1988] Crim LR 127. Whether there is a similar obligation on the part of defence counsel to draw to the judge's attention any error in his summing up is not certain. It used to be generally accepted that defence counsel could say nothing and seek to take advantage of an omission on appeal. This was seen as part of his duty to his client, but it is equally questionable whether a perceived duty to one's client should be allowed to result in the possible loss to that client of a chance of an acquittal by a jury as a result of an uncorrected judicial error. Defence counsel may note that of late the Privy Council has not been loath to comment on the failure of defence counsel in this regard as evidenced by *Jackson* (above).

At the end of the summing up, the trial judge will give specific directions on the verdict or possible verdicts in the matter. This will be dealt with in Chapter 16.

CHAPTER 15

THE JURY

The jury system remains the cornerstone of the criminal trial[1] in the Commonwealth Caribbean as it is in England and the US. This is so despite the fact that only a small minority of defendants qualify for jury trial, since most criminal offences are summary or may be tried summarily. Nonetheless, the right to trial by jury is regarded as basic to trials for all serious offences in democratic societies. In fact when, some 20 years ago, a trial judge in Bermuda purported to try a criminal matter in the Supreme Court without a jury because of the difficulty of obtaining an impartial jury in the small state, the Court of Appeal of Bermuda had this to say:

> There has been, and there is now, only one method of trying persons who have been committed for trial at the Supreme Court and that is by a judge sitting with a jury.[2]

Trial by jury in England is said to have originated during the eleventh century during the reign of Henry II. It eventually evolved from a powerless institution to one which shared even power with the judge and came into its own during the struggles in the reign of Charles I (who was beheaded) and James II.[3] Despite the established tradition of jury trial for serious offences in countries with the common law legal system, it has been the subject of attack as in this scathing denunciation by Oppenheimer:[4]

> We commonly strive to assemble 12 persons colossally ignorant of all practical matters, fill their vacuous heads with law which they cannot comprehend, obfuscate their seldom intellects with testimony which they are incompetent to analyse or remember, permit partisan lawyers to bewilder them with their meaningless sophistry, then lock them up until the most obstinate of their number coerce the others into submission, or drive them into open revolt.

Nonetheless, there have been many supporters of the system of jury trials who argue that juries are generally more right than judges. This type of comment has come from judges[5] themselves who have tried numerous cases with juries. In any event, trial by jury remains the one method of trying persons who have been charged with serious indictable offences such as murder, manslaughter and rape. While statute has intervened to permit summary trial by a magistrate for some indictable offences in specified circumstances,[6] this is only as regards those stipulated in the legislation, which never include capital offences and are usually less serious offences.

Originally a jury was required to return a unanimous verdict in all cases: *Winsor v R* [1866] LR 1 QB 289, p 303.[7] There was also no statutory time limit after which the judge could discharge a jury should they not agree. In *Winsor* it was argued on behalf of the defendant that she could not be legally tried before a second jury because, at her first trial,

---

1 Baldwin, J, and McConville, M, *Jury Trials*, 1979, Oxford: Clarendon, p 1.

2 Criminal Appeal, No 4 of 1980, p 7, discussed by Deosaran, R in 'Trial by jury in a post-colonial multiracial society ', *The Lawyer*, March 1981, p 5.

3 See analysis in Chadee, D, 'A short history of (the English and Trinidad and Tobago) trial by jury', *The Lawyer*, January 1994, p 17.

4 Oppenheimer, BS, 'Trials by jury', *University of Cincinnati Law Review*, vol 11, 1937, p 141, 142.

5 Such as Lord Halsbury (1903) and Lord Salmon (1974), as Baldwin and McConville (see fn 1) point out, p 3.

6 As discussed in Chapter 10.

7 Cited by the Court of Appeal in *R v David Michael* (1975) 27 WIR 307, pp 309–10.

the jury had been discharged from delivering a verdict on grounds other than necessity arising from illness, death or misconduct. The discharge was on failure to agree after some five hours of deliberation. It was argued that the jury should have been locked up over the weekend for consideration of the verdict. The Court of Queen's Bench rejected the argument. Nonetheless, the frequency of such contentions eventually led to the creation of modern statute to regulate the functioning of juries and jurors and the selection of jurors, among other matters. The English Juries Act 1870[8] which followed was enacted in large measure across the Commonwealth Caribbean region by the then colonies.

Since that time, the various legislatures have amended or replaced their law on juries so that, while there are many similarities in the legislation on juries across the region, there is great variation. These will be analysed in this chapter along with the growing case law.

Functions of the jury

As long ago as 1866 in *Winsor* (above), Cockburn CJ stated that one of the principles that lie at the foundation of [English] law is 'the maxim that judges shall decide questions of law and the juries questions of fact' (p 303). The main question of fact that the jury must determine is whether the defendant is guilty or not guilty. It is thus incumbent on the trial judge never to seek to usurp this function of the jury by seeking to persuade them to his point of view in relation to the credibility of the witnesses or the defendant. In both *Crosdale v R* (1995) 46 WIR 278, PC, and *Mears v R* (1993) 42 WIR 285, PC, the Privy Council held that the judge had intruded into the domain of the jury in this regard.

The jury as judges of fact have no functions to perform in respect of the determination of a submission of no case: *Crosdale* (above) and *Neil v R* (1995) 46 WIR 307, PC. As a consequence, it has been conclusively held in those cases that the jury must be required to withdraw during the hearing of the submissions. Similarly, the jury makes no determination on the admissibility of evidence, which plainly falls within the domain of the judge although the jury may be present when such objections are determined. The determination as to whether a confessional statement of the defendant was given voluntarily or not is made by the judge: *Ajodha v The State* (1981) 32 WIR 360, PC. This is usually in the absence of the jury so as to avoid possible prejudice to the defendant. In general, then, in cases where the judge must hear the evidence to determine its admissibility, it is advisable that the jury be asked to withdraw during arguments.

On the other hand, the jury must try issues such as whether the defendant is mute by malice or visitation of God, as was done in *Ricketts* (1996) 55 WIR 269, PC. In addition, it is the jury who determines the defendant's fitness to plead if this is an issue in the trial: *R v Podola* [1960] 1 QB 325. Where a special plea in bar such as autrefois is raised, a jury may be selected to determine issues of fact if they arise: *R v Rodriguez* (1973) 22 WIR 504. It is of significance to note that in general, where a jury has been selected to try a preliminary issue, the same jury[9] may be used, if there is no objection, in trying other issues, including the general issue of guilt or not.

The jury is expected to listen to all the evidence, the speeches and the summing up without response until their verdict. Sometimes after retirement, the foreman may request further directions to clarify some matter.[10] It has, however, been suggested that at any stage

8 This Act enacted the first provision for refreshment for jurors: discussed in ibid, p 310.

9 As, e.g., Bahamas, Juries Act, No 7 of 1998, s 16.

10 As was done in *Berry v R* (1992) 41 WIR 244, PC, when they returned to court after about an hour with a query.

after the prosecution closes its case, the jury may indicate that its members wish to stop the proceedings and acquit the defendant: *R v Falconer-Atlee* (1973) 58 Cr App R 348. This would be highly unusual and in that case, the English Court of Appeal stated that if the evidence is so tenuous, it is for the judge to take upon himself the responsibility of stopping the case, rather than leaving it to the jury. It is also permissible for members of the jury to be invited, through their foreman,[11] at the end of the evidence of a witness, to ask questions: *R v Lillyman* [1896] 2 QB 167. This right is limited to merely clearing up ambiguous matters and is less than that of the judge to ask questions. Certainly, the jury cannot be seen to be creating an imbalance in the proceedings. The questions should be channelled through the judge so as to avoid the danger of adducing inadmissible or prejudicial evidence. In the trial of James Fletcher and Pamela Fletcher for murder in St Vincent in July–August 1997, the foreman of the jury was allowed to ask questions directly of two of the witnesses for the prosecution. This is not a common practice in the rest of the Commonwealth Caribbean.

MEMBERSHIP OF THE JURY

Statute, usually in the form of a Jury Act or Juries Act, stipulates the qualifications and disqualifications for jurors as well as those who are exempted from jury service.

Qualifications and disqualifications

In general, any person who is an adult[12] and has not passed the age of 60 or 70,[13] as the case may be, is qualified to be a juror once he is legally resident or a citizen of the particular country. There are other requirements, and although they may be specified differently as qualifications in some jurisdictions and disqualifications in others, it appears that the basic requirements for jury service across the Commonwealth Caribbean[14] are very alike.

The juror is expected to have either some property or an earning capacity[15] but the requirements are very minimal, such that very few adults would not qualify. He is expected to be able to read, write and understand English, which is the primary and official language in all Commonwealth Caribbean jurisdictions. A person who has had a previous conviction for a serious offence for which he was imprisoned (the legislation may vary as to whether he

11 The foreman may be either male or female.

12 In some jurisdictions such as the Bahamas, Juries Act No 7 of 1998, s 3, the qualifying age is still 21. Also, see the qualifying ages provisions for Dominica, Grenada, Guyana and St Kitts and Nevis referred to below.

13 In Antigua, Jury Act 2009, s 4, provides that the upper age limit is 70.

14 See: Antigua, Jury Act 2009 (Act No 6 of 2009), ss 4, 6; Bahamas, Juries Act, No 7 of 1998, ss 3–4;
Barbados, Juries Act, Cap 115B, ss 4–5;
Dominica, Juries Act, Chap 5:70, ss 4, 6;
Grenada, Jury Act, No 31 of 2015, ss 4, 6;
Guyana, Criminal Law (Procedure) Act, Cap 10:01, ss 19–20;
Jamaica, Jury Act, s 2;
St Kitts and Nevis, Jury Act, Cap 3.15, ss 4, 7;
St Lucia, Criminal Code, ss 925–27;
St Vincent, Jury Act, Cap 28, ss 4–6;
Trinidad and Tobago, Jury Act, Chap 6:53, ss 4–5.

15 This requirement has been abolished in Antigua in the 2009 Jury Act.

must have been imprisoned for a specified time) is disqualified from jury service unless he has been granted a 'free' pardon, presumably wiping off the conviction. A bankrupt person may not serve on a jury and neither may a person who is insane, deaf, blind or (in some jurisdictions) who otherwise has a permanent infirmity of body, as some statutory provisions proclaim. The latter disqualifications may be queried as being discriminatory today. In fact, it was not until fairly recently that women[16] were deemed to qualify for jury service, which in itself exemplifies how restrictive the qualifying provisions for jury service were. The original property qualifications, which today appear minimal, were prohibitive at the time they were passed decades ago. Over time, the legislature has sought to widen the field of qualified jurors by removing restrictions to service and it is possible that the disability disqualifications may in time be revised. In this regard, it is worthy to note that whereas most jurisdictions such as Antigua[17] and Trinidad and Tobago[18] disqualify persons with permanent infirmity of the body from qualifying for service, the same is not true for Barbados.

Consequences of disqualification

If a person who is disqualified or unqualified as a juror sits in a jury, this will not in itself lead to the quashing of a conviction. This is provided for in some jurisdictions such as Barbados where s 8 of the Juries Act provides that the verdict or finding of a jury shall not be set aside on the ground that any member was disqualified or exempt from jury service. Even where the Juries Act does not so specify, it has been held that the provisions relating to making up of the jury lists, which are extensive in all jurisdictions, are meant to give finality to the certified jury list. This is so as to preclude any objection being taken to the qualification of a juror whose name appears on the list: *R v Singh* (1962) 5 WIR 61, a decision of the Court of Appeal of Jamaica. The court in that case followed the English case of *R v Kelly* [1950] 1 All ER 806 on this point, and distinguished *Ras Behari Lal v King-Emperor* (1933) 30 Cox CC 17, a decision of the Privy Council. In *Singh* it was discovered after the conclusion of the trial that one of the jurors who sat on the case was, by virtue of a previous conviction for a felony, disqualified from service. The appeal was dismissed on the basis that no miscarriage of injustice had occurred to the defendant. The court considered that in *Ras Behari Lal* (above), where one juror was found to know no English while certain others did not understand English sufficiently when the proceedings were in English, the Privy Council set aside the conviction not simply because of the disqualification, but on the basis of natural justice. In that case, the inability of the juror to understand English at all deprived the accused person of his fundamental right to that juror's determination of the issues in the trial. The same could not be said of the defendant in *Singh*.

In *Chapman* (1976) 63 Cr App R 75, the English Court of Appeal also considered *Ras Behari Lal* in an appeal based on the contention that one of the jurors in the trial was deaf and did not hear half the evidence or the summing up. The deafness only came to light afterwards. The court found that where only one juror was involved who could have been discharged and where the trial could have proceeded to a majority verdict, there was no miscarriage of justice. The defendant had been charged with burglary and a unanimous verdict had been returned on the charge. The conviction was affirmed.

16 E.g., it was only in 1966 by Act No 22 of 1966 that women could qualify for jury service in St Kitts and Nevis.

17 Jury Act 2009 s 6(b).

18 Jury Act, Chap 6:53, s 5(b).

It would seem that there should be no objection to a trial judge asking prospective jurors before jury selection to bring to his attention any disqualification from which they may suffer. In this vein, the trial judge in *Naresh Boodram and Ramiah v The State* (1997) 55 WIR 304 asked prospective jurors to bring to his attention any inability to return a true verdict in the case, for any good reason of conscience or acquaintance with the accused, the deceased, or their families. The Court of Appeal of Trinidad and Tobago held that the trial judge was acting properly within his powers to ensure a fair trial. It would seem to be even less objectionable for a trial judge to ask prospective jurors if they can read and write English, are resident, or have convictions and the like.

Exemptions

Throughout the region statutory provisions also enumerate lists of persons who are exempted or excused from service. The types of person exempted are similar in most jurisdictions and include judges, lawyers, magistrates, police officers, Members of Parliament, ministers of religion and diplomats, for obvious reasons. Their connection with the system of the administration of justice might lead to a perception of bias on their part one way or the other. Others who are exempted, for less obvious reasons, include teachers, nurses and fire officers. In many instances medical practitioners and bank managers are also exempted. The possible rationale is that these persons perform what may be regarded as essential public duties so that they cannot be spared from that employment. However, it may be thought that the consequence of these exemptions is that the resulting pool is too small or that the very persons who may perform well as jurors are prevented from participating in the criminal justice system. The law in the US provides an interesting contrast. There, very few persons are exempted from jury service, so that even lawyers and police officers may be called to serve.

In some jurisdictions even chemists,[19] pilots[20] and pharmacists are exempt. The Jamaica Jury Act in Schedule A specifically exempts teachers in the University of the West Indies and any tertiary institution. The first Schedule to the Criminal Law (Procedure) Act of Guyana, Cap 10:01 exempts all public officers. The Trinidad and Tobago Jury Act, Chap 6:53 does not appear to exempt nurses like most other jurisdictions, while spouses of judges and lawyers are entitled to be excused if they wish. On the other hand, in many other jurisdictions, spouses of all those who are exempt are also exempted. In contrast, the St Lucian Criminal Code in its list of exempt persons (s 927) does not include any spouses of exempt persons.

It is evident that there is need for revision of the list of exempt persons in legislation throughout the region. It should be determined whether there is any basis for exemption of the variety of personnel listed, as there may have been decades ago when the respective provisions were enacted. It may well be thought preferable to reduce the list of exempt persons and permit those who have difficulty or concerns to make individual application for exemption to a judge as is currently permitted in respect of qualified jurors.

It is a practice that on a specified day before the start of a criminal session, jurors who have been summoned for service may personally or by attorney seek special exemption. Most judges, if they entertain the exemption, may require the juror to serve at another time when he has less pressing commitments. A juror who is otherwise qualified for service and is not an exempt person is not entitled to be specially exempted because of his objection to 'judging a person': *Re Darien, A Juror* (1974) 22 WIR 323. In that case, a juror asked to be excused when

19 As in Antigua, e.g., Jury Act 2009, First Schedule.
20 Grenada Jury Act, No 31 of 2015, s 5; Jamaica Jury Act, Sch A.

his time came to be sworn on the ground of conscience. He was not excused and then refused to be sworn. He was fined by the trial judge and applied to the Supreme Court of Jamaica, claiming that his constitutional rights to freedom of conscience had been infringed. It was held that trial by jury, being reasonably required in the interest of public order, overrode the defendant's personal enjoyment of his freedom of conscience in the particular situation.

The Barbados Court of Appeal has, however, sanctioned the decision of a trial judge to exempt persons who have objections to the death penalty, prior to jury selection in a capital case: *Hinds v R* (1999) 58 WIR 38.

SELECTION OF THE JURY

Statute requires that a list of qualified jurors should be made and revised annually or biennially, as the case may be. The first list is prepared either by the Registrar of the Supreme Court, as for instance in Antigua and Dominica, or by the Chief Elections Officer, chiefly from the list of electors, as in Jamaica and Trinidad and Tobago. In the Bahamas a revising panel comprising the Registrar and two others both prepare and revise the list. In other jurisdictions the initial list is subsequently revised, usually by the magistrate of the District, or in Trinidad and Tobago by a magistrate who is appointed as the reviser. The reviser eliminates those jurors who are disqualified or exempt from the list. It has been held that the verdict of a jury will not be set aside on account of irregularities in the due revision of the jury list unless the applicant proves that he has been prejudiced thereby: *Montreal Street Railway Co v Normadin* [1917] AC 170, PC.

The revised list of jurors is eventually entered into the jurors book kept by the Registrar. From that book the names of jurors are randomly selected each month by the Registrar or his staff. Summonses are issued to prospective jurors by the staff of the registry of the Supreme Court. The jurors are served in sufficient time before the criminal session, either by the marshals or police officers, as statute provides. In one study[21] in 1976–1978 of selection of jurors in Trinidad and Tobago, it was found that half of the jurors who were presumed eligible were unavailable for reasons such as death, change of address, migration or disqualification. Of that half, a significant portion was unavailable at the time of the criminal session for service and sought exemptions either on the day fixed for granting such or before the court on the first court day of the sessions.

The Registrar must cause sufficient numbers of jurors to be served to ensure that panels of at least 36 or, in some jurisdictions, 48 jurors are present in each criminal court for the month. If several accused persons are expected to be tried jointly, a greater number of jurors may be summoned to that court to ensure that there is a sufficient pool from which to choose a jury. On the first day of the criminal sessions, the panel of jurors who are qualified and have been served to appear will attend the relevant criminal court. Unless any are excused on that day, these are the jurors from among whom juries will be constituted to try cases during that session. A session may comprise a month, as in Trinidad and Tobago, or two or three months. Each juror will be assigned a number and counters or balls, numbered from one to the number of jurors served to be present in court, will be placed in a jury box. One counter or ball is pulled at a time from the box by the Registrar or a member of his staff, when the time comes for selection of the actual jury to try a particular case that is to be heard. After a jury has tried a case and is discharged, the counters with the names of those

21 Op. cit., Deosaran, fn 2, p 5.

jurors will be replaced in the jury box with those of the other jurors. They are eligible for selection for subsequent trials.[22]

The issue as to the need for proper preparation of the jurors' register came up for consideration before the Privy Council in *DPP of the Virgin Islands v Penn* [2008] UKPC 29. In that case, while the Jury Act 1914 of the British Virgin Islands required preparation of a jurors list to be copied into a jurors book to form a register based on which a jury would be selected, the practice of the last 15 years had been very different. In impanelling juries successive Registrars had used the voters list prepared under the Elections Act. This had occurred at the trial of the appellant. There was no objection to this at trial but the question was raised on appeal. The Court of Appeal held that the Registrar had no jurisdiction to impanel based other than on the jurors register. The DPP appealed to the Privy Council. After careful scrutiny of the relevant legislation the Board followed its earlier decision in *Montreal Street Railway* (above). It held that there was nothing in the Jury Act 1914 to compel a conclusion that either the array or the trial should be regarded as a nullity. Where at trial such failures went unobserved by those responsible for trying the issues of law and fact and all appeared entirely in order there was 'no ground for considering that the default had or could have had any impact on the eligibility to serve, randomness, impartiality or ultimate decision of all or any of the members of the jury'.

Composition of jury

The number of jurors that constitute a jury varies among jurisdictions and also may differ depending on whether the charge is capital or non-capital. In the Bahamas,[23] Guyana,[24] St Kitts and Nevis[25] and now Antigua[26] the number of members (sometimes called the array) in a jury is 12 for all types of offences. In contrast, in Dominica,[27] the jury consists of nine jurors in all cases. In Barbados, Grenada, St Lucia, St Vincent and Trinidad and Tobago a jury comprises nine jurors in the trial of a non-capital case and 12 in the trial of a capital matter. A jury in Jamaica[28] consists of 12 persons to try a capital offence but only seven to try a non-capital matter.

Alternate jurors

Statute in Antigua, Grenada, St Lucia and Trinidad and Tobago has created the system of alternate jurors. This is a new phenomenon to countries that follow the English common law. As was observed by the Court of Appeal in Trinidad and Tobago in *Nankissoon Boodram v The State* (1997) 53 WIR 352, p 380: 'by introducing alternate jurors into our system [in the Caribbean] we followed American rather than English precedent'.

The provisions in Section 21A of Trinidad and Tobago, s 953 of the St Lucia Criminal Code 2004 and s 19 of the Grenada Jury Act[29] are all similar. The provisions are

22 In exceptional cases, a trial judge may relieve members of a jury who have sat on a long and difficult case from service for a specified time.

23 Juries Act, No 7 of 1998, s 18.

24 Criminal Law (Procedure) Act, Cap 10:01, s 33.

25 Jury Act, Cap 3.15, s 26.

26 Jury Act 2009, s 22 (1).

27 Juries Act, Chap 5:70, s 21.

28 Jury Act, s 31(2).

29 The Antigua provisions in s 22 (3) and 22 (4) of the Jury Act 2009 are very succinct and do not detail how the alternates would function.

substantially the same as the provisions relating to alternate jurors in Delaware, a state in the US: *Nankissoon Boodram* (above), p 380. The statute enables the court to direct that not more than six jurors may be empanelled in addition to the common jury to sit as alternate jurors. The alternates may replace jurors who, prior to the time for retirement, 'become or are found to be unable or disqualified to perform their duty'. Where an alternate does not replace a common juror up to the time of retirement, he will be discharged as soon as the jury retires to consider its verdict. In practice, a court may decide to use any number of alternate jurors (up to six), or none at all. This usually will depend on the length of time the trial is expected to take. The longer the time, the greater the likelihood that a juror may become unable to perform his duties and thus the more likely that alternate jurors will be selected. *Nankissoon Boodram* (above) was the first trial in Trinidad and Tobago in which alternate jurors were utilised and in that case a full slate (six) of alternates were chosen, since nine accused were being tried jointly for murder.

In that case, after the defendants were convicted they appealed on the ground, inter alia, 'that the alternate jurors were allowed to mingle with the common jurors who constituted the jury' and this was a breach of the prohibition against members of a jury mingling with outsiders, especially a jury that was sequestered. The Court of Appeal of Trinidad and Tobago followed authority from the Supreme Court of Delaware and held that the defendants had not been prejudiced by the mingling of the alternates with the regular jurors. The court also based its decision on the fact that, under statute, alternate jurors had the same functions, privileges and powers as common jurors. They were selected in the same manner and had to be similarly qualified. Any reference in the legislation to 'jurors' must therefore include alternates. The prohibition against mingling with outsiders must mean persons who were not jurors and did not include alternates.

It seems apparent that alternate jurors are not meant to be used willy-nilly to replace common jurors for reasons of expediency or mere absenteeism. The relevant statutory provisions in both Grenada and Trinidad and Tobago stipulate that alternates will replace any jurors 'found to be unable or disqualified to perform their duties'. It would seem that alternate juries are meant to replace those who may be properly discharged under the common law or statute. The usual reasons are for death, illness or other sufficient cause (s 19(3) of the Trinidad and Tobago Jury Act). In other words, where a juror could validly have been discharged under the law previously he still may be, but if so he will now be replaced by an alternate. It may thus be argued, then, that there is no likelihood in these jurisdictions (Grenada and Trinidad and Tobago) of a jury retiring without its full complement, as any discharged juror may be replaced. It must be pointed out, however, that alternates are not chosen in all cases, but only in some, usually capital cases.

Challenges

Both the prosecutor and the defence have the right to challenge prospective jurors called, before a jury is finally selected. This right to challenge, from very early times,[30] was dictated by the common law and later by statute in England. In Commonwealth Caribbean jurisdictions the right is stipulated in the provisions in legislation on juries. There are two types of challenge: peremptory challenge and challenge for cause. In some jurisdictions there

30 See *R v Chandler* [1964] 1 All ER 761, pp 763–64.

exists the right of the prosecution of 'standing by' jurors, usually when they have no right to peremptory challenges.

A peremptory challenge is one for which no reason need be given. When the prospective juror is about to be sworn (in the jury box) as a juror he may be peremptorily challenged simply by an indication 'challenge'. In all jurisdictions the defence has the right of peremptory challenge, but the maximum number of such challenges which may be made varies among the jurisdictions. In Antigua, Barbados, Dominica and St Kitts and Nevis the prosecution has no right of peremptory challenge, but has the right to 'stand by' as in England. In all jurisdictions, both sides may challenge for cause without restriction in number.

Peremptory challenges

In Antigua,[31] Dominica[32] and St Kitts and Nevis[33] the defence alone has the right of making peremptory challenges and, while in Antigua each accused has the right of up to five such challenges, in the other two jurisdictions the maximum is three. The St Vincent[34] Jury Act permits the Crown and each accused person to have the right to challenge peremptorily three jurors but the Crown also has the right of stand by. This is also the case in Barbados. In the Bahamas[35] each side, the prosecutor and each accused person, may challenge peremptorily up to ten jurors. The Criminal Law (Procedure) Act, Cap 10:01, of Guyana[36] permits the prosecution and each defendant the right to three peremptory challenges. In these six jurisdictions, the number of peremptory challenges are fixed regardless of the type of offence and the number of accused.

The position is somewhat different in other jurisdictions. In Barbados[37] a 'person arraigned' may object to up to seven prospective jurors by way of peremptory challenge. If, however, several accused persons are arraigned together, the sum total of the peremptory challenges available varies. Each person does not have a separate right to challenge seven. Instead, if five persons or fewer are arraigned together, a total of ten peremptory challenges are available to the defence, whereas if more than five persons are arraigned, each has only two peremptory challenges.

The Jamaica provisions[38] are less complicated. For persons arraigned for murder or treason, statute confers a right of peremptory challenge of seven to each accused person. For other offences the number is five to each accused person. The prosecution has the right of peremptory challenge to the same number in respect of every person arraigned as that person has. Thus, if two persons are jointly tried for murder, the prosecution has 14 peremptory challenges while each defendant has seven. The St Lucia statute[39] is also very simple. The prosecution and each accused person have up to four peremptory challenges each for trial of a capital offence, and three for a non-capital offence. The number of possible challenges available to the prosecution does not increase with the number of defendants.

31 Jury Act 2009.

32 Juries Act, Chap 5:70, s 22.

33 Jury Act, Cap 3.15, s 27 (a).

34 Jury Act, Cap 28, s 16.

35 Juries Act 1998, s 19.

36 Criminal Law (Procedure) Act, Cap 10:01, s 38.

37 Juries Act, Cap 115B, s 28(1) and (2).

38 Jury Act, s 33 (amended by Act No 13 of 2016, which adds a new subsection 2A, allowing four peremptory challenges where offences other than murder or treason are tried jointly).

39 Criminal Code, ss 959–68.

In Grenada, Section 21(a) of the Jury Act, No 31 of 2015 enables every accused person to challenge peremptorily any number of jurors not exceeding four. Section 21(b) also allows the prosecution to challenge peremptorily any number of jurors not exceeding four in respect of each accused person but not exceeding eight jurors in all.

The Jury Act of Trinidad and Tobago, Chap 6:53, was amended by Act No 10 of 1996. The new s 23 quite simply provides that every accused person is entitled to peremptory challenges of up to three while the prosecution is entitled to three in respect of each person charged. In the light of the introduction of alternate jurors, however, the new s 21A(5) permits both the prosecution and the defence an additional peremptory challenge in respect of each defendant in relation to the alternate jurors. It seems that if alternate jurors are selected, each side may utilise any peremptory challenges they have left, after selection of the jury, plus one additional challenge per defendant when challenging the alternates.

Peremptory challenges constitute the preferred type of challenge, since the party utilising them may do so without giving any reason for the challenge. It would seem irrelevant should a defendant choose to utilise his peremptory challenges to avoid particular jury members whether on the basis of class, gender or even race. This kind of usage is nonetheless curtailed by the fact that peremptory challenges are limited in number.

'Stand by'

In England, the right of the Crown to peremptory challenge was first abolished in 1305.[40] In its place evolved a right at common law for the prosecution (the Crown) to go through the panel of jurors present to 'stand by' jurors in order to see if an acceptable jury could be sworn without having to resort to challenge for cause. If the panel is 'gone through' and a full jury has not been sworn, then it would become necessary to recall the prospective jurors who had been stood down. If the prosecution still objected to any of these jurors, they would have to show cause why each such juror should be rejected. In *Chandler* (see note 40) Lord Parker CJ considered the history of the practice of 'stand by' in England in a case where the defendant claimed the right of stand by in addition to his right of peremptory challenge. The court held that where an accused person had the right of peremptory challenge, he could not claim the common law right to 'stand by' jurors which the prosecution, who had no right of peremptory challenge, enjoyed at common law.

In the Commonwealth Caribbean, statute in those jurisdictions where the prosecution has no right of peremptory challenge confers on the prosecution the entitlement to ask jurors to 'stand by until the panel has gone through'. The statutory provisions in most cases actually refer to the right 'as in England', thus making it clear that the right is exercised in the same way. As indicated above, the St Vincent Jury Act confers on the prosecution both the right of peremptory challenge and the right to stand by jurors as does the Barbados Juries Act Cap 115B.[41] Both rights are given by statute so the prohibition in *Chandler* (above) does not apply.

40 *R v Chandler* [1964] 1 All ER 760, p 764.
41 Section 28(5).

Challenge for cause

In selecting a jury, both the prosecution and the defence have the right to unlimited challenges of jurors (the polls) once they show cause. The party, be it the prosecution or the defence, who seeks to exercise this type of challenge must first lay a foundation of fact in support of the ground of his challenge: *Chandler* (above), p 767. In that case the defendant sought to contend that if he had been allowed to cross-examine a particular juror he would have been able to establish a prima facie case of bias. The Court of Criminal Appeal held that a defendant cannot simply allege that a prospective juror is antagonistic. According to Lord Parker CJ: 'There must be a foundation of fact creating a prima facie case before the juror can be cross-examined'.

Thus the party making the challenge is not entitled to question the juror to justify making the challenge: *David James v The State* Cr App 43 of 1977 (unreported), p 7, a decision of the Court of Appeal of Trinidad and Tobago. In *R v Renford Solomon* (1971) 18 WIR 65, the defence had challenged several jurors for cause during the jury selection process in which the defendant was charged for murder. On appeal after conviction, the defence contended that they should have been allowed to examine on the voir dire the jurors who were challenged before any steps were taken to adduce evidence in support of the challenges. The Court of Appeal of Jamaica dismissed the appeal, holding that a prima facie case must be made out in support of a challenge for cause before a juror could be questioned on the voir dire. It is clear, then, that the challenging party must bring other evidence in support of his challenge rather than expect to establish cause simply by cross-examining the challenged juror. Furthermore, a juror on the trial of the challenge cannot be made to answer questions which may discredit him although he may be asked about his qualifications or his feelings of possible bias: *R v Martin* [1848] 6 St Tr (NS) 925.

It is apparent that it is for the challenging party to bear the burden of proving the cause as alleged. Since the challenge for cause is usually by the defence, the standard of proof required is only on a balance of probabilities. The Court of Appeal of Trinidad and Tobago in *Nankissoon Boodram v The State* (1997) 53 WIR 352 implicitly acknowledged that it was for the defence who had made numerous challenges for cause, 34 of which were rejected by the trial judge, to show from the evidence that there was a real possibility of bias on the part of the challenged jurors.

The grounds for challenge for cause were well established at common law before they were enacted in statute, as they have now been in some jurisdictions.[42] A juror may be successfully challenged for cause on the basis that he is biased, 'not indifferent' between the prosecution and the accused person. This is sometimes called propter affectum. In addition, he may be challenged for cause in that he does not satisfy the qualification requirements, such as the residency or language requirements (propter defectum). The jury legislation[43] in countries such as the Bahamas, Grenada, Guyana, St Lucia and Trinidad and Tobago enumerates the several bases for challenge for cause in almost identical terms. They are the same as the grounds at common law, propter affectum and propter defectum.

42 As in the Jury Act, Chap 6:53, s 23A of Trinidad and Tobago.

43 Bahamas: Juries Act, 1998, s 20;
Grenada: Jury Act, No 31 of 2015, s 22;
Guyana: Criminal Law (Procedure) Act, Cap 10:01, s 39;
St Lucia: Criminal Code, s 957;
Trinidad and Tobago: Jury Act, Chap 6:53, s 23A, as amended by Act 10 of 1996.

In wholly exceptional cases, the trial judge may permit challenge for cause of prospective jurors without laying a foundation of fact individually against each juror. This may occur where there has been widespread and prejudicial pre-trial publicity[44] sufficient to establish the probability of prejudice on the part of anyone who had read that kind of information: *R v Kray* (1969) 53 Cr App R 412. It was held by the English Central Criminal Court that because of the 'wholly exceptional nature' of that case, counsel was entitled to examine the jurors as they came to be sworn. Similarly, in Trinidad and Tobago in the trial of *Nankissoon Boodram* (above) and eight others, the trial judge permitted challenges for cause against numerous jurors because of proof of widespread and pervasive negative pre-trial publicity. In a previous constitutional motion on the issue, the Privy Council had found that the pre-trial publicity was prejudicial in that it suggested that the first defendant was a notorious drug smuggler, that he had previously been charged with murder, and that he and his associates were such threats to the security of witnesses that they had to be specially protected while giving evidence at the preliminary hearing: *Nankissoon Boodram v AG* (1996) 47 WIR 459, PC. The Privy Council, however, refused to grant constitutional relief since they felt that this was a matter to be dealt with by the trial judge. It was in fact raised at trial where one of the measures the trial judge utilised was allowing the defence to challenge extensively for cause without having to lay an individual basis of bias for each individual juror: *Nankissoon Boodram v The State* (1997) 53 WIR 352.

It is the trial judge who makes the determination as to whether the objection to the juror should be upheld and the prospective juror discharged. In *Nankissoon Boodram v The State* (above), the court held that despite a statutory provision that there should be no appeal against a decision of the trial judge on a challenge for cause, this does not prevent the defendant from contending on appeal that the judge wrongly rejected the challenge. The defence may argue that this caused a real danger of bias on the part of one or more of the subsequently selected members of the jury so as to prejudice the fair trial of the defendant. All the provision meant was that a defendant could not hold up a trial while he appealed on the failure of his challenge for cause. The court went on to say that in determining such an imponderable as the risk of bias, the impression given by the person challenged and his general demeanour will be just as helpful as the answers given. The trial judge may thus be in the best position to make an assessment of possible bias of prospective juries. On the evidence before the court, they found no reason to reject the trial judge's decision in each case to reject 34 of the challenges for cause by the defendant.

Challenge to the array

In some jurisdictions, statute still enables challenge to the entire array or panel of prospective jurors summoned. This was a right always available at common law. The ground for this challenge is bias on the part of the officer responsible for listing and summoning jurors. He may, for instance, have deliberately selected jurors of a particular religion or from a particular group of people. Challenge to the array is rarely if ever made because alleged partiality on the part of the responsible officer is difficult to sustain and because of the detailed statutory procedure established for constitution of jury lists and selection of jury panels.

In general, the mere fact that an array or panel of prospective jurors is disproportionately representative of the society either in terms of gender or race is not a sufficient basis for challenging the array: *R v Ford* (1989) 89 Cr App R 278. Nonetheless, in the Trinidad and

44 See Seetahal, DS, 'Pre-trial publicity and a fair trial', *Caribbean Journal of Criminology and Social Psychology*, Vol 4, Nos 1 and 2 January/July 1999, pp 192–209.

Tobago San Fernando Assizes in November 1999, the prosecutor took the point[45] that the jury panel in the Second Assize Court was disproportionately representative of women. In a panel of some 61 jurors summoned, there were only two men. Similar disproportionality existed in the panel for the First and Third Assizes Courts. Section 15(4) of the Trinidad and Tobago Jury Act, Chap 6:53, provides that the number of women whose names are contained in a panel 'shall be in the same proportion as nearly as may be to the number of men whose names are so contained'. Although the section required that women must constitute at least 20 per cent of a panel, there was no such requirement for men. The Director of Public Prosecutions decided, in the interests of justice, to seek an enlargement of time, under s 40 of the Act, to constitute the panels. This he did by making an application by notice of motion to the High Court (ex parte). The motion was granted and fresh summonses were then issued by the Registrar to prospective male jurors. This was so as to ensure that men were more proportionally represented on the panels and thus avoid arguments being made that the constitution of the panels was in breach of the statute.

Jury vetting

It is not unconstitutional for the prosecuting authorities to cause the jury panel to be vetted to ensure that its members are qualified to serve: *R v McCann et al.* (1991) 92 Cr App R 239. In that case the court did not follow the dicta of Denning MR in *R v Sheffield Crown Court ex p Brownlow* (1980) 71 Cr App R 19 to the contrary. Since persons with serious convictions are in general disqualified from serving as jurors, it is a common law right of the prosecutor to be provided with information concerning the conviction of potential jurors so as to facilitate challenges for cause: *R v Mason* (1980) 71 Cr App R 157. In preparing the list of qualified jurors, the revising officer may not have had available all the information pertaining to the conviction of potential jurors. Additionally, some persons may become disqualified after the jurors' lists were prepared. In *R v Sheffield Crown Court ex p Brownlow*, the English Court of Appeal did not disagree with the order of the trial judge requiring the police to supply the defence with a list of jurors who had convictions.

Praying the tales

It may sometimes transpire that because of the exercise of peremptory challenges and challenges for cause by both sides, the panel is exhausted before a jury is selected. In the Jamaican case of *R v Renford Solomon* (1971) 18 WIR 65, the Court of Appeal of Jamaica sanctioned the practice of judges requiring jurors assigned to another court to be present for service in the court where the jurors assigned have been exhausted (by challenges).

Statute across the region has nevertheless provided for this eventuality by sanctioning the old established practice of 'praying the tales'. This enables the court upon application by the designated court official or upon request by either party to the trial to

> command the marshal to name and appoint, as often as need requires, so many of such persons then present as will make up a full jury; and the marshals shall, at such command of the court, return such persons duly qualified as are present or can be found to serve upon such jury.[46]

45 At the trial of *State v Harrison Baisden* on 29 November 1999.

46 Jury Act, Chap 6:53, s 36, Trinidad and Tobago.

Thus, in cases of need, jurors may be recruited from persons in or around the court. With slight variations, this entitlement to pray the 'tales', add to the jury panel virtual bystanders, is contained in most jury legislation in the Commonwealth Caribbean.[47] It seems that, except for Jamaica where s 43 of the Jury Act specifies otherwise, it is not necessary first to ensure that these talesmen are qualified as jurors. Presumably, they may be challenged afterwards on lack of qualification. In *Nankissoon Boodram v The State* (1997) 53 WIR 352, one of the grounds of appeal was that the marshal of the court had created an artificial pool of talesmen by summoning batches of persons on the jury list to attend the court. In that case it became apparent soon after the trial began that the panel of jurors would be exhausted. At that time 66 jurors had been successfully challenged for cause, 20 had been challenged peremptorily, and one excused. The prosecution made an application for the praying of the tales. The judge granted the application and made an order to that effect. The marshals were only able to locate 16 persons within the vicinity of the courthouse and, of these, 14 were not qualified. Thereafter, the marshal decided to send out notices to batches of jurors to attend at the courthouse. From these numbers, the remaining jurors were selected after questioning and various challenges, particularly on the part of the defence. It was argued by the defence that the court officials had merely summoned a new panel of jurors and had not prayed the 'tales'.

The Trinidad and Tobago Court of Appeal applied the old English case of *R v Dolby* [1823] 2 B&C 104 in holding that it was 'not necessary that tales should be selected out of persons accidentally present: they may be selected out of persons whose presence the sheriff or the coroner has taken previous means to obtain'. The court also considered that as the statutory provision allowed the marshals to retain persons who were 'present or can be found', the court officials were within their rights to summon persons (who could be found) to attend to create a pool of talesmen. The court made it clear, however, that there was no sanction available if these persons had disobeyed the summons, since they were not prospective jurors as such. Furthermore, talesmen were not entitled to be exempted from service on application to the court as were regular jurors.

The decision in *Nankissoon Boodram* as to selection of talesmen is clearly applicable to Guyana, whose statutory provision[48] on the tales is identical to that of Trinidad and Tobago. In Barbados and the Bahamas the statutory provisions are similar. In the relevant statutory provision of Dominica and St Kitts and Nevis mention is only made of selection of persons who are 'present'. Nevertheless, it would seem that the decision of *Dolby* in this regard permits the court officers to cause persons (talesmen) to be present in court to serve as jurors.

It is highly unusual in the Commonwealth Caribbean for resort to be had to praying of the tales, so it is of note to mention that the decision of the Court of Appeal in *Nankissoon Boodram* on this issue (as well as all other grounds) was considered by the Privy Council to give rise to no arguable grounds of appeal, so that leave to appeal by the nine applicants against their conviction for murder was refused.

---

47 Antigua: Jury Act 2009, s 20(4);
Bahamas: Juries Act 1998, s 17;
Barbados: Juries Act, Cap 115B, s 27(1);
Dominica: Juries Act, Chap 5:70, s 24(1)(a);
Guyana: Criminal Law (Procedure) Act, Chap 10:01, s 40(1);
Jamaica: Jury Act, s 43;
St Lucia: Criminal Code, ss 944, 961;
Trinidad and Tobago: Jury Act, Chap 6:53, s 36.

48 Criminal Law (Procedure) Act, Cap 10:01, s 40(1).

Exemption after selection

It has been held that where a juror has been properly selected and not challenged it is wrong for a trial judge to exempt him on the basis that he does not wish to be sequestered: *Abdool Salim Yaseen and Thomas v The State* (1990) 44 WIR 219. The Court of Appeal of Guyana held that a court could not deprive a defendant of the services of persons selected according to law – except for sufficient reasons. Such reasons would be equivalent to those which permit discharge during the course of a trial (illness or necessity).[49]

AT THE TRIAL

After a jury is selected, including alternates where permitted and utilised, the defendant is put in the charge of the jury who will determine whether he is guilty or not guilty. The judge may decide at that stage whether to sequester the jury or not. It is not permissible for a judge to discharge a juror simply because of the possibility of his ruling at some later stage of the trial that the jury should be sequestered: *Abdool Salim Yaseen and Thomas v The State* (1990) 44 WIR 219. In that case, the Court of Appeal of Guyana held that after a jury had been selected, jurors could only be excused as provided for by statute and common law. Fear of being sequestered was not a sufficient reason for excusing a juror from service.

There are many matters which a court must take into account after a jury is selected to ensure that the jury is able to consider the evidence and eventually the verdict independently and in a comfortable environment. For instance, the judge must ensure that the jury is provided with adequate refreshment during the course of the hearing as stipulated by legislation. Apart from such basic requirements, there are particular issues to which the trial judge should have regard. These are discussed below.

Previous arraignment

A defendant should not be put on trial more than once in one criminal session since it is likely that jurors who are to serve on the second trial most likely will be present in court when the first jury is chosen. This is so since all members of the panel should be present in court for selection from among their number. The presence of even some of the jurors, who are empanelled to try a defendant, in court on a previous occasion when the defendant was tried or even arraigned for another offence is bound to cause prejudice to the defendant: *Howe v R* (1974) 19 WIR 517. In that case from St Vincent, the defendant was tried with murder. At least some of the jurors who heard the murder charge had been present in court shortly before the hearing of the murder case, when the defendant was convicted of rape. The Court of Appeal of the West Indies Associated States considered this was a prejudicial event which created a situation prejudicial to the defendant. The court held that if a judge becomes aware, when a jury is empanelled to try an accused person, that there are jurors thereon who were present in court when the accused person was convicted shortly before, and it was not possible to choose a jury that had not been compromised, then he should discharge the jury and adjourn the trial to the next Assizes.

The Court of Appeal in Trinidad and Tobago had to deal with a similar situation in *Lester v The State* (1996) 50 WIR 452. In that case, while the defendant was awaiting trial

49 See below, 'Discharge of a Juror'.

on a charge of shooting with intent, he was taken to court on an unrelated charge of robbery. The trial in that matter proceeded before a jury. The next day the defendant was called on to answer the charge of shooting in the presence of the jury members who were sitting in court on that occasion. The shooting case was adjourned, but the robbery hearing continued and the defendant was convicted. The Court of Appeal allowed the appeal on the basis that the defendant did not have proper service of the indictment in accordance with the law. The court also stated per curiam that it was doubtful whether the conviction could be sustained in the light of the jury having been in court when the defendant was called on to plead on the shooting charge. The court opined that the jury empanelled for the robbery should have been put out of court before the matter was called. This not having been done, it was clear that the knowledge that the defendant was on another (unrelated and serious) charge must have operated to create some prejudice against the defendant in the minds of the jurors. The court said that it was uncertain if this kind of prejudice could have been counteracted by directions of the trial judge, which in any case was not given in this trial. In *Howe* (above), the court considered that the prejudice to the defendant was not overcome by the judge's warnings against holding such prejudice.

Decision to sequester

Where a trial commences, the jury empanelled to try the case may be permitted to separate and leave the court upon any adjournment of the case and before they retire to consider their verdict. On the first occasion that the jury separates, the trial judge should warn them not to speak about the case to anyone outside their number: *Prime* (1973) 57 Cr App R 632. If it is shown that a juror has misbehaved himself in this respect, an irregularity affecting the trial occurs. It is entirely within the discretion of the trial judge as to whether the jury should be permitted to separate or not. The statutory provisions in this regard throughout the region serve to underscore the fact that it is only if the interests of justice will not be adversely affected that the jury should be allowed to separate. In practice, however, the trial judge usually will allow the jury to separate on adjournment unless the interests of justice suggest that they should be kept together.

In Mohammed et al. v The State Cr App Nos 42, 47–49 of 1989 (unreported), the Court of Appeal of Trinidad and Tobago stated (Ibrahim J) that the purpose of sequestering a jury is to prevent unlawful communication with jurors so that their minds would not be affected by extraneous matters when they come to consider their verdicts. Thus a judge will usually only sequester a jury if he has some basis for believing that a fair trial would not be likely if the jury were permitted to separate and go at large.

Where a jury is sequestered, administrative arrangements must be made to ensure that there is no opportunity for interference with the jurors. Sequestered jurors must be protected from outside interference and communication in much the same way as if they had retired to consider their verdict. In *Mohammed* (above) the court considered and applied the Canadian case of *R v Ryan* [1951] 4 WWR 32. In that case a sequestered jury was allowed to go to the cinema accompanied by the sheriff. It was stated by the court that if a (sequestered) jury is permitted by the judge to go to a theatre or a game it should only be on condition that the jury is free from contact with the audience or crowd and is effectively supervised.

It is evident that once a decision is made to sequester a jury, it is to be assumed that the jury needs to be protected from outside interference in a way that a jury that is permitted to separate does not require. To do otherwise would be to erode the rationale for the very decision to sequester the jury. *Roberts v R* (1968) 13 WIR 50, which concerned a trial for murder in Grenada,[50] is instructive in this regard. The jury was sequestered to try the case on 2 November, but on 3 November a juror who had taken ill during the night had to be taken to the hospital for treatment. He was left at the hospital waiting room with other persons and was subsequently placed in a ward with other patients in the hospital. There he was kept for two days, after which the trial proceeded. On appeal after conviction, it was argued for the defence that the juror had ample opportunity to discuss the case with members of the public, whether he in fact did so or not. The Court of Appeal held that this was an irregularity that contravened the statutory provisions (s 176 of the Grenada Procedure Code) which mandated that proper arrangements should be made to prevent sequestered jurors from holding communication with anyone on the subject of the trial.

While, in general, a jury may separate on adjournments (usually day to day) during the trial, once an order of sequestration is made the jury must be supervised during any interaction with persons outside their members, other than designated officers of the court. There must be no opportunity afforded to jurors to communicate unsupervised with other persons. Any failure in this regard will defeat the purpose behind the sequestration order, which is to prevent the likelihood of interference and may vitiate the trial.

Jury protection

At common law, the trial judge has a discretion to order police protection for the jury should he think it necessary. It is a discretion which must be carefully exercised and only if there is danger of attempts at jury interference or intimidation. The issue usually arises upon application by the prosecution, who must state in the presence of the defence the reasons for making it and call evidence in support if necessary. In *R v Comerford* [1998] 1 Cr App R 235, it was held that once the judge is satisfied that there are attempts at jury interference, he may, to ensure a fair trial, order protection for the jurors. Additionally, he may order that the names of the jurors be withheld and that they be designated by numbers. This is to reduce the risk of direct contact with the jurors by outsiders by making them difficult to identify. The English Court of Appeal stated that provision in the juries legislation which referred to procedures to be followed after a juror's name 'has been drawn' did not impose a mandatory requirement that the names of jurors were to be called. They may be called by number. This latter practice is frequently utilised by judges in the Assizes in Trinidad and Tobago, who also find it more convenient.

It is incumbent on the trial judge to make it clear to the jury that they must not blame the defendant for the fact that they need police protection. Otherwise the defence may justifiably argue that they have been prejudiced by the order. As a corollary it must be considered whether police protection is appropriate when a main issue in the case is whether police witnesses have been honest. On the other hand, if the defendant is a police officer and there is evidence of a real danger of intimidation, the judge has to be very careful in making an order for protection to perhaps designate the selection of such protection. Police officers who are to protect the jurors must be those who clearly have no connection to the case and are without bias to the defendant. Otherwise, the problem of intimidation could be exacerbated by those who are meant to offer protection.

50 Criminal Procedure Code, Cap 72B, s 176 of Grenada stipulates that a jury in capital cases shall be kept together.

Once there is evidence that there is a probability of jury interference (there need not be actual interference), the judge will usually order sequestration of the jury. In these circumstances, he may order police protection as well as supervision by designated officers of the court. Upon occasion, however, judges have allowed the jury to go at large on adjournment and ordered limited protection for them while they are in the vicinity of the courthouse.

Intimidation

Intimidation of a member of a jury is a criminal contempt whether it is in court or out of court, once it is done in relation to his functions as a juror. A jury should be free to return a verdict without fear or favour from the defendant, counsel, witnesses or even the judge.[51] In *R v McKenna et al.* (1960) 44 Cr App R 63, the judge told the jury that if they did not arrive at a verdict by a certain time, he would keep them all night and resume court after 11 the next morning. The judge said this at 2:38 pm to the jury, after which they again retired and were back at 2:45 pm with a verdict. On appeal, the conviction was quashed; the Court of Criminal Appeal held that this could be considered intimidation.

Even a statement made after the jury has returned a verdict may be considered contempt if it amounts to threatening the jury or a juror for what he has done in the performance of his duty as a juror. This would constitute a clear attempt to interfere with the due administration of justice: *Moore v Clerk of Assize* [1971] 1 WLR 1669, just as reprehensible as an attempt to bribe or influence a juror. A juror may not seek to influence his fellow jurors by corrupt or improper means such as bribery or threats. This will clearly amount to a contempt on the part of that juror. By the same token, if a jury arrives at a verdict capriciously by the tossing of a coin, this will be considered (literally) a contempt of court.[52]

Bias – notes

Should there be any indication that the jury or a member of the jury is biased, this will constitute grounds for challenge for cause. The test in deciding this issue is that enunciated in *Re Medicaments and Related Classes of Goods (No 2)* [2001] 1 WLR 7000[53] approved by the House of Lords in *Porter v Magill* [2002] AC 357 HL: would a fair minded and informed observer conclude that there is a real possibility that the defendant may not have a fair trial as a result of the alleged bias? There must be a factual basis for the allegation, although bias itself need not be proven. If the issue of bias arises during the trial, the judge will have to consider the need to discharge[54] a juror or the jury.

During the course of a trial, jurors in the Commonwealth Caribbean, as in England, are, unlike their counterparts in the US, not usually allowed to take notes. This practice may be based on the desire to ensure full concentration of the jury on the evidence as adduced in the trial. It may be thought that individual jurors may place unnecessary weight on the parts of the evidence of which they took notes. Some jurors will not have mastered the art of taking notes while at the same time focussing on a witness's demeanour and so note taking could constitute a distraction. Possibly more pertinently, a juror may have recorded some evidence

---

51 See Chapter 16 for further discussion on pressure on the jury to arrive at a verdict.

52 *Langdell v Sutton* [1737] Barnes 32.

53 The *Medicaments* test is now the standard test for bias, and the authorities in the issue of jury misconduct and the test for discharge must all be adjusted with this in mind.

54 Discussed below.

wrongly and might be tempted to allow his notes to override the official record of the evidence in assessing the credibility of witnesses and the weight to be given to their evidence. A notable exception to this practice is the Bahamas, where jurors are not only permitted to take notes during the trial but are also provided with pen and paper so to do. It is uncertain from where this custom originated, but it is not from English practice. In recent times some judges in Trinidad and Tobago have allowed jurors to take notes during a trial.

A judge is, however, entitled to supplement his summing up with written directions given to the jury on specific issues of law. This may occur in long and complicated cases where the judge's summing up is also lengthy, such that it is unreasonable to expect a jury to remember all the salient directions in law. This practice has been sanctioned by the English courts as in *R v McKechnie* [1992] Crim LR 194, in which it was stated that the written directions must be actually used in the summing up, not just handed to the jury. In his summing up the judge may also list a number of pertinent questions that arise in the case for the consideration of the jury. If he proposes to supplement his summing up with this list of questions, the judge must submit the list to counsel to possibly enable them to make corrections, but also perhaps to address them in closing speeches.

This practice was followed in Trinidad and Tobago by Deyalsingh J in the joint trials of Indravani Ramjattan, Haniff Hilaire and Denny Baptiste DPP No 9/93, for murder, in May 1995. The trial began on 8 May and was completed on 29 May, during which time issues of joint enterprise, straying outside the joint enterprise and incriminating statements made by co-defendants, among others, arose. It was in these circumstances that the trial judge summed up the case for two days and supplemented his summing up with some written directions on particularly complicated issues to the jury. This conduct was not a source of contention on appeal subsequent to conviction, either at the Court of Appeal or the Privy Council. In more complicated cases it continues to be the practice by some judges.

DISCHARGE OF A JUROR

Sometimes during the course of a trial a situation might occur which could result in the judge having to discharge a juror. In this case the jury will have been sworn (12, nine or seven jurors as the case may be) and the question of challenge is no longer relevant. For instance, during the hearing a juror may die or become ill or some possible misconduct will be revealed. Statute[55] permits that, in such a case, the juror may be discharged and the trial may proceed and the verdict shall have the same effect as if given by the whole number. In Grenada all parties and in St Lucia the defence must consent to proceeding with the case if a juror is discharged. In the other jurisdictions this is a matter for the trial judge, presumably upon consideration of the interests of justice. Alternatively, statute and common law enable

55 As in Antigua: Jury Act, 2009, s 25;
Bahamas: Juries Act 1998, s 28(3);
Barbados: Juries Act, Cap 115B, ss 34–35;
Dominica: Juries Act, Chap 5:70, s 28;
Grenada: Jury Act, No 31 of 2015, s 27(3);
Guyana: Criminal Law (Procedure) Act, Cap 10:01, s 33;
Jamaica: Jury Act, s 31(3);
St Kitts and Nevis: Jury Act, Cap3,15, s 33;
St Vincent: Jury Act, Cap 28, s 15;
Trinidad and Tobago: Jury Act, Chap 6:53, s 19(3).

the trial judge to discharge the entire jury from returning a verdict even if one juror becomes incapable of continuing. Statute specifies the maximum number of jurors that may be discharged[56] from the jury while still enabling the return of a legitimate verdict. In Antigua up to three jurors may be discharged but only in non-capital matters,[57] while in Barbados, Grenada and Guyana as many as two jurors may be discharged and a valid verdict returned by the reduced number. In the Bahamas, Dominica, Jamaica, St Kitts and Nevis, St Vincent and Trinidad and Tobago a verdict may be taken from a jury comprising no more than one short of the statutory number after discharge. The grounds for discharge are, however, not limited to death or illness, which are stipulated in statute. Most statutes state that a juror may also be discharged for some 'other cause' or incapacity. In *State v Baichandeen* (1978) 26 WIR 213, p 218, the Court of Appeal of Guyana said that the power to discharge a juror is not conferred by statute, but rather the legislature presumes the existence of the power of challenge at common law. Statute, therefore, does not limit that power. The power to discharge a juror, it was said, arises from a high degree of need to discharge the juror: evident 'necessity'. Death or illness are merely examples of such necessity.

The relevant provisions in the St Lucia Code[58] seem to be predicated on the assumption that alternate jurors will replace any that are discharged or another juror from the panel may do so. Section 923(1)(c), however, still seems to contemplate a discharge without replacement.

The decision to discharge a juror

This decision to discharge is made by the judge on application by either side or on his own initiative if there appear to be grounds for justifying it. Where a juror is discharged and a conviction ensues, the exercise of the discretion by the trial judge to discharge a juror is subject to challenge in the appellate courts. The defence may contend, as was done in *Baichandeen* (above), that an improper exercise of the discretion deprived them of one voice in the jury which may have been to the possible benefit of the defendant. Thus a court of appeal may consider if, in the circumstances, the discharge was really a 'necessity', or otherwise permitted by statute. If a judge appears to have wrongly exercised his discretion in this regard, an ensuing conviction may be quashed on the basis of a material irregularity. Statutes across the region use somewhat different terms in describing the general grounds for discharge. Illness is usually common. Some statutes may simply state 'incapacity to serve' which may arise from a number of causes, including bias, death or some 'necessity'.

In *Baichandeen*, the trial judge discharged an absent juror on a trial for arson upon agreement on both sides. The juror had been absent for one day without explanation. It was held on appeal that the circumstances did not fall within the law permitting discharge of a juror. The statute provides that a juror may be discharged by the court 'as being through illness incapable of continuing to act, or for any other reason'. There was no evidence of either death, illness or great need to justify the discharge. The juror was later found to have had transport difficulties. It was held that the judge had acted without jurisdiction and that judge, counsel and the defendant could not effectively get together and agree to disregard a rule which was fundamental to a fair trial.

56 In those jurisdictions with provisions for alternate jurors, discharged jurors may properly be replaced by the alternates and after the alternates are exhausted only then will the question of accepting a verdict from a jury not comprising the statutory number arise.

57 Jury Act 2009, s 25(3).

58 Criminal Code, ss 963, 964.

In contrast, in the English case of *R v Hambery* [1977] 1 QB 924, the Court of Appeal considering a statutory provision identical to Guyana held that the judge was entitled to infer that it was important to a juror, whom he discharged, that she went on holiday on the date planned. Accordingly, there was nothing capricious about the exercise by the trial judge of his discretion to discharge a female juror who had plans to go on a pre-arranged holiday, where the trial extended beyond the three or four days originally anticipated. There was a high degree 'of need to do so'. The Court of Appeal opined that trial by jury depends on the willing co-operation of members of the public. Those summoned to serve as jurors are entitled to such consideration as it is within the power of the court to give them. *Hambery*, then, may be distinguished on the basis that the trial judge made a conscious informed decision to discharge the juror. It was not a case of her merely absenting herself without explanation.

In the Jamaican case of *R v Anderson* (1961) 3 WIR 402, the Federal Supreme Court confirmed, as a matter of no doubt, that a juror who falls ill during the trial may be discharged by the judge, leaving the remaining jurors to bring in the verdict.

In *Spence v R* (1999) 59 WIR 216 PC, the Privy Council had to consider s 15 of the St Vincent Jury Act which provides for discharge of a juror for illness, absence or 'if he becomes incapable of serving'. In that case, during the trial of the appellant for murder, a juror was discharged following a request by both the juror and her fiancé, the latter who wrote two strong letters to the judge complaining of the cost of cancelling their prearranged vacation.

Upon conviction the accused appealed complaining that he was entitled to a verdict of 12 jurors; the discharge in the circumstances resulted in the jury not being properly constituted. The Privy Council agreed and concluded that, there being no evidence that the juror was 'incapable' of serving, she had been improperly discharged. The court observed that the St Vincent statutory provision was unlike that of England which permitted discharge 'for any other reason' apart from incapacity. The Privy Council recommended amendment of the legislation to reflect the wider English law.

A discharge, then, must be for good cause such as in *R v Richardson* [1979] 1 WLR 1316, where the juror's husband had died the night before. It is rare that a juror will be discharged after retirement, but this is possible on account of illness which manifests itself then: *R v Hornsey* [1990] Crim LR 731. It is not always required that the discharge of a juror for necessity be done in court. In exceptional cases, such as in *Richardson*, it appears that such discharge may even be done in the judge's chambers.

Acquaintanceship with parties

Upon occasion, it may be discovered during the course of the trial that a juror is acquainted with either the accused or the alleged victim or their family. Where this occurs, it might be felt the acquaintanceship might lead to bias on the part of the juror in favour or against one side or the other. The judge is obliged to consider whether a fair trial will be possible despite the presence of the juror on the jury.

In *David James v The State*, CA, No 43 of 1977 (unreported), it was held by the Court of Appeal of Trinidad and Tobago that the fact that one juror was friendly with the brother of the defendant was insufficient to discharge the juror once there was nothing to show that he could not be impartial. In *Gibson v R* (1963) 5 WIR 450, on the other hand, where the defendant was charged for murder, a juror was discharged because it was discovered on the second day of the trial that he was the brother of the deceased. The juror admitted the fact, but explained that he was not aware of the procedure to bring this to the attention of anyone. Despite the objection of defence counsel, the trial proceeded with 11 jurors and the defendant was convicted. The Court of Appeal of Trinidad and Tobago, applying *R v Twiss* [1918] 2 KB 853, held that there was no conduct on the part of the juror which could lead to the inference that some injustice had been done. There was nothing to show that the presence of the discharged juror for one day of the trial could have influenced the other jurors in any way. In *Twiss* it had been held that there must be some indication that there is likely to be prejudice to a fair trial from a juror's acquaintance with a party to the case. In that case, it was the victim.

Even if a juror has knowledge that an accused person has previous convictions, this should not lead to his automatic discharge after the trial has commenced: *R v Box* [1964] 1 QB 1. The test to be applied now is that identified in *Medicaments* (above); whether a fair-minded and informed observer would conclude that there was a real possibility of bias on the part of the juror, approved in *Porter v Magill* [2002] AC 357 HL. In *R v Hood* [1968] 2 All ER 56, it was discovered during the trial, by the wife of the defendant, that a juror lived in the same road as her (the wife's) mother, whom she visited. She believed that the juror must have known that her husband had previous convictions. The juror was unknown to the defendant. The Court of Appeal upheld the trial judge's decision to discharge neither the juror nor the jury, although it was held that the prudent course might have been to discharge the entire jury and order a new trial. In this case, there was no evidence that a miscarriage of justice had occurred.

Misconduct/enquiry

If there is any realistic suspicion that the jury or one of its members has been approached, tampered with or intimidated, it is the duty of the trial judge to investigate the matter: *R v Blackwell* [1995] 2 Cr App R 625. The judge must enquire into contamination or possible contamination of the juror or jurors. The Court of Appeal of England held in that case that such investigation would probably include questioning of individual jurors or even the jury as a whole. The questioning must be directed towards ascertaining whether the jury's independence has been compromised. The judge, after completing his enquiry, will then decide whether he should discharge the whole jury, an individual juror or continue with the entire jury. In making the determination, the judge must apply the *Medicaments* test approved in *Porter v Magill* [2002] AC 357 HL.

The test is whether a fair-minded and informed observer, having considered all the relevant facts, would conclude that there was a real possibility that the juror(s) were biased. In *Blackwell* (above), upon allegations that there had been contact between a female juror and a male member of the public sitting in court, which gave rise to suspicion, the judge bluntly refused to investigate the matter. He instead discharged the juror and continued with the remaining jurors. It was held that the judge had improperly exercised his discretion. He deprived himself of information required to make a valid determination whether to discharge the whole jury. He should have held an enquiry into the allegations of contamination of the one juror he discharged and also in respect of the 11 remaining others. His failure to do so amounted to a serious irregularity in the trial.

It is apparent that even though statute may not specify misconduct as a ground for discharge at common law, in the interest of a fair trial the trial judge has inherent discretion to discharge a juror or the entire jury for misconduct. This will constitute evident 'necessity' or 'sufficient cause', as some statutory provisions stipulate. Before he makes a decision to continue with the trial, however, the judge must hold an enquiry into allegations of misconduct. In *Chaitlal v The State* (1985) 39 WIR 295, the Court of Appeal of Trinidad and Tobago held that the fact that one of the jurors had held a conversation with a witness was not fatal to the trial. The trial judge had held an enquiry into the incident. The court confirmed that it was not necessary that the evidence should be taken on oath in the conduct of the enquiry, nor did it matter that it was held in the judge's chambers. Both counsel were present and the juror, the marshal of the court (who made the complaint) and the witness were all questioned by the judge in investigating the complaint.

Allegations that a juror or jurors have had conversations or other improper contact with any party who has an interest in the case should be enquired into by the judge. These allegations clearly amount to suggestions of impropriety or other misconduct on the part of the juror. An example of such an allegation is that in *R v Twiss* [1918] 2 KB 853, where it was revealed that a juror had been seen to converse with the virtual complainant and two other prosecution witnesses. Upon enquiry by the judge, the juror indicated that the conversation related to the duration of the case and the length of a previous trial which had been mentioned in the course of the proceedings. The judge accepted the explanation and continued the trial with the juror. In *R v Prime* (1973) 57 Cr App R 632, the allegation was that a person, E, who had asked to be excused from jury service, during the lunch break had jokingly said to the wife and mother of the defendant, whom he knew: 'He is guilty'. This was said while E was walking along the street with two jurors near the courthouse. E had sought to be excused on the basis that he knew the defendant. It was held that in the circumstances of the case where the jury was not sequestered, that mere close contact between a member of the outside public and a juror was not an irregularity to affect the trial unless it could be shown that the person had, for instance, tried to pass information to the juror which should not be passed.

In *Ramlogan (Arnold) v The State* (2000) 58 WIR 374, it was found that approaches had been made to a juror by relatives of the two co-accused. The juror rebuffed the approaches and immediately reported the matter to the foreman who in turn told the judge. The judge held an enquiry in his chambers questioning in turn the juror and then the relatives. Having been told that the other jurors knew of the approaches he referred to the incident in open court and warned them against possible prejudice. He questioned each juror to ascertain if the juror could deliver a fair verdict. On appeal it was held that the investigation was meticulous. In the circumstances there was no need for the judge to ask each juror what account they had been given of the incident. The Court of Appeal adopted and followed the principles in *Blackwell.*

It is difficult to contend, where jurors are allowed to separate, that contact between jurors and parties in the case must necessarily amount to misconduct because it is observed. In *Sawyer* (1980) 71 Cr App R 283, it was alleged that two prosecution witnesses had spoken to three jurors in the court canteen. The trial judge ordered all concerned to be questioned on oath and it was elicited that the witnesses (customs officers) had merely passed the time of the day with the jurors and nothing material had been discussed. The case continued with the jury intact. On appeal the (English) Court of Appeal held that it was unbelievable that a mere exchange of words could in any way have influenced the jury to believe the witnesses. There was no real danger of bias in the instant case. In *Spencer and Smails* [1985] 1 All ER 673, the Court of Appeal approved the test in *Sawyer*, in a case where the judge had discharged one juror for possible bias against the defendant. The House of Lords in *Spencer and Smails* [1986] 2 All ER 928, HL, affirmed the decision of the Court of Appeal in dismissing the appeal. There was nothing to show that there was a real danger that the remaining jurors were prejudiced against the defendant because of contact with the discharged juror.

In contrast, in *Putnam* (1991) 93 Cr App R 281, the Court of Appeal, applying the same test in *Sawyer*, considered that there was evidence that jurors had been tampered with and since the source of the 'poison' could not be dealt with as it was unknown at the time of trial, the verdicts were unsafe. In that case one juror was assaulted twice during the trial and had to be hospitalised. After the trial it was discovered that another juror had been improperly approached by a juror in waiting to bring in a not guilty verdict. Eight other jurors were questioned and although none admitted to any similar approach, two of those questioned declined to make any statement at all. It was held that it had to be assumed that members of the jury had been tampered with and, as a consequence, there was a real danger that the defendants had been prejudiced. The test in *Sawyer* was in effect the same test for bias enunciated later in *R v Gough* [1993] 2 All ER 724, HL. Once there is anything to suggest that the alleged misconduct of a juror may lead to a real danger of prejudice, the juror, and in some cases the jury, if the possibility of contamination is real, should be discharged. This test must be adjusted in the light of the *Medicaments* test, approved in *Porter and Magill* (above).

To make that determination, however, the trial judge is bound to hold an enquiry in the matter. Those principles were reiterated by the Privy Council in the Trinidad and Tobago case of *Papan v The State* (1999) 54 WIR 451, PC. In that case it was alleged that the foreman of the jury had been seen to hold a conversation with the father of the deceased in the course of the trial for some 12 minutes. The judge summoned a meeting to consider the matter. The meeting was attended by attorneys in the matter, the foreman and the father of the deceased and the sister of the defendant who had made the accusation. The defendant was not present. The judge made short notes of the meeting, but did not take any action. Furthermore, he gave no reasons for his decision, nor did he make any findings of fact. The Privy Council found that 'the judge's notes inspired no confidence that the judge examined or considered the matter properly'. Prima facie there had been established more than fleeting contact between the foreman and the deceased father whom the foreman said he had known for eight years and with whom he 'frequently had morning coffee ... at a cafeteria'. In the final analysis, therefore, any allegation of misconduct on the part of a juror must be properly investigated by the trial judge. Whether evidence is taken on oath or not (in *Chaitlal* it was not), it behoves the trial judge to make a proper determination of the issues raised which includes making findings of fact and stating reasons for his subsequent action.

In *Jason Lawrence v The Queen* [2014] UKPC 2, failure to hold a *Blackwell* enquiry in circumstances which called for the holding of same did not vitiate the accused's conviction for murder. The deceased's mother had alleged that during the trial four members of the jury had been communicating with relatives of the appellant and that the foreman of the jury had also spoken to members of the appellant's family before the jury was empanelled. When the issue was raised, the judge did not send the jury out of the courtroom but had the mother of the deceased identify the members of the jury of whom she spoke. The judge asked those jurors about the allegation and each denied it. He then decided to proceed with his summing up. In the Board's view the judge's method of investigation was inappropriate yet eventually concluded that this did not cause any prejudice to the appellant. The Board held that the allegations which the deceased's mother made were far from clear; they were denied by the jurors; and there was therefore no reason to think that the making and the court's handling of the allegations had an improper influence on the jury in the performance of their duty.

DISCHARGING THE WHOLE JURY

The jury as a whole may be discharged before returning a verdict. This may be done where the jury is likely to have been influenced or 'contaminated' as in *Putnam* (above); where in a capital case, in a few jurisdictions,[59] a juror falls ill or dies or becomes incapacitated; or where more than one juror (or two in some jurisdictions)[60] has to be discharged on the

59 Antigua: Jury Act 2009, s 25(1), s 28; Dominica: Juries Act, Chap 5:70, s 28; St Kitts and Nevis: Jury Act, Cap 3.15, s 33.

60 As discussed above, some jurisdictions permit up to two jurors to be discharged and the case to continue in that eventuality; others provide for only one.

ground of illness, death or other sufficient cause. In addition, without fault on the part of any members of the jury, the judge might have to abort the trial and discharge the jurors. This may occur, for instance, if prejudicial evidence is inadvertently adduced in the course of the trial. Where a jury fails to agree on a verdict after a time set by statute, the judge may discharge the jury from further deliberations if he thinks that there is no prospect of the jury agreeing.[61] Where a jury is so discharged, a new trial will then be ordered to be held at a future criminal session.

Improper influences

In the same way that an enquiry should be held if it is alleged that a juror has misconducted himself, an enquiry must be held if it is suggested that the entire jury has been contaminated by improper influences, whether from its own misconduct or outside causes. In *Thorpe et al.* [1996] 1 Cr App R 269, three attempts were made to influence the jury. The defendants were being tried with conspiracy to defraud customers of a bank of over £11.7m by means of forged cheques. In separate incidents different jurors were approached by persons who apparently had interests in the case, in attempts to influence their decision. In each case, the juror immediately rejected the advance and reported the matter to the trial judge. The judge heard the explanation of each juror and then directly enquired of the entire jury whether they were likely to be influenced by what they had heard. The judge also heard submissions from counsel. Having considered all these matters, he decided to continue with the case. On appeal, it was held by the English Court of Appeal that the trial judge had properly considered the matter and had applied the relevant test – was there a real danger of prejudice against the defendants? – following *Sawyer* (above) and *Putnam* (above). On the facts of the case, there was no real risk of injustice. This finding was supported by the fact that the jurors had all rejected the advances and immediately reported them to the judge.

In R v Porter and Williams (1965) 9 WIR 1, the defence made an original argument that the large crowds which had assembled daily outside the court house in Jamaica must have intimidated the jury by their hostile behaviour against the defendants and thus caused bias against them. The crowds were on occasion heard to say 'They are murderers, they must hang' and 'Any jury who let go this man because he is a policeman, it would be serious'. The defendants, who were policemen, were charged with murder arising from an incident occurring during patrol. The judge had warned the foreman of the jury to inform him of any conduct tending to intimidate members of the jury. No such complaint was made. It was held on appeal that in the absence of any complaints from the jury members, there was no basis to infer that the jury were in any way influenced by the crowd behaviour.

Prejudicial evidence

If inadmissible and seriously prejudicial evidence against the defendant is given against him, the court has a discretionary power to discharge the jury from returning a verdict in the case. The judge has to determine whether there is a real possibility of injustice occurring because the jury, having heard the prejudicial matters, might be biased: *Docherty* [1999] 1 Cr App R 274 applying the test in *Gough* (above). In *Docherty* the defendant was charged with six counts

61 As specified in most jurisdictions, such as: Antigua: Jury Act 2009, s 29, s 31; Bahamas: Juries Act 1998, s 25; Barbados: Juries Act, Cap 115B, s 43; Jamaica: Jury Act, s 45(1); Trinidad and Tobago: Jury Act, Chap 6:53, s 28(3).

of sexual offences against his stepdaughter. He was found guilty of one count, acquitted on another and the judge directed acquittals on the four other counts. He appealed against the conviction on the ground, inter alia, that a prosecution witness had given prejudicial evidence that he, the defendant, had told her he had 'been in prison or something' and the judge had wrongly refused to discharge the jury. The Court of Appeal held that having regard to the circumstances of the case, where the prosecution had skilfully and immediately passed on to another matter after the unfortunate remark and where the jury had acquitted the defendant on another count, it was apparent that they were not affected by the prejudicial statement even if they understood it. The appeal was dismissed.

In making his assessment of whether a statement has serious prejudicial impact or not, the judge should approach the issue on the basis of the most prejudicial meaning that could reasonably be placed on the statement. In other words, the judge ought not to assume without more that the jury will not give the worst possible construction to the statement. The judge may also take it upon himself to discharge the jury if such an occasion demands rather than await an application from the defence. In *Charles James v R* (1959) 1 WIR 177, a case from (then) British Guiana, the Supreme Court, by a 2:1 majority, dismissed the appeal where an unrepresented defendant asked for the trial to proceed despite advice by the trial judge that he had a right to have the trial aborted. In that case, a prosecution witness in giving evidence had blurted out words to the effect that the defendant was a known thief. The defendant did not wish to have the trial stopped, and in the circumstances on appeal the court dismissed his claim of prejudice. It is suggested, nonetheless, that since the defendant was undefended, the trial judge should have taken it upon himself to discharge the jury if he considered the impact of the words to have been seriously prejudicial. It is unlikely that appellate courts today would take such a view of the course of conduct in the light of the *Medicaments* principles approved in *Porter v Magill*. A fair-minded and informed observer might well conclude that the prejudicial evidence could have resulted in a real possibility that the defendant would not obtain a fair trial.

In contrast, where the defendant is represented and elects to proceed with the trial, the court will frown upon a subsequent attempt to use the failure to discharge the jury on the admission of the prejudicial evidence as a ground of appeal. In *Hamilton v R* (1963) 5 WIR 361, it was accidentally disclosed by a prosecution witness that one F, whom the prosecutor alleged had acted in concert with the defendant, was executed. The evidence was inadmissible and prejudicial to the defendant as it portrayed him as a close associate of a man of violent character. The judge invited counsel to decide if he elected to proceed and he did so. The judge gave directions to the jury then and later in his summing up that they should disregard this disclosure. It was held that in the circumstances, the defendant had no right thereafter to complain of prejudice.

Peckham (1935) 25 Cr App R 125 is another case where a prejudicial statement was inadvertently made with regard to a defendant's criminal record. In that case, however, defence counsel's application for a fresh trial was refused by the judge. The defendant was convicted, but on appeal the English Court of Criminal Appeal quashed the conviction, holding that the judge ought to have discharged the jury and ordered a fresh trial.

In *Duporte v The Queen* [2015] UKPC 18 it was argued on appeal from a conviction for murder that the prosecution had wrongly and prejudicially produced before the jury a gun (with one spent bullet in the chamber) when there was no evidence of any kind linking that gun to the appellant. It was contended that in these circumstances, the jury should have been discharged once this evidence was given. The Board in dismissing the appeal held that there was no requirement for the jury to be discharged in spite of the fact that there may have existed heightened local sensitivity about gun crime. The crucial fact already before the jury was that the deceased had been shot dead by use of a gun. It followed that to produce a gun unconnected with the murder at trial could not have caused irremediable prejudice to the appellant.

Internal problems among the jury

Sometimes it may become clear that one or more jurors may not be able to fulfil their duty because of dissension in the ranks. In *R v Orgles et al.* [1993] 4 All ER 533, half way through the trial, two members of the jury complained to court staff about friction among the jury as a whole that was affecting their concentration. The court reported the matter to counsel in an attempt to determine the appropriate course to take. In the absence of any consensus, the court chose to question each juror individually in the presence of counsel and the defendants. The questions were designed to ensure that the jury did not reveal what had occurred in the jury room. The judge then caused the full jury to be brought into court and addressed them on the matter. He asked them to retire for some minutes and consider whether they could properly continue to carry on their duties. The jury returned and indicated that they could do so and the trial proceeded. The defendants were convicted and appealed, challenging the procedure adopted by the court.

The English Court of Appeal agreed that the procedure was incorrect and laid down certain guidelines for the approach that the trial court should adopt in such circumstances. When circumstances arise which raise an inference that one or more jurors may not be able to fulfil their oath, several matters will influence the approach of the court. The guidelines include the following:

- the court must consider whether the circumstances are external or not;
- external circumstances include, as discussed above, where a juror becomes ill; recognises a key witness as an acquaintance; or family problems make it difficult to continue. Less frequently, the circumstances may involve improper approaches made to a juror or suspect conversations between a juror and a stranger to the case;
- internal problems may occasionally arise where one or more members of a jury cannot fulfil their duty because of individual characteristics or problems of interaction with fellow jurors;
- whether the circumstances are external or internal, the judge must be primarily guided by the duty to ensure a fair trial;
- if the problems are external to the jury, the judge is within his rights to question the individual jurors concerned separately from the rest of the jury (as discussed in *R v Blackwell* [1995] 2 Cr App R 625);
- such separate questioning cannot be justified if the circumstances are internal to the jury. The judge is concerned here with the capacity of the jury as a whole to continue. He should question the whole jury in open court through their foreman to ascertain whether they can bring a true verdict according to the evidence; and
- it will be a matter for the exercise of the judge's discretion whether he chooses to discharge the entire jury or individual jurors (up to the number he is entitled to discharge by law).

Following *Orgles*, the law is more settled as to how a judge should deal with problems internal to the functioning of the jury. Whereas previously principles had been laid down as regards external problems such as jury acquaintanceship with strangers to the jury or misconduct (discussed above), there was little guidance on internal problems affecting the jury. Even though problems may have always existed, they had rarely ever come to the fore. A more recent situation concerning internal problems of a kind which usually arise at the selection stage (as in *Re Darien* (1974) 22 WIR 323) arose for consideration by the English Court of Appeal in *Schot and Barclay* [1997] 2 Cr App R 383. The issue related to how far the judge could go in questioning the jurors as to internal matters. In that case, after the jury had retired, a note was sent to the judge that they were unable to agree because of strong 'conscious beliefs' of some jurors. They were asked to clarify and stated that some jurors felt that they should not judge others. The judge discharged the entire jury and then asked for the names of the relevant jurors. He cited them for contempt and subsequently found them in contempt.

It was held that the judge should not have enquired as to what occurred in the jury room. This was contrary to the long-established practice that the happenings in the jury room are secret. What the judge might have done was to enquire as to the names of the two jurors who were having difficulty and assess whether it was possible to discharge them instead of the whole jury. The court also expressed the view that consideration should be given to excusing persons on grounds of conscientious objection to jury service. This is yet to be done in Commonwealth Caribbean jurisdictions.

Rationale and consequences

The decision to discharge a jury, other than for failure to agree or after the verdict is delivered, is one that must always be made in the interest of ensuring a fair trial. The procedure invoked in resolving any problems external or internal to the jury must also be guided by that consideration. In any event, if the whole jury is likely to be influenced by prejudicial or other issues not relevant to the trial, all jury members must be questioned or consulted. However, any such enquiry must never intrude on the sanctity of discussions in the jury room, whether during the case or on retirement. The decision to discharge is not open to review by the appellate courts on a subsequent trial: *R v Gorman* [1987] 2 All ER 435. After a trial is aborted by discharge of the jury or where the jury fails to agree and the jury is discharged, the trial judge should order a new trial. This will result in a newly constituted jury trying the defendant at a future date: *Payne* [1979] Crim LR 393. Where, however, there has been more than one failure by the jury to agree, it may be argued that proceeding with a fresh trial is oppressive: *Charles, Carter and Carter v The State* (1999) 54 WIR 455, PC; *Flowers v R* [2000] 1 WLR 2396, PC.

SEPARATION OF THE JURY

Jurors are permitted to separate from each other at the end of every day of hearing unless they are sequestered. This is provided for in most jury legislation in the region. Where a jury is sequestered, its members are not permitted to separate to go among members of the public unsupervised. Similarly, when a jury retires, the jury is kept in the safe custody of the marshals or other officers of the court and jurors ought not to separate until the jury is discharged. If a juror for some necessity is allowed to separate if the jury has retired or where sequestered,[62] he must have no communication with any other person except with the leave of the court. The issue of jurors separating from others after sequestration or retirement has engaged the attention of the courts on many occasions. It has been held that once the jury is charged to return a verdict, the jury

62 This common law principle is contained in a few statutes as in s 26(1) and 26(2) of the Bahamas Juries Act 1998.

must be kept together and under supervision: *R v Alexander* [1974] 1 WLR 422. If it is necessary for the juror to separate, he must remain in the charge of the bailiff. In *Alexander* the jury retired in the charge of two bailiffs and having left the court room was only a very short distance away when one juror returned to the court room on his own. It turned out that his purpose was to fetch the exhibits for the jury which the judge had referred to in his summing up as being available for their perusal. The juror's arrival was observed by defence counsel, who was in the court room. The juror was stopped and the judge was sent for. The rest of the jury came back into the court room and the jury again retired without any further incident. It was held by the Court of Appeal that the irregularity was so minimal that there was no possibility of prejudice to the defence. It is clear that in *Alexander* the juror had no opportunity to communicate with anyone. In contrast, in *R v Goodson* [1975] 1 All ER 760, a juror was given permission by the bailiff to leave the court room. He was subsequently discovered by prosecuting counsel making a telephone call in a booth in a public corridor. At that time the jury bailiff was present and observed what was taking place. The juror was prevented from returning to the jury room and the matter reported to the court. The court investigated and was told that the jury desired to speak to 'people' on the telephone and had been given permission by the bailiff to do so. It was agreed that this was an irregularity. Nevertheless it was established that the juror had not had any opportunity to speak to the other jurors about his conversation with anyone on the telephone. The court decided to discharge the juror because of the irregularity and proceed with the 11 others. On appeal, it was held that the separation by the juror in the circumstances amounted to a material irregularity. The court did not go on to consider whether at that stage of the trial it was possible under the then Criminal Justice Act 1965 to discharge a single juror and proceed with the other 11. It was instead held that the appropriate course should have been to discharge the entire jury, because the irregularity was so serious.

It may be thought that the decision in *Goodson* was made without full analysis of the principles for discharging a juror or a jury discussed above. If there was no real danger of prejudice (*Sawyer; Spencer and Smails*), should the entire jury have been discharged? The juror did separate, but it is arguable that separation simpliciter should not be the determinant, nor the fact that the defendant was deprived of one voice in the jury room, a factor to which the Court of Appeal referred. In fact in *R v Knott* (1992) *The Times*, 6 February, the Court of Appeal suggested that where a juror had been drinking and had caused criminal damage in a hotel where the jury had been sent after retirement, the wise course would have been to discharge the individual juror concerned. In addition, in *R v Hornsey* [1990] Crim LR 731, the English Court of Appeal sanctioned the judge's discretion to discharge a juror on account of illness after retirement.

It seems that the uncertainty as to how the appellate courts may view the fact of separation of a juror after retirement has led to conflicting decisions by trial judges. It is suggested, however, that in the light of the House of Lords' decision in *Spencer and Smails* [1986] 2 All ER 928, which sanctioned the test in *Sawyer*, that the determinant should be: has the juror's conduct in separating led to a real danger that the rest of the jurors will be prejudiced? If not, the entire jury need not be discharged. Factors to take into account would be the opportunity of the juror to communicate with members of the public and to influence his fellow jurors as a consequence. This appeared to have been the underpinning of the decision in *Alexander* (above) where even the separated juror was not discharged. The principle would seem to be in keeping with the older Guyanese decision of *Roberts v R* (1968) 13 WIR 50, where the juror, after sequestration, was left at the hospital in a waiting room for hours along with other members of the public. This was considered a material irregularity because of the opportunity to communicate with members of the public.

Telecommunications

More recent phenomena may have a serious impact on the issue of communication by jurors when sequestered or after retirement. Modern technology has created the mobile (or cellular) telephone and the electronic pager which can be carried about the person undetected. After retirement, then, a juror may yet be capable of making telephone calls in the jury room or receiving messages on his pager. This may well lead to undesirable (or the suspicion of such) communication between jurors and outside elements at critical stages of a trial when they should have no such contact. The matter came up for consideration by the English courts in *R v McCluskey* [1994] 98 Cr App R 216.

In that case, after the jury had retired to consider their verdict, the usher went to the jury room to remove the luncheon remains. At that time one of the jurors received a telephone call on his mobile telephone. He did not answer it, but the usher thereupon removed the batteries and the matter was reported to the judge. The judge called counsel to his chambers and informed them of the incident. It was stated that if there was to be any investigation it had to be done before any verdict was sought. Both counsel, however, agreed that there was no need for an investigation which might distract the jury and in circumstances where there was no evidence of attempted malign influence. Later, on appeal, evidence was tendered to show that the juror had admitted making one telephone call to his place of business while in the jury room.

The Court of Appeal stated:

- It was clearly an irregularity for a mobile telephone to be used once the jury had retired. This is in keeping with the clear principle that once a jury had been sent out to consider their verdict they must not separate from each other or the bailiffs and must be held incommunicado.
- The literature issued to prospective jurors should be amended to deal with the question of mobile phones.

This decision must logically apply to all forms of communication, including electronic pagers or mini-computers. Commonwealth Caribbean Courts should therefore take the necessary steps to ensure that a retired or sequestered jury is kept incommunicado in this age of fast-developing telecommunication technology.

ISSUES AFTER RETIREMENT

Additional evidence

The jury, once they have retired to consider their verdict, may not be supplied with additional evidence although they may ask and are entitled to see any of the exhibits already tendered as evidence in the trial. Where the jury ask to see exhibits, the request should usually be ventilated in open court, so as to ensure that the correct exhibits are supplied to them.

Jurors are not entitled to equipment to conduct experiments since they may be considered as permitting the introduction of new evidence. It has been held that equipment such as maps and scales[63] were wrongly supplied to the jury after retirement. In such

63 As in *R v Stewart and Sappleton* [1989] Crim LR 653; consider also *R v Maggs* [1990] Crim LR 654.

situations a conviction may be quashed as a consequence of irregularity. Things of a more general nature which a person may normally have in his possession may be made available to the jury if requested. Items such as a tape measure or a ruler are not considered objectionable, since the jury are not expected to be able to carry out experiments with those items. It seems that these are considered articles basic to everyday life.

Communications to judge

It is considered a cardinal principle of law that once a jury retires there must be no secret communication between the jury and anyone, not even the judge: *Ramstead v R* [1999] 2 WLR 698, PC, applying *R v McCluskey* [1994] 98 Cr App R 216. Any communication between the judge and the jury should take place in open court in the presence of the entire jury, both counsel and the defendant. The judge should state in open court the nature and content of the communication which he has received from the jury and, if necessary, seek the assistance from counsel: *R v Gorman* [1987] 2 All ER 435. This assistance should be sought normally before the jury is invited to return to the court room. When the jury does return to the court, the communication will be dealt with by the judge. The reason for these procedures is said to be to ensure that there is no suspicion of private or secret communication between the court and the jury, and to enable the judge to give proper and accurate assistance to the jury on any matter of fact or law which troubles them: *Ramstead* (above) applying *R v Pearson* [1996] 3 NZLR 275, p 279.

In *Ramstead*, an appeal from New Zealand, the jury, after deliberating for some time, sent two notes to the judge. In the first note they stated that they intended to return verdicts of not guilty in respect of two of the manslaughter counts on the indictment but guilty on another such count. In the second note they recorded a rider to their first note. The rider was to the effect that although due care, skill and knowledge were breached, the failures were not the essential cause of death of the victim. The judge did not inform counsel, but saw the foreman in his chambers where the foreman confirmed that the verdicts were unanimous despite the rider. The judge and jury then returned to the court where the jury delivered their verdicts as stated in the first note. The judge proceeded to discharge the jury and then informed counsel about the rider.

It was held on appeal to the Privy Council that the private discussion between the judge and jury amounted to a material irregularity. The rider was relevant to the issues and should have been shown to counsel before the jury announced their verdict. Their assistance should have been invited and the procedure endorsed in *Gorman* (above) ought to have been followed. The failure to follow the established procedure was held to have been so substantial that the conviction was quashed.

If a jury seeks clarification on issues or further directions, as they are entitled to, the judge should do all he can to ensure that they receive proper guidance. He must seek to understand clearly what is the confusion in the minds of the jurors, whether in terms of the law or the facts, and his further directions must aim to clarify the issue or issues. His further directions will naturally be arrived at after consultation with counsel on both sides. In *Ramstead*, the Privy Council criticised the trial judge for failing to appreciate that the second note (the rider), coming as it did after previous questions on the point by the jury, raised doubt as to whether the jury had understood the law on causation as it related to the issues. In the Jamaican case of *Berry v R* (1992) 41 WIR 244, PC, the Privy Council stated that the jury in that case did not receive proper guidance from the trial judge on a factual problem which they indicated to him they had when they returned to court about an hour after retirement for that express purpose. Instead, the trial judge summarised the conflict in the prosecution evidence and referred to the burden of proof without ever having ascertained what exactly their problem was with the evidence. This neglect by the trial judge contributed to the lack of fairness in the trial of the defendant, the Privy Council stated.

There are a few exceptional situations in which a communication (usually a note) from the jury need not be disclosed or be disclosed in full to the parties. This was acknowledged in *Ramstead* (above, at 702), although the court emphatically stated that the circumstances in that case did not fall within the narrow exceptions. It is only when the communication raises something unconnected with the trial that the judge can deal with the matter himself without reference to counsel or bringing the jury back to court: *Gorman* (above). In that case, Lord Lane CJ gave as an example of something unconnected with the trial a request that some message be sent to a relative of one of the jurors. Presumably, arrangements to pick up children after school, arrange transport or deal with the parking of vehicles could all fall within the few exceptions. Lord Lane made it clear, however, that these were exceptions to the established rule that applies 'in almost every other case' that the judge must consult counsel for the defence and the prosecution in open court as to the nature and content of communications with the jury.

Secrecy of the jury room

The sanctity of jury deliberations has long been recognised in English law. In *R v Hood* [1968] 2 All ER 56, an affidavit of a juror, stating that he only recognised the wife of the defendant when she gave evidence, was filed on appeal, in which it was contended that the jury should have been discharged because the juror knew the defendant before. The Court of Appeal (p 57) emphasised that 'the court will not ordinarily enquire into what passes between jurors, either in the jury box or in the jury room and will certainly not enquire as to the means by which they arrive at their verdict'. In the instant case, however, the affidavit dealt with a matter that was entirely extrinsic from what took place in the jury room. It in no way concerned the deliberations.

Caribbean courts continue to follow the English tradition in holding jury deliberations sacrosanct. In *Lalchan Nanan v The State* (1986) 35 WIR 358, PC, the Privy Council affirmed the decision of the Trinidad and Tobago Court of Appeal[64] to this effect. This case involved joint appeals from the decision of the Court of Appeal dismissing the appeal against the conviction of murder and its separate decision refusing to admit evidence of jurors in a constitutional motion. The relevant facts were that the jury returned through the foreman a verdict against the defendant of 'guilty' of murder, he (the foreman) having affirmatively stated that the verdict was unanimous. No other juror protested on the foreman's assertion. Nevertheless, on the following day the foreman and another juror visited the Registrar of the Supreme Court and indicated that four jurors had had doubts about the guilt of the defendant and that the foreman did not know the meaning of the word 'unanimous'. The foreman had thought that the clerk meant a majority verdict when he (the clerk) asked if the verdict was unanimous. It was in these circumstances that it was contended on behalf of the defendant that the affidavits of the four jurors (who allegedly had doubt) should be admitted as evidence in the constitutional motion brought by the defendant in which he alleged that there was a breach of his right not to be deprived of life except by due process of law.

The Privy Council in *Lalchan Nanan* had no hesitation in dismissing the appeal and maintaining the well-established general principle per Atkin LJ in *Ellis v Deheer* [1922] 2 KB 113, p 121:

64 *Lalchan Nanan v Registrar of the Supreme Court* (1979) 30 WIR 420.

> The court does not admit evidence of a juryman as to what took place in the jury room either by way of explanation of the grounds upon which the verdict was given, or by way of statement as to what he believed its 'effect to be'.

This principle applies to discussions between jurors in the jury box itself. The court indicated that there are two reasons of policy underlying the principle. They are:

(a) the need to ensure that the decision of juries are final;

(b) the need to protect jurymen from inducement or pressure either to reveal what had happened in the jury room, or to alter their views.

The effect of *Lalchan Nanan* is to confirm that what takes place in the jury room is secret and their decision given in open court is final. No evidence would be allowed as to any mistaken impression that a juror had or what informed his decision. As stated by Harman LJ in *Boston v Bagshaw* [1966] 1 WLR 1135, p 1137: 'It would be destructive of all trials by jury if one were to accede to this application [evidence of what passed in the jury room]. There would be no end to it'.

There are situations where evidence may be given by a juror as to certain matters connected with a trial in which the juror sat (as in *Hood*, above). In *Lalchan Nanan* the Privy Council recognised (p 367) that evidence may be given:

- that the verdict was not pronounced in sight nor sound of one or more members of the jury who did not agree. The confidence of the jury room may only be breached in so far as the juror, outside of whose sight and hearing the verdict was pronounced, may attest that he did or did not agree with the verdict;
- that a juror was not competent to understand the proceedings, in which case the verdict would be void (see *Ras Behari Lal* [1933] All ER 723, PC, where at least one juror understood no English, in which language the trial was conducted).

While these are not exhaustive situations, the Privy Council made it clear that evidence may only be given to rebut the presumption that all jurors assented to the verdict in certain cases. Such evidence may not be given where the verdict was given in sight and hearing of an entire jury, consisting of qualified jurors, who expressed no dissent.

There is no right of anyone to enquire into what occurred in the jury room.[65] This is a long-established principle at common law: *Schot and Barclay* [1997] 2 Cr App R 383, which is now encapsulated in England in the Contempt of Court Act 1981. It may be a contempt[66] then for anyone to obtain or disclose statements made and opinions expressed by members of a jury during the course of their deliberations. Any of these actions may be considered as calculated to interfere with the due administration of justice.

---

65 This relates to anything connected with the deliberations. It is thus not improper for a juror to indicate, as in *R v McCluskey* [1994] 98 Cr App R 216, that while in the jury room he made only one call on his mobile telephone to an employee.

66 *R v Armstrong* [1922] 2 KB 555.

CHAPTER 16

THE VERDICT

A jury is entitled to return a verdict of not guilty, guilty of the offence charged or guilty of a possible alternative offence. The jury may also fail to agree on a verdict. If a jury in the Commonwealth Caribbean delivers a verdict of guilty to a capital charge, it must be a verdict on which they all agree, but for one jurisdiction.[1] Otherwise, in non-capital cases, a majority verdict may be accepted. This chapter focusses on the issues that may arise from the judge's exhortation to the jury including specific directions on verdict. Problems that may flow from the attempts of the jury to arrive at a verdict and its delivery are also examined.

It must be pointed out at the outset that in general,[2] while no time limit is set for deliberations, there is provision in most jurisdictions[3] for the judge to discharge the jury after a certain time period of deliberations if he feels that the jury is unlikely to agree. This does not confer on the defendant a right to make an application for a discharge in such an event. It is merely a discretion to the trial judge to mitigate the rigours of the jury.[4]

Time of retirement

It has been held that the late retirement in the day of a jury, especially in capital cases, is undesirable: *Holder v The State* (1996) 49 WIR 450, PC. In that case the defendant was tried for murder in Trinidad and Tobago. The judge completed his summing up late in the evening and shortly afterwards, at 6.40 pm, the jury was directed to retire and deliberate. It was argued on appeal that this could have resulted in pressure on the jury, presumably to arrive at a verdict in a short space of time. In the circumstances of the case, however, where the jury retired for more than an hour, the Privy Council held that it was demonstrated that the jury did not feel under undue pressure to arrive at a verdict.

Nevertheless, the Board opined that such late retirement was undesirable. It follows, therefore, that where a judge realises that his summing up is likely to extend until late in the day, he should adjourn the case and begin his summing up afresh the next day so as to avoid the possibility of a late retirement which may place hardship on the jury.

PRESSURE

A judge must say nothing to convey to the part of the jury that they must bring in a particular verdict or even that they must bring in a verdict at all. Any such statement or direction may be considered a form of pressure on the jury, whose verdict is required to be given by the jurors of their own free will. In *R v Watson* [1988] 2 WLR 1156, p 1163, the English Court of Appeal held that it is a basic proposition that 'a jury must be free to deliberate without any form of

---

1 In St Kitts and Nevis, the Jury Act, Cap 3:15, s 35, allows ten jurors to agree on a verdict on a capital charge.

2 Except in Barbados, where the Juries Act, Cap 115B, s 41 sets a limit of three hours.

3 There appears to be no such specified period in statute in Guyana or St Vincent.

4 *R v David Michael* (1975) 27 WIR 307, p 313.

pressure being imposed on them, whether by way of promise or threat or otherwise'. A judge may exhort a jury to reach a verdict as long as he applies no pressure.[5]

No obligation to agree

It is a misdirection to imply an obligation on the jury to agree, since the jury has a right to disagree. In the Canadian case of *Harrison v R* [1974] 18 CCC (2d) 129, a decision of the Supreme Court of Canada, the court held by a majority judgment (6–3) that a trial judge is not obligated to tell a jury that they may disagree. In that case, the court held that the direction of the trial judge was not improper. The direction included:

> You must be unanimous as to any verdict that you bring back or as to an acquittal. All 12 of you must agree to convict or acquit.

The Supreme Court held that in its context, the direction simply meant that a verdict to convict or to acquit must be unanimous. In his dissenting judgment, Spence J concluded that the words could have conveyed to the jury that they were under an obligation to bring in a verdict.

The matter has been considered by the Court of Appeal of Trinidad and Tobago. In *Mohammed et al. v The State* Cr App Nos 42, 47–49 of 1989 (unreported), Ibrahim J stated that the test to be applied in determining whether the right to disagree was taken away was that enunciated in the Canadian case of *R v Latour* [1950] 98 CC 258, which was applied in *Harrison* (above). That test is whether any of the jurors could have reasonably understood from the direction that there was an obligation to agree on a verdict. If so, the direction would be bad in law.

In *Daniel Davis v The State* No 75 of 1988 (unreported), the Court of Appeal of Trinidad and Tobago considered as objectionable the judge's words: 'Your verdict must be unanimous. I am certain you know what "unanimous" means. This is it means that you must all agree one way or the other ... that he is guilty or not guilty'. In the trial of the defendant for robbery with aggravation, a non-capital offence, the court held that the direction was bad. In contrast is the decision in *Evans Xavier v The State* Cr App No 78 of 1988 (unreported[6]), where the Court of Appeal of Trinidad and Tobago considered a direction to the jury on a trial for murder. In that case the impugned words were: 'your verdict must be unanimous. And by "unanimous" I mean this: that all of you (12 of you) must be agreed one way or other'. The court held that there was nothing in the direction which expressly or impliedly suggested that the jury was precluded from failing to agree on a verdict. *Mohammed* (above) was distinguished on the basis that, in that case, the jury was told that in considering their verdict: 'there is no intermediary in this; it is either the accused is guilty as charged or not guilty'.

In *Xavier* the court emphasised that a verdict of a jury can only be one of guilty or not guilty. A disagreement by the jury is not a verdict. It appears, then, that the dividing line between the cases is that once it is clear that it is the verdict that must be agreed upon, the direction is unimpeachable. The trial judge may tell the jury that the verdict must be one upon which they all agree. He ought not simply to emphasise that they must agree one way or the other. This is so even for non-capital offences where the verdict need not be unanimous, since majority directions are only to be given after the stipulated statutory time after deliberations.

5 *Shoukatallie v R* (1961) 4 WIR 111, PC.

6 At the Privy Council this ground was not renewed, see *Xavier v The State* (1998) 57 WIR 342, PC.

Retirement or not

It has been the common practice in Commonwealth Caribbean countries for the trial judge at the end of his summing up in a criminal trial to ask the jury: 'Have you arrived at a verdict upon which you all agree or do you wish to retire to consider your verdict?'[7]

In *Crosdale v R* (1995) 46 WIR 278, PC, in considering an appeal from Jamaica, the Privy Council strongly disapproved of this practice. In that case the trial judge asked the jury to consult among themselves whether or not they wished to go to the jury room to consider their verdict. The Board held that this breached the cardinal rule that a trial judge must avoid any hint of pressure on the jury to reach a particular verdict. In the circumstances of the case the conviction was quashed, the court ruling that the defendant did not have a fair trial applying *Watson* (above). The Board held that the question could have conveyed to the jury that there was nothing to discuss. This could amount to coercion to return a particular verdict and was a material irregularity. In *Winston Solomon v The State* [1997] UKPC 59, the Privy Council confirmed that it was unfair to the defendant for the reasons given in *Crosdale* for the jury to be asked at the end of the summing up: 'Do you wish to retire?' Similarly, in *Lincoln De Four v The State* [1999] 1 WLR 1731, PC, the Board again followed *Crosdale* in holding that the question amounted to an irregularity in that it at least created the seeds of pressure upon the jury to reach a verdict 'because there was really nothing to discuss'. It is of note to point out that s 26(2) of the Trinidad and Tobago Jury Act, Chap 6:53 enables that the verdict of the jury may be given in the jury box. The section provides:

> The verdict of jury, whether on consultation in the jury box or after the jury have retired and been enclosed, shall be returned by the mouth of the foreman of the jury in the presence of the other jurors. When the jury are not immediately prepared to return their verdict, the court may direct them to retire and be enclosed.

Similarly, statutory provisions exist in Barbados (s 37(1) of the Juries Act, Cap 5 115B) and Guyana (s 155 of the Criminal Law (Procedure) Act, Cap 10:01). The clear inference from these propositions is that the jury is entitled to return a verdict without retiring. In contrast, no similar provision exists in the Jamaican Jury Act. In the light of the decisions above, in many trial courts the jury is simply informed of their right to return a verdict without retirement or to retire to deliberate. It is of interest to note that the English Court of Appeal in *R v Rankine* [1997] Crim LR 757 agreed that while it is not unlawful for a judge to ask the jury if they wished to consider their verdict without retiring, it would be better if he did not do so.

Pressure of time

In some instances, a jury may spend hours deliberating and yet not agree on a verdict. In such cases it may be difficult for a trial judge to determine what he should or could properly do or say to the jury. In the Guyanese case of *Shoukatallie v R* (1961) 4 WIR 111, PC, the jury had retired at 4.40 pm. At 8.40 pm they returned and said that they could not agree. In the course of his further address to them, the judge told the jury that it was a

7 See discussion in Seetahal, DS, 'Do you wish to retire?', *The Criminal Lawyer*, Vol 85, July/August 1998, p 5.

straightforward case, they must accept reason and not bring disgrace on their community. This was not considered an impermissible exhortation by the Privy Council since the jury retired for another four and a half hours, so it was clear that they were not pressured. It is suggested that, following the decision in *R v Watson* [1988] 1 All ER 897, however, this type of exhortation might well be considered unacceptable. In that case, the English Court of Appeal emphasised that since a jury must be free to deliberate without any form of pressure, the use of a direction warning them that it might cause public inconvenience or expense if they cannot agree should not be given, because it might impose pressure on the jurors to express agreement. The court in *Watson* disapproved of an earlier decision of *R v Walheim* (1952) 36 Cr App R 167 to the contrary.

In the Commonwealth Caribbean, statute in most cases stipulate a time period after which the jury may be discharged if no verdict seems likely. In respect of capital cases where there is no possibility of a majority verdict (but for St Kitts and Nevis), the trial judge merely needs to form the opinion that no verdict is probable before he discharges the jury. If the offence is noncapital, he may then inform the jury of the possibility of a majority verdict after the statutory set time has expired.[8]

In Barbados[9] the jury 'shall' be discharged after three hours of deliberations without a verdict. In St Lucia the maximum period is set at six hours: s 923(3), Criminal Code. In other jurisdictions it appears to be at the discretion of the court. In Antigua,[10] Dominica[11] and St Kitts and Nevis[12] the jury may be discharged after four hours if there is no prospect of agreement. In Grenada and St Lucia the relevant provisions[13] stipulate the time period as three hours, after which the judge may discharge the jury if there is no likelihood of agreement. In Jamaica[14] that period is set at one hour and, as for the Bahamas, the Juries Act allows for discharge 'after the expiration of a reasonable time from the conclusion of the summing up'.[15] In Trinidad and Tobago the relevant time period is four hours.[16]

There appears to be no statutory set time for deliberations after which the judge may discharge the jury in either Guyana or St Vincent. Those jurisdictions, however, enable majority verdicts for non-capital verdicts after two hours[17] so that in practice this may be the time after which the judge may choose to make an assessment as to whether a verdict is possible or not.

The Court of Appeal of Eastern Caribbean Supreme Court in *Flavia Richardson v R* HCRAP 2009/019 (unreported), judgment delivered 1 September 2011, held that in the absence of provisions in the Jury Act or Criminal Procedure Code of St Vincent regulating jury management and the time when a majority verdict must be given to the jury, the practice and procedure observed by the Crown Court of England must be applied.[18] In that regard the current practice and procedure specified in *Practice Direction (Criminal Proceedings: Consolidation)* [2002] 1 WLR 2870 is applicable.[19] This allows the trial

8 The Bahamas Juries Act appears to permit a majority verdict for non-capital offences to be given at any time: Juries Act 1998, s 24(2).

9 Juries Act, Cap 115B, s 41.

10 Jury Act, 2009, s 29.

11 Juries Act, Chap 5:70, s 31.

12 Jury Act, Cap 3:15, s 36.

13 Grenada: Jury Act, No 31 of 2015, s 25; St Lucia: Criminal Code, s 923(2);

14 Jury Act, s 45(1).

15 Juries Act 1998, s 25.

16 Trinidad and Tobago: Jury Act, Chap 6:53, s 28(3).

17 Guyana: Criminal Law (Procedure) Act, s158; St Vincent: Jury Act, Cap 28, s 14.

18 This is in accordance with the savings law provision in s 3 of the Criminal Procedure Act.

19 See discussion below on these Directions.

judge to send for a jury after two hours and ten minutes 'or such longer time as the judge thinks reasonable, and enquire if the members have reached a verdict'. If it appears they are not unanimous they should be asked to retire once more and told they should continue to endeavour to reach a unanimous verdict. Even though statute may set a time after which the judge may discharge a jury, this does not mean that he must do so. It is a matter for his discretion: *R v David Michael* (1975) 27 WIR 307, a decision of the Court of Appeal of Trinidad and Tobago. If the judge chooses to exhort the jury to attempt to arrive at a verdict, however, he must not set a time limit for their deliberations: *David Michael* (above). In that case, the court held that the unprecedented course adopted by the judge in fixing a definite period for further deliberation (half an hour) and the fact that the jury returned a verdict of guilty in that time was sufficient to invalidate the verdict. In the circumstances of the case, this course adopted by the judge amounted to coercion of the jury. In the more recent case of *Lincoln De Four v The State* [1999] 1 WLR 1731, PC, the judge (in Trinidad and Tobago) imposed a similar time limit of 30 minutes after the jury had deliberated for the mandatory three hours. After three hours of deliberation, when the jury returned to the court room (as is required), the foreman indicated that they were troubled by the sufficiency of the evidence. The judge said: 'I am going to give you an additional 30 minutes', after he had ascertained that a verdict was likely if the jury was given more time. The jury returned with a verdict of guilty in 20 minutes.

The Privy Council considered *David Michael* (above) and held that the imposition of a time limit for deliberations by the trial judge was a material irregularity. There was an appreciable risk that this could have placed the jurors under pressure to reach a verdict to which they would not have otherwise subscribed. The Board also felt that the judge should have reminded the jury, when the foreman referred to matters that troubled them, that it was their duty if they had an irreconcilable disagreement to say so. The Board felt that the conviction was unsafe.

In the English case of *R v McKenna* [1960] 1 QB 411, the trial judge went even further. After the jury in that case had deliberated for over two hours, the judge ordered that they be brought back into the court room and threatened them that if in ten minutes the jury 'had not arrived at a conclusion in this case you will have to be kept all night and we will resume this matter at quarter to 12 tomorrow'. Not unexpectedly, the jury returned in less than ten minutes with a guilty verdict. The Court of Criminal Appeal held that the conviction should be quashed since it was of fundamental importance that in their deliberation, a jury should be free to take such time as they felt they needed subject to the right of the judge to discharge them.

DIRECTIONS ON VERDICT – GENERAL

It follows from the foregoing that in directing the jury to consider their verdict, the trial judge must be very careful never to put any pressure on a jury to arrive at a verdict. In particular, he must avoid seeming to set a time limit, denying them the right to disagree or suggesting a particular verdict as desirable. In Commonwealth Caribbean jurisdictions, unlike in England,[20] there still exists the need for unanimity in respect of certain types of offence. These are capital offences. In such cases, no majority directions need be given and

20 Juries Act 1974, s 17.

a trial judge must be extra careful as to how he addresses the jury, especially when they appear to be in disagreement. In respect of non-capital offences, the availability of majority directions makes the situation less complex.

Capital cases – verdict

In St Kitts and Nevis[21] a majority verdict may be taken in capital cases. In Jamaica by the Jury (Amendment) Act No 24 of 2010, amending s 31, a majority verdict of nine (after two hours) is permissible only in respect of certain categories of murder. Otherwise statute, in keeping with previous common law where originally verdicts in all cases had to be unanimous,[22] demands that verdicts in capital cases throughout the Commonwealth Caribbean must be unanimous. All jurors must agree on the verdict.[23] It is for this reason that a trial judge, at the conclusion of his summing up, must tell the jury that any verdict which they arrive at must be a verdict on which they all agree. As indicated above[24] he need not specifically tell the jury that they have a right to disagree.

It seems that in appropriate circumstances the judge may direct the jury in accordance with the guidelines in *R v Watson* [1988] 1 All ER 897, which case was applied in both *Crosdale* (above) and *Lincoln De Four* (above). The approved direction is:[25]

> they have each taken an oath to return a true verdict according to the evidence and no juror must be false to that oath but that the jury has a duty to act not only as individuals but collectively by giving their own views and listening to the views of the others in arriving at a verdict.

The court stated that this direction, if given at all, is best included in the summing up. It is suggested that in capital cases it is inappropriate to give this direction at any time after the summing up, or it may be considered some form of coercion.

Should the jury return and indicate that they have not agreed, the judge must enquire of them whether, given more time, they are likely to agree upon a verdict. In keeping with the decision in *Lincoln De Four* (above) it is suggested that the judge must tell the jury that if they have irreconcilable differences, even after the mandatory time for deliberations, they must say so. Except for Guyana, St Vincent and the Bahamas the jury must deliberate for a minimum statutory set time period before they may be discharged by the trial judge. If the judge forms the opinion after enquiries of the jury that they are unlikely to agree even if given more time, he should discharge them. It is a matter of his discretion. Even in those jurisdictions without a minimum time set for deliberations, if the jury has not returned with a verdict after a reasonable time, the judge may discharge them if he feels that they are unlikely to agree.

If the jury returns to the court room and indicates that the members are not agreed, the judge may ask them to retire again and deliberate. If they ask for further direction on the law, he must assist them. If they indicate that they have a problem with the evidence, the judge must ask them to state if their differences are irreconcilable (*Lincoln De Four*). If

21 Cap 3:15, s 35.

22 *R v David Michael* (1975) 27 WIR 307.

23 If a juror (or jurors if statute permits) is validly discharged, the verdict agreed to by the remaining jurors will be considered a unanimous verdict.

24 Under the rubric: 'No obligation to agree'.

25 *R v Watson* [1988] 1 All ER 897, p 903.

they so indicate, the judge must discharge them once the minimum time for deliberations has expired. Otherwise he may then ask them to retire again and attempt to arrive at a verdict. In Barbados, the total time limit for retirement is three hours, after which the jury must be discharged. In the other jurisdictions there is no time limit. Once the judge reasonably forms the opinion that the jury is likely to agree on a verdict, he may allow them to deliberate. Further, he must stipulate no time limit for their deliberations even though he may himself be guided by considerations of time in exercising his discretion to discharge or not.

MAJORITY VERDICTS

In respect of all non-capital offences, the jury may return a majority verdict. Except for the Bahamas,[26] statute stipulates a time period for deliberations before a majority verdict is accepted. Similar statutory provisions in Antigua, Dominica, Grenada, Guyana, St Kitts and Nevis and St Vincent set the period of time that must elapse as two hours.[27] In Jamaica and Barbados it is one hour.[28] In Trinidad and Tobago, the time stipulated is three hours.[29] In St Lucia, statute[30] specifies that, after one hour, a minority of one may disagree, after two hours, a minority of two and so on, as long as six jurors agree one way or the other.

Non-capital or capital charge

In respect of capital charges, a majority verdict (of guilty) is acceptable on the lesser alternative offence, as in the case of manslaughter instead of murder.[31] The minimum number of jurors who must agree on a majority verdict for a non-capital offence on a capital charge varies among the different jurisdictions. In Dominica, there is no difference from a majority verdict on a non-capital charge, since the number of jurors in a jury is always nine whether the offence charged is capital or non-capital. The Juries Act provides that seven jurors must agree to a majority verdict.[32] This would mean that on a charge of murder after two hours, a verdict of manslaughter may be accepted if seven jurors are agreed on manslaughter.

In Barbados, Jamaica and Trinidad and Tobago if nine jurors[33] out of the 12 (selected to try the capital charge) agree on manslaughter after the statutory time period has elapsed, the verdict may be accepted. In Guyana, St Lucia and St Vincent, at least ten of the 12 jurors selected to try the capital offence must agree on an alternative lesser offence impliedly included in the capital charge. The Grenada Jury Act provides that at least ten jurors must agree on 'any offence less

---

26 Juries Act 1998, s 24(2).

27 Antigua: Jury Act, Cap 2009, s 28 (2) Dominica: Juries Act, Chap 5:70, s 30; Grenada: Jury Act, No 31 of 2015, s 24(2); Guyana: Criminal Law (Procedure) Act, Cap 10:01, s 158(c); St Kitts and Nevis: Jury Act, Cap 3:15, s 35; St Vincent: Jury Act, Cap 21, s 13.

28 Barbados: Juries Act, Cap 115B, s 40(2); Jamaica: Jury Act, s 44(2). Act No 13 of 2016 amended s 44 to now provide for different majorities in subsections 1A and 2, replacing majorities of '9 to 3' with '5 to 2'.

29 Trinidad and Tobago: Jury Act, Chap 6:53, s 28(1).

30 St Lucia: Criminal Code, s 923.

31 A majority verdict as regards manslaughter should only be accepted if the jury agrees on a not-guilty verdict on the murder charge. In most jurisdictions this may only occur after the expiration of the satisfactory fixed time for deliberations.

32 See above, fn 27.

33 Barbados: Juries Act, Cap 115B, s 39(1); Jamaica: Jury Act, s 31(4)(a); Trinidad and Tobago: Jury Act, Chap 6:53, s 28(2).

than murder of which they are entitled by law to convict'[34] on a murder charge. The Bahamas Juries Act 1998 enables a verdict of guilty of a non-capital offence to be returned by eight[35] of the 12 jurors already empanelled. The Antigua Jury Act 2009 provides at s 28 that a judge may accept 'any verdict' after two hours in which at least ten jurors agree.

St Kitts and Nevis

The St Kitts and Nevis statute in this regard is peculiar. Previously it provided that nine jurors would sit on any type of case (including murder). Section 26 of the Jury Act (now Cap 3:15) was amended first in 1998 and later by Act No 6 of 2000 to provide that a jury shall consist of 12 persons to try 'any proceedings'. It appears, however, that no consequential amendments were made in ss 9 and 33 which are still premised on the existence of a nine-member jury. As such the Act appears to allow a trial to proceed with eight jurors (s 33) after discharge but yet s 35 requires a verdict to be agreed by at least ten jurors.

Section 35 has been amended to read, in so far as is noteworthy:

> after the expiration of two hours from the conclusion of the summing up any verdict in which at least ten of them agree, may be accepted as the verdict of the whole.

The intention behind the amendment, it seems, was to permit a majority verdict of ten in respect of any offence, but the Jury Act seems at s 33 to allow a trial to proceed with eight jurors. The law in St Kitts and Nevis is, in this regard, anomalous and calls for legislative intervention.

Non-capital cases

In respect of non-capital charges, the jury in each jurisdiction must first deliberate for the same statutorily fixed minimum time required before it brings in a verdict of a noncapital offence on a capital charge, as discussed above. This means that in the Bahamas there is no such stipulated time period, whereas for the other jurisdictions the time varies between three hours and one hour. In St Kitts and Nevis the time period fixed is similar to that of Antigua and Dominica, which is two hours.[36] Any verdict delivered before the time period for deliberation has expired must be unanimous even for non-capital offences. It should be pointed out that where one or more jurors are discharged in accordance with the statutory provisions in that regard, a verdict agreed to by all the remaining jurors will be considered a unanimous verdict.

But for Antigua, Bahamas, Guyana and St Kitts and Nevis where the jury comprises 12 jurors in all cases, in most other jurisdictions for non-capital offences the array consists of nine jurors. Thus the number of jurors who can bring in a majority verdict in respect of the offences is determined by this fact in these jurisdictions. In Barbados, Dominica and Grenada the majority must constitute at least seven. This means that seven jurors must then agree on the (majority) verdict if it is to be valid. In St Lucia, s 923 of the Criminal Code, a majority verdict is acceptable in trial of a non-capital offence provided that the minority does not exceed two and at least six jurors agree on the verdict. If, for instance, two

34 Jury Act, No 31 of 2015, s 24(3).

35 Bahamas: Juries Act 1998, s 24(2): in the Bahamas, 12 jurors are selected to try any offence.

36 Jury Act, Cap 3:15, s 35.

jurors are discharged for illness or other necessity, this means that of the remaining seven, six must be agreed on the verdict. The Trinidad and Tobago statute is not dissimilar. The Jury Act provides[37] that a majority verdict may be given by at least six jurors (if one is discharged) or seven jurors (if all are present). The minority, thus, must not exceed two.

The St Vincent statute permits a majority of at least seven[38] to return a verdict on a noncapital charge. In that country, however, a non-capital charge may be joined on an indictment with a capital charge if they are founded on the same facts or form part of a series, despite the fact that the number of jurors in the jury varies with capital and noncapital offences. Section 13 of the Jury Act gives explicit sanction to this type of joinder in that it provides that 'where a count for a non-capital offence is joined in an indictment with a count on a capital offence the jury shall consist of twelve persons'. In such cases a verdict on the non-capital charge, if delivered more than two hours after its consideration, shall be received if at least ten jurors agree.

The Jamaica statute[39] is unique as regards the number of jurors constituting the jury for non-capital offences, which is seven. A verdict is acceptable once it is agreed upon by at least five jurors, after the lapse of one hour from retirement. In Guyana, where 12 jurors form the array even for trials of a non-capital offence, at least ten jurors must agree on the verdict.[40] In contrast, the Bahamas Juries Act is more liberal and a majority verdict may be accepted from 'two-thirds of the panel empanelled'.[41] This means that regardless of the possibility of discharge, eight jurors may return a verdict on a non-capital charge in the Bahamas.

Directions for majority verdict

Since, but for the Bahamas, statute throughout the Commonwealth Caribbean specifies that a verdict must be unanimous if it is delivered before the statutory time period, that time period must first expire before directions on the majority verdicts are given. To do otherwise would be in breach of the statutory requirements. As a majority verdict may only be taken after the stated time, it follows that the court should not direct the jury to consider a majority verdict until after the expiration of the stated time.

Section 40 of the Barbados Juries Act, Cap 115B is similar to s 17(3) and (4) of the English Juries Act in this regard. A verdict will not be accepted unless the jury has had no less than one hour for deliberation or such longer period as the judge thinks reasonable 'having regard to the nature and complexity of the case'. This type of provision is unusual in the Commonwealth Caribbean, which merely requires deliberation for a set time before a majority verdict can be validly taken. In considering this provision, the Court of Appeal of Barbados in *Hobbs and Mitchell v R* (1992) 46 WIR 42 advised that a presiding judge, to avoid 'highly technical points' on appeal, should allow an ample margin over the prescribed period of time before recalling a jury for directions on the possibility of a majority verdict in accordance with s 40(2).

Even before the majority direction, the judge may in his summing up indicate to the jury in general terms that the law permits a majority verdict. The English Court of Appeal in

37 Jury Act, Chap 6:53, s 28(1).
38 Jury Act, Cap 28, s 13.
39 Jury Act, s 31(4)(b).
40 Criminal Law (Procedure) Act, Cap 10:01, s 158(c).
41 Juries Act 1998, s 24(2).

Practice Direction (Criminal Proceedings: Consolidation) [2002] 1 WLR 2870 at IV. 46.1 advised that the judge should direct the jury along these lines before they retire:

> As you may know the law permits me in certain circumstances to accept a verdict which is not the verdict of you all. Those circumstances have not yet arisen so that when you retire I must ask you to reach a verdict upon which each one of you is agreed. Should, however, the time come when it is possible for me to accept a majority verdict, I will give you a further direction.

It is suggested that this direction is fully appropriate in the Commonwealth Caribbean as regards non-capital offences. It makes for a uniform practice in directing a jury on this issue in the summing up.

Taking the majority verdict

The *Practice Direction* (above) also sets out a procedure for the taking of a majority verdict when the jury returns. If they return before the two or three hours as set by statute, and the verdict is not unanimous, they should be sent out again with a further direction to arrive at a verdict on which they all agree. When the jury returns after the expiration of the statutory time set for mandatory deliberation, they must first be asked if they have arrived at a verdict on which they are all agreed. They must be directed to answer yes or no. If yes, they are then asked what is the verdict and it is delivered.

If, however, at this point the jury (through its foreman)[42] indicates that the verdict is not unanimous, the judge should ask them to retire once more and continue to try to reach a unanimous verdict. He must tell them that if they cannot, he will accept a majority verdict. The judge must then inform the jury of the type of majority that he is mandated by law to accept. That is, he will say: 'I will accept a majority verdict in which at least seven [or six or five or ten, as the case may be as statute in the various jurisdictions dictate] of you agree'.

When the jury finally returns they should be asked: 'Have at least seven [or whatever number is stipulated as above] of you agreed upon your verdict?' If the foreman replies in the affirmative, then the verdict must be stated as guilty or not guilty. If guilty, the foreman must then be asked whether it is a verdict of all or a majority. If a majority, then the foreman must specify the number who agreed and who dissented. This is so as to ensure that the statutory minimum number of jurors have agreed to the verdict.

This *Practice Direction* (above) has been followed throughout the Commonwealth Caribbean with adaptations to the particular jurisdiction in terms of the number of jurors in each case. Even though, in general, there is no requirement by statute for the foreman to state in open court[43] the number of jurors who agree and who dissent on a guilty verdict, this practice is followed. This appears to be a reasonable course in the interests of fairness to the defendant.

If the jury fails to return a verdict even after they are told that they may return a majority verdict, the judge may discharge them.[44] At this stage it is technically permissible to give a *Watson* direction[45] as to the 'duty to act not only as individuals but collectively'. In *R v Morgan* [1997] Crim LR 593, however, the English Court of Appeal stated that if the *Watson*

42 A foreman is elected before the trial actually starts, and it is through him that the jury communicates in court to the judge. The foreman may be of either gender.

43 Barbados is an exception in that the English law has been adopted in this regard.

44 He must, in Barbados, if three hours have expired after retirement.

45 See *R v Watson* [1988] 1 All ER 897, p 903 (cited above).

direction is given, it must be given some time after the majority directions and the terms of the direction laid down in that case must be precisely followed. To do otherwise may lead to an argument that improper pressure was exerted on the jury to reach a verdict. Interestingly enough, the commentary on that case in the *Criminal Law Review* (1997) p 595 suggests that a *Watson* direction may be something of an anachronism and if it is improper to give it earlier on, 'it is unclear why it may become proper later'.

It is suggested, then, that in the Commonwealth Caribbean, if a *Watson* direction is to be given at all, whether in capital or non-capital trials, it is best that it be given during the summing up.

RETURN OF THE VERDICT

It is a contempt of court at common law for a jury to refuse to deliver a verdict[46] unless it is to state that they cannot agree. Such a refusal may presumably be considered conduct calculated to interfere with the due administration of justice as defined in *AG v Times Newspapers Ltd* [1973] 3 All ER 54, HL; *AG v Newspaper Publishing plc* [1987] 3 All ER 276. A jury therefore must either return a verdict or state that they disagree.

Fortunately, in most cases juries do return verdicts, and in general the verdict must be accepted by the trial judge even if he disagrees with it. A verdict may on occasion constitute a finding of guilt to an offence which is not specifically included in the indictment. This is possible in the case of an offence that is implicitly charged because it is included in a greater offence as, for instance, manslaughter on a charge of murder/larceny or theft in robbery. On occasion, a jury may bring in a special verdict of insanity if the defence is successfully raised on behalf of the defendant. Separate verdicts must be returned in relation to each count in an indictment and each defendant, if there is a joint trial. The jury is entitled to find different verdicts as regards each defendant or each count as long as each is justified by the evidence and the law. Where the counts are in the alternative, the jury should be asked as to a verdict on the most serious first. If the verdict is guilty, they should then be discharged from returning a verdict on the other counts.

Finality of the verdict

Once the foreman of the jury has returned a verdict on behalf of the jury that is clear and unequivocal, the trial judge must accept the verdict. If there is any challenge to the effect of the verdict it may be rectified promptly once the jury has left the jury box. It is for the jurors to rectify any uncertain verdict. If the verdict is incomplete and the trial judge discharges the defendant before the jury have finished dealing with the possible alternatives left to them, the purported acquittal is a nullity: *R v Carter and Carnavan* (1964) 48 Cr App R 122.

In that case the jury were asked if the defendants were guilty or not guilty of 'robbery being armed'. The foreman replied: 'not guilty'. The judge then purported to discharge the accused persons whereupon the foreman remained standing. He then said to the trial judge 'we thought there were two charges here, robbery being armed with an offensive weapon and robbery without being armed'. The latter charge having then been specifically put to the jury, they returned a verdict of guilty of robbery with aggravation. It was held on an appeal that the discharge by the trial judge in the circumstances was a

46 It is also a contempt to refuse to deliver a directed verdict of acquittal: *Bushell's Case* [1670] Vaugh 135.

complete nullity, since the jury had not yet dealt with all the possible verdicts arising from the indictment. The verdict had been incomplete at the time and the jury were entitled to complete it.

Once a jury has pronounced a full verdict in general, they are considered functus officio in that their functions have expired. The converse issue came up for consideration in *Cummings et al. v The State* (1995) 49 WIR 406, by the Court of Appeal of Trinidad and Tobago, as regards a statement that the jury could not agree. The jury returned and upon enquiry informed the judge that they had failed to agree on a decision in respect of any of the three accused. The judge then ordered a new trial. The foreman then voiced the opinion that the jury could agree if given more time. The judge gave more time and the jury eventually returned with verdicts of guilty. On appeal, the court found that the jury became functus officio when the trial judge made the order for a retrial. They could not then retire again. This decision may be justified on the basis that there was nothing to correct in the earlier statement that the jury had failed to agree. It was not ambiguous. When the presiding judge ordered a retrial, this meant that the functions of the jury were to be considered discharged, even if they were still in the jury box and had not been formally discharged. If a juror dissents from a verdict, delivered by the foreman on behalf of the entire jury, he must say so in open court at the time of delivery. This is not to say that the minority jurors in a majority verdict must voice their disagreement in open court. Since their disagreement has already been counted in the minority, they are not expected to raise the matter again. Where, however, the juror or jurors wish to assert that the verdict delivered by the foreman is not the verdict of the jury, the time to do so is immediately after its delivery: *Sanker and Pitts v R* (1982) 33 WIR 64, a decision of the Court of Appeal of Belize. In that case the defence alleged that the verdict was not as had been stated by the foreman, but there was agreement in a proportion which was not allowed by statute for the return of a verdict. The court in dismissing the appeal held that when a verdict was delivered by the foreman of the jury in the sight and hearing of all the jurors without their protest, their assent to the verdict was conclusively presumed. The court distinguished the English case of *R v Vodden* (1853) 6 Cox CC 226 on the basis that the dissent in the instant case was made known the day after the delivery of the verdict (even though sentence had not yet been passed), whereas in *Vodden* the court held that once dissent is made clear before the jurors left the box, the verdict could be challenged.

It is clear that if a juror wishes to challenge a verdict delivered by the foreman, he must do so without delay. Any delay in challenging the verdict could suggest that external factors led to the questioning of the verdict especially if the jurors have already left the court room. In *Lalchan Nanan v The State* (1986) 35 WIR 358, PC, the day after the jury had returned a verdict of guilty of murder against the defendant, two jurors (one of whom was the foreman) visited the Registrar of the Supreme Court to say that the foreman had thought that 'unanimous' meant 'majority' at the time he delivered the verdict; that in fact the jury were divided 8:4 in favour of conviction. This foreman and three other jurors swore affidavits to that effect. On the joint appeal in the criminal matter and subsequent constitutional motion, the Privy Council upheld the decisions that none of the affidavits should be admitted as evidence. The Board confirmed that (p 366):

> where a verdict had been given in the sight and hearing of an entire jury without any expression of dissent by any member of the jury, there was a rebuttable presumption that all members of the jury assented to it and the court would not thereafter receive evidence from a member of the jury that he did not agree with the verdict, or that his apparent disagreement with the verdict resulted from a misapprehension on his part.

In *Nanan* the Privy Council emphasised that there are two reasons of policy behind this underlying principle. They are:

(a) the need to ensure that decisions of the jury are final (the body of jurors themselves may not challenge it except in open court at the time of its delivery);
(b) the need to protect jurors from inducements or pressure either to reveal what has passed in the jury room or to alter their view (see *Ellis v Deheer* [1922] 2 KB 113, p 121, per Atkin LJ).

The Board commended the statement of Denning MR in *Boston v Bagshaw* [1966] 1 WLR 1135:

> Once a jury have given their verdict, and it has been accepted by the judge and they have been discharged they are not at liberty to say that they meant something different.

This principle was reiterated again in *R v Qureshi* [2002] 1 WLR 518 where a member of the jury three days after the delivery of a verdict alleged that some jurors had been racially prejudiced against the defendant and had made up their minds as to his guilt at the outset of the trial. The court emphasised that any complaints about what occurred during the trial cannot properly be made after the verdict was delivered. Following *Nanan* it was held that if trial by jury is to be preserved some allegations can only be investigated if made *before* the jury's part in the trial has come to an end.

Inconsistent verdict

A judge is entitled to reject a verdict which appears to be ambiguous or verdicts which are inconsistent. He may then ask the jury to reconsider the matter. In such a case he may give the jury further directions and ask them to retire again. There have been many cases in which it was alleged that a verdict was ambiguous or verdicts were inconsistent, but few which may be considered so obviously unacceptable as the verdicts in *R v Shirley* (1964) 6 WIR 561. In that case, from Jamaica, the jury having retired were asked if they had 'arrived at a verdict'. After ascertaining that the verdict was unanimous the Registrar asked: 'Is the prisoner Vincent Shirley guilty or not guilty of murder?' The foreman said 'guilty', whereupon the Registrar proceeded to ask if the prisoner was guilty or not guilty of manslaughter, to which the foreman replied: 'not guilty of manslaughter'. The Court of Appeal of Jamaica held that the two verdicts could not stand: 'They are mutually inconsistent for the reason that a verdict of not guilty of manslaughter must of necessity negative an unlawful killing which is an essential element in the offence of murder'. The defendant therefore could not be at the same time guilty of the greater offence but not guilty of the lesser. In the circumstances of the case, the trial judge should not have allowed the Registrar to put the second question to the jury. A lesser alternative offence did not arise if the defendant was already found guilty of the greater offence.

In *R v Sweetland* (1957) 42 Cr App R 62, the defendants were charged with conspiracy to cheat and defraud and also jointly with the specific officer relating to the fraud (four other counts of obtaining by false pretences). The defendants were convicted of the completed offences but acquitted of the conspiracy. Since the case against the defendants on the completed officers hinged on the allegation that they acted together, it was held that the verdicts on the counts charging the specific offences were necessarily inconsistent with the not guilty verdict on the conspiracy (and contra wise).

It was stated that where the jury returns a verdict which appears to be inconsistent with another, it was proper for the trial judge to put questions to the jury in an attempt to clear up the apparent inconsistency. It may even be desirable that he should give the jury a further direction on the constituencies of the offences concerned. The judge must, however, ensure from the evidence and the law that the verdicts are truly inconsistent. Merely because the offences arose from the same incident does not mean that the verdicts in respect of all the offences must be one way. In *R v Steele* (1975) 24 WIR 317, the defendant was tried for four counts, the first two with regard to a Miss A for (a) indecent assault and (b) robbery with aggravation arising out of the same incident. The other two counts emanated from what was purportedly similar fact evidence in respect of another woman. As regards Miss A, the jury found the defendant not guilty on the robbery, but guilty of the indecent assault. The trial judge claimed that the verdicts were inconsistent and represented a compromise. He directed the jury to reconsider the verdicts. The jury found verdicts adverse to the defendant on all counts. On appeal, the court held that even though the offences arose from one incident, the verdicts were not inconsistent with each other or the evidence. The defendant could have indecently assaulted the victim, but not intended to rob her (the items were recovered near the scene).

Even if two verdicts are held to be inconsistent, this does not necessarily make the verdict complained of unsafe: *R v McCluskey* [1994] 98 Cr App R 216. In that case the defendant was charged with murder and affray arising out of the same incident. The offences arose out of a fact situation where the defendant allegedly stabbed the deceased in a fight in which they and two other men were involved. The defendant claimed to have been acting in self-defence. The charge of affray was based on the threat of unlawful violence arising from the use of the knife. Thus, once the jury found the defendant used the knife other than in self-defence, the affray was proved. Nevertheless, the jury brought in a verdict of guilty of manslaughter but acquitted the defendant of affray. It was held on appeal that the two verdicts were clearly inconsistent. The English Court of Appeal nevertheless held that the fact that two verdicts were shown logically to be inconsistent did not make the verdict complained of unsafe unless the only explanation for the inconsistency must, or might, have been that the jury was confused and/or adopted the wrong approach. The court concluded that the jury, having convicted the defendant on a very serious crime, must have considered the second count academic. In the circumstances of that case, the verdict in relation to manslaughter (guilty) stood. It is perhaps tempting to rationalise the facts in *Shirley* (above) in the same way, but in that case, since the legal definition of murder includes manslaughter, it was not possible for the two verdicts to stand together. The defendant could not be both guilty of murder and not guilty of manslaughter on the same charge.

Alternative verdicts

At common law (and now in some cases by statute in the Commonwealth Caribbean) there are certain offences which are implicitly included in a count for a greater offence. This is so where the greater offence necessarily includes the lesser offence and they are both indictable offences: *Shirley* (above) in relation to murder and manslaughter. It is thus permissible for a jury to return a verdict of guilty in respect of the implicitly included lesser offence[47] even though there is no specific count in the indictment for that offence. The jury ought properly to first find the defendant not guilty of the greater offence before going on to confirm the lesser. In *R v Saunders* [1988] AC 148, HL, the House of Lords specifically stated that it was

47 *R v Hollingberry* [1825] 4 B&C 329.

not desirable to abandon the long-established practice of indicting only for murder in cases where manslaughter may be left to the jury. Other offences which are in the alternative at common law may include wounding with intent and unlawful wounding; rape and indecent assault; robbery and theft. Furthermore, it has always been permissible to convict of an attempt on a charge of the full offence and vice versa.

Statute has in some cases[48] intervened to dictate that a charge of a greater offence (or specific offence) may allow conviction for another offence. In relation to a motor manslaughter charge, statute across the region[49] now provides that a defendant may be found guilty of dangerous driving on a charge of manslaughter. Similarly, in some countries on a charge of trafficking illegal narcotics, a person may be found guilty of simple possession.

Even where the offence charged may allow for the jury to bring in a verdict of another offence, the trial judge need not advise the jury of this option unless it arises from the evidence. In *Fazal Mohammed* (1990) 37 WIR 438, PC, the defendant was charged with murder. The trial judge did not leave manslaughter to the jury. The Privy Council held that on the facts of that case, there was no duty to leave such a verdict to the jury. The medical evidence established beyond any possible doubt that the terrible injury to the throat of the victim could not have been accidentally inflicted; the woman's throat had been cut down to the level of her backbone. It was clear that whoever inflicted the injury must have intended to kill or at least cause serious injury. Since the defence was that the defendant was not present and they did not raise the issue of manslaughter, the Board considered that for the judge to leave the issue of manslaughter to the jury would have been wholly unrealistic and might have led to unnecessary confusion. The clear-cut decision that the jury had to make was whether the prosecution had proved that the appellant was the attacker. A contrary finding was made by the English Court of Appeal in *Williams* [1994] 99 Cr App R 163. In that case the defendant, who was charged with murder, alleged that the deceased had committed suicide by jumping. The prosecution contended that the defendant had deliberately caused the deceased to fall from a 12th-floor flat by throwing or pushing her. The judge told the jury they could consider whether the defendant may not have held the deceased over the balcony to frighten her and as a result she accidentally fell. This would make him guilty of manslaughter. The court held that the judge was justified to leave the manslaughter alternative to the jury, who in fact convicted for manslaughter.

Sometimes an indictment may contain two counts which are specifically in the alternative. That is, the ingredients of one offence are not included in the other, but if the jury finds the defendant guilty of one offence they must acquit him of the other. Two such offences are larceny (or theft) and receiving. If the defendant is found to be the thief and guilty of larceny/theft, he may not also be found to be the receiver. He must be discharged of at least one of the offences. A finding of guilt on both will be inconsistent verdicts. This is in contrast to alternative offences like murder and manslaughter, where the latter is implicitly included in the other. If a jury finds the defendant guilty of the greater offence (murder) they should not be asked to return a verdict on the lesser alternative offence, because guilt of the lesser offence is in fact already included in the greater by implication: *Shirley* (above).

---

48 The St Lucia Criminal Code has extensive provisions in this regard, ss 982–95;
The following provisions are also of note:
Barbados: Criminal Procedure Act, Cap 127, s 9;
Guyana: Criminal Law (Procedure) Act, Cap 10:01, ss 100–03;
Jamaica: Criminal Justice (Administration) Act, s 15;
Trinidad and Tobago: Criminal Procedure Act, Chap 12:02, s 30.

49 As in Motor Vehicles and Road Traffic Act, Trinidad and Tobago, Chap 48:50, s 80.

Special verdict of insanity

The jury is entitled to return a special verdict in respect of the defence of insanity once they find that the defendant has proved the defence on a balance of probabilities.[50] In general, in Commonwealth Caribbean jurisdictions, if insanity is proved the jury may find the defendant 'guilty by reason of insanity'[51] of the offence charged. This is the only defence which, if successfully raised, leads to a verdict of guilty, albeit a special verdict.

The situation is somewhat different in Barbados, Dominica and St Vincent. In those jurisdictions, legislation now permits the return of a verdict of 'not guilty' by reason of insanity of the offence charged. This new entitlement in Barbados was created by Act 25 of 1998 which amended the Criminal Procedure Act, Cap 127, creating a new s 9A. In St Vincent, the law contained in s 120(1) of the Code appears to have existed for some time. In respect of Dominica, s 39(3) of the Eastern Caribbean States Supreme Court (Dominica) Act, Chap 4:02 refers to the special verdict established of 'not guilty by reason of insanity'.

It is the duty of the defendant to point to sufficient evidence to raise a prima facie case that he was at the time of the incident suffering from legal insanity. This is because the onus is on the defence to prove insanity, as distinct from other common law defences where he need merely raise a reasonable doubt. Unless the defence adduces sufficient evidence to establish a prima facie case of insanity, the defence need not be left to the jury: *James v R* (1997) 54 WIR 86. In that case the Barbados Court of Appeal, in applying *McNaghten's case* (1843) 10 Cl & Fin 200, held that the defence must show that the defendant was labouring under a defect of reason from disease of the mind and that, in consequence of the defect thereof, he either did not know what he was doing or, if he did, he did not know what he was doing was wrong. Once the defence brings sufficient evidence of insanity, the judge must give special directions on the issue, defining insanity and the burden of proof and the standard among other things. In the St Lucian case of *Tench v R* (1992) 41 WIR 103, the trial judge did not direct the jury as to the possibility of bringing in a special verdict of insanity although it was specifically raised by the defence. The medical evidence brought by the defendant did not relate to the time of the incident and other evidence suggested that the defendant was not mentally retarded or otherwise legally insane. The Court of Appeal suggested that the trial judge should have directed the jury as to the possibility of the special verdict of insanity, but on the facts of the case this was not fatal to the conviction.

If the defendant is in fact found guilty (or not guilty, as the case may be) but 'insane' in relation to the offence charged, he is specially sentenced as provided for by statute. He is in general sent to the mental institution, usually a public institution, and is to remain there at the 'pleasure' of the Head of State. This would suggest that he at some time in the future may be discharged, if he is deemed to be no longer insane, at the behest of the Head of State.

Insanity is rarely used as a defence in the Commonwealth Caribbean (and elsewhere), presumably because of the still-existing stigma attached to a finding that one is insane. Most

---

50 *Woolmington v DPP* [1935] AC 462, HL.

51 Antigua: Criminal Procedure Act, Cap 117, s 53;
Bahamas: Criminal Procedure Code, Ch 91, s 191;
Grenada: Criminal Procedure Code, Cap 72B, s 181;
Guyana: Criminal Law (Procedure) Act, Cap 10:01, s 178;
Jamaica: Criminal Justice (Administration) Act, s 25(2);
St Kitts and Nevis: Criminal Procedure Code, Cap 4:06, s 64;
St Lucia: Criminal Code, s 1019;
Trinidad and Tobago: Criminal Procedure Act, Chap 12:02, s 66.

defendants who may arguably be insane seem to rely on defences such as provocation, sane automatism (which leads to an acquittal) or, in some jurisdictions, where it is available, diminished responsibility (as a defence to murder).

Post-verdict

After the jury returns a verdict, the jury is discharged from further participation in the case. This is also true where the jury is unable to agree and the judge feels that a verdict is unlikely. If the verdict of the jury is one of 'not guilty', the defendant is deemed acquitted of the charge and is released unless he is required to be held in custody on another matter. If the defendant is found guilty of any offence permissible under the law, the judge will then proceed to sentencing according to law.

CHAPTER 17

CRIMINAL APPEALS

Appeal from the Criminal High Court (or Supreme Court or Circuit Court as it may be variously termed) lies to the Court of Appeal. In the Eastern Caribbean States the countries which subscribe to the Eastern Caribbean Supreme Court Act[1] share a joint Court of Appeal which sits as a Circuit Court in the various countries.[2] The other Commonwealth Caribbean States each have their own Court of Appeal which in some cases (as in Jamaica and Trinidad and Tobago, for instance) may have more than one court sitting at a time.

The appellate procedure is determined by statute[3] which, in many instances, is based on old or more current English legislation. As such, the English common law is particularly relevant in defining the applicable local law. The variation in the law among the jurisdictions in large measure depends on which English statute has been followed. There exist in each jurisdiction very detailed Court of Appeal Rules which amplify the statutory provisions by providing for formalities in relation to notice of appeal or leave to appeal, time limits, and also specify the duties of the court officials in processing the appeal as well as the necessary forms.

In Barbados, Guyana, Belize and Dominica the Caribbean Court of Justice is the final appellate court, but the Privy Council still has that distinction in other Commonwealth Caribbean jurisdictions. A duly constituted Court of Appeal in the Commonwealth Caribbean is composed of three justices of appeal sitting together as one court. This is specified by relevant statute in the jurisdictions.

RIGHT OF APPEAL

Initially, only a person convicted could appeal on indictable trial. This was dictated by statute and is still the law in several Commonwealth Caribbean jurisdictions. Some jurisdictions have amended the law to include a right of appeal by the prosecution in specified instances.

Person convicted

In general, a person convicted of any offence upon indictable trial may appeal to the Court of Appeal. He may appeal against conviction, sentence or both. A person who has been found 'guilty' by reason of insanity (or not guilty as the case may be in Barbados, Dominica and St Vincent) may now as provided for by statute across the region appeal against this special verdict.[4] In addition, s 12 of the Barbados Criminal Appeal Act, Cap 113A enables a person who has been found unfit to plead by a jury to appeal against the finding.

---

1 The Eastern Caribbean Supreme Court Act, which is adapted to meet the legislative needs of each subscribing State, creates the Supreme Court, which comprises the High Court and the Court of Appeal. Each State has its own division of the High Court sitting in that State.

2 The independent States which subscribe to the Eastern Caribbean Supreme Court are Antigua, Dominica, Grenada, St Kitts and Nevis, St Lucia and St Vincent.

3 As emphasised in relation to Jamaica by the Privy Council in *DPP v White* (1977) 26 WIR 482, PC. The law in the Commonwealth Caribbean in relation to criminal appeals is statutorily based and is very similar.

4 Previously there was no appeal, as this verdict was regarded as tantamount to an acquittal: *R v Browne* (1963) 6 WIR 303.

Appeal on a question of law alone may be without leave of the court. Otherwise the convicted person must seek leave of the court to appeal, whether on questions of fact alone, mixed fact and law, or sentence. In all jurisdictions a time limit for appealing is stipulated. Except for the Bahamas and Barbados where it is 21 days,[5] in all other jurisdictions the convicted person must appeal within 14 days of conviction and/or sentence. An extension of time to appeal may be granted upon application to the court except in cases of capital convictions. This is discussed below. If the convicted person dies before the appeal is heard, the right of appeal dies with him: *R v Kearley* (No 2) [1994] 3 All ER 246, HL.

The prosecution

Legislation in several jurisdictions has now intervened to grant to the prosecution a limited right of appeal usually against sentence or a directed verdict of acquittal. They are[6] Antigua, the Bahamas, Barbados, Dominica, Grenada, Guyana, St Kitts and Nevis, St Vincent and Trinidad and Tobago. Previously any 'appeal' by the prosecution was by way of case stated (as in the other jurisdictions) in which case the determination of the case is not affected. The new statutory provisions enable the Court of Appeal to overturn sentences or verdicts of acquittals in those specified cases. Thus the defendant, now the respondent, must be served to appear. In other respects, the appeal is treated like a usual appeal.

The Bahamas provision simply enables the Attorney General, on behalf of the Crown, to appeal, with leave of the Court Appeal only, against sentence of the convicted person. The Court of Appeal may, as with other appeals against sentence, vary the sentence by increasing or decreasing it.

The Barbados law is similar. Although it refers to a 'reference' for a 'review' of the sentence, the Court of Appeal may in the same way vary the sentence. Although the law only came into effect in 2002 it has been utilised by the DPP on several occasions. In *DPP's Reference No 1 of 2003* (*R v Skeete (Kurt)*) (2004) 66 WIR 94 the Chief Justice of Barbados referred to the previous reviews by the Director under the new law in the course of giving judgment in the then latest review.

The Dominica law on prosecution appeal, on the other hand, makes no mention of appeal against sentence. Section 37(2) of Chap 4:02 allows the DPP to appeal by way of special case to the Court of Appeal against a judge's decision on a point of law or evidence unless 'a jury has deliberated and returns a verdict of not guilty'. It would seem, then, that the appeal is restricted to cases where, as a result of an error in law by the judge, a no-case submission is upheld and the jury directed to return a not guilty verdict. In such a case the jury would not 'have deliberated'. In *John v DPP for Dominica* (1982) 31 WIR 150, for the first time, the provision was utilised in Dominica. The Court of Appeal held that the trial judge was in all the circumstances wrong to accede to the submission of no case in respect of all three accused persons. Accordingly, the appeal was allowed and a retrial was ordered. This

5 Bahamas: Court of Appeal Act, Ch 40, s 13; Barbados: Criminal Appeal Act, Cap 113A, s 19. The section stipulates 14 days in capital cases and 21 for all others.

6 Antigua: Criminal Procedure (Amendment) Act No 14 of 2004; Bahamas: Criminal Appeal Act, Ch 40, s 11 (3), amended by Act 4 of 1989; Barbados: Act No 5 of 2000, the Criminal Appeal (Amendment) Act (proclaimed July 2002); Dominica: Eastern Caribbean Supreme Court (Dominica) Act, Chap 4:02, s 37(2); Grenada: Act No 21 of 2012 creating a new Section 40A in the West Indies Associated States Supreme Court (Grenada) Act 2012; Guyana: Court of Appeal (Amendment) Act No 4 of 2010; St Kitts and Nevis: Eastern Caribbean Supreme Court (Saint Christopher, Nevis) Act, Cap 3:11, s 42; St Vincent: Act No 10 of 2007, creating a new Pt IIA in the Eastern Caribbean Supreme Court (St Vincent and the Grenadines) Act; Trinidad and Tobago: Supreme Court of Judicature Act, Chap 4:01, ss 65E–65Q.

decision was affirmed by the Privy Council in *John v DPP* (1985) 32 WIR 230, PC. In that case the Board confirmed that the right of the DPP to determine how the special case required for his appeal should be stated should be exercised after consultation with defence counsel and even the trial judge. It seems, however, that failure to consult will not vitiate the right of appeal. The Board also confirmed that the legislation was constitutional even though it put an onus (as distinct from a discretion) on the Court of Appeal to order a retrial if the court believed the decision of the trial judge was wrong in law.

The West Indies Associated States Supreme Court Grenada (Amendment) Act 2012 amended Cap 336 to provide for the right of appeal by the DPP as well as provision for an Attorney General's reference. The new s 40A now allows the DPP to appeal an acquittal, on various grounds, to the Court of Appeal and the Privy Council. These grounds include: where a no-case submission was upheld, a material irregularity committed in the course of the trial or where the trial judge had given the jury a substantial misdirection on the law or facts.

Where an accused has been acquitted, the new s 40B allows the Attorney General to refer a point of law to the Court of Appeal for an opinion. The AG is also allowed to refer important questions of law or fact to the Court of Appeal on areas including constitutional or legislative interpretation.

In 1996, the Trinidad and Tobago legislature amended the Supreme Court of Judicature Act, Chap 4:01 by the Administration of Justice (Miscellaneous Provisions) Act 1966. That Act created a new Part IIIB of the Supreme Court of Judicature Act, which includes ss 65E to 65Q. The effect of this new Part is to confer on the DPP the right to appeal to the Court of Appeal (s 65E):

(a) against a judgment or verdict of acquittal that is the result of a decision by the trial judge to uphold a no-case submission or otherwise withdraw the case from the jury, on the ground that the decision of the trial judge is erroneous in point of law;
(b) with leave, to appeal against sentence passed by the trial judge, unless it is a sentence fixed by law (mandatory).

The Trinidad and Tobago law thus seems to encompass the combination of rights given to the prosecution to appeal in the Bahamas and Dominica law. As in Dominica, no leave is required to appeal against a verdict resulting from a directed verdict of acquittal. A notable difference, however, is that whereas the appeal in Dominica may be on a point of law or evidence, in Trinidad and Tobago it is only possible on a point of law. In St Vincent legislation was passed in 2007 to give the DPP powers similar to those of the prosecution in Trinidad and Tobago. By Act No 10 of 2007 the DPP is given the power to appeal a directed verdict by a jury following a successful no-case submission and a sentence. Leave must be obtained for appeals involving mixed fact and law as well as sentence.

There have been several instances where the DPP in Trinidad and Tobago has appealed against seemingly light sentences and the Court of Appeal has increased those sentences. There have, however, been fewer appeals against directed verdicts. Nonetheless, the few that there have been have served to demonstrate some inadequacies in the Trinidad and Tobago law as regards the procedure to be adopted when the DPP appeals against an acquittal where a defendant has already been discharged. In one case, the discharged defendants were already out of the country when the Court of Appeal ordered a retrial, holding that the judge erred in upholding a no-case submission. Despite the fact that the court issued warrants for the arrests of the defendants, it is unlikely that they will be executed as the whereabouts of the defendants, who are non-nationals, are unknown. The Trinidad and Tobago legislation was thus shown to be deficient in securing the attendance of the defendant, who has been discharged on a directed verdict, at the Court of Appeal. If the Court of Appeal allows the appeal and orders a retrial (as statute permits), it will be virtually impossible to give effect to such order as it relates to defendants who live abroad.

It appears that this problem was contemplated by the legislature in St Kitts and Nevis. Act No 10 of 1998[7] confers wide powers on the DPP to appeal both an acquittal and sentence of an accused person. The provision also requires that the DPP, if he chooses to exercise the right of appeal, shall, before the trial judge discharges the accused or makes an order (such as a sentencing order), serve notice of his intention to appeal to the Court and inform the court orally that he intends to appeal against the verdict of the court. An appeal under this section has the effect of suspending the execution of the decision, judgment or order until the final determination of the appeal. The accused person thus remains in custody unless the court, having regard to the gravity of the offence, releases him on bail on condition sufficient to ensure that he attends the appeal proceedings and abides by the results thereof.[8]

The right of appeal granted to the DPP in St Kitts and Nevis and, since 2010, in Guyana, is clearly the widest in terms when compared with similar legislation in the Commonwealth Caribbean. The DPP may appeal against both acquittal and sentence without leave. He may appeal on acquittals in respect of a wide variety of offences which are listed in the statute and appears to include all serious indictable offences. He may appeal not only where acquittals have resulted from a directed verdict, but also where such acquittal results from:

- a submission upheld on the basis of a defect in the depositions or the committal of the accused person for trial or the indictment;
- the exclusion of material evidence sought to be adduced by the prosecution;
- a substantial misdirection by the trial judge in the course of his summation;
- a material irregularity in the trial.

Furthermore, the DPP in St Kitts and Nevis may appeal against sentence not only on the basis of inadequacy but also that the sentence is one that the court had no power to pass or that it is wrong in principle. The respective provisions in the Bahamas and Trinidad and Tobago as to appeals against sentence, while not restricted to inadequacy, are not as comprehensive as those of St Kitts and Nevis.

In 2010, Act No 4 of 2010 was passed in Guyana to amend the Court of Appeal Act. It is identical to the St Kitts and Nevis law in relation to appeals by the DPP to the Court of Appeal. It provides for appeals against both acquittals and sentence in exactly the same terms as the St Kitts and Nevis law.

Legislation in Antigua appears to convey in simple terms full powers of appeal to the DPP. Act No 14 of 2004 amending the Criminal Procedure Act, enables the DPP to appeal on 'acquittal or sentence' passed by a magistrate or judge. The only qualification is that the appeal against the acquittal must be on a 'point of law' which in itself conveys little restriction.

The constitutionality of legislation conferring a right of appeal to the State was subject to challenge on another basis than that in *John v DPP* (above). In Trinidad and Tobago, on an appeal[9] in this regard the respondent challenged the constitutionality of the amendment by Act No 28 of 1996 to the Supreme Court of Judicature Act, Chap 4:01 allowing an appeal against an acquittal. One of the grounds of appeal was that the statute was in breach of the existing due process rights of an accused person not to be subject to double jeopardy; that is,

7 Creating a new s 38A, now s 42, of Cap 3:11: Eastern Caribbean Supreme Court (Saint Christopher and Nevis) Act.

8 Cap 3:11, s 42(5).

9 *The State v Boyce (Brad)* (2001) 65 WIR 283.

he should not be retried following a verdict of acquittal (even one directed by the trial judge). The Court of Appeal of Trinidad and Tobago held that the law was unconstitutional on this basis: *The State v Boyce (Brad)* (2001) 65 WIR 283.

The DPP appealed to the Privy Council and in *The State v Brad Boyce* (2006) 68 WIR 437, PC, the Board reversed the Court of Appeal's finding. It held that there was nothing particularly unfair or unjust about a statutory rule that enabled an appellate court to correct an error of law by which an accused person was wrongly discharged or acquitted and order that his guilt or innocence be properly determined by law. Such a rule existed in most countries. The Board considered that the (previous) absence of a right of appeal by the prosecution could not be said to constitute part of an individual's right to fundamental due process. The Court of Appeal was wrong, the Privy Council said, in holding the legislation unconstitutional.

The courts have already considered what appeal on a question of law means. In *Smith v R* (2000) 56 WIR 145, PC, the Privy Council considered the effect of s 17(2) to the Bermuda Court of Appeal Act. That section allows the Attorney General of Bermuda to appeal to the Court of Appeal against the judgment of the Supreme Court 'on any ground of appeal which involves a question of law alone'. In that case, the trial judge had upheld a no-case submission taking the view that the circumstantial evidence, on which the prosecution case was based, was 'inconclusive to connect the [appellant] with the commission of the crime'. The prosecution appealed, concluding that the judge erred in law in so doing and in directing a verdict of not guilty. The Privy Council held that in the circumstances of that case, the judge's decision was on a question of mixed law and fact, taking the Crown's argument at its highest. The Board said that it is a settled principle of law that an acquittal recorded by a court of competent jurisdiction, although erroneous on a point of law, cannot generally be questioned before any other court. An acquittal is final. To abolish or qualify this principle the legislature must do so in clear and specific language. Since the Bermuda statute permitted appeal by the Attorney General on 'a question of law alone', the provision could not be interpreted to include any point in relation to the evidence (the facts). It followed that the Attorney General in Bermuda had no right of appeal on a question of mixed fact and law which arose in that case.

The decision in *Smith* as well as its possible implications on the Trinidad and Tobago legislation was considered by the Privy Council in *The State v Brad Boyce* (above). The Board held that the basis for the conclusion in the *Smith* case that the law excluded questions of mixed law and fact was because the Bermudan statute used the term 'questions of law *alone*', unlike the Trinidad and Tobago statute, which read 'erroneous in point of law'. The Board held that this referred to all questions of law that were for the judge and any ruling made by a judge could be challenged under the latter statute.

Other reviews by the Court of Appeal

Apart from an appeal by the convicted person or by the DPP (or Attorney General in the Bahamas) there are other means by which a decision or judgment in a jury trial may be tested by the Court of Appeal. This all depends on the statutory provisions in the respective jurisdictions, but what is certain is that an acquittal of a defendant may not be upset by means of any of these challenges. Procedurally, the reviews are effected in the same manner as a regular appeal in indictable trial.

The most usual reference to the Court of Appeal is that made by the DPP (or Attorney General as statute stipulates) on a point of law following an acquittal. Whatever the decision of the Court of Appeal, it has no effect on the acquittal. Nevertheless, the acquitted person has a right to appear in person or at the hearing to argue in person. In many jurisdictions, legislation enables this type of reference.[10] Soon after the change of law in Guyana in 1978 to grant this right to the DPP, the Court of Appeal heard *DPP's Reference* (No 1 of 1980) (1980) 29 WIR 94, the first matter in the exercise of its new jurisdiction, as the court itself observed. In that case, the defendant was acquitted on a trial for robbery. During the course of the trial, the defendant gave unsworn evidence and called no witnesses. His counsel did not address the jury. The trial judge denied the prosecution the right to make a closing address. It was on this point of law that the DPP referred the case to the Court of Appeal:

> Does the State have a right of reply (under the relevant statute) in a case where the accused in his defence makes an unsworn statement from the dock and counsel for the defence declines to sum up the evidence.

The Court of Appeal answered in the affirmative. *DPP's Reference* (No 1 of 1980) is an example of the use that the DPP may properly make of his power of reference to the Court of Appeal even when a verdict cannot be reasonably impugned. The *Reference* may be utilised to clarify any aspect of the law that during the course of the hearing is shown to be uncertain.

The power to state a case at the instance of the trial judge for consideration by the Court of Appeal may be similarly utilised. It is up to the trial judge, not the DPP, to state the case. It may thus be possible to argue that this power may be less frequently utilised, since the judge may be less inclined to hold himself up to challenge by the Court of Appeal than the defendant or the DPP may be. Whether this is so or not, there have been equally as few References by the DPP to the Court of Appeal in the Commonwealth Caribbean as there have been cases stated by the trial judge. Nonetheless, one example of the latter is that of *R v Ramcharan* (1970) 17 WIR 407. In that case, a trial judge in Trinidad and Tobago sentenced a defendant who was convicted of receiving stolen goods to a fine of $1,500 and ordered him to sign a bond to keep the peace. After having done so, but upon considering the matter further, the judge stated a case for consideration to the Court of Appeal pursuant to s 60(1) of the Supreme Court of Judicature Act 1962 which read:[11]

> Where any person is convicted on indictment the trial judge may state a case or reserve a question of law for the consideration of the Court of Appeal and the Court of Appeal shall consider and determine such case stated or question of law reserved and may either –
>
> (a) confirm the judgment given upon the indictment;
> (b) order that the judgment be set aside and quash the conviction and direct a judgment and verdict of acquittal to be entered;

10 As evidenced in the following statutory provisions: Bahamas: Court of Appeal Act, Ch 40, s 27, as amended by Act 4 of 1989; Barbados: Criminal Appeal Act, Cap 113A, s 18; Guyana: Court of Appeal Act, Cap 3:01, s 32A, as amended by Act 21 of 1978; St Kitts and Nevis: Cap 3:11, s 43; Trinidad and Tobago: Supreme Court of Judicature Act, Chap 4:01, s 63.

11 Identical provisions exist in most of the Commonwealth Caribbean, such as in:
Antigua: Eastern Caribbean Supreme Court Act, Cap 143, s 57;
Barbados: Criminal Appeal Act, Cap 113A, s 34;
Dominica: Eastern Caribbean Supreme Court (Dominica) Act, Chap 4:02, s 55;
Grenada: West Indies Associated States Supreme Court (Grenada) Act, Cap 336, s 58;
Guyana: Court of Appeal Act, Cap 3:01, s 27;
Jamaica: Criminal Justice (Administration) Act, s 55;
St Kitts and Nevis: Eastern Caribbean Supreme Court (St Christopher and Nevis) Act Cap 3:11, s 61;
St Lucia: West Indies Associated States Supreme Court (Saint Lucia) Act No 17 of 1969, s 52;
St Vincent: Eastern Caribbean Supreme Court (St Vincent and the Grenadines) Act, Cap 24, s 57.

(c) order that the judgment be set aside, and give instead thereof the judgment which ought to have been given at the trial;
(d) require the Judge by whom such case has been stated or question has been reserved to amend such statement or question when specially entered on the record; or
(e) make such other order as justice requires.

The Court of Appeal in *Ramcharan* was required to consider whether as a matter of law a judge of the High Court had power to impose a fine for the offence of receiving stolen goods which was a felony. The court determined that there was no such power and accordingly remitted the fine and substituted the sentence to one of five years' imprisonment, holding that a bond was inappropriate. It is apparent, then, that a case stated may result in the sentence of a defendant who has already been convicted being varied so that he may receive a harsher sentence. This is not possible with a Reference by the DPP referred to above, which is only permissible if the defendant has been acquitted (no matter how erroneously). A judge may thus utilise a 'case stated' to the Court of Appeal to change a sentence that is legally wrong when he himself may not do so after he has passed sentence (he may be considered functus officio). Otherwise, the defendant may in general forestall the exercise of his power by the judge by himself appealing his conviction.

Executive intervention

Throughout the Commonwealth Caribbean, statute[12] also provides in many jurisdictions for intervention by the executive in the person of the Head of State, acting on the advice of the appropriate minister, to refer a case to the Court of Appeal. This may be done[13] where the convicted person has petitioned the Head of State asking for a 'pardon' claiming that new evidence has been found, after he has exhausted his appeals, which may impact on the validity of his conviction or even sentence (except sentence of death). If the Head of State refers a case to the Court of Appeal under his statutory authority,[14] it will be treated in like manner as an appeal from the convicted person. This power has until recently rarely been used in the Commonwealth Caribbean. In *Ramdeen (Angela) v The State* (2000) 56 WIR 485, PC, the Privy Council took the unusual step of granting the appellant leave to file a second appeal to the Privy Council even though her (first) appeal against conviction for murder to the Board had already been heard and dismissed. Subsequent to the dismissal of the appeal, the appellant was interviewed by an English psychiatrist, who reported that, in her opinion, the appellant at the time of the incident was suffering from diminished responsibility. On the basis of this 'fresh' evidence, the Board granted leave to appeal. In doing so the Board opined that s 64(2) of the Supreme Court of Judicature Act of Trinidad and Tobago could be utilised by the Head of State, the President, to refer the case back to the Court of Appeal to consider the 'fresh' evidence.

Subsequently, in *Clarke v R* (2004) 64 WIR 191, PC, the Privy Council had to consider an 'appeal' from a decision of the Court of Appeal of Jamaica, dismissing a reference by the

12 The statutory provisions are based on the old English Criminal Appeal Act 1907, s 19, replaced by the Criminal Appeal Act 1968, s 17.

13 See *R v Secretary of State for the Home Department ex p Hickey and Others* (No 2) [1995] 1 WLR 734 where the English court considered the similar English provision in the Criminal Appeal Act 1968, s 17.

14 Examples of this statutory authority include: Antigua: Cap 143, s 59; Guyana: Cap 3:01, s 31; Jamaica: Judicature (Appellate) Jurisdiction Act, s 29; St Vincent: Cap 24, s 59; Trinidad and Tobago: Chap 4:01, s 64.

Governor General to the Court of Appeal. The court considered the fresh evidence and decided it was not capable of belief. The Privy Council agreed and the appellant's second set of appeals was dismissed.

In Trinidad and Tobago there have been several such references to the Court of Appeal following referrals through the President. One such reference that resulted in the eventual acquittal of the appellant was *Wilberforce Bernard v The State* (2007) 70 WIR 255, PC, in which the Board held that the conviction must be set aside because 'the appellant was deprived of the proper protection by the appointment of inexperienced counsel and the failure on the part of the court to afford him the necessary materials and opportunity to prepare himself properly'. This was in a case where the appellant had been represented at trial on a charge of murder by counsel of three months' standing.

INITIATING THE APPELLATE PROCESS

In order to activate the appellate process, an appellant must either file a notice of appeal, notice of application for leave to appeal or notice of application for extension of time to appeal. In whichever instance, the notice must be filed within 14 days (or 21 days in the Bahamas and Barbados) of the conviction and/or sentence. If the sentence is on a different date from the finding of guilt, the time must be counted from the date of sentence.[15] The notice of appeal or application for leave to appeal must usually be accompanied by the grounds of appeal.

Notice of appeal/notice of application for leave to appeal

As indicated above, if an appeal is on a matter of law alone, a notice of appeal is sufficient. No leave is required to appeal which is of right on a question of law as the Court of Appeal is considered a court of review of the law. This may explain why the DPP requires no leave to appeal against an acquittal, in those jurisdictions where he may appeal, since his grounds usually relate to issues of law.

Once the appeal involves questions of fact[16] or is against sentence, the appellant must obtain leave from the Court of Appeal to appeal. This is provided for in the relevant statutes in the jurisdictions which Rules thereof, in general, also stipulate that a notice of application for leave to appeal, if granted, shall be deemed to be a notice of appeal. This is significant because it means that although a single judge may grant leave to appeal, this procedure is rarely followed.[17] Since the appellant must file just as extensive grounds for the leave application as for the full hearing, the Court of Appeal will frequently hold only one hearing in the matter by a properly constituted court. This not only permits the court to treat the leave application as the full hearing if it wishes, but also saves time and repetition in avoiding the appellant having to seek a review of his leave application by a fully constituted court, if leave is refused by a single judge.

In practice, the appellant will file notice of application for leave to appeal and append his grounds (at the same time or supplemented later). On the date of the hearing, he will argue the application for leave on the same grounds that he intends to pursue the full appeal. In

15 A conviction is not complete until sentence has been passed: *Richards v R* (1992) 41 WIR 263, PC.

16 Even if the grounds are mixed with law, leave is required for the appeal: *R v Robinson* [1953] 1 WLR 872.

17 The position is slightly different in Jamaica where a single judge deals with the leave application in chambers except in cases involving the death penalty, where it is heard and determined by the Court of Appeal. Where a single judge refuses leave, the Court of Appeal may hear the application.

giving judgment, if the Court of Appeal grants leave, it will state that the court treats the notice of application for leave as the notice of appeal and proceed to hearing and judgment. There is usually no separate hearing of the application for leave to appeal and the hearing of the appeal.

Signing the notice

The relevant Court of Appeal Rules in Commonwealth Caribbean jurisdictions provide that all notices of appeal, applications for leave or application for extension of time must be signed by the appellant. Other notices (including grounds) may be signed by his lawyer. Generally, if the appellant cannot write or it is contended that he is insane, then the notice of appeal, application for leave or application for extension may be signed by his legal representative. An unsigned notice generally is taken to mean that there is no valid appeal before the court. The appellate process has not been properly activated.

A poignant example of this occurred in *Pollard v R* (1995) 47 WIR 185, PC. In that case, an appellant and his co-defendant were convicted for murder and sentenced to death in the St Vincent Supreme Court. An appeal by the co-defendant was successful. The appellant also attempted to appeal and a notice for application for leave to appeal on his behalf was taken to the registry for filing in the prescribed time of 14 days. The notice was returned because it was signed by counsel and not the defendant, as required by the Court of Appeal Rules. The appellant's counsel sought an extension of time, but this was refused by the Court of Appeal of the Eastern Caribbean because there exists no jurisdiction in the court to extend time to appeal in capital cases.[18] The appellant appealed to the Privy Council. The Board conceded that there could be no extension of time on capital cases. It held, however, that it would treat the failure of the appellant to sign as a mere non-compliance with r 44(1) of the West Indies Associated States Court of Appeal Rules 1968, which required the personal signature of the appellant, except if he was insane or a body corporate. Since non-compliance with the Rule could be waived by the court under r 11 once remedied by the applicant, the Board decided to waive the non-compliance from the date of the lodging of the notice.

The Board felt that on the facts of the case, the lack of the appellant's signature on the notice amounted to no more than a technical non-compliance with the Rules, since clearly it was not wilful on the part of the applicant. The Board considered that it would have been in the interests of justice to waive the non-compliance at the time of the hearing of co-defendant's appeal which was on similar if not identical grounds to the appellant. Even more significant was the fact that since that time, the conviction of the co-defendant had been quashed and this indicated that the appellant's conviction would be similarly vitiated. In all the circumstances, the Board felt, there were compelling reasons in the interests of justice why r 11 should be applied to relieve the defendant of his technical non-compliance with r 44.

Pollard is authority, then, for the proposition that a court may waive noncompliance with the Rules in exceptional cases. It is evident that the factors which must have been paramount in influencing the decision of the Board included the facts that the case was capital in nature and that the appeal was likely to succeed. Furthermore, there was no fault on the part of the appellant. All of these enabled the Board to waive non-compliance with the Rules. If the requirement for personal signature had been set in statute, however, it is doubtful whether it could have been so easily waived.

---

18 Eastern Caribbean Supreme Court (Saint Vincent and the Grenadines) Act, Cap 24, s 48(2).

Extension of time

In general, but for the Bahamas,[19] statute throughout the Commonwealth Caribbean permits the Court of Appeal to grant extensions of the time to appeal, set by statute, except in cases involving conviction of death. The relevant Bahamas provision (s 13 of the Court of Appeal Act, Ch 40) does not limit the right to seek extension of time to appeal in noncapital cases. It has been emphasised, even in *Pollard* (above), that there are very good reasons for imposing a rigid time limit on appeals in cases involving death sentences: *R v Twynham* (1920) 15 Cr App R 38, p 39, per Lord Reading CJ. In that case it was stated that the mere giving of notice of appeal or application for leave has the effect of postponing the execution. If it were possible to extend time, it would be open to a convicted murderer, having failed in one appeal, to give notice asking for an extension of time in order to bring some other matter before the court. Alternatively, the convicted person may delay giving notice until the last possible minute to provide for a further extension of time. To prevent this abuse, the legislature denied extension of time in capital cases. Appeals in capital cases therefore admit of no extension of time.[20] However, to prevent any prejudice to a person convicted and sentenced to death, a practice has evolved to require such a person, immediately after he is taken in custody at the prison after conviction, to sign a notice of application for leave to appeal. Even though no grounds are contained in the notice at that time, the Court of Appeal will not generally deem this a serious irregularity once grounds are eventually served.

As regards non-capital convictions, and it seems all convictions in the Bahamas, a prospective appellant may seek an extension of time to appeal by filing a notice of application for extension of time. The notice must state:

- the name of the applicant, his address and, if in prison, the name of the prison;
- essential details of the appeal;
- the court at which he was convicted and the sentence;
- whether the applicant proposes to appeal against conviction or sentence or both, and if he is applying for bail pending the hearing of the appeal;
- the proposed grounds of appeal.

An application for an extension of time is usually heard and determined by a single judge of the Court of Appeal. If refused, the applicant may seek leave from the full Court of Appeal as duly constituted (three judges sit as a court) under statute. An applicant seeking an extension of time must give good reasons for the delay before the court will exercise its power to extend the time to file a notice of appeal or notice of application for leave to appeal. Obviously, the longer the delay, the more difficult it will be to convince the court to grant the application. In *R v Marsh* (1953) 25 Cr App R 49, the English Court of Appeal refused applications for extension of time which was made after considerable delay and only after the convictions of two other co-defendants had been quashed. The court held that this was not a sufficient ground to allow the application. The applicants themselves had to show that there was merit, in that their appeal would probably succeed, to justify the Court of Appeal from departing from its usual practice not to grant any considerable extension of time.

19 Court of Appeal Act, Ch 40, s 13(2), the Bahamas.

20 Currently this is achieved by the condemned person by bringing a constitutional motion citing an alleged breach of some fundamental human (constitutional) right.

Marsh exemplified some of the usual considerations that the Court of Appeal will take into account and these were evident in *Sahadath Ali v R* (1969) 15 WIR 399, a case from Trinidad and Tobago. In that case, the applicant was convicted in May for unlawful wounding and gave notice of appeal against conviction on the same day as conviction. Six months later, in October, he sought to appeal instead against sentence. He applied for extension of time to file a notice of application of leave to appeal against sentence and gave as the main reason for his delay the fact that he was unrepresented and did not appreciate the difference. The Court of Appeal, holding that substantial grounds must be given for delay to cause it to intervene, stated that such intervention would occur where the judge had exceeded his jurisdiction in imposing a sentence. In this case, he had not done so, therefore no extension of time to appeal against sentence would be granted.

If delay was due substantially to the fault of his lawyer, and this was shown by the applicant, the court may consider these good and substantial reasons: *Martin v Chow* (1984) 34 WIR 379. In that case, the Court of Appeal of Trinidad and Tobago considered (in an application in a civil matter) that the applicant had shown that exceptional circumstances existed for his failure to file a notice of appeal within the stipulated time. The application was granted. In *Ali* (above) it was emphasised that if it appears that the appeal will succeed, the extension for time will usually be given. On the facts of that case, however, no good grounds were shown to exist for the appeal.

Since the Privy Council's decision in *Cannonier v Director of Public Prosecutions Isaac and others v Director of Public Prosecutions* (2012) 80 WIR 260, a decision from St Christopher and Nevis, criminal appeals in capital cases under the Eastern Caribbean Supreme Court Act carry a discretionary time limit. In appropriate cases therefore, the Court of Appeal may grant extensions of time to appeal in capital cases. In *Cannonier*, the Privy Council stated that appellate review of convictions and sentences of death was obviously of crucial importance given the final and irrevocable nature of the penalty. Also, since the death penalty was discretionary in St Kitts, appellate review by the Court of Appeal was necessary to ensure the consistent application of the death penalty and to safeguard against arbitrariness and excessive use. The Board stated that the fixed 14-day time limit to appeal served no legitimate purpose, but rather had the capacity to cause injustice. The Board concluded that the need for expeditious disposals of appeals in capital cases could be equally met by a discretionary time limit.

Bail pending appeal

An appellant has a right to apply for bail pending the hearing and determination of his appeal. In his notice of appeal or notice of application for leave to appeal, he must indicate if he is so applying. The application is made to a single judge of the Court of Appeal. In Trinidad and Tobago, the Bail Act No 18 of 1994 prohibits the granting of bail for murder, treason, piracy and hijacking and in certain specified circumstances such as where the defendant has three or more previous convictions for specified serious offences within a stipulated time of ten years. Otherwise, the principles determining the grant of bail on appeal are, like in the other Commonwealth Caribbean jurisdictions, based on the common law. The common law principles were reviewed by the Court of Appeal of Guyana in *State v Scantlebury* (1976) 27 WIR 103, pp 105–07. In *Sinanan et al. v The State* (No 1) (1992) 44 WIR 359, the Court of Appeal of Trinidad and Tobago commended these principles as applicable to most, if not all, Commonwealth countries (p 371).

In *Scantlebury* (above), the Court of Appeal confirmed that while a court has jurisdiction to admit an appellant to bail, the appellant had no common law, constitutional nor statutory right to bail. Normally bail would not be granted to an appellant (or a prospective one) after his conviction by a jury. Bail on appeal is not to be lightly allowed. An applicant for such bail must show that there are special circumstances in his case 'that make it the just thing to do to put him on bail pending the hearing of his appeal'.

A crucial consideration and an exceptional circumstance would be that there is a real likelihood that the appeal would come up for hearing after the appellant has served his sentence. Another exceptional circumstance would be that the conviction was plainly wrong, so that the appeal had every prospect of success. To some extent this requires the appellant to argue before the court some (if not all) of the grounds of appeal that should have been filed with the notice of appeal or notice of application for leave. The rationale for granting bail pending appeal is that if an appeal succeeds after an appellant has served most of his sentence, justice might not appear to have been done.

On the other hand, the gender of the appellant should not be a factor influencing the decision to grant bail. Neither is the hardship likely to be imposed on the family of an appellant an exceptional factor. The ill health of the appellant (or a member of his family) will not generally justify the grant of bail. In *Scantlebury*, the court did concede that while it was conceivable that the state of health of the appellant himself ought to be a ground in certain circumstances to admit him to bail, the ill health of his spouse could hardly be a consideration. The court must look at all the reasons advanced by the appellant cumulatively in deciding whether bail should be granted pending an appeal. It must weigh the factors outlined above against the fact that the presumption of innocence no longer applies to a person who has been convicted. He has no right to bail that a person still charged with, but not convicted of, an offence arguably has.

GROUNDS OF APPEAL

A prospective appellant activates the appellate process by completing: (a) a notice of appeal (b) notice of application for leave to appeal or (c) notice of application for extension of time (accompanied by either notice (a) or (b)). In each case, the form of notice contains various questions which include his name, the offence for which he is convicted and the date, among other things. Of crucial importance is the requirement to stipulate the grounds for the appeal (or the application) in the notice of appeal. If there are many grounds, they may be specified in a separate form accompanying the notice. The various notices are prepared forms supplied by the Registry of the Supreme Court, but the detailed grounds themselves are prepared separately by counsel for the appellant.

The Registrar's duties

The notice of appeal or other notice to initiate the appeal is submitted to the Registrar. It is the duty of the Registrar, as set out in the relevant Court of Appeal Rules, to notify the respondent of the notice. This will usually be the prosecution through either the DPP or the Attorney General, as the case may be. If the prosecution appeals, the defendant or his lawyer is notified. In practice, the appellant serves a copy of all his notices to the respondent in the matter (as well as to the Registrar).

After the Registrar has received the appropriate notice, he must prepare at least four copies of the record of proceedings in the court below and of the summing up of the judge of the court below. The record of proceedings should contain:

- the indictment and the plea;
- the verdict, any evidence given thereafter and the sentence (if any);

- notes of any particular part of the evidence relied on as a ground of appeal;
- other such notes of evidence as the Registrar may require to be included;
- in capital cases, copies of the notes of all evidence and
- in other cases, copies of any part/the whole of the notes of evidence, as the appellant or respondent may require.

Any interested party in the trial may, usually on behalf of the appellant or respondent, apply for and shall be furnished with a copy of the record of proceedings and the summing up. The Registrar may also take custody of any exhibits in the matter and the original transcripts of the proceedings, including tapes or other electronic records.

Statutory grounds

It is usual for counsel for the appellant, after he has received and studied the summing up and notes of the proceedings, to amplify or otherwise amend the Grounds of Appeal. This should usually be done with leave, but it is a mere formality at the hearing to seek such leave, which may even be dispensed with. The grounds or allegations go towards establishing one or more of the bases of appeal stipulated by statute. There are four statutory bases[21] which common legislation throughout the region specifies.[22] They are:

(a) appeal against conviction on any ground which involves a question of law alone;
(b) appeal against conviction on any ground which involves a question of fact alone or mixed law and fact;
(c) appeal against conviction on any ground which appears (to the court) to be a sufficient ground of appeal;
(d) appeal against sentence.

The drafting of the grounds

Every ground of appeal must be set out in separate numbered paragraphs. The real grounds seek to establish one or more of the statutory bases. Clearly, they need not include the words of the statute. In drafting grounds of appeal, counsel for the appellant must clearly state the misdirection or irregularity or other error of law which he alleges. For instance, he may state as a ground of appeal 'The trial judge failed to give a correct direction on the burden of proof as it relates to alibi'. Counsel must also set out concisely the particulars of the alleged non-direction or misdirection. General grounds are of little assistance to the court: *R v Nicco* [1972] Crim LR 420. In *R v Fielding* (1938) 26 Cr App R 211, the English Court of Criminal Appeal emphasised that it was unsatisfactory that grounds of appeal should be drawn with vagueness:

> If misdirection is complained of, it must be stated whether the alleged misdirection is one of law or fact, and its value must also be stated. If omission is complained of, it must be stated what is alleged to have been omitted.

---

21 As stated, e.g., in: Antigua: Eastern Caribbean Supreme Court Act, Cap 143, s 39; Jamaica: Judicature (Appellate) Jurisdiction Act, s 13(1); Trinidad and Tobago: Supreme Court of Judicature Act, Chap 4:01, s 43.

22 Act No 26 of 1996, which replaces Court of Appeal Act, Ch 40, s 11 of the Bahamas, specifies seven grounds which are variations of the usual four bases in the other jurisdictions.

The court considered that it was unfair to both the court and the prosecution to ask that they search through the summing up and transcripts to find out of what there may be to complain. Thus, some grounds of appeal against conviction may begin:

- The trial judge wrongly admitted ... [specify item] as evidence.
- The trial judge in his summing up misdirected the jury in that he ... [specify the direction].
- The trial judge wrongly or improperly commented on the defence of alibi raised by the defendant in saying that ... [state comment].
- There was a material irregularity at the trial when the jury were permitted to separate when juror X ... [state what he did].

In respect of appeal against sentence, the ground may include:

- In passing sentence, the trial judge was wrongly influenced by ... [state irrelevant factors].
- The sentence was too severe in all the circumstances of the case.
- The sentence passed is not permissible in law.

It is also said to be the duty of counsel in drafting grounds of appeal to act responsibly and not to make sweeping and unjustified attacks on the summing up unless he justifies those attacks in his grounds: *R v Morson* (1976) 62 Cr App R 236. It is expected that counsel will comply with the Court of Appeal Rules and so a ground that is not stated in the notice should be pointed out before argument and leave sought to include it.

Skeleton arguments

With the emphasis by the Court of Appeal on the need for particulars of grounds and detailed references, practice in most jurisdictions has evolved a requirement for skeleton arguments to be served by the parties to the court and exchanged between each other. This removes the unnecessary burden on the court to sift through the summing up and also clarifies the issues of appeal. Practice Directions have not yet been issued by the Supreme Court in most jurisdictions to give effect to this custom,[23] which emanated following verbal requests by the Courts of Appeal. The nature of skeleton arguments which are filed in criminal appeals (usually with a set time before the hearing of the appeal) appears to be in keeping with the requirements for perfected grounds referred to in *Guide to Proceedings in the Court of Appeal Criminal Division* (1983) 77 Cr App R 138: 'Perfected grounds should consist of a fresh document containing references by page number and letter to all relevant passages in the transcript. Authorities on which counsel relies should be cited'. The skeleton arguments, then, will amplify each ground of appeal by summarising the misdirection, omission or error complained of citing the passage in the summing up or evidence complained of and also the authorities which support the contention argued. Skeleton arguments are filed separately, as a fresh document, from the grounds of appeal.

It is unarguable that the practice of preparing and filing skeleton arguments considerably reduces the time taken in the hearing of an appeal.

23 One jurisdiction where Practice Directions have been issued is in Trinidad and Tobago – Practice Direction, dated 28 May 1996.

On a plea of guilty

While there is no doubt that an appellant may appeal on the severity of the sentence passed when he pleads guilty, he may wish also, or alternatively, to appeal against conviction. It was stated in *R v Forde* [1923] 2 KB 40 that once a plea of guilty is recorded, an appeal against conviction should only be entertained if: (a) the appellant did not appreciate the nature of the offence or did not intend to plead guilty; or (b) on the admitted facts he could not in law have been convicted of the offence charged. While these remain two of the circumstances in which an appeal against conviction may be pursued on a plea of guilty, it was held in *R v Lee* [1984] 1 All ER 1080 that those are not exhaustive circumstances. Even where a defendant has been convicted on his unequivocal plea of guilty, the Court of Appeal may allow the appeal if it finds the conviction to be unsafe. In that case, the defendant pleaded guilty to numerous counts of manslaughter and arson contained in some 11 different indictments. The pleas were by reason of diminished responsibility and after consultation with experienced counsel and expert evidence, which indicated he was fit to plead. Subsequently it was discovered, following inquiries by the *Sunday Times* newspaper and the police, that at least some of the arsons could not have been committed by the appellant. Fresh evidence was tendered of this on an application for leave along with evidence from the appellant which showed that he was of low intelligence and was of a deprived or institutionalised background and may have been motivated to plead guilty out of a desire for notoriety and publicity. In the 'wholly unusual circumstances' of the case, the court decided to admit the evidence and hear the appeal to determine if the convictions could stand as regards, initially, the charges in the first indictments. Submissions would also be heard as to the charges in the other ten indictments.

R v Whitehouse [1977] 2 WLR 925 is more representative of the kind of matter in which the Court of Appeal may entertain an appeal against conviction despite a guilty plea. In that case, the defendant pleaded guilty to two charges of inciting his 15-year-old daughter to commit incest. He was convicted and appealed against sentence. At the hearing, the court took the view that inciting the victim of an offence (incest) to commit the offence could not be a crime. Thus the defendant had pleaded guilty to an offence not known to law and the decision of the trial judge to accept the guilty plea was erroneous in law.

In *Shawn Parris v The State* Cr App No 12 of 2004 (unreported) from Trinidad and Tobago the appellant had pleaded guilty to manslaughter on a charge of murder. He was sentenced to life imprisonment not to be released for 30 years. He sought to appeal both his conviction and sentence, claiming he had been pressured into pleading guilty with a promise of a lighter sentence. The Court of Appeal dismissed his appeals and held, after hearing evidence *de bene esse* to decide if the evidence was capable of belief, that the plea was freely given and was without improper inducement.

Question of law

Most appeals against conviction involve a mixture of law and facts. There are, however, grounds which may involve issues of law alone. This includes jurisdictional issues such as that the indictment is defective;[24] or the committal for trial was irregular and thus the indictment is invalid: *R v Gee et al.* (1936) 25 Cr App R 198. Where it is alleged that a trial in which three indictments are tried together is a nullity,[25] this involves an issue of law alone: lack of jurisdiction of the court.

24 If it is unsigned, as in *R v Morais* [1988] 87 Crim App R 9.

25 See *Olivo* (1942) 28 Cr App R 173.

An allegation that a count in an indictment is duplicitous usually involves a question of law alone: does the count charge more than one offence? Similarly a misdirection that, on a charge of murder, the defence bears a burden of proof that the incident was an accident is an error in law: *Woolmington v DPP* [1935] AC 462, HL.

AT THE HEARING

An appeal involves legal submissions. Evidence is rarely given at this level having regard to the fact that the Court of Appeal is not a court of re-hearing. Having submitted grounds of appeal and skeleton arguments, each counsel appears on the appointed day before the court, which comprises a panel of three judges. The appellant goes first and argues his submissions. He may choose to disregard certain grounds and pursue the rest. The President of the court (usually the most senior judge) or any other judge may directly put questions to counsel as to the issues he raises in his submissions. The court may even indicate how it is thinking on certain grounds and ask counsel to respond. It may ask for clarification on the applicability of the authorities, statute or case law. The hearing is interactive and does not simply constitute a presentation of legal submissions. This is accommodated by the fact that the skeleton arguments of both sides are already known to each other and the court.

Counsel for the respondent will reply to the submissions put forward by the appellant. The Court of Appeal may request a reply only on grounds that it considers may have merit. The court (any one of the judges) will also question counsel for the respondent so as to obtain clarification of his submissions or elicit a direct response to any specific argument raised by the appellant. After hearing both sides, the court may allow the appellant to respond to new matters raised by the respondent, if any. The court at the end of the hearing may immediately deliver an oral judgment with reasons. Alternatively, it may indicate its decision and deliver the actual reasons on a subsequent date. Finally, it may reserve judgment to a future date. It has been held that if an appellant wishes to object to the composition of the court, he must do so before or at the hearing of the appeal: *Berry v DPP* (1995) 48 WIR 193.

Representation and appearance

Statute throughout the region provides that legal assistance must be assigned to an appellant in a criminal appeal if 'it appears desirable and in the interests of justice that the appellant should have legal aid and that he has not sufficient means to enable him to obtain that aid'.[26] This means that definitely in all capital cases, an appellant will be provided with legal aid at the expense of the State. The same is usually true in jurisdictions that have legal aid institutionalised for all serious offences where the defendant is tried indictably.

Although, generally, a defendant is not entitled to switch from one counsel to another, especially if the legal aid is provided for by the State, the court may allow this in certain circumstances on appeal. In *Thomas v The State* (1997) 52 WIR 491, PC, a case from Trinidad and Tobago, counsel who appeared for the appellant, who had been convicted of murder, had been briefed by the Legal Aid Authority. When the matter was called before the Court of Appeal, he sought leave to withdraw. He indicated that, after carefully studying the summing up, he had concluded that there were no grounds of substance. He had so

26 Eastern Caribbean Supreme Court Act, Cap 143, s 51, Antigua, which is reflective of almost identical provisions in the relevant Court of Appeal legislation in the Commonwealth Caribbean.

informed the appellant, who had asked that he return the brief so he could retain other counsel. The Court of Appeal refused to give leave to counsel to withdraw.

The Privy Council, while dismissing the petition for leave to appeal, expressed the view that the appellant did not have an opportunity either in person or through alternative counsel to put before the Court of Appeal any points that he might have sought to have raised. This was undesirable if counsel had been asked to return the brief. At the time the matter was called, there was no counsel appearing on behalf of the appellant since counsel had no authority to so announce himself.

The decision in *Thomas* highlights another matter of practice at the hearing of a criminal appeal. Unlike at a hearing of a summary appeal, an appellant in a criminal appeal need not be present. An appeal may be proceeded with, and this is often done, in the absence of the appellant. This is so only if he is represented by counsel, since otherwise there will be no one to argue the appeal on his behalf. The Board in *Thomas* seemed to be suggesting that if counsel, who has been instructed to withdraw, appears and the appellant is himself absent, then the appellant is virtually unrepresented. Throughout the region, the Court of Appeal legislation provides that an appellant may be present at the (final) hearing of his appeal, though not at an application for leave or extension of time. This is usually only if the appellant so desires and indicates that wish when he files his notice of appeal or application for leave.

Thus, if an appellant is dissatisfied with counsel and requests his withdrawal, the court should not force the counsel to proceed in the absence of the appellant. The appellant himself must be given the opportunity to instruct alternative counsel or to address the court himself, whichever is more appropriate. The Court of Appeal has a discretion to request the attendance of the appellant at any hearing pertaining to him at the court, whether it be the final hearing or an application for leave or extension of time.

Abandonment of the appeal

An appellant may serve notice of abandonment of his appeal to the Registrar of the Supreme Court. This may be done at any time after he has filed his notice to activate the appellate process: notice of appeal, notice of application for leave or notice of application for extension of time. Once a notice of abandonment is served, the appeal 'shall be deemed to have been dismissed by the court'.[27] The relevant Court of Appeal Rules in the jurisdictions of the Commonwealth Caribbean all contain such a provision.

If an appellant seeks to resuscitate his appeal after abandonment, he may not do so by asking to withdraw his notice of abandonment: *R v Medway* [1976] Crim LR 118. In that case the English Court of Appeal confirmed that it had no jurisdiction to allow a notice of abandonment to be withdrawn. This is because the appeal would have already been dismissed. Where, however, the appellant in making the determination to abandon is shown not to have acted as a result of an informed and deliberate decision, the court may treat the notice of abandonment as a nullity. The result would be that the notice of appeal or application for leave or application for extension of time would subsist. The onus lies on the appellant to show that either he did not appreciate what he was doing because of his mental condition at the time, or that he did not act deliberately, but was influenced by substantial misinformation.

27 As specified in r 59(1) of the Court of Appeal Rules 1968 of the West Indies Associated States (now Eastern Caribbean States).

Fresh evidence

Statute across the Commonwealth Caribbean provides that, in certain circumstances, the Court of Appeal may receive fresh evidence. Legislative provisions in this regard are almost identical in stipulating that the Court of Appeal may receive the evidence of any witness who would have been competent to give evidence at trial, whether he was called at trial or not. The grounds on which this fresh evidence should be received are:

- if it appears to the court that the evidence is likely to be credible and would have been admissible at trial on an issue that is the subject of the appeal; and
- if the court is satisfied that though it was not adduced at the trial, there is a reasonable explanation for the failure to adduce it.[28]

Even if the grounds are not specified in statute, as in Jamaica and Trinidad and Tobago, the same grounds will be applicable, since they represent the usual bases on which fresh evidence may be admitted at common law as enunciated in *Parks* [1961] 1 WLR 1484. The evidence must be:

- evidence that was not available at the trial;
- relevant to the issue in the case;
- credible – capable of belief; and
- sufficient to have raised a reasonable doubt in the minds of the jury if it had been given at trial together with the other evidence.

In that case, the Court of Appeal granted leave to the defence to call the prosecutrix in a case where the appellant had been convicted of indecent assault, to cross-examine her on previous convictions of dishonesty, which were unknown to the defence at the trial. In similar vein, the Court of Appeal of Trinidad and Tobago in *Glenroy Bishop v The State* (2000) 60 WIR 370 had to consider fresh evidence that one of the prosecution witnesses, Jacobs, had previous convictions, a fact which only became known to the defence just prior to the appeal to the Privy Council. The case had been remitted by the Privy Council to the Court of Appeal to consider this evidence.

In *Forde v R* (1979) 36 WIR 127, PC, the Privy Council upheld the decision of the Court of Appeal to refuse to admit as fresh evidence statements allegedly made to two persons, F and D, who claimed that a third party, G, had admitted to the offence for which the appellant was convicted. The court held that the evidence was inadmissible as hearsay and would not have been admissible even at trial in any event. The question was whether the evidence was credible in the circumstances of the case. The Privy Council held that the Court of Appeal had asked itself the proper question under s 29 (above) of the Barbados Criminal Appeal Act. The evidence would not be admitted.

The usual practice in seeking leave to tender fresh evidence is for the party so desiring to serve an affidavit containing the evidence to the Registrar, after he has stipulated in his notice of appeal that he wishes to call such fresh evidence. It is for the Court of Appeal itself (and not a single judge thereof) to determine if the evidence should be admitted. If the court decides to admit the evidence, the witness will be called and examined by the party in whose favour he is giving the evidence and then cross-examined by counsel for

28 Criminal Appeal Act, Cap 113A, s 29(2)(a) and (b) of Barbados, whose provisions are identical to those of many Commonwealth Caribbean jurisdictions such as Antigua: Cap 143, s 45; Dominica, Chap 4:02, s 43.

the opposing party. The practice is thus the usual one for adducing evidence from witnesses.

In *The Director of Public Prosecutions v Nelson* [2015] UKPC 7, an appeal from Antigua and Barbuda, the Privy Council examined the procedure to admit fresh evidence in the Court of Appeal. The Board held that, under Section 45 of the Eastern Caribbean Supreme Court Act, the Court of Appeal is required to receive fresh evidence unless it is satisfied that the evidence if received would not afford any ground for allowing the appeal. At the hearing of the appeal, the court would decide whether the evidence affected the validity of the conviction. This allowed the court at the determination at the appeal, to determine whether the fresh evidence affected the validity of the conviction, including whether it would, if accepted, be such as might reasonably have affected the outcome of the trial. The Board noted that this procedure was comparable with that adopted by the English Court of Appeal, Criminal Division, under Section 23 of the Criminal Appeal Act 1968 (UK); namely that the fresh evidence is admitted (if the other conditions for doing so are met) *de bene esse* with the court then proceeding to examine in the context of the appeal as a whole whether the fresh evidence is such as to impact adversely on the safety of the conviction.

In a line of cases from the Commonwealth Caribbean, the Privy Council has remitted a number of cases back to the Court of Appeal in the relevant jurisdictions, to consider the reception of evidence of diminished responsibility. In each case, the evidence related to the issue of diminished responsibility which was either not raised at trial at all or not properly investigated by the defence at that stage. In doing so, the Privy Council acted in like manner to English courts in *Ahluwahlia* [1992] 4 All ER 889 and *R v Thornhill* (No 2) [1996] 2 All ER 1023. In *Williams v R* (No 1) (1998) 53 WIR 162, PC, the appellant was convicted of murder of his common law wife in St Vincent. At the trial, evidence disclosed that he was also responsible for the deaths of their two infant children. The defence called a psychiatrist to give evidence, but his evidence was unhelpful to the defence as regards the issue of diminished responsibility. As a result, the judge withdrew this issue from the jury. The appeal to the Court of Appeal was dismissed. Subsequent to that, a 'distinguished English forensic psychiatrist' (*Williams*, p 169) went to St Vincent and interviewed the appellant in person 'for over five hours on 19 February 1998', some three and a half years after the incident. Dr NLG Eastman, the psychiatrist, nevertheless purported to be able to express an opinion on the appellant's mental condition at the time of the killing. The Privy Council considered that Dr Eastman's evidence was likely to be credible and so passed the threshold test for admissibility under s 45(a)[29] of the Eastern Caribbean Supreme Court (St Vincent and the Grenadines) Act. The Privy Council accordingly remitted the case back to the (Eastern Caribbean) Court of Appeal to decide how best to deal with the evidence, which the Board ruled was admissible. The Court of Appeal, it said, could either order a retrial at which the evidence would be admitted or receive the evidence itself, allowing cross-examination and rebutting evidence if necessary.

As a footnote to this, it is instructive to consider the judgment of the Privy Council in *Williams v R* (No 2) (2000) 56 WIR 269, PC. That appeal came before the Privy Council consequent on the majority judgment of the Court of Appeal of the Eastern Caribbean States who allowed Dr Eastman's evidence to be admitted but dismissed it as speculative, based as it was merely on what the appellant had reported. The Court of Appeal accordingly refused to permit oral evidence-in-chief or cross-examination and did not order a retrial. The Privy Council disapproved of this course, and sent the matter back to a differently constituted Court of Appeal to hear the evidence.

29 This section is identical to the Criminal Appeal Act, Cap 113A, s 29(2), Barbados, cited above.

In another appeal, this time from Trinidad and Tobago, the Privy Council took the same course as in *Williams v R* (No 1) (above). In *Campbell v The State* (1999) 55 WIR 439, PC, the appellant was convicted of murder alleged to have occurred on 28 February 1993. At his trial, the defence called evidence of a psychiatrist, who had never examined the appellant, to give evidence. She was only able to give evidence of his medical history where it was contended that he had at some time in the past ingested poison. On the appeal before the Privy Council, counsel for the appellant sought to tender new evidence in the form of a report by 'Dr NLG Eastman, a distinguished English psychiatrist' (*Campbell*, p 445). This time Dr Eastman had interviewed the appellant for four hours some six years after the incident. Despite resistance from the counsel for the State to the effect that it was undesirable to admit fresh evidence so late in the day where the evidence itself could be of little assistance (the opinion was based largely on what the appellant told the doctor), the Board decided that the matter should be remitted to the Court of Appeal. The Board felt that it might be necessary in the interests of justice to admit the evidence. The Board said that having regard to what it had been told were 'limited facilities for the psychiatric examination of accused persons in Trinidad and Tobago and the difficulty of advancing a defence based upon a thorough psychiatric examination and report on that jurisdiction' (*Campbell*, p 446), it felt that there was a reasonable explanation for the failure to adduce such evidence previously. Unlike what had occurred in *Williams* (above), however, the Privy Council did not itself decide that the evidence should be admitted but, probably having regard to the issues raised by counsel for the State, decided to remit the case to the Court of Appeal to consider admissibility of the fresh evidence.

Whether it is indeed a fact that it is difficult to obtain psychiatric examination of defendants in the Commonwealth Caribbean, it is clear that the Privy Council will have no hesitation in directing the admission (or at least consideration) of fresh evidence by the Court of Appeal once the case is capital and involves allegations of diminished responsibility. Another instance of this was in *Ramdeen (Angela) v The State* (2000) 56 WIR 485, PC, an appeal from the Court of Appeal of Trinidad and Tobago on conviction for murder. Again it appeared that the 'fresh' evidence of diminished responsibility only became available years after the incident following interviews by an English psychiatrist. The psychiatrist first saw the appellant after conviction and, in this case, after an appeal to the Privy Council had been dismissed. The Privy Council granted leave for a second appeal on learning of this 'fresh' evidence.

Subsequently, in *Clarke v R* (2004) 64 WIR 191 PC, the Privy Council took a more hard-line approach in relation to purported fresh evidence which involved a key prosecution witness recanting his testimony. The Board considered that the Court of Appeal was in a better position to determine whether such evidence was 'capable of belief'. The Privy Council also sanctioned the practice outlined in *Pendleton* [2002] 1 WLR 72 HL to admit fresh evidence *de bene esse* if the court could not be sure at the outset whether it should be admitted or not. After hearing the witness the Court of Appeal could then determine whether to admit the evidence or not. Similarly in *Pitman v R* (2008) 73 WIR 404, PC the Board referred the matter back to the local Court of Appeal in Trinidad and Tobago to consider the impact of the fresh evidence of a forensic psychiatrist and psychologist admitted at the Privy Council on behalf of the appellant. The Court of Appeal was directed to hear the evidence of the witnesses who would be subject to cross-examination as well as any other evidence and make a determination as to whether the conviction was safe.

In an early indication of its views on the issue of fresh evidence at the appellate level, the CCJ in *Cadogan v R* [2007] 69 WIR 249, CCJ (AJ) decided that fresh evidence on the issue of diminished responsibility and misconduct of the trial attorney should not be admitted. The court held that, on one hand, the evidence was not sufficiently cogent and, on the other, it was not reliable.

Recently the Privy Council in *Lester Pitman v The State, Neil Hernandez v The State* [2017] UKPC decided that the admission of fresh evidence on appeal is a matter of discretion. Not only must the evidence appear credible but the explanation for its absence at trial is very relevant to the exercise of the discretion. Even where fresh evidence is late, it may be sufficiently compelling, such that justice requires its admission. The Board further held that the best prevention of late medical evidence lay in the regular early expert examination of all defendants facing murder charges.

DETERMINATION OF APPEALS

The Court of Appeal on any criminal appeal against conviction is entitled to allow the appeal or dismiss the appeal. In either case, the court may make consequential orders. The court may also vary the sentence passed. In an appeal against sentence, the Court of Appeal may increase or decrease the sentence.

Allowing an appeal

The Court of Appeal may allow the appeal if it finds that any one of the statutory grounds for allowing an appeal is satisfied. If the appeal is allowed, the Court of Appeal must quash the conviction and either direct an acquittal or order a retrial for the same offence or an alternative, implicitly included, offence in the indictment. The Court of Appeal must do one or the other: *DPP v White* (1977) 26 WIR 482, PC. In that case the Jamaican Court of Appeal allowed an appeal where the verdict of the jury was delivered on two counts in 27 minutes, well under the statutory period for deliberations before which a majority verdict may not be given. Only one count was unanimous, but the jury never indicated which. The Court of Appeal held the trial was a nullity and quashed the conviction. The court felt that, since the first trial was a nullity, they had no power to order a 'new' trial. The DPP appealed against the failure to make an order. The Privy Council held that the powers of the Court of Appeal in allowing an appeal were circumscribed by statute. The court must either enter a verdict of acquittal or order a retrial. It cannot decline to do both. The position is the same in other Commonwealth Caribbean jurisdictions where the jurisdiction of the Court of Appeal in each case is wholly statutory.

The decision whether to enter a verdict of acquittal or order a retrial is dictated by the consideration as to whether it is in the interests of justice[30] to order a retrial (as stated in relevant statutory provision): *Johnson v The State* (1999) 55 WIR 410, p 421, PC. In that case the Privy Council allowed an appeal from the Trinidad and Tobago Court of Appeal, quashed the conviction and remitted the case to the Court of Appeal to consider whether a retrial should be ordered. One of the chief determinants in deciding if a retrial should be ordered is the length of time which has elapsed since the date of the incident. Another related factor is whether the defendant would be prejudiced in defending the charge by the lapse of time: *Glenroy Bishop v The State* (2000) 60 WIR 370, a decision of the Court of Appeal of Trinidad and Tobago. In that case, the Court of Appeal decided to order a retrial because the time lapse had not been significant and the case for the prosecution was strong. In *Johnson* (above), it was the strength of the case which influenced the Court of Appeal eventually to order a retrial. It is significant to

30 See *Reid v R* (1978) 27 WIR 254, PC, for a list of common factors to be considered in determining whether or not to order a retrial.

note that if the Court of Appeal allows the appeal and orders a retrial, the Privy Council will not lightly interfere with such an order: *Holder v R* (1978) 31 WIR 98, PC. The Board will only do so if it is clear that in making its order the Court of Appeal erred by either taking into account matters to which it ought not to have had regard or did not take into account matters to which it should have paid attention.

In *Krishna Persad and Ramsingh Jairam v The State* (2001) 58 WIR 433, PC, the Board considered an appeal against an order for retrial. It held that on the facts of that case, where the Court of Appeal did not expressly hear the appeal before it made the order and so did not consider pertinent matters like the 15-year delay, the order of retrial would be quashed and the case remitted to the Court of Appeal to hear the appeal fully. The Court of Appeal had not taken into account matters that it ought to in making the decision to order a retrial.

Allowing in part

The Court of Appeal has power to allow the appeal in part on 'some count or part of the indictment',[31] but dismiss the appeal on another count or part of the indictment. This power is generally only utilised if there is more than one count charged and the court finds that the conviction on one (or more) charge may stand, whereas another may not. If this occurs, the court may affirm the sentence passed on the appellant at trial or substitute such sentence as it thinks proper and as warranted by the law.

More usual, however, is the decision of the Court of Appeal to substitute, instead of the verdict found, a verdict of guilty of an alternative offence of which the appellant could, on the indictment, have been found guilty. The court must find that the jury must at least have been satisfied of the facts which prove him guilty of that other offence. In *Stafford and Carter v The State* (1998) 53 WIR 417, PC, the Privy Council considered the application of the relevant statutory provision in s 45(2) of the Trinidad and Tobago Supreme Court of Judicature Act:[32]

> Where an appellant has been convicted of an offence and the jury could on the indictment have found him guilty of some other offence, and on the finding of the jury it appears to the Court of Appeal that the jury must have been satisfied of facts which proved him guilty of that offence, the Court of Appeal may, instead of allowing or dismissing the appeal, substitute for the verdict found by the jury a verdict of guilty of that other offence.

In that case, the Board found that the evidence, when taken with the jury's verdict, was sufficient to show that they must have been satisfied that the facts would justify the conviction of the appellants for manslaughter. The Board decided that the evidence in the case did not go towards proving that the appellants had the necessary mens rea for murder. However, the Board considered that the verdict of the jury (guilty of murder) showed that they rejected the appellants' evidence. This meant that the jury must have been satisfied that each appellant was a party to a scheme to carry out a robbery (from which death resulted). There was enough evidence to show that the appellants at least had mens rea to do an unlawful act likely to cause harm. A verdict of manslaughter in each case was held to be appropriate. The cases were remitted to the Court of Appeal to pass sentence.

---

31 As stated in relevant legislation in the region, e.g., Eastern Caribbean Supreme Court Act, Cap 143, s 41(1), Antigua; Supreme Court of Judicature Act, Chap 4:01, s 45(1), Trinidad and Tobago.

32 Such a provision is common in all Commonwealth Caribbean jurisdictions.

In deciding whether the court should substitute a verdict which the jury did not return, the court must apply different considerations from those used in applying the proviso and dismissing an appeal: *Moses v The State* (1996) 49 WIR 455, p 469, PC. The Privy Council in that case emphasised that the decision to substitute involves more an assessment of the verdict than the evidence. The proper approach where a misdirection is given is to assume that the jury understood the direction and reached a verdict of guilty in the light of it. The appellate court must then deduce from putting the two together what findings of the jury must lie behind the verdict. In *Moses*, as compared with *Stafford and Carter*, the court determined that all the verdict showed was that the jury 'must have been satisfied' that the appellant was a party to a scheme to rob. This was insufficient to ground a substitution of a manslaughter verdict for the murder conviction, which the Board found could not stand because of a misdirection on the felony-murder rule that, the Board found, had been abolished.

Furthermore, an appellate court may only substitute a verdict of which the jury could have found the appellant plainly guilty on the indictment. In other words, the lesser alternative offence must necessarily constitute part of the greater offence charged. On the facts in *Moses*, the Board determined that the jury's verdict clearly showed that they were satisfied the appellant was a party to a robbery. However, an indictment for murder does not include a tacit indictment for robbery as it does for manslaughter, the lesser offence to murder. Since robbery was not included as a count in the indictment, the Board could not substitute that verdict for the murder. The appeal in *Moses* was thus allowed in its entirety.

Dismissing the appeal and the proviso

The Court of Appeal may dismiss the appeal if it finds no merit in any of the grounds of appeal argued by the appellant. Alternatively, the court may find merit in one or more grounds but decide to apply the 'proviso' and dismiss the appeal. The Privy Council will not normally review the application of the proviso by the Court of Appeal unless the court has misdirected itself in important respects: *Stafford and Carter v The State* (1998) 53 WIR 417, PC. The proviso is one which is common to Commonwealth Caribbean jurisdictions in legislation relating to the grounds on which the Court of Appeal may allow an appeal. The common proviso stipulates:

> Provided that the Court may, notwithstanding that they are of the opinion that the point raised in the appeal might be decided in favour of the appellant, dismiss the appeal if they consider that no substantial miscarriage of justice has actually occurred.[33]

Apart from grammar, the only variation to this typical proviso in Commonwealth Caribbean jurisdictions is the lack of qualification to 'miscarriage of justice' in some jurisdictions. Just as the Jamaica proviso (above), legislation[34] in Barbados, Guyana, St Kitts and Nevis and Trinidad and Tobago refers to 'a substantial miscarriage of justice' occurring. It is debatable whether this qualification makes a difference in the approach of the courts in the region in their application of the provisos in the different jurisdictions of the Commonwealth Caribbean. In both cases the ultimate question is whether the appellant has lost a chance of acquittal that was fairly open to him.

33 Proviso to the Jamaica Judicature (Appellate Jurisdiction) Act, s 14(1).

34 Barbados: Criminal Appeal Act, Cap 113A, s 4(2);
Guyana: Court of Appeal Act, Cap 3:01, s 13;
St Kitts and Nevis: Eastern Caribbean Supreme Court (Saint Christopher and Nevis) Act, s 44;
Trinidad and Tobago: Supreme Court of Judicature Act, Chap 4:01, s 44.

In *Moses* (above) it was emphasised that applying the proviso involves a question of assessing the evidence that was before the jury. The criteria for the application of the proviso where the court has misdirected itself is if the jury had received the appropriate directions, whether they would, without doubt, have convicted the appellant on a consideration of the whole of the admissible evidence, omitting from consideration evidence which clearly the jury did not believe: *Stafford and Carter v The State* (above). In the latter case, the Privy Council found that the trial judge had misdirected the jury on important aspects of the case, intent and joint enterprise. Omitting the appellants' evidence in the box which the jury clearly did not believe, the 'untainted' evidence included separate statements by each appellant, the post mortem report and evidence of the finding of the body. This did not constitute sufficient evidence on which it could be said that a reasonable jury would inevitably have convicted the appellants for murder. Accordingly the Board held that the proviso could not be implied and the conviction for murder in each case must be quashed. Verdicts of manslaughter were substituted.

In *Chitrah and Malharri Dookran v The State* [2007] UKPC 15, the Privy Council overturned the convictions of the two appellants where the Court of Appeal had applied the wrong test in applying the proviso. The Board emphasised that the true test to be applied was not whether a reasonable jury might well have convicted, which was the test the Court of Appeal evidently applied, but whether they would have 'inevitably' convicted.

In *Fazal Mohammed v The State* (1990) 37 WIR 438, PC, on the other hand, the Privy Council endorsed the application of the proviso on the facts and evidence in the case. The appellant was convicted of murder of one GM. The evidence called at trial disclosed that one MB had sharpened a razor for the appellant on the morning of the incident. That night, the victim was discovered bleeding with her throat cut lying on the road outside her home. She subsequently died from the wound. The next morning the appellant gave himself up to the police and later gave a voluntary confession in which he confessed to cutting the throat of the deceased victim. He admitted that a razor case found outside his mother's house was his. In addition to all of this, the daughter of the deceased also gave evidence that she witnessed the incident. Although she was not 14 at the time, she was allowed to give sworn evidence without an appropriate enquiry being held by the judge to determine whether she was capable of giving sworn evidence. It was agreed on appeal that the clear rule of practice made it mandatory that an enquiry should be held as to the competency of a child under 14 to take the oath. The evidence was thus not admissible. Nevertheless, the Court of Appeal and later the Privy Council considered that this was a fit case for the application of the proviso. As the Board indicated, the case for the prosecution 'was very convincing' even excluding the testimony of the daughter of the deceased, based as it was on the appellant's own confession supported by the evidence of the possession and sharpening of a razor on the day of the incident and the forensic evidence. The Board went further to emphasise that the injury to the throat was so severe that the question of manslaughter did not arise once the jury found the appellant was the attacker.

Sometimes, application of the proviso is declined because a particular fault (omission, irregularity) is so serious that even though the Court of Appeal believes the evidence is sufficient to justify a reasonable jury inevitably finding the defendant guilty, the deserved conviction must be sacrificed to the general principle of fairness in a criminal trial. Such was the case in *R v Badjan* (1966) 50 Cr App R 141, where the court on the trial of the appellant for inflicting grievous bodily harm failed to refer to the defence of self-defence raised on behalf of the appellant. The English Court of Criminal Appeal held that it was generally impossible to apply the proviso (the same in terms as those in Commonwealth Caribbean jurisdictions) where a defence which the appellant was entitled to have left to the jury was not mentioned. This was so no matter that the defence in the light of the evidence might have been regarded as 'tenuous'. Similarly, in *R v Mckenna* (1960) 44 Cr App R 63, the English Court of Appeal declined to apply the proviso, despite the strength of the evidence, in a case where the trial judge had intimidated the jury by threatening to keep them overnight for deliberations if they had not arrived at a verdict by a certain time. The court pointed out that the judge's conduct was contrary to the fundamental principle that a jury should deliberate in complete freedom.

In cases depending on identification evidence, a significant failure to give the requisite directions (a *Turnbull* direction)[35] to the jury to apply caution in considering that evidence, will generally result in a substantial miscarriage of justice, necessitating the quashing of the conviction: *Douglas v R* (1995) 47 WIR 340, PC, an appeal from Jamaica. While the Privy Council recognised that there are rare cases where the evidence is so compelling that it is plain that a conviction was inevitable, it followed a long line of its own previous cases involving identification evidence in quashing convictions.

The question whether to apply the proviso or not then generally hinges on the strength of the evidence and whether a conviction would have been inevitable despite the flaw in the trial or summing up. Although the Privy Council may be reluctant to review the application of the proviso by the local Courts of Appeal, it has had no hesitation in doing so on many occasions in the past. The decision whether to apply the proviso is never an easy one, depending as it does on a balance between ultimate fairness to a defendant and the obvious strength of the evidence against him.

Reasons by Court of Appeal

When a Court of Appeal dismisses an appeal it is expected that the court should give its reasons for refusing the appellant's appeal. The situation becomes more critical where the appellant wishes to appeal to a higher court. In *Teerathraj Maharaj v The State* [2008] UKPC 28 the Privy Council stressed that they took a very serious view of the failure of the local Court of Appeal to give its reasons in that case. Nonetheless, they held that, if a conviction were otherwise sound, it would not be quashed simply because of the failure of the Court of Appeal to give their reasons for dismissing an appeal against that conviction. If the Board considered that there might be merit in the appeal it would grant special leave to appeal and would, in due course, give a reasoned judgment allowing or dismissing the appeal, which would, in substance, remedy the failure by the Court of Appeal.

The Board, in determining whether there was merit in that case, considered the transcript of the summing-up as well as a transcript of the hearing before the Court of Appeal. They were able to determine that there was no merit.

Special verdict

There are particular statutory provisions in criminal appeal legislation throughout the region dealing with appeals involving a special verdict of insanity. The provisions are more or less similar. If a person appeals against a finding of a special verdict, the Court of Appeal is entitled to substitute the special verdict with guilty of the offence charged (or an alternative offence) and pass sentence[36] accordingly. Otherwise, the court may substitute the special verdict for a verdict of acquittal.

35 As in *R v Turnbull* [1976] 3 All ER 549, whose principles on directions in cases depending largely on identification evidence have been adopted and followed throughout the Commonwealth Caribbean.

36 In such a case, sentence will be deemed to run from the time it would have run if passed in the proceedings.

Conversely, if on the hearing of an appeal the Court of Appeal is of the opinion that the proper verdict should have been a special verdict of insanity, it may so substitute the verdict. Thereafter, the court may direct that the appellant may be kept in custody as a prisoner of unsound mind is dealt with when the special verdict is found by the jury. It would seem that in such cases, for the Court of Appeal to make such a finding it would have to hear evidence. In effect, this is similar to what the Privy Council asked of the respective Courts of Appeal in the Commonwealth Caribbean in *Williams v R* (No 1) (1998) 53 WIR 162, PC, and *Campbell v The State* (1999) 55 WIR 439, PC. In each case, the court could hear the psychiatric evidence and itself make a determination that the appellant at the time of the offence was suffering from diminished responsibility. It follows that the same procedure may be followed if the new evidence relates to insanity.

Appeals involving sentence

On an appeal against conviction, if the Court of Appeal allows the appeal in part so as to substitute the verdict or acquit on part of the indictment as discussed above, most courts in the Commonwealth Caribbean may not impose a more severe sentence than was imposed on the original verdict. The sentence on appeal against conviction, therefore, may only be varied by the Court of Appeal so as to impose a less severe sentence.[37]

If the court on an appeal against conviction dismisses the appeal, the sentence is not varied. On an appeal against sentence, on the other hand, the Court of Appeal:

> shall, if it thinks that a different sentence should have been passed, quash the sentence passed at trial, and pass such other sentence warranted in law by the verdict (whether more or less severe) in substitution therefor as it thinks ought to have been passed and in any other case shall dismiss the appeal.[38]

This provision exists both in those jurisdictions where the prosecution has no right of appeal and in others where the prosecution now has a right of appeal against sentence. It is clear, therefore, that it applies to an appellant who has appealed against the severity of his sentence. The provision permits a Court of Appeal in such case to vary the sentence to one of greater severity. This is, indeed, a punitive power granted to the Court of Appeal and it has been exercised in cases of appeal against sentences for offences related to illegal narcotics to increase the sentence. It is arguable that this provision is designed to discourage frivolous

37 An exception is that in Guyana: Court of Appeal Act, Cap 3:01, s 13(3), as amended by Act No 21 of 1978, which permits variation just as on an appeal against sentence.

38 This same provision exists in the Criminal Appeal legislation throughout the Commonwealth Caribbean: Antigua: Eastern Caribbean Supreme Court Act, Cap 143, s 40(4); Bahamas: Court of Appeal Act, Ch 40, s 12(3), as amended by Act 26 of 1996; Barbados: Criminal Appeal Act, Cap 113A, s 14; Dominica: Eastern Caribbean Supreme Court (Dominica) Act, Chap 4:02, s 38(4); Grenada: West Indies Associated States Supreme Court (Grenada) Cap 336, s 41(3);

Guyana: Court of Appeal Act, Cap 3:01, s 13(3);

Jamaica: Judicature (Appellate) Jurisdiction Act, s 14(3);

St Kitts and Nevis: Eastern Caribbean States Supreme Court (Saint Christopher, Nevis) Act, Cap 3:11, s 44(4);

St Lucia: West Indies Associate States Supreme Court (Saint Lucia) Act No 17 of 1969, s 35(3);

St Vincent: Eastern Caribbean States Supreme Court (Saint Vincent and the Grenadines) Act, Cap 24, s 40(7);

Trinidad and Tobago: Supreme Court of Judicature Act, Chap 4:01, s 44(3).

appeals against sentence. On the other hand, it may serve to discourage defendants who have justifiable grounds from exercising their rights for fear of an increased sentence.

In *Williams v The State* (2005) 66 WIR 313, PC, the Privy Council, in an appeal from Trinidad and Tobago, considered the case of a police officer who, having been convicted of rape and sentenced to 25 years, had his sentence increased to 30 years on appeal. The Board found that since the Court of Appeal had refused the appellant leave to appeal against sentence the court had no jurisdiction to increase the sentence. Such a power only arose where there was an appeal before them and refusal to grant leave meant that there was no valid appeal. Further the Board was quite emphatic that

> an appellate court which has power to increase a sentence and is considering the exercise of that power should invariably give the applicant leave to appeal against sentence or his counsel an indication to that effect and an opportunity to address the court on the increase or to ask for leave to withdraw the application.

In *Marco Oliver v R* (2007) 70 WIR 1, PC, the Privy Council reiterated these principles in an appeal from the Bahamas. The practical effect of these decisions therefore is that the court's power to increase a sentence on appeal will be rendered nugatory since any appellant faced with the choice of an increased sentence or withdrawal of the appeal will invariably withdraw.

It is also now settled that where the prosecution appeals against an unduly lenient sentence the respondent to the appeal (the convicted person) is entitled to be present at the hearing and to be legally represented: *Campbell v R* (2006) 69 WIR 26, PC.

Computation of sentence

Once the Court of Appeal affirms a conviction and stipulates a sentence of imprisonment, the next question is: from when is the term of the sentence deemed to run? Legislation across the region varies as to what should be the norm.

In some jurisdictions, if leave to appeal was granted by the Court of Appeal or the trial judge certified that the case was one fit for appeal against conviction, time in custody pending determination of the appeal must be reckoned as part of the term of the sentence. Otherwise, the time may be counted at the discretion of the Court of Appeal. If the court directs otherwise, it must give reasons for so doing.[39]

In contrast, statute in other jurisdictions such as the Bahamas, Jamaica and Trinidad and Tobago provides that the sentence shall be deemed to run from the date on which the appeal is determined, or the day the application for leave is refused, or the day the appellant is returned in custody, if he is on bail, after the appeal is determined. These provisions[40] on computation of sentence are therefore much harsher than in other jurisdictions.

The provisions[41] in this regard in Barbados and Guyana are more detailed, but are similar to those of Antigua and like jurisdictions. In general, time in custody will be counted as part of the sentence except that six weeks of the time in custody after conviction may be disregarded on computing the term. If, however, leave was granted to appeal or the trial

39 See statutory provisions to this effect in: Antigua: Cap 143, s 47 (above); Dominica: Chap 4:02, s 45 (above); Grenada: Cap 336, s 48 (above); St Kitts and Nevis: Cap 3:11, s 51 (above); St Lucia: Act No 17 of 1969, s 42 (above); St Vincent: Cap 24, s 47 (above).

40 As in: Bahamas: Ch 40, s 25(3) (above); Jamaica: Judicature (Appellate) Jurisdiction Act, s 31(3); Trinidad and Tobago: Chap 4:01, s 49(1) (above).

41 Barbados: Cap 113A, s 33 (above); Guyana: Cap 3:01, s 18 (above).

judge certified the case as fit for appeal, the entire period in custody shall be counted in computing the term of the sentence.

The legislation suggests that an appellant from the Bahamas, Jamaica or Trinidad and Tobago who appeals against sentence may suffer a harsher fate than his counterpart in other jurisdictions if his appeal is dismissed: *Jagessar and Bhola Nandlal v The State* (No 2) (1990) 41 WIR 373.

In *Kumar Ali v The State; Leslie Tiwari v The State* (2005) 67 WIR 309 in considering two appeals on sentence from Trinidad and Tobago that were heard together, the Board examined the issue of how appellate courts should determine the date from which an appellant's sentence should run, if his appeal is dismissed. The Board considered the implications of Section 49(1) of the Supreme Court of Judicature Act, which it recognised, mirrored the Section 14 (3) of the repealed English Criminal Appeal Act 1907. The Board also emphasised that most Caribbean jurisdictions emulated the modern English law in this area, which had reversed the presumption that a sentence should run from the date of dismissal. The Privy Council held that a Court of Appeal should consider each case in the light of the relevant facts in deciding whether to exercise a discretion whether to backdate. The Board was firm that orders backdating sentences should not be restricted to exceptional cases. Furthermore, it was wrong to take into account the heinous nature of the offence as a factor in determining if to backdate. In the instant matters the Board found that in the case of Tiwari it could not be said that his appeal was so devoid of merit as to justify loss of time and in the case of Ali no account had been taken of the fact that the hearing of his appeal was delayed through no fault of his by four years. Both appellants' sentences were backdated to the date of conviction.

It is clear from the *Ali–Tiwari* judgment therefore, that the law on computation of sentences following the dismissal of an appeal will now be guided by the same principles throughout the region. This position was affirmed in the more recent judgment of *Young v The State* (2008) 74 WIR 467, PC. The issue arose in that case as to whether the time between conviction and appeal should count as part of the time served if the appeal is devoid of merit. The Board reiterated that orders backdating sentences to the date of conviction should not be restricted to exceptional cases and affirmed its decision in *Tiwari* that where an appeal is devoid of merit the appellate court 'should impose a penalty for bringing or persisting with a frivolous application which fairly reflects the need to discourage wasting the court's time without inflicting an unfairly long extension of imprisonment upon the applicant'. In other words, the court could order 'loss of time' in a proportionate manner. In *Young* the Board did not conclude that the appeal was devoid of merit contrary to the finding of the Court of Appeal so the sentence was ordered to run from the date of conviction.

Despite the Board's concession that loss of time is possible it is difficult to imagine, consequent on the decisions of *Tiwari* and *Young*, that the Board would ever be likely to consider it fair to order a sentence to run from the date of the dismissal of an unsuccessful appellant's appeal.

Prosecution appeal

In the few jurisdictions where the prosecution now has a right to appeal from an order on an indictable trial if the appeal is allowed, the Court of Appeal has few recourses. The court has no power to substitute a conviction for an acquittal, so where an appeal against acquittal or other related order succeeds, it may only order a retrial. A successful appeal by the prosecution against sentence entitles the Court of Appeal to vary the sentence to more or less severe, just as on appeal by a convicted person who appeals against severity of sentence.

BASES FOR ALLOWING AN APPEAL

While counsel for the appellant may argue many grounds of appeal, each ground should be crafted so as to enable him to contend that one of the statutory grounds for allowing the appeal has been satisfied. Alternatively, counsel may argue that the cumulative effect of several misdirections or irregularities support one of the statutory grounds for allowing the appeal. In general, there are three grounds for allowing an appeal as stipulated in statute across the region. A conviction may only be quashed if one of the grounds as stipulated in statute is satisfied: *DPP v Shannon* [1974] 3 Env LR 144, HL; *DPP v White* (1977) 26 WIR 482, PC.

Question of law

In all jurisdictions, the Court of Appeal may allow an appeal on the basis that the judgment of the court before which the appellant was convicted should be set aside on the ground of a wrong decision in law. A wrong decision in law could be one to allow inadmissible evidence to be admitted or to refuse to make an order for separate trials where the justice of the case so requires. A failure to put the defence adequately or at all: *R v Badjan* (1966) 50 Cr App R 141, or unsatisfactory directions on how to treat identification evidence: *Reid, Dennis and Whylie v R* (1989) 37 WIR 346, PC, admits of an error in law. In *Moses v The State* (1996) 49 WIR 455, PC, it was held that an incorrect direction in law was given by the trial judge when he directed the jury on the application of the felony-murder rule in a trial in Trinidad and Tobago where felonies had been abolished. The error in *Moses* is a rare example of a direction that could be said to satisfy the only ground for allowing an appeal: a wrong decision on a question of law. In general, most successful grounds of appeal may satisfy more than one ground for allowing the appeal.

Unsafe or unsatisfactory

In most Commonwealth Caribbean jurisdictions, a conviction may be quashed if the verdict of the jury is found to be 'unsafe or unsatisfactory' in all the circumstances. This is in keeping with the appellate powers of the English Court of Appeal under s 3 of the Criminal Appeal Act 1968 (before it was amended by the Criminal Appeal Act 1995 to read just 'unsafe'). Guyana, Jamaica and Trinidad and Tobago retain the old ground[42] under the English Criminal Appeal Act 1907, which legislation they followed. This is that a conviction may be quashed if the verdict of the jury is 'unreasonable or cannot be supported having regard to the evidence' (s 4(1)). Section 12 of the Court of Appeal Act, Ch 40, of the Bahamas as amended by Act No 26 of 1996, contains both grounds.

The test to be applied in deciding if a conviction is unsafe or unsatisfactory is whether in the whole of all of the circumstances of the trial, the Appeal Court has a 'lurking doubt' as to the correctness of the conviction: *R v Cooper* (1969) 53 Cr App R 82. Many matters may contribute to this determination: some actual irregularity, mistake of law or weakness in the case for the prosecution, among others. The reaction of the court need not be based strictly on the evidence but may be caused by the 'general feel of the case': *John v R* (1994) 47 WIR 122. In that case, the Court of Appeal of the Eastern Caribbean States applied *Cooper* and

42 The effect of the two provisions was considered by the Privy Council in *Daley v R* [1993] 4 All ER 86, PC, an appeal from Jamaica.

held that, considering all the circumstances of the verdict, including the evidence and the summing up, they were left in doubt as to whether justice was done by the verdict of guilty. The conviction was quashed on the basis that it was unsafe or unsatisfactory.

This ground thus enables the Court of Appeal to consider any matter including the evidence in deciding the conviction is unsafe or unsatisfactory.

Unreasonable or cannot be supported

The old English ground for allowing an appeal, which still exists in Guyana, Jamaica and Trinidad and Tobago, provides that an appeal may be allowed if the verdict of the jury is 'unreasonable or cannot be supported having regard to the evidence'.[43] In *Daley v R* [1993] 4 All ER 86, PC, the Privy Council stated that this provision was understood to mean that an appellate court would intervene to quash a conviction only if there was no evidence on which a properly directed jury could convict. It is evident, then, that this ground is narrower than the newer ground that a conviction should be quashed if the verdict is unsafe or unsatisfactory. This latter ground entitles the appellate court to quash a conviction even if there is evidence once the court has a lurking doubt or feels uncomfortable about the conviction.

To succeed on the ground that the verdict is unreasonable or cannot be supported having regard to the evidence, it is insufficient for an appellant to show that the case against him is weak: *R v McNair* (1908) 2 Cr App R 2. Even if members of the court feel some doubt as to the correctness of the verdict, this is insufficient to allow an appeal on this ground: *R v Crook* (1910) 4 Cr App R 60; *R v Graham* (1910) 4 Cr App R 210. The decisions are in contrast to the decision in *Cooper* (above), where it was held that such doubt was sufficient to allow an appeal on the ground that the verdict is unsafe or unsatisfactory.

As discussed in Chapter 14, in analysing *Daley* (above), the approach in considering a submission of no case[44] is to consider whether there is any evidence on which a properly directed jury could properly convict. This approach is founded on the interpretation of the provision that a verdict will be quashed if it is unreasonable or unsupported by the evidence. The approach of the Court of Appeal in deciding whether to quash a conviction on this ground ought to be the same. The court ought only to quash a conviction on this ground if there is evidence on which a reasonable jury if properly directed could have convicted. This is so even if the evidence in the opinion of the appellate court is 'thin': *Taibo v R* (1996) 48 WIR 74, PC. The Court of Appeal ought not to substitute its own view of the evidence for that of the jury unless the jury's verdict is clearly perverse.

R v Nembhard (1974) 22 WIR 362 is an example of a rare instance when a Court of Appeal (of Jamaica) allowed an appeal on this ground alone. In that case, N was convicted for the murder of his young son and sentenced to death. The doctor who examined the body did only an external examination. He gave as his opinion that death was from a broken neck. He did not dissect the body, however, but opined that death could alternatively have resulted from asphyxiation caused by an indentation on the back of his neck. He could not say what caused the indentation. The defence was that, when being carried by the appellant, the child had fallen and suffered injury. The Court of Appeal allowed the appeal. The medical evidence was clearly equivocal in that, while it led to grave suspicion, there was no proof

43 See: Guyana: Court of Appeal Act, Cap 3:0, s 13(1); Jamaica: Judicature (Appellate) Jurisdiction Act, s 14 (1); Trinidad and Tobago: Supreme Court of Judicature Act, Chap 4:01, s 44(1).

44 See Chapter 14, sub-heading 'No-case submission'.

beyond reasonable doubt that the appellant murdered his son. The verdict of guilty of murder was therefore held to be unreasonable on the facts.

Material irregularity

The third basis on which an appeal may be allowed is that there was a material irregularity in the course of the trial. This was the third ground of appeal stipulated in s 2(1) of the English Criminal Appeal Act 1968, which was adopted by most jurisdictions in the Commonwealth Caribbean, replacing the previous ground that there was a miscarriage of justice. This latter ground, miscarriage of justice, is that which still exists in Guyana, Jamaica and Trinidad and Tobago, which countries still retain the provisions identical to s 4(1) of the old Criminal Appeal Act of England 1907.

In *DPP v Shannon* [1974] 3 WLR 155, HL, the House of Lords emphasised that the power to quash a conviction on the ground of material irregularity in the course of the trial is narrower in scope than the power conferred by s 4(1) of the 1907 Act to quash a conviction on the ground that there has been a miscarriage of justice. A material irregularity is usually a procedural irregularity, that is, a mistake in the procedure at trial short of defects in the summing up. Examples of a material irregularity include where a juror improperly separates from others while the jury is sequestered: *Roberts v R* (1968) 13 WIR 50, or where the judge fails to hold an enquiry upon allegations that jurors were tampered with: *R v Blackwell* [1995] 2 Cr App R 625.

Even where there has been a material irregularity (in the jurisdictions which permit this ground for the allowing of appeal), the conviction may not be quashed unless it is shown that the irregularity resulted in a miscarriage of justice (or substantial miscarriage of justice as the case may be): *R v Ash* [1984] Crim LR 45. In that case, the Clerk of the Courts was allowed to explain to the jury how certain cheques, evidence in the case, were categorised, in the absence of the judge, counsel and the defendant. The English Court of Appeal, while stating that it was extraordinary that such a procedure had been adopted, held that, in the absence of any suggestion that anything improper had occurred and in the face of the fact that the evidence was overwhelming, the irregularity, albeit a material irregularity, did not result in a miscarriage of justice.

Miscarriage of justice

In Guyana, Jamaica and Trinidad and Tobago the third basis, following the English Criminal Appeal Act 1907, for allowing an appeal is on any ground that there was a miscarriage of justice, as indicated above. In each case in these jurisdictions, the proviso may be applied if the court considers that there was nevertheless no substantial miscarriage of justice.

As identified in *Shannon* (above), miscarriage of justice is much wider in scope than material irregularity. This occurs by reason of a mistake, omission or irregularity on the trial of the appellant. A miscarriage of justice therefore includes a material irregularity. In *R v Haddy* (1944) 29 Cr App R 182, the English Court of Appeal stated that a 'substantial miscarriage of justice', within the meaning of the proviso in the 1907 Act, occurred where by reason of a mistake, omission or irregularity during the trial the appellant has lost a chance of acquittal which was fairly open to him.

The conjoint effect of the miscarriage of justice ground and the proviso in those jurisdictions that retain the 1907 provision, then, is very similar to the meaning attributed to where a verdict is found to be 'unsafe or unsatisfactory', discussed above in *R v Cooper*

(1969) 33 Cr App R 82. In that case it was held that a verdict may be considered unsafe or unsatisfactory if, considering all the circumstances and evidence in the trial, the court is left in doubt as to whether justice was done by the verdict of guilty.

The effect of the different statutory bases

It follows, then, that the decision by the Court of Appeal in the various jurisdictions whether to allow on a criminal appeal is, in the final analysis, the same. The central issue is whether the verdict of guilty can properly stand having regard to the errors, irregularities and the evidence given in the trial of the appellant. If the appellant can be said to have lost the fair chance of an acquittal in that there is a lurking doubt as to whether justice was done, the conviction should be quashed. It will be considered unsafe or unsatisfactory or amounting to a substantial miscarriage of justice.

Lincoln De Four v The State [1999] 1 WLR 1731, PC, is indicative of the fact that the Privy Council considers the same test is applicable in deciding whether to allow a criminal appeal, whether the appellate process of the Court of Appeal relates to substantial miscarriage of justice or that the verdict is unsafe. That case was an appeal from Trinidad and Tobago, where the statutory powers of the Court of Appeal to allow an appeal are as under the 1907 provision. The statutory bases[45] therefore include the finding that a verdict is unreasonable or cannot be supported by the evidence; or where there is a miscarriage of justice; or a wrong decision in law (unless the Court of Appeal finds no substantial miscarriage of justice has resulted). In *De Four*, the Privy Council found that there were two irregularities involving the delivery of the verdict by the jury: the judge imposed a time limit for further retirement and the clerk asked the jury whether they 'wished' to retire. The Board considered that these matters could have constituted pressure on the jury. Accordingly, they considered that 'the conviction was unsafe and should be quashed'.

Although the Privy Council has the same jurisdiction and powers[46] possessed by the Court of Appeal in relation to any case coming before it, the Board made no reference to whether a substantial miscarriage of justice had occurred. It was sufficient to find the conviction 'unsafe', a term that does not appear in the appellate powers granted by statute of the Court of Appeal of Trinidad and Tobago. This type of finding, which is not atypical,[47] makes it clear that in allowing an appeal, courts across the Commonwealth Caribbean are essentially guided by the same test.

FINAL COURT OF APPEAL

The Judicial Committee of the Privy Council was established by the Judicial Committee Act 1833 to hear appeals from colonies and dominions. The Act was later amended by the Judicial Committee Act 1844. Section 24 of the 1833 Act provided for the making of rules by the Privy Council 'regulating the mode, form and time of appeal'. The Rules made

45 See Supreme Court of Judicature Act, Chap 4:01, s 44(1) of Trinidad and Tobago.

46 See, for instance, the Constitution of Trinidad and Tobago, s 109(7), relating to appeals to the Judicial Committee of the Privy Council.

47 In *Crosdale v R* (1995) 46 WIR 278, PC, the Privy Council concluded that the judge's question whether the jury wished to retire was a 'material irregularity'. This term is not contained in the relevant Jamaican provision, which relates to 'miscarriage of justice'.

thereunder are common[48] to all Commonwealth Caribbean countries who, becoming independent, individually accepted the jurisdiction of the Privy Council.

In all but four Commonwealth Caribbean jurisdictions the Judicial Committee of Her Majesty's Privy Council remains the ultimate legal Court of Appeal. In *Mitchell v DPP* (1985) 32 WIR 241, PC, the Privy Council recognised the right of any Member State of the six Caribbean States of the West Indies Associated States to preclude any right of appeal to the Privy Council which was preserved by s 3 of the West Indies Associated States (Appeals to Privy Council) Order 1967 in the West Indies Associated States. Any State may abolish appeals to the Privy Council by amendment of its own Constitution. The Board found that Grenada had in fact done so in relation to that country by Act 1 of 1985.[49] In *Logan v R* [1996] 4 All ER 190, PC, the Privy Council was at pains to point out on an appeal from Belize that the function of the Privy Council can be abolished or modified in Belize only by amending the Constitution.[50] So long as the Constitution remains unamended, no law can validly curtail the constitutional right of citizens to apply to the Judicial Committee for special leave to appeal or the right of the Judicial Committee to grant such an application. The same is obviously true for the rest of the Commonwealth Caribbean.

In April 2005 the Caribbean Court of Justice (CCJ) was formally established. The CCJ is to act as a court of original jurisdiction for most countries in the Caricom in respect of Caribbean Single Market and Economy (CSME) matters on the interpretation and application of the relevant trade treaties. However, it is so far the final Court of Appeal only in respect of Barbados, Belize, Dominica[51] and Guyana. The relevant and necessary legislation in this regard in Jamaica and Trinidad and Tobago has not been passed, although attempts have been made. The first criminal appeal from Barbados was heard in 2006.

Leave to appeal

To the Privy Council

In respect of criminal matters for those jurisdictions who retain the Privy Council, appeal lies with special leave of the Privy Council. This is provided for in the relevant statutory provisions which accepted the jurisdiction of the Privy Council in each jurisdiction. In *Lesmond v R* (No 2) (1967) 10 WIR 259, the appellant sought to contend that the Court of Appeal of the West Indies Associated States had jurisdiction to grant him leave to appeal to Her Majesty in Council (the Privy Council) against a refusal by the Court of Appeal to grant leave to appeal a conviction for murder. The Court of Appeal confirmed that in relation to criminal matters, the Court of Appeal has no jurisdiction to grant such leave.

This point was made clear by the Privy Council itself in relation to an application for special leave to appeal to the Privy Council from an applicant from Barbados: *Holder v R* (1978) 31 WIR 98, PC. In that case, the Court of Appeal of Barbados purported to grant leave to an appellant to appeal against an order for retrial made by the Court of Appeal in allowing his appeal against conviction. The Privy Council starkly made the point that the

48 Judicial Committee (General Appellate Jurisdiction) Rules Order 1982.

49 Appeals to the Privy Council were reinstated in Grenada, on the same terms as before, by Act No 19 of 1991, the Constitutional Judicature (Restoration) Act 1991. Act No 20 of 1991 also re-enacted the West Indies Associated States Supreme Court (Grenada) Act.

50 In 2010 Belize, by Act No 4 of 2010, amended its Constitution to abolish all appeals to the Privy Council, replacing it with the Caribbean Court of Justice.

51 The Constitution of Dominica (Amendment) Act 2014, Act 4 of 2014 allowed appeals to the CCJ.

Court of Appeal of Barbados under its own laws had no power 'to grant leave in a criminal matter and their decision to do so is consequently a nullity'.

In *Logan* (above) the Privy Council considered a case where an appellant whose appeal was dismissed by the Court of Appeal sought leave to appeal to the Privy Council some 15 months afterwards (January 1995), only after his petition to the Governor General to exercise the prerogative of mercy had been dismissed. The Privy Council granted leave and at the hearing of the substantive appeal sometime later, commented on the right of an appellant to seek the exercise of the prerogative as distinct from his right to seek leave to appeal his conviction. The Board acknowledged the judgment of the Court of Appeal in *Lauriano v AG of Belize* (1995) 47 WIR 74 (*Logan*, p 195). In that case the Chief Justice of Belize declared that:

(a) The Privy Council had no jurisdiction to grant special leave to appeal after the expiry of periods of time stipulated in local Rules;
(b) In any event, the Privy Council had no such jurisdiction after a plea of mercy by a man sentenced to death had been rejected by the Advisory Committee.

To do otherwise, the Chief Justice said, would mean that the Privy Council would be seeking to 'arrogate' a power it did not have and that would amount to 'rule by decree by Her Majesty in Council'.

In an unusually strong statement, the Board contended that a confusion between the roles of the Advisory Committee on Mercy and of the Judicial Committee seemed to be at the root of the Chief Justice's decision. The Board made it clear that: 'the Judicial Committee has no function in relation to the prerogative of mercy. What it does have under the Constitution of Belize is the function of being the ultimate legal Court of Appeal'. So long as the Constitution is unamended, no law can validly curtail the constitutional right of the citizens to apply to the Judicial Committee in compliance with the rules made under the 1833 and 1844 Acts. Accordingly, the Privy Council had power to grant special leave to appeal which was not curtailed by a specific time limit for application for such leave. Special leave to appeal would be granted at the discretion of the Privy Council.

The Jamaica Judicature (Appellate) Jurisdiction Act entitles the Court of Appeal to grant leave to the DPP or the defendant to appeal from a decision of the Court of Appeal where the decision involves a point of law of exceptional public importance. Application to the Privy Council for leave to appeal against the decisions of the Court of Appeal is initiated by notice of an intention to apply to the Privy Council for special leave to appeal and evidence of service of the notice supported by affidavit of counsel. This notice is usually filed on both the DPP and the Attorney General. In most cases where the convicted person is a pauper, the State/Crown pays the costs of the petitioner in his appeal to the Privy Council.

Entitlement to appeal to the Privy Council is a constitutionally enshrined right in those countries that have retained its jurisdiction. The laws governing the procedure of appealing to the Privy Council are comprised principally of the Judicial Committee Act.[52] The Judicial Committee (Appellate Jurisdiction) Rules,[53] Practice Directions of the Judicial Committee,[54] and the Constitutions, Orders in Council and relevant legislation of the countries from which appeals are received.

For independent republic countries, namely Trinidad and Tobago,[55] appeals lie to the Judicial Committee of the Privy Council itself. In the other Commonwealth Caribbean

52 The Judicial Committee Act 1844, s 1.
53 Judicial Committee (Appellate Jurisdiction) Rules 2009.
54 Judicial Committee Practice Direction 1, Rule 2.4.
55 Fn 54, Rule 2.4.

territories that retain the Queen as Head of State, namely Antigua and Barbuda, The Bahamas, Grenada, Jamaica, St Kitts and Nevis, St Lucia and St Vincent and the Grenadines, an appeal lies to her Majesty in Council. Leave to appeal to the Privy Council, or to her Majesty in Council as the case may be, lies as of right in limited circumstances. Alternatively, appellants may appeal to the Privy Council with special leave.

Appeal as of right

In all the Commonwealth Caribbean countries which retain the Privy Council as their apex court, appeals lie as of right in the case of final decisions in criminal proceedings which involve a question of interpretation of the constitution.[56] In the Constitutions of Antigua and Barbuda, Jamaica, St Lucia, Grenada, St Kitts and Nevis and St Vincent and the Grenadines identical provisions are found save for the substitution of the words 'Her Majesty in Council' for the words 'the Judicial Committee'.

In instances where an appeal lies as of right, the Court of Appeal must be satisfied that the proposed appeal raises an arguable issue under the statutory or constitutional provision before it grants leave to the appellant to petition the Judicial Committee.[57] Where an appeal lies as of right, the process of first seeking the leave of the court below has been described as a 'gatekeeping exercise' as there is no discretion vested in the Court of Appeal to withhold leave on the ground that the appeal lacks merit.[58] Moreover, where the constitution of a particular territory creates an appeal as of right, the Court of Appeal may not in the exercise of its inherent jurisdiction impose further terms and conditions not contained in legislative instrument conferring that right.[59]

The role of the Court of Appeal in these cases is simply to establish that a right to appeal exists and only impose such conditions as are attendant on the exercise of that right.[60] In criminal cases this means simply determining whether the matter also involves an issue of constitutional interpretation.

Appeal with leave of the Court of Appeal

Appeals may also lie to the Privy Council with the leave of the Court of Appeal in cases as prescribed by Parliament.[61] Similar provisions are common to all Commonwealth Caribbean constitutions listed above, enabling the legislatures of each country to prescribe other categories of cases eligible for transmission to the Privy Council.

Appeal with special leave of the Privy Council

A common theme across the respective constitutions is the preservation of a general right to directly petition the Privy Council for special leave to appeal. This right exists as a discrete

56 In Trinidad and Tobago the relevant provision is Section 109 of the Constitution.

57 *Alleyne-Forte v The Attorney General of Trinidad and Tobago and Others* [1997] UKPC 49.

58 *Griffith v Guyana Revenue Authority and Another* [2007] 3 LRC 324.

59 *Crawford and others v Financial Institutions Services Ltd (Jamaica)* [2003] UKPC 49.

60 *Electrotech Services Ltd v Issa Nicholas (Grenada) Ltd* [1998] 1 WLR 202.

61 Bahamian Constitution, s 105.

entitlement that cannot be circumscribed by Parliament. For example, s 110 of the Jamaican Constitution states:

> (3) Nothing in this section shall affect any right of Her Majesty to grant special leave to appeal from decisions of the Court of Appeal to Her Majesty in Council in any civil or criminal matter.

Identical language is adopted in the constitutions of each of the countries referred to above, the only material exception being Trinidad and Tobago, in which case the constitution provides:

> An appeal shall lie to the Judicial Committee with the special leave of the Judicial Committee from decisions of the Court of Appeal in any civil or criminal matter in any case in which, immediately before the date on which Trinidad and Tobago became a Republic, an appeal could have been brought with the special leave of Her Majesty to Her Majesty in Council from such decisions.

The modification in language was necessary to preserve the right to appeal directly to Her Majesty's Privy Council after the transition to republican status. Ultimately, the Judicial Committee possesses a complete and general discretion whether to grant special leave.[62]

In cases where an appeal lies as of right and the court below withholds leave, the Judicial Committee will only refuse special leave in exceptional cases such as instances where the appeal is wholly devoid of merit.[63]

The Board may also refuse to grant special leave where it considers that the case raises important constitutional issues that are best ventilated by the local courts from which special leave to appeal is sought.[64] Moreover, the fact that the court below has refused to grant leave to appeal to the Privy Council will 'always be a relevant, and often no doubt decisive, consideration for the Board to consider when deciding whether or not to grant special leave'.[65]

Procedure on appeal

The process of appealing to the Privy Council is governed by the Privy Council (Appellate Jurisdiction Rules), Privy Council Practice Directions and Orders in Council in respect of the territories falling under its jurisdiction. An appeal is typically commenced in the court below by an application seeking leave by way of motion or petition within 21 days of the date of the judgment being appealed from.[66] The application may be heard by a single judge of the Court of Appeal and may be granted conditionally with any orders the Court considers necessary and reasonable to impose to ensure the timely preparation and dispatch of the record of appeal for the Privy Council.[67]

In the exercise of this supervisory 'gatekeeping' jurisdiction the Court of Appeal may (after it has granted leave) also dismiss the appeal for want of prosecution if in the Court's

62 Practice Direction 1, Rule 2.1.

63 *Crawford v Financial Institution Services* (fn 59).

64 *Marie and Vencadsamy and others v The Electoral Commissioner, The Electoral Supervisory Commission and The State of Mauritius* [2011] UKPC 45.

65 *Noel Campbell v The Queen (Jamaica)* [2010] UKPC 26.

66 Bahamas (Procedure in Appeals to Privy Council) Order 1964 (S.I. 1964 No. 2042), S. 3; The Trinidad and Tobago (Procedure in Appeals to Privy Council) Order in Council 1962/1976, S. 2.

67 Trinidad and Tobago Order in Council 1962, s 5.

opinion the appellant fails to show due diligence in procuring the record of appeal for transmission to the Privy Council.[68]

If the court below refuses to grant leave to appeal or leave is not obtained, the applicant may seek the permission (or special leave) of the Privy Council to appeal. Rule 11 of the Privy Council Appellate Jurisdiction Rules states that 'An application for permission to appeal must be filed within 56 days from the date of the order or decision of the court below or the date of the court below refusing permission to appeal (if later)'.[69]

Where leave to appeal has been granted by the court below, the procedure is slightly different. In that case, the notice of appeal must be filed within 56 days of the decision of the court below and must be accompanied by a copy of the order granting leave as well as the decision or order appealed.[70] The Privy Council may extend the time for bringing an appeal where the statutory period has expired. An application made out of time must be accompanied by an explanation. The longer the delay in filing, the more convincing and weighty the explanation will need to be. The applicant must satisfy the Board that, having regard to all the circumstances, it is in the interests of justice that the time limit should be extended.[71]

To the CCJ

It is now settled that appeal to the CCJ is not a right in a criminal matter unless the issue revolves around the interpretation of the Constitution. In *R v Lewis* (2007) 70 WIR 75, CCJ (AJ), a case from Barbados, the Crown appealed to the CCJ as of right under s 6(c) of the Caribbean Court of Justice Act 2003 against the decision of the Court of Appeal of Barbados on 5 January 2006 quashing the conviction of the respondent, Mitchell Ken O'Neal Lewis, for murder, setting aside the sentence of death and ordering a retrial. It was raised as a preliminary issue whether the prosecution had the right to appeal as of right in the circumstances. It was held that the right of appeal to the CCJ conferred by s 6(c) of the CCJ Act is available to the prosecution in criminal cases when a conviction has been quashed by the Court of Appeal, just as it is to a person whose conviction has been upheld by that court. In so far as an appeal as of right is concerned, the prosecution only had such a right in criminal proceedings which involved a question as to the interpretation of the Constitution. In the instant matter the Court of Appeal, in reaching its determination, was not engaged in the interpretation of the Constitution and so the Crown was not entitled to appeal as of right against the decision of the Court of Appeal. Section 104 of the Belize Constitution, amended by Act No 4 of 2010, appears to make this clear. Another route to the CCJ in criminal matters appeal is with special leave of the CCJ.[72]

Special leave to appeal to the CCJ

As a general rule, special leave to appeal is required when a convicted person seeks to challenge his/her conviction and/or sentence before the CCJ. The entitlement to seek special leave 'exists independently of whether the applicant enjoys an appeal as of right or

68 Fn 67, s 11.
69 Judicial Committee Rules, Rule 11.
70 Judicial Committee Rules, Rule 18(2).
71 *Carlos Hamilton and Jason Lewis v The Queen* [2012] UKPC 31.
72 Agreement Establishing the Caribbean Court of Justice, Article 25, s 4.

has sought and been refused leave from the Court of Appeal'.[73] In *Andrew Leroy Lovell v The Queen* [2014] CCJ 19 (AJ) the CCJ held that the applicable test in determining whether special leave ought to be granted by the CCJ to appeal a criminal conviction is whether the case merits a further appeal. The court emphasised that in criminal matters that requirement would primarily be met by demonstrating that there is possibility of a miscarriage of justice if special leave is withheld.

In *Tyrone Da Costa Cadogan v The Queen* [2006] CCJ 4 (AJ), the applicant was convicted of murder and his appeal against conviction was dismissed by the Court of Appeal of Barbados. In dismissing his application for special leave to appeal to the CCJ, the court held that the grant of special leave was a matter of discretion. Special leave would be granted where to refuse leave would result in a realistic possibility of a miscarriage of justice.

Special leave may also be granted in the public interest where an 'arguable' point of law of public importance is raised and a full hearing is required to establish accurate precedent.[74]

Procedure and time limits

The procedure governing appeals to the CCJ is set out in Parts 10–11 of the Appellate Rules. As a general rule, an appeal is commenced by filing a notice of appeal (appeal as of right), unless leave has been granted by the court below or special leave to appeal has been granted by the CCJ. Where an appeal lies as of right (as in criminal appeals involving matters involving constitutional issues) the notice of appeal must be filed (in writing) within 42 days of the date of the judgment sought to be appealed. Similarly, an application for special leave to appeal to the CCJ may be made to the CCJ in writing within 42 days of the date of the judgment from which special leave to appeal is sought. If special leave is granted, the applicant must then file his notice of appeal within 21 days of the order of the CCJ. Where leave to appeal to the CCJ has been sought from the appellate court below and consequently refused, the application for special leave to appeal to the CCJ must be filed within 21 days of the refusal.

Appeals out of time

Where the prescribed time for the seeking of special leave to appeal has lapsed, an application for an extension of time to seek special leave must be made demonstrating good and substantial reasons for the variation of the time limits.[75] It was held in the case of *Ramnarine Somrah v The Attorney General of Guyana, The Police Service Commission* [2009] CCJ 5 (AJ) that, additionally, the applicant is required to demonstrate that the appeal has a realistic chance of success. The CCJ also held in *June Blackman aka June Gill v Elma Carmen Gittens – Blackman, Marcia Annette Gittens – Grant* [2014] CCJ 17 (AJ) that, generally, the Court will not excuse non-compliance with the time limits set out in the Appellate Rules unless it is necessary to avert a clear miscarriage of justice. The court further held that, in the absence of an application to extend time, the CCJ has no jurisdiction to entertain an out-of-time application for special leave.

---

73 *Mark Royden Williams v The Director of Public Prosecutions* [2016] CCJ 16 (AJ).

74 *Jippy Doyle v The Queen* [2011] CCJ 4 (AJ).

75 Appellate Rules, Rule 5.4.

Powers of the CCJ

The powers exercisable by the CCJ in its appellate jurisdiction are identical to those possessed by the appellate court in the contracting party from which the appeal is brought. Generally, these powers include the power to quash, set aside or substitute verdicts; substitute sentences; order retrials and grant bail pending the hearing of an appeal.[76]

Renewing the application

Even though a petition for special leave to appeal has been dismissed by the Privy Council, a second petition may be made: *Bethel v The State* (1998) 55 WIR 394, PC. In that case the Board pointed out that there is no procedural bar to a second petition for leave, but the Board would not normally entertain a second petition based upon matters which could have been raised in the first. The Privy Council granted leave on the second petition and treated it as the hearing of the appeal. The case was considered exceptional as it was based on misconduct by the petitioner's counsel at trial, where evidence of such misconduct was only obtained after the first petition for leave has been dismissed. It was in effect in the nature of 'fresh' evidence and, the Board held, justified the decision of the Board to regard the case as exceptional.

It may transpire, even more rarely, that after an appeal has been fully heard and determined by the Privy Council, leave to appeal may be granted to hear a second appeal. Such was the case in *Angela-Ramdeen v The State* (2000) 56 WIR 485, PC, where the Privy Council granted leave to appeal on a second petition to set aside the judgment of the Judicial Committee delivered on 1 December 1999. In that judgment, the Board had dismissed the appellant's appeal against the decision of the Court of Appeal of Trinidad and Tobago affirming her conviction for murder of two young children.

The Privy Council in *Ramdeen* acknowledged that there is a strong authority against the bringing of a second appeal in that there should be finality to legal proceedings. Nonetheless, where compelling fresh evidence is discovered in a case where an appellant is sentenced to death, the interests of justice may demand that the case could be reheard on appeal. In the circumstances, the Board granted leave to appeal without making any decision in the cogency of the evidence in support of the issue of diminished responsibility. It is of note to recall that the House of Lords, some of whose members sit in the Privy Council from time to time, granted leave to appeal and heard a second appeal in *R v Bow Street Metropolitan Stipendiary Magistrate et al. ex p Pinochet Ugarte* (No 2) [1999] 1 All ER 577, HL, when new evidence was discovered that one of the Law Lords had ties with a third party in the case.

Who appeals?

A defendant in a criminal trial is entitled to seek leave to appeal to the Privy Council where his appeal has been dismissed by the Court of Appeal. In Jamaica, the Director of Public Prosecutions or the defendant may, with leave of the Court of Appeal, appeal to the Privy Council from any decision of the court where in the opinion of the court, the decision involves 'a point of law of exceptional public importance and it is desirable in the public interest that a further appeal should be brought': s 35 of the Judicature (Appellate

76 Agreement Establishing the Caribbean Court of Justice, Art 25, s 6.

Jurisdiction) Act. This provision confers an additional right of a defendant to appeal to the Privy Council and a usual right to the DPP to appeal in criminal cases.

This right of the DPP in Jamaica has been exercised on several occasions. One such instance is in *DPP v White* (1977) 26 WIR 482, PC. In that case the Court of Appeal quashed the convictions of the defendant on the basis that the trial amounted to a nullity. The court, however, refused to make an order for acquittal or retrial, holding that it was incompetent to do so since there had in effect been no real trial.

Nevertheless the court, considering the matter to be of exceptional public importance, granted time to appeal to the Privy Council and in doing so certified four questions. The Privy Council answered the certified questions to the effect that the jurisdiction of the Court of Appeal is wholly statutory and in the circumstance it must either order an acquittal or a retrial.

Act No 10 of 1998 of St Kitts and Nevis created a new s 38A, now s 42 to the Eastern Caribbean Supreme Court (Saint Christopher and Nevis) Act Cap 3:11. Sub-section (1) thereof provides that:

> (1) The Director of Public Prosecutions may without leave of Court appeal to the Court of Appeal or the Privy Council against the acquittal of an accused person where the accused has been acquitted by reason of . . . [a list of grounds included].

Those provisions appear to confer on the DPP the right to appeal without leave to the Privy Council against the dismissal of appeal by the Court of Appeal. It is also arguable that this law can be read to mean that the DPP may (unusually) appeal directly to the Privy Council against an acquittal in the High Court.

In Trinidad and Tobago, Act No 28 of 1996[77] created a right of appeal from a decision of the Court of Appeal where the prosecution has appealed the decision at trial. This appeal as of right would seem to accrue to both the defence and the prosecution. This section clearly does not confer on the prosecution an additional right to appeal to the Privy Council from a decision of the Court of Appeal as in Jamaica in cases where the defendant initiates the appellate process.

Act No 4 of 2010 of Guyana amended the Criminal Appeal Act to provide, at Section 33L, for an appeal from a decision of the Court of Appeal 'under this Part' to lie with the Caribbean Court of Justice as of right. The new Part created by the Amendment Act deals with appeals by the DPP so this means that the DPP or accused person, the respondent in the DPP appeal, requires no leave to appeal to the CCJ, just as the DPP of St Kitts and Nevis requires no leave to appeal to the Privy Council. In contrast, however, as indicated above, in the usual type of appeal, those by convicted persons, an appellant to either the CCJ or the Privy Council requires leave of the court.

The existing right of the prosecution

In *Krishna Persad and Ramsingh Jairam v The State* (2001) 58 WIR 433, PC, the appellants appealed against a decision of the Trinidad and Tobago Court of Appeal to order a (second) retrial for murder. In the course of its judgment, the Privy Council referred to the 'cross-appeal' of the State in which a restoration of the convictions had been suggested. This was the first time in recent history in Trinidad and Tobago that the historic right of the prosecution to appeal to the Privy Council (not based on statute as in Jamaica) had been exercised.

77 Now Section 650 of the Supreme Court of Judicature Act, Chap 4:01.

This right of appeal by the Crown in a criminal matter was confirmed in *AG for Ceylon v Perera* [1953] AC 200, PC.[78] In that case, it was held that Her Majesty in Council (the Privy Council) has power to entertain an appeal from any dominion or dependency of the Crown 'in any matter, whether civil or criminal, by whichever party to the proceedings the appeal is brought, unless that right has been expressly removed': p 203.

Commonwealth Caribbean jurisdictions that allow appeals[79] to the Privy Council have not expressly renounced the right of the prosecution, the Crown or State, to appeal to the Privy Council. In fact, the various constitutions preserve the right of appeal to the Privy Council with special leave of the Privy Council, from any decision of the Court of Appeal in any criminal matter. The right of appeal is preserved to any party in a criminal matter,[80] as in a civil matter.

However, within recent memory the prosecution has not exercised this historical right to initiate an appeal to the Privy Council. In *Persad and Jairam* (above), the appeal by the State was in fact a cross-appeal. Many jurists in the Caribbean are reluctant to accept that the prosecution should still exercise this right as they feel that it can be said to have fallen into desuetude.

The appeal

In exercising its jurisdiction to hear an appeal, the Privy Council has all the jurisdictions and powers possessed by the Court of Appeal in relation to the case. It considers the same grounds of appeal and determines an appeal on the same statutory bases. If fresh evidence is sought to be tendered, however, the Privy Council remits the case to the Court of Appeal with directions to hear the evidence itself[81] or to determine if the evidence should be admitted.[82]

While it may seem obvious that where a convicted person appeals against conviction or sentence to the Privy Council the prosecution must appear at the hearing, the Board has had to reiterate this more than once. In *R v Eiley and others* [2009] UKPC 40 the appellants who had been convicted of murder appealed against the dismissal of their appeals, by the Court of Appeal of Belize, to the Privy Council. At the hearing before the Privy Council the prosecution did not appear. The Board observed,

> Prosecuting authorities of countries that have preserved the right of appeal to Her Majesty in Council should recognise the importance that the Board attaches to receiving appropriate assistance where appeals are brought against criminal convictions, especially where these are against convictions for an offence as serious as murder.

The role of the Privy Council is not to act as a second court of criminal appeal: *Gayle v R* (1996) 48 WIR 287, PC, an appeal from Jamaica. Matters such as weight to be given to evidence, inferences that may legitimately be drawn from the evidence and whether a presumption or final burden of proof has been discharged are matters to be determined by the local court of appeal. Save in exceptional circumstances, the Privy Council will not enter

78 Following *AG v Bertrand* (1867) LR 1 PC 520.

79 As do most except for Guyana.

80 See the following provisions of the Constitutions of: Antigua: s 122(3); Bahamas: s 105; Barbados: s 88; Dominica: s 106(3); Grenada: s 104(3); Jamaica: s 110(3); St Kitts and Nevis: s 99(3); St Lucia: s 108(3); St Vincent: s 99(3); Trinidad and Tobago: s 109(3).

81 As in *Williams v R* (No 1) (1998) 53 WIR 162, PC.

82 See *Campbell v The State* (1999) 55 WIR 439, PC.

into a re-hearing of these issues. In essence, then, the Privy Council is not expected to duplicate the role of the Court of Appeal or the trial court. Questions relating to evaluation of the evidence are considered essentially a matter for the local courts: *John et al. v DPP* (1982) 32 WIR 230, PC. In *Baughman v R* (2000) 56 WIR 198, PC, in a split decision, the Privy Council dismissed an appeal from the Court of Appeal of the Eastern Caribbean States on a conviction for murder. The Board emphasised that in the absence of new evidence or an argument not considered by the courts below, an appellant, to be successful before the Privy Council, needed to show some error of law or of principle by the Court of Appeal. On the most favourable view of the appellant's arguments, all that had been shown was that there was more than one view as to the strength of the prosecution case. That was insufficient, as the Privy Council would not generally review the evidence.

Generally, the Privy Council will not review the order of the Court of Appeal to order a retrial: *Holder* (above), nor a decision to apply the proviso: *Stafford and Carter v The State* (1998) 53 WIR 417, PC. In the latter case, the Privy Council nevertheless stated that it would reconsider the application of the proviso where the Court of Appeal appeared to have misdirected itself in important respects. The Privy Council considered that the Court of Appeal had misdirected itself on the principles relating to the abolition of felony-murder rule in *Stafford and Carter* and allowed the appeal in part, substituting verdicts of manslaughter for murder.

More recently, in *Krishna Persad and Ramsingh Jairam v The State* (2001) 58 WIR 433 PC, the Privy Council considered a case where the appellant had appealed against the decision of the Court of Appeal to order a retrial. In that case, on a third trial, the appellants were convicted for murder in 1995 which had been committed in 1985. At the appeal in 1998, the Trinidad and Tobago Court of Appeal recognised that the prosecution had failed to disclose material relating to charges and disciplinary proceedings at the time pending against a crucial prosecution witness, a police inspector. Without actually hearing the appeal, the Court of Appeal allowed the appeal and ordered a retrial. The court said they were not hearing the matter, but made the order nevertheless. Both the appellants and the State appealed. The appellants appealed against the propriety of ordering a retrial in the circumstances and the State against the jurisdiction of the Court of Appeal to make any such order in the circumstances.

In remitting the case back to the Court of Appeal, the Board asserted:

(a) The determination of the consequences of setting aside the conviction and sentence is a distinct and separate exercise from the decision to set aside. The decision to quash a conviction should not be influenced by considerations of the propriety of ordering a new trial.

(b) The court had power to quash the conviction and sentence and order a new trial if they felt the trial was unfair, but there should be some indication of the reasons for ordering a new trial.

(c) The Board itself would not determine the substance of the two appeals but would remit the case back to the Court of Appeal to consider whether there was a miscarriage of justice, and whether the provision should be applied or a new trial ordered.

(d) In deciding whether to order a new trial, the Court of Appeal should take into account the fact that 15 years had passed since the date of the verdict.

It is clear from *Persad and Jairam* that the Privy Council preferred the Court of Appeal itself to examine whether a retrial should be ordered after actually hearing the appeal. Presumably if the court had made the order for retrial after such hearing only then, in the exceptional circumstances of that case, might the Privy Council have reviewed the order.

CHAPTER 18

SENTENCING

A defendant may only be sentenced if he has been found guilty of an offence by the magistrate or the jury as the case may be, or if he has pleaded guilty to the offence. He may then be sentenced in accordance with whatever sentence the law provides for the particular offence. In general, the maximum penalty for an offence is stipulated by the particular statute creating that offence.[1] In addition, an offender is subject to the range of sentences, created by specific legislation, that may apply to all offences, such as probation or community service. As well as summary[2] or indictable procedure, legislation may provide for sentences peculiar to that level of trial.

This chapter will focus on the principles that are applied by the court in determining which sentence to fix in any particular instance and the range of sentencing options available. Before that, however, it is relevant to consider the procedure to be adopted by the court after the finding or the admission of guilt by a defendant.

PROCEDURE ON SENTENCING

Before sentence is passed on a defendant in an indictable trial, the allocutus must first be put to him. This is a direct invitation to mitigate. He is asked by the relevant court official whether he has anything to say as to why sentence should not be passed on him in accordance with the law. Statute[3] in some jurisdictions specifically includes this requirement as part of the procedure prior to sentencing. Where this is so and the allocutus is not put, any subsequent sentence passed is void and the defendant remains unsentenced: *R v Porter* (1961) 3 WIR 551, a decision from the Federal Supreme Court arising from Trinidad and Tobago. Furthermore, it is arguable that a sentence passed in such circumstances, even in jurisdictions without such a statutory provision, is not a valid sentence. This is because the defendant has been denied his inherent right to mitigate the harshness of a probably serious sentence.

At trial in the magistrates' court, a formal allocutus is not usually put to the defendant, but he is asked whether he has anything to say in mitigation. It is important that an unrepresented defendant be invited by the magistrate to make a plea in mitigation of his sentence, since he may not be aware of this privilege. Where a defendant is represented, while the magistrate need not specifically invite counsel to mitigate on his client's behalf, he must certainly do nothing to stop him.

Mitigation

The plea in mitigation is made either by counsel if the defendant is represented or by the defendant himself if he is not. If the sentence is one fixed by law, as in the case of murder, in Barbados and Trinidad and Tobago the defendant will usually say nothing, although he should

---

1 As, e.g., offences constituted in the Offences Against the Persons Act or the Larceny/Theft Act in most jurisdictions. Otherwise, Criminal Codes may provide for the creation and sentencing of common offences.

2 As in Summary Courts Act, Chap 4:20, s 71 of Trinidad and Tobago, which relates to a magistrate's power to discharge an offender absolutely or conditionally.

3 As in Criminal Procedure Code, Ch 91, Bahamas, s 183; Criminal Procedure Act, Chap 12:02, s 46(1), Trinidad and Tobago.

be invited to say why sentence should not be passed on him in accordance with the law: *Porter* (above). The defence in the plea in mitigation will usually attempt to relate the principles of sentencing to the defendant's particular situation in an attempt to secure the least harsh sentence for the defendant. Where appropriate, mitigating circumstances in the commission and investigation of the crime itself may be pointed out. These may include the fact that no violence was actually used (for example, in a robbery) or that the defendant pleaded guilty.

It is not unusual for the defence to call character witnesses to testify as to the good standing of the defendant in the community or to his change of character from the time of commission of the offence, as the case may be. Reference may be made to the family background of the defendant, including any dependants he may have. On occasion, at the request of the defence or on its own initiative, the court may direct that a probation report be prepared as to the background of the defendant and the circumstances of the commission of the offence. The court may then utilise this report in determining what sentence should be imposed. This is a frequent occurrence where the defendant is a child or a young person.

Newton hearing

Where a defendant pleads guilty, but there is a conflict on questions of fact between the defence and the prosecution as to the circumstances of the commission of the offence, the court must accept the defence account or hold an enquiry into the facts of the offence: *R v Newton* (1983) 77 Cr App R 13. This is not to say that the court will accept the guilty plea where the defence version admits of a valid defence to the charge. In such a case, the plea will be considered equivocal:[4] *Lewis v Commissioner of Police* (1969) 13 WIR 186. If the defendant's explanation does not amount to a possible defence, but his version of the facts is inconsistent with that of the prosecution, the court should hold an enquiry if the discrepancy may significantly affect the sentence (though not the verdict). This usually will be the case where the defence denies aggravating features of the offence (such as being armed during a rape). A *Newton* hearing is effectively a trial within a trial for the express purpose of resolving such differences. Although usually utilised at indictable trial, there is no reason why this procedure may not be adopted in the magistrates' court as well, where the court may listen to evidence to resolve the issue.

The procedure is set out in *Newton* (above) as elaborated in *Tolera* (1999) 1 Cr App R 29. Once the prosecution and/or the court feels unable to accept the defence version, evidence should be called to resolve the conflicts. The issues needing resolution should be crystallised by the trial judge: *R v Beswick* (1995) 160 JP 33. It has been held that during the course of such an enquiry, evidence is called in the normal way and the rules of evidence should be followed: *R v Gandy* (1989) 11 Cr App R(S) 564. The prosecution may call any witness they wish and the witness may be cross-examined by the defence. The defendant would usually give evidence consistent with his version of the facts and his evidence may be challenged by the prosecutor. It is for the prosecution to prove beyond a reasonable doubt that the defence version is wrong. The judge is the trier of facts in a *Newton* hearing and determines which version he accepts, bearing in mind the usual burden and standard of proof. He must consider whether the matters put forward really amount to a contradiction of the prosecution case or merely go towards mitigation. If the judge rejects the defence version, he may then proceed to sentence in the usual way and his decision will rarely give rise to a basis of appeal: *R v Ahmed* (1984) 6 Cr App R(S) 391. Furthermore, any discount that the judge may have been minded initially to give to the defendant for pleading guilty may be reduced: *Beswick* (above).

4 See Chapter 6 in this regard.

In *Tolera* (above) the English Court of Appeal differentiated between a situation where a defendant gives an account different from that of the prosecution to the court, and one given to a probation officer for the purposes of a pre-sentence report. In the latter situation, the court held, it is unnecessary for the sentencing judge to pay attention to the part of the report which conflicts with the prosecution case unless the defendant expressly draws reference to it and asks that it be treated as a basis for sentencing. The prosecution should be forewarned of this request by the defence. If the issue of fact is contested, then the matter should be determined at an enquiry by calling evidence. In *Tolera*, the Court of Appeal approved the procedure set out by the judge in this regard in a case where the judge did not accept the defendant's version of facts contained in the pre-sentence report.

Taking offences into consideration

It is a recognised practice that offences which have not been tried may be 'taken into account' in imposing sentence for some other offence of which an accused person has been found guilty or to which he has pleaded guilty. This was recognised by the Guyana Court of Appeal in *State v Vibert Hodge* (1976) 22 WIR 303 as a procedure which has been given statutory recognition at indictable trial in that jurisdiction. Otherwise, as in England and in most Commonwealth Caribbean jurisdictions, this is a procedure which has no statutory underpinning: *James Murphy v The State* (1996) 50 WIR 457, a decision of the Court of Appeal of Trinidad and Tobago. It is available at both indictable and summary trial. In *Hodge* (above), it was held that the trial judge was wrong to have allowed an accused person to plead guilty to six other outstanding charges (not before the court) after he had been convicted of the offence with which he had been tried. The correct procedure would have been merely to ask the accused person if he admitted guilt on the outstanding matters as opposed to pleading guilty. If he did, the court would have considered that, but would sentence him only in respect of the offence for which he had been tried and found guilty. This was 'taking the offences into consideration'. In *Murphy* (above) the Court of Appeal of Trinidad and Tobago sought to distinguish *Hodge* on the basis that in that case the defendant was unrepresented and the trial judge had adopted a course at variance with that which the accused person wished or intended. The defendant had wanted the other offences to be taken into account without actually pleading to them. In *Murphy*, on the other hand, the Court of Appeal said, the defendant was represented and had been advised by counsel. In upholding the procedure adopted by the trial judge, the Court of Appeal said that it was clear that the defendant actually wished to plead guilty to the other offences as a manifestation of his contrition. On the facts of *Murphy*, it is difficult to appreciate this reasoning of the court. The defendant had been found guilty of breaking and entering a fast food outlet. Counsel asked for time to persuade his client to 'take a certain course' in relation to two other pending matters, to wit: office breaking and entering, and larceny of a motorcar. To these offences the defendant eventually pleaded guilty. The trial judge taking this plea into account and also his previous convictions for arrestable offences sentenced the defendant to 12 years' imprisonment (the usual maximum of 10 years being increased to any term of years because of the previous indictable convictions)[5] on the main offence and five years each in respect of the others, the sentences to run consecutively. The defendant would therefore be liable to serve 20 years' imprisonment. There was no benefit that accrued to the defendant from having pleaded guilty to the other offences. It is hard to

5 Criminal Procedure Act, Chap 12:02, s 50, Trinidad and Tobago. Such a provision is common to the Commonwealth Caribbean.

believe that contrition alone would have caused him to want to plead guilty to his disadvantage rather than having these offences taken into consideration.

The practice of taking offences into consideration allows for a defendant to admit outstanding offences to the court who will take them into account in pronouncing sentence on the offence on the indictment. In so doing, the court may give a longer sentence than it would usually give if it were considering only the charge on the indictment. While the sentence passed by the court is passed only for the offence in the indictment before the court, the actual sentence reflects an acknowledgment of the fact that the defendant is guilty of other offences. There is no conviction on the offences taken into consideration, but it will constitute an abuse of process to attempt to proceed on them subsequently: *R v Nicholson* (1947) 32 Cr App R 98. It is evident, therefore, that the defendant in *Murphy* (above) secured no benefit from the alternative procedure of pleading guilty separately to the different offences to which he was separately sentenced, such sentences to run consecutively.

The procedure to have offences taken into consideration is first for the prosecution to prepare a list of charges which the defendant has outstanding. This list will be served on the defendant, who will indicate, after time for consideration, to which offence he admits liability. Only those offences which the court has power to try may be considered. For instance, a judge may not take into account summary offences. In general, the offences must be of a similar kind to that which is on the indictment before the court. It is apparent that it may not be in the public interest to take into consideration an offence of violence to the person in sentencing on an offence involving dishonesty. After the list has been served on the defendant, he must sign to the list or to those offences which he admits. Thereafter, he must admit the offences personally before the court. The court will then proceed to sentence the defendant and must stipulate what offences have been 'taken into consideration' in passing the single sentence.

Role of the prosecution

The prosecutor has a very limited role to play in sentencing. He is expected to be aware of the maximum sentence for the offences on the indictment so as to be able to provide that information to the court, if necessary. As a minister of justice, he should not urge a particular sentence or a severe sentence. In relation to plea bargaining, however, statute, as in Trinidad and Tobago in the Criminal Practice (Plea Discussion and Plea Agreement) Act No 11 of 1999, permits the prosecutor to recommend or agree to a specific sentence on a plea agreement only. This statute so far is rarely used and in the absence of a plea agreement, the prosecutor must act in accordance with the accepted practice.

The prosecutor must have available the record of any previous convictions of the defendant and should produce this to the court at the time for sentencing. If the defendant does not admit to any conviction, it must be proved before the court in any way that is stipulated by statute, but otherwise by the police officer who has charge of the records of the police department or who can attest to the convictions. On occasion, and in the case of an unrepresented defendant, it is not unusual for the prosecutor as a minister of justice to remind the court of any mitigating factor in favour of the defendant who has been found guilty or who has pleaded guilty.

Victim impact statements

The English courts have sanctioned the tendering by the prosecution for consideration by the sentencing court a statement by the victim as to the impact of the offence on him: *AG's*

Reference (No 2 of 1995) (R v S) [1995] Crim LR 835. In fact, in England, the Court of Appeal has even gone to the extreme of saying that in the absence of such evidence, the court should not draw any inference about the harm done to the victim: *O's case* (1992) 14 Cr App R(S) 632. It seems that where the defendant challenges the victim's evidence on this issue, he may be cross-examined as to the matters alleged in the statement: Commentary [1995] Crim LR 836 (to *AG's Reference*, above). It has thus become a growing practice in English courts to admit victim impact statements as matters to which the court should have regard. The use of victim impact statements has been recommended as 'a useful vehicle to enhance justice in adversarial criminal justice systems'.[6]

In 2002 the English Court of Appeal issued its first *Practice Direction* [2002] Cr App R 8 on Victim Impact Statements. This gives formal recognition to the victim's role in sentencing. The Bahamas legislature in Act No 35 of 2011 repealed and replaced s 185 of the Criminal Procedure Code to permit a victim to make representations before sentence is handed down. Victim is stated to mean the person who suffers harm as well as the spouse or relative of such a person.

Although victim statements are not usually tendered in the Commonwealth Caribbean, it is not uncommon for the courts to enquire orally of the victim, after a finding of guilt has been made, as to matters he may wish to raise. In *AG's Reference* (above), the English Court of Appeal disagreed with the trial judge that it was inappropriate for him to receive evidence which would aggravate the impact which the offences had on the victim. The Court of Appeal (despite the absence of statutory sanction for the practice) expressed the view that it was wholly appropriate that a trial judge should receive factual information as to the impact of the offences on a victim. The judge was well equipped to determine what matters were relevant and what were merely inflammatory.

It follows, therefore, that in the Commonwealth Caribbean it is possible to utilise victim impact statements to inform a sentencing decision along the same lines as a probation report. Copies of the statement should be available to the defence, the prosecution and the court. This is entirely in keeping with the international recognition that the victim does have a place in the criminal justice system, other than as a witness.

PRINCIPLES OF SENTENCING

There has always been concern in the region over apparent disparities in sentencing. In addition, it is felt that sentences should demonstrate the expectations of society in inflicting punishment whether as a deterrent or as a purely punitive measure. Over time, certain general principles of sentencing have evolved to reflect these concerns and they serve to guide courts in deciding what sentence to impose.

Five objects

In *Benjamin v R* (1964) 7 WIR 459, Wooding CJ of the Court of Appeal of Trinidad and Tobago accepted as correct a statement in the *Modern Law Review* of September 1964 that there are really five objects which constitute the aims of punishment. They are:

6 Erez, E, 'Who's afraid of the big bad victim' (1999) Crim LR 545, p 555.

(a) Retribution – this is in recognition that punishment is intended to reflect the denouncement by the society and legislature of the offence and the offender.
(b) Deterrence vis à vis potential offenders – the offender must be punished appropriately to deter other like-minded offenders from engaging in that form of deviant behaviour.
(c) Deterrence vis à vis the particular offender – here, the purpose is to seek to ensure that the offender himself is deterred from future criminal conduct by the punishment inflicted on him.
(d) Preventive – this is aimed at preventing the particular offender from offending against the law by incarcerating him.
(e) Rehabilitation – the aim is to rehabilitate the offender so that he may reform his ways to become a contributing member of society.

In *Edwin Farfan v The State* Cr App No 34 of 1980 (unreported) 7 May 1984, a decision of the Court of Appeal of Trinidad and Tobago, it was stated that in some cases one object may be predominant while in other cases other objects may prevail. The court felt that the objects of sentencing (as declared in *Benjamin*) should not be 'overstrained'. Each case must depend on its own circumstances and various factors must be considered by the court in deciding which principle of sentencing should predominate.

Factors to take into account

Among the factors which should be taken into account is the prevalence of the offence in the society. Where the offence is prevalent, the overriding consideration should be deterrence of both potential offenders and the particular offender: *Farfan*. In that case, the court stated that the prevalence of rape in the society (in the 1980s) was such that courts

> owe a duty not only to the victim but indeed to the society as a whole to impose such punishment as would reflect its utter abhorrence of the deed and which at the same time would serve as a deterrent to other would be perpetrators of this abominable crime.

In the English case of *Davies* (1978) 67 Cr App R 207, the court felt that where a solicitor breached his client's trust and used their money to further his business deals, both the retributive and deterrent aspects had to be considered. Despite the fact that the solicitor pleaded guilty and co-operated with the police, the Court of Appeal rejected any consideration that hardship to his family should be a matter for consideration in reducing sentence. The court considered that the solicitor had 'brought all this on himself', that is, being struck off the rolls, having to live on social security and take jobs such as 'playing the piano for somebody and working as a clerk'.

In *Davies*, the court examined what it termed the classical considerations relevant to sentences: retribution, deterrence, prevention and rehabilitation. Lawton LJ expressed the view that the retributive element was an important one in that case. The judge compared the sentence with that which was then imposed on those indulging in organised crime where the approved policy was for sentences of six to eight years, even where the amount of money involved was less than in the current case, where it was £0.26m. It was important to keep a sense of proportion in ensuring proper retribution for the type of crime. As to the deterrent element, the court felt that what had to be maintained was that all persons who are in certain positions of trust must know that if they are in breach of that trust, they must be punished and punished severely. 'No criminal could be in greater breach of trust than a solicitor acting as such', stated Lawton CJ. In the final analysis the court held that it was in the interest of the (legal) profession and the public that the sentences imposed (a maximum of four years) should be upheld. The appeal was dismissed.

Similar sentiments to the English Court of Appeal in *Davies* (above) may have been behind the decision of the trial judge in the trial of Patrick Jagessar and Bhola Nandlal in May 1988 to sentence them to the maximum penalty of two years for corruption. The case involved a magistrate, the first defendant, who solicited and received bribes from the second defendant to dismiss his cases. The Court of Appeal in *Jagessar and Bhola Nandlal v The State* (No 2) (1990) 41 WIR 373 refused to allow calculation of the sentences of the appellants from the date of conviction, 10 May 1988, instead of the date of dismissal of the appeal, 30 June 1989. Despite the fact that the appellants would have served greater than the maximum sentence of two years possible for that crime if sentence were to run from 30 June 1989, the Court of Appeal considered that there were no exceptional circumstances to order otherwise.

Another factor that determines which principle of sentencing should prevail is the nature and circumstances of the offence. In *Farfan* (above), the court considered that the conduct of the appellant was reprehensible. He was the 44-year-old uncle-in-law of the victim, who was 11 years old at the time of the incident. The court said that he had betrayed the confidence reposed on him and felt that the incident could leave psychological scars on the victim for the rest of her life.[7] It is clear that not only should the type of offence be relevant in determining sentence, but the aggravating circumstances as well.

On 7 December 1995 in the trial of Oscar Wilson at the Port of Spain Assizes (Trinidad and Tobago), the defendant was sentenced to six years' imprisonment for unlawful carnal knowledge of an 11-year-old girl. The defendant had pleaded guilty to the offence on facts that could be said to amount to extreme depravity in that the defendant forced the victim to drink his urine after raping her, bit her about her body and robbed her of jewellery and $10 in cash. Yet the trial judge described the 21-year-old man as having committed 'an act of stupidity' and said he felt sorry for him. The judge's sentence and accompanying statements created an uproar in the society and eventually led to the passing of legislation[8] enabling the State to appeal against sentences imposed by trial judges that were perceived to be lenient. The sentence passed on Oscar Wilson in 1995 may be compared with that confirmed by the Court of Appeal in *Farfan* (above) in not unlike circumstances. In the latter case the sentence was 14 years' imprisonment and 15 strokes of the birch.

Another aggravating factor which operates against the defendant would be where he has previous convictions for like or other serious offences. This could lead the court to decide that the offender should be kept away from society as long as possible. In the sentencing of Natasha De Leon in the Port of Spain Assizes (Trinidad and Tobago) on 1 March 2001, the trial judge made this clear. The defendant, who had been found guilty of manslaughter, had a previous conviction for murder for an offence committed in the same month. The trial judge described her as a 'menace to society' who needed 'intense rehabilitation'. The judge said that society needed to be protected from the defendant and sentenced her to life imprisonment, not to be released before the expiration of 20 years.

Conversely, a defendant who has a clean record would be considered less of a danger to society, especially if violence was minimal in the commission of the offence. The court may be more inclined to concern itself with the rehabilitative aspect of punishment along with the basic need for deterrence of other potential offenders. Where a defendant is young, this must

7 It is evident here that the Court of Appeal of Trinidad and Tobago in 1984 was taking into account the impact of the offence on the victim in deciding the sentence.

8 Act No 28 of 1996 of Trinidad and Tobago, the Administration of Justice (Miscellaneous Provisions) Act, amending the Supreme Court of Judicature Act, Chap 4:01.

be a significant consideration, since it may be considered that he has his whole life before him and so should be given a chance. In *R v Bird* (1992) 157 JP 488, the defendant took a vehicle without the consent of the owner and committed several driving offences. The English Court of Appeal weighed the fact that the defendant had accelerated towards police cars and collided with two of them against the fact that he was a young man of only 17 who had pleaded guilty. His custodial sentence of 15 months was substituted for one of 12 months since the mitigating factors were not overwhelming.

Time spent on remand

Where an appellant has spent time in custody awaiting his trial, a sentencing court should factor the time spent into its determination as to what sentence it imposes. In *Mohammed Iqual Callachand et al. v The State* [2008] UKPC 49 the Privy Council made it clear that any such period should be fully taken into account in assessing the length of the sentence to be served from the date of sentencing. Where, however, a defendant deliberately delayed the proceedings to ensure that a large part of whatever sentence he ultimately received would be served on remand or where he is in custody for more than one offence he should not expect the advantage of time spent in custody to be considered.

In *da Costa Hall v R* (2011) 77 WIR 60 the CCJ held, following *Callachand*, that upon sentencing full credit should be given for any time spent in custody prior to sentencing, particularly where conditions endured by prisoners on remand were more onerous than those after sentence. This would be subject to a residual discretion in the sentencing judge not to apply the primary rule, as for example: (i) where the defendant had deliberately contrived to enlarge the amount of time spent on remand; (ii) where the defendant was on remand for some other offence unconnected with the one for which he was being sentenced; (iii) where the period of pre-sentence custody was less than a day or the post-conviction sentence was less than two or three days; (iv) where the defendant was serving a sentence of imprisonment during the whole or part of the period spent on remand; and (v) generally where the same period of remand in custody would be credited to more than one offence. Those examples were not an exhaustive list of instances where the judge might depart from the prima facie rule, and other examples might arise in actual practice.

The court made it clear that the time spent in pre-sentence custody should be taken into account by reduction of the term of the actual sentence passed, as distinct, for instance, from backdating a sentence, as in the case of sentences fixed on appeal.

Double jeopardy in sentencing

Where the prosecution appeals a sentence on the grounds of leniency the appellate court, if it does decide to increase the sentence, may apply a discount to the sentence on the basis of 'double jeopardy'. This discount has been applied by the Barbados Court of Appeal in references by the DPP such as in *DPP's Reference No. 1 of 2003 (R v Skeete)* [2003] 66 WIR 94). In *Attorney General's References Nos. 14 and 15 of 2006 (R v French and Webster)* [2007] 1 Cr App R. (S.) 40 a full court of the English Court of Appeal reconsidered the established principles and said the following:

> 57 Our conclusions thus far would lead us to increase [the respondent's sentence]. ... The question then arises of whether we should make a further reduction to reflect the fact that he has been subject to 'double jeopardy'. The procedure whereby the Attorney-General can seek to refer a sentence for reconsideration by the Court of Appeal on the ground that it is unduly

> lenient was introduced by s. 36 of the Criminal Justice Act 1988. Almost from the start it has been the practice of the Court, when considering whether to substitute a heavier sentence and, if so, the length of such sentence, to have regard to the fact that the procedure subjects the defendant to anxiety which should normally be reflected by some discount in the sentence which would otherwise be imposed. This consideration has been described as 'double jeopardy'.
>
> 59 The principle is recognised not only in this jurisdiction but in a number of other common law jurisdictions where the prosecution enjoys a right to appeal against sentence. In this jurisdiction the practice of giving a discount from what would otherwise be the appropriate sentence to reflect double jeopardy is well established where this Court increases a sentence on a reference by the Attorney-General. The range of discount is wide, generally lying between 12 per cent and 30 per cent.

Pleading guilty

It is always a mitigating factor if the defendant pleads guilty. This saves the court time and expense, both of which are relevant considerations. More importantly, the fact that the defendant has waived his right to require the prosecution to prove its case may be taken to be indicative of remorse and/or a desire to reform. This itself might influence the court in favour of the defendant in that the court might feel that there is little need to keep the defendant away from society or to deter him from committing further crimes. In *Farfan* (above), the term of imprisonment was reduced from 20 years to 14 years because of the plea of guilty. Thus, while there is no set discount for a plea of guilty in statutory rules in the Commonwealth Caribbean, the practice is that in determining the appropriate sentence recognition is always given to a guilty plea. Where a defendant pleads guilty, his sentence should be less, all things being equal, than that of a co-defendant who is found guilty on trial. The defendant is entitled to a sentence discount for saving the parties in the criminal justice system time and expense and the victim the trauma of giving evidence.[9]

In *Tyack v The State* [2006] UKPC 18 the Privy Council clarified that the proper starting point in sentencing is the normal range of sentences for the particular offence and not the maximum sentence. The Board also acknowledged that a defendant is entitled to a suitable discount for a plea of guilty.

Sentencing guidelines

In the region there have been many calls for sentencing guidelines to be provided for judges and magistrates. Among the concerns voiced is the perceived disparity in sentences meted out by the courts for like offences, as highlighted above. In addition, concerns about recidivism and the graduation of offenders from committing less serious offences to more serious offences have resulted in laws providing for alternatives to custodial sentences. In what circumstances and in reference to whom these alternatives should be utilised are matters which may be properly addressed by sentencing guidelines.

The legislatures in some jurisdictions across the region have attempted to lay down specific sentencing guidelines. Section 35 of the Barbados Penal Systems Reform Act No 50 of 1998, which in material aspects is similar to the English Criminal Justice Act 1991,

9 Samuels, A, 'The discount for guilty plea: the judicial principles' (1999) 163 JPN 792.

provides for certain specific circumstances when custodial sentences, other than those fixed by law, should be imposed. Furthermore, the Act also stipulates that courts should give reasons for certain custodial sentences and sets out the procedure for such. Section 41 of the Act contains general guidelines for the court. Section 41(2) states:

> Those guidelines are as follows:
>
> 1 The rehabilitation of the offenders is one of the aims of sentencing except where the penalty is death.
> 2 The gravity of the punishment must be commensurate with the gravity of the offence.
> 3 The offender must not be sentenced except for an offence of which the offender has been convicted or for another offence or other offences which the offender has asked the court to take into consideration in passing sentence.
> 4 Where a fine is imposed, the court in fixing the amount of the fine must take into account, among other relevant considerations, the means of the offender so far as these are known to the court, regardless whether this will increase or reduce the amount of the fine.

While these guidelines reflect some of the usual factors taken into account in sentencing in Barbados prior to the statutory codification, the enactment in statute means that courts are now bound to consider these matters in passing sentence. The guidelines serve to focus the attention of the courts on issues that they might otherwise ignore. Statutory guidelines such as these are enacted with the anticipation that they will result in greater consistency in sentencing without removing the discretion of a court ultimately to decide on what is appropriate. If the judge or magistrate is harsher or more lenient than expected, he may be required to provide reasons for his decision.

In *DPP's Reference No 1 of 2003 (R v Skeete (Kurt))* 66 WIR 94 the Barbados Court of Appeal considered the implications of section 36 (2) of the Penal System Reform Act and its impact on a case where a defendant had been given four years' imprisonment after pleading guilty to manslaughter on a charge of manslaughter. Although the defendant had accepted responsibility and had been in custody for two years pending trial the court held that the sentence was too lenient. The court opined that the sentencing court had put too little weight on the fact that the offence was a violent one (as required by the Penal System Reform Act), involving the possession and use of an unlicensed firearm. This was a very grave offence of manslaughter and in the interests of protecting the public the sentence was increased to 13 years. This case illustrates the utility of having sentencing guidelines specified in statute and the impact they ought to have in generating some 'consistency in sentencing practice', as described by the Chief Justice in delivering the judgment of the court.

In *R v Lorde* (2006) 73 WIR 28 the Court of Appeal of Barbados reviewed the guidance given on sentencing in respect of manslaughter. The court held that the bottom of the scale for a grave case of manslaughter without the use of a firearm was 16 years' and the top of the scale was 20 years' imprisonment. A sentencing court must balance the aggravating and the mitigating factors in arriving at a sentence that was commensurate with the seriousness of the offence. See also the judgment of the Barbados Court of Appeal in *DPP's Reference No 2 of 2010* (unreported) on sentencing principles in manslaughter.

In contrast, in *R v Mayers* (2009) 74 WIR 82 the court, while opting to give no guidelines in a case of rape, recognised that rape was a serious sexual offence with a maximum penalty of life imprisonment and would therefore normally qualify on conviction for an automatic custodial sentence. The aggravating factors in the particular case were: (i) the restraint of and threats to the complainant; (ii) the complainant was particularly vulnerable as an employee of the appellant, who abused the trust of the complainant; (iii) the complainant was feeling ill at the time as her stomach was hurting and her menstrual period was due; (iv) the appellant impressed the complainant with his financial superiority and willingness to help her family; (v) the location and time of the commission of the offence, in an isolated place at night; (vi) the appellant had unprotected sex; and (vii) the age of the appellant and the disparity in ages between the appellant and the complainant. The only mitigating factor the court said was that the appellant had no previous criminal convictions.

The St Lucia Criminal Code 2004 contains similar provisions to those of Barbados both in relation to custodial sentencing and guidelines: ss 1096–98, 1102–03, Criminal Code.

The Dominica Criminal Justice (Reform) Act, Chap 12:35, while it is much less extensive in both scope and content than the Barbados Penal Systems Reform Act, also attempts to limit the power of a court to pass sentences of imprisonment. A judge or magistrate who passes such a sentence is required to give reasons for imprisoning offenders between the ages of 18 and 23 years.

There is now legislation in the Bahamas and Trinidad and Tobago for enabling the development of sentencing guidelines in general, and for specific offenders. Act No 1 of 2000, the Criminal Procedure Amendment Act of the Bahamas, provides for the Chief Justice to make and issue sentencing guidelines. In Trinidad and Tobago, the Sentencing Commission Act No 80 of 2000 became law[10] in November 2000. That Act establishes a body to be known as the Sentencing Commission which, inter alia, will have responsibility to develop sentencing guidelines and periodically review them as well as to develop a framework for the setting of maximum penalties and ranges of sentences. At the time of writing, the Commission has only recently been constituted and is not yet functioning.

Sentencing structure

In *Aguillera, Ballai, Ballai and Ayow v The State* Crim App Nos 5, 6, 7, 8 of 2015, the Court of Appeal of Trinidad and Tobago set out the recommended sentencing methodology to be used for all criminal offences, whether indictable and summary, which is supposed to be in keeping with the modern trend of requiring full transparency in sentencing. Accordingly, the overall sentencing structure should, generally, reflect the following matters:

(i) The calculation of the starting point which takes into account the aggravating and mitigating factors of the offence only; these are the objective circumstances which relate to the gravity of the offence itself and which assist in gauging its seriousness, that is, the degree of harmfulness of the offence;
(ii) An appropriate upward or downward adjustment of the starting point (or, dependent on the circumstances, and if there is in effect a cancelling out, no adjustment at all), which takes into account the aggravating and mitigating factors relative to the offender; these are the subjective circumstances of the offender which in turn inform the degree of the culpability of the particular offender;
(iii) (Where appropriate) a discount for a guilty plea; any deviation from the usual discount requires particularly careful justification and an explanation which is clearly expressed; and
(iv) Credit for the period of time spent in pre-trial custody.

10 Act No 80 of 2000 (which required proclamation) was proclaimed by Legal Notice 214 on 6 November 2000.

TYPES OF SENTENCING

In general, provision is made by legislation for the penalties which are available on criminal conviction. The specific legislation relating to particular crimes will spell out the maximum penalties possible for those offences. For murder, death is the penalty fixed by law across the Commonwealth Caribbean countries. Otherwise, the maximum penalty is usually a term of imprisonment. For serious offences this may run into years, whereas for summary offences the maximum term of imprisonment may comprise months or days, which invariably represent the alternative to the maximum fine stipulated. Summary procedure legislation identifies some of the sentencing alternatives available on summary trial, while relevant indictable procedure legislation refers to those available at indictable trial. In addition, in many countries of the Commonwealth Caribbean there has been a host of new legislation providing for alternative sentences to custody which have been created by specific statute relating to that mode of punishment. Sentences such as community service and parole fall within that type. The growing trend in the region appears to be towards community-based punishment as opposed to custodial sentence. This is exemplified by the major changes in the law in this regard in the St Lucia Criminal Code 2004. Nonetheless, in respect of indictable offences, the punishment inflicted by courts in the case of an adult is more often than not one of imprisonment. Children and other juveniles are, as provided by statute, dealt with specially and there are more sentencing options utilised for juvenile offenders.

Absolute discharge

A court may, where it considers that it is inexpedient to inflict punishment and a probation order is not appropriate, discharge an offender absolutely. In such a case no conviction is recorded against the defendant, even though he is guilty of the offence. The power to discharge an offender absolutely appears to derive from statute and should be imposed in accordance with the terms of the provision. Section 3 of the Penal Systems Reform Act 1998 of Barbados and s 1182 of the St Lucia Criminal Code 2004 provide for absolute discharge by any court, which means it is available at both summary and indictable trial. Section 61 of the Grenada Criminal Procedure Code, Cap 72B, on the other hand, allows a discharge without proceeding to conviction if it appears to the court that the offence 'was in the circumstances of the case so trifling in nature that it is inexpedient to inflict any punishment . . .'. Presumably a trifling offence would be a summary offence although the statute does not so restrict the use of the power of the court. In some jurisdictions, such as Trinidad and Tobago, the power to grant an absolute discharge seems to be a power of the magistrate on summary trial.[11] There is no reference to such a power in the legislation relating to indictable trials. Interestingly, in some jurisdictions, the power of absolute discharge is contained in the Probation Act.[12]

Even if a judge of the High Court can claim to have a power of absolute discharge, in the absence of statutory underpinning, it would be an extremely rare case in which absolute discharge would be appropriate for a defendant who is guilty of an indictable offence. The usual rationale for an absolute discharge is that the nature of the offence and character of the offender are such that no conviction should be recorded, nor any punishment inflicted. The court will weigh the antecedents of the offender against the facts of the case. It is

11 Guyana: Summary Jurisdiction (Procedure) Act, Cap 10:02, s 42(1) (a); Trinidad and Tobago: Summary Courts Act, Chap 4:20, s 71(1) (a); St Vincent: Probation of Offenders Act, Cap 179, s 3(1) (a).

12 As in St Vincent: Probation of Offenders Act, Cap 179, s 3(1) (a).

unlikely that it can be rationally determined that it is inexpedient to inflict punishment and record no conviction on a defendant guilty of other than a trifling offence.

Conditional discharge

Instead of an absolute discharge, a court may discharge an offender on condition that he commits no offence during a specified period. In such a case, the court must explain to the offender the consequences of the order in that should he commit another offence during the period of the conditional charge, he will be liable to be sentenced for the original offence.[13] Once no offence is committed, the defendant is absolutely discharged with no offence recorded against him.

In a conditional discharge, the defendant signs no bond of good behaviour and the only condition is non-commission of any offence for the specified period. This type of order is rarely used and is frequently confused with a binding-over order or a conviction resulting in a 'reprimand and discharge', in which case no punishment is inflicted, but a conviction is recorded. Power to grant a conditional discharge must be founded in statute and it is usually stated as an alternative to absolute discharge.

Binding-over order

Frequently, a court may impose a binding-over order on an offender. Such an order may be one of two types, both of which involve the offender signing a bond to be of good behaviour for a specified time.

The first type of bond is one where the offender is bound over for a specified period (usually not exceeding three years) to keep the peace and be of good behaviour. The bond is a recognisance in a specific sum which may be protected with sureties. It is usual to ask the offender if he consents to being bound over, but in the absence of any assertion by the defendant to the contrary, this will be assumed: *R v Central Criminal Court ex p Boulding* [1984] 2 WLR 321. With this type of bond, if the defendant fails to keep the peace during the time specified, he may be called upon to forfeit the sum stipulated in the bond. There is in general no condition that he must come up for sentencing if he breaks the bond. It appears that power to impose this type of bond must originate in statute.[14]

In *Ex p Boulding* (above) it was made clear that in imposing a bond, the court must give the defendant a right to be heard as to amount of the recognisance contemplated. In that case, the English Queen's Bench Division found that a figure of £500 was very high having regard to the means of the applicant/defendant. He should have been allowed the opportunity to make representations as to the sum involved. It is a rare instance that a defendant who is offered a choice of being bound over in lieu of any other punishment will refuse it. If he refuses the condition (keeping the peace), the court may inflict another penalty. If he agrees, but later refuses to sign the bond, it may be that he will be in contempt of court. A bond to keep the peace is more appropriate in respect of offences where the defendant has shown a tendency to violence or breaches of the peace.

The other type of bond is that by which a defendant agrees to be bound over on condition that he comes up for judgment when required. It has been held that this is an old

13 See, e.g.: Barbados: Penal Systems Reform Act 1998, s 3(2), (3); St Lucia: Probation Act No 11 of 1960, s 20.

14 This power was first available to magistrates by the English Justice of the Peace Act 1361, s 115.

common law power, so that it is available to judges on indictable trial (without statutory authorisation): *Williams* (1982) 75 Cr App R 378. Some summary procedure legislation in the region[15] also makes provision for this type of binding-over order. It is in combination with the first type of bond described above. Under the legislation the defendant signs a bond in a specified sum on conditions. One of those is that he comes up for judgment (conviction or sentence), but meanwhile must be of good behaviour. Under the common law, the conditions could include being of good behaviour or that he move to another place, presumably for the purpose of rehabilitation. It is vital that the defendant consents to the conditions and this should be made clear to him, even on threat of imprisonment otherwise.

In *Williams* (above), the defendant, a British citizen, was released on a bond on condition that he leave for Jamaica within ten days and remain there for three to five years. Although his parents were Jamaican, the defendant had never been to Jamaica and had been born in England. The defendant resisted the conditions, but it was nevertheless imposed by the sentencing judge. It was held that the sentence must be quashed since the power to impose conditions on a binding-over order can be exercised only if the subject consents or acknowledges himself to be bound by the terms. This is clear from the fact that the defendant 'comes up for judgment' if he breaks the bond. The Court of Appeal distinguished the case of *Vincent* (unreported, 3 November 1981) in which a young man 'who was anxious to return to Trinidad, where his parents were in a comfortable way of business', was made the subject of a similar order to last ten years.

The effect of a bond, then, is that the offender is not sentenced. In this regard it is different from a suspended sentence where the offender is first sentenced and the sentence is thereafter suspended having regard to the circumstances of the case. In that situation, there is no question of consent to conditions or a bond. Bonds are avidly sought on behalf of their clients by defence counsel. In some jurisdictions, such as Trinidad and Tobago, it is not unusual for a court to make a binding-over order where the defendant has paid compensation to the victim, particularly in cases where the parties knew each other before. It does not, however, appear to be the practice of police officers or other officials to follow up the order to ensure that the terms of the order are observed. This may have more to do with lack of manpower than lack of interest on the part of the officials concerned.

Suspended sentence

The suspended sentence is a creation of statute and exists as a sentencing alternative only in some jurisdictions. These include Barbados, Dominica, Guyana and Jamaica.[16] A suspended sentence is a term of imprisonment of up to two or three years (depending on the jurisdiction) which does not take effect immediately. Sentence is passed on a person on the same basis that ordinary imprisonment would be. In other words, imprisonment is considered the appropriate sentence. The only difference is that the offender is not asked to serve the time because of exceptional circumstances operating in his favour. Youth, good character and the fact of pleading guilty are not, in isolation, considered exceptional circumstances so

15 Guyana: Summary Jurisdiction (Procedure) Act, Cap 10:02, s 42(1)(b); St Lucia: Criminal Code, s 1240;

16 Barbados: Penal Systems Reform Act 1998, s 6;
Dominica: Criminal Justice (Reform) Act, Chap 12:53, s 6;
Guyana: Criminal Law Reform Act 1988, ss 3–6;
Jamaica: Criminal Justice (Reform) Act, ss 6–7 as amended by Act No 6 of 2001, Criminal Justice Reform (Amendment) Act;
St Lucia: Criminal Code, ss 1184–86.

as to justify the imposition of a suspended sentence. The mental health of the defendant, on the other hand, may amount to such an exceptional circumstance, *Khan* (1994) 15 Cr App R (S) 320, as would attempts by the defendant to make reparation to the victim. The court will consider all the circumstances of the case to determine if they can be said to amount to 'exceptional' circumstances. One consideration may be whether the defendant's personal situation will make it difficult for him to serve the sentence in prison.

A suspended sentence may be combined with a financial order such as (monetary) compensation so as to make it clear to the community that the defendant is not being 'let off' the consequences of his actions. Legislation provides, however, that a suspended sentence may not be given with a probation order since the latter is a supervisory form of release given in lieu of other sentences.[17] In general, statute across the region also provides that a suspended sentence is not available to a person convicted of a firearm offence.

If the defendant should commit another offence (not a trifling offence) during the period of the sentence, the sentence may be activated. The other offence need not be of the same type. Thus if an offender, having been granted a suspended sentence for theft, for instance, assaults someone during the period of the sentence (even though it is suspended), he may be called upon to serve the whole term of his sentence. The court, however, has power in deserving cases to substitute a lesser period of imprisonment for the original sentence, previously suspended. It is usual and, in some cases, required by statute, that a court should explain to the defendant the nature and consequences of the suspended sentence, in particular his liability if he commits a further offence during the period of the sentence.

Probation

This is a form of supervisory sentence for which statute specifically provides in Commonwealth Caribbean jurisdictions. It is widely used for juveniles in lieu of any other sentence across the Commonwealth Caribbean, but rarely used for adults, although the relevant statutes do not proscribe its use for adults.

A probation order simpliciter is usually made in lieu of other forms of punishment. In *R v Brown* (1964) 7 WIR 47, the Court of Appeal of Jamaica confirmed that s 3 of the Jamaica statute authorises the making of a probation order in lieu of imprisonment and not in lieu of any other sentence. This highlights the fact that the terms of the legislation must be strictly followed in this regard. Since the passage of the original probation legislation,[18] statute has intervened in some cases to provide for combination orders consisting of community service and probation orders or other forms of community sentencing and probation. In those jurisdictions which now provide for some form of community service, a combination order may be made by the court. These jurisdictions include Barbados, Dominica, Jamaica, St Lucia and Trinidad and Tobago. While some jurisdictions specifically provide for the

17 The Criminal Justice (Reform) Act, Chap 12:53, s 9 of Dominica provides, however, that the court may make a suspended sentence supervision order, consequent on a suspended sentence.

18 Antigua: Probation of Offenders Act, Cap 345; Barbados: Probation of Offenders Act, Cap 146; Dominica: Probation Act, Chap 12:33; Grenada: Probation Act, Cap 256; Guyana: Probation Act, Cap 11:04; Jamaica: Probation of Offenders Act; St Kitts and Nevis: Probation Act, Cap 4:27; St Lucia: Criminal Code; St Vincent: Probation of Offenders Act, Cap 179; Trinidad and Tobago: Probation of Offenders Act, Chap 13:51.

combination order,[19] the relevant statutes enacting community service in all jurisdictions make it clear that community service orders fall under the probation department.

A probation order may be imposed either at summary or indictable trial. While some statutes simply provide that a convicted person may be granted probation in lieu of other punishment, certain jurisdictions permit probation on summary conviction without any conviction being recorded (St Vincent, Trinidad and Tobago). This is not the case with respect to indictable offences and it appears that the defendant's conviction will be recorded if he is found liable on indictable conviction, even though he is put on probation. A probation order in general ought not to be for longer than three years. If the order is breached during that time, the defendant will be brought before the court for sentencing in accordance with statute.

In deciding whether to impose probation, a court, as directed by statute, must consider the nature of the offence[20] and the character of the offender. Other factors which may be taken into account include the age, health or mental condition[21] of the offender and the seriousness of the offence. As mentioned above, it is unusual for the court in the Commonwealth Caribbean to place adult offenders on probation, although probation reports may be requested as part of the pre-sentence process.

In imposing a probation order, the court must explain to the offender the duration and requirements of the order. The requirements are meant to ensure proper supervision by the probation department and may include stipulations as to how often and where the defendant should submit to the supervision of the probation officer who is assigned to supervise him. The order may also require that the defendant (probationer) satisfy certain requirements as to residence as the court directs and can also prohibit his association with undesirable persons. Other conditions may include abstention from intoxicating liquor and from frequenting certain (undesirable) places. A copy of the probation order is usually provided to the probationer so that he remains cognisant of the conditions of the order during the period of his supervisory sentence.

Probation officers have been part of the criminal justice system for decades. Statute recognises their role in ensuring that the supervisory sentence is effected. The role of the probation officer includes visiting the probationer and receiving reports at reasonable intervals as to his progress. This may be specified in the order or may be as the officer thinks fit. The officer also ensures that the conditions of the order are observed and reports to the court on the behaviour of the probationer. Where necessary he advises, assists and may even befriend the probationer. The court may also request of a probation officer a report on a defendant who has been found guilty or who has pleaded guilty, to inform its determination as to an appropriate sentence, which need not eventually include probation.

Community service order

The community service order represents one of the new alternatives to custodial sentences which grew out of the clamour for new ideas in the late twentieth century to serve the needs of the criminal justice system. The community service order may be used when an adult offender is before the courts for the first time. It promotes the ideas of rehabilitation and making reparation to the victim, but does not convey the impression that the offender is

19 Barbados: Penal Systems Reform Act 1998–50, s 17; Trinidad and Tobago: Community Services Orders Act No 19 of 1997, s 24; Dominica: Act No 3 of 2013 creating a new s 11C.

20 In *AG's Reference* (No 2 of 1995) (R v S) [1995] Crim LR 835, the Court of Appeal of England considered that a probation order was an unduly lenient sentence in a case where an offender had committed several sexual offences against his daughter when she was between five and six years old.

21 As stated in Probation of Offenders Act, Cap 179, s 3, St Vincent.

being 'let off'. Community service was introduced into Britain by s 14 of the Powers of the Criminal Courts Act 1973. That legislation was followed in the Commonwealth Caribbean in Dominica and Jamaica, which jurisdictions passed statute to create[22] the new sentencing alternative along the lines of the 1973 English Act. The English law was revised in 1991 by the Criminal Justice Act, which provided that community service orders could be combined with probation supervision. This legislation forms the basis of the law[23] passed in Barbados and Trinidad and Tobago introducing community service and was included in the Dominica Act by Act No 3 of 2013.

Community service is a measure available to persons over 16 (Barbados, Trinidad and Tobago) or over 17, as the law provides. Presumably it is not available for children because the order may be viewed as sanctioning child labour. Community service allows a convicted offender to serve the whole or part of a sentence in lieu of imprisonment by performing unpaid work. There is thus no question of not recording a sentence; it is simply that the sentence is served through specific work or labour in the community which is specified by the court in sentencing. The number of hours which must be served should be stated and, in most jurisdictions, a maximum is set in statute (Barbados – 240 hours; Trinidad and Tobago – 240 hours as well as a minimum 80 hours in Barbados).

A defendant must consent to community service. If he does not consent, another sentence will be passed. In general, statute prohibits the imposition of community service for offences involving violence[24] or firearms. The Schedule to the Trinidad and Tobago Community Service Orders Act lists a range of offences for which community service is not available. In any event, before a community service order is made, the court will request a probation report as to its suitability as a sentence. It is only after the court has received this report and ensured that practical arrangements can be made for the performance of the work that a community service order will be made.

The probation department is responsible for supervising the performance of community service by the offender. The probation officer assigned will instruct the offender as to the performance of the work assigned on the job. Supervision may be provided by persons designated by the probation officer to so supervise. Usually, specific times will be specified for the work to be done. If the offender fails to comply with the terms of the order, he will be summoned to court. Unlike probation orders or binding-over orders, the commission of another offence during the time of community service is not a breach of the community service order. The focus here is more on reparation than behaviour per se. Failure to perform the work assigned will definitively amount to a breach.

The breach of a community service order without reasonable excuse may lead to the court revoking the order and dealing with the offender as provided for by statute. Since community service is a statutory creation, the provisions of the statute must be strictly followed in this regard. In general, the court has an option to impose a fine on the defendant in lieu of the (breached) community service order, or a sentence of imprisonment where appropriate (as in the case of indictable offences). Unusually, the Trinidad and Tobago Community Service Orders Act provides that the community service order is in the form of a suspended sentence. Section 3(1) states that the court, in a case where imprisonment for the

22 Dominica: Criminal Justice (Reform) Act, Chap 12:35, as amended by Act No 3 of 2013, s 10; Jamaica: Criminal Justice (Reform) Act, s 10 as amended by Act No 6 of 2001, now enabling other sentences such as electronic monitoring and mediation.

23 Barbados: Penal Systems Reform Act 1998, ss 13–14, 17–18; Trinidad and Tobago: the Community Service Orders Act 1997.

24 As in Criminal Justice (Reform) Act of Jamaica, s 10(1).

offence is less than 12 months, 'may pass sentence but may order the operation of the whole or part of the sentence[25] to be suspended for a period not exceeding two years and may then make a community service order'. The effect of this provision is that where a defendant breaches a community service order, the sentence of imprisonment which was suspended may be activated. This is without prejudice to the power of the court to impose a fine or make an additional order.

Even though community service has existed for some time in a few Commonwealth Caribbean jurisdictions and, more recently, in Barbados and Trinidad and Tobago, it is not often utilised as a mode of punishment. The reason for this may be that the defendant and defence counsel prefer to argue for a binding-over order or even a fine rather than a form of supervised release that involves unpaid labour, which is what community service is. Alternatively, the many restrictions and requirements[26] connected to its imposition may lead to delay in actually implementing community service as a sentence, since this militates against quick disposition of cases. In St Lucia the law enabling community service appears to have been superseded by other community sentences including a sentence involving 'extra mural services' in lieu of imprisonment.[27] It involves working and serving a sentence outside of prison.

Monetary penalties

Fines

A fine is the most frequent form of punishment imposed on offenders who have committed summary offences, particularly where the offences are merely regulatory, such as traffic breaches. It has been held that there is no common law power in a judge trying a felony (or arrestable offence) to impose a fine: *R v Ramcharan* (1970) 17 WIR 407. In that case it was stated that the power of a judge in England to impose a fine on trial in the High Court had been removed as far back as 1848. Thereafter it was necessary for statute to confer on a judge (in the same way as a magistrate for summary trial) power to inflict a fine on indictable conviction. Statute throughout the Commonwealth Caribbean now includes this power of a judge to impose a fine, though in practice it is one that is rarely exercised.

An alternative period of imprisonment is stipulated for default in payment of any fine imposed, whether the fine is not paid at all or not paid in time. In general, both the maximum amount of the fine and the alternative period of imprisonment are set by the statute defining the offence for which the offender has been convicted. Otherwise, for summary trial, summary procedure legislation relating to powers of magistrates in sentencing may outline the appropriate alternative periods of imprisonment for the range of fines that the magistrate may set.[28]

In determining the amount of the fine, the court should take into account matters such as the means of the defendant, his employment record (what he earns or his potential) and, if the case is one for drug trafficking, perhaps the market value of the illegal drugs seized from him: *Authority Cambridge v Brown Mag* App No 34 of 1983 (a decision of the Court of Appeal of Trinidad and

25 In May 2005 in *The State v Roxanne Headley* Cr App No 56 of 2003, the Trinidad and Tobago Court of Appeal imposed a 'community service sentence' for the first time. The court imposed a sentence of nine months on a defendant and suspended six months to enable the defendant to do community service.

26 For probation officer's report and proof that arrangements can be made for the defendant to work under supervision.

27 Criminal Code ss 1174–76.

28 As, e.g., Summary Courts Act, Chap 4:20, s 68(2), Trinidad and Tobago.

Tobago). In the case of a poor defendant, a high fine might mean that he will have to serve the alternative period of imprisonment for default, but a rich defendant can evade imprisonment as he can with impunity afford very high fines. A fine in his case is no true punishment. Other factors such as previous convictions and the age of the defendant will also be relevant.

Statute has intervened to permit courts to allow a deserving defendant time to pay the fine. This 'time allowed' must be requested by the defendant, usually upon enquiry by the sentencing magistrate if he wishes such time. Practice in any event dictates that the court should take into account the age and means of the defendant in setting the time allowed to exercise the option of a fine. If a defendant cannot pay the fine in the time set, he may ask for an extension of time. In *Mills v Byron* (1968) 12 WIR 301, the Antigua High Court considered a case where a defendant pleaded guilty to two traffic charges. He was ordered to pay the respective fines of $100 and $60 forthwith. The defendant appealed, contending that the magistrate should not have ordered him to pay forthwith. The Chief Justice of the West Indies Associated States held that before a magistrate can make an order to require payment forthwith, he must go through the procedure set out by statute, which involved inquiry of the convicted defendant as to whether he desired time to be allowed for payment. Only if the defendant expressed no such desire, or shows he has no fixed place of abode, or the magistrate identifies some other special reason, should no time be allowed. The law expressly forbids a magistrate from sending a person to prison for failure to pay a fine forthwith without giving him the option permitted by statute of time to be allowed for payment.

Costs, compensation and restitution

Other monetary penalties, which may be made by a court against a defendant, include costs, compensation and restitution. A defendant may be asked to pay costs to the complainant/victim as may be determined by the court as 'just and reasonable'.[29] Alternatively, the court may award the defendant costs where it dismisses a complaint if it finds the complaint to have been vexatious or frivolous. This latter power is provided for in most summary procedure legislation across the region, but is rarely used. The payment of costs to the victim may be awarded in indictable trials as well once statute so provides. Compensation is a payment to be made to a victim who has suffered at the hands of a convicted defendant. The amount of the compensation (as in the case of costs) is determined by the sentencing court subject to any statutory maximum specified.[30] It is not unusual for a compensation order to be made in addition to another sentence, but invariably this is done if the other sentence is not harsh such as a binding-over order or a suspended sentence. In *R v Wylie* [1974] Crim LR 608, the English appellate court suggested that it is undesirable to make a compensation order where the defendant had been sentenced to a substantial term of imprisonment. Unless the defendant is required to make the payments after his release, the award would be of little use. This is so because a monetary award (as distinct from a fine) is generally enforced as a civil debt, so that the defendant would have served the alternative term of imprisonment for non-payment while in prison serving his sentence of imprisonment. Furthermore, if the payments are required to be made after release, this might result in the defendant committing other crimes to pay the compensation. A compensation order should thus be made only in uncomplicated cases where the amount of the damage does not exceed the defendant's needs: Commentary [1974] Crim LR 609.

29 As stipulated, e.g., in the Grenada Criminal Procedure Code, Cap 72B, s 32.

30 Criminal Procedure Act, Chap 12:02, s 54 of Trinidad and Tobago was amended by Act No 28 of 1996 to increase the maximum compensation possible, consequent on conviction of the defendant, from $480 to $50,000.

The acceptance of an award of compensation on the part of the victim precludes his ability to bring a civil action for damages for injuries or loss arising from the offence. The victim is thus entitled to refuse to accept compensation so as to preserve his rights under the civil law.

The Barbados Penal Systems Reform (Amendment) Act, 2010–10 is somewhat different in this regard. Under a new s 16A, where detailed provisions are made for compensation orders, the beneficiary may still bring a civil action arising from the same cause/matter but the amount he may recover is reduced.

The power to award restitution, although confirmed by statute in most cases, does not depend on statute for its existence. A court may simply make an order when a defendant is convicted and otherwise sentenced that stolen or dishonestly obtained goods, the subject of the charge, should be returned to their owner. If the defendant has been convicted of the offence, this presupposes that he has no right of ownership of the goods. Even if the defendant appeals, it seems that unless the defendant is contending that he has a claim of right or owns the articles, the goods in question may be restored to the owner.

Imprisonment

Imprisonment is the usual mode of punishment passed on a defendant convicted of an indictable offence. The maximum period of imprisonment for any offence is determined by the statute that either creates the particular offence or provides the penalty for the particular offence. However, the power of a magistrate to impose imprisonment is determined by the maximum provided in the relevant summary procedure or summary offences legislation. In practice, a magistrate will rarely impose a sentence of imprisonment for a purely summary offence. Where an indictable offence is tried summarily, however, imprisonment is more frequently utilised for these more serious offences that include possession of firearms, possession or trafficking of illegal narcotics and certain offences to the person. In respect of such offences, the maximum sentence of imprisonment on summary conviction is invariably much higher than six months, the usual maximum for summary offences.

Section 37 of the Barbados Penal Systems Reform Act, which requires a court to obtain a pre-sentence report before passing a custodial sentence, was considered in *R v Gittens* (2010) 75 WIR 126 and subsequently by the Court of Appeal in *Damien Omar Cummins v Commissioner of Police* Mag Appeal No 6 of 2011 (unreported).

Life imprisonment is available in most jurisdictions for offences such as manslaughter, rape or trafficking of dangerous narcotics such as cocaine or heroin. It is a sentence imposed on dangerous offenders who may be considered a 'menace to society'. In *Edwin Farfan v The State* Cr App No 34 of 1980, a decision of the Court of Appeal of Trinidad and Tobago, it was stated that the Commissioner of Prison had reported that, in that jurisdiction, a term of life imprisonment did not on average exceed 13–15 years. This finding prompted an amendment to the Interpretation Act, Chap 3:01, creating s 69A. That section enables a court (in Trinidad and Tobago) on sentencing an offender to life imprisonment to declare at the same time a period before the expiration of which, in its view, the offender shall not be released.

Where life imprisonment is specified as the sentence in the ordinary way, the prisoner's case (and sentence) comes up for review in accordance with practice established by Prison Rules, usually every four years. This was the basis for the statement in *Farfan* that a sentence of 'life imprisonment' meant 13–15 years. Such sentences are in general treated as if they were 20-year sentences and accordingly reduced. If a judge wishes to impose a sentence greater than 20 years for an offence where the maximum penalty is life imprisonment he should, in jurisdictions other than Trinidad and Tobago, specify a term of years.

Prison Rules[31] across the region dictate that an offender earns an almost automatic remission of up to one-third of any term of imprisonment to which he is sentenced. Thus an offender who is sentenced to 24 months' imprisonment may serve only 16 months, unless he forfeits the remission by bad conduct. Furthermore, even if statute specifies a minimum sentence for an offence, this may not be enforceable in the face of a provision such as s 68(2) of the Interpretation Act, Chap 3:01 of Trinidad and Tobago:

> Where in any Act or statutory instrument provision is made for a minimum penalty or fine ... such Act or statutory instrument shall have effect as though no such minimum penalty or fine had been provided.

In *Grant v Jack* (1971) 19 WIR 123, the Court of Appeal of Trinidad and Tobago held that the effect of this provision was that a mandatory minimum sentence was unenforceable in Trinidad and Tobago. This is of course unless Parliament prescribes punishment and specifically provides that it overrides the Interpretation Act. In jurisdictions such as St Lucia, statute may expressly provide for a minimum punishment (in accordance with s 1104 of the Criminal Code of St Lucia). It is relevant to note that in the US the Supreme Court has sanctioned mandatory minimum sentencing statutes: *Chapman v US* [1991] 500 US 453, 111 S Ct 1919.

In general, a sentence of imprisonment is imposed with hard labour. The chief exceptions to this are where the sentence is in respect of criminal contempt or if the health or age of the offender dictates otherwise. These would be considered exceptional circumstances. 'Hard labour' refers to work as determined by the prison authorities, which may include cooking duties or cleaning duties, hardly in the realm of 'labour'. Persons who are in custody not having been sentenced or those who are on Death Row are not required to do hard labour whilst in prison.

Consecutive/concurrent sentences

Where a defendant is convicted of two or more offences each for which he is sentenced to imprisonment or where he is already serving a sentence of imprisonment, the sentencing court will have to decide whether the sentences should run concurrently or consecutively. Usually, if the offences arise out of the same incident, the court will order that they run concurrently: they are to be served together.

If the sentence of imprisonment is imposed on a defendant who is serving another sentence which is unrelated, the new sentence will generally be ordered to run consecutively to the existing

---

31 Prison Rules across the region provide that a prisoner is entitled to remission not exceeding one-third of the term as long as the term does not fall below 31 days. In Jamaica this one-third remission entitlement is only for first-time offenders; others are only entitled to one-quarter remission. The following rules demonstrate the similarity in provisions across the regions although the rules were made at different times.

Antigua: r 211, Prison Rules to Cap 341;

Dominica: r 36, Prison Rules to Chap 12:70;

Grenada: r 303, Prison Rules to Cap 254;

Guyana: r 256, Prison Rules to Cap 11:01;

Jamaica: r 178 of the 1991 Rules to the Corrections Act;

St Vincent: rr 42–44, Prison Rules to Cap 281;

Trinidad and Tobago: r 285 of the Prison Rules made under the West Indies Prison Rules 1838.

This Rule was amended in 1991 to permit remission of up to one-half for sentences of 12 months or less once the period to be served does not fall under 30 days.

sentence. If the defendant is serving more than one sentence, the new sentence should be consecutive to the total period of imprisonment to which the prisoner is then subject.

When dealing with sentences for different offences, the court should always clarify if the sentences are concurrent or consecutive. The CCJ considered the propriety of consecutive sentences in *Vishnu Bridgelall v Hardat Hariprashad* [2017] CCJ 8 (AJ). The appellant had been convicted on two charges of trafficking narcotics and sentenced to serve two consecutive terms of imprisonment. The court decided that, barring special circumstances, where a person is convicted of multiple offences which arise out of the same set of facts or the same incident, it will be appropriate to impose concurrent, and not consecutive, sentences. Consecutive sentences would be appropriate where the offences arose out of unrelated facts or incidents, or where the offences were of the same or similar kind but where the overall criminality will not sufficiently be reflected by concurrent sentences. In the present case, however, only a single act of possession of narcotics found at one address, albeit in two different places, had been proved.

Corporal punishment

This is a form of physical punishment which may be imposed on male persons who have been convicted of violent crimes such as sexual offences, wounding and robbery. This is invariably on indictable conviction. It is in addition[32] to another sentence, usually a period of imprisonment, and is not in lieu thereof. Persons convicted of and sentenced for capital offences are not liable to corporal punishment. Corporal punishment is intended to show society's abhorrence for the crime and the circumstances of the crime committed by the convicted offender.

Corporal punishment as a penalty for crime has been abolished in the Bahamas by s 117 of the Penal Code, Ch 77, and in Jamaica by the Law Reform (Flogging and Whipping) (Abolition) Act, No 5 of 2013. In Trinidad and Tobago it has been abolished in respect of offenders aged 18 and under in that the Corporal Punishment (Offenders Not Over Sixteen) Act, Chap 13:03, has been repealed.[33] Furthermore, the Corporal Punishment (Offenders Over Sixteen) Act, Chap 13:04, has been amended to read 'Offenders over Eighteen'.[34] This means that only persons over 18 may be liable to corporal punishment in Trinidad and Tobago.

Corporal punishment may involve a flogging with the cat-o'-nine-tails,[35] use of which is rare today, or a whipping with a tamarind or birch rod. The maximum number of 'strokes' possible is stipulated in statute and does not usually exceed 24. The administering of the punishment may only be done after medical examination of the offender and on supervision by a prison official. These matters are provided for in the legislation dealing with corporal punishment across the region. In some jurisdictions there are specific Corporal Punishment Acts.[36]

32 See, e.g., Corporal Punishment Act, Cap 106, s 5 of Antigua.

33 Act No 66 of 2000, the Miscellaneous Provisions (Children) Act 2000, s 6.

34 Part V of Act No 66 of 2000.

35 Statutory provisions for flogging still remain in jurisdictions such as Antigua: Corporal Punishment Act, Cap 106, s 13.

36 As in:
Antigua: Corporal Punishment Act, Cap 106;
Barbados: Corporal Punishment Act, Cap 125;
Dominica: Corporal Punishment Act, Chap 12:73;
Grenada: Corporal Punishment (Caning) Act No 10 of 1960;
St Kitts and Nevis: Corporal Punishment Act, Cap 3:09;
St Lucia: Corporal Punishment (Caning) Act No 26 of 1980;
St Vincent: Corporal Punishment of Juveniles Act, Cap 170;
Trinidad and Tobago: Corporal Punishment (Offenders Over 18) Act, Chap 13:04, as amended.

It has been held that it is desirable that a judge, before passing a sentence of corporal punishment, should invite counsel to address the court on the issue: *R v Pryce* (1994) 47 WIR 336. In that case, the Jamaica Court of Appeal made it clear that until it was repealed, corporal punishment remained part of the law of Jamaica, which was preserved by the savings law clause. On the facts of the case, the defendant's conduct in stabbing his mother-in-law (who was defending his wife from his attack) was 'callous, cold and brutish and plainly called for condign punishment'. It was in these circumstances that corporal punishment was imposed together with four years' imprisonment for wounding with intent. The Court of Appeal (Carey J) considered that, in the interests of justice, counsel should have been invited to address the court on the issue of corporal punishment. The failure to do so, however, did not on the facts of that case require that the sentence should be quashed.

Parole

This is a measure which works in combination with incarceration so that part of the term of imprisonment is served outside the institution under supervised release.

A prisoner sentenced to a specific period of imprisonment will be eligible for parole usually after he has served one-third of his term. He will be granted a parole hearing after he submits a written application for same to the Parole Board, constituted under the relevant statute. Usually, the defendant will be interviewed by the Board or a panel of the Board who will have studied the offender's history beforehand as well as any representation made on his behalf. If the Board considers that the applicant, if granted parole, will not constitute a danger to society and that his rehabilitation will be assisted by reintroduction into society, he may be granted parole. Variables such as the seriousness of the crime itself, the age of the offender, his background and his behaviour in prison will be taken into account in deciding if parole should be granted.

Parole is really a means of serving the remaining part of a sentence in the community. The offender is not exempt from serving that part of the sentence; he just serves it in a different way. If he should violate the parole order, whose conditions invariably include reporting to a parole officer and non-conviction of another crime during the time on parole, parole will be revoked and the offender must return to prison to serve the balance of his sentence.

Both Jamaica, by Act No 8 of 1978,[37] and St Lucia[38] introduced parole into their respective criminal justice systems. Despite this, the measure is hardly a popular one and this may be because of the perception that it amounts to condoning criminality.[39] Until effective supervision is assured for parolees and measures instituted to assist in the plight of victims of crime in the region, parole is unlikely to be viewed in a positive light. The growth in violent and gang-related crimes in the region militates against this. Reports from the US of early release of persons convicted of violent crimes who have killed while out on parole do not contribute to recommending parole as an alternative measure. One noteworthy case is that of Kenneth Mcduff, who killed three teenagers in Texas and was sentenced to death by electric chair in 1966. His sentence was commuted to life imprisonment in 1972 when the Texas Supreme Court held the death penalty, as it was then effected, to be unconstitutional.

---

37 As amended by Act 19–2010.

38 Criminal Code ss 1136–55.

39 Seetahal, DS, 'Towards a better future in corrections: sentencing alternatives', *The Lawyer*, January 1993, p 31.

In 1990, Mcduff was released on parole only to be charged shortly thereafter for two murders allegedly committed within a month of his release.

The death penalty

The death penalty was for years considered the mandatory sentence for murder throughout the region. Though also a discretionary penalty[40] for treason, prosecutions for treason are virtually unknown in the Commonwealth Caribbean. So all capital sentences are invariably for murder. The sentence of death is executed by hanging. During the 1980s there was a virtual moratorium on executions in the Commonwealth Caribbean and most sentences were commuted to life imprisonment by the respective Advisory Committees on Mercy usually constituted in constitutions of countries of the Commonwealth Caribbean. The moratorium arose because of the many constitutional motions filed by condemned prisoners citing various breaches of their fundamental human rights, including cruel and unusual punishment occasioned by delay. The execution of the death penalty had to be stayed again and again pending the hearing of these motions. In *Pratt and Morgan v AG* (1993) 43 WIR 340, PC, the Privy Council commuted the death sentences of the appellants on the grounds that delay in carrying out the sentences amounted to cruel and unusual punishment. *Pratt and Morgan* and *Guerra v Baptiste* (1995) 47 WIR 439, PC, confirmed that sentences of death should be carried out within two years after conviction. If the prisoner files constitutional motions and seeks the intervention of international human rights bodies, the time period should be no more than five years, discounting any period of delay occasioned by the fault of the prisoner (such as escape from custody).

The decisions of the Privy Council in this regard led to speedier hearings in murder cases across the region. Almost farcically, in one case[41] the appellant argued on complaint to the Human Rights Committee that he was prejudiced by the speedy disposal of his case from trial through the appellate process. Thus the decisions of the Privy Council, while not always approved in the region, resulted in the removal one by one of the hindrances to carrying out the death penalty.

Between 2001–2006 there was a series of challenges to the constitutionality of the mandatory death penalty across the region from Belize to Trinidad and Tobago with differing results.[42]

In *R v Hughes* (2001) 60 WIR 156 PC, the Privy Council considered the St Lucia constitution and its legislation authorising the infliction of the death penalty. The Board concluded that the mandatory death sentence amounted to inhuman or degrading punishment and contravened the constitutional protection against such a breach of his human rights. There was no room for mitigation or the consideration of individual circumstances of the accused or the offence by the court. Accordingly, the law mandating the death sentence would be modified to render the death sentence discretionary. The Privy Council approved the decisions of the Eastern Caribbean Court of Appeal in *Newton Spence v R, Peter Hughes v R*, ECCA, Cr Appeals No 20 of 1998 and No 14 of 1997 (unreported), 2 April 2001. The

40 As in Treason Act, Chap 11:03, s 2, Trinidad and Tobago.

41 *Nankissoon Boodram v Baptiste (No 2)* (1999) 55 WIR 404, PC: the defendants were executed by hanging in June 1999.

42 Ramgoolam, R, 'The mandatory death penalty for homicide in Trinidad and Tobago: a critique', *The Journal of Comparative Law*, Vol 11, No 1, 2016.

Board, however, held that it was the task of the judge after hearing submissions and evidence to determine the sentence.

In *Reyes v R* (2002) 60 WIR 42 PC, a decision of the Privy Council given at the same time, the court considered the law in Belize and also concluded on the bases of the constitution and law of that country that the mandatory death penalty was unconstitutional. Furthermore, the distinction in Belize between Class A (capital) and Class B (non-capital) murders was not tightly enough drawn to provide discrimination between one murder and another.

In *Forrester Bowe et al. v R* (2006) 68 WIR 10 the Board considered their previous decision in *Jones v AG of the Bahamas* [1995] 1 WLR 891 PC in respect of the imposition of the death penalty in the Bahamas. In that case it was held that the wording of s 312 of the Penal Code providing that 'Whoever commits murder shall be liable to suffer death', imposed a mandatory sentence of death. The Board pointed out, however, that the issue in *Jones* related to the interpretation of s 312 and not to its constitutionality, which was not challenged. Having considered the constitutionality of the provision in *Forrester* the Board held that s 312 should be construed as imposing a discretionary and not a mandatory sentence of death.

These cases serve to confirm that the mandatory death penalty is unconstitutional in most Commonwealth Caribbean jurisdictions.

In a trilogy of judgments given in 7 July 2004 a nine-member panel of the Privy Council overruled its 2003 decision in *Balkissoon Roodal v The State* (2003) 64 WIR 270 PC and specified the law for Barbados, Trinidad and Tobago and Jamaica.

In *Boyce and Joseph v R* (2004) 64 WIR 37 PC and *Matthew v The State* (2004) 64 WIR 412 PC, the Privy Council held in the case of Barbados and Trinidad and Tobago respectively that the mandatory death sentence was not unconstitutional. The relevant provision of the Offence Against the Person Act in each country was immune from constitutional challenge on the ground that such law could not be held to be inconsistent with the constitution. The mandatory death sentence was preserved. The courts could not take into account the question of international obligations in interpreting the statute because the provisions were unambiguous.

In so far as Jamaica was concerned, however, the Privy Council considered that the 1992 Offences Against the Persons (Amendment) Act had repealed s 2 of the 1864 Offences Against the Person Law. The 1992 Amendment Act was not a mere modification of the law. It was effectively new law and so was not 'existing' at the time of the 1962 constitution. Any mandatory death sentence in Jamaica was therefore unconstitutional.

But for Barbados and Trinidad and Tobago the death sentence is no longer mandatory for murder or other capital offences such as treason.

Guyana passed the Criminal Offences (Amendment) Act 2010, Act No 21 of 2010, to remove the death penalty for some less aggravated types of murder and, in any event, made the death penalty discretionary for aggravated murder: the sentence is death or life imprisonment. In 2011 the Bahamas, by Penal Code (Amendment) Act 2011, amended s 290 and replaced s 291 of the Penal Code to make special provisions for sentencing for murder in almost identical terms as Guyana, but for an upward trend in terms of imprisonment. As with the Guyanese law, a convicted murderer is liable to the death penalty only in respect of certain types of aggravated murders, specified in the statute. Further, a defendant convicted of such a murder is liable to be sentenced to either 'death or to imprisonment for life', thus requiring a sentencing hearing when applicable.

Even so, the Privy Council has held that in Trinidad and Tobago the death penalty is not mandatory for 'violent arrestable murder', murder during the course or furtherance of a violent arrestable offence: *Miguel v The State* [2011] UKPC 14. The Board in analysing the effect of s 2A (1) of the Criminal Law Act found that this law, which sought to reintroduce the felony murder rule (after its repeal by implication by a 1979 law which abolished the concepts of felony and misdemeanour), was not a saved law (as other types of murder covered by the Offences Against the Person Act: see *Matthew*, above) and accordingly the penalty for this type of murder was cruel and unusual punishment and therefore unconstitutional. The Board held that the 1997 law was not the same as the old. It held that

> although in respect of some offences the 1997 Act reintroduced the felony murder rule at common law, some violent arrestable offences were not felonies at common law, and in these circumstances section 2A is in some respects wider than the felony murder rule at common law.

A person found guilty of murder where the death sentence is discretionary is entitled to make representations at a sentencing review to seek to have another sentence imposed on him.

The discretion

In determining whether to exercise its discretion to impose the death sentence a court must take into account two fundamental factors: (1) the facts and circumstances surrounding the commission of the offence and (2) the character and record of the convicted person: *Pipersburgh v R* (2008) 72 WIR 108, PC. In that case the Board approved the principles enunciated by the OECS Court of Appeal in *Mitcham v R* (unreported), 3 November 2003, in particular that the death penalty should only be imposed in the most exceptional and extreme cases of murder.

These principles were reinforced in *Trimmingham v R* [2009] UKPC 25 where the Board emphasised that the death sentence should be reserved for (a) the worst of the worst type of cases and (b) where there was no reasonable prospect of reform and the object of punishment could not be achieved by any other means.

In further development of the principles to be applied in determining when to impose the death penalty, the Board in *Lockhart v R* [2011] UKPC 13 considered how best the sentencing court could make this determination. The Board reiterated that the first step is to determine if the killing is to be regarded as occupying a place in the worst category of murder. This would require primarily an assessment of the nature of the crime and the surrounding circumstances. If it is determined that the case is one of the worst of the worst then the question of the possibility of reform needs be addressed. In making such a determination the Board concluded that in every case in which the death penalty is being considered, the report of a consultant psychiatrist is needed before the question of whether there is reasonable possibility of reform can be properly addressed. Further, in some cases, a report from a clinical psychologist might also be necessary. Where a sentencing court considers that it is impossible to decide whether the first aspect of the second principle in *Trimmingham* can be fulfilled without the assistance of a clinical psychologist, a report from such an expert will be indispensable to the proper consideration of that question.

Juveniles

Legislation across the region prohibits the pronouncement of sentence of death on a person who was under 18 at the time he committed the (capital) offence. In some jurisdictions this provision is contained in the relevant Children's or Juveniles Act,[43] while in others it is contained in the Offences Against the Person Act.[44] The old s 29 of the Jamaica Juveniles Act merely provided that sentence of death was not to be passed on 'a person under the age

43 As in the Bahamas: Children and Young Persons (Administration of Justice) Act, Ch 90, s 41; Barbados: Juvenile Offenders Act, Cap 138, s 14; Trinidad and Tobago: Children Act, Chap 46:01, s 79.

44 As in Offences Against the Person Act, Cap 4:21, s 3(1), St Kitts and Nevis.

of eighteen years'. In *Baker v R* (1975) 23 WIR 463, PC, the Privy Council held that this could only mean that as long as the offender was 18 at the time of conviction, he could be sentenced to death. Accordingly, s 29 was amended by Act No 39 of 1975 and it is now specified in s 78(1) of the Child Care and Protection Act that the relevant date is when the offence was committed. This is in line with the rest of the Commonwealth Caribbean.

Statute provides for the alternative disposition of the case in such circumstances where the person is convicted of murder but was under 18 at the time of the commission of the offence. Section 14 of the Juvenile Offenders Act, Cap 138 of Barbados is representative of similar provisions in this regard throughout the Commonwealth Caribbean. In so far as is relevant, that section reads:

> in lieu thereof the court shall, notwithstanding anything in this or any other Act sentence him [the offender] to be detained during Her Majesty's pleasure, and if so sentenced he shall be liable to be detained in such place and under such conditions as the Governor General may direct and whilst so detained shall be deemed to be in legal custody.

In Trinidad and Tobago, Guyana and other jurisdictions where the Queen is not the titular Head of State, the word 'President' is substituted where relevant.

In *Browne v R* (1999) 54 WIR 213, PC, the Privy Council considered the meaning and effect of an identical provision in s 3(1) of the Offences Against the Person Act, then Cap 56 of St Kitts and Nevis. The case involved an offender who was convicted of murder in 1994, when he was 16 years old, for an offence committed in 1993 when he was 15 years old. He was sentenced under s 3(1) to be detained at the Governor General's pleasure, but on appeal challenged the legality of the sentence as being in contravention of the constitution. The Privy Council held:

- The detention during the Governor General's pleasure was not a life sentence but was a wholly discretionary sentence: following *R v Secretary of State for the Home Department ex p Venables* [1998] AC 407, HL where the House of Lords had made a similar finding on the meaning of the words 'detention during Her Majesty's pleasure'. One of the purposes of the detention at 'pleasure' was to maintain flexibility so as to assess, during the detention, the desirability of reintegrating the young offender in society as well as his developing maturity through his formative years. Even though the order of detention involved the power to detain indefinitely, from time to time the relevant authority must, taking into account punishment, which was another purpose of the sentence, decide if detention was still justified.
- The selection of punishment is an integral part of the administration of justice and should not be committed to the hands of the executive of which the Governor General is part (or Her Majesty or the President, as the case may be). Punishment is a matter for the courts.
- Unlike other Caribbean countries, the constitution of St Kitts and Nevis did not in general preserve the validity of previous laws. Existing laws (from 19 September 1983) were to be construed with such modifications, adaptations, qualifications and exceptions to bring them in conformity with the constitution. In the circumstances the sentence to be detained 'during the Governor General's pleasure' must be set aside, since it contravened the constitutional requirement for the separation of powers in sentencing and this was unlawful.

The case was remitted to the Court of Appeal of the Eastern Caribbean States for the court to exercise its power and determine the proper sentence to be substituted.

'Child'/Death

In *DPP v Mollison* (2003) 64 WIR 140 PC, the Privy Council considered an appeal from Jamaica made on the same basis as *Browne.* The appellant who was 16 at the time of the offence was sentenced to detention 'during the Governor General's pleasure' pursuant to s 29 of the Juveniles Act. The court held that s 29 of the Juveniles Act was unconstitutional. It was incompatible with the separation of powers doctrine on which the constitution was founded. The savings law clause, which related to existing legislation that breached the fundamental human rights section of the constitution, did not operate to save legislation that breached the separation of powers doctrine. The two issues were separate.

Accordingly, s 29 of the Juveniles Act had to be modified to bring it into conformity with the constitution. This would be achieved, as in the case of *Browne,* by reading into the statute detention 'at the court's pleasure'. The court and not the executive would review the defendant's sentence. The Child Care and Protection Act that repealed the Juveniles Act provides that a child murderer in Jamaica is now liable to be imprisoned for life.

In *Chuck Attin v AG* HCA 2175 of 2003, the High Court of Trinidad and Tobago adopted and followed the principles enunciated in *Mollison.* The Children Act was accordingly modified by the court. As far as Barbados is concerned the law was clarified by the Privy Council in *Tennyson Winston Griffith v R* PC [2004] UKPC 58. The Privy Council followed its earlier decision on *Mollison.* Throughout the region, then, it is now clear that the appropriate sentence for a child murderer is detention at the court's pleasure, to be followed by periodic reviews. Such period would be determined by the age of the child at the time of the offence.

The legislature of Barbados has amended s 14 of its Juvenile Offenders Act in the Criminal Appeal (Amendment and Miscellaneous Provisions) Act, 2009–2012 to replace the phrase 'during Her Majesty's pleasure' with 'during the Court's pleasure' and made consequential amendments to its Offences Against the Person Act.

The Advisory Committee on Mercy

In each Commonwealth Caribbean country there exists an Advisory Committee, or Council, on the Prerogative of Mercy (Mercy Committee) to determine whether a condemned person should be granted mercy and his execution permanently stayed. The Committee is usually constituted under the constitution[45] and invariably comprises the minister responsible for national security, the Attorney General, the Director of Public Prosecutions and several other members who are respected citizens. It was made clear in *Logan v R* [1996] 4 All ER 190, PC, an appeal from Belize to the Privy Council, that the roles of the Mercy Committee and the Privy Council are separate. The decision to grant mercy is contingent on the facts of the offences. Where the circumstances of the crime are particularly heinous, no authority would be inclined to exercise the prerogative of mercy. On the other hand, even if the facts of the crime are odious, if the trial leading to the conviction is legally unsatisfactory, the conviction cannot stand no matter how strong the evidence. The appellate court should quash the conviction. As the Board stated in *Logan,* p 199: 'It is for the courts to rule on the legality of the conviction and for the Advisory Council to decide whether to exercise the prerogative of mercy in relation to a person lawfully convicted. These are two separate functions'.

Although this did not occur in *Logan,* it is the practice to exhaust all criminal appeals first before having recourse to the Mercy Committee. That committee will consider information

45 See, e.g., Constitution of Barbados, s 92; Constitution of Trinidad and Tobago, ss 88–89.

derived from the record of the case, the trial judge's report and representations made by the condemned person. The committee's advice will then be tendered to the Head of State (the Governor General or the President), who is actually the authority to grant mercy. There is no appeal against a refusal to exercise mercy, although this refusal may be followed by an appeal to the Privy Council against the dismissal of the criminal appeal by the Court of Appeal (*Logan*).

Appeal against sentence

The procedure and consequences of an appeal against sentence were discussed in Chapter 17. Nonetheless, it is relevant to note here that while failure to follow the statutory procedure may render a sentence invalid, an invalid sentence in itself does not render the entire criminal proceedings null and void: *R v Porter* (1961) 3 WIR 551. Similarly, an excessive sentence which is invalid may be simply substituted by another sentence: *R v Uxbridge JJ ex p Clarke* [1968] 2 All ER 992.

Even if there is no formal appeal against sentence, where an appellant has been jointly charged and his circumstances are similar to his co-defendant who was sentenced differently (to a lesser sentence), the court may equalise the sentences: *R v Montriou* (1921) 16 Cr App R 74.

CHAPTER 19

JUVENILES

In the twentieth century, the law evolved to provide for special treatment of juvenile offenders within the criminal justice system. The law in the Commonwealth Caribbean was initially based largely on the English Children and Young Persons Act 1933. Since then, several countries have amended their laws to make them less harsh as regards juveniles and also more in keeping with the United Nations Convention on the Rights of the Child.[1] Consequently, not only is the procedure following upon arrest of a juvenile different from that for adults, but also the likely punishment for a juvenile offender is different. This short chapter focusses on the basic differences in the trial of a juvenile as compared with the trial of an adult. These differences are in general specified by statute.

Who is a juvenile?

The term juvenile includes both a 'child' and a 'young person' and is used to refer to persons under 16.[2] This is still the law in some Commonwealth Caribbean jurisdictions, but in other jurisdictions the law has been amended to increase the age. In the Bahamas, Dominica, St Kitts and Nevis and Trinidad and Tobago a juvenile is a person under 18.[3] In Guyana it is a person under 17.[4] Grenada appears to have neither a Juveniles Act nor a Children and Young Persons Act,[5] and the relevant law on procedure for trial of a child is contained in s 84 of the Criminal Procedure Code in which the child, for the purposes of that section, is designated as a person under 14 years. In general, while a child is under 14 years old, a 'young person' is 14 to under 16, 17 or 18, as the case may be. The Child Care and Protection Act 2004 of Jamaica, which repealed the Juveniles Act and came into effect in 2005, defines 'child' as a person under 18. There is thus no separate definition of juvenile or young person in Jamaica.

Under the relevant Juvenile or Children and Young Persons Act, special provision is made for trial of a juvenile charged with an offence. The age of criminal responsibility varies across the region. The minimum age is (above) seven years (Barbados, Grenada and Trinidad and Tobago), which is the original common law position. In Guyana it is ten years and in St Lucia and Jamaica 12 years. In other jurisdictions the age of criminal responsibility appears to be over eight years old. The age is usually determined by provision in the relevant statute on juvenile offenders.

---

1 The Convention on the Rights of the Child was adopted unanimously by the United Nations General Assembly on 20 November 1989. Under the Convention, a child is a person under the age of 18 years.

2 Antigua: Juvenile Act, Cap 229, s 2; Barbados: Juvenile Offenders Act, Cap 138, s 2; St Lucia: Children and Young Persons Act, 11 of 1972, s 2; St Vincent: Juveniles Act, Cap 231, s 2.

3 Bahamas: Children and Young Persons (Administration of Justice) Act, Ch 90, s 2; Dominica: Children and Young Persons Act, Chap 37:50, s 2; St Kitts and Nevis: Juvenile Act, Cap 4:15, s 2; Trinidad and Tobago: Children Act, Chap 46:01 (as amended), s 2.

4 Guyana: Juvenile Offenders Act, Cap 10:03, s 2.

5 There is a Child Protection Act and Adoption Act 2010, which repealed the previous Act, No 17 of 1998. It deals mainly with protection of children and children's homes as well as adoption.

On arrest

There are fairly similar provisions[6] across the region for dealing with juveniles following arrest. First of all, a juvenile who is detained in a police station must be kept separate from adults. Even before and after court attendance he must be prevented from associating with adult prisoners. This is expected to be achieved through arrangements made by the Commissioner of Police. A juvenile who is arrested for any offence not involving homicide or other grave crime and who cannot be brought before a court immediately should be released in the care of his parent or guardian unless this would defeat the ends of justice. This is a special type of 'bail' allowed to a juvenile charged with an offence. If a juvenile is not released on bail, he must be remanded in a place of detention that is not a prison. This may be in a children's home or other place of detention for youthful offenders. In Guyana, the Juvenile Offenders Act was amended by Act No 18 of 2007 to provide for the establishment and maintenance of Holding Centres for juveniles.

The law also requires that parents or guardians of juveniles who have been arrested and charged attend the court where the juvenile will appear. They are either warned to attend, or may be compelled by process to attend.

Trial of juvenile

Juveniles are invariably tried in a juvenile court, which is a special type of court established by the relevant statute pertaining to juvenile trials. In some jurisdictions[7] it is provided that juvenile courts are not to be held in the regular magistrates' court buildings while in others the same buildings are used on special days. Juvenile court hearings are usually held in camera in that no persons other than the juvenile, his lawyer, the parties to the case and members and officers of the court are present, except by leave of the court. A juvenile is also entitled to have his parents present in court with him. There is restricted reporting of proceedings in the juvenile court and the names of the victim and offenders are not usually publicised.

Trial in the juvenile court involves summary trial by a magistrate and in general a juvenile who is charged for any offence other than homicide may be tried summarily[8] in the juvenile court. In Jamaica, where a child is at least 14 and the offence is one listed in the Fourth Schedule (which includes murder, treason and firearm offences), the matter is heard indictably.

In some jurisdictions, a distinction is drawn between a child and a young person in respect of a trial for more serious indictable offences, but in all jurisdictions a child (usually a person

6 Antigua: Juvenile Act, Cap 229, ss 15–18;
Bahamas: Children and Young Persons (Administration of Justice) Act Ch 90, ss 33–35;
Barbados: Juvenile Offenders Act Cap 138, ss 4–6;
Dominica: Children and Young Persons Act, Chap 37:50, ss 19–21;
Grenada: Criminal Procedure Code, Cap 72 B, ss 6–7;
Guyana: Juvenile Offenders Act, Cap 10:03, ss 5–7;
Jamaica: Child Care and Protection Act, s 66;
St Kitts and Nevis: Juvenile Act, Cap 4:15, ss 15–17;
St Lucia: Children and Young Persons Act, 11 of 1972, ss 19–21;
St Vincent: Juveniles Act, Cap 231, ss 22–24;
Trinidad and Tobago: Children Act, Chap 46:01, ss 71–74.

7 E.g., Antigua: Juveniles Courts Act, Cap 230, s 2.

8 See, e.g., Antigua: Magistrate's Code of Procedure Act, Cap 255, s 43; Bahamas: Children and Young Persons Act, Ch 90, s 8(3); Barbados: Juvenile Offenders Act, Cap 138, s 8; Guyana: Juvenile Offenders Act, Cap 10:03, s 9; Trinidad and Tobago: Summary Courts Act, Chap 4:20, s 99.

under 14) must be tried summarily for offences other than homicide. Thus, in these jurisdictions, for all indictable offences but homicide, a child is tried by a magistrate sitting in the juvenile court.

A young person may, however, be tried indictably for an indictable offence other than murder. This is because most jurisdictions provide that the young person may be asked if he consents to the trial of an indictable offence summarily. In the case of a child, there is no question of consent by the child. The matter (other than homicide) is dealt with summarily as a matter of course, unless statute gives the right to the parents to elect indictable trial,[9] which is the case in a few jurisdictions.

If a juvenile is jointly charged with an adult, different considerations apply.[10] The procedure is determined by statute, but in general the juvenile may be tried with the adult who has been committed for trial. It appears that the preliminary enquiry in respect of the juvenile may be heard in the juvenile court. In practice, if the juvenile is at least a young person, he may be tried as an adult for an indictable offence. For summary offences, even if he is alleged to have committed the offence with an adult, he may yet be tried in the juvenile court. The procedure in trial at the juvenile court is not as strict in the regular magistrates' courts. For instance, in some cases the parents of the juvenile may ask questions of the witnesses. At the end of the prosecution case, the juvenile is allowed to make a statement in lieu of giving evidence on oath. The court relaxes the rules of evidence in an effort to make the proceedings more friendly and the parties more at ease.

Methods of disposal of cases

As has already been discussed,[11] a person who is convicted of murder committed when he was under 18 may not be sentenced to death, but must be otherwise detained. A child who is found guilty of any offence may not be sentenced to imprisonment. He may be sent to a training school or other place of detention for a specific period, usually not exceeding three years. A young person who is convicted in a juvenile court may in general be sentenced to imprisonment, but a maximum period is set by statute and this is usually no more than three months.[12]

The Jamaica legislation makes detailed provision in s 76 of the Child Care and Protection Act for dealing with child offenders, including detention at a child correctional centre. For instance, s 79 provides that 'a court shall not order a child under the age of twelve years to be sent to a juvenile correctional centre unless for any reason the court is satisfied that the child cannot suitably be dealt with otherwise'. It is unclear whether this means that a child may only be sent to a correctional centre if he cannot be dealt with otherwise. Furthermore, although the Act states that a child shall not be sentenced to imprisonment for any offence, it permits under s 78(5)

9 See, e.g.:
Dominica: Magistrate's Court of Procedure Act, Chap 4:20, s 40;
St Vincent: Criminal Procedure Code, Cap 172, s 15.

10 Grenada: Juvenile Justice Act No 24 of 2012, s 47;
St Kitts: Juvenile Act, Chap 4:15, s 19;
St Lucia: Children and Young Persons Act, Chap 3.09, s 22.

11 See Chapter 18.

12 As in: Barbados: Juvenile Offenders Act, Cap 138, s 9(6); Dominica: Magistrate's Code of Procedure Act, Chap 4:20, ss 90–94; St Kitts and Nevis: Magistrate's Code of Procedure Act, Cap 3:17, s 102.

> where a child under the age of fourteen years is convicted of an offence specified in the Fourth Schedule and the court is of opinion that none of the other methods in which the case may legally be dealt with is suitable, the court may sentence the child to be detained for such period, not exceeding twenty-five years, as the court may determine.

The provisions of these sections, on the face of it, appear to be ambiguous to some extent.

Other than the rare instance of custodial sentencing, a juvenile who is tried summarily is liable to a range of other sentences which are identical across the region.[13]

Even if the juvenile offender is found guilty, the court may dismiss the case. Alternatively, the court may make a probation order under the Probation Act or place the offender under supervision of a probation officer or other person for up to three years. Other forms of punishment include discharging the offender on his entering into a recognisance for good behaviour; committing him to the care of a fit person; ordering the parents/guardian to give security for the good behaviour of the child; ordering the offender or the parent/guardian to pay a fine; sending the offender to an industrial school or committing him to another place of detention. In deciding what punishment to impose, the court will have regard to the nature of the offence, the age of the offender and the interests of justice in general.

If the juvenile is discharged or placed on probation, a conviction should not be recorded against him if he does not misbehave. Where, however, he is sentenced to a place of detention, this means that he has been convicted, so a conviction will usually be recorded.

There have been recent changes in the law across the region to improve the treatment of juvenile offenders. For instance, in Trinidad and Tobago the law was changed to provide that no person under 18[14] should be subjected to corporal punishment. In St Kitts and Nevis, Act No 6 of 1998 amended the Juvenile Act to provide for committal of juvenile offenders to a juvenile rehabilitation centre. This type of centre was also created by that Act. Jamaica brought its Child Care and Protection Act into effect in 2005 primarily to provide for the care, protection and education of children. Among the new provisions of the Act are the institution of the Children's Court and the creation of the office of Children's Advocate. Guyana, through its Juvenile Offenders (Amendment) Act 2007, provided for the establishment of Holding Centres for juveniles, which must be certified by the Minister. Juveniles are held in these centres while in custody and awaiting release. The significant difference in policy in the treatment of juvenile offenders as against adult offenders is that, in respect of the former, the law is truly moving towards rehabilitation and reform of the offender.

In Trinidad and Tobago, Judges' Rules for children came into effect in November 2016, which declare that they are to be treated as a code of practice for the guidance of police officers. The rules deal with such pre-trial matters as stop and search, and questioning before search. There are also rules on arrest and interrogation of children, including the recording of confessions. Rules on gathering evidence include fingerprinting, identification parades, and the taking of intimate and non-intimate samples from a child. Where the rules are breached, it will not automatically invalidate any procedure but its effect will be a matter for the court to decide.

---

13 Barbados: Juvenile Offenders Act, Cap 138, ss 13–16;
Dominica: Magistrate's Code of Procedure Act, Chap 4:20, ss 92–94;
Grenada: Juvenile Justice Act, No 24 of 2012, ss 55, 56 and 61;
St Lucia: Children and Young Persons Act, Chap 3.09, ss 16–18;
Trinidad and Tobago: Children Act, Chap 46:01, s 59.

14 Act No 66 of 2000.

Jurisdiction over children's matters

In Trinidad and Tobago, since the commencement of The Children and Family Division Act of 2016,[15] the authority and jurisdiction in children matters exercisable by the High Court and Courts of Summary Jurisdiction is now exercisable by the Children Court. Children Court judges and masters hear criminal matters in the Children Court and exercise powers (in addition to the powers conferred under the Supreme Court of Judicature Act) usually exercisable by a magistrate in children matters under the Summary Courts Act. The judges and masters may also hear and determine maintenance matters and applications for protection orders under Domestic Violence legislation.

Sentencing options

Under The Children Act, Chap 46:01, the court's sentencing options[16] include:

a) dismissal of the charge;
b) discharge of the offender and placing him under the supervision of a probation officer;
c) committal of the offender to a Community Residence appropriate to the age of the child;
d) ordering the offender to pay a fine, damages and costs.

First offenders

Where a child is convicted of any offence and the offence is his first offence, the court may pronounce a custodial sentence only in certain circumstances, such as if the court is convinced that the offence is so grave that no other punishment or course of action that it is authorised to impose under the Act is sufficient and, having regard to relevant information, it is in the best interests of the child that he be placed in an appropriate Community Residence.[17]

Peer resolution

Where a child who is charged with an offence, other than those offences prescribed in Schedule 4 (murder, conspiring or soliciting to commit murder, manslaughter), enters a plea of guilty, the Children Court may, with the agreement of the child and the consent of the parent, guardian or person with responsibility for the child, refer the matter to Court-annexed Peer Resolution to seek a recommendation as to the appropriate measures or sanctions to be employed for the offence.[18]

Appeals

An appeal shall lie from any judgment or order of a Children Court master or a Children Court judge to the Court of Appeal in like manner and to like extent as an appeal from any judgment or order of a judge.[19]

15 Act No.6 of 2016.
16 Chap 46:01, s 59(2)).
17 Fn. 16, s 59(3).
18 Fn. 15, s 40.
19 Fn. 15, s 58.

CHAPTER 20

EXTRADITION

David West[1]

Extradition is the legal process whereby a person accused or convicted of an extraditable offence in one State is found in another State (the requested State) and the foreign State (the requesting State) seeks the return of that person through diplomatic channels to be tried or to serve his sentence in the requesting State.

The conduct of extradition proceedings is governed entirely by statute. Failure to comply with the relevant statute will render the order committing a person for extradition void: *US Government v Bowe* (1989) 37 WIR 9, PC. The lawyer must therefore follow the extradition legislation to the letter. A wrong step in the extradition process can invalidate the whole request which can be a great embarrassment to a government.

BACKGROUND

All Commonwealth Caribbean extradition legislation have their genesis in the UK Extradition Act of 1870, which made reference to the colonies. In 1966 Commonwealth Law Ministers met in London and devised an extradition scheme for the 'rendition' of fugitive criminals within the Commonwealth. This scheme was known as 'scheme for the Rendition of Fugitive Offenders within the Commonwealth' (Cmnd 3008). This scheme, often referred to as 'the London Scheme' was revised in 1983. Some Commonwealth Caribbean jurisdictions still rely on the Fugitive Offenders Act 1967 as a basis for their extradition legislation.[2]

Extradition legislation has been improved significantly within the Commonwealth Caribbean. Canada passed a new Extradition Act in 1999[3] which for the first time allowed evidence to be admissible via a Record of Case method, which allows hearsay evidence instead of the cumbersome method of authentication of documents by a judge, magistrate or officer in the requesting state. Trinidad and Tobago has also followed this method of admissibility of evidence with great success.[4]

Going a step further, Caricom countries have now agreed in principle to an extradition scheme amongst Caricom countries known as 'the Caricom Arrest Warrant Treaty'. This revolutionary process of rendition will allow an arrest warrant backed by the signature of a judge to be the basis of a request to another country. On receipt of the arrest warrant, the person wanted would be arrested, taken before a magistrate and returned to the requesting State. There would be no need for formal authenticated evidence.

Extradition and Mutual Legal Assistance are two important tools in the fight against transnational crime. Mutual Assistance is a relatively new concept that involves countries rendering assistance to each other in order to facilitate the successful prosecution of offences in the respective country. Some examples of assistance include:

a) taking the testimony or statements of persons;
b) providing documents, records and articles of evidence;

---

1 David West, an attorney at law, was head of the Central Authority of Trinidad and Tobago for over 10 years until 2009. He is now in private practice.

2 St Vincent & the Grenadines.

3 1999 Extradition Act (SC 1999, c 18).

4 Extradition (Commonwealth and Foreign Territories) Act 1986 as amended, s 19A(5).

c) locating or identifying persons;
d) serving documents;
e) transferring persons in custody for testimony or other purposes;
f) executing requests for searches and seizures;
g) assisting in proceedings related to restraint, confiscation, forfeiture of assets, restitution and collection of fines and
h) examining objects and sites.

Many countries have signed bi-lateral and multi-lateral treaties that allow for evidence to be transmitted from one country to the other. The department/unit involved in this process is designated the Central Authority, which is usually based either in the Ministry of the Attorney General or the Director of Public Prosecutions Department.

BASIC EXTRADITION PROCEDURE

The request

When the requesting state knows the whereabouts of an accused person or a person convicted of an extraditable offence who has fled its jurisdiction, the police, usually INTERPOL, contacts the Central Authority/Director of Public Prosecutions Department (DPP) of the country in which the person is to be found to make a request for the extradition of that person. The Central Authority/DPP will contact their counterparts in the requested State to inform them that a request for extradition will be forthcoming.

When the request arrives at the Central Authority/DPP in the requested State, counsel at that department will prepare the arrest warrant (provisional or full), the Authority to Proceed (ATP) and any other necessary documentation. A copy of the provisional/full request with the warrant of arrest and ATP, if necessary, is forwarded to the magistrates' court for signature by a magistrate. Normally the complainant takes the documentation from the Central Authority/DPP to the magistrate and swears to the warrant of arrest. When the person accused or convicted of the extradition crime is arrested he is brought before the magistrates' court as soon as practicable.

Hearing before the magistrate

The hearing of an extradition case is similar to a committal/preliminary enquiry.[5] The parties before the court are the requesting State (who has initiated the matter) and the

5 Antigua and Barbuda: Extradition Act No 12 of 1993, s 11(1);
Bahamas: Act No 8 of 1994, s 10 (1);
Barbados: Cap 189, Act No 21 of 1979, s 13(3);
Belize: Extradition Act, Cap 112 Revised Edition 2000, s 3;
Dominica: Act No 6 of 1981, s 13(3);
Grenada: Extradition Act, Cap 98, s 11(1);
Guyana: Fugitive Offenders Act No 15 of 1998, s 15;
Jamaica: Extradition Act No 7 of 1991, s 10(1);
St Lucia: Extradition Act No 12 of 1986, s 12(3);
St Kitts and Nevis: Extradition Act 1870, s 9;
St Vincent: Fugitive Offenders Act, Cap 175, s 12;
Trinidad and Tobago: Extradition Act No 36 of 1985, s 12(2).

accused. A good practice is for counsel representing the requesting State to furnish a copy of the domestic charges to the accused.[6] This is because the ATP is addressed to the magistrate, however the person accused or convicted is entitled to know what charges he has to meet.[7] If the requesting State has only made a provisional request, then it will have a period of time to produce the extradition documents.[8] Normally the time allowed is 60 days (this time limit will differ from treaty to treaty). However, the requesting State can ask for an extension of time, once good cause can be shown to the magistrate. There is a duty on the magistrate to fix a date to receive the ATP.[9] Counsel representing the requesting State will call at least two main witnesses: (1) the person who received the documents from the requesting State to tender the evidence and certificate of specialty[10] and (2) the arresting police officer to identify the accused.

After the witnesses for the requesting State have been cross examined but before the case for the prosecution is closed, counsel for the requesting State tenders the ATP into evidence as a court exhibit. At this stage counsel for the accused can make a submission of no case to answer. If the magistrate overrules the submission the defence has the option of calling witnesses and/or the accused can even go into the witness box and testify.[11] If the magistrate finds that a prima facie case has been made out then the magistrate commits the accused into custody. If the magistrate is of the opinion that a prima facie case is not made out then he must discharge the accused forthwith.

Sometimes the accused person may have knowledge that a request for his extradition will be made by a requesting State. The accused person will then make representations to the relevant Minister and the Chief Magistrate that an ATP should not be issued and a warrant taken out for his arrest. It was held in *R v Home Secretary ex p Norgren (DC)* [2000] QB 817, 826H, that:

---

6 *Charron v Government of the United States of America and anor* (2000) 56 WIR 27, PC.

7 In the matter of *Javid Nagdhi* [1989] Crim LR 825.

8 Antigua: Extradition Act No 12 of 1993, s 11(4);
Bahamas: Act No 8 of 1994, s 10(3);
Barbados: Cap 189, Act No 21 of 1979, s 10 does not differentiate between provisional and full warrants;
Belize: Extradition Act, Cap 112 Revised Edition 2000, s 6;
Dominica: Act No 6 of 1981, s 10 does not differentiate between provisional and full warrants;
Grenada: Extradition Act, Cap 98 s 11(4); Guyana: Fugitive Offenders Act No 15 of 1998, s 15(4);
Jamaica: Extradition Act No 7 of 1991, s 10(3)(4);
St Lucia: Extradition Act No 12 of 1986, s 9 does not differentiate between provisional and full warrant;
St Kitts and Nevis: Extradition Act 1870, s 8;
St Vincent: Fugitive Offenders Act, Cap 175, s 2(3);
Trinidad and Tobago: Extradition Act 1985 Act No 36 of 1985, s 12(3).

9 *Government of the Federal Republic of Germany v Sotiriadis* [1975] AC 1.

10 Form of certificate should be in terms of:
Antigua: Extradition Act No 12 of 1993, s 8(4);
Bahamas: Act No 8 of 1994, s 7(3);
Barbados: Cap 189, Act No 21 of 1979, s 7(2);
Belize: Extradition Act, Cap 112 Revised Edition 2000, s 3;
Dominica: Act No 6 of 1981, s 7(2);
Grenada: Extradition Act, Cap 98, s 8(4);
Guyana: Fugitive Offenders Act No 15 of 1998, s 8 (3);
Jamaica: Extradition Act No 7 of 1991, s 7(3);
St Lucia: Extradition Act No 12 of 1986, s 6(3);
St Kitts and Nevis: Extradition Act 1870, s 3(2);
St Vincent: Fugitive Offenders Act, Cap 175, s 7(3);
Trinidad and Tobago: Extradition Act No 36 of 1985, s 8(3).

11 *R v Governor of Brixton Prison, ex p Gross* [1999] QB 538.

> The statutory scheme makes no provision for representations to be made by the object of an extradition request before an order to proceed is issued.

Therefore, the person accused or convicted of an extraditable offence has no statutory authority to make any representations at this stage and the relevant Minister or magistrate should ignore such a request. In *Jack Austin Warner v The Attorney General of Trinidad and Tobago*, Claim No CV 2015-04091, dated 27 September 2017, the Honourable Mr Justice Aboud held that a person facing extradition did not have a right to be heard before the issuance of an ATP. Justice Aboud in his judgment quoted from ex p Norgren (above).

Can an interested party intervene in judicial review proceedings?

In the case of *Jack Austin Warner v The Attorney General of Trinidad and Tobago*, Claim No CV 2015-04091, dated 17 June 2016, the United States Government filed an application to be an interested party in Mr Warner's judicial review claim. The claimant, Jack Warner, objected. In ruling on the application, Justice Aboud held:[12]

> In my opinion the requirement of sufficient interest is not necessarily satisfied when an applicant only has an interest in the outcome or result of the claim. The quality or sufficiency of the interest must be examined. It should be an interest that is connected to and important to the fair resolution of the subject matter of the claim. Being affected by the eventual ruling is not, it seems to me, the critical or sole consideration. If an applicant with such an interest was excluded from participating and the exclusion would potentially cause damage to it or lead to an unjust result ... then that, of course, is an abrogation of its natural justice right to be heard in its own cause. A sufficient interest would normally be evident in a case like that.

Justice Aboud[13] found that the following factors would constitute 'sufficient interest' to link an interested party in extradition proceedings:

(1) if 'the Judicial Review concerned or was partially connected to a dispute between the claimant and the applicant as to the viability of the record of the case before the Chief Magistrate'.
(2) where it was alleged that the applicant acted improperly in making its extradition request; or
(3) whether there was a question as to whether the applicant was seeking to extradite the claimant for improper purposes.

Justice Aboud concluded that the applicant United States Government did not show a sufficient interest to be allowed to intervene. He elaborated that this was not a situation where the USA had indicated that its position was different from that of the Attorney General, or that the Attorney General was unwilling or unable to represent their viewpoint (assuming that the viewpoints were different).

12 at para 17.
13 at para 22.

Must an extradition treaty be in conformity with the act?

In *Jack Austin Warner v The Attorney General of Trinidad and Tobago*, Claim No. CV 2015-04091, dated 27 September 2017, the claimant, Mr Warner, attacked the validity of the Extradition Treaty made between the USA and Trinidad and Tobago. He claimed that the Treaty was not in conformity with the Extradition Act, and therefore, since the Attorney General was required to certify the conformity before making the Order declaring the United States of America as a foreign territory, the AG had exceeded his jurisdiction under the Act when he made the Order. The claimant's argument concluded that the Order was void and consequently an ATP could not be issued pursuant to the Order.

It is important to set out Section 4 of the Trinidad and Tobago Extradition Act 1985 as amended. (Note the 2004 amendment Act did not affect the wording of Section 4.)

> (1) Where a Treaty has been concluded, whether before or after the commencement of this Act, between Trinidad and Tobago and any foreign territory in relation to the return of fugitive offenders, the Attorney General may, by Order subject to negative resolution of Parliament, declare that territory to be a foreign territory (hereafter referred to as a declared foreign territory) in relation to which this Act applies, and where any such Order so declares, this Act applies in relation to that territory; and any such Order may provide that this Act applies in relation to that territory subject to such exceptions, adaptations, modifications or other provisions as may be specified in the Order and, where any such Order so provides, this Act applies in relation to that territory subject to such exceptions, adaptations, modifications or other provisions.
>
> (2) An Order shall not be made under subsection (1) unless the Treaty –
>
> (a) **is in conformity with the provisions of this Act, and in particular with the restrictions on the return of fugitive offenders contained in this Act**; and
>
> (b) provides for the determination of the Treaty by either party to it after the expiration of a notice not exceeding one year.
>
> (3) An Order made under subjection (1) shall recite or embody the terms of the Treaty and shall not remain in force for any longer period than the Treaty; **and the Order shall be conclusive evidence that the Treaty complies with the requisitions of this Act and that this Act applies in relation to the foreign territory mentioned in the Order, and the validity of the Order shall not be questioned in any legal proceedings whatever.** (Emphases added.)

Justice Aboud held that Section 4(3) of the Act did not prevent the judiciary from reviewing the validity of the USA Order and the conclusive evidence clauses. Having held that the courts had the power to enquire into the validity of the Order made between Trinidad and Tobago and the USA, Justice Aboud went on to consider whether or not the Act was in conformity with the Treaty.

Justice Aboud premised his decision on the fact that extradition statutes ought to be given a broad and general construction in order to facilitate extradition rather than obstruct it. He cited well-known cases such as *Kindler v Canada* (1991) 84 DLR (4th) 438 at 488; and *Cartwright v Superintendent of Her Majesty's Prison* [2004] 1 WLR 902, para. 15. Justice Aboud held that the issue to be decided was whether or not the differences between the Treaty and the Act were so severe – or so out of conformity with the 1985 Act (or the 2004 Act) – that the Order made by the Attorney General was void.

After concluding his review of the alleged inconsistencies between the Treaty and the Act (see paras 58 to 96 of the judgment), Justice Aboud determined that the Order was valid.

The Claimant has since appealed this decision to the Court of Appeal.

Bail

When the accused person is brought before the magistrates' court he is entitled to apply for bail.[14] A court's primary concern in deciding whether or not to grant bail is whether the fugitive would surrender to the custody of the court when called upon.[15] If there is an objection to bail the onus of proof is on counsel for the requesting state and the standard of proof is on a balance of probabilities.[16] In most cases the person accused or convicted of the extraditable offence has fled from the requesting jurisdiction, is found in the requested jurisdiction and an extradition request has been made for his return. This in itself would constitute evidence against granting bail.

All Commonwealth Caribbean jurisdictions have their respective Bail Acts which cover instances when bail should or should not be granted. In extradition cases when a magistrate or judge is considering whether or not to grant bail, in addition to the factors outlined in the Bail Act there should be a special need for care and caution in the grant of bail. However, a major factor which courts take into consideration when deciding whether to grant bail to a fugitive are the treaty obligations of the countries.[17]

The factors that a court will take into account in deciding whether or not to grant bail are similar to the circumstances if the offence had been committed in the requested State. Some of the factors are:

- The seriousness of the offence.
- Whether the person wanted or convicted is a national of the requested country.
- Whether the person wanted or convicted would fail to surrender to custody.
- Whether the person wanted or convicted would commit an offence whilst on bail.
- Whether the person wanted or convicted would interfere with witnesses, or obstruct the course of justice.

---

14 Antigua and Barbuda: Extradition Act No 12 of 1993, s 11(2).
Bahamas: Act No 8 of 1994, s 10(2);
Barbados: Cap 189, Act No 21 of 1979, s 14(1)(2);
Belize: Extradition Act, Cap 112 Revised Edition 2000, s 3;
Dominica: Act No 6 of 1981, s 14(1)(2);
Grenada: Extradition Act, Cap 98, s 11(2);
Guyana: Fugitive Offenders Act No 15 of 1998, s 15(2);
Jamaica: Extradition Act No 7 of 1991, s 10(2);
St Lucia: Extradition Act No 12 of 1986, s 13(1)(2);
St Kitts and Nevis: Extradition Act 1870, s 9;
St Vincent and the Grenadines: Fugitive Offenders Act, Cap 175 s 12(2);
Trinidad and Tobago: Extradition Act No 36 of 1985, s 12(2).

15 *Re Gordon Young*, 1 Belize Law Reports 220.

16 *R v Governor of Canterbury Prison, ex p Craig* [1991] 2 QB 195.

17 *Re Gordon Young* (above); *R v Phillips* (1922) 27 Cox CC 160; *R v Spilsbury* [1898] 2 QB 615; *United Mexican States v Cabal* (2001) HCA 60.

- The wanted or convicted person's social ties to the community, his associations or antecedents.
- The length of time the person has been in the requested jurisdiction.

In 2005 the Privy Council held in *Knowles v Supt of Fox Hill Prison* (2005) 69 WIR 1, PC 11:

> Mere residence and having a family in the country do not necessarily lead to the conclusion that there will be no attempt to flee the jurisdiction, particularly in a case where it is possible that substantial sums of money may be available from drug smuggling.

If bail is granted to a person wanted or convicted of an extraditable offence then there are usually very stringent conditions attached. Such conditions may include, for example, a large sum to secure bail, reporting conditions and surrender of all travel documents.

After committal proceedings a question may arise as to whether a person accused or convicted of an extraditable offence can obtain bail before applying for a writ of habeas corpus. Unusually the Antigua legislation provides for bail immediately after the committal stage.[18] In the Trinidad and Tobago case of *Ishwar Galbaransingh and Steve Ferguson v The Commissioner of Prisons*, CV2008-02848 and CV2008-02849, High Court T&T, Pemberton J, held that the 'application for and the grant of bail cannot predate the application for habeas corpus'. In contrast, in *Launder v Governor of Brixton Prison* [1998] EWHC Admin 214, Mance J was of the view that habeas corpus was available to a person even though granted bail. Paragraph 51 of the judgment provides:

> Habeas corpus addresses in origin the situation of persons wrongly detained in another's custody, and the prescribed forms for use in habeas corpus cases still refer to the respondent 'having the custody or body of the applicant' and to the body of the applicant being 'taken and detained under your custody' (c.f. prescribed forms 87–90 in Section A of Part 2 of the Supreme Court Practice). **Nevertheless, in the context of extradition at least, it is clear that habeas corpus will lie, although the person being sought to be extradited has been committed on bail, rather than in custody.** In other contexts, too, as Simon Brown L.J. has pointed out, there is authority that the bailing of a person seeking habeas corpus is no bar to the issue of the writ. (Emphasis added.)

The Court of Appeal of Trinidad and Tobago in *Steve Ferguson and Ishwar Galbaransingh v The Commissioner of Prisons* Civil Appeal No. 108 of 2009 Justice of Appeal Smith followed the reasoning in *Launder v Governor of Brixton Prison* (above) and expressly stated that habeas corpus proceedings are available to persons already on bail in extradition proceedings.

THE AUTHORITY TO PROCEED

This is the pivotal document in extradition proceedings. It has been held in *R v Governor of Brixton Prison and Another Ex parte Cuoghi* [1998] 1 WLR 1513 that the Attorney General may grant an Authority to Proceed (ATP) in the absence of duly authenticated documents. However, at the committal proceedings the documents must be duly authenticated to be admissible in evidence. Once the Attorney General receives the extradition request and

18 Antigua: Extradition Act No 12 of 1993, s 11(9).

issues his ATP, extradition proceedings have begun.[19] If a person wanted or convicted of an extradition offence was detained pursuant to a provisional arrest warrant the ATP takes over and validates anything that was incorrect.[20]

More than one ATP may be issued on the same request for extradition.[21] It would, however, be an abuse of process to continuously re-arrest a person accused or convicted of the extraditable offence until the requesting State obtains a committal.[22]

There are conflicting views on whether or not it is necessary to issue a warrant of arrest (for a person accused or convicted of an extraditable offence who was previously arrested on a provisional warrant) once the ATP has been signed. In *Athanassiadis v Government of Greece* [1971] AC 282 and *Edwards v Director of Public Prosecutions* (1994) 47 WIR 302, the courts held that it would be 'as unnecessary as would be the issue of a warrant for the arrest of a person serving a sentence of imprisonment'. Lord Diplock, however, stated in *Sotiriadis* (at p 29C–D):

> If an order of the Secretary of State is received before the date (fixed by the Magistrate for the production of the order to proceed), the prisoner should be brought before the magistrate without delay. He should be informed of the charges made against him in the requisition and if, as would usually be the case, the judicial hearing cannot start immediately, he should be told that he is being remanded in custody pending the hearing of the case against him for his extradition on those charges.

In the Trinidad and Tobago case of *Judicial Review application by Ibrahim Noumeh (TT)* HCA No 1160 of 1998, the court was of the view that out of an abundance of caution the accused should be arrested and brought before the magistrate if only to be informed of the President's Authority to Proceed (now ATP) and what crimes/offences he has to answer.

The offences listed in the ATP should be the equivalent local offences to those which the accused is charged with abroad. Counsel who is drafting the ATP should transpose the foreign offences into local offences since the magistrate does not take into account foreign law.[23] In *Alain Charron v The Government of the United States and The Superintendent of Her Majesty's Prison*, Commonwealth of the Bahamas, CA Crim App No 16 of 1998, Gonsalves-Sabola P stated:

> In fact, in the ATP which gave jurisdiction to the court of committal, the equivalent Bahamian offences were identified by the responsible minister as conspiracy to possess dangerous drugs with intent to supply, and conspiracy to export dangerous drugs contrary to Sections 14 (4) and 29 (1) respectively of the Dangerous Drugs Act of the Bahamas.

In Jamaica and Guyana it appears that the ATP may list the foreign offences. In *Emmanuel v Commissioner of Correctional Services and another* (2007) 73 WIR 291, Harrison P stated:

> Nowhere in this section or under any other provision in the Act is the Minister required in his authority to proceed, to translate offences framed in terms of foreign law in a requesting state's indictment, in terms of Jamaican law.

19 *Gov't of the Federal Republic of Germany v Sotiriadis* [1975] AC 1.

20 *R v Governor of Pentonville Prison ex p Osman* (No 3) [1990] 1 WLR 878; *R v Bow Street Magistrates' Court ex p Van Der Holst* (1985) 83 Cr App Rep 114.

21 *US Government v Bowe* (1989) 37 WIR 7, PC; *Rees v Sec of State for the Home Dept* [1986] AC 937; HCA No 3388/2001 *Leon Paul Williams v The AG of T&T*.

22 HCA No 3388/2001 *Leon Paul Williams* (above).

23 *Government of Denmark v Neilsen* [1984] AC 606 at 619.

Harrison P went on to state that it is up to the magistrate to determine 'in his opinion' whether the offences charged in the foreign indictment can be translatable into corresponding offences under Jamaican law.

DISCLOSURE

It is entirely up to the requesting State what material it discloses to the person accused or convicted of an extraditable offence. There is no statutory requirement of disclosure so any disclosure is voluntary;[24] even where the material exists in the requested country there can be no compulsion of disclosure. The courts have resisted imposing domestic criminal procedure into extradition proceedings.[25]

There is, however, a duty of candour on the requesting State. Failure to disclose material beneficial to the accused or convicted person could render the extradition proceedings an abuse of process. It is settled law that the requesting State should disclose any material that 'destroys or very severely undermines the evidence on which it relies': *Samuel Knowles Jr v The Government of USA* (2006) 69 WIR 1, PC at 3. It is up to the person being extradited to raise the issue of non-disclosure and that person must show that the material is in the hands of the requesting state.[26]

In *Ralston Wellington v The Government of the United States of America* [2004] EWHC 418 (Admin), a decision of the Divisional Court, endorsed by the Privy Council in *Knowles* (above), Mitting J stated six propositions governing disclosure in extradition proceedings:

1. It is for the requesting State alone to determine the evidence upon which it relies to seek a committal.
2. The requesting State is not under any general duty of disclosure similar to that imposed on the prosecution at any stage in domestic criminal proceedings.
3. The magistrates' court has the right to protect its process from abuse of process and the requesting State has a duty not to abuse that process. That is no different from saying that the requesting State must fulfil the duty, which it has always had, of candour in making applications for extradition.
4. In fulfilment of that duty, the requesting State must disclose any evidence which would render worthless the evidence on which it relies to seek committal.
5. It is for the person subject to the extradition process to establish that the requesting State is abusing the process of the court.
6. The requested State may be given power to request further evidence under the relevant Order in Council but, in the absence of evidence of abuse, the court is entitled to, and should generally, refuse to request the UK authorities to exercise that power or to adjourn to permit it to be exercised.

24 *Re Proulx* [2001] 1 All ER 57.
25 *R v Governor of Pentonville Prison ex p Lee* [1993] 1 WLR 1294.
26 *Michael Haroo v Commr of Prisons*, CV 2006–03583 (TT).

EXTRADITABLE OFFENCE

In order to constitute an extraditable offence the conduct alleged against the person accused or convicted, as described by the requesting State, must correspond with an offence which is punishable under the laws of the requested State, usually for a specified minimum period. In all Commonwealth Caribbean extradition legislation there exists a comprehensive definition of what is an extraditable offence.[27] Some Commonwealth Caribbean countries still have what is known as a list of extraditable offences and other countries have a minimum penalty clause. In deciding what is an extraditable offence, the courts look at the *conduct* of the person accused or convicted of the extraditable offence.[28] Since most of the conduct takes place outside of the requested State the conduct has to be transposed to the requested State, i.e., if the conduct took place in the requested country would that amount to an offence?[29] A warrant of arrest should only be issued if the offence is an extraditable offence and the offence is alleged to have taken place within the jurisdiction of the requesting State.

In addition, for an offence to be deemed an extraditable offence, it has been held in *R v Bow Street Magistrates Court ex p Pinochet (No 3)* [2000] 1 AC 147, HL, that the conduct must be punishable at the time the offence was committed and not the date of the request.

ADMISSIBILITY OF EVIDENCE

A case for extradition against the accused or the person convicted of an extraditable offence cannot be made out unless the documents accompanying the extradition package are admitted into evidence under the relevant extradition legislation.[30] There will invariably be a challenge to

---

27 Antigua and Barbuda: Extradition Act No 12 of 1993, s 4;
Bahamas: Act No 8 of 1994, s 5;
Barbados: Cap 189, Act No 21 of 1979, s 4;
Belize: Extradition Act, Cap 112 Revised Edition 2000, s 3. See also: Art 2 of Treaty with USA;
Dominica: Act No 6 of 1981, s 4;
Grenada: Extradition Act, Cap 98, s 4;
Guyana: Fugitive Offenders Act No 15 of 1998, s 5;
Jamaica: Extradition Act No 7 of 1991, s 5;
St Lucia: Extradition Act No 12 of 1986, s 3;
St Kitts and Nevis: Extradition Act 1870, s 26;
St Vincent: Fugitive Offenders Act, Cap 175, s 6;
Trinidad and Tobago: Extradition Act No 36 of 1985, s 6.

28 *Government of Denmark v Neilsen* [1984] AC 606.

29 *Al-Fawwaz v Governor of Brixton* [2002] 1 AC 556.

30 Antigua and Barbuda: Extradition Act No 12 of 1993, ss 28 and 29;
Bahamas: Act No 8 of 1994, s 14;
Barbados: Cap 189, Act No 21 of 1979, ss 15 and 16;
Belize: Extradition Act, Cap 112 Revised Edition 2000, s 3 and Art 7 USA Treaty;
Dominica: Act No 6 of 1981, ss 15 and 16;
Grenada: Extradition Act, Cap 98 ss 30 and 31;
Guyana: Fugitive Offenders Act No 15 of 1998, s 24;
Jamaica: Extradition Act No 7 of 1991, s 14;
St Lucia: Extradition Act No 12 of 1986, ss 14 and 15;
St Kitts and Nevis: Extradition Act 1870, ss 14 and 15;
St Vincent: Fugitive Offenders Act, Cap 175, s 26;
Trinidad and Tobago: Extradition Act No 36 of 1985, s 19A.

authentication and admissibility of the documents. All Caribbean Commonwealth territories except Trinidad and Tobago[31] require that documents purporting to contain sworn testimony of evidence must be 'duly authenticated' if the document purports to be certified by a judge, magistrate or officer of the requesting State.

As Harrison P in *Ramcharan v Commr. of Correctional Services and anor* (2007) 73 WIR 312 at 321, stated:

> Authentication under the Act is therefore a dual purpose, namely:
>
> (a) certification, by the relevant judicial or diplomatic authority of the requesting state, vouching for the genuine nature of the documents as being either originals or true copies of originals, and
>
> (b) authentication, by the oath of the witness or the formal affixing of a seal by the relevant minister in the requesting state. This is in essence a subsidiary authentication.

It has been held that a Public Prosecutor is 'plainly an officer of the Netherlands'[32] and that certification is 'to declare or attest by formal legal certificate'.[33] Duly authenticated documents do not make the evidence admissible. The evidence must still satisfy all the legal rules. Generally the rules against hearsay apply.[34] In Trinidad and Tobago, however, following Canadian precedent, statute provides that evidence that would otherwise be inadmissible is admissible under the Extradition Act. For a valid authentication it is not necessary for every document to have a valid certificate by a judge, magistrate or officer of the foreign territory testifying as to its authenticity. If all the statements are tied together and authenticated by a certificate identifying the statements, that would be a valid means of authentication.[35]

This dual method of certification and authentication was thought to be cumbersome and time consuming. Canada in 1999 changed their method of certification whereby a prosecuting authority would sign the document stating that the evidence was available for trial in the requesting State. This was deemed sufficient certification.[36] Trinidad and Tobago in 2004 amended its legislation to along similar lines as the Canadian law except that the certification must confirm admissibility rather than availability. Certification by an Assistant United States Attorney has been challenged as not being that of a prosecuting authority. In *Steve Ferguson and Ishwar Galbaransingh v Attorney General of Trinidad and Tobago and Chief Magistrate*, CV 2006–2959 (TT), Bereaux J stated at page 29:

> There was no such specificity in *Warris*. Moreover, there is evidence from Mr. Alexander Acosta, the United States Attorney for the Southern District of Florida, that Mr. Axelrod is a prosecuting authority. In my judgment, it is sufficient for the purposes of Section 19 A (3) that the certificate states on the face of the record that '*I am a prosecuting authority*'. ... Once the document recites that the official is a prosecuting authority on its face it is admissible.

31 Trinidad and Tobago amended its Extradition Act by Act No 12 of 2004.

32 Per Lloyd J in *R v Bow Street Magistrates' Court ex p Van der Holst* (1985) 83 Crim App Rep 114.

33 Per Watkins LJ in *Re Espinoza* [1986] Crim LR 684, DC.

34 *R v Governor of Pentonville Prison ex p Kirby* [1979] 1 WLR 541, DC; *R v Governor of Pentonville Prison ex p Osman* [1989] 3 All ER 701.

35 *Oskar v Government of the Commonwealth of Australia* [1988] AC 366.

36 *United States of America v Ferras* (above).

TEST FOR COMMITTAL[37]

There are different elements that the requesting State must prove in order to secure a committal.

First, the requesting State must show that the offence in the ATP is an extraditable offence. Second, there must be evidence that if the *conduct* had taken place in the requested State, there is sufficient evidence to find a prima facie case. Thirdly, the identification of the person accused or convicted in the requesting State must be proved.

The first element has already been discussed. In relation to the second, in Canada the test for sufficiency of evidence and the role of the extradition magistrate was considered in *United States of America v Ferras; United States of America v Latty* [2006] SCR 77, [2006] SCC 33. In that case McLachlin CJ stated at paragraph 20:

> It follows that before a person can be extradited, there must be a judicial determination that the requesting state has established a *prima facie* case that the person sought committed the crime alleged and should stand trial for it.

McLachlin CJ went on to say at paragraphs 25–26:

> the extradition judge must judicially consider the facts and the law and be satisfied that they justify committal before ordering extradition. The judge must act as a judge, not a rubber stamp. I conclude that the principles of fundamental justice applicable to an extradition hearing require that the person sought for extradition must receive a meaningful judicial determination of whether the case for extradition prescribed by s. 29 (1) of the Extradition Act has been established – that is whether there is sufficient evidence to permit a properly instructed jury to convict. This requires an independent judicial phase, an independent and impartial judge and a judicial decision based on an assessment of the evidence and the law.

McLachlin CJ at paragraph 40 of the judgment further stated that the extradition judge had power to exclude evidence that was unreliable and dangerous. In Commonwealth Caribbean jurisdictions the test for committal is *Regina v Galbraith* [1981] 1 WLR 1039, where Lord Lane analyses how a judge should approach a submission of 'no case'. This analysis was followed in *R v Governor of Pentonville Prison ex p Osman* [1989] 3 All ER 701, where Lloyd LJ stated:

> It is the duty of a magistrate in an extradition case to consider the evidence as a whole and to reject any evidence which he considers worthless, but he is neither entitled nor obliged to determine the amount of weight to be attached to any evidence or to compare one witness with another, since that would be for the jury at any subsequent trial. It follows, therefore,

37 Antigua and Barbuda: Extradition Act No 12 of 1993, s 11(7);
Bahamas: Act No 8 of 1994, s 10(5);
Barbados: Cap 189, Act No 21 of 1979, s 17(1);
Belize: Extradition Act, Cap 112 Revised Edition 2000, s 3;
Dominica: Act No 6 of 1981, s 17(1);
Grenada: Extradition Act, Cap 98, s 11(7);
Guyana: Fugitive Offenders Act No 15 of 1998, s 15(4);
Jamaica: Extradition Act No 7 of 1991, s 10(5);
St Lucia: Extradition Act No 12 of 1986, s 16(1);
St Kitts and Nevis: Extradition Act 1870, s 10;
St Vincent: Fugitive Offenders Act, Cap 175, s 12(4);
Trinidad and Tobago: Extradition Act No 36 of 1985, s 12(4).

> that the magistrate is not concerned with any inconsistencies or contradictions in a witness's evidence unless they are such as to justify rejecting or eliminating his evidence as a whole, nor is he concerned with whether the witness's evidence is corroborated.

These authorities demonstrate that before a magistrate can rule that there is sufficient evidence to commit, there must be evidence in the admissible documents to prove all the elements of the offence. The magistrate may take into consideration inconsistencies and contradictions in the evidence only if they demonstrate that the evidence is manifestly unreliable. In such a case the magistrate must reject the evidence of the requesting State.

Identification

Identification is usually proved by a photograph attached to the extradition package.[38] The Extradition Act of Trinidad and Tobago has to some extent made identification of the person wanted or convicted of an extraditable offence easier by allowing the fact that the name of the person is similar to that on the warrant and the use of fingerprints and other means of description identifying the person sought.[39]

For prosecutors and persons preparing the extradition package it is necessary that there be evidence in the prima facie evidence of identity of the person sought, not simply evidence of the person whose extradition is requested.

The magistrate at the extradition hearing following a submission of no case to answer may give the prosecution leave to re-open the prosecution case so that the prosecution can tender supplemental evidence to bolster the identification evidence already admitted. In such a case, the magistrate should allow the defence the opportunity to cross examine the witness who adduced the supplemental evidence and to make a further no-case submission (*Keron Pierre v The Commissioner of Prisons* Claim No CV 2011-01865).

Where a person has been convicted of an extraditable offence and is deemed unlawfully at large by the requested State certain additional facts must be proved by requesting State. The requesting State must not only prove the person was convicted of an extraditable offence but *also* that person is 'unlawfully at large'. The term 'unlawfully at large' is not defined in the Extradition Acts of Commonwealth Caribbean jurisdictions and is wide enough to include persons who have escaped custody, persons who have failed to answer bail, and persons who have failed to appear for sentence. There must be direct evidence of the person being unlawfully at large.[40]

In *Anderson* [1993] Crim LR 954, DC, the court identified the test for unlawfully at large:

> The court ... must be satisfied that the offence constitutes an extradition crime as defined by Section 2 of the Act. To that end, it is enjoined to hear representations made by both sides – such representations being, one would suppose, almost invariably no more than legal argument. Once so satisfied, it is clear that the next stage is that the court must be satisfied of the two factual matters ... firstly, that the person concerned has been convicted of the offence; second that he appears to be unlawfully at large. [These being questions of fact] it must necessarily follow that the court must receive evidence in an acceptable form.

38 *Re Bradshar*, 28 February 1984 (unreported); *R v Governor of Pentonville Prison ex p Rodrigues*, *The Times*, 29 November 1984, DC; *R v Governor of Pentonville Prison ex p Voets* [1986] 2 All ER 630; *Kajala v Noble*(1982) 75 Cr App R 149; *Sealy v Government of the United States of America* (1992) 47 WIR 23.

39 Act No 12 of 2004, s 19B.

40 *Urru v The Governor of HMP Brixton and the Government of Italy*, CO/4009/99 DC.

The prosecution bears the burden of proof to show that the person is unlawfully at large. Once the court finds that the person has been 'convicted' of the extraditable offence, the magistrate shall then determine whether there are any prohibitions to his committal. In Commonwealth Caribbean jurisdictions persons convicted in their absence whose convictions are not final are treated as persons accused of the extraditable offence.

APPLICATION FOR HABEAS CORPUS

All of the Commonwealth Caribbean jurisdictions have sections in their legislation that allow for an application for habeas corpus if the person accused or convicted is committed.[41] A magistrate on committing a person to custody *must* inform him of his right to apply for habeas corpus within 15 days of committal. The 15-day period starts from the day of committal.

Extradition from all of the Caribbean Commonwealth countries is barred if it appears to the High Court or relevant Minister that, in respect of the offence of which the person is accused or convicted, it is not warranted because:

> (a) by reason of the trivial nature of the offence; or
> (b) by reason of the passage of time since he is alleged to have committed it or to have become unlawfully at large, as the case may be; or
> (c) because the accusation against him is not made in good faith in the interest of justice, it would, having regard to all the circumstances, be unjust and oppressive to return him.[42]

These are gateways by which the issue of unjust and oppressive must be proved. In Trinidad and Tobago, however, the addition of the words 'or any other sufficient cause' in s 13 of the 1985 Act as amended effectively gives the court a very wide discretion if on any ground it would be unjust or oppressive to return the person. Section 17(2)d of the Fugitive Offenders Act of Guyana makes similar provision.

The authorities are clear that a High Court hearing an application for habeas corpus cannot retry or rehear the case. The High Court is also not an appeal court.[43] In this regard Lord Reid[44] has stated:

> The court does not hear the case by way of appeal so as to reverse the magistrate's decision on fact or alter a discretion properly exercised.

---

41 Antigua and Barbuda: Extradition Act No 12 of 1993, s 13;
Bahamas: Act No 8 of 1994, s 11;
Barbados: Cap 189, Act No 21 of 1979, s 19;
Belize: Extradition Act, Cap 112 Revised Edition 2000, s 3;
Dominica: Act No 6 of 1981, s 19;
Grenada: Extradition Act, Cap 98, s 13;
Guyana: Fugitive Offenders Act No 15 of 1998, s 16;
Jamaica: Extradition Act No 7 of 1991, s 11;
St Lucia: Extradition Act No 12 of 1986, s 18;
St Kitts and Nevis: Extradition Act 1870, s 11;
St Vincent: Fugitive Offenders Act, Cap 175, s 14;
Trinidad and Tobago: Extradition Act 1985, Act No 36 of 1985, s 13.

42 *Extradition Law and Practice* (2nd edn), Ivor and Clive Stanbrook.

43 *R v Governor of Pentonville Prison ex p Osman* [1989] 3 All ER 701 at 72.

44 *Armah v Government of Ghana* [1966] 3 All ER 177 at 184, [1986] AC 192 at 230.

In *Armah's* case [1966] 3 All ER 177, 184, Lord Reid and Lord Pearce adopted a straightforward *Wednesbury*[45] test, 'whether there was evidence on which a reasonable magistrate, properly directing himself in law could commit'.

In many instances the person accused or convicted of an extraditable offence would argue that it is unjust and oppressive to return them to the requesting country. The burden of proof is on them and the standard of proof is a balance of probabilities.

In *Kakis v Government of Cyprus* [1978] 1 WLR 779, the House of Lords considered the relationship between the terms 'unjust' and 'oppressive' in the context of s 8(3) of the Fugitive Offenders Act 1967 (UK). Lord Diplock said (at 782–83):

> 'Unjust' I regard as directed primarily to the risk of prejudice to the accused in the conduct of the trial itself, 'oppressive' as directed to hardship to the accused resulting from changes in his circumstance that have occurred during the period to be taken into consideration; but there is room for overlapping, and between them they would cover all cases where to return him would not be fair.

The person accused or convicted of the extradition offence may also wish to argue that, due to the passage of time, it would be unfair to now extradite him. The onus is upon the applicant to adduce cogent evidence that it would be unjust and oppressive to extradite him. The courts, in determining whether or not it is unjust and oppressive to return the person accused or convicted of the extraditable offence, are limited to cases where it appears by reason of the passage of time it is unjust and oppressive to return him.[46] The courts will not rely on mere speculation or assertions.[47] In *Woodcock v Government of New Zealand* [2003] EWHC 2668 (Admin), the Divisional Court held that the statutory test of 'unjust or oppressive' was directed to the *return* rather than the *trial* itself:

> requires this court to have regard to whatever safeguards may exist in the domestic law of the requesting state to ensure that the accused would not be subjected to an unjust trial there. There are, it should be borne in mind, clear advantages in having the question whether or not a fair trial is now possible decided in the domestic court, rather than by us.

Recently in the UK the House of Lords in *Gomes v Government of Trinidad and Tobago* [2009] UKHL 21, had to give careful attention to what was meant by the phrase *unjust or oppressive*. In that case Lord Brown said:

> 32. With regard to the concept of injustice, the law has moved on since *Kakis*, in part because of the developing abuse of process jurisdiction over the past 30 years. It is unnecessary to rehearse this at length. Rather it is sufficient to refer to the judgment of the Privy Council delivered by Lord Bingham of Cornhill in *Knowles* v *Government of the United States of America* [2007] 1 WLR 47, in particular at Para. 31 where the Board approved the Divisional Court's judgment in *Woodcock* v *Government of New Zealand* [2004] 1 WLR 1979 from which it extracted and endorsed the propositions:
>
> First, the question is not whether it would be unjust and oppressive to try the accused but whether . . . it would be unjust or oppressive to extradite him (Para. 20). Secondly, if the court of the requesting state is bound to conclude that a fair trial is impossible, it would be unjust or oppressive for the requested state to return him (Para. 21). But, thirdly, the court of the requested state must have regard to the safeguards which exist under the domestic law of the requesting state to protect a defendant against a trial rendered unjust or oppressive by the passage of time (Paras. 21–22). Fourthly, no rule of thumb can be applied to determine whether the passage of time has rendered a fair trial no longer possible: much will turn on the

45 *Associated Picture Houses Ltd v Wednesbury Corp* [1947] 2 All ER 680.

46 *R v Governor of Pentonville Prison ex p Narang* [1978] AC 247 at 271 F–G.

47 *R v Bow Street Magistrates' Court ex p Odoli* CO/1998/93 Unrep Transcript 26 January 1994 at 16A–B.

> particular case (Paras. 14–16, 23–25). Fifthly, there can be no cut-off point beyond which extradition must inevitably be regarded as unjust or oppressive. (Para. 29)
>
> 33. The second of those propositions, it will be noted invites consideration of whether, in any particular case, 'a fair trial is impossible', and that indeed we regard as the essential question underlying any application for a Section 82 bar on the ground that the passage of time has made it unjust to extradite the accused.

Lord Brown went on to say:

> we would nevertheless stress that the test of establishing the likelihood of injustice will not be easily satisfied. The extradition process, it must be remembered, is only available for returning suspects to friendly foreign states with whom this country has entered into multilateral or bilateral treaty obligations involving mutually agreed and reciprocal commitments. The arrangements are founded on mutual trust and respect. There is a strong public interest in respecting such treaty obligations. As has repeatedly been stated, international co-operation in this field is ever more important to bring to justice those accused of serious cross-border crimes and to ensure that fugitives cannot find safe havens abroad. We are told that the Section 82 (or Section 14) 'defence' is invoked in no fewer than 40% of extradition cases. This seems to us an extraordinarily high proportion and we would be unsurprised were it to fall following the Committee's judgment in the present case.

Bad faith is another ground on which the person accused or convicted may wish to rely on. However, this is very difficult to prove. In this regard see: *R v Governor of Pentonville Prison ex p Tarling* [1979] 1 WLR 1417, which held there must be evidence of bad faith and not mere speculation and suspicion.[48] The court also considered the meaning of 'good faith' *in Samuel Knowles Jr v The Gov't of USA*.

ABUSE OF PROCESS

It has been held in *Rhett Allen Fuller v The Attorney General of Belize* [2011] UKPC 23 that an applicant may be granted a writ of habeas corpus if the application can fall within the narrow definition of abuse of process as outlined by their Lordships. Three categories of 'abuse of process' were identified:

> (i) making use of the process of the court in a manner which is improper, such as adducing false evidence or indulging in inordinate delay, or
>
> (ii) using the process of the court in circumstances where it is improper to do so, as for instance where a defendant has been brought before the court in circumstances which are an affront to the rule of law, or
>
> (iii) using the process of the court for an improper motive or purpose, such as to extradite a defendant for a political motive.

Further, their Lordships re-confirmed the position that the magistrate has no jurisdiction to entertain an application for an abuse of process. This jurisdiction rests solely with the High Court.

48 *Charron v Government of the United States of America and Anor*, CA No. 54 of 1998 (2000).

ORDER FOR RETURN[49]

No Commonwealth Caribbean jurisdiction except Trinidad and Tobago and the Bahamas allows for the return of the person accused or convicted of the extraditable offence if he is serving a sentence of imprisonment or detention or is charged with a local offence. Section 26(3) of the Guyana Fugitive Offenders Act permits the temporary transfer of the fugitive who is to be extradited to the requesting State even if he is serving a sentence or charged in Guyana. Otherwise the legislation is quite clear in relation to the other jurisdictions that these impediments have to be removed first before the person can be surrendered.

The legislation goes on to state that the relevant Minister shall inform the person to be surrendered forthwith of his decision of surrender. The person to be surrendered is entitled to make representations to the relevant Minister as to why he should not be surrendered. It should also be noted that the person to be surrendered may file for judicial review of the Minister's decision.[50]

However, in Trinidad and Tobago, the Attorney General can make an order of surrender if the person is serving a sentence of imprisonment or is charged with an offence.[51] In *Steve Ferguson and Ishwar Galbaransingh v The Attorney General of Trinidad and Tobago and Chief Magistrate* Civil Appeal No 60 of 2007, the appellants were indicted in the US for certain fraud and money laundering charges arising out of investigations by the Immigration Customs and Enforcement Bureau (ICE). A request for extradition was made for their return and the Attorney General duly signed the ATP in 2006. However, the same appellants were charged locally in Trinidad for the same conduct arising out of fraud and bid-rigging arising out of the Piarco Airport Construction Project in 2004. The appellants argued that an ATP should not have been issued by the Attorney General and hence no order for extradition could be made whilst the defendants were facing local charges in Trinidad and Tobago. The Court of Appeal held that s 16(2) of the Act was the complete answer which makes provision for extradition while local charges were pending. The court further agreed with Bereaux J when their Lordships stated that the question of forum should be decided after the Attorney General makes an order for return. In his judgment Bereaux J had specifically stated that extradition proceedings may continue while local charges are pending. Bereaux J said at page 39:

> In my judgment unless the criminal proceedings have concluded with a verdict of guilt or innocence, criminal proceedings can be discontinued at any stage to facilitate extradition, unless it

49 Antigua: Extradition Act No 12 of 1993, ss 14 and 15;
Bahamas: Act No 8 of 1994, s 12;
Barbados: Cap 189, Act No 21 of 1979, ss 26 and 27;
Belize: Extradition Act, Cap 112 Revised Edition 2000, s 3;
Dominica: Act No 6 of 1981, ss 26 and 27;
Grenada: Extradition Act, Cap 98 ss 15 and 16;
Guyana: Fugitive Offenders Act No 15 of 1998, s 26;
Jamaica: Extradition Act No 7 of 1991, s 12;
St Lucia: Extradition Act No 12 of 1986, ss 25 and 26;
St Kitts and Nevis: Extradition Act 1870, s 11;
St Vincent: Fugitive Offenders Act, Cap 175 ss 16–20;
Trinidad and Tobago: Extradition Act No 36 of 1985, s 11.

50 *R v Secretary for State for the Home Dept ex p Warren* [2003] EWHC 1177 (Admin).

51 Extradition Act 1985, s 16(2) as amended by Act No 12 of 2004.

> shows that such discontinuance is effected to obstruct or forestall a likely acquittal (which may become apparent during a trial) . . . Until such trial is concluded the order to proceed can be issued and the committal proceedings commence.

In a case where the same conduct complained of can or is being charged locally, for extradition to be ordered the Attorney General will have to make a *Cotroni*[52] decision so that an order for extradition can be made. The Supreme Court of Canada set out factors which the Attorney General would have to take into consideration when determining which forum is appropriate. La Forest J in *Cotroni* (1989) 48 CCC (3d) 193, SCC, at para 40 stated the factors as follows:

- where the impact of the offence felt or likely to have been felt,
- which jurisdiction has the greater interest in prosecuting the offence,
- which jurisdiction has laid charges,
- which jurisdiction has the most comprehensive case,
- which jurisdiction is ready to proceed to trial,
- where is the evidence located,
- whether the evidence is mobile,
- the number of accused involved and whether they can be gathered together in one place for trial,
- in what jurisdiction were most of the acts in furtherance of the crime committed,
- the nationality and residence of the accused,
- the severity of the sentence the accused is likely to receive in each jurisdiction.

Once the Attorney General takes account of the above factors in making his decision, it would be very difficult for a court to find on an application for judicial review that the Attorney General had acted *Wednesbury* unreasonably. However, in a later decision of *Steve Ferguson and Ishwar Galbaransingh v The Attorney General of Trinidad and Tobago* CV 2010-04144, Boodoosingh J after weighing the *Cotroni* factors held that the appropriate forum to try the claimants was Trinidad and Tobago. Justice Boodoosingh further held that failure of the Attorney General to disclose correspondence between himself and the Director of Public Prosecutions denied the claimants the opportunity to fully put their case before the Attorney General for due consideration.

CHECKLIST FOR EXTRADITION TO A REQUESTING STATE

1. Ensure there is a valid extradition Act (referring to the requesting State) or Treaty between the requested and requesting State.
2. Determine whether the conduct alleged is an extraditable offence under the law of the requested State.

52 *United States v Cotroni* (1989) 48 CCC (3d) 193 (SCC).

3. Ensure that the alleged offence was committed within the jurisdiction of the requesting State. See *Liangsiriprasert v Government of the United States of America* [1991] 1 AC 225, PC and *Libman v The Queen* (1985) 21 CCC (3d) 206.
4. Ensure that there are no bars to extradition and that the rule of speciality will be observed, e.g., the offence is not a political offence, the offence is not statute barred and no pleas in bar could be raised, i.e., autrefois acquit and autrefois convict.
5. Ensure that the extradition package is complete and disclose copies to the defence. Also disclose the ATP (if available) and certificate of speciality, if applicable. If the ATP is not disclosed then disclose the schedule of charges. Disclosure of the witness statements are at the discretion of the prosecutor.
6. If the person is alleged to be convicted (as opposed to accused) of an extraditable offence, prove the conviction by the certificate of conviction or other duly authenticated judicial documents as well as any other evidence demonstrating that the person was present at the conviction hearing and is now unlawfully at large.

APPENDICES

THE BAHAMAS

No 01/1999

In the Supreme Court

Criminal Side

The Queen versus

NE

To Wit:

NE is charged with the following offence(s):

Statement of Offence

MURDER, contrary to section 312 of the Penal Code, Chapter 77.

Particulars of Offence

That you, **NE**, on Thursday, 20th August, 1998 at New Providence, did murder **RE**.

/s/ BT (Director of Public Prosecutions)

(for) and on behalf of the Attorney-General

Dated this . . . . .day of 1999

BARBADOS

THE QUEEN

v

JD

THE SUPREME COURT

(High Court)

JD is charged with the following offences:

FIRST COUNT

STATEMENT OF OFFENCE

Robbery, contrary to section 8(1) of The Theft Act, Chapter 155.

PARTICULARS OF OFFENCE

JD, on the 26th day of July, 2000, in the parish of St Michael in this Island, robbed **BK** of one watch, one chain, one wallet and $15.00 Barbados Currency, the property of the said **BK**.

SECOND COUNT

STATEMENT OF OFFENCE

Wounding with intent, contrary to section 16 of the Offences against the Person Act, Chapter 141.

PARTICULARS OF OFFENCE

JD, on the 26th day of July, 2000, in the parish of St Michael in this Island, unlawfully wounded **BK** with intent to do him serious bodily harm, or to maim, disfigure or disable him.

____

Director of Public Prosecutions

DOMINICA

IN THE EASTERN CARIBBEAN SUPREME COURT

No 30 of 2001

IN THE HIGH COURT OF JUSTICE

(CRIMINAL)

COMMONWEALTH OF DOMINICA

THE STATE

v

BJ

INDICTMENT by the Director of Public Prosecutions of the Commonwealth of Dominica.

BJ is charged with the following offence:

STATEMENT OF OFFENCE

MURDER

PARTICULARS OF OFFENCE

BJ, on the 6th day of October, 2000 at Jones Street, Castletown in the Parish of St George, Commonwealth of Dominica, murdered CZ.

Dated this 15th day of March 2001.

____

DIRECTOR OF PUBLIC PROSECUTIONS

GRENADA

IN THE SUPREME COURT OF GRENADA
AND THE WEST INDIES ASSOCIATED
STATES IN THE HIGH COURT OF JUSTICE
(CRIMINAL)

CASE NO 9 OF 2000

THE QUEEN

v

AR

FIRST COUNT

Her Majesty's Director of Public Prosecutions in and for the State of Grenada and its Dependencies for and on behalf of Our Sovereign Lady the Queen presents that YOU,

AR of Boca in the parish of St George and State aforesaid, on Wednesday the 4th day of March 2000 at Boca aforesaid, DID HAVE IN YOUR POSSESSION a prohibited weapon, to wit, a 9mm sub machine gun: contrary to Section 20(1)(a) of the Firearms Act No 42 of 1968 of the Laws of Grenada.

SECOND COUNT

And Her Majesty's Director of Public Prosecutions aforesaid, further presents that YOU, the said AR of Boca aforesaid, on Wednesday the 4th day of March 2000 at Boca aforesaid, DID HAVE IN YOUR POSSESSION A FIREARM, to wit, one 9mm pistol except under and in accordance with the terms and conditions of a Firearm User's Licence: contrary to section 20(1)(b) of the Firearms Act No 42 of 1968 of the Laws of Grenada.

Dated this 22nd day of November 2000.

____

DIRECTOR OF PUBLIC PROSECUTIONS

GUYANA

THE STATE

v

DM

IN THE HIGH COURT OF THE SUPREME COURT OF JUDICATURE OF GUYANA.

(Criminal Jurisdiction)

County of DEMERARA

PRESENTMENT OF THE DIRECTOR OF PUBLIC PROSECUTIONS FOR GUYANA.

DM is charged with the following offence:

STATEMENT OF OFFENCE

Murder, contrary to section 100 of the Criminal Law (Offences) Act, Chapter 8:01.

PARTICULARS OF OFFENCE

DM, on the 26th day of April, 2000, in the county of Demerara murdered SC.

____

Director of Public Prosecutions

JAMAICA

The Queen vs AH and MM

In the Supreme Court of Judicature for Jamaica

In the Circuit Court Division of the Gun Court for the Island of Jamaica

IT IS HEREBY CHARGED on behalf of Our Sovereign Lady the Queen:

STATEMENT OF OFFENCE

Capital Murder, contrary to Section 2(1)(a)(i) of the Offences Against the Person (Amendment) Act.

PARTICULARS OF OFFENCE

AH and MM on the 5th day of November, 1998 in the parish of St Andrew murdered GD, a member of the security forces acting in the execution of his duties.

/s/ CL
Deputy Director of Public Prosecutions
for Director of Public Prosecutions
March 9, 2000

SAINT VINCENT AND THE GRENADINES

In the High Court of Justice

(Criminal)

Case No 2 of 2001

The Queen

v

AB

AB is charged as follows:

STATEMENT OF OFFENCE

Robbery contrary to Section 216 of the Criminal Code Cap 124 of the Laws of Saint Vincent and the Grenadines, Revised Edition 1990.

PARTICULARS OF OFFENCE

AB on the 6th day of October, 2000 at Joneston Drive, Castletown in Saint Vincent and the Grenadines stole one handbag valued at EC$150, jewellery and cash together worth EC $2,500, the property of Z and at the time of so doing and in order so to do used force on the said Z.

Dated the 2nd day of February, 2001.

____

Director of Public Prosecutions

ST LUCIA

IN THE HIGH COURT OF JUSTICE

(CRIMINAL)

Dated the 1st day of April 2001 Session

THE QUEEN

v

BA

HB

TJ

The Director of Public Prosecutions presents that the accused BA, HB and TJ on the 6th day of October 2000 at Ericcson Drive, Castletown in the State of Saint Lucia did commit Robbery upon ZK by stealing from her person, a bag valued at $150 as well as jewellery and cash together worth $2,500 contrary to Section 364 of the Criminal Code of Saint Lucia.

SECOND COUNT

And the said Director of Public Prosecutions further presents that BA at the place and date aforesaid did commit robbery upon ZK by stealing from her a Motorola cellular telephone contrary to Section 364 of the Criminal Code of St Lucia.

Dated this 1st day of April 2001.

____

Director of Public Prosecutions

TRINIDAD AND TOBAGO

THE STATE **v** **AB**
DC

IN THE HIGH COURT OF JUSTICE

PORT OF SPAIN

INDICTMENT BY THE DIRECTOR OF PUBLIC PROSECUTIONS

AB and DC are charged with the following offences:

FIRST COUNT

STATEMENT OF OFFENCE

ROBBERY WITH AGGRAVATION, contrary to Section 24(1)(a) of the Larceny Act, Chap 11:12, as amended.

PARTICULARS OF OFFENCE

AB and DC, on the 2nd day of February, 1995, at Barataria, in the County of St George, being armed with a gun, together robbed LJ of one pair of gold bracelets, one bangle and three gold jingles.

SECOND COUNT

STATEMENT OF OFFENCE

ROBBERY WITH AGGRAVATION, contrary to Section 24(1)(a) of the Larceny Act, Chap 11:12; As amended.

PARTICULARS OF OFFENCE

AB and DC, on the 2nd day of February, 1995, at Barataria, in the County of St George, being armed with a gun, together robbed EN of one wedding band valued at $500.

THIRD COUNT

STATEMENT OF OFFENCE

POSSESSION OF FIREARM, contrary to section 6(1) of the Firearms Act, Chap 16:01.

PARTICULARS OF OFFENCE

AB, on the 2nd day of February, 1995, at Barataria, in the County of St George, had in his possession a firearm, to wit, one 7.62mm rifle he not being the holder of a Firearm User's Licence with respect to such firearm.

DC has been previously convicted of an arrestable offence, to wit, House-breaking and Larceny on the 22nd day of January, 1991, at the Arima Magistrates' Court.

____

Director of Public Prosecutions

46/98

REPUBLIC OF TRINIDAD AND TOBAGO

No . . . .

COMPLAINT

Corporal JK, 900 . . . .
. . . . . *Complainant*
XY . . . . *Defendant*
The complaint of JK, Corporal 900 of Morvant Police Station who comes before me the undersigned and [saith on oath] that XY of . . . . did on . . . . day of. . . . ., 20 . . . . at . . . .
in the County of St George* . . . .
. . . .

And the said JK prays that the said XY may be summoned to answer the said complaint.

/s/ JK

. . . .
Signature of Complainant

Taken before me at the .Court this . . . . .day of . . . ., 20

. . . .
Magistrate of Justice

* Here state concisely the nature of complaint.

REPUBLIC OF TRINIDAD AND TOBAGO

INFORMATION, INDICTABLE OFFENCE, PRELIMINARY ENQUIRY

Chap 12:01

(Indictable Case)

No . . . .

COUNTY OF . . . .

WH, Police Sergeant No 1000 . . . . .of . . . . .Central Police Station
informs the undersigned Magistrate that . . . . .XY . . . .
of 105 Woodford Street, Port of Spain . . . .
on Friday . . . . .the 8th . . . . .day of September
in the year of Our Lord two thousand . . . .
at Collins Street, Maraval, Port of Spain . . . .
and within the limits of the said County of St George . . ..
did . . . .
. . . .
. . . .
. . . .
. . . .
. . . .

Taken and at the
Office, this day of 20

____

Magistrate

REPUBLIC OF TRINIDAD AND TOBAGO

CASE

No.

SEARCH WARRANT

(Chap 4:20, Sec 41)

County of

To
WHEREAS it appears, on the oath of
of
that there is reasonable ground for believing that*

are concealed in

at

This is therefore to authorize and require you to enter into the said premises at any time and to search for the said things and to bring the same before me or some other Magistrate or Justice.

Dated this day of 20

Magistrate or Justice

* Insert description of the things to be searched for and of the offence in respect of which the search is made.

INFORMATION USED TO SUPPORT SEARCH WARRANT
REPUBLIC OF TRINIDAD AND TOBAGO

Case No

COMPLAINT UPON OATH

(Part 1, Form 2, Section 33, Chap 4:20)

COUNTY OF

Informant
Defendant

The information of

of who saith on his oath*

of

that

†

‡

And the said prays that

the

said may be summoned

to answer the said information §

Taken and sworn to before me this day of 20

at

____

Magistrate

* Or Affirmation. †State concisely the substance of the information. ‡Add, for the arrest of a witness – And he further saith that of can give material evidence, but is not likely to attend voluntarily; or, and wilfully avoids service of the summons.

§ Or, if a warrant is desired in the first instance – may be apprehended for the said offence, and dealt with according to law. Or, for sureties for the peace – And he lays this information for the safety of his person and property and not from malice or revenge against the said . . . . . .

JAMAICA

INFORMATION

Parish of St Ann's

The Information and Complaint

of the parish of . . . . made and taken upon oath before the undersigned this . . . . .day of . . . . .In the year of Our Lord two thousand and . . . . .who saith that on . . . . the . . . . day of . . . . in the year aforesaid one . . . . .of the said parish of . . . . .with force . . . . at . . . . and within the jurisdiction

against the form of the Statute in such case made and provided, and against the Peace of Our Sovereign Lady the Queen Her Crown and Dignity, and thereupon the said Complainant prays that the said . . . . . . .may be summoned to answer unto the said Complaint according to Law.

Taken and sworn to before me at . . . . in the parish of . . . . .this . . . . day of . . . . .two thousand and . . . .

____

Justice of the Peace or Clerk of the Courts
for the Parish of St Anns

REPUBLIC OF TRINIDAD AND TOBAGO

No . . . ., 20 . . . .

Recognizance of Bail instead of Remand on an Adjournment of Preliminary Examination

(Ch 12:01 Sec 29(3))

BE it remembered, that on the 15th day of March in the year of Our Lord two thousand
JT of 6 Thomas Lane, Arouca in the county of St George and
XY of
personally came before me, one of the State's Magistrates for the said County and severally acknowledged themselves to owe to the State the several sums following; that is to say: the said JT the sum of
dollars, Trinidad and Tobago currency and the said XY the sum of
dollars like money to be made and levied of their several Goods and Chattels, lands and tenements respectively, to the use of the State, if he the said

fails in the Condition endorsed.

Taken and acknowledged the say and year first above-mentioned, at the Magistrate's Court of Before me

____

Magistrate

Condition

The Condition of the within-written Recognizance is such, that whereas the within-bounden was on the day of 20

charge before me the undersigned (the Magistrate's Court)

for that he on the day of 20

Did

And whereas the examination of the witnesses for the prosecution in this behalf is

At the Magistrates Court if therefore the said Shall appear before the said Court

Said day of 20

At nine o'clock in the forenoon, or at an earlier day if so required and at every date, time and place to which during the course of the proceedings this enquiry may be from time to time adjourned, then the said Recognizance to be void, or else to stand in full force and virtue.

____

Magistrate

RECOGNIZANCE OF BAIL ON COMMITTAL

(Chap 12:01)

THE STATE

against

XY

on the charge of

for (*state offence briefly*)

AT

in the said Island, on this day of

in the year of Our Lord two thousand

in the said

Island, acknowledges himself to be indebted to our State of Trinidad and Tobago, in the sum of

and

acknowledges himself to be indebted to our State, in the sum of

like money; upon condition that, if the said XY

do personally appear before the Supreme Court, in the Town of

to answer to any indictment that shall be presented against him in the said Court in or about the premises within the term of twelve calendar months from the date of this acknowledgement, and do not depart the Court, without leave, and do accept service of any such indictment at the residence of

situate in

in the Town of

and that the said

in the meantime be of good behaviour, and keep the peace toward the State and all her citizens and especially towards

then this recognizance to be void, or else to remain in full force.

REPUBLIC OF TRINIDAD AND TOBAGO

Case No. . . . .

RECOGNIZANCE FOR APPEARANCE OF DEFENDANT WHERE THE CASE IS ADJOURNED OR NOT AT ONCE PROCEEDED WITH

(Chap 4:20, section 66 122, Part VII, Schedule III, Form 29)

County of St George

JUDICIARY/MAGISTRACY

BE it remembered that on the day of , 20 . . . .

of

and

of

before me, the undersigned Magistrate (or Justice) for the said district, and severally acknowledged themselves to the State the several sums following, namely, the said

as principal the sum of

and the said

as surety the sum of

To be levied on their several movable and immovable property respectively, if the said fails in the condition hereon endorsed.

Taken and acknowledged the day and year first above-mentioned, before me.

1 . . . .

. . . .

2 . . . .

. . . .

Justice of the Peace

CONDITION ENDORSED

The condition of the within written recognizance is such that if the within bounden appears before the Magistrate (or Justice) in the said Court, on the day of , 20. . . . . at nine o'clock, a.m. in the forenoon at Magistrate's Court (and at every time and place to which during the course of the proceedings against the said the hearing may be from time to time adjourned) to answer further the complaint made against him by
and to be further dealt with according to law, then the said recognizance shall be void, but otherwise shall remain in full force.

____

Justice of the Peace

STATUTORY DECLARATION TO BE MADE BY A SURETY OR SURETIES

[Section – Bail Act]

COUNTY OF . . . .

I the undersigned of . . . . do solemnly and sincerely declare as follows:
I/*We have agreed to offer myself/*ourselves as surety for . . . .
. . . . /defendant in the case State/Police vs . . . .
In this regard I/*we acknowledge to owe to the State the sum of . . . .
To be levied on my/*our several movable and immovable property if the said . . . .
Fails in the condition of the recognisance to be entered before . . . .
Magistrate/Justice of the Peace.

And for that purpose I/*we, the undersigned declare –

(a) that my*/our movable and immovable property including other financial assets consists of the following:
   (i) Particulars of immovable property – description of immovable property, date of the Deed and name address of the parties to the Deed
   (ii) Estimated value of immovable property
   (iii) Bank balances – name of the bank, account number and amount
   (iv) Any other movable property and its value;

(b) That the immovable property specified in subparagraph (a) (i) above is owned by me/us free from any encumbrances; or in consideration of;
(c) That I/we have not stood surety/sureties on the consideration of the aforesaid immovable/movable property in the case/cases noted below which case/cases has/have been determined;
(d) That I/we have not been convicted of any criminal offence. Further a criminal charge is pending against me/*us./*No criminal charge is pending against me/*us.

Signed . . . .

. . . .

Declarant/Declarants

I/*We make this declaration conscientiously believing the same to be true and according to the Statutory Declarations Act, and I/*we am/*are aware that if there is any statement in this declaration which is false in fact, which I/*we know or believe to be false or do not believe to be true, I/*we am/*are liable to fine and imprisonment.

Signed . . . .

. . . .

Declarant/Declarants

Declared before me day of 20

Signed . . . .

Magistrate, Justice of the Peace, Registrar

* Strike whichever is inapplicable

Magisterial Information No . . . .

TRINIDAD AND TOBAGO

IN THE MATTER OF THE CONSTITUTION OF THE

REPUBLIC OF TRINIDAD AND TOBAGO

AND

ON THE INFORMATION

OF

WS

Police Sergeant No 900

VS

EK also called ABDUL

FOR

MURDER

I, MM, Director of Public Prosecutions, pursuant to the provisions of section 90 of the Constitution of the Republic of Trinidad and Tobago and all powers in that behalf enabling, do grant immunity from prosecution to EK also called ABDUL relative to this matter, subject to the following conditions:

(1) That the Statutory Declaration made by EK also called ABDUL and sworn to on the 12th day of February, 2000 is true to the best of the knowledge and belief of the said EK also called ABDUL.
(2) That the said EK also called ABDUL shall give evidence in accordance with the Statutory Declaration referred to herein, when required to do so.
(3) That the said EK also called ABDUL not leave the State of Trinidad and Tobago without the permission of the Director of Public Prosecutions.
(4) That the said EK also called ABDUL subject himself to arrangements made by the State for his protection.

This immunity will be withdrawn in the event of a deliberate breach of any of the above conditions and not otherwise.

Dated this 12th day of February 2000

MM

Director of Public Prosecutions

[EK endorses a copy of the immunity in his own handwriting acknowledging receipt and agreement to its terms and conditions]

REPUBLIC OF TRINIDAD AND TOBAGO

No . . . .

THE COURT OF APPEAL

Criminal Form VI

NOTICE OF APPLICATION FOR LEAVE TO APPEAL AGAINST A CONVICTION UNDER SECTION 5(b)

To the Registrar of the Supreme Court

I, . . . HK . . ., having been convicted of the offence of . Murder . and (being now a prisoner in the State Prison) at . . . . Port of Spain . . . . and †now living at . . . . and being desirous of appealing against my said conviction, Do Hereby Give You Notice that I apply to the Court of Appeal for leave to appeal against my said conviction on the grounds hereinafter set forth.

(Signed).. . . . . .HK. . . . .

. . . .

(or Mark) . . . .

. . . .

Dated this 25th day of May 2000.

‡PARTICULARS OF TRIAL AND CONVICTION

Date of Trial: 25 May 2000
In what Court tried: High Court Port of Spain
Sentence: Death by Hanging

§GROUNDS FOR APPLICATION

Counsel will supply grounds

. . . .

. . . .

You are required to answer the following questions:

1 If you desire to apply to the Court of Appeal to assign you legal aid and on your appeal, state your position in life, amount of wages, or salary, etc., and any other facts which you submit show reasons for legal aid being assigned to you.
2 If you desire to be present when the Court of Appeal considers your present application for leave to appeal, state the grounds on which you submit that the Court of Appeal should give you leave to be present thereat.
3 The Court of Appeal will, if you desire it, consider your case and argument if put in writing by you or on your behalf, instead of your case and argument being presented orally. If you desire to present your case and argument in writing, set out here as fully as you think right your case and argument in support of your appeal.

State if you desire to be present at the final hearing of your appeal.

_ Here state the offence, e.g., Larceny, Murder, Forgery
† Where applicant for any reason not in custody.
‡ Fill in all these particulars.
§ Here state as clearly and concisely as possible the grounds on which you desire to appeal against your conviction.

NOTICE OF INTENTION TO APPLY FOR LEAVE TO PRIVY COUNCIL

IN THE PRIVY COUNCIL
ON APPEAL FROM THE
COURT OF APPEAL
OF TRINIDAD AND TOBAGO

BETWEEN:

VK
Petitioner
And
THE STATE OF
TRINIDAD AND TOBAGO
Respondent

TAKE NOTICE that the above-mentioned VK intends to apply to the Judicial Committee of the Privy Council for Special Leave to Appeal against the Judgment of the Court of Appeal dated 26 April 1996 in the above-mentioned cause.

Dated this 10th day of March 1999.

____

Counsel for the Petitioner

TO: The Director of Public Prosecutions
16–18 Sackville Street
Port of Spain; and to

The Attorney General of Trinidad and Tobago
Richmond Street
Port of Spain

SUPPORTING AFFIDAVIT TO NOTICE OF INTENTION

IN THE PRIVY COUNCIL

ON APPEAL FROM THE

COURT OF APPEAL

OF TRINIDAD AND TOBAGO

BETWEEN:

VK

Petitioner

And

THE STATE OF

TRINIDAD AND TOBAGO

Respondent

I, KC, Attorney-at-Law, of 1 St Vincent Street, in the City of Port of Spain, in the Island of Trinidad, MAKE OATH and SAY as follows:

1 The facts disposed herein are true and correct and within my personal knowledge, except where stated to be otherwise.
2 I am an Attorney at Law of 1 St Vincent Street, aforesaid.
3 That I did on the 10th day of March 1999 at Knox Street, in the City of Port of Spain, in the Island of Trinidad, personally serve a true and correct copy of a Notice of Intention to apply to the Judicial Committee of the Privy Council for Special Leave to Appeal in this matter on the Attorney General at the office of the Ministry of National Security at Knox Street, in the City of Port of Spain, aforesaid, by leaving a copy thereof with one OP, an employee of the office of the said Ministry.
4 That I did on the said 10th day of March 1999 endorse on a true copy of the said Notice of Intention to apply to the Judicial Committee of the Privy Council the date and month of the year.

SWORN AT

THIS DAY OF 1999.

Before me,

____

Commissioner of Affidavits

BIBLIOGRAPHY

Acker, JR and Brody, DC, *Criminal Procedure: A Contemporary Perspective*, 1999, Gathersbury, MD: Aspen.

Archbold Criminal Pleading: Evidence and Practice, 38th edn, 1973, London: Sweet & Maxwell.

Archbold Criminal Pleading: Evidence and Practice, 41st edn, 1981, London: Sweet & Maxwell.

Archbold Criminal Pleading: Evidence and Practice, 47th edn, 1999, London: Sweet & Maxwell.

Archbold Criminal Pleading: Evidence and Practice, 2006 edn, London: Sweet & Maxwell.

Archbold Criminal Pleading: Evidence and Practice, 2009 edn, London: Sweet & Maxwell.

Archbold Criminal Pleading: Evidence and Practice, 2013 edn, London: Sweet & Maxwell.

Archbold Magistrates' Courts Criminal Practice, 2011 edn, London: Sweet & Maxwell.

Baldwin, J and McConville, M, *Jury Trials*, 1979, Oxford: Clarendon.

Bell Antoine, R, *Commonwealth Caribbean Law and Legal Systems*, 1999, London: Cavendish Publishing.

Belnavis, GA, *Criminal Procedure in the Resident Magistrates' Court and Petty Sessions Court: A Practical Look*, (unpublished), 2000, Jamaica: Norman Manley Law School.

Blackstone's Criminal Practice 2008, 2007, Oxford: Oxford University Press.

Bryant, MJ, 'Doing time for the community', *Justice of the Peace and Local Government Law*, 8 March 1997, p 233.

Burke, J, *Osborne's Concise Law Dictionary*, 6th edn, 1976, London: Sweet & Maxwell.

Chadee, D, 'A short history of (the English and Trinidad and Tobago) trial by jury', *Journal of Law Association of Trinidad and Tobago, The Lawyer*, January 1994, p 17.

Chuck, D, 'The role of sentences in dealing with criminal offenders in the Commonwealth Caribbean', *West Indian Law Journal*, March 1981, vol 5, p 25.

Corre, N, 'Abuse of process and the power to stay a prosecution', 1991, 155 JPN, 27 July 1991, p 469.

Davies, FG, 'Abuse of process: an expanding experimental doctrine', 1999, 163 JPN and (1999) 163 JPN, p 309.

Demerieux, M, *Fundamental Rights in Commonwealth Caribbean Constitutions*, 1992, Barbados: Faculty of Law Library, University of the West Indies.

Deosaran, R, 'Trial by jury in a post-colonial multi-racial society', *Journal of Law Association of Trinidad and Tobago, The Lawyer*, March 1981.

Emmins on Criminal Procedure, 7th edn, 1997, London: Blackstone.

Erez, E, 'Who's afraid of the big bad victim?', 1999, Crim LR 545.

Green, G, 'The concept of uniformity in sentencing', 1996, ALJ, February 1996, p 112.

Hilson, CS, 'Discretion to prosecute and judicial review', 1993, Crim LR 739.

Niblett, J, *Disclosure in Criminal Proceedings*, 1997, London: Blackstone.

Oppenheimer, BS, 'Trials by jury', *University of Cincinnati Law Review*, vol 11, 1937, pp 141, 142.

Pattenden, R, 'Abuse of process in criminal litigation', 1990, JCL 341.

Ramgoolam, R, 'The mandatory death penalty for homicide in Trinidad and Tobago: a critique', *The Journal of Comparative Law*, Vol 11, No 1, 2016.

Reeves, P, 'The Judicial Committee of the Privy Council: a court with power over life and death', 1999, 163 JPN, p 964.

Report of the Commission appointed to enquire into and report and make recommendations on the machinery for the Administration of Justice in the Republic of Trinidad and Tobago, October 2000, unpublished report, Trinidad and Tobago Government.

Richards, S, 'Reform in the magistrates' courts in Barbados', *Journal of the Law Association of Trinidad and Tobago, The Lawyer*, July 1994.

Samuels, A, 'The discount for guilty plea: the judicial principles', 1999, 163 JPN, p 792.

Seetahal, DS, 'Towards a better future in corrections: sentencing alternatives', *Journal of the Law Association of Trinidad and Tobago, The Lawyer*, January 1993.

Seetahal, DS, 'The jury: Tobago or Trinidad?', *Journal of the Law Association of Trinidad and Tobago, The Lawyer*, January 1994.

Seetahal, DS, 'The case for plea bargaining in the Caribbean', *Caribbean Journal of Criminology and Social Psychology*, Vol 1, No. i, January 1996, Trinidad and Tobago: The University of the West Indies, St Augustine.

Seetahal, DS, 'Do you wish to retire?', in *The Criminal Lawyer*, Vol 85, July/August 1998, Butterworths.

Seetahal, DS, 'Can a juror change her mind?', *Bench and Bar of Minnesota*, Vol LVI, No 111, March 1999.

Seetahal, DS, 'Pre-trial publicity and a fair trial', *Caribbean Journal of Criminology and Social Psychology*, Vol 4, Nos 1 and 2, January/July 1999, Trinidad: The University of the West Indies, St Augustine.

Seetahal, DS, Report on the Reform of the Criminal Law and Procedure of Saint Lucia, (unpublished), November 1999, consultancy for the Government of St Lucia.

Smith, JC, *Smith and Hogan, Criminal Law*, 8th edn, 1996, London: Butterworths.

Stanbrook, I and Stanbrook, C, *Extradition Law and Practice*, 2nd edn, 2000, Oxford: Oxford University Press.

INDEX

Page numbers in **bold** refer to the appendices.

Made in United States
Orlando, FL
07 April 2024

45538480R00285